Highly Recommended

New Edition

OSWAAL BOOKS®

LEARNING MADE SIMPLE

AF731501

NCERT TEXTBOOK SOLUTIONS

CLASS 12

CHEMISTRY

Strictly based on the Latest NCERT Textbook

Powered by

oswaal.ai

LEARNING MADE SMARTER

Smart guidance that helps you learn, practise and improve.

Your Path to Academic Excellence:

1

100% Updated

ith the Latest
CERT Textbook

2

Comprehensive Coverage

with all NCERT concepts

3

Visual Learning Tools

with Concept Videos

4

Extensive Revision Tools

with Crisp Revision Notes, Mind Maps & Mnemonics

5

Complete Question Coverage

with all NCERT textbook questions

OSWAAL BOOKS®
LEARNING MADE SIMPLE

This Edition: 2026

ISBN: 9789359588650

Disclaimer

This publication has been prepared by qualified subject matter experts with rigorous editorial review. Despite our best efforts, errors may exist. Readers are encouraged to report any by scanning the QR code on the Table of Contents page so corrections can reach all users.

This book is a study aid. Examination results depend on multiple factors including individual preparation and the specific examination conducted. No particular outcome is guaranteed.

Links in this book provide access to supplementary content. Accessibility depends on internet connectivity and device compatibility. Third-party content linked herein was verified at the time of printing; however, the Publisher does not guarantee that such content will remain accurate, available, or appropriate over time.

Views expressed by individual contributors are their own and do not represent the Publisher's position. The Publisher does not endorse personal opinions or political statements contained herein.

All maps, boundaries, and diagrams are artistic representations for educational reference only and are not geographically or politically authoritative.

For details on personal data processing, see our Privacy Policy at www.oswaalbooks.com/privacy. This publication is governed by the laws of India. Disputes shall be subject to the exclusive jurisdiction of courts in Agra, Uttar Pradesh.

Published by: Oswaal Books and Learning Private Limited, Oswaal House, 1/11, Sahitya Kunj, M.G. Road, Agra-282002 (U.P.), India

contact@oswaalbooks.com

+91-562-2857671

Printed at: Upkar Print House Pvt. Ltd., Agra

Contents

PREFACE

"Education is the passport to the future, for tomorrow belongs to those who prepare for it today." – Malcolm X

In the pursuit of academic excellence, the journey often begins with curiosity. As students embark on the path to success in the exams, the Oswaal NCERT Textbook Solutions Book for the academic year stands as an invaluable companion, illuminating the way forward.

Success in any exam goes beyond memorization; it involves developing a deep understanding of every concept. The NCERT textbooks provide the essential foundation. Introducing the Oswaal NCERT Textbook Solutions Book, a vital tool to unlock the full potential of every student.

Let's uncover what this book covers for you:

1) **Updated for –** The books are 100% updated for the academic year, adhering strictly to the latest NCERT guidelines.

2) **Comprehensive Coverage -** We cover all concepts and topics outlined in the most recent NCERT textbooks.

3) **Visual Learning Aids -** Explore theoretical concepts and concept videos that offer a brief description of the topic and help visualize complex concepts.

4) **Effective Revision Tools -** Benefit from crisp Revision Notes, Mind Maps, and Mnemonics designed to facilitate efficient and effective review.

5) **Complete Question Coverage -** All questions from the NCERT textbooks are covered in our solutions, providing a thorough grasp of the subject matter.

What sets this book apart is the expertise behind its creation. The solutions within are the result of the meticulous efforts of expert faculty, individuals with a profound understanding of the curriculum, and the dedication to maintaining the highest quality standards.

May this book be your guide, encouraging you to not just study but to explore and understand.

Wishing you a fulfilling and successful academic journey.

Team,

Oswaal Books

How To Talk To AI

Crafting the Perfect Prompt

oswaal.ai
LEARNING MADE SMARTER

Think of AI as your super-smart study buddy — **the better you ask, the better it answers.** A **prompt** is simply the question or instruction you give to AI. Master this skill, and you'll unlock a powerful tool for learning.

The Basic Prompt Structure

[Role] + [Task] + [Context] + [Format]

Element	What It Means	Example
Role	Tell it who to be	*"Act as a Subject "........" teacher."*
Task	What you want it to do	*"...explain the concept of..."*
Context	Give background details	*"For Class ...., Chapter ...."*
Format	How you want the answer	*"...using bullet points and a diagram."*

Weak Prompt vs. Strong Prompt

☒ **Weak Prompt**
Tell me about this topic "..........".

☑ **Strong Prompt**
"Act as a subject "........" teacher. Explain the topic "........" clearly for school students. Use simple language, include key points, and give one example."

Pro Tips for Better Prompts

Be Specific
Say exactly what you need, not vague requests

Set the Level
Mention your class & board

Ask Examples
Add "with real-life examples" to remember better

Request Format
Ask for tables, flowcharts, or mnemonics

Iterate
Ask follow-ups to simplify or expand

Other Useful AI Tools for Students

ChatGPT
Explains concepts, solves questions, makes notes & projects
chatgpt.com

Google Gemini
Great for diagrams, visuals & numerical explanations
gemini.google.com

Perplexity AI
Research tool with verified info & sources
perplexity.ai

Photomath
Solves Maths problems with step-by-step solutions
photomath.com

Notion AI
Creates notes, organizes syllabus & project structure
notion.so

Quizlet AI
Makes flashcards & quizzes from any chapter
quizlet.com

Canva AI
Makes posters, charts, covers & PPTs easily
canva.com

Otter.ai
Records lectures & converts to written notes
otter.ai

Remember: AI doesn't read minds — it reads prompts. The clearer you are, the more it helps!

Exclusive School Books Suppliers

	KARNATAKA
BANGALORE	Pride Book World, 9448685507, Tanwer Books and Garments, 9916049273, Jipsy, 9620325985
MYSORE	Ragavendra Book Agency, 9591911489
	TELANGANA
HYDERABAD	Shri Sharada store Books & Stationers, 9700768789, Sri Balaji Book Depot, 9676996199, Vishal Book Distributors, 9246333166, Pranavi Publishers, 919948853126, Shri Sharada store Books & Stationers, 9700768789
	TAMIL NADU
CHENNAI	M.K. Stores, 9840030099, Sivaa Book Centre, 9952933315, Kamal Book House, 9841077369
ERODE	Selvam Book Centre, 919843199697
MADURAI	Selvi Book Shoppe, 9345037977, Madurai Book Shop, 9751937519
COIMBATORE CUDDALORE	Indian Book Centre, 9443093053
	MAHARASHTRA
PUNE	Madhusheela Books & Stationers, 7875899892, Pravin Sales, 8888038889
NANDED	Vijay Book Centre, 9822994436
JALNA	Anil Paper Mart, 919422722522
CHHATRAPATI SAMBHAJINAGAR	AARTI BOOK CENTRE, 919422203836
NAGPUR	Sandeep Book Depot, 9371078789
VASAI	Dinvin Books Excellence PVT. LTD. , 9867561128
MUMBAI	New Student Agencies LLP, 8355965098, Ravechi Book Stationery, 9769002371
	ANDHRA PRADESH
VISAKHAPATNAM	VKML Books, 8125168946
NANDYAL	Sathyam Book Store & Fancy, 9052439300
NELLORE	S V S Book Centre, 9347100774
VIJAYAWADA	VKML Books, 9966639957
	HARYANA
ROHTAK	Babu Ram Pradeep Kumar, 9813214692
VIZIANAGARAM	Himamsu Book Distributor, 9493434777
	MADHYA PRADESH
INDORE	Mahesh Book Depot, 9893855543
SHAHDOL	Anjali Book Centre, 917067572992

	JHARKHAND
DEOGHAR	Navyug Sahitya Mandir, 919031917035
BOKARO STEEL CITY	Bokaro Student Friends Pvt. Ltd, 919234628152
	MEGHALAYA
SHILLONG	New Book Centre, 9774088719
	WEST BENGAL
KOLKATA	Oriental Pub. Dist. Pvt. Ltd., 919903879153, United Book House, 9831344622
	UTTAR PRADESH
PRAYAGRAJ	Saraswati book depot, 7706855403
KANPUR	Raj Book, 9235616506
MATHURA	Sapra Traders, 9410076716, Agrawal Book House, 7906527213
GHAZIABAD	Vani Enterprises, 919891276834
	DELHI
DELHI	Mittal Books, 919810133323, Prakash Brothers, 919811179840, R.D. Chawla & Sons, 9810045752, Ameen Global Services, 919716028892, Need Prakashan Pvt Ltd, 9968383261
	GUJARAT
VADODARA	Career Skills Education and Research Foundation, 8469149288
BHARUCH	J.D. Agency, 9099944480
	KERALA
ERNAKULAM	Novel House School Supplies, 8792342807
	ASSAM
GUWAHATI	Central Book Agency, 9954707165
SILCHER	New Book Stall, 919435712617
JORHAT	Bajrang stationery, 9706978968
	RAJASTHAN
ANUPGARH	City Pride Departmental Store, 919414095677
BARMER	Dev Indra Enterprises, 7073282106
	MANIPUR
IMPHAL	Global Agencies, 917641814494
	PUNJAB
TARN TARAN	Sital Di Hatti, 919988206890
KHAMMAM	Sri Nivasa Book Stall, 919948247838
	CHHATTISGARH
RAIPUR	Central Book House, 9406016308

Our Distributors

	ANDHRA PRADESH
VISAKHAPA-THAM	Sri Rajeshwari Book Link, 9848036014,
VIJAYAWADA	Sree Vidya Book Depot, 9491830839
	ANDAMAN & NICOBAR ISLAND
PORTBLAIR	Krishna Book Centre, 9474205570
	ARUNACHAL PRADESH
NAHARLAGUN	New Pothi Ghar, 8731832947
	ASSAM
SILCHAR	Book Emporium, 9675972993, 6000763186, New Book Stall, 9435712617
GUWAHATI	Kayaan Enterprises, (0361) 2630443,
	BIHAR
PATNA	Nova Publisher & Distributors, (0612) 2666404, Gyan Ganga Limited, 9304826651, Rishu Pustak Bhandar, 8294576789, Sri Durga Pustak Mandir, 9334477386, Vikas Book Depot, 919504780402, Bokaro Student Friends Pvt. Ltd, 7277931285
BIHAR SHARIF	Good Books , 8210685462
MUZAFFARPUR	Pustak Bhandar, 7870834225
	CHATTISGARH
AMBIKAPUR	M.P Department Stores, 9425254264
BOKARO	Bokaro Student Friends Pvt. Ltd, Bokaro, 7277931285
DURG	Bhagwati Bhawani Book Depot, 0788-2327620, 9827473100
RAIPUR	Gupta Pustak Mandir, 7974220323,
BILASPUR	Pustak Bhawan, 9300667909
	DELHI
DELHI	Mittal Books, (011) 23288887, 9899037390, A One Books, New Delhi, 8800497047, Batheja Super Store, 9871833924, 9811182352, Zombozone, 9871274082, LDS Marketing, 9811182352/9999353491, R.D. Chawla & Sons, 9810045752, Janta Book Depot, 9313046321, Bokaro Student Friends Pvt. Ltd, 7004074900

	GUJARAT
AHMEDABAD	Patel Book Agencies, 9898184248, 9824386112, 9825900335, Shalibhadra Stationers, 9904477855
VAPI	Goutam Book Sellers, 9081790813
VADODARA	Shree ji Book Depot, 9824649375, Nilesh Book Centre. 9924458748, Umakant Book Sellers & Stationer, 6359396370
AHMEDNAGAR	Hira Stationers, 9970150300
	HARYANA
ROHTAK	Swami Kitab Ghar, 9355611088, Babu Ram Pradeep Kumar, 9813214692
GURGAON	Book Care Centre Venture, 9654564783
REWARI	Repro Books Ltd, 8657315914, Annu book depot, 9053246268
	JHARKHAND
BOKARO	Bokaro Student Friends Pvt. Ltd. (0654) 2233094, 7360021503, Bharati Bhawan Agencies, 06542-265302, 9431740797
HAZARIBAGH	Khandelwal Book Depot, 9708607489
DEOGHAR	Navyug Sahitya Mandir, 9031917035
RANCHI	Pustak Mandir, 9431115138, Agarwal Book Depot, 9334869210, Jayshree Book House, 8434430311, Bokaro Student Friends Pvt. Ltd, 7360021508
DHANBAD	Bokaro Student Friends Pvt. Ltd, 6202834756
	KARNATAKA
HUBLI	Renuka Book Distributor, (0836) 2244124, Vidyamandir Book Distributors, 9980773976
BANGLORE	Krishna book house, 9739847334, Sapna Book House Pvt. Ltd., 9980513242, Sree Sai Ram Book Traders, 9738881088
	MADHYA PRADESH
INDORE	Pustak Bhawan, 8982150100, Bhaiya Store, 9425318103, S.P. & Publication, 7000025933
GWALIOR	Agarwal Book Depot, 9425116210
JABALPUR	Vinay Pustak Sadan, 8962362667, Anand Books and Stationers, 9425323508, Akash Book Distributor, 8989111444, Bharat Book House, 9826541542
KATNI	Shri Mahavir Agency, 9425363412

24/01/26

Our Distributors

MAHARASHTRA

AMRAVATI	Delta Pen House, 9890350073
PUNE	Vikas Book House, 9921331187, Pravin Sales, 9890683475, New Saraswati Granth Bhandar, 9422323859 Sai Book Collection, 9623224343 Yash Agencies, 9850956542
MUMBAI	New Student Agencies, 7045065799, Shivam Books & Stationery, 8619805332
KOLHAPUR	Jai Book Co. 9404671543
NAGPUR	Laxmi Pustakalay and Stationers, (0712) 2727354, Vijay Book Depot, 9860122094 Renuka Book Distributor, 9765406133, Novelty Book Depot, 9657690220, Shree Mahalaxmi Pustakalaya, 7507099360
DHULE	Navjeevan Book Stall, 7020525561
YAVATMAL	Shri Ganesh Pustkalaya, 9423131275
NASHIK	Vishal Book Centre, Nashik - 8208249434
VASAI	Prime Book Centre, Vasai, 9890293662

ODISHA

CUTTACK	A. K. Mishra Agencies, 9437025991, 9437081319
BHUBANESHWAR	M/s Pragnya, 8847888616, 9437943777, Padmalaya, 9437026922,
KEONJHAR	Students Corner, 7008435418
KORAPUT	Ambica Book Centre, 7008585008

PUNJAB

AMBALA	Bharat Book Depot, 7988455354
PATIALA	Goel Sons, 9463619978, Adarsh Enterprises, 9814347613
JALANDHAR	Cheap Book Store, 9872223458, 9878258592, City Book Shop, 9417440753, Subhash Book Depot, 9876453625, Gaurav Book world, 9478821183
LUDHIANA	Amit Book Depot, 9815807871, Bhatia Book Centre, 9815277131, Gupta Brothers, 9888200206
CHANDIGARH	Mohindra Book Depot, 9814920226
BATHINDA	Goyal Sons , 9464478362, Bhagwati Book Depot, 9463120564

RAJASTHAN

AJMER	Laxmi General Store, Ajmer, 0145- 2428942 9460652197
KOTA	Raj Traders, 9309232829
BHILWARA	Nakoda Book Depot, (01482) 243653, 9214983594,
JAIPUR	Saraswati Book House, (0141) 2610823, 9829811155, Goyal Book Distt., 9460983939, 9414782130
JODHPUR	Kitab Mahal, 9460957875

TRIPURA

AGARTALA	Books Corner, 8794894165, 8984657146

TAMIL NADU

COIMBATORE	Majestic Book House, 9791966665
CHENNAI	M.R. Book Store (044) 25364596, Kalaimagal Store, (044) 5544072, 9940619404, Vijaya Stores, 9381037417, Bookmark It-Books & Stat. Store, 7305151653, M.K. Stores, 9840030099, Tiger Books Pvt. Ltd., 9710447000,
MADURAI	Selvi Book Shoppe, 9843057435

KERALA

ERNAKULAM	Academic Book House, (0484) 2376613, H & C Store, 9864196344
KOTTAYAM	Asad Book Centre, (0481) 2566992
CALICUT	Aman Book Stall, (0495) 2721282,
KOZHIKODE	T.B.S. Publishers Distributors, 7559822223

TELANGANA

HYDERABAD	Sri Balaji Book Depot, (040) 27613300, 9866355473 Vishal Book Distributors, 9246333166

UTTARAKHAND

DEHRADUN	Inder Book Agencies, 9634045280 Brothers Pustak Bhandar, 9897833882

UTTAR PRADESH

AGRA	Sparsh Book Agency, 9412257817, Sanjay Publication, 8126699922 Arti book centre, 8630128856, Om Pustak Mandir, (0562) 2464014, 9319117771 Panchsheel Books, 9412257962, 9412257961 Manav Book World, 9760316933
MATHURA	Sapra Traders, 9410076716
PRAYAGRAJ	Mehrotra Book Agency, (0532) 2266865, 9415636890
AZAMGARH	Sasta Sahitya Bhandar, 9450029674
ALIGARH	K.B.C.L. Agarwal, 9897124960,
NAJIBABAD	Gupta News Agency, 8868932500
KANPUR	Radha News Agency, 8957247427, Raj Book Dist., 9235616506, H K Book Distributors, 9506033137/9935146730
GORAKHPUR	Vidyarthi Sahitya Bhandar, 6394026706
LUCKNOW	Om Book Depot, 7705871398, Azad Book Depot Pvt. Ltd., 7317000250, Ashirwad Book Depot, 9235501197, Book.com, 7458922755, Universal Books, 9450302161, Sheetla Book Agency, 9235832418, Vidyarthi Kendra Publisher & Distributor Pvt Ltd, 9554967415, Tripathi Book House, 9415425943, Navyug Book Agencies, 8073564410, Pustak Vatika, 7905317119
MEERUT	Ideal Book Depot, (0121) 4059252, 9837066307
NOIDA	Goyal Books Overseas Pvt.Ltd., 1204655555, 9873387003
PRAYAGRAJ	Kanhaiya Pustak Bhawan, 9415317109
RENUKOOT	Om Stationers, 7007326732
VARANASI	Bokaro Student Friends Pvt. Ltd , 9798050654

WEST BENGAL

KOLKATA	Oriental Publishers & Distributor (033) 40628367, Katha 'O' Kahini, (033) 22196313, 22419071, Saha Book House, (033), 22193671, 9333416484, United Book House, 9831344622, Bijay Pustak Bhandar, 8961260603,
NORTH DINAJPUR	Sarkar Book Suppliers, 9830949359
COOCH BEHAR	S.B. Book Distributor, Cooch Behar, 9002670771
KHARAGPUR	Subhani Book Store, 9046891334
SINGRAULI	Ambedkar Book Depot, 9826115292
KANPUR	Lamba Book Stall, 9839024277
KARNAL	Chopra Book Store, 8950322681

24/01/26

SOLUTIONS

CHAPTER 1

Solution

A homogeneous mixture of two or more pure substances is known as a solution. There are two constituents in the solution, i.e., solute which is present in lesser amount (e.g., sugar, salt, etc.) and solvent which is present in larger amount in solution (e.g., water, milk, etc.).

If the constituents of the solution are two, it is called binary, if three then ternary, if four then quaternary and so on.

Note: *Solvent determines the physical state of the solution.*

Types of Solutions

- Any state of matter (solid, liquid or gas) can act both as a solvent and solute during the formation of a solution. Therefore, depending upon the physical states of solute and solvent, we can have following nine different types of solutions:

S. No.	Types of Solution	Solute	Solvent	Examples
1.	Solid – Solid	Solid	Solid	Alloys like brass, bronze, etc.
2.	Solid – Liquid	Solid	Liquid	Solution of sugar, salt, urea, etc., in water.
3.	Solid – Gas	Solid	Gas	Sublimation of substances like iodine, camphor, etc., into air, dust or smoke particles in air.
4.	Liquid – Solid	Liquid	Solid	Hydrated salts, mercury in amalgamated zinc, etc.
5.	Liquid – Liquid	Liquid	Liquid	Alcohol in water, benzene in toluene.
6.	Liquid – Gas	Liquid	Gas	Aerosol, water vapour in air.
7.	Gas – Solid	Gas	Solid	Hydrogen adsorbed in Palladium.
8.	Gas – Liquid	Gas	Liquid	Aerated drinks.
9.	Gas – Gas	Gas	Gas	Mixture of gases, etc.

Aqueous solution: A solution containing water as a solvent is known as aqueous solution. For example, sugar solution.

Non-aqueous solution: A solution containing solvent other than water is known as non-aqueous solution. For example, iodine dissolved in alcohol.

Saturated solution: A solution in which no more solute can be dissolved at the same temperature is known as saturated solution.

Unsaturated solution: A solution in which more amount of solute can be dissolved at the same temperature is known as unsaturated solution.

Solubility

Solubility can be defined as the maximum amount of solute that can be dissolved in 100 g of solvent to form a saturated solution at a given temperature.

Causes of Solubility:

(i) Inter-ionic attraction in the solute molecules: Molecules are stabilised in the lattice due to electrostatic forces and the energy released is known as lattice energy.

(ii) Inter-molecular attraction between solvent molecules.

(iii) **Solvation:** It denotes the force of attraction between solute and solvent molecules.

(iv) Temperature.

- **Factors affecting Solubility:**

  (i) **Nature of Solute and Solvent:** "Like dissolves like", *i.e.*, polar solvents like water and ammonia can dissolve polar solutes or ionic solutes while non-polar solvents can dissolve non-polar organic solutes.

  (ii) **Temperature:** Solubility increases with increase in temperature. It increases for endothermic reaction while it decreases for exothermic reaction.

  (iii) **Pressure:** The solubility of solid in liquid is not affected significantly by pressure because solids and liquids cannot be compressed.

  (iv) **Hydration Energy:** It is the amount of energy released when 1 mol of ions gets hydrated. It is an exothermic process.

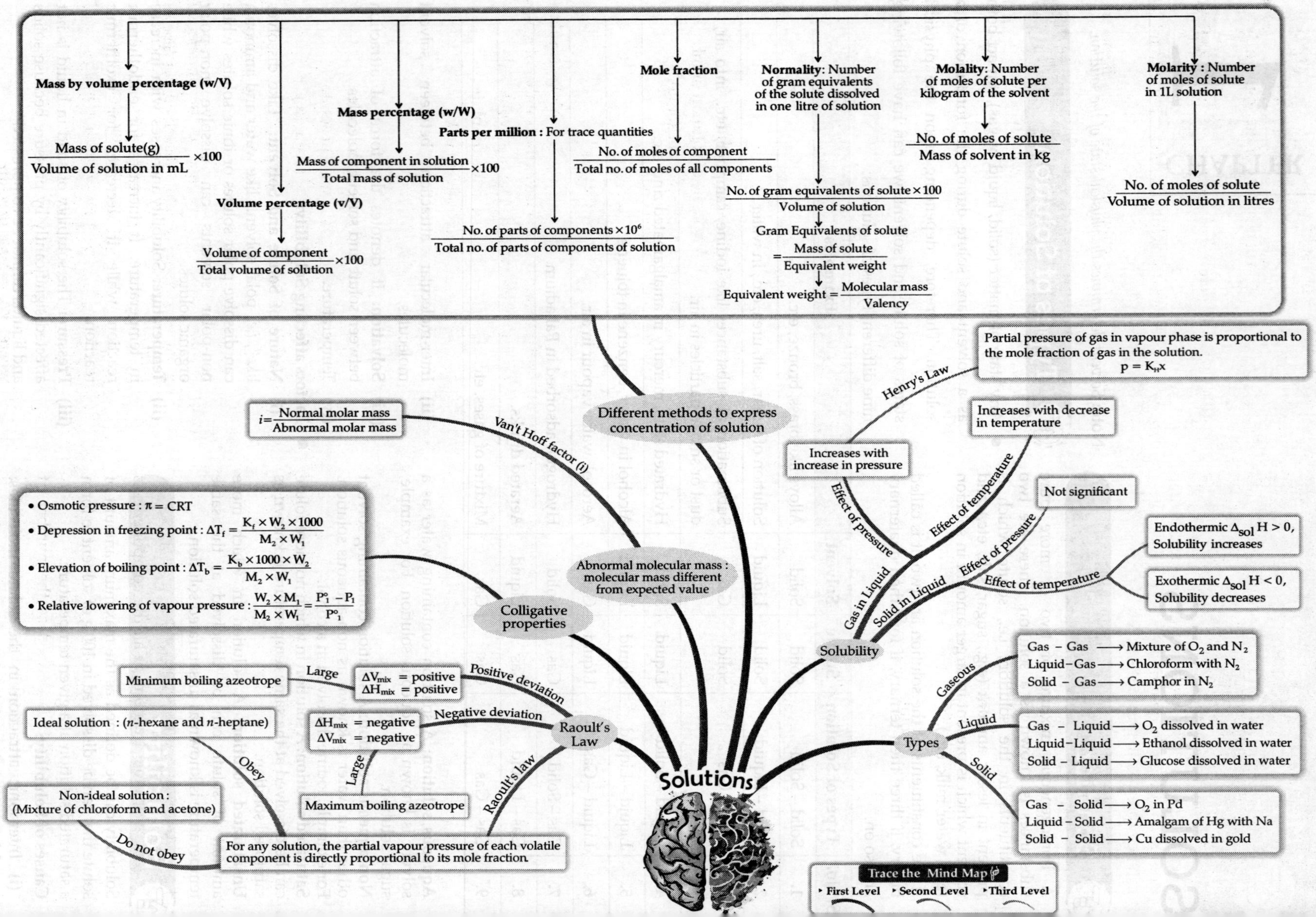
Solutions
Different methods to express concentration of solution
Mass by volume percentage (w/V)
Mass of solute(g) / Volume of solution in mL × 100
Mass percentage (w/W)
Mass of component in solution / Total mass of solution × 100
Volume percentage (v/V)
Volume of component / Total volume of solution × 100
Parts per million : For trace quantities
No. of parts of components × 10^6 / Total no. of parts of components of solution
Mole fraction
No. of moles of component / Total no. of moles of all components
Normality: Number of gram equivalents of the solute dissolved in one litre of solution
No. of gram equivalents of solute × 100 / Volume of solution
Gram Equivalents of solute = Mass of solute / Equivalent weight
Equivalent weight = Molecular mass / Valency
Molality: Number of moles of solute per kilogram of the solvent
No. of moles of solute / Mass of solvent in kg
Molarity : Number of moles of solute in 1L solution
No. of moles of solute / Volume of solution in litres
Henry's Law
Partial pressure of gas in vapour phase is proportional to the mole fraction of gas in the solution.
p = K_H x
Increases with decrease in temperature
Increases with increase in pressure
Effect of pressure
Effect of temperature
Gas in Liquid
Solid in Liquid
Not significant
Endothermic Δ_sol H > 0, Solubility increases
Exothermic Δ_sol H < 0, Solubility decreases
Solubility
Types
Gaseous
Liquid
Solid
Gas – Gas ⟶ Mixture of O2 and N2
Liquid – Gas ⟶ Chloroform with N2
Solid – Gas ⟶ Camphor in N2
Gas – Liquid ⟶ O2 dissolved in water
Liquid – Liquid ⟶ Ethanol dissolved in water
Solid – Liquid ⟶ Glucose dissolved in water
Gas – Solid ⟶ O2 in Pd
Liquid – Solid ⟶ Amalgam of Hg with Na
Solid – Solid ⟶ Cu dissolved in gold
Van't Hoff factor (i)
i = Normal molar mass / Abnormal molar mass
Abnormal molecular mass : molecular mass different from expected value
Colligative properties
• Osmotic pressure : π = CRT
• Depression in freezing point : ΔTf = Kf × W2 × 1000 / M2 × W1
• Elevation of boiling point : ΔTb = Kb × 1000 × W2 / M2 × W1
• Relative lowering of vapour pressure : W2 × M1 / M2 × W1 = P°1 – P1 / P°1
Raoult's Law
Positive deviation
ΔVmix = positive
ΔHmix = positive
Large
Minimum boiling azeotrope
Negative deviation
ΔHmix = negative
ΔVmix = negative
Large
Maximum boiling azeotrope
Raoult's law
For any solution, the partial vapour pressure of each volatile component is directly proportional to its mole fraction.
Obey
Ideal solution : (n-hexane and n-heptane)
Do not obey
Non-ideal solution : (Mixture of chloroform and acetone)
Trace the Mind Map
First Level
Second Level
Third Level

Methods of Expressing Concentration of a Solution

- The concentration of a solution is the amount of solute present in the given quantity of solute or solvent. It can be expressed in any of the following types:

(i) Mass percentage $\left(\frac{w}{W}\right)$: It is the amount of solute in grams dissolved per 100 g of solution.

$$\text{Mass\% of a solute} = \frac{\text{Mass of solute in the solution}}{\text{Total mass of the solution}} \times 100$$

(ii) Volume percentage $\left(\frac{v}{V}\right)$: It is defined the as volume of a solute dissolved per 100 mL of solution.

Volume% of a solute

$$= \frac{\text{Volume of solute}}{\text{Total volume of the solution}} \times 100$$

(iii) Mass by volume percentage $\left(\frac{w}{v}\right)$: It is defined as the mass of solute dissolved per 100 mL of solution. It is commonly used in medicine and pharmacy.

Mass by volume % of solute

$$= \frac{\text{Mass of solute}}{\text{Volume of solution}} \times 100$$

(iv) Parts per million ***(ppm)***: It can be defined as the parts of a component per million (10^6) parts of the solution. It is used to express the concentration of a solute present in trace quantities.

$$ppm\text{ (A)} = \frac{\text{Number of the parts of the component (A)}}{\text{Total number of parts of all the components of the solution}} \times 10^6$$

Parts per million can be expressed in three ways:

(a) Mass to mass

$$ppm\text{ (mass to mass)} = \frac{\text{Mass of a component}}{\text{Total mass of solution}} \times 10^6$$

(b) Volume to volume

ppm (volume to volume)

$$= \frac{\text{Volume of a component}}{\text{Total volume of solution}} \times 10^6$$

(c) Mass to volume

ppm (mass to volume)

$$= \frac{\text{Mass of a component}}{\text{Volume of solution}} \times 10^6$$

(v) Mole Fraction: It is the ratio of number of moles of a particular component to the total number of moles of all the components. e.g., mole fraction of component A.

$$\chi_A = \frac{n_A}{n_A + n_B},$$

where n_A is the number of moles of component 'A' and n_B is the number of moles of component 'B'.

Similarly,

$$\chi_B = \frac{n_B}{n_A + n_B}$$

Sum of mole fractions of all the components is always one.

$$\chi_A + \chi_B = 1$$

(vi) Molarity (M): It is defined as the number of moles of solute dissolved per litre (or one cubic decimetre) of solution.

$$\text{Molarity} = \frac{\text{Number of moles of solute}}{\text{Volume of solution in litres}}$$

$$M = \frac{W_B \times 1000}{M_B \times V}$$

where, W_B = Weight of solute

V = Volume of solution in mL

M_B = Molar mass of solute.

Unit is mol L^{-1} or M (molar).

And $\frac{\text{Weight of solute }(W_B)}{\text{Molar mass of solute }(M_B)}$ = Moles of solute

(vii) Molality (m): It is defined as the number of moles of solute per 1000 g or 1 kg of solvent.

$$\text{Molality} = \frac{\text{Number of moles of solute}}{\text{Mass of solvent in kg}}$$

$$m = \frac{W_B \times 1000}{M_B \times W}$$

where, W_B = Weight of the solute

M_B = Molar mass of solute

W = Mass of solvent in g

Unit is mol kg^{-1} or molal (*m*).

Molality and mole fraction do not change with change in temperature.

(viii) Normality (N): It is defined as the number of gram equivalents of solute dissolved per litre of solution.

$$\text{Normality} = \frac{\text{Number of gram equivalent of solute}}{\text{Volume of solution in litre}}$$

$$N = \frac{W_B \times 1000}{E_B \times V}$$

where, W_B = Mass of solute

E_B = Equivalent weight of solute

V = Volume of solution in mL

Relationship between Molarity (M) and Molality (m)

Relationship between Molarity (M) and Molality (m):

$$\frac{1}{m} = \frac{d}{M} - \frac{M_B}{1000}$$

where, m = Molality of solution

M = Molarity of solution

M_B = Molar mass of solute

d = Density of solution in g mL^{-1}

- **Relationship between Mole fraction of solute (χ_B) and Molality (m):**

$$m = \frac{\chi_B \times 1000}{(1-\chi_B)\times M_A}$$

where χ_B is mole fraction of solute, m is molality and M_A is molar mass of solvent.

Henry's Law

- The relationship between pressure and solubility is guided by Henry's Law. According to this law, 'The mass of a gas dissolved in given volume of the liquid at a constant temperature depends upon the pressure applied."

It can also be stated as the partial pressure of the gas (p) in vapour phase is proportional to the mole fraction of the gas (χ) in the solution.

$$p = K_H\chi,$$

where K_H = Henry's constant.

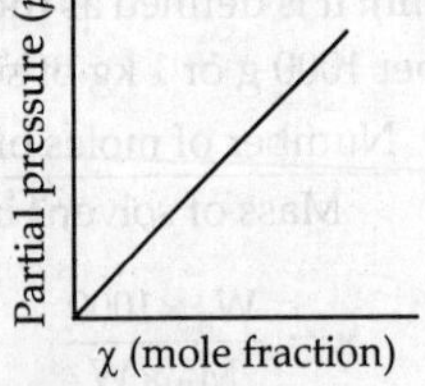

Fig. 1: The slope of the line is the Henry's constant, K_H

- **Applications of Henry's law:**
  - **(i)** To increase the solubility of CO_2 in soda water and soft drinks, the bottle is sealed under high pressure.
  - **(ii)** To avoid the toxic effects of high concentration of nitrogen in blood, the tanks used by scuba divers are filled with air diluted with Helium (11.7%), Nitrogen (56.2%) and Oxygen (32.1%).
  - **(iii)** At high altitudes, low blood oxygen causes climber to become weak and make them unable to think clearly, which are symptoms of a condition known as *anoxia*.
- **Limitations of Henry's law:** This law is applicable only when:
  - **(i)** The pressure of gas is not too high, and temperature is not too low.
  - **(ii)** The gas should not undergo any chemical change.
  - **(iii)** The gas should not undergo association or dissociation in the solution.

Mnemonics

Concept: Henry's Law

Mnemonics: Reserve Personal Secretary

Interpretations: Relation between pressure and solubility of gas.

The relationship between pressure and solubility is guided by Henry's Law. According to this law, "The mass of a gas dissolved in a given volume of the liquid at a constant temperature depends upon the pressure applied."

- Vapour pressure is the pressure exerted by vapour over a liquid at equilibrium state at constar temperature.
- Vapour pressure depends on the following factors:
  - **(i)** Nature of the liquid.
  - **(ii) Temperature:** Vapour pressure of a liqui increases with increase in temperature.

Raoult's Law

Scan to know more about this topic

Raoult"s law

Raoult's law for a solution of volatile liquids: It states that for a solution of volatile liquids, the partial vapour pressure of each component of the solution is directly proportional to its mole fraction in solution.

Suppose, a solution is prepared by mixing two volatile liquids A and B. Let χ_A and χ_B respectively, be their mole fractions and let p and p_B be their partial vapour pressures respectively, i the solution at a particular temperature.

If $p^0{}_A$ and $p^0{}_B$ are their vapour pressures in the pure stat respectively, then according to Raoult's law:

$$p_A = p^0{}_A\,\chi_A$$

$$p_B = p^0{}_B\,\chi_B$$

Considering Dalton's law of partial pressure,

$$p_{total} = p_A + p_B$$

Substituting values of p_A and p_B,

$$p_{total} = \chi_A\, p^0{}_A + \chi_B\, p^0{}_B$$

$$= (1-\chi_B)\, p^0{}_A + \chi_B\, p^0{}_B$$

$$= p^0{}_A + (p^0{}_B - p^0{}_A)\chi_B$$

The composition of the vapour phase in equilibrium wit the solution can be determined from the partial pressur of the two components. If χ_A and χ_B are the mole fraction of components A and B respectively, in the vapour phase then,

$$p_A = \chi_A p_{total}$$

and $$p_B = \chi_B p_{total}$$

In general, $$p_i = \chi_i\, p_{total}$$

- **Raoult's law as a special case of Henry's law** According to Raoult's law, the vapour pressure c volatile component (A) in a given solution is given as

$$p_A = p^0{}_A\,\chi_A$$

According to Henry's law, in the solution of a gas in liquid, the gaseous component is normally so volatil that it exists as a gas and solubility depends upon Henry's law to which:

$$p_A = K_H \chi_A$$

On comparing both the expressions p^0_A is equal to K_H.

- **Raoult's law for non-volatile solute:** For a solution containing non-volatile solute present in a volatile solvent, Raoult's law may be stated as the relative lowering of vapour pressure for a solution is equal to the mole fraction of solute.

$$\chi_B = \frac{p^0_A - p_A}{p^0_A},$$

where, χ_B = Mole fraction of solute,

$p^0_A - p_A$ = Lowering of vapour pressure.

Ideal and Non-ideal Solutions

Ideal solution: A solution is called an ideal solution if it obeys Raoult's law over a wide range of concentration at a specific temperature.

(i) Raoult's law is obeyed, $p_A = p^0_A \chi_A$, $p_B = p^0_B \chi_B$

(ii) $\Delta_{mix}H = 0$,

(iii) $\Delta_{mix}V = 0$,

(iv) The force of attraction between A-A and B-B is nearly equal to A-B.

Some examples of ideal solutions are:

(i) *n*-hexane and *n*-heptane,

(ii) Ethyl bromide and ethyl chloride,

(iii) Benzene and toluene,

(iv) Chlorobenzene and bromobenzene.

Non-ideal solution: A solution which does not obey Raoult's law for all the concentrations is called a non-ideal solution.

(i) Raoult's law is not obeyed, i.e., $p_A \neq p^0_A \chi_A$ and $p_B \neq p^0_B \chi_B$

(ii) $\Delta_{mix}H \neq 0$,

(iii) $\Delta_{mix}V \neq 0$,

(iv) The force of attraction between A-A and B-B is not equal to A-B.

Some examples of non-ideal solutions are: (i) Water and ethanol (ii) Chloroform and acetone (iii) Ethanol and cyclohexane.

A non-ideal solution can show either positive or negative deviation from Raoult's law.

Positive deviation from Raoult's law: In this type of deviation, A-B interactions are weaker than the interactions between A-A or B-B and leads to increase in vapour pressure.

Some examples are: (i) Water and ethanol, (ii) Chloroform and water, (iii) Ethanol and CCl_4, (iv) Methanol and chloroform, (v) Benzene and methanol, (vi) Acetic acid and toluene.

Negative deviation from Raoult's law: In this type of deviation in non-ideal solutions, the intermolecular attractive forces between A-A and B-B are weaker than those between A-B and leads to decrease in vapour pressure.

Some examples are: (i) Chloroform and acetone, (ii) Chloroform and methyl acetate, (iii) H_2O and HCl, (iv) H_2O and HNO_3, (v) Acetic acid and pyridine, (vi) Chloroform and benzene.

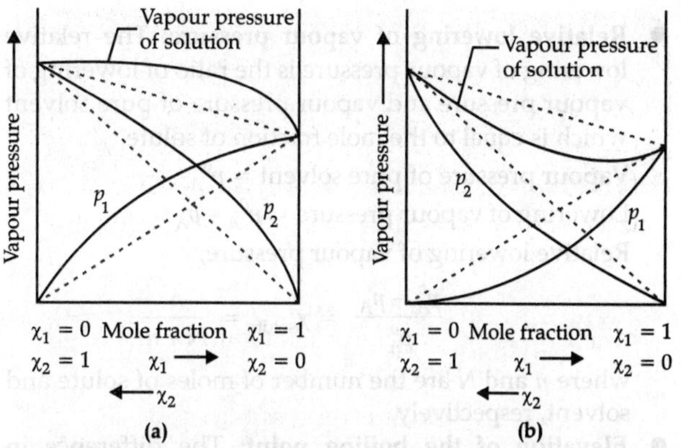

Fig. 2: The vapour pressures of two component systems as a function of composition: (a) A solution that shows positive deviation from Raoult's law, and (b) A solution that shows negative deviation from Raoult's law.

- **Azeotropes:** Liquid mixtures which distil over without change in composition are called constant boiling mixtures or azeotropes or azeotropic mixtures.
- **Minimum boiling azeotropes:** Non-ideal solutions showing large positive deviation from Raoult's law form minimum boiling azeotropes at a specific composition, e.g., water and benzene, chloroform and methanol.
- **Maximum boiling azeotropes:** Non-ideal solutions showing large negative deviation from Raoult's law form maximum boiling azeotropes which boil at temperature higher than the boiling points of its components, e.g., mixture of HNO_3 and H_2O.

Mnemonics

Concept: Raoult's law for Non-volatile Solute

Mnemonics: R.L. is Very Poor Student = Most Failure Student

Interpretations: Relative lowering of vapour pressure for a solution is equal to the mole fraction of solute.

Concept: Ideal solution

Mnemonics: ISRaeL

Interpretations: Ideal solution obeys Raoult's law

Concept: Non-Ideal solution

Mnemonics: Nano Scale Device Research Laboratory

Interpretations: Non-Ideal solution does not obey Raoult's law

Colligative Properties

Certain properties of solutions depend only on the number of particles of the solute (molecules or ions) and do not depend on the nature of solute, such properties are called colligative properties. These are:

(i) Relative lowering of vapour pressure.

(ii) Depression of freezing point.

(iii) Elevation of boiling point.

(iv) Osmotic pressure of the solution.

- **Relative lowering of vapour pressure:** The relative lowering of vapour pressure is the ratio of lowering of vapour pressure and vapour pressure of pure solvent which is equal to the mole fraction of solute.

  Vapour pressure of pure solvent = $p^0{}_A$

  Lowering of vapour pressure = $p^0{}_A - p_A$

  Relative lowering of vapour pressure,

$$\frac{p_A^o - p_A}{p_A^o} = \chi_{solute} = \frac{n}{N+n}$$

  where n and N are the number of moles of solute and solvent, respectively.

- **Elevation of the boiling point:** The difference in boiling point of solution and pure solvent is called elevation of the boiling point.

  Boiling point of pure solvent = $T^0{}_b$

  Boiling point of solution = T_b

  Increase in boiling point $\Delta T_b = T_b - T^0{}_b$ is known as the elevation of boiling point for dilute solution.

$$\Delta T_b \propto \frac{\Delta p}{p^\circ} = x_B$$

$$\Delta T_b = K_b m$$

$$\Delta T_b = \frac{K_b \times 1000 \times w_2}{M_2 \times w_1}$$

  Where, w_2 = weight of solute in g

  M_2 = Molar mass of solute

  w_1 = weight of solvent in g

  $\Delta T_b = K_b m$

  K_b = Boiling point elevation constant or molal elevation constant or **Ebullioscopic constant.**

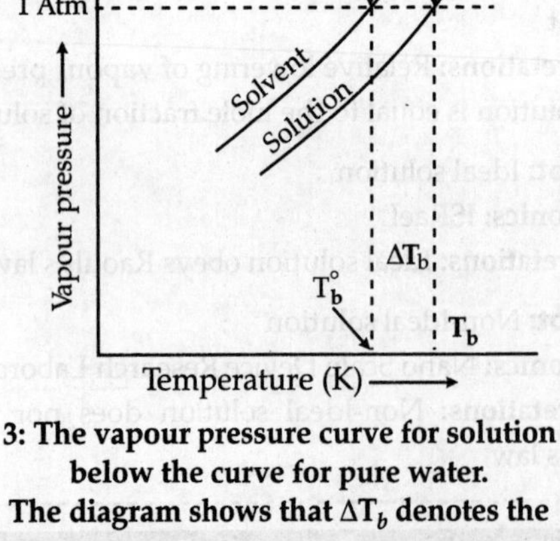

Fig. 3: The vapour pressure curve for solution lies below the curve for pure water. The diagram shows that ΔT_b denotes the elevation of boiling point of a solvent in solution.

- **Depression of freezing point:** According to Raoult's law, when a non-volatile solid is added to the solvent, its vapour pressure decreases and it would become equal to that of solid solvent at lower temperature. Thus, the difference in the freezing point of pure solvent and that of the solution is known as depression in freezing point.

  The freezing point of pure solvent = $T^o{}_f$

  The freezing point when non-volatile solute is dissolved in it = T_f (Freezing point of solution)

  The decrease in freezing point $\Delta T_f = T^o{}_f - T_f$ is know as depression in freezing point.

  For dilute solution,

$$\Delta T_f = K_f \chi_B$$

$$\Delta T_f = K_f \chi_B$$

$$\Delta T_f = K_f \frac{W_B}{M_B} \times \frac{M_A}{W_A}$$

$$\Delta T_f = K_f m.$$

  We know,

  (i) $\frac{W_B \times 1000}{M_B \times W_A}$ = molality

  (ii) $\Delta T_f = K_f m$

  K_f = Freezing point depression constant or mola depression constant or **Cryoscopic constant.**

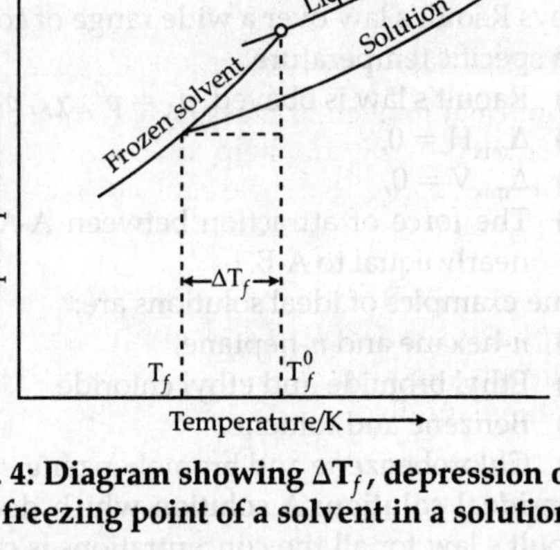

Fig. 4: Diagram showing ΔT_f, depression of the freezing point of a solvent in a solution.

- **Osmosis:** The process in which there is net flow o solvent to the solution by a semi-permeable membran is called osmosis.

  Osmotic pressure: The extra pressure that is applied t stop the flow of solvent to solution across a semi-permeabl membrane is called osmotic pressure of the solution.

  For a dilute solution, osmotic pressure is proportiona to the molar concentration (C) of the solution at given temperature T.

  Thus π = CRT as π is the osmotic pressure and R is th gas constant.

$$\pi = \frac{n}{V} RT$$

  (n is the number of moles, V is the volume of solutior

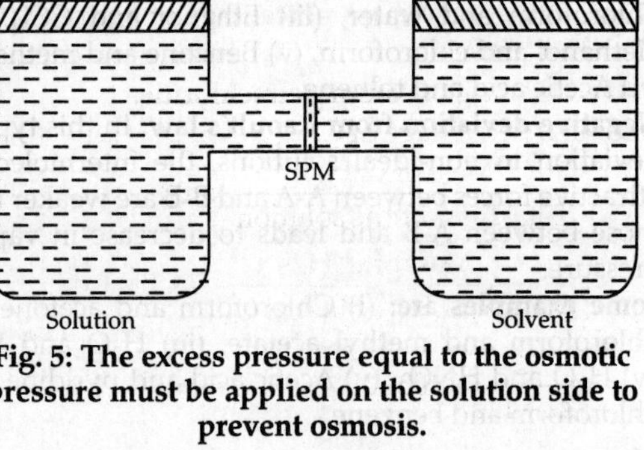

Fig. 5: The excess pressure equal to the osmotic pressure must be applied on the solution side to prevent osmosis.

- **Reverse Osmosis:** The direction of osmosis can be reversed, if a pressure larger than the osmotic pressure is applied to the solution side. Now the pure solvent flows out of the solution through the semi-permeable membrane. This phenomenon is called reverse osmosis.

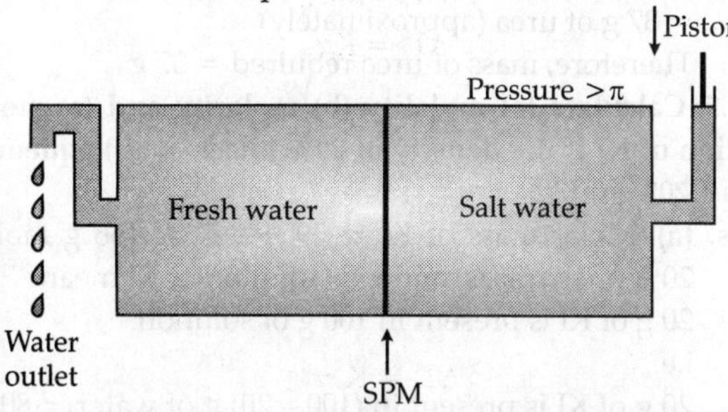

Fig. 6: Reverse osmosis occurs when a pressure larger than the osmotic pressure is applied to the solution.

Abnormal and Molecular Masses

- **Abnormal molecular mass**: When the molecular mass calculated with the help of colligative property is different from theoretical molecular mass, it is called abnormal molecular mass
- **Van't Hoff factor:** The ratio of the observed (experimental) value of a colligative property to the normal (calculated) value of the same property is called as van't Hoff factor.

Mathematically,

$$i = \frac{\text{Observed (experimental) value of a colligative property}}{\text{Normal (calculated) value of the same colligative property}}$$

Or, $$i = \frac{\Delta_{obs}}{\Delta_{cal}},$$

where Δ_{obs} and Δ_{cal} respectively, represent the observed and calculated value of a colligative property.

Thus,

(i) For lowering of vapour pressure, $i = \frac{(\Delta p)_{obs}}{(\Delta p)_{cal}}$;

(ii) For elevation of boiling point, $i = \frac{(\Delta T_b)_{obs}}{(\Delta T_b)_{cal}}$;

(iii) For depression of freezing point, $i = \frac{(\Delta T_f)_{obs}}{(\Delta T_f)_{cal}}$;

(iv) For osmotic pressure, $i = \frac{\pi_{obs}}{\pi_{cal}}$;

Since a colligative property is proportional to number of particles of solute:

$$i = \frac{\text{Normal molecular mass}}{\text{Observed molecular mass}}$$

Normal molecular mass = $i \times$ calculated molecular mass

$$i = \frac{\text{Total number of moles of particle after association/dissociation}}{\text{Total number of moles of particle before association/dissociation}}$$

- **Hypertonic solution:** A solution is called hypertonic, if its concentration is higher than that of the solution separating it by a semi-permeable membrane.
- **Hypotonic solution:** A solution is called hypotonic, if its concentration is lower than that of the solution separating it by a semi-permeable membrane.
- **Isotonic solution:** Two solutions are called isotonic, if they exert the same osmotic pressure at a given temperature. Isotonic solutions have same molar concentration. When such solutions are separated by semi-permeable membrane, no osmosis occurs between them.

Mnemonics

Mnemonics: RLVP_DFP_EBP_OP

Interpretations:

— Relative lowering of Vapour pressure
— Depression in Freezing Point
— Elevation of Boiling Point
— Osmotic Pressure

NCERT CORNER

Intext Questions

Page - 5

Q. 1.1. Calculate the mass percentage of benzene (C_6H_6) and carbon tetrachloride (CCl_4) if 22 g of benzene is dissolved in 122 g of carbon tetrachloride.

Ans. Mass percentage of C_6H_6

$$= \frac{\text{Mass of } C_6H_6}{\text{Total mass of the solution}} \times 100$$

$$= \frac{\text{Mass of } C_6H_6}{\text{Mass of } C_6H_6 + \text{Mass of } CCl_4} \times 100$$

$$= \frac{22}{22+122} \times 100$$

$$= 15.28\ \%$$

Mass percentage of CCl_4

$$= \frac{\text{Mass of } CCl_4}{\text{Total mass of the solution}} \times 100$$

$$= \frac{\text{Mass of } CCl_4}{\text{Mass of } C_6H_6 + \text{Mass of } CCl_4} \times 100$$

$$= \frac{122}{22+122} \times 100$$

$$= 84.72\ \%$$

Q. 1.2. Calculate the mole fraction of benzene in solution containing 30% by mass in carbon tetrachloride.

Ans. Let the total mass of the solution be 100 g and the mass of benzene be 30 g.

$\therefore$ Mass of carbon tetrachloride

$= (100 - 30)\text{ g} = 70\text{ g}$

Molar mass of benzene (C_6H_6)

$= (6 \times 12 + 6 \times 1)\text{ g mol}^{-1}$

$= 78\text{ g mol}^{-1}$

$\therefore$ Number of moles of $C_6H_6 = \frac{30}{78}\text{ mol}$

$= 0.3846\text{ mol}$

Molar mass of carbon tetrachloride (CCl_4)

$= 1 \times 12 + 4 \times 35.5 = 154\text{ g mol}^{-1}$

$\therefore$ Number of moles of $CCl_4 = \frac{70}{154}\text{ mol}$

$= 0.4545\text{ mol}$

Thus, the mole fraction of C_6H_6 is given as:

$$\frac{\text{Number of moles of } C_6H_6}{\text{Number of moles of } C_6H_6 + \text{Number of moles of } CCl_4}$$

$= \frac{0.3846}{0.3846 + 0.4545}$

$= 0.458$

Q. 1.3. Calculate the molarity of each of the following solutions: (a) 30 g of $Co(NO_3)_2.6H_2O$ in 4.3 L of solution (b) 30 mL of 0.5 M H_2SO_4 diluted to 500 mL.

Ans. Molarity is given by:

$$\text{Molarity} = \frac{\text{Moles of solute}}{\text{Volume of solution in litre}}$$

(a) Molar mass of

$Co(NO_3)_2.\,6H_2O = 59 + 2(14 + 3 \times 16) + 6 \times 18$

$= 291\text{ g mol}^{-1}$

Therefore, moles of $Co(NO_3)_2 = \frac{30}{291}\text{ mol}$

$= 0.103\text{ mol}$

So, molarity $= \frac{0.103\text{ mol}}{4.3\text{ L}}$

$= 0.023\text{ M}$

(b) Number of moles present in 1000 mL of 0.5 M H_2SO_4

$= 0.5\text{ mol}$

$\therefore$ Number of moles present in 30 mL of 0.5 M

$H_2SO_4 = \frac{0.5 \times 30}{1000}\text{ mol}$

$= 0.015\text{ mol}$

Molarity $= \frac{0.015}{0.5}\text{ L}$

$= 0.03\text{M}$

Q. 1.4. Calculate the mass of urea (NH_2CONH_2) required in making 2.5 kg of 0.25 molal aqueous solution.

Ans. Molar mass of urea (NH_2CONH_2)

$= 2(1 \times 14 + 2 \times 1) + 1 \times 12 + 1 \times 16$

$= 60\text{ g mol}^{-1}$

0.25 molal aqueous solution of urea means:

1000 g of water contains 0.25 mol

$= (0.25 \times 60)$ g of urea

$= 15$ g of urea

i.e., (1000 + 15) g of solution contains 15 g of urea

Hence, 2.5 kg (2500 g) of solution contains

$= \frac{15 \times 2500}{1000 + 15}\text{ g}$

$= 36.95\text{ g}$

$= 37$ g of urea (approximately)

Therefore, mass of urea required $= 37$ g

Q. 1.5. Calculate (a) molality (b) molarity and (c) mole fraction of KI if the density of 20% (mass/mass) aqueous KI is 1.202 g mL^{-1}.

Ans. (a) Molar mass of KI $= 39 + 127 = 166\text{ g mol}^{-1}$

20% (mass/mass) aqueous solution of KI means 20 g of KI is present in 100 g of solution.

i.e.,

20 g of KI is present in (100 – 20) g of water = 80 g of water

Hence, molality of the solution

$= \frac{\text{Moles of KI}}{\text{Mass of water in kg}}$

$= \frac{20}{166 \times 0.08}\text{ m}$

$= 1.506\text{ m}$

$= 1.51$ m (approximately)

(b) It is given that the density of the solution

$= 1.202\text{ g mL}^{-1}$

Therefore, volume of 100 g solution

$= \frac{\text{Mass}}{\text{Density}}$

$= \frac{100\text{ g}}{1.202\text{ g mL}^{-1}}$

$= 83.19\text{ mL}$

$= 83.19 \times 10^{-3}\text{ L}$

Hence, molarity of the solution

$= \frac{20}{166 \times 83.19 \times 10^{-3}}$

$= 1.45\text{ M}$

(c) Moles of KI $= \frac{20}{166} = 0.12\text{ mol}$

Moles of water $= \frac{80}{18} = 4.44\text{ mol}$

Hence, mole fraction of KI

$= \frac{\text{Moles of KI}}{(\text{Moles of KI} + \text{Moles of water})}$

$= \frac{0.12}{(0.12 + 4.44)}$

$= 0.0263.$

Page - 9

Q. 1.6. H_2S, a toxic gas with rotten egg like smell, is used for the qualitative analysis. If the solubility of H_2S in water at STP is 0.195 m, calculate Henry's law constant.

Ans. The solubility of H_2S in water at STP is 0.195 m, i.e 0.195 mol of H_2S is dissolved in 1000 g of water.

Moles of water $= \frac{1000}{18}$

$= 55.56\text{ mol}$

$\therefore$ Moles fraction of H_2S,

$$x = \frac{\text{Moles of } H_2S}{\text{Moles of } H_2S + \text{Moles of water}}$$

$$= \frac{0.195}{0.195 + 55.56}$$

$$x = 0.0035$$

At STP, pressure (P) = 0.987 bar

According to Henry's law:

$$p = K_H x$$

$$k_H = \frac{p}{x} = \frac{0.987}{0.0035} \text{ bar}$$

$$= 282 \text{ bar}$$

Q. 1.7. Henry's law constant for CO_2 in water is 1.67 × 10^8 Pa at 298 K. Calculate the quantity of CO_2 in 500 mL of soda water when packed under 2.5 atm CO_2 pressure at 298 K.

Ans. It is given that:

$$K_H = 1.67 \times 10^8 \text{ Pa}$$

$$p_{CO_2} = 2.5 \text{ atm} = 2.5 \times 1.01325 \times 10^5 \text{ Pa} = 2.533125 \times 10^5 \text{ Pa}$$

According to Henry's law:

$$p_{CO_2} = K_H x$$

$$x = \frac{p_{CO_2}}{K_H} = \frac{2.533125 \times 10^5}{1.67 \times 10^8}$$

$$= 0.00152$$

$$x = \frac{n_{CO_2}}{n_{CO_2} + n_{H_2O}} = \frac{n_{CO_2}}{n_{H_2O}}$$

[Neglect the amount of soda present]

In 500 mL of soda water, the volume of water = 500 mL

We can write: 500 mL of water = 500 g of water

$$= \frac{500}{18} \text{ mol of water}$$

$$= 27.78 \text{ mol of water}$$

Now, $\frac{n_{CO_2}}{n_{H_2O}} = x$

$$\frac{n_{CO_2}}{27.78} = 0.00152$$

$$n_{CO_2} = 0.042 \text{ mol}$$

∴ Quantity of CO_2 in 500 mL of soda water

$$= (0.042 \times 44)\text{g}$$

$$= 1.848 \text{ g}$$

Page - 15

Q. 1.8. The vapour pressure of pure liquids A and B are 450 and 700 mm Hg respectively, at 350 K . Find out the composition of the liquid mixture if total vapour pressure is 600 mm Hg. Also find the composition of the vapour phase.

Ans. It is given that:

$$P^o_A = 450 \text{ mm of Hg}$$

$$P^o_B = 700 \text{ mm of Hg}$$

$$P_{total} = 600 \text{ mm of Hg}$$

$$P_{total} = P^o_A x_A + P^o_B (1 - x_A)$$

$$P_{total} = P^o_A x_A + P^o_B - P^o_B x_A$$

$$P_{total} = (P^o_A - P^o_B) x_A + P^o_B$$

$$\Rightarrow 600 = (450 - 700)\, x_A + 700$$

$$\Rightarrow -100 = -250 x_A$$

From Raoult's law, we have:

$$P_A = P^o_A x_A$$

$$P_B = P^o_B x_B = P^o_B (1 - x_A)$$

$$\Rightarrow x_A = 0.4$$

Hence, $x_B = 1 - x_A = 0.6$

Now, $P_A = P^o_A x_A$

$$= 450 \times 0.4 = 180 \text{ mm of Hg}$$

$$P_B = P^o_B x_B$$

$$= 700 \times 0.6$$

$$= 420 \text{ mm of Hg}$$

Now, in the vapour phase: Mole fraction of liquid A

$$= \frac{P_A}{P_A + P_B}$$

$$= \frac{180}{180 + 420} = \frac{180}{600} = 0.30$$

Mole fraction of liquid B = 1 – 0.30

$$= 0.70$$

Page - 23

Q. 1.9. Vapour pressure of pure water at 298 K is 23.8 mm Hg. 50 g of urea (NH_2CONH_2) is dissolved in 850 g of water. Calculate the vapour pressure of water for this solution and its relative lowering.

Ans. It is given that vapour pressure of pure water,

$$P^o_1 = 23.8 \text{ mm of Hg}$$

Weight of water taken,

$$w_1 = 850 \text{ g}$$

Weight of urea taken,

$$w_2 = 50 \text{ g}$$

Molecular weight of water,

$$M_1 = 18 \text{ g mol}^{-1}$$

Molecular weight of urea,

$$M_2 = 60 \text{ g mol}^{-1}$$

Now, we have to calculate vapour pressure of water in the solution. We take vapour pressure as P_1.

Now, from Raoult's law, we get:

$$\frac{p^o_1 - p_1}{p^o_1} = \frac{n_2}{n_1 + n_2}$$

$$\Rightarrow \frac{p^o_1 - p_1}{p^o_1} = \frac{\frac{w_2}{M_2}}{\frac{w_1}{M_1} + \frac{w_2}{M_2}}$$

$$\frac{23.8 - p_1}{23.8} = \frac{\frac{50}{60}}{\frac{850}{18} + \frac{50}{60}}$$

$$\Rightarrow \frac{23.8 - p_1}{23.8} = \frac{0.83}{47.22 + 0.83}$$

$$\frac{23.8 - p_1}{23.8} = 0.0173$$

$$p_1 = 23.4 \text{ mm of Hg}$$

Hence, the vapour pressure of water in the given solution is 23.4 mm of Hg and its relative lowering is 0.0173.

Q. 1.10. Boiling point of water at 750 mm Hg is 99.63°C. How much sucrose is to be added to 500 g of water such that it boils at 100°C.

Ans. Here, elevation of boiling point,

$$\Delta T_b = (100 + 273) - (99.63 + 273)$$

$$= 0.37 \text{ K}$$

Mass of water,

$$w_1 = 500 \text{ g}$$

$$M_2 = 12 \times 12 + 22 \times 1 + 11 \times 16$$

$$= 342 \text{ g mol}^{-1}$$

Molal elevation constant,

$$K_b = 0.52 \text{ K kg mol}^{-1}$$

As we know that:

$$\Delta T_b = \frac{K_b \times 1000 \times w_2}{M_2 \times w_1}$$

$$\Rightarrow \quad w_2 = \frac{\Delta T_b \times M_2 \times w_1}{K_b \times 1000}$$

$$= \frac{0.37 \times 342 \times 500}{0.52 \times 1000}$$

$$= 121.67 \text{ g (approximately)}$$

Therefore, 121.67 g of sucrose is to be added.

Q. 1.11. Calculate the mass of ascorbic acid (Vitamin C, $C_6H_8O_6$) to be dissolved in 75 g of acetic acid to lower its melting point by 1.5°C.

K_f = 3.9 K kg mol^{-1}.

Ans. Mass of acetic acid, $w_1 = 75$ g

Molar mass of ascorbic acid ($C_6H_8O_6$),

$$M_2 = 6 \times 12 + 8 \times 1 + 6 \times 16$$

$$176 \text{ g mol}^{-1}$$

Lowering of melting point,

$$\Delta T_f = 1.5 \text{ K}$$

We know that:

$$\Delta T_f = \frac{K_f \times w_2 \times 1000}{M_2 \times w_1}$$

$$w_2 = \frac{\Delta T_f \times M_2 \times w_1}{K_f \times 1000}$$

$$= \frac{1.5 \times 176 \times 75}{3.9 \times 1000}$$

$$= 5.08 \text{ g (approximately)}$$

Therefore, 5.08 g of ascorbic acid is needed to be dissolved.

Q. 1.12. Calculate the osmotic pressure in pascals exerted by a solution prepared by dissolving 1.0 g of polymer of molar mass 185,000 in 450 mL of water at 37°C.

Ans. It is given that:

Volume of water, V = 450 mL = 0.45 L

Temperature, T = (37 + 273) K = 310 K

Number of moles of the polymer,

$$n = \frac{1}{185000} \text{ mol}$$

We know that:

Osmotic pressure,

$$\pi = \frac{n}{V} \text{RT}$$

$$= \frac{1}{185000} \text{ mol} \times \frac{1}{0.45 \text{ L}} \times 8.314 \times 10^3 \text{ Pa L K}^{-1} \text{ mol}^{-1} \times 310 \text{ K}$$

$$= 30.96 \text{ Pa}$$

$$= 31 \text{ Pa (approximately)}$$

Exercise Questions

Q. 1. Define the term solution. How many types of solutions are formed? Write briefly about each type with an example. [NCERT Ex. Q. 1.1, Page 27]

Ans. A solution is a homogeneous mixture of two or more than two substances on molecular level. The constituent of the mixture present in a smaller amount is called the solute and the one present in larger amount is called the solvent. Example: Small amount of sugar (solute) dissolved in water (solvent). There are nine types of solutions formed. They are:

S. No.	State of Solute	State of solvent	Examples
1.	Gas	Gas	Air
2.	Gas	Liquid	Oxygen in water
3.	Gas	Solid	H_2 in Palladium
4.	Liquid	Gas	Moisture
5.	Liquid	Liquid	Alcohol in water
6.	Liquid	Solid	Water and sodium carbonate
7.	Solid	Gas	Camphor in N_2 gas
8.	Solid	Liquid	Sugar in water
9.	Solid	Solid	Stainless steel (carbon in Iron)

Out of these nine types of solution, solid in liquid, liquid in liquid and gas in liquid are very common. When the components of the solution are mixed, the resulting solution may be in the solid, liquid or gaseous state. They are:

(i) Gaseous solution: The solution in which the solvent is a gas is called a gaseous solution. In these solutions, the solute may be liquid, solid, or gas. For example, a mixture of oxygen and nitrogen gas is a gaseous solution.

(ii) Liquid solution: The solution in which the solvent is a liquid is known as a liquid solution. The solute in these solutions may be gas, liquid, or solid.

(iii) Solid solution: The solution in which the solvent is a solid is known as a solid solution. The solute in these solutions may be a gas, liquid or solid. For example, a solution of copper in gold is a solid solution.

Q. 2. Give an example of a solid solution in which the solute is a gas. [NCERT Ex. Q. 1.2, Page 27]

Ans. Solution of hydrogen and palladium: In this hydrogen (which is a gas) is solute and palladium is solvent.

Q. 3.Define the following terms: [NCERT Ex. Q. 1.3, Page 27]

(i) Mole fraction (ii) Molality (iii) Molarity (iv) Mass percentage.

Ans.

(i) Mole Fraction: It is defined as the ratio of number of moles of one component to the total number of moles of solute and solvent present in the solution.

Mole fraction

$$= \frac{\text{Number of moles of the component}}{\text{Total number of moles of all components}}$$

It is a denoted by x.

Take it as binary solution, the number of the moles of solute will be n_A and the number of moles of solvent will be n_B, then the mole fraction of the solute in the solution is given as:

$$x_A = \frac{n_A}{n_A + n_B}$$

In the same manner, the mole fraction of the solvent in the solution is given as:

$$x_B = \frac{n_B}{n_A + n_B}$$

(ii) Molality: It is the number of moles of the solute dissolved per kilogram of the solvent. It is denoted by m.

$$\text{Molality} = \frac{\text{mole of solute}}{\text{mass of solvent in kg}}$$

Unit for molality is mol kg^{-1}.

(iii) Molarity: It is the number of moles of the solute dissolved per litre of the solution. It is represented by M.

$$\text{Molality} = \frac{\text{mole of solute}}{\text{volume of solute in litres}}$$

Unit for molarity is mol L^{-1}.

(iv) Mass Percentage: The mass percentage of a component in a given solution is the mass of the component per 100 g of the solution.

Mass percentage of the component

$$= \frac{\text{Mass of the component in the solution}}{\text{Total mass of the solution}} \times 100$$

Q. 4.Concentrated nitric acid used in laboratory work is 68% nitric acid by mass in aqueous solution. What should be the molarity of such a sample of the acid if the density of the solution is 1.504 g mL^{-1}?

[NCERT Ex. Q. 1.4, Page 27]

Ans. Concentrated nitric acid used in laboratory work is 68% nitric acid by mass in an aqueous solution. This means that 68 g of nitric acid is dissolved in 100 g of the solution.

Molar mass of nitric acid (HNO_3)

$= 1 \times 1 + 1 \times 14 + 3 \times 16$

$= 63\ \text{g mol}^{-1}$

Then, number of moles of HNO_3

$= \frac{68}{63}$ mol

$= 1.08$ mol

Also density $= 1.504\ \text{g/mL}^{-1}$ (given)

Therefore from the formula, density $= \frac{\text{Mass}}{\text{Volume}}$

Volume of solution $= \frac{100}{1.504} = 66.49$ mL

Therefore molarity of nitric acid

$= \left(\frac{1.08}{66.49}\right) \times 1000 = 16.24$ M

Q. 5.A solution of glucose in water is labelled as 10% w/w, what would be the molality and mole fraction of each component in the solution? If the density of solution is 1.2 g mL^{-1}, then what shall be the molarity of the solution? [NCERT Ex. Q. 1.5, Page 28]

Ans. 10% w/w solution of glucose in water means that 10 g of glucose is present in 100 g of the solution i.e., 10 g of glucose is present in (100 – 10) g = 90 g of water.

Molar mass of glucose ($C_6H_{12}O_6$)

$= (6 \times 12) + (12 \times 1) + (6 \times 16) = 180\ \text{g mol}^{-1}$

The, number of moles of glucose

$= \frac{10}{180}$ mol $= 0.056$ mol

$\therefore$ Molarity of solution $= \frac{0.056}{0.09} = 0.62\ \text{mol L}^{-1}$

Number of moles of water $= \frac{90}{18} = 5$ mol

Mole fraction of glucose $(x_g) = \frac{0.056}{(0.056 + 5)}$

$= 0.011$

And, mole fraction of water $x_w = 1 - x_g$

$= 1 - 0.011$

$= 0.989$

If the density of the solution is 1.2 g mL^{-1}, then the volume of the 100 g solution can be given as:

$= \frac{100\ \text{mL}}{1.2\ \text{g mL}^{-1}}$

$= 83.33$ mL

$= 83.33 \times 10^{-3}$ L

$\therefore$ Molarity of the solution $= \frac{0.056}{83.33 \times 10^{-3}}$

$= 0.67$ M

Q. 6.How many mL of 0.1 M HCl are required to react completely with 1 g mixture of Na_2CO_3 and $NaHCO_3$ containing equimolar amounts of both?

[NCERT Ex. Q. 1.6, Page 28]

Ans. Let the amount of Na_2CO_3 be x and that of $NaHCO_3$ be $1 - x$

Firstly, calculating molar mass of Na_2CO_3 and $NaHCO_3$, we get

$Na_2CO_3 = (2 \times 23) + (1 \times 12) + (3 \times 16) = 106\ \text{g mol}^{-1}$

$NaHCO_3 = (23 \times 1) + 1 + 12 + (3 \times 16) = 84\ \text{g mol}^{-1}$

Now, moles of $Na_2CO_3 = \frac{x}{106}$

and moles of $NaHCO_3 = \frac{1-x}{84}$

Now according to question, number of moles of Na_2CO_3 = number of moles of $NaHCO_3$

Therefore $\frac{x}{106} = \frac{1-x}{84}$

$84x = 106 - 106x$

$84x + 106x = 106$

$190x = 106$

$x = \frac{106}{190} = 0.558$

$\therefore$ moles of $Na_2CO_3 = \frac{0.558}{106} = 0.00526$

And moles of $NaHCO_3 = \frac{1 - 0.558}{84}$

Now, HCl reacts with Na_2CO_3 and $NaHCO_3$ as follows:

$$Na_2CO_3 + 2HCl \rightarrow 2NaCl + H_2O + CO_2$$

$$NaHCO_3 + HCl \rightarrow NaCl + H_2O + CO_2$$

From the above reactions, 1 mol of Na_2CO_3 will react with 2 mol of HCl.

$\therefore$ 0.00526 mol of Na_2CO_3 will react with 2 × 0.00526 mol of HCl and similarly 0.00526 mol of $NaHCO_3$ will react with 0.00526 mol of HCl

Total moles of HCl required to react with mixture of $NaHCO_3$ and Na_2CO_3

$= 2 \times 0.00526 + 0.00526 = 0.01578$ mol

Also, according to question

0.1 mol of 0.1 M HCl is present in 1000 mL

or 0.01578 mol of 0.1 M HCl is present in

$$\left(\frac{1000}{0.1}\right) \times 0.01578 = 158 \text{ mL}$$

Hence, 158 mL of 0.1 M of HCl is required to react completely with 1 g mixture of Na_2CO_3 and $NaHCO_3$ containing equimolar amounts of both.

Q. 7.A solution is obtained by mixing 300 g of 25% solution and 400 g of 40% solution by mass. Calculate the mass percentage of the resulting solution.

[NCERT Ex. Q. 1.7, Page 28]

Ans. Total amount of solute present in the mixture is given by,

$$300 \times \frac{25}{100} + 400 \times \frac{40}{100}$$

$= 75 + 160$

$= 235$ g

Total amount of solution = 300 + 400 = 700 g

Hence, mass percentage (w/W) of the solute in the resulting solution $= \frac{235}{700} \times 100\%$

$= 33.57\ \%$

Mass percentage *(w/W)* of the solvent in the reuslting solution,

$= (100 - 33.57)\%$

$= 66.43\ \%$

Q. 8.An antifreeze solution is prepared from 222.6 g of ethylene glycol ($C_2H_6O_2$) and 200 g of water. Calculate the molality of the solution. If the density of the solution is 1.072 g mL^{-1}, then what shall be the molarity of the solution? [NCERT Ex. Q. 1.8, Page 28]

Ans. Calculation of Molality:

Mass of ethylene glycol = 222.6 g (Given)

Molar mass of ethylene glycol $[C_2H_4(OH)_2]$

$= 2 \times 12 + 6 \times 1 + 2 \times 16$

$= 62$ g mol^{-1}

Therefore moles of ethylene glycol

$$= \frac{222.6 \text{ g}}{62 \text{ g mol}^{-1}}$$

$= 3.59$ mol

Mass of water = 200 g (Given)

Therefore molality of the solution is

$$= \frac{\text{moles of ethylene glycol}}{\text{mass of water}} \times 1000$$

$$= \left(\frac{3.59}{200}\right) \times 1000$$

$= 17.95$ mol kg^{-1}

Calculation of Molarity:

Moles of ethylene glycol = 3.59 mol (already calculated)

Total Mass of solution = 200 + 222.6

= 422.6 g

$$\text{Volume of solution} = \frac{\text{Mass}}{\text{Density}}$$

$$= \frac{422.6}{1.072}$$

= 394.22 mL

now molarity of the solution

$$= \frac{\text{moles of ethylen glycol}}{\text{volume of solution}} \times 1000$$

$$= \frac{3.59}{394.22} \times 1000$$

= 9.11 M

Q. 9.A sample of drinking water was found to be severely contaminated with chloroform ($CHCl_3$) supposed to be a carcinogen. The level of contamination was 15 *ppm* (by mass):

(i) express this in percent by mass.

(ii) determine the molality of chloroform in the water sample. [NCERT Ex. Q. 1.9, Page 28]

Ans.

(i) 15 *ppm* means: 15 parts per million (10^6) of the solutions

$$\text{So, percent by mass} = \frac{\text{mass of chloroform}}{\text{total mass}} \times 100$$

$$= \left(\frac{15}{10^6}\right) \times 100$$

$= 1.5 \times 10^{-3}\ \%$

(ii) Molarity: Mass of chloroform = 15 g

Molar mass of chloroform ($CHCl_3$)

$= (1 \times 12) + (1 \times 1) + (3 \times 35.5)$

$= 119.5$ g mol^{-1}

$$\text{Moles of chloroform} = \frac{15}{119.5} = 0.1255 \text{ mol}$$

Mass of water = 10^6

$$\text{Therefore molality} = \frac{\text{moles of chloroform}}{\text{mass of water}} \times 1000$$

$$= \left(\frac{0.1255}{10^6}\right) \times 1000$$

$= 1.255 \times 10^{-4}$ mol kg^{-1}

Q. 10. What role does the molecular interaction play in a solution of alcohol and water?

[NCERT Ex. Q. 1.10, Page 28]

Ans. The lower members of alcohols are highly soluble in water, but the solubility decreases with increase in the molecular weight. The solubility of lower alcohols in water is due to formation of hydrogen bonds (Hydrogen bonding) between alcohols and water molecules.

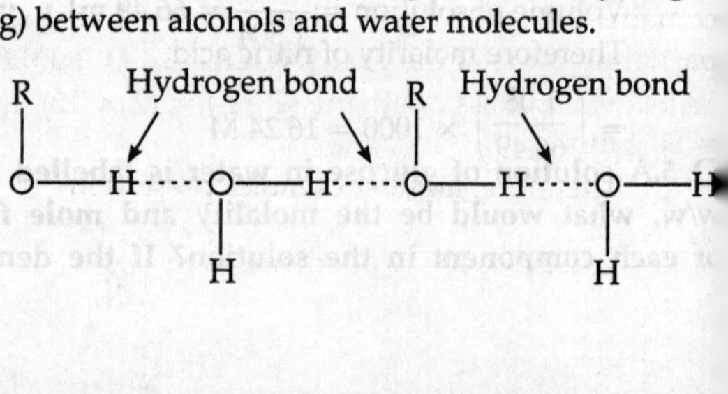

However, as the size of alcohol molecule increases, the alkyl groups become larger and prevents the formation of hydrogen bonds with water, hence the solubility goes on decreasing with increase in the length of carbon chain. Also, the interaction between the molecules of alcohol and water is weaker than alcohol–alcohol and water–water interactions. As a result, when alcohol and water are mixed, the intermolecular interactions become weaker, and the molecules can easily escape. This increases the vapour pressure of the solution, which in turn lowers the boiling point of the resulting solution.

Q. 11. Why do gases always tend to be less soluble in liquids as the temperature is raised? **[NCERT Ex. Q. 1.11, Page 28]**

Ans. When a gas is dissolved in liquid, it generates a small quantity of heat, so we can say that dissolution of gas in a liquid is an exothermic reaction.

Gas + liquid → solution + heat

According to Le Chatelier's principle, when we increase the temperature in an exothermic reaction, the reaction will move to backward direction that means solution will dissociate and will give gas. Hence, with the rise of temperature gas will become less soluble.

Q. 12. State Henry's law and mention some important applications. **[NCERT Ex. Q. 1.12, Page 28]**

Ans. Henry's law: The solubility of a gas in a liquid at a particular temperature is directly proportional to the pressure of the gas in equilibrium with the liquid at that temperature.

OR

The partial pressure of a gas in vapour phase is proportional to the mole fraction of the gas (x) in the solution. $p = K_H x$ where K_H is Henry's law constant.

Applications of Henry's law:

(i) In order to increase the solubility of CO_2 gas in soft drinks and soda water, the bottles are normally sealed under high pressure. Increase in pressure increases the solubility of a gas in a solvent according to Henry's Law. If the bottle is opened by removing the stopper or seal, the pressure on the surface of the gas will suddenly decrease. This will cause a decrease in the solubility of the gas in the liquid, i.e., water. As a result, it will rush out of the bottle producing a hissing noise or with a fizz.

(ii) As pointed above, oxygen to be used by deep sea divers is generally diluted with helium in order to reduce or minimise the painful effects during decompression.

(iii) As the partial pressure of oxygen in air is high, in lungs it combines with haemoglobin to form oxyhaemoglobin. In tissues, the partial pressure of oxygen is comparatively low. Therefore, oxyhaemoglobin releases oxygen in order to carry out cellular activities

Q. 13. The partial pressure of ethane over a solution containing 6.56 × 10⁻³ g of ethane is 1 bar. If the solution contains 5.00 × 10⁻² g of ethane, then what shall be the partial pressure of the gas? [NCERT Ex. Q. 1.13, Page 28]

Ans. Molar mass of ethane (C_2H_6) = (2 × 12) + (6 × 1) = 30 g mol⁻¹

Therefore, number of moles present in

$$6.56 \times 10^{-3} \text{ g of ethane} = \frac{6.56\times10^{-3}}{30}$$

$$= 2.187 \times 10^{-4} \text{ mol}$$

Let the number of moles of the solvent be x.

According to Henry's law,

$$p = K_H x$$

$$1 = K_H \frac{2.187\times10^{-4}}{2.187\times10^{-3}+x}$$

$$= K_H \frac{2.187\times10^{-4}}{x}$$

$$K_H = \frac{x}{2.187\times10^{-4}} \text{ bar}$$

(Since $x >> 2.187 \times 10^{-4}$)

Number of moles present in 5.00×10^{-2} g of ethane

$$= \frac{5.00\times10^{-2}}{30} \text{ mol}$$

$$= 1.67 \times 10^{-3} \text{ mol}$$

According to Henry's law,

$$p = K_H x$$

$$= \frac{x}{2.187\times10^{-3}} \times \frac{1.67\times10^{-3}}{(1.67\times10^{-3})+x}$$

$$= \frac{x}{2.187\times10^{-3}} \times \frac{1.67\times10^{-3}}{x}$$

(Since, $x >> 1.67 \times 10^{-3}$)

$$= 0.764 \text{ bar}$$

Therefore, partial pressure of the gas shall be 0.764 bar.

Q. 14. What is meant by positive and negative deviations from Raoult's law and how is the sign of $\Delta_{mix}H$ related to positive and negative deviations from Raoult's law? **[NCERT Ex. Q. 1.14, Page 28]**

Ans. According to Raoult's law, the partial vapour pressure of each volatile component in any solution is directly proportional to its mole fraction. The solutions which obey Raoult's law over the entire range of concentration are known as ideal solutions. The solutions that do not obey Raoult's law (non-ideal solutions) have vapour pressures either higher or lower than that predicted by Raoult's law (given in figure).

If the vapour pressure is higher, then the solution is said to exhibit positive deviation, and if it is lower, then the solution is said to exhibit negative deviation from Raoult's law.

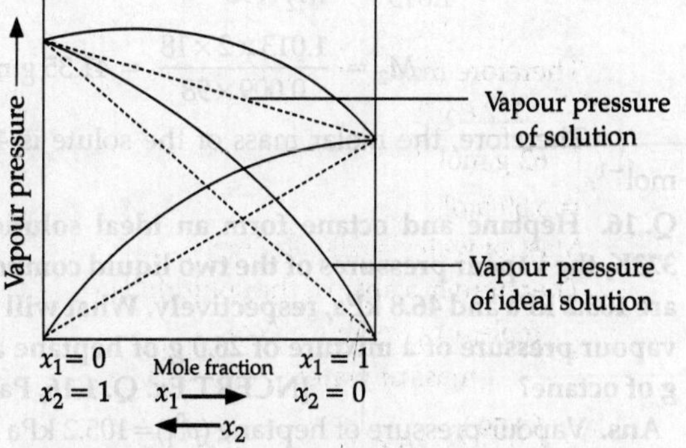

Vapour pressure of a two-component solution showing positive deviation from Raoult's law

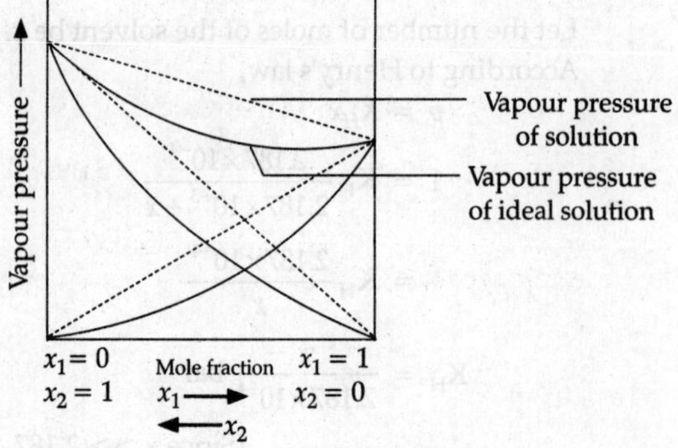

Vapour pressure of a two-component solution showing negative deviation from Raoult's law

In the case of an ideal solution, the enthalpy of the mixing of the pure components for forming the solution is zero.

$$\Delta_{sol}H = 0$$

In the case of solutions showing positive deviations, absorption of heat takes place.

So, $\Delta_{sol}H$ = Positive

In the case of solutions showing negative deviations, evolution of heat takes place.

So, $\Delta_{sol}H$ = Negative

Q. 15. An aqueous solution of 2% non-volatile solute exerts a pressure of 1.004 bar at the normal boiling point of the solvent. What is the molar mass of the solute?

[NCERT Ex. Q. 1.15, Page 28]

Ans. Here,

Vapour pressure of the solution at normal boiling point (p_1) = 1.004 bar

Vapour pressure of pure water at normal boiling point p^0_1 = 1.013 bar

Mass of solute, (w_2) = 2 g

Mass of solvent (water), (w_1) = 98 g

Molar mass of solvent (water), (M_1) = 18 g mol^{-1}

According to Raoult's law,

$$\frac{p_1^0 - p_1}{p_1^0} = \frac{w_2 \times M_1}{M_2 \times w_1}$$

$$\frac{1.013 - 1.004}{1.013} = \frac{2 \times 18}{M_2 \times 98}$$

$$\frac{0.009}{1.013} = \frac{2 \times 18}{M_2 \times 98}$$

$$M_2 = \frac{1.013 \times 2 \times 18}{0.009 \times 98} = 41.35 \text{ g mol}^{-1}$$

Therefore, the molar mass of the solute is 41.35 g mol^{-1}.

Q. 16. Heptane and octane form an ideal solution. At 373K, the vapour pressures of the two liquid components are 105.2 kPa and 46.8 kPa, respectively. What will be the vapour pressure of a mixture of 26.0 g of heptane and 35 g of octane? [NCERT Ex. Q. 1.16, Page 28]

Ans. Vapour pressure of heptane (p^0_1) = 105.2 kPa

Vapour pressure of octane (p^0_2) = 46.8 kPa

We know that,

Molar mass of heptane (C_7H_{16}) = 7 × 12 + 16 × 1

= 100 g mol^{-1}

∴ Number of moles of heptane = $\frac{26}{100}$ mol

= 0.26 mol

Molar mass of octane (C_8H_{18}) = 8 × 12 + 18 × 1

= 114 g mol^{-1}

∴ number of moles of octane = $\frac{35}{114}$ mol

= 0.31 mol

Mole fraction of heptane, $x_1 = \frac{0.26}{0.26 + 0.31}$

= 0.456

And, mole fraction of octane, x_2 = 1 – 0.456

= 0.544

Now, partial pressure of heptane,

$$p_1 = x_1 p_1^0$$

= 0.456 × 105.2

= 47.97 kP$_a$

Partial pressure of octane,

$$p_2 = x_2 p_2^0$$

= 0.544 × 46.8

= 25.46 kPa

∴ Vapour pressure of solution,

$$p_{total} = p_1 + p_2$$

= 47.97 + 25.46

= 73.43 kP$_a$

Q. 17. The vapour pressure of water is 12.3 kPa at 300 K. Calculate vapour pressure of 1 molal solution of a non-volatile solute in it. [NCERT Ex. Q. 1.17, Page 28]

Ans. 1 molal solution means 1 mol of the solute is present in 1000 g of the solvent (water). Molar mass of water = 18 g mol^{-1}

Therefore, number of moles present in 1000 g of water = $\frac{1000}{18}$

= 55.56 mol.

Hence, mole fraction of the solute in the solution is

$$x_2 = \frac{1}{1 + 55.56} = 0.0177$$

It is given that,

Vapour pressure of water

$$p_1^0 = 12.3 \text{ kP}_a$$

Applying the relation

$$\frac{p_1^0 - p_1}{p_1^0} = x_2$$

$$\Rightarrow \frac{12.3 - p_1}{12.3} = 0.0177$$

$$\Rightarrow p_1 = 12.0823$$

= 12.08 kP$_a$ (approximately)

Therefore, the vapour pressure of the solution is 12.08 kP$_a$.

Q. 18. Calculate the mass of a non-volatile solute (molar mass 40 g mol^{-1}) which should be dissolved in 114 g octane to reduce its vapour pressure to 80%.

[NCERT Ex. Q. 1.18, Page 28]

Ans. Let the vapour pressure of pure octane be p^0_1

Then, the vapour pressure of the octane after dissolving the non-volatile solute is

$$\frac{80}{100}p_1^0 = 0.8p_1^0$$

Molar mass of solute, $M_2 = 40$ g mol^{-1}

Mass of octane, $w_1 = 114$ g

Molar mass of octane, (C_8H_{18}),

$$M_1 = (8 \times 12) + (18 \times 1) = 114 \text{ g mol}^{-1}$$

Applying the relation,

$$\frac{p_1^0 - p_1}{p_1^0} = \frac{w_2 \times M_1}{M_2 \times w_1}$$

$$\frac{p_1^0 - 0.8p_1^0}{p_1^0} = \frac{w_2 \times 114}{40 \times 114}$$

$$\frac{0.2p_1^0}{p_1^0} = \frac{w_2}{40}$$

$$0.2 = \frac{w_2}{40}$$

So, $w_2 = 8$ g

Therefore, the required mass of the solute is 8 g.

Q. 19. A solution containing 30 g of non-volatile solute exactly in 90 g of water has a vapour pressure of 2.8 kPa at 298K. Further, 18 g of water is then added to the solution and the new vapour pressure becomes 2.9 kPa at 298K. Calculate:

(i) molar mass of the solute

(ii) vapour pressure of water at 298 *K*.

[NCERT Ex. Q. 1.19, Page 28]

Ans. (a) Let, the molar mass of the solute be M g mol^{-1}

Now, the no. of moles of solvent (water),

$$n_1 = \frac{90}{18} = 5 \text{ mol}$$

And, the no. of moles of solute,

$$n_2 = \frac{30}{M} \text{ mol}$$

$$p_1 = 2.8 \text{ kP}_a$$

Applying the relation:

$$\frac{p_1^0 - p_1}{p_1^0} = \frac{n_2}{n_1 + n_2}$$

$$\frac{p_1^0 - 2.8}{p_1^0} = \frac{\frac{30}{M}}{5 + \frac{30}{M}}$$

$$1 - \frac{2.8}{p_1^0} = \frac{\frac{30}{M}}{\frac{5M+30}{M}}$$

$$1 - \frac{2.8}{p_1^0} = \frac{30}{5M+30}$$

$$\frac{2.8}{p_1^0} = 1 - \frac{30}{5M+30}$$

$$\frac{2.8}{p_1^0} = \frac{5M+30-30}{5M+30}$$

$$\frac{2.8}{p_1^0} = \frac{5M}{5M+30}$$

$$\frac{p_1^0}{2.8} = \frac{5M+30}{5M} \quad \text{(i)}$$

After the addition of 18 g of water:

$$n_1 = \frac{90+18}{18} = 6 \text{ mol}$$

$$p_1 = 2.9 \text{ kP}_a \text{ (given)}$$

Again, applying the relation:

$$\frac{p_1^0 - p_1}{p_1^0} = \frac{n_2}{n_1 + n_2}$$

$$\frac{p_1^0 - 2.9}{p_1^0} = \frac{\frac{30}{M}}{6 + \frac{30}{M}}$$

$$1 - \frac{2.9}{p_1^0} = \frac{\frac{30}{M}}{\frac{6M+30}{M}}$$

$$1 - \frac{2.9}{p_1^0} = \frac{30}{6M+30}$$

$$\frac{2.9}{p_1^0} = 1 - \frac{30}{6M+30}$$

$$\frac{2.9}{p_1^0} = \frac{6M+30-30}{6M+30}$$

$$\frac{2.9}{p_1^0} = \frac{6M}{6M+30}$$

$$\frac{p_1^0}{2.9} = \frac{6M+30}{6M} \quad \text{...(ii)}$$

Dividing equation (i) by (ii), we have:

$$\frac{2.9}{2.8} = \frac{\frac{5M+30}{5M}}{\frac{6M+30}{6M}}$$

$$\frac{2.9}{2.8} \times \frac{6M+30}{6} = \frac{5M+30}{5}$$

$$2.9 \times 5 \times (6M + 30) = 2.8 \times 6 \times (5M + 30)$$

$$87 M + 435 = 84 M + 504$$

$$3 M = 69$$

$$M = 23u$$

Therefore, the molar mass of the solute is 23 g mol^{-1}.

(b) Putting the value of 'M' in equation (i), we have:

$$\frac{p_1^0}{2.8} = \frac{5 \times 23 + 30}{5 \times 23}$$

$$\Rightarrow \frac{p_1^0}{2.8} = \frac{145}{115}$$

$$\Rightarrow p_1^0 = 3.53$$

Hence, the vapour pressure of water at 298 K is 3.53 kP$_a$

Q. 20. A 5% solution (by mass) of cane sugar in water has freezing point of 271 K. Calculate the freezing point of 5% glucose in water if freezing point of pure water is 273.15 K. [NCERT Ex. Q. 1.20, Page 28]

Ans. Here, $\Delta T_f = (273.15 - 271)$ K = 2.15 K

Molar mass of sugar ($C_{12}H_{22}O_{11}$) = (12 × 12) + (22 × 1) + (11 × 16)

$$= 342 \text{ g mol}^{-1}$$

5% solution (by mass) of cane sugar in water means 5 g of cane sugar is present in (100 – 5) g = 95 g of water.

$$\text{Now, number of moles of cane sugar} = \frac{5}{342} \text{ mol}$$

$$= 0.0146 \text{ mol}$$

Therefore, molality of the solution,

$$m = \frac{0.0146}{0.095}$$

$$= 0.1537 \text{ mol kg}^{-1}$$

Applying the relation,

$$\Delta T_f = K_f \times m$$

$$\Rightarrow K_f = \frac{\varnothing T_f}{m}$$

$$= \frac{2.15}{0.1537}$$

$$= 13.99 \text{ K kg mol}^{-1}$$

Molar of glucose ($C_6H_{12}O_6$)

$$= (6 \times 12) + (12 \times 1) + (6 \times 16)$$

$$= 180 \text{ g mol}^{-1}$$

5% glucose in water means 5 g of glucose is present in (100 – 5) g = 95 g of water.

$$\therefore \text{Number of moles of glucose} = \frac{5}{180} \text{ mol}$$

$$= 0.0278 \text{ mol}$$

Therefore, molality of the solution,

$$m = \frac{0.0278}{0.095}$$

$$= 0.2926 \text{ mol kg}^{-1}$$

Applying the relation,

$$\Delta T_f = K_f \times m$$

$$= 13.99 \text{ K kg mol}^{-1} \times 0.2926 \text{ mol kg}^{-1}$$

$$= 4.09 \text{ K (approximately)}$$

Hence, the freezing point of 5% glucose solution is (273.15 – 4.09) K= 269.06 K.

Q. 21. Two elements A and B form compounds having formula AB_2 and AB_4. When dissolved in 20g of benzene (C_6H_6), 1 g of AB_2 lowers the freezing point by 2.3K whereas 1.0 g of AB_4 lowers it by 1.3 K. The molar depression constant for benzene is 5.1 K kg mol^{-1}. Calculate atomic masses of A and B.

[NCERT Ex. Q. 1.21, Page 28]

Ans. We know that,

$$M_2 = \frac{1000 \times w_2 \times K_f}{\Delta T_f \times w_1}$$

$$M_{AB_2} = \frac{1000 \times 1 \times 5.1}{2.3 \times 20}$$

$$= 110.87 \text{ g mol}^{-1}$$

$$\text{Then,} \quad M_{AB_4} = \frac{1000 \times 1 \times 5.1}{1.3 \times 20}$$

$$= 196.15 \text{ g mol}^{-1}$$

Now, we have the molar masses of AB_2 and AB_4 as 110.87 g mol^{-1} and 196.15 g mol^{-1}, respectively.

Let the atomic masses of A and B be x and y respectively. Now, we can write:

$$x + 2y = 110.87$$

$$x + 4y = 196.15$$

Subtracting equation (i) from (ii), we have

$$2y = 85.28$$

$$\Rightarrow y = 42.64$$

Putting the value of 'y' in equation (1), we have

$$x + (2 \times 42.64) = 110.87$$

$$\Rightarrow x = 25.59$$

Hence, the atomic masses of A and B are 25.59 u and 42.64 u, respectively.

Q. 22. At 300K, 36 g of glucose present in a litre of its solution has an osmotic pressure of 4.98 bar. If the osmotic pressure of the solution is 1.52 bars at the same temperature, what would be its concentration?

[NCERT Ex. Q. 1.22, Page 29]

Ans. Here,

$$T = 300 \text{ K}, p = 1.52 \text{ bar}$$

$$R = 0.083 \text{ bar L K}^{-1} \text{ mol}^{-1}$$

Applying the relation, $\pi = CRT$

$$\Rightarrow C = \frac{\pi}{RT}$$

$$= \frac{1.52}{0.083 \times 300}$$

$$= 0.061 \text{ mol}$$

Since the volume of the solution is 1 L, the concentration of the solution would be 0.061 M.

Q. 23. Suggest the most important type of intermolecular attractive interaction in the following pairs.

(i) *n*-hexane and *n*-octane

(ii) I_2 and CCl_4

(iii) $NaClO_4$ and water

(iv) methanol and acetone

(v) acetonitrile (CH_3CN) and acetone (C_3H_6O).

[NCERT Ex. Q. 1.23, Page 29]

Ans.

(a) Van der Waal's forces of attraction.

(b) Van der Waal's forces of attraction.

(c) Ion-dipole interaction.

(d) Dipole-dipole interaction.

(e) Dipole-dipole interaction.

Q. 24. Based on solute-solvent interactions, arrange the following in order of increasing solubility in n-octane and explain. Cyclohexane, KCl, CH_3OH, CH_3CN.

[NCERT Ex. Q. 1.24, Page 29]

Ans. *n*-octane is an organic solvent (liquid). Out of given examples, cyclohexane is the strongest organic solvent, so according to it like dissolves like, cyclohexane is most likely to be dissolved as a solute in *n*-octane. After cyclohexane, CH_3CN will be dissolved completely as a solute in *n*-octane, then CH_3OH and the least soluble will be KCl. Also, since *n*-octane and cyclohexane, both of them belongs to alkane category, their solubility will be maximum.

Therefore, the order of increasing solubility in n-octane is as follows:

KCl < CH_3OH < CH_3CN < Cyclohexane.

Q. 25. Amongst the following compounds, identify which are insoluble, partially soluble and highly soluble in water?

(i) phenol (ii) toluene (iii) formic acid (iv) ethylene glycol (v) chloroform (vi) pentanol.[NCERT Ex. Q. 1.25, Page 29]

Ans. (a) Phenol (C_6H_5OH) has the polar group $-OH$ and non-polar group $-C_6H_5$. Thus, phenol is partially soluble in water.

(b) Toluene ($C_6H_5-CH_3$) has no polar groups. Thus, toluene is insoluble in water.

(c) Formic acid (HCOOH) has the polar group $-OH$ and can form H-bond with water. Thus, formic acid is highly soluble in water.

(d) Ethylene glycol has polar $-OH$ group and can form H$-$bond. Thus, it is highly soluble in water.

(e) Chloroform is insoluble in water.

(f) Pentanol ($C_5H_{11}OH$) has polar $-OH$ group, but it also contains a very bulky nonpolar $-C_5H_{11}$ group. So, pentanol is partially soluble in water.

Q. 26. If the density of some lake water is 1.25 g mL^{-1} and contains 92 g of Na^+ ions per kg of water, calculate the molarity of Na^+ ions in the lake.

[NCERT Ex. Q. 1.26, Page 29]

Ans. Number of moles present in 92 g of Na^+ ions

$$= \frac{92\,g}{23\,g\,mol^{-1}}$$

$$= 4 \text{ mol}$$

Therefore, molality of Na^+ ions in the lake

$$= \frac{4\,mol}{1\,kg}$$

$$= 4 \text{ mol kg}^{-1}$$

Q. 27. If the solubility product of CuS is 6 × 10^{-16}, calculate the maximum molarity of CuS in aqueous solution. [NCERT Ex. Q. 1.27, Page 29]

Ans. Solubility product of CuS, $K_{sp} = 6 \times 10^{-16}$

Let s be the solubility of CuS in mol L^{-1}.

Now,

$$CuS \rightarrow Cu^{2+} + S^{2-}$$

$$K_{sp} = [Cu^{2+}][S^{2-}]$$

$$= s \times s = s^2$$

Then, we have, $s = \sqrt{K_{sp}}$

$$s = \sqrt{6 \times 10^{-16}}$$

$$= 2.45 \times 10^{-8} \text{ mol L}^{-1}$$

Hence, the maximum molarity of CuS in an aqueous solution is 2.45×10^{-8} mol L^{-1}.

Q. 28. Calculate the mass percentage of aspirin ($C_9H_8O_4$) in acetonitrile (CH_3CN) when 6.5 g of $C_9H_8O_4$ is dissolved in 450 g of CH_3CN. [NCERT Ex. Q. 1.28, Page 29]

Ans. 6.5 g of $C_9H_8O_4$ is dissolved in 450 g of CH_3CN.

Then, total mass of the solution = (6.5 + 450) g

= 456.5 g

$$\therefore \text{ mass percentage of } C_9H_8O_4 = \frac{6.5}{456.5} \times 100\%$$

$$= 1.424\ \%$$

Q. 29. Nalorphene ($C_{19}H_{21}NO_3$), similar to morphine, is used to combat withdrawal symptoms in narcotic users. Dose of nalorphene generally given is 1.5 mg. Calculate the mass of 1.5 × 10^{-3} m aqueous solution required for the above dose. [NCERT Ex. Q. 1.29, Page 29]

Ans. The molar mass of nalorphene ($C_{19}H_{21}NO_3$)

(19 × 12) + (21 × 1) + (1 × 14) + (3 × 16) = 311 g mol^{-1}

Moles of nalorphene ($C_{19}H_{21}NO_3$),

$= 1.5 \times 10^{-3}/311 = 4.82 \times 10^{-6}$ mol

$$\text{Now, molality} = \frac{\text{moles of solute}}{\text{mass of solvent}} \times 1000$$

Putting the values in above equation, we get

$$1.5 \times 10^{-3} = \frac{(4.82 \times 10^{-6})}{\text{mass of water}} \times 1000$$

$$\text{Mass of water} = \frac{(4.82 \times 10^{-6} \times 1000)}{1.5 \times 10^{-3}}$$

Hence, mass of water = 3.2 g

Q. 30. Calculate the amount of benzoic acid (C_6H_5COOH) required for preparing 250 mL of 0.15 M solution in methanol. [NCERT Ex. Q. 1.30, Page 29]

Ans. 0.15 M solution of benzoic acid in methanol means, 1000 mL of solution contains 0.15 mol of benzoic acid

Therefore, 250 mL of solution contains

$$= \frac{0.15 \times 250}{1000}$$

mol of benzoic acid = 0.0375 mol of benzoic acid

Molar mass of benzoic acid (C_6H_5COOH)

= (7 × 12) + (6 × 1) + (2 × 16)

= 122 g mol^{-1}

Therefore, required benzoic acid

= 0.0375 mol × 122 g mol^{-1}

= 4.575 g

Q. 31. The depression in freezing point of water observed for the same amount of acetic acid, trichloroacetic acid and trifluoroacetic acid increases in the order given above. Explain briefly. [NCERT Ex. Q. 1.31, Page 29]

Ans.

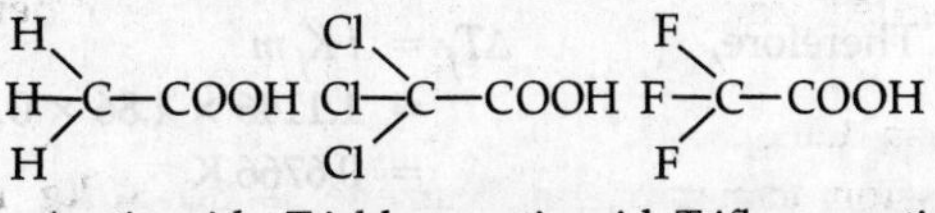

Acetic acid Trichloroacetic acid Trifluoroacetic acid

Among H, Cl, and F, H is least electronegative while F is most electronegative. Then, F can withdraw electrons towards itself more than Cl and H. Thus, trifluoroacetic acid can easily lose H^+ ions, that is, trifluoroacetic acid ionizes to the largest extent. Now, the more ions produced, the greater is the depression of the freezing point. Therefore, the depression in the freezing point increases in the order:

Acetic acid < trichloroacetic acid < trifluoroacetic acid

Q. 32. Calculate the depression in the freezing point of water when 10 g of $CH_3CH_2CHClCOOH$ is added to 250 g of water. $K_a = 1.4 \times 10^{-3}$, $K_f = 1.86$ K kg mol^{-1}.

[NCERT Ex. Q. 1.32, Page 29]

Ans. Molar mass of

$$CH_3CH_2CHClCOOH = 15 + 14 + 13 + 35.5 + 12 + 16 + 16 + 1$$

$$= 122.5 \text{ g mol}^{-1}$$

Therefore, number of moles present in 10 g of

$$CH_3CH_2CHClCOOH = \frac{10}{122.5}$$

$$= 0.0816 \text{ mol}$$

It is given that 10 g of CH_3 CH_2 CHClCOOH is added to 250 g of water

∴ Molality of the solution

$$= \frac{0.816}{250} \times 1000$$

$$= 0.3264 \text{ mol kg}^{-1}$$

Let α be the degree of dissociation of $CH_3CH_2CHClCOOH$.

Now if α is the degree of dissociation of $CH_3CH_2CHClCOOH$,

$$\text{So, } K_a = \frac{C\alpha \times C\alpha}{C(1-\alpha)}$$

$$K_a = \frac{C\alpha^2}{(1-\alpha)}$$

Since a very small with respect to 1, 1 − α = 1

$$K_a = C_\alpha{}^2$$

$$\alpha = \frac{\sqrt{K_a}}{C}$$

Putting the values, We get

$$\alpha = \frac{\sqrt{1.4 \times 10^{-3}}}{0.3264}$$

$$= 0.1146$$

Now at equilibrium, the Van't Hoff factor

$$i = \frac{1-\alpha+\alpha+\alpha}{1}$$

$$= 1 + 0.1146$$

$$= 1.1146$$

Hence, the depression in the freezing point of water is given as:

Therefore, $\Delta T_f = i\,K_f\,m$

$$= 1.1146 \times 1.86 \times 0.3264$$

$$= 0.6766 \text{ K}$$

Q. 33. 19.5 g of CH_2FCOOH is dissolved in 500 g of water. The depression in the freezing point of water observed is 1.00 C. Calculate the Van't Hoff factor and dissociation constant of fluoroacetic acid.

[NCERT Ex. Q. 1.33, Page 29]

Ans. Molecular mass of CH_2FCOOH

= 14 + 19 + 12 + 16 + 16 + 1 = 78 g/mol

Now, Moles of $CH_2FCOOH = \frac{19.5}{78}$

$$= 0.25$$

Taking the volume of the solution as 500 mL, we have the concentration:

$$C = \frac{0.25}{500} \times 1000$$

Therefore, Molality = 0.50 m

So now putting the value in the formula:

$$\Delta T_f = K_f \times m$$

$$= 1.86 \times 0.50 = 0.93 \text{ K}$$

Van't hoff factor

$$= \frac{\text{observed freezing point depression}}{\text{calculated freezing point depression}}$$

$$= \frac{1}{0.93} = 1.0753$$

Let α be the degree of dissociation of CH_2FCOOH

$$CH_2FCOOH \rightleftharpoons CH_2FCOO^- + H^+$$

Initial conc.	C mol L^{-1}	0	0	
At equilibrium	C(1 − α)	Cα	Cα	Total = C(1 + α)

Now total number of moles

$$= m(1-a) + ma + ma$$

$$= m(1+\alpha)$$

$$i = \frac{\alpha(1+\alpha)}{\alpha} = 1 + \alpha$$

$$= 1.0753$$

Therefore, α = 1.0753 − 1

$$= 0.0753$$

$$K_a = \frac{[CH_2FCOO^-][H^+]}{CH_2FCOOH}$$

$$= \frac{C\alpha \times C\alpha}{C(1-\alpha)}$$

$$= \frac{C\alpha^2}{1-\alpha}$$

$$K_a = \frac{0.5 \times (0.0753)^2}{1-0.0753}$$

$$= \frac{0.5 \times 0.00567}{0.9247}$$

$$= 0.00307 \text{ (approx.)}$$

$$= 3 \times 10^{-3}$$

Q. 34. Vapour pressure of water at 293K is 17.535 mm Hg. Calculate the vapour pressure of water at 293K when 25 g of glucose is dissolved in 450 g of water.

[NCERT Ex. Q. 1.34, Page 29]

Ans. Vapour pressure of water, p_1^0 = 17.535 mm of Hg

Mass of glucose, w_1 = 25 g

Mass of water, w_2 = 450 g

As we know that,

Molar mass of glucose

$(C_6H_{12}O_6)$, M_1 = 6 × 12 + 12 × 1 + 6 × 16

= 180 g mol^{-1}

Molar Mass of water,

M_2 = 18 g mol^{-1}

So, number of moles of glucose,

$$n_1 = \frac{25}{180}$$

$$= 0.139 \text{ mol}$$

And, number of moles of water $n_2 = \frac{450}{180}$

$= 25$ mol

We know, that

$$\frac{p_1^0 - p_1}{p_1^0} = \frac{n_1}{n_2 + n_1}$$

$$\frac{17.535 - p_1}{17.535} = \frac{0.139}{0.139 + 25}$$

$$17.535 - p_1 = \frac{0.139 \times 17.535}{25.139}$$

$$17.535 - p_1 = 0.097$$

$$p_1 = 17.44 \text{ mm of Hg}$$

Hence, the vapour pressure of water is 17.44 mm of Hg.

Q. 35. Henry's law constant for the molality of methane in benzene at 298K is 4.27×10^5 mm Hg. Calculate the solubility of methane in benzene at 298K under 760 mm Hg. [NCERT Ex. Q. 1.35, Page 29]

Ans. Here, $p = 760$ mm Hg, $K_H = 4.27 \times 10^5$ mm Hg

According to Henry's law,

$$p = K_H x$$

$$\Rightarrow x = \frac{p}{K_H} = \frac{760 \text{ mm Hg}}{4.27 \times 10^5 \text{mm Hg}} = 177.99 \times 10^{-5}$$

$= 178 \times 10^{-5}$ (approximately)

Therefore, the mole fraction of methane in benzene is 178×10^{-5}.

Q. 36. 100 g of liquid A (molar mass 140 g mol^{-1}) was dissolved in 1000 g of liquid B (molar mass 180 g mol^{-1}). The vapour pressure of pure liquid B was found to be 500 torr. Calculate the vapour pressure of pure liquid A and its vapour pressure in the solution if the total vapour pressure of the solution is 475 torr. [NCERT Ex. Q. 1.36, Page 29]

Ans. Number of moles of liquid A,

$$n_A = \frac{100}{140} \text{mol}$$

$$= 0.714 \text{ mol}$$

Number of moles of liquid B,

$$n_B = \frac{1000}{180} \text{mol}$$

$$= 5.556 \text{ mol}$$

Then, moles fraction of A,

$$x_A = \frac{n_A}{n_A + n_B}$$

$$= 0.114$$

And, mole fration of B,

$$x_B = 1 - 0.114 = 0.886$$

Now,

$$p_{total} = p_A + p_B$$

$$p_{total} = p^{\circ}_A x_A + p^{\circ}_A x_B$$

$$475 = p^{\circ}_A \times 0.114 + 500 \times 0.886$$

$$p^{\circ}_A = 280.7 \text{ torr}$$

Hence, vapour pressure of pure A = 280.7 torr

Vapour pressure of A in solution = 280.7 × 0.114

= 32 torr

Now, $p_A = p^{\circ}_A x_A$

$$p^{\circ}_A = \frac{p_A}{x_A}$$

$$= \frac{32}{0.114}$$

= 280.7 torr

Therefore, the vapour pressure of pure liquid A is 280.7 torr.

Q. 37. Vapour pressures of pure acetone and chloroform at 328K are 741.8 mm Hg and 632.8 mm Hg respectively. Assuming that they form ideal solution over the entire range of composition, plot p_{total}, $p_{chloroform}$, and $p_{acetone}$ as a function of $x_{acetone}$. The experimental data observed for different compositions of mixture is:

100 × $x_{acetone}$	$P_{acetone}$/mm Hg	$P_{chloroform}$/mm Hg
0	0	632.8
11.8	54.9	548.1
23.4	110.1	469.4
36.0	202.4	359.7
50.8	322.7	257.7
58.2	405.9	193.6
64.5	454.1	161.2
72.1	521.1	120.7

Plot this data also on the same graph paper. Indicate whether it has positive deviation or negative deviation from the ideal solution. [NCERT Ex. Q. 1.37, Page 30]

Ans. From the question, we get the following data:

100 × $x_{acetone}$	$P_{acetone}$/ mm Hg	$P_{chloroform}$/ mm Hg	P_{total} (mm Hg)
0	0	632.8	632.8
11.8	54.9	548.1	603.0
23.4	110.1	469.4	579.5
36.0	202.4	359.7	562.1
50.8	322.7	257.7	580.4
58.2	405.9	193.6	599.5
64.5	454.1	161.2	615.3
72.1	521.1	120.7	641.8

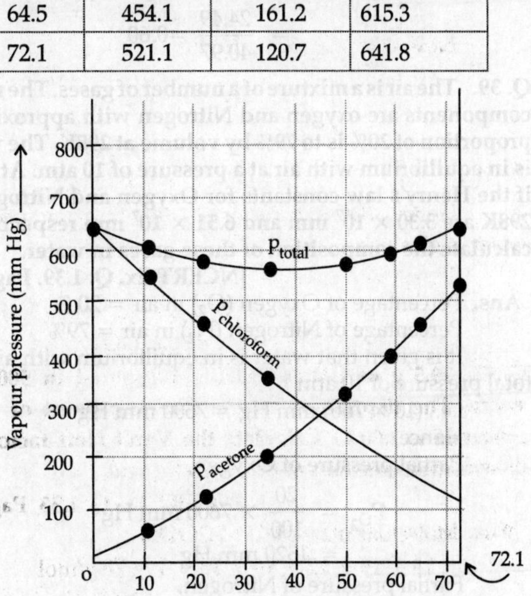

It can be observed from the graph that the plot for the P total of the solution curves downwards. Therefore, the solution shows negative deviation from the ideal behaviour.

Q. 38. Benzene and toluene form ideal solution over the entire range of composition. The vapour pressure of pure benzene and toluene at 300 K are 50.71 mm Hg and 32.06 mm Hg respectively. Calculate the mole fraction of benzene in vapour phase if 80 g of benzene is mixed with 100 g of toluene. [NCERT Ex. Q. 1.38, Page 30]

Ans. Molar mass of benzene (C_6H_6) = 6 × 12 + 6 × 1 = 78 g mol^{-1}

Molar mass of toluene($C_6H_5CH_3$) = 7 × 12 + 8 × 1 = 92 g mol^{-1}

Now, number of moles present in 80 g of benzene

$$= \frac{80}{78} = 1.026 \text{ mol}$$

Number of moles present in 100 g of toluene

$$= \frac{100}{92} = 1.087 \text{ mol}$$

Therefore, Mole fraction of benzene, x_B

$$= \frac{1.026}{1.026 + 1.087} = 0.486$$

And, mole fraction of toluene x_T

$$x_T = 1 - 0.486 = 0.514$$

$$p_b^0 = 50.71 \text{ mm Hg (given)}$$

$$p_t^0 = 32.06 \text{ mm Hg (given)}$$

It is given that vapour pressure of pure benzene,

And, vapour pressure of pure toluene,

$$p_b = x_b \times p_b^0$$

Therefore, partial vapour pressure of benzene,

$$= 0.483 \times 50.71$$
$$= 24.49 \text{ mm Hg}$$

And, partial vapour pressure of toluene,

$$p_t = x_t \times p_t^0$$
$$= 0.514 \times 32.06$$
$$= 16.479 \text{ mm Hg}$$

Total vapour pressure = 24.49 + 16.48

$$= 40.97 \text{ mm Hg}$$

Mole fraction of benzene in vapour phase

$$= \frac{24.49}{40.97} = 0.60$$

Q. 39. The air is a mixture of a number of gases. The major components are oxygen and Nitrogen with approximate proportion of 20% is to 79% by volume at 298K. The water is in equilibrium with air at a pressure of 10 atm. At 298K if the Henry's law constants for Oxygen and Nitrogen at 298K are 3.30 × 10^7 mm and 6.51 × 10^7 mm respectively, calculate the composition of these gases in water. [NCERT Ex. Q. 1.39, Page 30]

Ans. Percentage of Oxygen (O_2) in air = 20 %

Percentage of Nitrogen (N_2) in air = 79%

It is given that water is in equilibrium with air at a total pressure of 10 atm

i.e., (10 × 760) mm Hg = 7600 mm Hg

Hence,

Partial pressure of Oxygen,

$$P_{O_2} = \frac{20}{100} \times 7600 \text{ mm Hg}$$
$$= 1520 \text{ mm Hg}$$

Partial pressure of Nitrogen,

$$P_{N_2} = \frac{79}{100} \times 7600 \text{ mm Hg}$$
$$= 6004 \text{ mm Hg}$$

Now, according to Henry's law:

$$p = K_H x$$

For Oxygen:

$$p_{O_2} = K_H \cdot x_{O_2}$$

$$x_{O_2} = \frac{p_{O_2}}{K_H} = \frac{1520 \text{ mm Hg}}{3.30 \times 10^7 \text{ mm Hg}}$$

(Given K_H = 3.30 × 10^7 mm Hg)

$$= 4.61 \times 10^{-5}$$

For Nitrogen:

$$p_{N_2} = K_H \cdot x_{N_2}$$

$$x_{N_2} = \frac{p_{N_2}}{K_H} = \frac{6004 \text{ mm Hg}}{6.51 \times 10^7 \text{ mm Hg}}$$

$$= 9.22 \times 10^{-5}$$

Therefore, the mole fractions of oxygen and nitrogen in water are 4.61 × 10^{-5} and 9.22 × 10^{-5}, respectively.

Q. 40. Determine the amount of $CaCl_2$ (i = 2.47) dissolved in 2.5 litre of water such that its osmotic pressure is 0.75 atm at 27° C. [NCERT Ex. Q. 1.40, Page 30]

Ans. We know that,

$$\pi = i\frac{n}{V}RT$$

$$\pi = i\frac{w}{MV}RT$$

$$w = \frac{\pi MV}{iRT}$$

$$\pi = 0.75 \text{ atm}$$
$$V = 2.5\text{L}$$
$$i = 2.47$$
$$T = (27 + 273)\text{K} = 300\text{K}$$

Here,

$$R = 0.0821 \text{ L atm K}^{-1} \text{ mol}^{-1}$$
$$M = 1 \times 40 + 2 \times 35.5$$
$$= 111 \text{ g mol}^{-1}$$
$$= \frac{0.75 \times 111 \times 2.5}{2.47 \times 0.0821 \times 300}$$

Therefore, w = 3.42 g

Hence, the required amount of $CaCl_2$ is 3.42 g.

Q. 41. Determine the osmotic pressure of a solution prepared by dissolving 25 mg of K_2SO_4 in 2 litre of water at 25° C, assuming that it is completely dissociated. [NCERT Ex. Q. 1.41, Page 30]

Ans. If K_2SO_4 is completely dissociated then these ions are produced

Then, $K_2SO_4 = 2K^+ + SO_4^{2-}$

So total number of ions produced = 3

Therefore, i = 3

Now molecular mass of

K_2SO_4 = (2 × 39) + (1 × 32) + (4 × 16) = 174 g mol

Now $\pi = iCRT$

$$= \frac{iW_B \times RT}{M_B \times V}$$

$$= \frac{3 \times 25 \times 10^{-3} \times 0.082 \times 298}{174 \times 2}$$

$$= 5.27 \times 10^{-3} \text{ atm.}$$

□□

CHAPTER 2

ELECTROCHEMISTRY

- Chemical reactions can be used to produce electrical energy, conversely, electrical energy can be used to carry out chemical reactions that do not proceed spontaneously.
- **Electrochemistry** is the branch of chemistry which deals with the study of the production of electricity from energy released during spontaneous chemical reactions and the use of electrical energy to result in non-spontaneous chemical transformations.
- **Electrolytic conduction:** The flow of electric current through an electrolytic solution is called electrolytic conduction.
- **Electrolyte:** A substance that dissociates in solution to produce ions and hence, conducts electricity in dissolved state or molten state.
  Weak electrolyte – H_2CO_3, CH_3COOH, HCN.
  Strong electrolyte – NaCl, HCl, NaOH.
- **Degree of ionisation:** It is the ratio of number of ions produced to the total number of molecules in electrolyte.
- **Resistance** is defined as the property of a given substance to obstruct the flow of charge. It is directly proportional to the length (l) and inversely proportional to its area of cross-section (A).

$$R \propto \frac{l}{A} \text{ or; } R = \rho\frac{l}{A}$$

ρ = Resistivity or specific resistance.

- **Resistivity:** If a solution is placed in between two parallel electrodes having cross sectional area 'A' and distance 'l' apart, then

$$R = \rho\frac{l}{A}$$

where ρ = resistivity and its SI unit is Ohm-m or Ohm-cm is used as a unit.

- **Conductance:** The ease with which the current flows through a conductor is called conductance. It is reciprocal of resistance. *i.e.,*

$$C = \frac{1}{R} = \frac{A}{\rho l} = \kappa\frac{A}{l}$$

The SI unit of conductance is **Siemens (S).**

$$R = \rho\frac{l}{A},$$

$1S = 1\ \text{Ohm}^{-1} = 1\ \Omega^{-1}$

- **Conductivity:** It is reciprocal of resistivity and is denoted by κ (Greek Kappa).

$$\kappa = C \times \frac{l}{A},$$

where C = Conductance of the solution, l = Distance/length, A = Area of cross-section
Its SI unit is S m^{-1}. Also expressed as S cm^{-1}.
It depends upon the:
(i) Nature of the material
(ii) Temperature
(iii) The number of valence electrons per atom or size of the ions produced and their solvation (electrolytes).

- **Metallic conductance** is the electrical conductance in metals that occurs due to the movement of electrons. It depends upon the:
  (i) Nature and structure of the metal
  (ii) Number of valence electrons per atom
  (iii) Temperature

Conductance of Electrolytic Solutions

- **Electrolytic or ionic conductance** is the conductance of electricity that occurs due to ions present in the solution. It depends upon the:
  (i) Nature of electrolyte or interionic attractions
  (ii) Solvation of ions
  (iii) Nature of solvent and its viscosity
  (iv) Temperature
- Wheatstone bridge helps us to measure R_4.

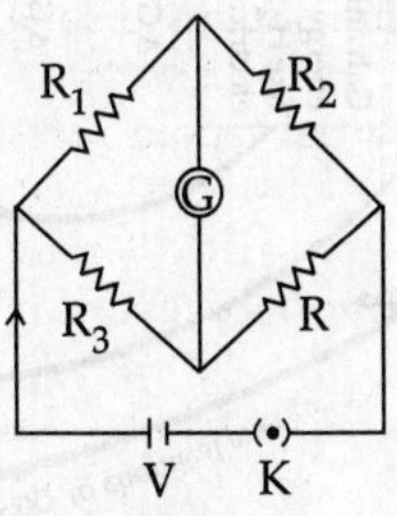

Fig. 1

$$R_4 = \frac{R_3R_2}{R_1}$$

- **Cell constant (G):** It is the ratio of distance between electrodes to the cross-sectional area between electrodes.

$$\text{Cell constant (G)} = \frac{l}{A} \text{ in cm}^{-1} \text{ or m}^{-1}$$

It depends on the:
(i) Distance between the electrodes.
(ii) Area of cross section.

- **Molar conductivity:** It is defined as the conducting power of all the ions produced by one gram mole of an electrolyte in a solution. It is denoted by Λ_m.

$$\Lambda_m = \frac{\kappa}{C} \times 1000 \text{ S cm}^2 \text{ mol}^{-1},$$

where κ = Conductivity, C = Concentration of solution.
SI unit of molar conductivity is S m^2 mol^{-1}.
Debye-Huckel-Onsager equation: It is only applicable for strong electrolytes:

$$\Lambda = \mathring{\Lambda} - A\sqrt{C},$$

where $\mathring{\Lambda}$ = Limiting molar conductivity, Λ = Molar conductivity, A = Constant and C = Concentration of solution.

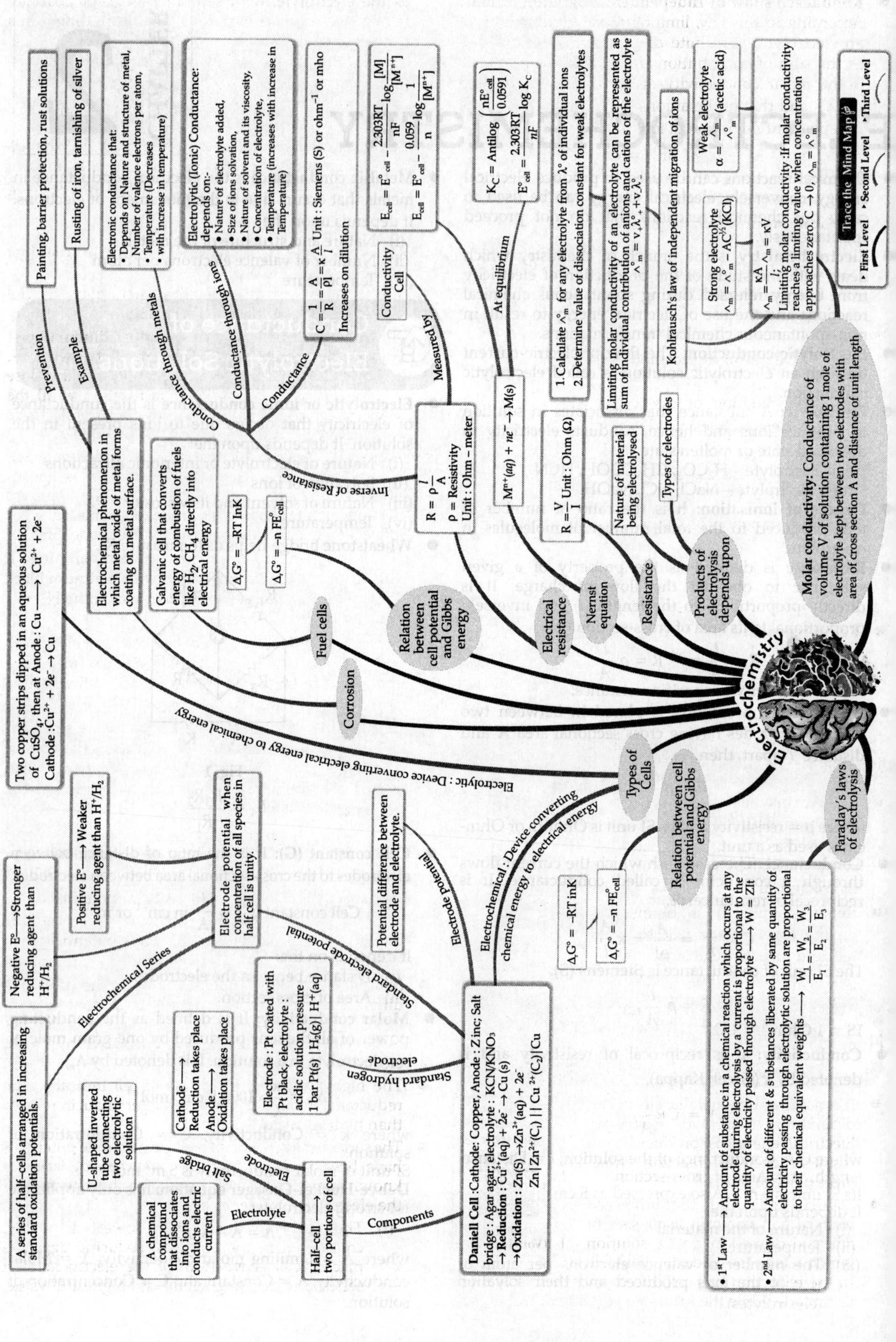
Electrochemistry
Trace the Mind Map ☞ • First Level • Second Level • Third Level
A series of half-cells arranged in increasing standard oxidation potentials.
Electrochemical Series
Negative E° ⟶ Stronger reducing agent than H^+/H_2
Positive E° ⟶ Weaker reducing agent than H^+/H_2
Two copper strips dipped in an aqueous solution of $CuSO_4$, then at Anode : $Cu \longrightarrow Cu^{2+} + 2e^-$ Cathode : $Cu^{2+} + 2e^- \rightarrow Cu$
Electrolytic : Device converting electrical energy to chemical energy
Electrochemical : Device converting chemical energy to electrical energy
Types of Cells
A chemical compound that dissociates into ions and conducts electric current
Electrolyte
U-shaped inverted tube connecting two electrolytic solution
Salt bridge
Cathode ⟶ Reduction takes place Anode ⟶ Oxidation takes place
Electrode
Half-cell ⟶ two portions of cell
Components
Electrode : Pt coated with Pt black, electrolyte : acidic solution pressure 1 bar $Pt(s)|H_2(g)|H^+(aq)$
Standard hydrogen electrode
Electrode potential when concentration of all species in half cell is unity.
Standard electrode potential
Potential difference between electrode and electrolyte.
Electrode potential
Daniell Cell : Cathode: Copper, Anode : Zinc; Salt bridge : Agar agar; electrolyte : KCN/KNO_3 → Reduction : $Cu^{2+}(aq) + 2e^- \rightarrow Cu(s)$ → Oxidation : $Zn(S) \rightarrow Zn^{2+}(aq) + 2e^-$ $Zn|Zn^{2+}(C_1)||Cu^{2+}(C_2)|Cu$
$\Delta_r G° = -RT \ln K$
$\Delta_r G° = -n FE°_{cell}$
Relation between cell potential and Gibbs energy
Faraday's laws of electrolysis
• 1st Law ⟶ Amount of substance in a chemical reaction which occurs at any electrode during electrolysis by a current is proportional to the quantity of electricity passed through electrolyte ⟶ $W = ZIt$
• 2nd Law ⟶ Amount of different & substances liberated by same quantity of electricity passing through electrolytic solution are proportional to their chemical equivalent weights ⟶ $\frac{W_1}{E_1} = \frac{W_2}{E_2} = \frac{W_3}{E_3}$
Painting, barrier protection, rust solutions
Prevention
Rusting of iron, tarnishing of silver
Example
Electrochemical phenomenon in which metal oxide of metal forms coating on metal surface.
Corrosion
Galvanic cell that converts energy of combustion of fuels like H_2, CH_4 directly into electrical energy
Fuel cells
$\Delta_r G° = -RT \ln K$
$\Delta_r G° = -n FE°_{cell}$
Relation between cell potential and Gibbs energy
Electronic conductance that: • Depends on Nature and structure of metal, Number of valence electrons per atom, • Temperature (Decreases with increase in temperature)
Conductance through metals
Electrolytic (Ionic) Conductance: depends on:- • Nature of electrolyte added, • Size of ions solvation, • Nature of solvent and its viscosity, • Concentration of electrolyte, • Temperature (increases with increase in Temperature)
Conductance through ions
$C = \frac{1}{R} = \frac{A}{\rho l} = \kappa \frac{A}{l}$ Unit : Siemens (S) or ohm^{-1} or mho Increases on dilution
Conductance
Inverse of Resistance
Conductivity Cell
Measured by
$R = \rho \frac{l}{A}$ ρ = Resistivity Unit : Ohm – meter
Electrical resistance
$E_{cell} = E°_{cell} - \frac{2.303RT}{nF} \log \frac{[M]}{[M^{n+}]}$
$E_{cell} = E°_{cell} - \frac{0.059}{n} \log \frac{1}{[M^{n+}]}$
$M^{n+}(aq) + ne^- \rightarrow M(s)$
Nernst equation
$K_C = \text{Antilog}\left(\frac{nE°_{cell}}{0.0591}\right)$
$E°_{cell} = \frac{2.303RT}{nF} \log K_C$
At equilibrium
$R = \frac{V}{I}$ Unit : Ohm (Ω)
Resistance
Nature of material being electrolysed
Types of electrodes
Products of electrolysis depends upon
1. Calculate $\Lambda°_m$ for any electrolyte from λ° of individual ions
2. Determine value of dissociation constant for weak electrolytes
Limiting molar conductivity of an electrolyte can be represented as sum of individual contribution of anions and cations of the electrolyte $\Lambda°_m = \nu_+\lambda°_+ + \nu_-\lambda°_-$
Kohlrausch's law of independent migration of ions
Strong electrolyte $\Lambda_m = \Lambda°_m - A C^{1/2}$ (KCl)
Weak electrolyte $\alpha = \frac{\Lambda^c_m}{\Lambda°_m}$ (acetic acid)
$\Lambda_m = \frac{\kappa A}{l}$; $\Lambda_m = \kappa V$
Limiting molar conductivity : If molar conductivity reaches a limiting value when concentration approaches zero. $C \rightarrow 0$, $\Lambda_m = \Lambda°_m$
Molar conductivity: Conductance of volume V of solution containing 1 mole of electrolyte kept between two electrodes with area of cross section A and distance of unit length

- **Kohlrausch's law of Independent Migration of ions:** According to this law, limiting molar conductivity of an electrolyte, at infinite dilution, can be expressed as the sum of contributions from its individual ions. If the molar conductivity of the cations is denoted by λ_+^∞ and that of the anions by λ_-^∞, then the law of independent migration of ions is

$$\Lambda_m^\infty = v_+ \lambda_+^\infty + v_- \lambda_-^\infty \text{ or } \mathring{\Lambda} = v_+ \lambda_+^\circ + v_- \lambda_-^\circ,$$

where, v^+ and v^- are the number of cations and anions per formula of electrolyte.

Applications of Kohlrausch's law:

(i) Calculation of molar conductivities of weak electrolyte at infinite dilution.

(ii) Calculation of degree of dissociation (α) of weak electrolytes:

$$\text{Degree of dissociation } (\alpha) = \frac{\Lambda_m^c}{\Lambda_m^\circ}$$

(iii) Determination of dissociation constant (K) of weak electrolytes:

$$K_a = \frac{C\alpha^2}{(1-\alpha)} = \frac{C\Lambda_m^2}{\Lambda_m^\circ(\Lambda_m^\circ - \Lambda_m^2)}$$

(iv) Determination of solubility of sparingly soluble salts:

$$\text{Solubility} = \frac{\kappa \times 1000}{\Lambda_m^\circ}$$

- **Redox reaction:** A chemical reaction in which oxidation and reduction both processes take place simultaneously is known as a redox reaction. Oxidation is a process in which any substance loses one or more electrons while reduction is the process in which one or more electrons are gained by another substance.

Electrochemical Cell

- A device in which the redox reaction is carried indirectly and chemical energy is converted to electrical energy. It is also called galvanic cell or voltaic cell.
- **Redox couple:** It is defined as having together the oxidised and reduced form of a substance taking part in an oxidation or reduction half reaction.

Scan to know more about this topic

Electrochemistry-Voltaic cell

Galvanic Cell or Voltaic Cell

- It consists of two metallic electrodes dipped in electrolytic solutions. Electrical energy is produced as a result of chemical reaction which takes place in this cell.
- **Daniell cell:** It is the improved form of galvanic cell. It consists of zinc rod dipped in $ZnSO_4$ solution which acts as the oxidation half-cell.

  In the reduction half-cell, the copper vessel itself acts as cathode while the saturated solution of $CuSO_4$ acts as the electrolyte. Both solutions are kept apart by taking zinc sulphate in porous pot and putting it in a copper sulphate solution.

Scan to know more about this topic

Galvanic cells (Voltaic cells)

$$Zn(s) + Cu^{2+} \rightleftharpoons Zn^{2+} + Cu$$

Cell is represented as,

$$Zn(s)\,|Zn^{2+}(aq)\,(C_1)\,||\,Cu^{2+}(aq)\,(C_2)|\,Cu(s)$$

- **Salt Bridge and its function:** It is an inverted U-shaped glass tube which contains a suitable salt in the form of a thick paste made in agar-agar. It performs following functions—
  (i) It completes inner cell circuit.
  (ii) It prevents transference of electrolyte from one half-cell to the other.
  (iii) It maintains the electrical neutrality of the electrolytes in the two half-cells.
- **Electrode Potential:** It is the potential difference set up between the metal and solution of its own ions. It shows the tendency of an electrode to either lose or gain electrons. When the concentration of all the species involved in a half-cell is unity, then the electrode potential is called standard electrode potential.
- **Standard Electrode Potential:** Electrode potential at 25°C, 1 bar pressure and 1 M solution is known as standard electrode potential (E°). The standard electrode potential of any electrode can be measured by connecting it to Standard Hydrogen Electrode (SHE).

  SHE has a standard potential at all temperatures. It consists of a platinum foil coated with platinum black dipped into an aqueous solution in which the H^+ = 1 M at 25°C and 1 bar pressure.

  The potential difference between the two electrodes of a galvanic cell is called the cell potential (measured in volts). It is also called the emf of the cell when no current is flowing through the circuit.
- **EMF of the cell:** Electromotive force is also called emf (denoted and measured in volts). It is the voltage developed by any source of electrical energy such as battery or dynamo. It is generally defined as the potential for a source in a circuit.

$$E_{cell} = E_{cathode} - E_{anode}$$

In terms of standard oxidation electrode potential,

$$E^\circ_{cell} = E^\circ_{anode} - E^\circ_{cathode},$$

Here, $E^\circ_{cathode}$ = standard electrode potential of cathode

E°_{anode} = standard electrode potential of anode

- **Standard oxidation potential:** It is the potential difference when given electrode is in contact with its ions having 1 molar concentration, undergoes oxidation when coupled with standard hydrogen electrode.
- The higher value of E° for a half-cell indicates that reductant in the half-cell is stronger reducing agent than hydrogen gas.
- The series in which all the standard electrode potentials have been arranged in order of increasing value is known as electrochemical series. The characteristics of the electrochemical series are:

  (i) The reducing agent with lowest E° value, considered as the strongest reducing agent, is placed well above (top) of the electrochemical series. The oxidising agent with highest E° value, considered as the strongest oxidising agent, is placed below (bottom) of the electrochemical series.

(ii) Oxidising power increases with increase in E° value.

(iii) Any metal of lower E° value can reduce other metal of higher E° value. Similarly, any metal of higher E° value can oxidise other metal of lower E° value.

- **Applications of Electrochemical series:** Important applications are as follows:
  (i) In comparing relative reducing or oxidizing power of the elements.
  (ii) In predicting the feasibility or spontaneity of a redox reaction.
  (iii) In predicting whether a metal can evolve hydrogen from an acid or not.
  (iv) Comparison of reactivities of metals and non-metals.
  (v) Determination of standard Gibbs energy change.
  (vi) Determination of equilibrium constant.

Nernst Equation

- If the concentration of species in the electrode reaction is not equal to 1 M, then we use Nernst equation. For a general electrode,

$$M^{n+}(aq) + ne^- \rightarrow M(s)$$

the Nernst equation can be written as:

$$E_{(M^{n+}/M)} = E^\circ_{(M^{n+}/M)} - \frac{RT}{nF} ln \frac{[M_{(s)}]}{[M^{n+}(aq)]}$$

where E° = Standard electrode potential, R = Gas constant (8.31 $JK^{-1}\ mol^{-1}$), T = Temperature (K), *n* = Number of moles of electrons and F = Faraday Constant (96500 C),

At equilibrium,

$$E^\circ_{cell} = \frac{0.059}{n} \log K_c$$

K_c = Equilibrium constant

$$K_c = \frac{[M]}{[M^{n+}]}$$

For the cell with the net reaction,

$$aA + bB \xrightarrow{ne^-} mM + nN$$

the Nernst equation at 298 K can be written as:

$$E_{cell} = E^\circ_{cell} - \frac{0.059}{n} \log \frac{[M]^m [N]^n}{[A]^a [B]^b}$$

where, $E^\circ_{cell} = E^\circ_{cathode} - E^\circ_{anode}$

- **Gibbs energy:**

$$\Delta G^\circ = -nFE^\circ_{cell}$$

For the cell reaction to be spontaneous, ΔG must be negative,

Calculations of $\Delta_r G^\circ$ and $\Delta_r G$:

$$\Delta_r G^\circ = -nF\, E^\circ_{cell}$$

and $$\Delta_r G = -nF\, E_{cell}$$

We also know that Gibbs energy change is equal to the useful work done.

Electrolytic Cells and Electrolysis

- **Electrolysis** is the process of decomposition of an electrolyte when electric current is passed through either its aqueous solution or molten (fused) state. This process takes place in an electrolytic cell.
- **Faraday's First Law of Electrolysis:** The amount of chemical reaction which occurs at any electrode during electrolysis by a current is proportional to the quantity of electricity passed through the electrolyte.

$$m = Z \times I \times t,$$

where Z = Electrochemical equivalent

- **Faraday's Second Law of Electrolysis:** Amount of various substances liberated by the same quantity of electricity passed through the electrolytic solution is proportional to their chemical equivalent weights.

$$\frac{w_1}{E_1} = \frac{w_2}{E_2}$$

- **Products of electrolysis depends on:**
  (i) Physical state of material.
  (ii) Types of electrode being used.
- Battery is a combination of galvanic cells in series and used as a source of electrical energy.

Batteries

Types of batteries:

(i) Primary battery are non-chargeable batteries such as Leclanche cell and Dry cell. In these batteries, the reaction occurs only once and after use over a period of time battery becomes dead and cannot be reused again.

(ii) Secondary battery are chargeable cells involving reversible reaction. Example, Lead storage battery and Nickel-Cadmium cells.

- **Dry cell (Leclanche cell):** The anode consists of a zinc container and the cathode is a graphite electrode surrounded by powdered MnO_2 and C. The space is filled with paste of NH_4Cl and $ZnCl_2$.

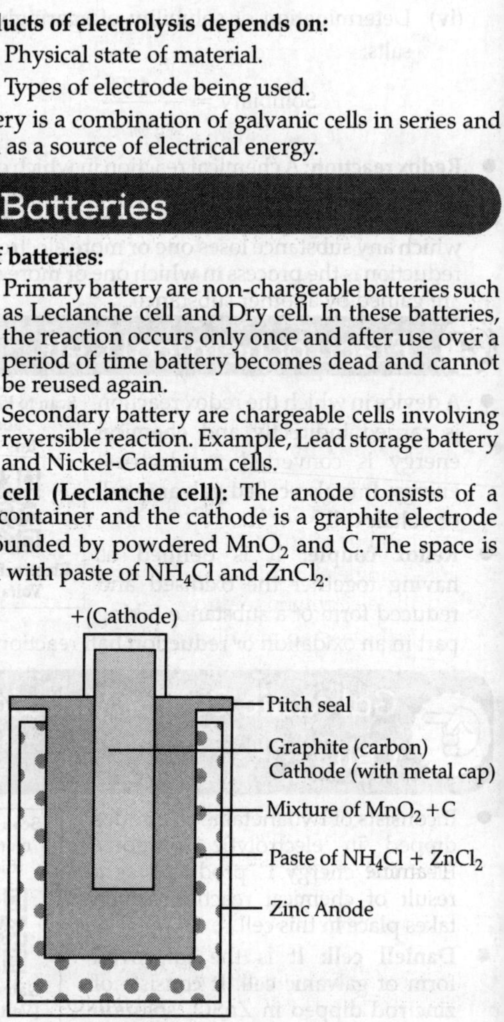

Fig. 2: A dry cell

At anode: $Zn(s) \rightarrow Zn^{2+}(aq) + 2e^-$.

At cathode: $MnO_2(s) + NH_4^+(aq) + 2e^- \rightarrow MnO(OH) + NH_3$

The net reaction: $Zn + NH_4^+(aq) + MnO_2 \rightarrow Zn^{2+} + MnO(OH) + NH_3$

- **Lead storage battery:**

  Anode – Spongy lead

  Cathode – Lead packed with lead dioxide

  Electrolyte – Aqueous solution of H_2SO_4 (38%)

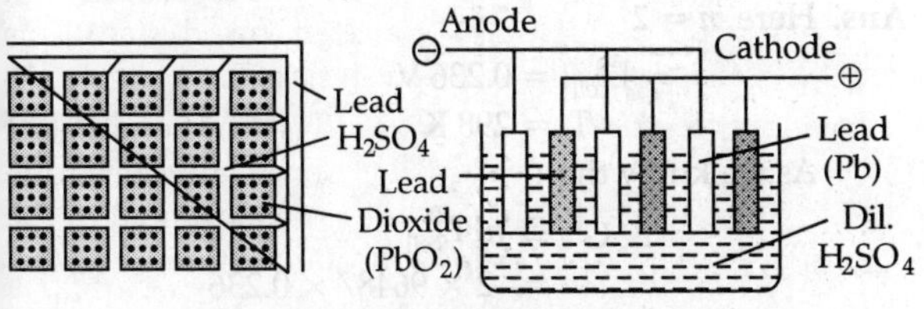

Fig. 3: Storage battery

Discharge reaction of cell:

At anode: Following reaction takes place at anode:

$$Pb(s) + SO_4^{2-}(aq) \rightarrow PbSO_4(s) + 2e^-$$

Reaction at cathode: PbO_2 filled in lead grid gets reduced to Pb^{2+} ions which combines with SO_4^{2-} ions to form $PbSO_4(s)$.

Complete cathode reaction is as follow:

$$PbO_2(s) + 4H^+(aq) + SO_4^{2-}(aq) + 2e^- \rightarrow PbSO_4(s) + 2H_2O(l)$$

Complete cell reaction: $Pb(s) + PbO_2(s) + 2H_2SO_4(aq) \rightarrow 2PbSO_4(s) + 2H_2O(l)$

Recharge reaction of cell: It changes the direction of electrode reaction $PbSO_4$ accumulated at cathode gets reduced to Pb.

At cathode, $PbSO_4 + 2e^- \rightarrow Pb(s) + SO_4^{2-}(aq)$

At anode, $PbSO_4$ gets oxidized to PbO_2

$$PbSO_4(s) + 2H_2O \rightarrow PbO_2(s) + 4H^+(aq) + SO_4^{2-}(aq) + 2e^-$$

Complete cell reaction would be as follow:

$$2PbSO_4(s) + 2H_2O(l) \xrightarrow{\text{charge}} Pb(s) + PbO_2(s) + 2H_2SO_4(aq)$$

- **Conventions for representing the Galvanic Cell:**

  (i) Double vertical line is used for salt bridge. Left hand side of the double line is anode and the cathode is on the right hand side.

  (ii) A single vertical line is used to separate metal and the electrolytic solution.

  (iii) If there is no metallic surface involved, we write Pt.

Example:

$$Zn(s) + Cu^{2+}(aq) \rightarrow Zn^{2+}(aq) + Cu(s)$$
$$Zn(s) \mid Zn^{2+}(aq) \mid\mid Cu^{2+}(aq) \mid Cu(s)$$

- **Fuel cells:** Electrical cells that are designated to convert the energy from the combustion of fuels such as hydrogen, carbon monoxide or methane directly into electrical energy are called fuel cells.

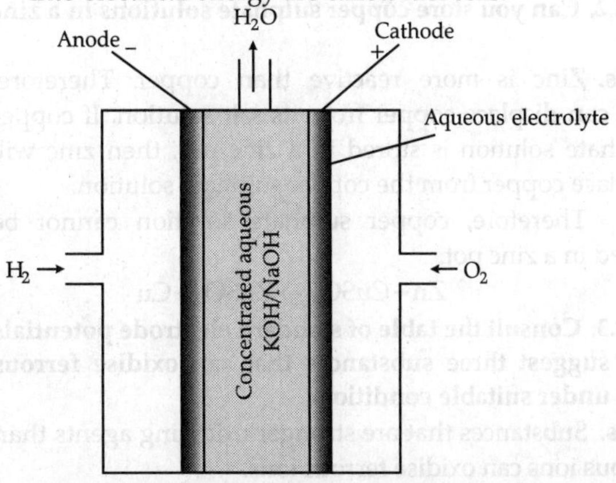

Fig. 4: Fuel cell using H_2 and O_2 produces electricity

In the cell:

Anode: $[H_2(g) + 2OH^-(aq) \rightarrow 2H_2O(l) + 2e^-] \times 2$

Cathode: $O_2(g) + 2H_2O(l) + 4e^- \rightarrow 4OH^-(aq)$

Net reaction: $2H_2(g) + O_2(g) \rightarrow 2H_2O(l)$.

Corrosion

- The process of slow conversion of metals into their undesirable compounds (usually oxide) by reaction with moisture and other gases present in the atmosphere.

Rusting of iron:

$$Fe(s) + 2H^+(aq) + \frac{1}{2}O_2(g) \rightarrow Fe^{2+}(aq) + H_2O(l)$$

$$2Fe^{2+}(s) + \frac{1}{2}O_2(g) + 2H_2O(l) \rightarrow Fe_2O_3(s) + 4H^+$$

$$Fe_2O_3 + xH_2O \rightarrow \underset{\text{Rust}}{Fe_2O_3.xH_2O}$$

Prevention of corrosion:

(i) **Barrier protection:** By covering the surface with paint or a thin film of grease or by electroplating.

(ii) **Sacrificial protection:** By galvanization.

(iii) Alloying.

NCERT CORNER

Intext Questions

Page - 36

Q. 2.1. How would you determine the standard electrode potential of the system $Mg^{2+} \mid Mg$?

Ans. The standard electrode potential of $Mg^{2+} \mid Mg$ can be measured with respect to the standard hydrogen electrode, represented by

$$Pt(s), H_2(g)\ (1\ atm) \mid H^+(aq)\ (1\ M).$$

Cell consisting of $Mg \mid MgSO_4$ (aq 1 M) as the anode and the standard hydrogen electrode as the cathode, is set up.

$$Mg \mid Mg^{2+}(aq, 1\ M) \mid\mid H^+(aq, 1\ M) \mid H_2\ (g, 1bar), Pt$$

Hence, this way the EMF of the cell is measured, and this measured EMF is the standard electrode potential of the magnesium electrode.

$$E^o = E^o_R - E^o_L$$

Here,

E^o_R for the standard hydrogen electrode is zero.

$$E^o = 0 - E^o_L$$
$$= -E^o_L$$

Q. 2.2. Can you store copper sulphate solutions in a zinc pot?

Ans. Zinc is more reactive than copper. Therefore, zinc can displace copper from its salt solution. If copper sulphate solution is stored in a zinc pot, then zinc will displace copper from the copper sulphate solution.

Therefore, copper sulphate solution cannot be stored in a zinc pot.

$$Zn + CuSO_4 \rightarrow ZnSO_4 + Cu$$

Q. 2.3. Consult the table of standard electrode potentials and suggest three substances that can oxidise ferrous ions under suitable conditions.

Ans. Substances that are stronger oxidizing agents than ferrous ions can oxidise ferrous ions.

$$Fe^{2+} \rightarrow Fe^{3+} + e^-, E^\theta = -0.77 \text{ V}$$

This indicates that the substances having higher reduction potentials than + 0.77 V can oxidise ferrous ions to ferric ions. Three substances that can do so are F_2, Cl_2 and O_2.

Page - 41

Q. 2.4. Calculate the potential of hydrogen electrode in contact with a solution whose pH is 10.

Ans. For hydrogen electrode, $H^+ + e^- \rightarrow \frac{1}{2}H_2$, it is given that

$$pH = 10$$
$$\therefore \quad [H^+] = 10^{-10} \text{ M}$$

Now, using Nernst equation

$$H_{\left(H^+/\frac{1}{2}H_2\right)} = E^o_{\left(H^+/\frac{1}{2}H_2\right)} - \frac{RT}{nF}\ln\frac{1}{[H^+]}$$
$$= E^o_{\left(H^+/\frac{1}{2}H_2\right)} - \frac{2.303RT}{nF}\log\frac{1}{[H^+]}$$
$$= E^o_{\left(H^+/\frac{1}{2}H_2\right)} - \frac{0.0591}{1}\log\frac{1}{[H^+]}$$
$$= 0 - \frac{0.0591}{1}\log\frac{1}{[10^{-10}]}$$
$$= -0.0591 \log 10^{10} = -0.591 \text{ V}$$

Q. 2.5. Calculate the emf of the cell in which the following reaction takes place:

$Ni(s) + 2Ag^+ (0.002 \text{ M}) \rightarrow Ni^{2+} (0.160 \text{ M}) + 2Ag(s)$

Given that $E_{cell} = 1.05$ V

Ans. $E_{(cell)} = E^\theta_{cell} - \frac{0.0591}{n}\log\frac{[Ni^{2+}]}{[Ag^+]^2}$

$$= 1.05 - \frac{0.0591}{2}\log\frac{(0.160)}{(0.002)^2}$$
$$= 1.05 - 0.02955 \log\frac{0.16}{0.000004}$$
$$= 1.05 - 0.02955 \log 4 \times 10^4$$
$$= 1.05 - 0.02955 (\log 10000 + \log 4)$$
$$= 1.05 - 0.02955 (4 + 0.6021)$$
$$= 0.914 \text{ V}$$

Q. 2.6. The cell in which the following reaction occurs: $2Fe^{3+}(aq) + 2I^-(aq) \rightarrow 2Fe^{2+}(aq) + I_2(s)$ has $E^0_{cell} = 0.236$ V at 298 K.

Calculate the standard Gibbs energy and the equilibrium constant of the cell reaction.

Ans. Here, $n = 2$

$$E^o_{cell} = 0.236 \text{ V},$$
$$T = 298 \text{ K}$$

As we know that:

$$\Delta_r G^\theta = -nFE^\theta_{cell}$$
$$= -2 \times 96487 \times 0.236$$
$$= -45541.864 \text{ J mol}^{-1}$$
$$= -45.54 \text{ kJ mol}^{-1}$$

Again $\Delta_r G^\theta = -2.30RT \log K_c$

$$\log K_c = \frac{\Delta rG^\theta}{2.303\,T} = -\left(\frac{-45.54 \times 10^3}{2.303 \times 8.314 \times 298}\right)$$
$$= +7.981$$
$$\therefore \quad K_c = \text{Antilog } (7.981)$$
$$= 9.57 \times 10^7$$

Page - 51

Q. 2.7. Why does the conductivity of a solution decrease with dilution?

Ans. The conductivity of a solution is the conductance of ions present in a unit volume of the solution. The number of ions which is responsible for carrying current decreases when the solution is diluted. Hence, the conductivity of a solution decreases with dilution.

Q. 2.8. Suggest a way to determine the Λ^o_m value of water.

Ans. Applying Kohlrausch's law of independent migration of ions, the value of water can be determined as follows:

$$\Lambda^o_m = \Lambda^o_{m\,(HCl)} + \Lambda^o_{m(NaOH)} - \Lambda^o_{m(NaCl)}$$

Hence, if we know the values of Λ^o_m for HCl, NaOH, and NaCl, then we can calculate the value of Λ^o_m for the water.

Q. 2.9. The molar conductivity of 0.025 mol L^{-1} methanoic acid is 46.1 S cm^2 mol^{-1}. Calculate its degree of dissociation and dissociation constant. Given $\lambda^0_{(H+)} = 349.6$ S cm^2 mol^{-1} and $\lambda^0_{(HCOO-)} = 54.6$ S cm^2 mol^{-1}.

Ans.

$$C = 0.025 \text{ mol L}^{-1}$$
$$\Lambda_m = 46.1 \text{ S cm}^2 \text{ mol}^{-1}$$
$$\lambda^o_{(H+)} = 349.6 \text{ S cm}^2 \text{ mol}^{-1}$$
$$\lambda^o_{(HCOO-)} = 54.6 \text{ S cm}^2 \text{ mol}^{-1}$$
$$\Lambda^o_{m\,(HCOOH)} = \lambda^o_{(H+)} + \lambda^o_{(HCOO-)}$$
$$= 349.6 + 54.6$$
$$= 404.2 \text{ S cm}^2 \text{ mol}^{-1}$$

Now, degree of dissociation:

$$\alpha = \frac{\lambda_m(HCOOH)}{\Lambda^o_m(HCOOH)}$$
$$= \frac{46.1}{404.2}$$
$$= 0.114 \text{ (approximately)}$$

Thus, dissociation constant:

$$K = \frac{C\alpha^2}{1-\alpha}$$

$$= \frac{(0.025)(0.114)^2}{(1-0.114)}$$

$$= 3.67 \times 10^{-4} \text{ mol L}^{-1}$$

Page - 54

Q. 2.10. If a current of 0.5 Ampere flows through a metallic wire for 2 hours, then how many electrons would flow through the wire?

Ans. $I = 0.5$ A

$t = 2$ hours

$= 2 \times 60 \times 60$ s $= 7200$ s

We know that,

$Q = It$

$= 0.5 \text{ A} \times 7200 \text{ s}$

$= 3600$ C

$\because$ If 96487 C $= 6.023 \times 10^{23}$ electrons.

$$\therefore \quad 3600 \text{ C} = \frac{6.023 \times 10^{23} \times 3600}{96487} \text{ electrons}$$

$= 2.25 \times 10^{22}$ electrons

Therefore, 2.25×10^{22} electrons will flow through the wire.

Q. 2.11. Suggest a list of metals that are extracted electrolytically.

Ans. The highly reactive metals having large negative E° values, which can themselves act as powerful reducing agents can be extracted electrolytically. Metals that are on the top of the reactivity series such as sodium, potassium, calcium, lithium, magnesium, aluminium is extracted electrolytically.

Q. 2.12. Consider the reaction:

$Cr_2O_7^{2-} + 14H^+ + 6e^- \rightarrow 2Cr^{3+} + 7H_2O$

What is the quantity of electricity in coulombs needed to reduce 1 mol of $Cr_2O_7^{2-}$?

Ans. The given reaction is;

$$Cr_2O_7^{2-} + 14\,H^+ + 6e^- \rightarrow 2Cr^{3+} + 7H_2O$$

The required quantity of electricity will be = 6 F

Hence, to reduce 1 mole of $Cr_2O_7 = 6 \times 96,487$ C

$= 5,78,922$ C

Page - 58

Q. 2.13. Write the chemistry of recharging the lead storage battery, highlighting all the materials that are involved during recharging.

Ans. A lead storage battery consists of a lead anode, a grid of lead packed with lead oxide (PbO_2) as the cathode, and a 38% solution of sulphuric acid (H_2SO_4) as an electrolyte.

When the battery is in use, the following cell reactions take place:

At anode: $Pb(s) + SO_4^{2-}(aq) \rightarrow PbSO_4(s) + 2e^-$

At cathode:

$PbO_2 + SO_4^{2-} + 4H^+ + 2e^- \rightarrow PbSO_4 + 2H_2O^-$

The overall cell reaction is given by,

$Pb + PbO_2 + 2H_2SO_4 \rightarrow 2PbSO_4 + 2H_2O$

When a battery is charged, the reverse of all these reactions takes place.

Hence, on charging $PbSO_4(s)$, present at the anode and cathode is converted into $PbO_2(s)$ and $Pb(s)$ respectively.

Q. 2.14. Suggest two materials other than hydrogen that can be used as fuels in fuel cells.

Ans. Methane CH_3 and methanol CH_3OH can be used as fuels in fuel cells.

Q. 2.15. Explain how rusting of iron is envisaged as setting up of an electrochemical cell.

Ans. In corrosion, due to the presence of air and moisture, oxidation takes place at a particular spot of an object made of iron. That spot behaves as the anode. The reaction at the anode is given by,

$$Fe \rightarrow Fe^{2+} + 2e^-$$

Electrons released at the anodic spot move through the metallic object and goes to another spot of the object. Therefore, in the presence of H^+ ions, the electrons reduce oxygen. This spot behaves as the cathode. These H^+ ions come either from H_2CO_3, which are formed due to the dissolution of carbon dioxide from air into water or from the dissolution of other acidic oxides from the atmosphere in water.

The reaction corresponding at the cathode is given by,

$$O_2 + 4H^+ + 4e^- \rightarrow 2H_2O$$

Now, the overall reaction will be:

$$2Fe + O_2 + 4H^+ \rightarrow 2Fe^{2+} + 2H_2O$$

Ferrous ions are further oxidized by atmospheric oxygen to ferric ions. These ferric ions combine with moisture, present in the surroundings, to form hydrated ferric oxide that is, rust ($Fe_2O.\ xH_2O$). Therefore, the rusting of iron is envisaged as the setting up of an electrochemical cell.

Exercise Questions

Q. 1. Arrange the following metals in the order in which they displace each other from the solution of their salts.

Al, Cu, Fe, Mg and Zn.

[NCERT Ex. Q. 2.1, Page 59]

Ans. The following is the order in which the given metals displace each other from the solution of their salts.

Mg, Al, Zn, Fe, Cu

Q. 2. Given the standard electrode potentials,

$K^+/K = -2.93V$, $Ag^+/Ag = 0.80V$,

$Hg^{2+}/Hg = 0.79V$

$Mg^{2+}/Mg = -2.37$ V, $Cr^{3+}/Cr = -0.74V$

Arrange these metals in their increasing order of reducing power. [NCERT Ex. Q. 2.2, Page 59]

Ans. Higher the oxidation potential more easily it is oxidized and hence greater is the reducing power. Thus, increasing order of reducing power will be Ag<Hg<Cr<Mg<K.

Q. 3. Depict the galvanic cell in which the reaction $Zn(s)+2Ag^+(aq) \rightarrow Zn^{2+}(aq)+2Ag(s)$ takes place. Further show:

(i) Which of the electrode is negatively charged?

(ii) The carriers of the current in the cell.

(iii) Individual reaction at each electrode.

[NCERT Ex. Q. 2.3, Page 59]

Ans. The galvanic cell in which the given reaction takes place is depicted as:

$$Zn \mid Zn^{2+} \mid\mid Ag^+ \mid Ag$$

(i) Zn electrode (anode) is negatively charged.

(ii) Ions are carriers of current in the cell and in the external circuit, current will flow from zinc to silver.

(iii) The reaction taking place at the anode is given by,

$$Zn \rightarrow Zn^{2+} + 2e^-$$

The reaction taking place at the cathode is given by,

$$Ag^+ + e^- \rightarrow Ag$$

Q. 4. Calculate the standard cell potentials of galvanic cell in which the following reactions take place:

(i) $2Cr(s) + 3Cd^{2+}(aq) \rightarrow 2Cr^{3+}(aq) + 3Cd$

(ii) $Fe^{2+}(aq) + Ag^+(aq) \rightarrow Fe^{3+}(aq) + Ag(s)$

Calculate the $\Delta_r G^0$ and equilibrium constant of the reactions. [NCERT Ex. Q.2.4, Page 59]

Ans. (i) $E^0_{Cr^{3+}/Cr} = -0.74$ V

$E^0_{Cd^{2+}/Cd} = -0.40$ V

The galvanic cell of the given reaction is depicted as:

$$Cr \mid Cr^{3+} \mid\mid Cd^{2+} \mid Cd$$

Now, the standard cell potential is

$$E^0 = E^0_R - E^0_L$$
$$= -0.40 - (-0.74)$$
$$= +0.34 \text{ V}$$
$$\Delta_r G^0 = -nFE^0_{cell}$$

In the given equation,

$$n = 6$$
$$F = 96500 \text{ C mol}^{-1}$$
$$E^0_{cell} = +0.34 \text{ V}$$

Then, $\Delta_r G^0 = -6 \times 96500 \text{ C mol}^{-1} \times 0.34 \text{ V}$

$$= -196860.48 \text{ CV mol}^{-1}$$
$$= -196860.48 \text{ J mol}^{-1}$$
$$= -196.86 \text{ kJ mol}^{-1}$$

Again

$$\Delta_r G^0 = -RT \ln K$$
$$\Rightarrow \Delta_r G^0 = -2.30 \text{ RT} \ln K$$
$$\Rightarrow \log K = -\frac{\Delta_r G}{2.303 \text{ RT}}$$
$$= \frac{(-196.83 \times 10^3)}{2.303 \times 8.314 \times 298}$$
$$= 34.496$$
$$K = \text{antilog}(34.496)$$
$$= 3.139 \times 10^{34}$$

(ii) $E^0_{Fe^{3+}/Fe^{2+}} = 0.77$ V

$E^0_{Ag^+/Ag} = 0.80$ V

The galvanic cell of the given reaction is depicted as:

$$Fe^{2+}_{(aq)} \mid Fe^{3+}_{(aq)} \mid\mid Ag^+_{(aq)} \mid Ag_{(s)}$$

Now, the standard cell potential is

$$E^0 = E^0_R - E^0_L$$
$$= 0.80 - 0.77 = 0.03$$

Here, $n = 1$

Then, $\Delta_r G^0 = -nFE^0_{cell}$

$$= -1 \times 96500 \text{ C mol}^{-1} \times 0.03 \text{ V}$$
$$= -2,895 \text{ Jmol}^{-1}$$
$$= -2.89 \text{ kJ mol}^{-1}$$

Again, $\Delta_r G^0 = -2.303 \text{ RT} \ln K$

$$\log K = \frac{Ø_r G}{2.303 \text{ RT}}$$
$$= \frac{-(-2894.61)}{2.303 \times 8.314 \times 298}$$
$$= 0.5073$$
$$K = \text{antilog}(0.5073)$$
$$= 3.2 \text{ (approx)}.$$

Q. 5. Write the Nernst equation and emf of the following cells at 298 K:

(a) $Mg(s) \mid Mg^{2+}(0.001 \text{ M}) \mid\mid Cu^{2+}(0.0001 \text{ M}) \mid Cu(s)$

(b) $Fe(s) \mid Fe^{2+}(0.001 \text{ M}) \mid\mid H^+(1\text{M}) \mid H_2(g)(1\text{bar}) \mid Pt(s)$

(c) $Sn(s) \mid Sn^{2+}(0.050 \text{ M}) \mid\mid H^+(0.020\text{M}) \mid H_2(g)(1 \text{ bar}) \mid Pt(s)$

(d) $Pt(s) \mid Br_2(l) \mid Br^-(0.010 \text{ M}) \mid\mid H^+(0.030 \text{ M}) \mid H_2(g)$ (1 bar) | Pt(s). [NCERT Ex. Q.2.5, Page 59]

Ans. (a) For the given reaction, the Nernst equation can be given as:

$$E_{cell} = E^\theta_{cell} - \frac{0.0591}{n} \log \frac{[Mg^{2+}]}{[Cu^{2+}]}$$
$$= \{0.34 - (-2.36)\} - \frac{0.0591}{2} \log \frac{0.001}{0.0001}$$
$$= 2.7 - \frac{0.0591}{2} \log 10$$
$$= 2.7 - 0.02955 = 2.67 \text{ V (approximately)}$$

(b) For the given reaction, the Nernst equation can be given as:

$$E_{cell} = E^\theta_{cell} - \frac{0.0591}{n} \log \frac{[Fe^{2+}]}{[H^+]^2}$$
$$= \{0 - (-0.44)\} - \frac{0.0591}{2} \log \frac{0.001}{1^2}$$
$$= 0.44 - 0.02955(-3)$$
$$= 0.52865 \text{ V} = 0.53 \text{ (approximately)}$$

(c) For the given reaction, the Nernst equation can be given as:

$$E_{cell} = E^\theta_{cell} - \frac{0.0591}{n} \log \frac{[Sn^{2+}]}{[H^+]^2}$$
$$= \{0 - (-0.14)\} - \frac{0.0591}{2} \log \frac{0.050}{(0.020)^2}$$

$= 0.14 - 0.0295 \times \log 125$
$= 0.14 - 0.062$
$= 0.078$ V
$= 0.08$ V (approximately)

(d) For the given reaction, the Nernst equation can e given as:

$$E_{cell} = E^{\theta}_{cell} - \frac{0.0591}{n}\log\frac{1}{[Br^-]^2[H^+]^2}$$

$$= (0-1.09) - \frac{0.0591}{2}\log\frac{1}{(0.010)^2(0.030)^2}$$

$$= -1.09 - 0.02955 \times \log\frac{1}{0.00000009}$$

$$= -1.09 - 0.02955 \times \log\frac{1}{9\times10^{-8}}$$

$= -1.09 - 0.02955 \times \log(1.11 \times 10^7)$
$= -1.09 - 0.02955(0.0453 + 7)$
$= -1.09 - 0.208$
$= -1.298$ V

Q. 6.In the button cells widely used in watches and other devices the following reaction takes place:

$Zn(s) + Ag_2O(s) + H_2O(l) \rightarrow Zn^{2+}(aq) + 2Ag(s) + 2OH^-$ (aq)

Determine Δ_rG^o and E^o for the reaction.

[NCERT Ex. Q.2.6, Page 59]

Ans. $Zn(s) \rightarrow Zn^{2+} + 2e^-$; $E^o = 0.76$ V

$$\frac{Ag_2O + H_2O + 2e \rightarrow 2Ag + 2OH^- \quad E^o = 0.344\,V}{Zn + Ag_2O + H_2O \rightarrow Zn^{2+} + 2Ag + 2OH^- \quad E^o = 1.104\,V}$$

$E^o = 1.104$ V

We know that,

$\Delta_rG^o = -nFE^o$
$= -2 \times 96487 \times 1.104$
$= -213043.296$ J
$= -213.04$ kJ

Q. 7.Define conductivity and molar conductivity for the solution of an electrolyte. Discuss their variation with concentration. [NCERT Ex. Q.2.7, Page 59]

Ans. Conductivity of a solution is defined as the conductance of a solution of 1 cm in length and area of cross-section 1 sq cm. The inverse of resistivity is called conductivity or specific conductance. It is represented by the symbol κ. If ρ is resistivity, then we can write:

$$\kappa = \frac{1}{\rho}$$

The conductivity of a solution at any given concentration is the conductance (G) of one-unit volume of solution kept between two platinum electrodes with the unit area of cross-section and at a distance of unit length.

$$G = \kappa\frac{A}{l} = \kappa.1 = \kappa$$

$A = 1, l = 1,$

Since, conductivity always decreases with a decrease in concentration, both for weak and strong electrolytes. This is because the number of ions per unit volume that carry the current in a solution decreases with a decrease in concentration.

Molar conductivity:

Molar conductivity of a solution at a given concentration is the conductance of volume V of a solution containing 1 mole of the electrolyte kept between two electrodes with the area of cross-section *A* and distance of unit length.

$$\Lambda_m = \kappa\frac{A}{l}$$

Now, $l = 1$ and A = V (volume containing 1 mole of the electrolyte).

$$\Lambda_m = \kappa V$$

Molar conductivity increases with a decrease in concentration. This is because the total volume V of the solution containing one mole of the electrolyte increases on dilution.

The variation of Λ_m with for strong and weak electrolytes is shown in the following plot:

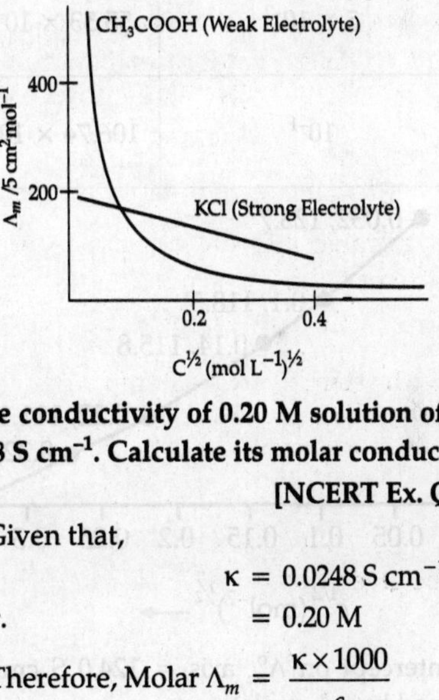

Q. 8.The conductivity of 0.20 M solution of KCl at 298 K is 0.0248 S cm^{-1}. Calculate its molar conductivity.

[NCERT Ex. Q.2.8, Page 59]

Ans. Given that,

$\kappa = 0.0248$ S cm^{-1}

∴ $c = 0.20$ M

Therefore, Molar $\Lambda_m = \dfrac{\kappa \times 1000}{c}$

$= \dfrac{0.0248 \times 1000}{0.2}$

$= 124$ S cm^2 mol^{-1}

Q. 9.The resistance of a conductivity cell containing 0.001M KCl solution at 298 K is 1500 Ω. What is the cell constant if conductivity of 0.001M KCl solution at 298 K is 0.146 × 10^{-3} S cm^{-1}. [NCERT Ex. Q.2.9, Page 59]

Ans. Given, Conductivity, $\kappa = 0.146 \times 10^{-3}$ S cm^{-1}; Resistance, R = 1,500 Ω

We know that,

Cell constant = κ × R
$= 0.146 \times 10^{-3} \times 1{,}500$
$= 0.219$ cm^{-1}

Q. 10. The conductivity of sodium chloride at 298 K has been determined at different concentrations and the results are given below:

Concentration/M	0.001	0.010	0.020	0.050	0.100
$10^2 \times \kappa$/S m^{-1}	1.237	11.85	23.15	55.53	106.74

Calculate Λ_m for all concentrations and draw a plot between Λ_m and c½. Find the value of Λ_m^0.

[NCERT Ex. Q.2.10, Page 60]

Ans. $\dfrac{1\,\text{S cm}^{-1}}{100\,\text{S m}^{-1}} = 1$ (unit conversion factor)

Concentration (m)	κ(S cm^{-1})	$\Lambda_m = \dfrac{1000 \times \kappa}{\text{Molarity}}$(S cm^2 mol^{-1})	$C^{1/2}$ ($M^{1/2}$)
10^{-3}	1.237×10^{-4}	$\dfrac{1000 \times 1.237 \times 10^{-4}}{10^{-3}} = 123.7$	0.0316
10^{-2}	11.85×10^{-4}	$\dfrac{1000 \times 11.85 \times 10^{-4}}{10^{-2}} = 118.5$	0.100
2×10^{-2}	23.15×10^{-4}	$\dfrac{1000 \times 23.15 \times 10^{-4}}{2 \times 10^{-2}} = 115.8$	0.141
5×10^{-2}	55.53×10^{-4}	$\dfrac{1000 \times 55.53 \times 10^{-4}}{5 \times 10^{-2}} = 111.1$	0.224
10^{-1}	106.74×10^{-4}	$\dfrac{1000 \times 106.74 \times 10^{-4}}{10^{-1}} = 106.7$	0.316

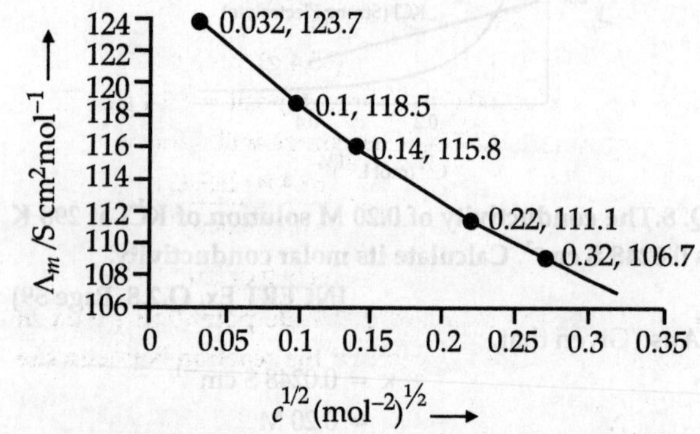

Λ^o = Intercept on Λ_m^o axis = 124.0 S cm^2 mol^{-1}, which is obtained by extrapolation to zero concentration.

Q. 11. Conductivity of 0.00241 M acetic acid is 7.896×10^{-5} S cm^{-1}. Calculate its molar conductivity. If Λ_m^0 for acetic acid is 390.5 S cm^2 mol^{-1}, what is its dissociation constant? [NCERT Ex. Q.2.11, Page 60]

Ans. Given,

$$\kappa = 7.896 \times 10^{-5} \text{ Sm}^{-1}$$

$$C = 0.00241 \text{ mol L}^{-1}$$

molar conductivity,

$$\Lambda_m = \frac{\kappa}{C} = \frac{7.896 \times 10^{-5}}{0.00241} \times \frac{1000}{1}$$

$$= 32.76 \text{ S cm}^2 \text{ mol}^{-1}$$

$$\Lambda_m^o = 390.5 \text{ S cm}^2 \text{ mol}^{-1}$$

Again,

$$\alpha = \frac{\Lambda_m}{\Lambda_m^o} = \frac{32.76}{390.5}$$

$$= 0.084$$

$$K_a = \frac{C\alpha^2}{(1-\alpha)}$$

∴ Dissociation constant

$$= \frac{(0.00241)(0.084)^2}{(1-0.084)}$$

$$= 1.86 \times 10^{-5}$$

Q. 12. How much charge is required for the following reductions:

(i) 1 mol of Al^{3+} to Al?

(ii) 1 mol of Cu^{2+} to Cu?

(iii) 1 mol of MnO_4^- to Mn^{2+}?

[NCERT Ex. Q.2.12, Page 60]

Ans. (i) $Al^{3+} + 3e^- \rightarrow Al$

Required charge = 3F

= $3 \times 96{,}500$ C

= 2.89×10^5 C

(ii) $Cu^{2+} + 2e^- \rightarrow Cu$

Required chrge = 2F

= $2 \times 96{,}500$ C

= 1.93×10^5 C

(iii) $MnO_4^- \rightarrow Mn^{2+}$

$Mn^{7+} + 5e^- \rightarrow Mn^{2+}$

∴ Required charge 5F

= $5 \times 96{,}500$ C

= 4.825×10^5 C

Q. 13. How much electricity in terms of Faraday is required to produce

(i) 20.0 g of Ca from molten $CaCl_2$?

(ii) 40.0 g of Al from molten Al_2O_3?

[NCERT Ex. Q.2.13, Page 60]

Ans. (a) According to the question,

$$Ca^{2+} + 2e^- \rightarrow Ca$$

$\because$ Electricity required to produce 40 g of calcium

$$= 2F$$

$\therefore$ Hence, electricity required to produce 20 g of calcium

$$= \frac{2 \times 20}{40} F$$

$$= 1F$$

(b) According to the question

$$Al^{3+} + 3e^- \rightarrow Al$$
$$27g$$

$\because$ Electricity required to produce 27 g of Al

$$= 3 F$$

$\therefore$ Hence, electricity required to produce 40 g of Al

$$= \frac{3 \times 40}{27} F$$

$$= 4.44 F$$

Q. 14. How much electricity is required in coulomb for the oxidation of

(i) 1 mol of H_2O to O_2?

(ii) 1 mol of FeO to Fe_2O_3?

[NCERT Ex. Q.2.14, Page 60]

Ans. (i) According to the question,

$$O^{2-} \rightarrow \frac{1}{2}O_2 + 2e$$

Electricity required for the oxidation of 1 mol of H_2O to O_2 = 2 F

$$= 2 \times 96{,}500 \text{ C}$$
$$= 1{,}93{,}000 \text{ C}$$

(ii) Here, according to the question,

$$Fe^{2+} \rightarrow Fe^{3+} + e$$

Electricity required for the oxidation of 1 mol of FeO to Fe_2O_3 = 1 F

$$= 96{,}500 \text{ C}$$

Q. 15. A solution of $Ni(NO_3)_2$ is electrolysed between platinum electrodes using a current of 5 amperes for 20 minutes. What mass of Ni is deposited at the cathode?

[NCERT Ex. Q. 2.15, Page 60]

Ans. Given, Current = 5 A

Time = 20 × 60 = 1,200 s

Formula used: Charge = Current × Time

= 5 × 1,200

= 6,000 C

So, according to the reaction

$$Ni^{2+} + 2e^- \rightarrow Ni$$
$$58.7 \text{ g}$$

Nickel deposited by 2 × 96500 C = 58.71 g

Therefore, nickel deposited by 6,000 C

$$= \frac{58.71 \times 6{,}000}{2 \times 96500} \text{g}$$

$$= 1.825 \text{ g}$$

Therefore, 1.825 g of Nickel will be deposited at the cathode.

Q. 16. Three electrolytic cells A, B, C containing solutions of $ZnSO_4$, $AgNO_3$ and $CuSO_4$, respectively are connected in series. A steady current of 1.5 amperes was passed through them until 1.45 g of silver deposited at the cathode of cell B. How long did the current flow? What mass of copper and zinc were deposited?

[NCERT Ex. Q.2.16, Page 60]

Ans. According to the reaction:

$$Ag^+ + e^- \rightarrow Ag$$
$$108g$$

$\because$ 108 g of Ag is deposited by 96,487 C.

$\therefore$ 1.45 g of Ag is deposited by $= \frac{96{,}487 \times 1.45}{107}$ C

$$= 1295.43 \text{ C}$$

given,

Current = 1.5 A

$$t = \frac{1295.43}{1.5} \text{s}$$

$\therefore$ Time = 863.6 s = 864 = 14.40 min

Again,

$$Cu^{2+} + 2e^- \rightarrow Cu$$
$$(63.5 \text{ g})$$

$\because$ 2 × 96500 C of charge deposit = 63.5 g of Cu

$\therefore$ 1295.43 C of charge will deposit

$$= \frac{63.5 \times 1295.43}{2 \times 96500} = 0.426 \text{ g of Cu}$$

$$Zn^{2+} + 2e^- \rightarrow Zn$$
$$(65.4 \text{ g})$$

i.e., 2 × 96500 C of charge deposit = 65.4 g of Zn

Therefore, 1295.43 C of charge will deposit

$$= \frac{(65.4 \times 1295.43)}{(2 \times 96500)} \text{g}$$

$$= 0.439 \text{ g of Zn}$$

Q. 17. Using the standard electrode potentials given in Table 3.1 (of NCERT), predict if the reaction between the following is feasible:

(i) Fe^{3+}(aq) and I^-(aq)

(ii) Ag^+ (aq) and Cu(s)

(iii) Fe^{3+} (aq) and Br^- (aq)

(iv) Ag(s) and Fe^{3+} (aq)

(v) Br_2 (aq) and Fe^{2+} (aq).

[NCERT Ex. Q.2.17, Page 60]

Ans. (i) $Fe^{3+} + e^- \rightarrow Fe^{2+}] \times 2$; $E^o = +0.77$ V

$2I^- \rightarrow I_2 + 2e^-$; $E^o = -0.54$ V

$2Fe^{3+} + 2I^- \rightarrow 2Fe^{2+} + I_2$; $E^o = +0.23$ V

Since E^θ for the overall reaction is positive, the reaction between Fe^{3+} and I^- is feasible.

(ii) $Ag^+ + e^- \rightarrow Ag] \times 2$; $E^o = +0.80$ V

$Cu \rightarrow Cu^{2+} + 2e^-$; $E^o = -0.34$ V

$2Ag^+ + Cu \rightarrow 2Ag + Cu^{2+}$; $E^o = +0.46$ V

Since E^θ for overall reaction is positive, the reaction between Ag^+ and Cu is feasible.

(iii) $Fe^{3+} + e^- \rightarrow Fe] \times 2$; $E^o = +0.77$ V

$2Br \rightarrow Br_{2(l)} + 2e^-$; $E^o = -1.09$ V

$2Fe^{3+} + 2Br \rightarrow 2Fe^{2+}$ and $Br_{2(l)}$; $E^o = -0.32$ V

Since E° for the overall reaction is negative, the reaction between Fe^{3+} and Br^- is not feasible.

(iv) $Ag \rightarrow Ag^+ + e^-$; $E^o = -0.80$ V

$Fe^{3+} + e^- \rightarrow Fe^{2+}$; $E^o = +0.77$ V

$Ag + Fe^{3+} \rightarrow Ag^+ + Fe^{2+}$; $E^o = -0.03$ V

Since E° for the overall reaction is negative, the reaction between Fe^{3+} (aq) and Ag(aq) is not feasible.

(v) Br_2 (aq) + $2e^- \rightarrow 2Br^-$(aq) $E^o = +1.09$ V

Fe^{2+} (aq) $\rightarrow Fe^{3+}$(aq) + $e^- \times 2$ $E^o = -0.77$ V

$Br_2 + 2Fe^{2+} \rightarrow 2Br^- + 2Fe^{3+}$

$E^{\circ}_{cell} = 1.08 - 0.77 = 0.31$ V (feasible)

Q.18. Predict the products of electrolysis in each of the following:

(i) An aqueous solution of $AgNO_3$ with silver electrodes.

(ii) An aqueous solution of $AgNO_3$ with platinum electrodes.

(iii) A dilute solution of H_2SO_4 with platinum electrodes.

(iv) An aqueous solution of $CuCl_2$ with platinum electrodes. [NCERT Ex. Q.2.18, Page 60]

Ans. (i) At cathode: The following reduction reactions compete to take place at the cathode.

$Ag^+ + e^- \rightarrow Ag$; $E^o = 0.80$ V

$H^+ + e^- \rightarrow \frac{1}{2}H_2$; $E^o = 0.00$ V

The reaction with a higher value of E^0 takes place at the cathode. Therefore, deposition of silver will take place at the cathode.

At anode: The Ag anode is attacked by NO_3^- ions. Therefore, the silver electrode at the anode dissolves in the solution to form Ag^+.

(ii) At cathode: The following reduction reactions compete to take place at the cathode.

$Ag^+ + e^- \rightarrow Ag$; $E^o = 0.80$ V

$H^+ + e^- \rightarrow \frac{1}{2}H_2$; $E^o = 0.00$ V

The reaction with a higher value of E° takes place at the cathode. Therefore, deposition of silver will take place at the cathode.

At anode: Since Pt electrodes are inert, the anode not attacked by NO_3^- ions. Therefore, OH^- or NO_3^- ion can be oxidized at the anode. But OH^- ions having a lower discharge potential and get preference and decompose to liberate O_2.

$OH^- \rightarrow OH + e^-$

$4OH^- \rightarrow 2H_2O + O_2$

(iii) At cathode, the following reduction reaction occurs to produce H_2 gas.

$H^+(aq) + e^- \rightarrow ½ H_2(g)$

At anode, the following processes are possible

$2H_2O \rightarrow O_2 + 4H^+ + 4e^-$;

$E^o = +1.23$ V (i)

$2SO_4^{2-} \rightarrow S_2O_6^{2-} + 2e^-$;

$E^o = +1.96$ V (ii)

For dilute sulphuric acid, reaction (i) is preferred to produce O_2 gas. But for concentrated sulphuric acid reaction (ii) occurs.

(iv) At cathode: The following reduction reaction compete to take place at the cathode.

$Cu^{2+} + 2e^- \rightarrow Cu$; $E^o = 0.34$ V

$H^+ + e^- \rightarrow \frac{1}{2}H_2$; $E^o = 0.34$ V

The reaction with a higher value of E^0 takes place at the cathode. Therefore, deposition of copper will take place at the cathode.

At anode: The following oxidation reactions are possible at the anode.

$Cl^- \rightarrow \frac{1}{2}Cl_2 + e^-$; $E^o = 1.36$ V

$2H_2O(1) \rightarrow O2 + 4H^+ + 4e^-$; $E^o = +1.23$ V

At the anode, the reaction with a lower value of E is preferred. But due to the over-potential of oxygen, Cl^- gets oxidized at the anode to produce Cl_2 gas.

CHAPTER 3

CHEMICAL KINETICS

Rate of Chemical Reaction

Chemical Kinetics: It is the branch of physical chemistry which deals with study of the rate of chemical reaction and the mechanism by which the reaction occurs.

Scan to know more about this topic

Kinetics

Rate of Reaction: The rate of reaction is the change of concentration of any reactant or product with time, for a reaction.

$$A + B \rightarrow C$$

Rate of reaction, A =

$$\frac{\text{Decrease in concentration of A}}{\text{Time taken}} = \frac{-\Delta[A]}{\Delta t}$$

Similarly, $B = \frac{-\Delta[B]}{\Delta t}$

and for product $C = \frac{\Delta[C]}{\Delta t}$

where, [A], [B] and [C] are molar concentrations of the reactants and the product, respectively.

- **Unit of rate of reaction:** mol L^{-1} s^{-1} or mol L^{-1} min^{-1} (in liquid), atm s^{-1} or atm min^{-1} (in gaseous form).
- **Instantaneous rate of reaction:** Instantaneous rate is defined as the rate of change in concentration of any one of the reactant or products at a particular time.

Instantaneous rate

$$= \frac{dx}{dt} = \frac{-d[A]}{dt} = \frac{-d[B]}{dt} = \frac{+d[C]}{dt}$$

- **Average rate of reaction:** The rate of reaction measured over a long-time interval is called average rate of a reaction.

$$\text{Average rate} = \frac{\Delta x}{\Delta t},$$

where, Δx = change in concentration in given time and Δt = time taken.

Factors Affecting the Rate of a Chemical Reaction

(i) **Concentration of reactants:** Rate of reaction is directly proportional to the concentration of the reactants. Thus, to increase the rate of a reaction the concentration of the reactants has to be increased.

(ii) **Temperature:** The rate of a reaction increases with the increase in temperature because the kinetic energy of the molecules increases the rate of reaction.

(iii) **Pressure:** Pressure affects the rate in only gaseous reactions. Increase in pressure decreases the volume and increases concentration. Increase in concentration increases the rate of reaction.

(iv) **Presence of catalyst:** The rate of many reactions is greatly affected by the presence of a catalyst. In the presence of a catalyst, the activation energy of a reaction decreases due to which the reaction proceeds at a faster rate.

(v) **Nature of the reactants:** In a chemical reaction, some bonds are broken while some new bonds are formed. Thus, if the molecules are simpler, then fewer bonds will rupture and the rate of reaction becomes fast while in complex molecules, more bonds will rupture and the velocity of reaction decreases.

(vi) **Surface area of the reactants:** In some heterogeneous reactions, the reaction takes place at the surface of the reactant. Thus, in such reactions, the reaction rate is greatly affected by the surface area. Marble powder reacts faster than marble chips.

(vii) **Effect of radiations:** Those reactions which are initiated by the radiations of wavelengths are termed as photochemical reactions. These reactions generally proceed at a faster rate than normal thermal reactions.

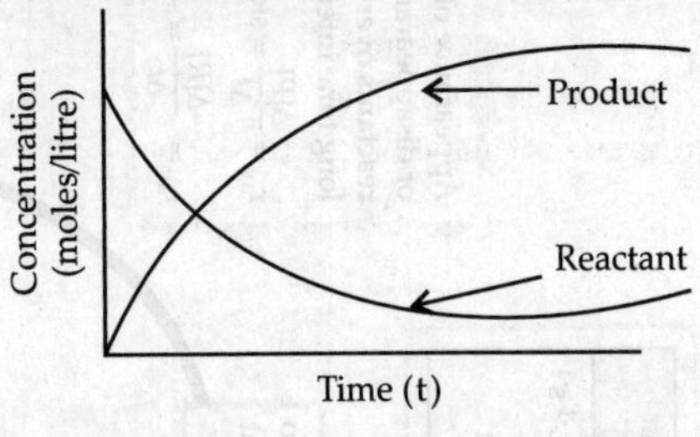

(viii) **Effect of physical state:** Rate of reaction depends upon physical state of the reactant, *e.g.*, $I_2(g)$ reacts faster than $I_2(s)$. $AgNO_3(aq)$ reacts with NaCl but $AgNO_3(s)$ does not react with NaCl.

- **Rate Law:** Rate law or rate equation is the expression which relates the rate of reaction with concentration of the reactants. The constant of proportionality 'k' is known as rate constant. The rate law states that the rate of reaction is directly proportional to the product of molar concentration of reactants and each concentration is raised to some power which may or may not be equal to stoichiometry coefficients of reacting species.

$$\text{Rate} = k[A]^m [B]^n$$

Chemical Kinetics

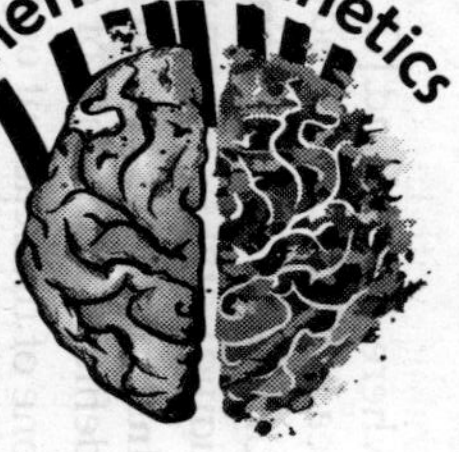

Rate of Chemical Reaction

Change in concentration of reactants or products in unit time; Unit : mol L^{-1} s^{-1} or atm s^{-1}

$R \rightarrow P$

Rate of appearance of P $= \frac{\text{Increase in concentration of P}}{\text{Time taken}} = +\frac{\Delta[P]}{\Delta t}$

Rate of disappearance of R $= \frac{\text{Decrease in concentration of R}}{\text{Time taken}} = \frac{-\Delta[R]}{\Delta t}$

Average Rate

Appearance of products or disappearance of reactants over a long time interval.

$r_{av} = \frac{\Delta[P]}{\Delta t}$ = slope

$r_{av} = \frac{-\Delta[R]}{\Delta t}$ = –slope

Factors Influencing rate of reaction

Concentration : Higher the concentration of reactants, faster is the rate of reaction.

Temperature : Increases with increase in temperature. Becomes almost double with 10°C rise.

Catalyst : Increases with a catalyst.

Surface Area : Greater is the surface area, faster is the rate of reaction.

Activation Energy : Lower the activation energy, faster is the reaction.

Instantaneous Rate

Rate of change in concentration of reactant/product at a particular time.

$r_{inst} = \frac{-d[R]}{dt} = \frac{+d[P]}{dt}$

Rate Law

Expression in which reaction rate is given in terms of molar concentration of reactants with each term raised to power which may or may not be same as stoichiometric coefficient of reactants in a balanced chemical equation.

$aA + bB \rightarrow cC + dD$

Rate $= k [A]^a [B]^b = \frac{d[R]}{dt}$

$k = \frac{[C]^c [D]^d}{[A]^a [B]^b}$

Rate Constant: Rate of a reaction when concentration of each of the reactant in unity.

Order	Unit
0	mol $L^{-1}s^{-1}$
1	s^{-1}
2	$mol^{-1}L\ s^{-1}$

Order of a Reaction

Sum of powers of concentration of the reactants in the rate law.

Collision Theory : Rate of reaction depends on the collision frequency and effective collisions.

Effective Collision

Collision in which molecules collide with sufficient kinetic energy and proper orientation for breaking of bonds and formation of new bonds.

E_a and proper orientation of the molecules determine the criteria for an effective collision.

Rate $= PZ_{AB}e^{-Ea/RT}$

P is Steric or Probability factor

Collision Frequency

Number of collisions per unit volume of reaction mixture

Rate $= Z_{AB}e^{-Ea/RT}$

Integrated Rate Equation

Integration of differential rate equation to give a relation between concentrations at different times and rate constant.

Order	Integrated Rate Law	Straight Plot	Unit (k)
0	$kt = [R]_0 - [R]$	[R] vs t	mol L^{-1} s^{-1}
1	$kt = \ln\{[R]_0/[R]\}$	ln[R] vs t	s^{-1}

Half-life of a Reaction

Time in which the concentration of a reactant is reduced to one half of its initial concentration.

First Order: $t_{1/2} = \frac{0.693}{k}$

Zero Order: $t_{1/2} = \frac{[R]_0}{2k}$

Molecularity of a Reaction

Number of reacting species taking part in an elementary reaction colliding to bring out a reaction.

Pseudo First Order Reaction

Not truly of first order but under certain conditions behave as first order reaction. In such reaction, one reactants is in excess.

- Acid hydrolysis of ethyl acetate
- Inversion of sugar

Arrhenius Equation

$k = Ae^{-Ea/RT}$

$\log k = \log A - \frac{E_a}{2.303RT}$

$\log \frac{k_2}{k_1} = \frac{E_a}{2.303RT}\left[\frac{T_2 - T_1}{T_1 T_2}\right]$

Activation Energy, E_a : Energy required to form an intermediate called activated complex (C)

E_a = Threshold energy - Average Kinetic energy of reacting molecules

Trace the Mind Map

First Level ▸ Second Level ▸ Third Level

Rate Constant: Rate constant is also called specific reaction rate. When concentration of both reactants is unity (one), then the rate of reaction is known as rate constant. It is denoted by 'k'.

Molecularity: Total number of atoms, ions or molecules of the reactants involved in the reaction is termed as molecularity. It is always a whole number. It is never more than three. It cannot be zero.

An example is the decomposition of N_2O_4.

Elementary Reaction: An elementary reaction is a chemical reaction in which one or more of the chemical species react directly to form products in a single reaction step and with a single transition state.

For a complex reaction generally, molecularity of the slowest step is same as the order of the overall reaction.

Initial rate of reaction: The rate at the beginning of the reaction when the concentrations have not changed appreciably is called initial rate of reaction.

Scan to know more about this topic

Kinetics- Initial rates and Integrated Rate laws

Rate Determining Step: The slowest step in the reaction mechanism is called rate determining step.

Order of reaction: Order is defined as the sum of powers of concentration of the reactants in the experimentally derived rate equation or rate law expression. Order of reaction is experimentally determined and is not written from the balanced chemical equation. Order of reaction can be whole number, zero or fractional.

- **Zero order reaction:** The rate of reaction does not change with the concentration of the reactants. *i.e.*

$$\text{Rate} = k[A]_0,$$

$$k = \frac{[A]_0 - [A]}{t},$$

where 'k' is rate constant, $[A]_0$ is initial concentration of reactant.

- Unit of the rate constant k is mol L^{-1} s^{-1}. This reaction will be zero order reaction. Decomposition of gaseous ammonia on hot platinum, thermal decomposition of HI on gold surface and photochemical reaction between hydrogen and chlorine are examples of zero order reaction.
- **First order reaction:** The rate of reaction is directly proportional to the first power of the concentration of reacting substance. Rate constant of the first order reaction is

$$k = \frac{2.303}{t}\log\frac{a}{a-x}$$

$$\Rightarrow \quad k = \frac{2.303}{t}\log\frac{[A_0]}{[A]},$$

where 'a' is initial concentration and $(a - x)$ is the concentration after time 't'. Unit of 'k' is s^{-1} or min^{-1}. Decomposition of N_2O_5 and N_2O are examples.

- **Pseudo first order reaction:** If a reaction is not truly of the first order but under certain conditions becomes reaction of first order is called pseudo first order reaction, *e.g.*, acidic hydrolysis of ester (ethyl acetate)

$$CH_3COOC_2H_5 + H_2O \xrightleftharpoons{H+} CH_3COOH + C_2H_5OH$$

- **Second order reaction:** The reaction in which sum of powers of concentration terms in rate law or rate equation is equal to 2.

$$\frac{dx}{dt} = k[A][B]$$

Unit of rate constant is mol^{-1} L s^{-1} or M^{-1} s^{-1}, where M is molarity.

Reaction	Order	Unit of rate constant	Example
Zero order	0	mol^{-1} L^{-1} s^{-1}	$H_2 + Cl_2 \xrightarrow{\text{Sunlight}} 2HCl$
First order	1	s^{-1}	$2N_2O_5 \rightarrow 4NO_2 + O_2$
Pseudo first order	1	s^{-1}	$C_{12}H_{22}O_{11} + H_2O \xrightarrow{H^+} C_6H_{12}O_6 + C_6H_{12}O_6$
Second order	2	mol^{-1} L s^{-1}	$H_2 + I_2 \rightarrow 2HI$

- **Equation for typical first order gas phase reaction:**

$$A(g) \rightarrow B(g) + C(g)$$

$$k = \frac{2.303}{t}\log\frac{p_i}{p_A}$$

$$k = \frac{2.303}{t}\log\frac{p_i}{(2p_i - p_t)}$$

where p_i is the initial pressure of A at time, $t = 0$ and p_t is the total pressure at time t.

- **Half-life of a reaction:** The time taken for a reaction when half of the initial value has reacted is called **half-life of a reaction.**

For zero order reaction, $t_{1/2} = \frac{[A]_0}{2k}$,

where $[A]_0$ is initial and last concentration of reaction it means there is no change in concentration and 'k' is rate constant.

For 1st order reaction, $t_{1/2} = \frac{0.693}{k}$

nth order reaction: In general, for nth order reaction of the type

$$A \rightarrow \text{products, where, } \frac{dx}{dt} = k[A]^n$$

$$k_n = \frac{1}{t(n-1)}\left[\frac{1}{[A]^{n-1}} - \frac{1}{[A]_0^{\,n-1}}\right]$$

where $[A]_0$ is initial concentration, [A] is final concentration after time t and n can have all the values except 1.

- **Half-life of a reaction of nth order:**

$$t_{1/2} \propto \frac{1}{[A]_0^{n-1}}$$

$t_{1/2} \propto [A]$ for zero order

$t_{1/2}$ is independent of [A] for 1st order

$$t_{1/2} \propto \frac{1}{[A]} \text{ for } 2^{nd} \text{ order}$$

$$t_{1/2} \propto \frac{1}{[A]^2} \text{ for } 3^{rd} \text{ order}$$

Amount of substances left after n half-lives = $\frac{[A]_0}{2^n}$

- **Integrated rate laws for the reactions of zero and first order:**

Order	Reaction type	Differential rate law	Integrated rate law	Straight line plot	Half Life	Units of k
0	$A \rightarrow P$	$\frac{d[A]}{dt} = -k$	$kt = [A]_0 - [A]$	[A] Vs. t	$\frac{[A]_0}{2k}$	conc. time^{-1}
1	$A \rightarrow P$	$\frac{d[A]}{dt} = -k[A]$	$[A] = [A]_0 e^{-kt}$ $kt = \frac{ln[A]_0}{[A]}$	ln [A] Vs. t	$ln\frac{2}{k}$	time^{-1}

- **Lifetime:** The time in which 98% of the reaction is completed is called lifetime.
- The rate of reaction is dependent on temperature. This is expressed in terms of temperature coefficient.

$$\text{Temperature coefficient} = \frac{\text{Rate constant at 308 K}}{\text{Rate constant at 298 K}}$$

It is observed that for a chemical reaction with rise in temperature by 10°, the rate constant is nearly doubled.

- **Activation energy:** It is an extra energy which must be possessed by reactant molecules so that collision between reactant molecules is effective and leads to the formation of product molecules.
- Activation energy (E_a) for a reaction cannot be zero. It is not possible that every collision between molecules will be effective. E_a cannot have negative value.
- **Threshold energy:** The minimum energy that the reacting species must possess in order to undergo effective collision to form product molecules is called threshold energy.
- **Arrhenius equation:** Activated complex is defined as unstable intermediate formed between reacting molecules. It is highly unstable and readily changes into product. Arrhenius equation gives the relation between rate of reaction and temperature.

$$k = Ae^{-E_a/RT}$$

where k = rate constant, A = Frequency factor (Arrhenius factor), E_a = Activation Energy, R = Gas constant, T = Temperature in Kelvin

$$\ln K = \ln A - \frac{E_a}{RT}$$

$$\log k = \log A - \frac{E_a}{2.303\, RT}$$

A plot of log k with 1/T gives a straight line with slope $= -\frac{E_a}{2.303\, R}$

If k_2 and k_1 are rate constants at temperature T_2 and T_1 respectively, then

$$\log\frac{k_2}{k_1} = \frac{E_a}{2.303\, R}\left[\frac{T_2 - T_1}{T_1 \cdot T_2}\right]$$

- Those collisions which lead to the formation of produc molecules are called effective collisions.

Rate of reaction = $f \times z$,

where 'z' is collision frequency and 'f' is fraction o collisions, which are effective.

- The number of collisions that take place per second pe unit volume of the reaction mixture is called collisior frequency. It is represented by 'Z'.
- Activated complex is defined as unstable intermediate formed between reacting molecules. It is highly unstable and readily changes into product.
- According to the collision theory, rate of reactior depends on the collision frequency and effective collisions.

$$\text{Rate} = Z_{AB}e^{-E_a/RT},$$

where Z_{AB} represents the collision frequency of reactants A and B. $e^{-E_a/RT}$ represents the fraction of molecules with energies equal to or greater than E_a.

- **Catalyst:** A catalyst is a substance that alters the rate of reaction without itself undergoing any chemical change at the end of reaction.
- **Intermediate complex theory:**

$$\underset{\text{Reactants}}{A + B} + \underset{\text{Catalyst}}{X} \longrightarrow A \cdots B \longrightarrow A \longrightarrow \underset{\text{Product}}{B} + \underset{\text{Catalyst}}{X}$$

(X: Intermediate complex)

Characteristics of catalyst:

(i) Catalyses only the spontaneous reaction.

(ii) Does not change the equilibrium constant.

(iii) Catalyses both the forward and backward reactions.

(iv) Does not alter the free energy change (ΔG) of a reaction.

(v) A small amount of the catalyst can catalyse large amount of reactions.

NCERT CORNER

Intext Questions

Page - 66

Q. 3.1. For the reaction R → P, the concentration of a reactant changes from 0.03M to 0.02M in 25 minutes. Calculate the average rate of reaction using units of time both in minutes and seconds.

Ans. Average rate of reaction,

$$= \frac{\Delta[R]}{\Delta t} = \frac{[R]_2 - [R]_1}{t_2 - t_1}$$

$$= \frac{0.02 - 0.03}{25} \text{ M min}^{-1}$$

$$= -\frac{-0.01}{25} \text{ M min}^{-1}$$

$$= 4 \times 10^{-4} \text{ M min}^{-1}$$

$$= \frac{4 \times 10^{-4}}{60} \text{ M s}^{-1}$$

$$= 6.67 \times 10^{-6} \text{ M s}^{-1}$$

Q. 3.2. In a reaction, 2A → Products, the concentration of A decreases from 0.5 mol L^{-1} to 0.4 mol L^{-1} in 10 minutes. Calculate the rate during this interval?

Ans. Average rate,

$$= \frac{1}{2}\frac{\Delta[A]}{\Delta t} = \frac{1}{2}\frac{[A]_2 - [A]_1}{t_2 - t_1}$$

$$= \frac{1}{2} \times \frac{0.4 - 0.5}{10} = \frac{1}{2} \times \frac{-0.1}{10}$$

$$= 0.005 \text{ mol L}^{-1} \text{ min}^{-1}$$

$$= 5 \times 10^{-3} \text{ M min}^{-1}$$

Q. 3.3. For a reaction, A + B → Product; the rate law is given by $r = k[A]^{1/2}[B]^2$. What is the order of the reaction?

Ans. The order of the reaction

$$\frac{1}{2} + 2 = 2\frac{1}{2} = 2.5$$

Q. 3.4. The conversion of molecules X to Y follows second order kinetics. If concentration of X is increased to three times how will it affect the rate of formation of Y?

Ans. Initial rate $= k[X]^2$

When concentration is increased 3 times,

then new rate $= k[3X]^2$

$= k \times 9[X]^2$

Therefore, the rate of reaction will become 9 times i.e., the rate of formation of Y will increase by q times.

Page - 78

Q. 3.5. A first order reaction has a rate constant 1.15 × 10^{-3} s^{-1}. How long will 5 g of this reactant take to reduce to 3 g?

Ans. Given:

Initial amount = 5 g

Final concentration = 3 g

Rate constant = 1.15 × 10^{-3}s^{-1}

We know that for a first order reaction,

$$t = \frac{2.303}{k}\log\frac{[R_{initial}]}{[R_{final}]}$$

$$= \frac{2.303}{1.15 \times 10^{-3}}\log\frac{5}{3}$$

$$= \frac{2.303}{1.15 \times 10^{-3}} \times 0.2219$$

$= 444.3$ s

Q. 3.6. Time required to decompose SO_2Cl_2 to half of its initial amount is 60 minutes. If the decomposition is a first order reaction, calculate the rate constant of the reaction.

Ans. Given, $t½ = 60$ min.

$$k = \frac{0.693}{t^{1/2}} = \frac{0.693}{60}$$

$$= 1.155 \times 10^{-2} \text{ min} = \frac{1.155 \times 10^{-2}}{60}$$

$$= 1.925 \times 10^{-4} \text{ s}^{-1}$$

Page - 84

Q. 3.7. What will be the effect of temperature on rate constant?

Ans. The rate constant $K = Ae^{-Ea/RT}$ of a chemical reaction increases with increase in temperature. It is observed that the rate constant of a reaction is nearly doubled when the temperature is increased by 10°C.

$$k = Ae^{-Ea/RT}$$

where, A = Arrhenius factor or the frequency factor.

T = temperature

R = 8.31.4 JK^{-1} mol^{-1}

E_a = Activation energy

Q. 3.8. The rate of the chemical reaction doubles for an increase of 10K in absolute temperature from 298K. Calculate E_a.

Ans. Given T_1 = 298 K

T_2 = (298 + 10) K = 308 K

As given above that rate of reaction doubles when temperature increased by 10°C.

Take value of $k_1 = k$ and that of $k_2 = 2k$.

Also, R = 8.314 J K^{-1} mol^{-1}

Now, substituting above values in the equation:

$$\log\frac{k_2}{k_1} = \frac{E_0}{2.303\,R}\left[\frac{T_2 - T_1}{T_1 T_2}\right]$$

We obtain:

$$\log\frac{k_2}{k_1} = \frac{E_0}{2.303 \times 8.314}\left[\frac{10}{298 \times 308}\right]$$

$$\log 2 = \frac{E_0}{2.303 \times 8.314}\left[\frac{10}{298 \times 308}\right]$$

$$\therefore \quad E_0 = \frac{2.303 \times 8.314 \times 298 \times 308 \times \log 2}{10}$$

$$= 52897.78 \text{ J mol}^{-1} = 52.9 \text{ kJ mol}^{-1}$$

Q. 3.9. The activation energy for the reaction

2 HI(g) → H_2 + I_2 (g)

is 209.5 kJ mol^{-1} at 581K. Calculate the fraction of molecules of reactants having energy equal to or greater than activation energy?

Ans. As given,

$$E_a = 209.5 \text{ kJ mol}^{-1} = 209{,}500 \text{ J mol}^{-1}$$
$$T = 581 \text{ K}$$
$$R = 8.314 \text{ JK}^{-1} \text{ mol}^{-1}$$

Fraction of molecules of reactants having energy equal to or greater than activation energy is given as follows:

$$x = e^{-E_a} \times RT$$

$$\Rightarrow \ln x = -E_a/RT$$
$$\Rightarrow \log x = -\frac{E_a}{2.303\,RT}$$
$$\Rightarrow \log x = -\frac{209{,}500}{2.303 \times 8.314 \times 581} = 18.8323$$

Now, x = Antilog (18.8323)
= Antilog $\overline{19}.1677$
= 1.471×10^{-19}

Exercise Questions

Q. 1. From the rate expression for the following reactions, determine their order of reaction and the dimensions of the rate constants.

(i) $3NO(g) \rightarrow N_2O(g)$; Rate = $k[NO]^2$

(ii) $H_2O_2(aq) + 3I^-(aq) + 2H^+ \rightarrow 2H_2O(l) + 3I^-$; Rate = $k[H_2O_2][I^-]$

(iii) $CH_3CHO(g) \rightarrow CH_4(g) + CO(g)$; Rate = $k[CH_3CHO]^{3/2}$

(iv) $C_2H_5Cl(g) \rightarrow C_2H_4(g) + HCl(g)$; Rate = $k[C_2H_5Cl]$

[NCERT Ex. Q. 3.1, Page 85]

Ans. (i) As given that,
rate = $k[NO]^2$

Therefore, order of the reaction = 2

$$\text{Dimension of } k = \frac{\text{Rate}}{[NO]^2} = \frac{\text{mol L}^{-1}\text{s}^{-1}}{(\text{mol L}^{-1})^2}$$
$$= \frac{\text{mol L}^{-1}\text{s}^{-1}}{\text{mol}^2\text{L}^{-2}} = \text{L mol}^{-1}\text{ s}^{-1}$$

(ii) Given rate = $k[H_2O_2][I^-]$

Hence, order of the reaction = 2

$$\text{Dimension of } k = \frac{\text{Rate}}{[H_2O_2][I^-]}$$
$$= \frac{\text{mol L}^{-1}\text{s}^{-1}}{(\text{mol L}^{-1})(\text{mol L}^{-1})}$$
$$= \text{L mol}^{-1}\text{s}^{-1}$$

(iii) Given, rate = $k[CH_3CHO]^{3/2}$

$\therefore$ Order of reaction = $\frac{3}{2}$

$$\text{Dimension of } k = \frac{\text{Rate}}{[CH_3CHO]^{3/2}}$$
$$= \frac{\text{mol L}^{-1}\text{s}^{-1}}{(\text{mol L}^{-1})^{3/2}} = \frac{\text{mol L}^{-1}\text{s}^{-1}}{\text{mol}^{3/2}\text{L}^{-3/2}}$$
$$= \text{L}^{1/2}\text{ mol}^{-1/2}\text{ s}^{-1}$$

(iv) Given, rate = $k[C_2H_5Cl]$

Hence, order of the reaction = 1

$$\text{Dimension of } k = \frac{\text{rate}}{[C_2H_5Cl]}$$
$$k = \frac{\text{mol L}^{-1}\text{s}^{-1}}{\text{mol L}^{-1}}$$
$$k = \text{s}^{-1}$$

Q. 2. For the reaction:

$$2A + B \rightarrow A_2B$$

the rate = $k[A][B]^2$ with $k = 2.0 \times 10^{-6}$ mol^{-2} L^2 s^{-1}. Calculate the initial rate of the reaction when [A] = 0.1 mol L^{-1}, [B] = 0.2 mol L^{-1}. Calculate the rate of reaction after [A] is reduced to 0.06 mol L^{-1}.

[NCERT Ex. Q. 3.2, Page 85]

Ans. The initial rate of the reaction is:

$$\text{Rate} = k[A][B]^2$$
$$= (2.0 \times 10^{-6}\text{ mol}^{-2}\text{ L}^2\text{s}^{-1})(0.1\text{ mol L}^{-1})(0.2\text{ mol L}^{-1})^2$$
$$= 8.0 \times 10^{-9}\text{ mol}^{-2}\text{ L}^2\text{ s}^{-1}$$

when [A] is reduced from 0.1 mol L^{-1} to 0.06 mol^{-1}, the concentration of A reacted

$$= (0.1 - 0.06)\text{ mol L}^{-1} = 0.04\text{ mol L}^{-1}$$

Hence, concentration of B consumed

$$= \frac{1}{2} \times 0.04\text{ mol L}^{-1} = 0.02\text{ mol L}^{-1}$$

So, concentration of B left behind

$$[B] = (0.2 - 0.02)\text{ mol L}^{-1} = 0.18\text{ mol L}^{-1}$$

After [A] is reduced to 0.06 mol L^{-1}, the rate of the reaction is given by,

$$\text{Rate} = k[A][B]^2$$
$$= (2.0 \times 10^{-6}\text{ mol}^{-2}\text{ s}^{-1})(0.06\text{ mol L}^{-1})(0.18\text{ mol L}^{-1})^2$$
$$= 3.89\text{ mol L}^{-1}\text{ s}^{-1}$$

Q. 3. The decomposition of NH_3 on platinum surface is zero order reaction. What are the rates of production of N_2 and H_2 if $k = 2.5 \times 10^{-4}$ mol^{-1} L s^{-1}?

[NCERT Ex. Q. 3.3, Page 85]

Ans. Decomposition of ammonia (NH_3) on platinum (Pt) surface is represented by the following reaction:

$$2NH_3(g) \xrightarrow{Pt} N_2(g) + 3H_2(g)$$

$$\therefore \text{Rate} = -\frac{1}{2}\frac{d[NH_3]}{dt} = \frac{d[N_2]}{dt} = \frac{1}{3}\frac{d[H_2]}{dt}$$

However, it is given that the reaction is of zero order. Hence,

$$-\frac{1}{2}\frac{d[NH_3]}{dt} = \frac{d[N_2]}{dt} = \frac{1}{3}\frac{d[H_2]}{dt} = k$$
$$= 2.5 \times 10^{-4}\text{ mol L}^{-1}\text{ s}^{-1}$$

Hence, the rate of production of N_2 is

$$\frac{d[N_2]}{dt} = 2.5 \times 10^{-4}\text{ mol L}^{-1}\text{ s}^{-1}$$

The rate of production of H_2 is

$$\frac{d[H_2]}{dt} = 3 \times 2.5 \times 10^{-4} \text{ mol L}^{-1} \text{ s}^{-1}$$
$$= 7.5 \times 10^{-4} \text{ mol L}^{-1} \text{ s}^{-1}$$

Q. 4.The decomposition of dimethyl ether leads to the formation of CH_4, H_2 and CO and the reaction rate is given by

$$\text{Rate} = k\,[CH_3OCH_3]^{3/2}$$

The rate of reaction is followed by increase in pressure in a closed vessel, so the rate can also be expressed in terms of the partial pressure of dimethyl ether, i.e.,

$$\text{Rate} = k(P_{CH_3OCH_3})^{3/2}$$

If the pressure is measured in bar and time in minutes, then what are the units of rate and rate constants?

[NCERT Ex. Q. 3.4, Page 85]

Ans. If pressure is measured in bar and time in minutes, then

$$\text{Unit of rate} = \text{bar min}^{-1}$$
$$\text{Rate} = k(P_{CH_3OCH_3})^{3/2}$$
$$k = \frac{\text{Rate}}{(P_{CH_3OCH_3})^{3/2}}$$

Hence, unit of rate constant (k)

$$= \frac{\text{bar min}^{-1}}{\text{bar}^{3/2}}$$
$$= \text{bar}^{-1/2} \text{ min}^{-1}$$

Q. 5.Mention the factors that affect the rate of a chemical reaction. [NCERT Ex. Q. 3.5, Page 85]

Ans. The factors that affect the rate of a reaction are as follows:

(a) Concentration of reactants
(b) Temperature
(c) Presence of a catalyst
(d) Exposure to radiations
(e) Nature of reactants

Q. 6.A reaction is second order with respect to a reactant. How is the rate of reaction affected if the concentration of the reactant is

(i) doubled
(ii) reduced to half ? [NCERT Ex. Q. 3.6, Page 85]

Ans. Let the concentration of the reactant be $[A] = a$

Rate of reaction, $R = k\,[A]_2 = ka^2$

(i) If the concentration of the reactant is doubled, *i.e.*, $[A] = 2a$,

then the rate of the reaction would be $R' = k(2a)^2 = 4ka^2 = 4R$

Hence, the rate of the reaction is increased by 4 times.

(ii) If the concentration of the reactant is reduced to half, *i.e.*, $[A] = 1/2\,a$ then the rate of the reaction would be

$$R'' = k\left(\frac{1}{2}a\right)^2 = \frac{1}{4}ka^2 = \frac{1}{2}R$$

Hence, the rate of the reaction is reduced to 1/ 4.

Q. 7. What is the effect of temperature on the rate constant of a reaction? How can this effect of temperature on rate constant be represented quantitatively?

[NCERT Ex. Q. 3.7, Page 85]

Ans. The rate constant is nearly doubled with a rise in temperature by 10°C for a chemical reaction.

The temperature effect on the rate constant can be represented quantitatively by Arrhenius equation,

$$k = Ae^{-Ea/RT}$$

where, k is the rate constant.
A is the Arrhenius factor or the frequency factor.
R is the gas constant.
T is the temperature.
Ea is the energy of activation for the reaction

Q. 8. In a pseudo first order reaction in water, the following results were obtained:

t/s	0	30	60	90
[Ester] mol L^{-1}	0.55	0.31	0.17	0.085

(i) Calculate the average rate of reaction between the time interval 30 to 60 seconds.

(ii) Calculate the pseudo first order rate constant for the hydrolysis of ester. [NCERT Ex. Q. 3.8, Page 85]

Ans. (i) Average rate of reaction between the time interval, 30 to 60 seconds,

$$= \frac{d(\text{ester})}{dt}$$
$$= \frac{(0.31 - 0.17)}{(60 - 30)}$$
$$= \frac{0.14}{30}$$
$$= 4.67 \times 10^{-3} \text{ mol L}^{-1} \text{ s}^{-1}$$

(ii) For a pseudo first order reaction,

$$k = \frac{2.303}{t} \log \frac{[R]_0}{[R]}$$

$$\text{For } t = 30 \text{ s}, k_1 = \frac{2.303}{30} \log \frac{0.55}{0.31}$$
$$= 1.911 \times 10^{-2} \text{ s}^{-1}$$

$$\text{For } t = 60 \text{ s}, k_2 = \frac{2.303}{60} \log \frac{0.55}{0.17}$$
$$= 1.957 \times 10^{-2} \text{ s}^{-1}$$

$$\text{For } t = 90 \text{ s}, k_3 = \frac{2.303}{90} \log \frac{0.55}{0.085}$$
$$= 2.075 \times 10 \text{ s}^{-1}$$

Then, average rate constant,

$$k = \frac{(k_1 + k_2 + k_3)}{3}$$

$$\frac{1.911 \times 10^{-2} + 1.957 \times 10^{-2} + 2.075 \times 10^{-2}}{3}$$
$$= 1.98 \times 10^{-2} \text{ s}^{-1}$$

Q. 9. A reaction is first order in A and second order in B.

(i) Write the differential rate equation.

(ii) How is the rate affected on increasing the concentration of B three times?

(iii) How is the rate affected when the concentrations of both A and B are doubled?

[NCERT Ex. Q. 3.9, Page 85]

Ans. (a) The differential rate equation will be:

$$-\frac{d[R]}{dt} = k[A][B]^2$$

(b) If the concentration of B is increased 3 times, then

$$-\frac{d[R]}{dt} = k[A][3B]^2 = 9k[A][B]^2$$

Hence, the rate of reaction will be increased by 9 times.

(c) When the concentrations of both A and B are doubled,

$$-\frac{d[R]}{dt} = k[A][B]^2 = k[2A][2B]^2 = 8k\,[A][B]^2$$

Hence, the rate of reaction will be increased by 8 times.

Q. 10. In a reaction between A and B, the initial rate of reaction (r_0) was measured for different initial concentrations of A and B as given below:

A/mol L^{-1}	0.20	0.20	0.40
B/mol L^{-1}	0.30	0.10	0.05
r_0/mol L^{-1} s^{-1}	5.07×10^{-5}	5.07×10^{-5}	1.43×10^{-4}

What is the order of the reaction with respect to A and B? [NCERT Ex. Q. 3.10, Page 86]

Ans. Let the order of the reaction with respect to *A* be *x* and with respect to *B* be *y*. Therefore,

$$\therefore \quad r_0 = k[A]^x[B]^y$$

$$5.07 \times 10^{-5} = k[0.20]^x[0.30]^y \quad \text{...(i)}$$

$$5.07 \times 10^{-5} = k[0.20]^x[0.10]^y \quad \text{...(ii)}$$

$$1.43 \times 10^{-4} = k[0.40]^x[0.05]^y \quad \text{...(iii)}$$

Dividing equation (i) by (ii), we get

$$\frac{5.07\times10^{-5}}{5.07\times10^{-5}} = \frac{k[0.20]^x[0.30]^y}{k[0.20]^x[0.10]^y}$$

$$1 = \frac{[0.30]^y}{[0.10]^y}$$

$$\therefore \quad \left(\frac{0.30}{0.10}\right)^0 = \left(\frac{0.30}{0.10}\right)^y$$

Dividing equation (iii) by (ii), we obtain

$$\frac{1.43\times10^{-4}}{5.07\times10^{-5}} = \frac{[0.40]^x}{[0.20]^y} \left[\begin{array}{l}\text{since } y = 0 \\ [0.05]^y = [0.30]^y = 1\end{array}\right]$$

$$2.821 = 2x$$

$$\Rightarrow \quad \log 2.821 = x \log 2$$

(Taking log on both sides)

$$\Rightarrow \quad x = \frac{\log 2.821}{\log 2} = 1.496 = 1.5$$

(approx.)

Therefore, the order of the reaction with respect to A is 1.5 and with respect to *B* is zero.

Q. 11. The following results have been obtained during the kinetic studies of the reaction:

$$2A + B \rightarrow C + D$$

Experiment	[A]/ mol L^{-1}	[B]/ mol L^{-1}	Initial rate of formation of D/mol L^{-1} min^{-1}
I	0.1	0.1	6.0×10^{-3}
II	0.3	0.2	7.2×10^{-2}
III	0.3	0.4	2.88×10^{-1}
IV	0.4	0.1	2.40×10^{-2}

Determine the rate law and the rate constant for the reaction. [NCERT Ex. Q. 3.11, Page 86]

Ans. Let the order of the reaction with respect to *A* be *x* and with respect to *B* be *y*.

So, rate of the reaction is given by,

$$\text{Rate} = k[A]^x[B]^y$$

According to the details given in the question,

$$6.0 \times 10^{-3} = k[0.1]^x[0.1]^y \quad \text{(i)}$$

$$7.2 \times 10^{-2} = k[0.3]^x[0.2]^y \quad \text{(ii)}$$

$$7.88 \times 10^{-2} = k[0.3]^x[0.4]^y \quad \text{(iii)}$$

$$2.40 \times 10^{-2} = k[0.4]^x[0.1]^y \quad \text{(iv)}$$

Dividing equation (iv) by (i), we get

$$\frac{2.40\times10^{-2}}{6.0\times10^{-3}} = \frac{k[0.4]^x[0.1]^y}{k[0.1]^x[0.1]^y}$$

$$\Rightarrow \quad 4 = \frac{[0.4]^x}{[0.1]^x}$$

$$\Rightarrow \quad (4)^1 = 4^x$$

$$\therefore \quad x = 1$$

Dividing equation (iii) by (ii), we get

$$\frac{2.88\times10^{-1}}{7.2\times10^{-2}} = \frac{k[0.3]^x[0.4]^y}{k[0.3]^x[0.2]^y}$$

$$\Rightarrow \quad 4 = \left(\frac{0.4}{0.2}\right)^y$$

$$\Rightarrow \quad 4 = 2^y$$

$$\Rightarrow \quad 2^2 = 2^y$$

$$\Rightarrow \quad y = 2$$

$$\therefore \quad \text{Rate law} = k[A]\,[B]^2$$

$$\therefore \quad k = \frac{\text{Rate}}{[A][B]^2}$$

From experiment I, we get

$$k = \frac{6.0\times10^{-3}\,\text{mol L}^{-1}\,\text{min}^{-1}}{(0.1\,\text{mol L}^{-1})(0.1\,\text{mol L}^{-1})^2}$$

$$= =6.0\ \text{L}^2\,\text{mol}^{-2}\,\text{min}^{-1}$$

From experiment II, we get

$$k = \frac{7.2\times10^{-2}\,\text{mol L}^{-1}\,\text{min}^{-1}}{(0.3\,\text{mol L}^{-1})(0.2\,\text{mol L}^{-1})^2}$$

$$= 6.0\ \text{L}^2\,\text{mol}^{-2}\,\text{min}^{-1}$$

From experiment III, we get

$$k = \frac{2.88\times10^{-1}\,\text{mol L}^{-1}\,\text{min}^{-1}}{(0.3\,\text{mol L}^{-1})(0.4\,\text{mol L}^{-1})^2}$$

$$= 6.0\ \text{L}^2\,\text{mol}^{-2}\,\text{min}^{-1}$$

From experiment IV, we get

$$k = \frac{2.40\times10^{-2}\,\text{mol L}^{-1}\,\text{min}^{-1}}{(0.4\,\text{mol L}^{-1})(0.1\,\text{mol L}^{-1})^2}$$

$$= 6.0\ \text{L}^2\,\text{mol}^{-2}\,\text{min}^{-1}$$

Hence, rate constant, $k = 6.0\ \text{L}^2\,\text{mol}^{-2}\,\text{min}^{-1}$

Q. 12. The reaction between A and B is first order with respect to A and zero order with respect to B. Fill in the blanks in the following table:

Experiment	[A]/ mol L^{-1}	[B]/ mol L^{-1}	Initial rate / L^{-1} min^{-1}
I	0.1	0.1	2.0×10^{-2}
II	--	0.2	4.0×10^{-2}
III	0.4	.04	--
IV	--	0.2	2.0×10^{-2}

[NCERT Ex. Q. 3.12, Page 86]

Ans. The given reaction is of the first order with respect to A and of zero order with respect to *B*. Hence, the rate of the reaction is given by,

$$\text{Rate} = k[A]^1 [B]^0$$
$$\text{Rate} = k[A]$$

From experiment I, we get

$2.0 \times 10^{-2}\ \text{mol L}^{-1}\ \text{min}^{-1} = k(0.1\ \text{mol L}^{-1})$

$\Rightarrow k = 0.2\ \text{min}^{-1}$

From experiment II, we get

$4.0 \times 10^{-2}\ \text{mol L}^{-1}\ \text{min}^{-1} = 0.2\ \text{min}^{-1}\ [A]$

$\Rightarrow [A] = 0.2\ \text{mol L}^{-1}$

From experiment III, we get

$\text{Rate} = 0.2\ \text{min}^{-1} \times 0.4\ \text{mol L}^{-1} = 0.08\ \text{mol L}^{-1}\ \text{min}^{-1}$

From experiment IV, we get

$2.0 \times 10^{-2}\ \text{mol L}^{-1}\ \text{min}^{-1} = 0.2\ \text{min}^{-1}\ [A]$

So, $[A] = 0.1\ \text{mol L}^{-1}$

Q. 13. Calculate the half-life of a first order reaction from their rate constants given below:
(i) 200 s^{-1} (ii) 2 min^{-1} (iii) 4 $years^{-1}$

[NCERT Ex. Q. 3.13, Page 86]

Ans. (a) Half-life, $t_{1/2} = \dfrac{0.693}{k} = \dfrac{0.693}{200\ s^{-1}}$

$= 3.47 \times 10^{-3}$ s (approx)

(b) Half-life, $t_{1/2} = \dfrac{0.693}{k} = \dfrac{0.693}{2\ \text{min}^{-1}}$

$= 0.347$ min (approx)

(c) Half-life, $t_{1/2} = \dfrac{0.693}{k} = \dfrac{0.693}{4\ \text{years}^{-1}}$

$= 0.173$ years (approx)

Q. 14. The half-life for radioactive decay of 14C is 5730 years. An archaeological artifact containing wood had only 80% of the 14C found in a living tree. Estimate the age of the sample. [NCERT Ex. Q. 3.14, Page 86]

Ans. Here, $k = \dfrac{0.693}{t_{1/2}} = \dfrac{0.696}{5.730}\ \text{years}^{-1}$

It is known that,

$$t = \frac{2.303}{k}\log\frac{[R]_0}{[R]} = \frac{2.303}{\frac{0693}{5.730}}\log\frac{100}{80}$$

$= 1,845$ years (approx.)

Therefore, the age of the sample is 1,845 years

Q. 15. The experimental data for decomposition of N_2O_5

$[2N_2O_5 \rightarrow 4NO_2 + O_2]$

in gas phase at 318K are given below:

t/s	$10^2 \times [N_2O_5]$/mol L^{-1}
0	1.63
400	1.36
800	1.14
1200	0.93
1600	0.78
2000	0.64
2400	0.53
2800	0.43
3200	0.35

(i) Plot $[N_2O_5]$ against *t*.
(ii) Find the half-life period for the reaction.
(iii) Draw a graph between $\log[N_2O_5]$ and *t*.
(iv) What is the rate law ?
(v) Calculate the rate constant.
(vi) Calculate the half-life period from *k* and compare it with (ii). [NCERT Ex. Q. 3.15, Page 86]

Ans. (i) Shape of the graph of $[N_2O_5]$ versus *t* will be as follows:

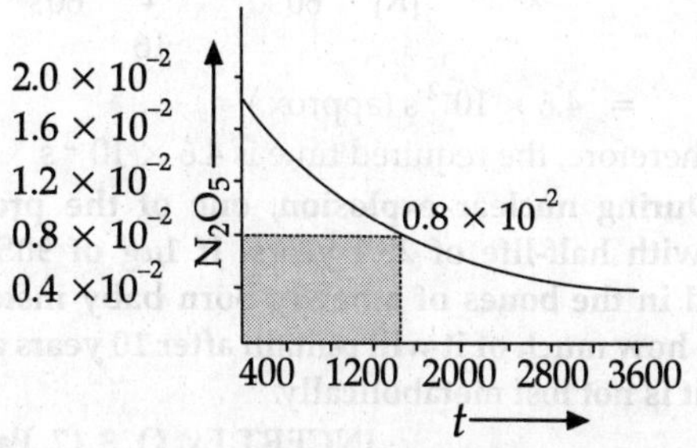

(ii) Half-life is the time in which initial concentration of N_2O_5 changes from 1.63×10^{-2} molar to half of its value, i.e., 0.815×10^{-2} molar and in the graph, it is equal to 1450 s.

(iii)

t/s	$10^2 \times [N_2O_5]$/mol L^{-1}
0	–1.7918
400	–1.8665
800	–1.9431
1200	–2.0315
1600	–2.1079
2000	–2.1933
2400	–2.2757
2800	–2.3752
3200	–2.4559

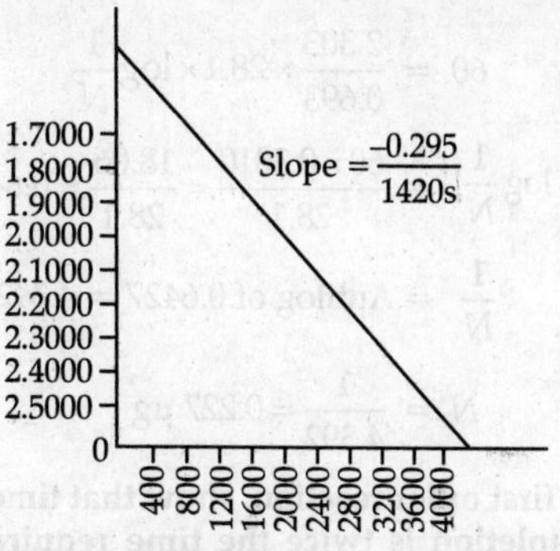

(iv) The graph of $\log[N_2O_5]$ versus *t* will be a straight line with negative slope.

Rate = $k[N_2O_5]$ as it is the first-order reaction.

(v) $\text{Slope} = \dfrac{-k}{2.303} = \dfrac{-0.67}{3200}$

$\Rightarrow \quad k = \dfrac{-0.67 \times -2.303}{3200}$

$\therefore \quad k = 4.82 \times 10^{-4}\ s^{-1}$

(vi) $t_{1/2} = \dfrac{0.693}{k} = \dfrac{0.693}{4.82 \times 10^{-4}}\ s = 1438\ s$

Q. 16. The rate constant for a first order reaction is 60 s^{-1}. How much time will it take to reduce the initial concentration of the reactant to its 1/16th value?

[NCERT Ex. Q. 3.16, Page 87]

Ans. It is known that

$$t = \frac{2.303}{k}\log\frac{[R]_0}{[R]} = \frac{2.303}{60\,s^{-1}}\log\frac{1}{\frac{1}{16}} = \frac{2.303}{60\,s^{-1}}\log 16$$

$$= 4.6 \times 10^{-2}\ \text{s (approx.)}$$

Therefore, the required time is 4.6×10^{-2} s.

Q. 17. During nuclear explosion, one of the products is 90Sr with half-life of 28.1 years. If 1μg of 90Sr was absorbed in the bones of a newly born baby instead of calcium, how much of it will remain after 10 years and 60 years if it is not lost metabolically.

[NCERT Ex. Q. 3.17, Page 87]

Ans. $$k = \frac{0.693}{t_{1/2}} = \frac{0.693}{28.1\ \text{years}}$$

Also, $$t = \frac{2.303}{k}\log\frac{[N]_0}{N}$$

When $t = 10$ years,

$$10 = \frac{2.303}{0.693} \times 28.1 \times \log\frac{1}{N} \qquad [\because N_0 = 1]$$

$$\Rightarrow \log\frac{1}{N} = \frac{10 \times 3.010}{28.1} = \frac{3.01}{28.1} = 0.1071$$

$$\Rightarrow \frac{1}{N} = \text{Antilog of } 0.1071$$

$$\Rightarrow \frac{1}{N} = 1.279$$

$$\Rightarrow N = \frac{1}{1.279} = 0.7818\ \mu g$$

When $t = 60$ years

$$60 = \frac{2.303}{0.693} \times 28.1 \times \log\frac{1}{N}$$

$$\Rightarrow \log\frac{1}{N} = \frac{60 \times 0.3010}{28.1} = \frac{18.06}{28.1} = 0.6427$$

$$\Rightarrow \frac{1}{N} = \text{Antilog of } 0.6427 = 4.392$$

$$\Rightarrow N = \frac{1}{4.392} = 0.227\ \mu g$$

Q. 18. For a first order reaction, show that time required for 99% completion is twice the time required for the completion of 90% of reaction.

[NCERT Ex. Q. 3.18, Page 87]

Ans. For a first-order reaction, the time required for 99% completion is

$$t_1 = \frac{2.303}{k}\log\frac{100}{100-99} = \frac{2.303}{k}\log 100 = 2 \times \frac{2.303}{k}$$

For a first-order reaction, the time required for 99% completion is

$$t_2 = \frac{2.303}{k}\log\frac{100}{100-90} = \frac{2.303}{k}\log 10 = \frac{2.303}{k}$$

Hence, $t_1 = 2t_2$

Therefore, the time required for 99% completion of a first-order reaction is twice the time required for the completion of 90% of the reaction.

Q. 19. A first order reaction takes 40 min for 30% decomposition. Calculate $t_{1/2}$.

[NCERT Ex. Q. 3.19, Page 87]

Ans. For a first-order reaction,

$$t = \frac{2.303}{k}\log\frac{[R]_0}{[R]}$$

$$\therefore\ t = \frac{2.303}{40\,\text{min}}\log\frac{100}{100-30}$$

$$= \frac{2.303}{40\ \text{min}}\log\frac{10}{7}$$

$$= 8.918 \times 10^{-3}\ \text{min}^{-1}$$

Hence, $t_{1/2}$ of the decomposition reaction is

$$t_{1/2} = \frac{0.693}{k} = \frac{0.696}{8.918 \times 10^{-3}}\ \text{min}$$

$$= 77.7\ \text{min (approx.)}$$

Q. 20. For the decomposition of azoisopropane to hexane and nitrogen at 543 K, the following data are obtained.

t (sec)	P(mm of Hg)
0	35.0
360	54.0
720	63.0

Calculate the rate constant.

[NCERT Ex. Q. 3.20, Page 87]

Ans. The decomposition of azoisopropane to hexane and nitrogen at 543 K is represented by the following equation.

$$(CH_3)_2CHN = NCH(CH_3)_2(g) \rightarrow N_2(g) + C_6H_{14}(g)$$

	$(CH_3)_2CHN = NCH(CH_3)_2(g)$	$N_2(g)$	$C_6H_{14}(g)$
At $t = 0$	P_0	0	0
At $t = t$	$P_0 - p$	p	p

After time t, total pressure,

$$P_1 = (P_0 - p) + p + p$$

$$\Rightarrow P_1 = P_0 + p$$

$$\Rightarrow p = P_1 - P_0$$

$$\therefore\ P_0 - p = P_0 - (P_t - P_0)$$

$$= 2P_0 - P_t$$

For a first-order reaction,

When $t = 360$ s,

$$k = \frac{2.303}{t}\log\frac{P_0}{P_0 - p} = \frac{2.303}{t}\log\frac{P_0}{2P_0 - Pt}$$

$$= \frac{2.303}{360\,s}\log\frac{35.0}{2 \times 35.0 - 54.0} = 2.175 \times 10^{-3}\,s^{-1}$$

When $t = 720\,s$,

$$k = \frac{2.303}{720\,s}\log\frac{35.0}{2 \times 35.0 - 63.0} = 2.235 \times 10^{-3}\,s^{-1}$$

Therefore, the average value of rate constant,

$$\therefore\ k = \frac{(2.175 \times 10^{-3}) + (2.235 \times 10^{-3})}{2}\,s^{-1}$$

$$= 2.21 \times 10^{-3}\,s^{-1}$$

Q. 21. The following data were obtained during the first order thermal decomposition of SO_2Cl_2 at a constant volume.

$$(SO_2Cl_2\ g) \rightarrow SO_2\ (g) + Cl_2\ (g)$$

Experiment	Time (s – 1)	Total pressure (atm.)
1	0	0.5
2	100	0.6

Calculate the rate of the reaction when total pressure is 0.65 atm.

[NCERT Ex. Q. 3.21, Page 87]

Ans. $SO_2Cl_2(g) \rightarrow SO_2(g) + Cl_2(b)$

p_i 0 0

p_i 0 x x

$p_i - x + x + x = p$

$$k = \frac{2.303}{t}\log\frac{p_i}{2p_i\ p_i} = \frac{2.303}{100}\log\frac{0.5}{(2\times 0.5 - 0.6)}$$

$$= \frac{2.303}{100}\log\frac{0.5}{0.4} = \frac{2.303}{100}[\log 5 - \log 4]$$

$$= \frac{2.303}{100}[0.6990 - 0.6021] = \frac{2.303}{100}[0.0969]$$

$$= 2.23 \times 10^{-3}\ s^{-1}$$

$$p_i = x + x + x = 0.65$$

$$0.50 + x = 0.65$$

$$\therefore \quad x = 0.15$$

$$\text{Rate} = kP_{(SO_2Cl_2)} = 2.23 \times 10^{-3}\ (0.50 - 0.15)$$

$$= 2.23 \times 10^{-3} \times 0.35$$

$$= 7.805 \times 10^{-4}\ \text{atm. s}^{-1}$$

Q. 22. The rate constant for the decomposition of N_2O_5 at various temperatures is given below:

T/°C	0	20	40	60	80
$10^5 \times K/S^{-1}$	0.787	1.70	25.7	178	2140

Draw a graph between ln K and 1/T and calculate the values of A and Ea. Predict the rate constant at 30°C and 50°C. **[NCERT Ex. Q. 3.22, Page 87]**

Ans. From the given data, we obtain

T/°C	0	20	40	60	80
T/K	273	293	313	333	353
$\frac{1}{T}/K^{-1}$	3.66×10^{-3}	3.41×10^{-3}	3.19×10^{-3}	3.0×10^{-3}	2.83×10^{-3}
$10^5\times K/S^{-1}$	0.0787	1.70	25.7	178	2140
ln k	–7.147	–4.075	–1.359	–0.577	3.063

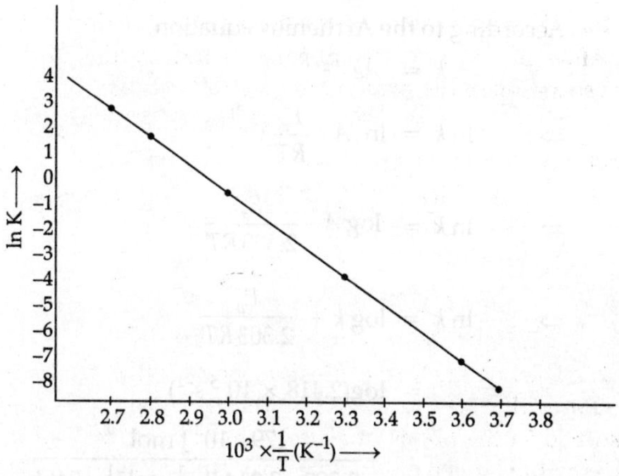

Slope of the line,

$$\frac{y_2 - y_2}{x_2 - x_1} = -12.301\ K$$

According to Arrhenius equation,

$$\text{Slope} = \frac{-E_a}{R} \Rightarrow E_a = -\text{Slope} \times R$$

$$= -(-12.301K) \times (8.314\ J\ K^{-1}mol^{-1})$$

$$= 102.27\ kJ\ mol^{-1}$$

Again,

$$\ln K = \ln A - \frac{E_a}{RT}$$

$$\ln A = \ln K + \frac{E_a}{RT}$$

When $T = 273$ K

$\ln K = -7.147$

$$\text{Then, } \ln A = -7.147 + \frac{102.27\times10^3}{8.314\times273}$$

$$= 37.911$$

Therefore, $A = 2.91 \times 10^6$

When $T = 30 + 273\ K = 303\ K$

$$\frac{1}{T} = 0.0033\ K = 3.3 \times 10^{-3}\ K$$

$$\text{Then, at } \frac{1}{T} = 3.3 \times 10^{-3}\ K$$

$$\ln K = -2.8$$

Therefore, $K = 6.08 \times 10^{-2}\ S^{-1}$

Again, when $T = 50 + 273\ K = 323\ K$

$$\frac{1}{T} = 0.0031\ K = 3.1 \times 10^{-3}\ K$$

$$\text{Then at } \frac{1}{T} = 3.1 \times 10^{-3}\ K$$

$$\ln K = -0.5$$

Therefore, $K = 0.6075^{-1}$

Q. 23. The rate constant for the decomposition of hydrocarbons is $2.418 \times 10^{-5}s^{-1}$ at 546 K. If the energy of activation is 179.9 kJ/mol, what will be the value of pre-exponential factor. **[NCERT Ex. Q. 3.23, Page 87]**

Ans.

$$k = 2.418 \times 10^{-5}\ s^{-1}$$

$$T = 546\ K$$

$$Ea = 179.9\ kJ\ mol.^{-1}$$

$$= 179.9 \times 10^3\ J\ mol.^{-1}$$

According to the Arrhenius equation,

$$k = Ae^{-E_a/RT}$$

$$\Rightarrow \quad \ln k = \ln A - \frac{E_a}{RT}$$

$$\Rightarrow \quad \ln k = \log A - \frac{E_a}{2.303\,RT}$$

$$\Rightarrow \quad \ln k = \log k + \frac{E_a}{2.303\,RT}$$

$$= \log(2.418 \times 10^{-5}\ s^{-1}) + \frac{179 \times 10^3\ \text{J mol.}^{-1}}{2.303 \times 3.314\ \text{Jk}^{-1}\text{mol}^{-1} \times 546k}$$

$$= (0.3835 + 5)\ 17.2082$$

$$= 12.5917$$

$$\therefore \quad A = \text{Antilog}\ (12.5917)$$

$$= 3.9 \times 10^{12}\ s^{-1}\ \text{(approx.)}$$

Q. 24. Consider a certain reaction A → Products with $k = 2.0 \times 10^{-2} s^{-1}$. Calculate the concentration of A remaining after 100 s if the initial concentration of A is 1.0 mol L^{-1}. [NCERT Ex. Q. 3.24, Page 87]

Ans. As unit of k is s^{-1}, the given reaction is a first-order reaction.

$$\therefore \quad k = \frac{2.303}{t} \log \frac{[A]_0}{[A]}$$

$$2.0 \times 10^{-2}\ s^{-1} = \frac{2.303}{100\ s} \log \frac{1.0}{[A]}$$

$$2.0 \times 10^{-2}\ s^{-1} = \frac{2.303}{100\ s}(-\log[A])$$

$$-\log[A] = \frac{2.0 \times 10^{-2} \times 100}{2.303}$$

$$[A] = \text{anti-log}\left(-\frac{2.0 \times 10^{-2} \times 100}{2.303}\right)$$

$$= 0.135\ \text{mol L}^{-1}\ \text{(approx.)}$$

Hence, the remaining concentration of A is 0.135 mol. L^{-1}.

Q. 25. Sucrose decomposes in acid solution into glucose and fructose according to the first order rate law, with $t_{1/2}$ = 3.00 hours. What fraction of sample of sucrose remains after 8 hours ? [NCERT Ex. Q. 3.25, Page 87]

Ans. For a first order reaction,

$$k = \frac{2.303}{t} \log \frac{[R]_0}{[R]}$$

It is given that, $t_{1/2}$ = 3.00 hours

$$\text{Therefore,} \quad k = \frac{0.693}{t_{1/2}} = \frac{0.693}{3} h^{-1} = 0.231 h^{-1}$$

$$\text{Then,} \quad 0.231\ h^{-1} = \frac{2.303}{8\text{h}} \log \frac{[R]_0}{[R]}$$

$$\Rightarrow \quad \log \frac{[R]_0}{[R]} = \frac{0.231 h^{-1} \times 8h}{2.303}$$

$$\Rightarrow \quad \frac{[R]_0}{[R]} = \text{Antilog}\ (0.8024) = 6.3445$$

$$= 0.1576\ \text{(approx.)}$$

$$= 0.158$$

Therefore the fraction of sample of sucrose that remains after 8 hours is 0.158.

Q. 26. The decomposition of hydrocarbon follows the equation

$$K = (4.5 \times 10^{11}\ S^{-1})\ e^{-28000K/T}$$

Calculate E_a. [NCERT Ex. Q. 3.26, Page 88]

Ans. Given, $K = (4.5 \times 10^{11}\ S^{-1})\ e^{-28000K/T}$ ...(i)

Arrhenius equation is given by

$$k = Ae^{-E_a/RT} \quad ...(ii)$$

From equation (i) and (ii), we get

$$E_a/RT = R \times 28000\ K$$

$$= 8.314\ \text{J K}^{-1}\ \text{mol}^{-1} \times 28000\ K$$

$$= 232792\ \text{J mol}^{-1}$$

$$= 232.792\ \text{kJ mol}^{-1}$$

Q. 27. The rate constant for the first order decomposition of H_2O_2 is given by the following equation:

$\log k = 14.34 - 1.25 \times 10^4 K/T$

Calculate E_a for this reaction and at what temperature will its half-period be 256 minutes? [NCERT Ex. Q. 3.27, Page 88]

Ans. Arrhenius equation is given by,

$$k = Ae^{-Ea/RT}$$

$$\Rightarrow \quad \ln k = \ln A - E_a/RT$$

$$\Rightarrow \quad \ln k = \log A - E_a/RT$$

$$\Rightarrow \quad \log k = \log A - E_a/2.303\ RT \quad ...(i)$$

The given equation is

$$\log k = 14.34 - 1.25 \times 10^4\ K/T \quad ...(ii)$$

From equation (i) and (ii), we obtain

$$E_a/2.303\ RT = 1.25 \times 10^4\ K/T$$

$$\Rightarrow \quad E_a = 1.25 \times 10^4\ K \times 2.303 \times R$$

$$= 1.25 \times 10^4\ K \times 2.303 \times 8.314\ \text{JK}^{-1}\ \text{mol}^{-1}$$

$$= 239339.3\ \text{J mol}^{-1}\ \text{(approx.)}$$

$$= 239.34\ \text{kJ mol}^{-1}$$

Also, when $t_{1/2}$ = 256 minutes,

$$k = \frac{0.693}{t_{1/2}}$$

$$= \frac{0.693}{256}$$

$$= 2.707 \times 10^{-3}\ \text{min}^{-1}$$

$$= 4.51 \times 10^{-5}\ s^{-1}$$

It is also given that,

$$\log k = 14.34 - 1.25 \times 104\ K/T \quad 3$$

$$\Rightarrow \quad \log(4.51 \times 10^{-5}) = 14.34 - \frac{1.25 \times 10^4 K}{T}$$

$$\Rightarrow \quad \log(0.654 \times 05) = 14.34 - \frac{1.25 \times 10^4 K}{T}$$

$$\Rightarrow \quad \frac{1.25 \times 10^4 K}{T} = 18.686$$

$$\Rightarrow \quad T = \frac{1.25 \times 10^4 \text{K}}{18.686}$$

$$= 668.95\ K$$

$$= 669\ K\ \text{(approx.)}$$

Q. 28. The decomposition of A into product has value of k as 4.5 × 10^3 s^{-1} at 10°C and energy of

activation 60 kJ mol^{-1}. At what temperature would k be $1.5 \times 10^4 s^{-1}$? [NCERT Ex. Q. 3.28, Page 88]

Ans. Given $k_1 = 4.5 \times 10^3 \text{ s}^{-1}$,
$T_1 = 10 + 273 \text{ K} = 283 \text{ K}$;
$k_2 = 1.5 \times 10^4 \text{ s}^{-1}$, $T_2 = ?$,
$E_a = 60 \text{ kJ mol}^{-1}$

Applying Arrhenius equation,

$$\log\frac{k_2}{k_1} = \frac{E_a}{2.303R}\left(\frac{T_2 - T_1}{T_1T_2}\right)$$

$$\log\frac{1.5\times10^4}{4.5\times10^3} = \frac{60000}{2.303\times8.314}\left(\frac{T_2-283}{283T_2}\right)$$

or, $$\log 3.333 = 3133.63\left(\frac{T_2-283}{283T_2}\right)$$

or, $$\frac{0.5228}{3133.63} = \frac{T_2-283}{283\,T_2}$$

or, $0.0472\,T_2 = T_2 - 283$ or $0.9528\,T_2 = 283$

or, $$T_2 = \frac{283}{0.9528} = 297 \text{ K} = 297 - 273$$
$$= 24°\text{C}$$

Q. 29. The time required for 10% completion of a first order reaction at 298K is equal to that required for its 25% completion at 308K. If the value of A is $4 \times 10^{10}s^{-1}$. Calculate k at 318K and E_a. [NCERT Ex. Q. 3.29, Page 88]

Ans. For a first-order reaction,

At 298 K,

$$t = \frac{2.303}{k}\log\frac{a}{a-x} = \frac{2.303}{k}\log\frac{100}{90}$$
$$= \frac{0.1054}{k}$$

At 308 K,

$$t' = \frac{2.303}{k'}\log\frac{100}{75} = \frac{2.2877}{k'}$$

As per detail given in the question

$$t = t'$$

$$\Rightarrow \frac{0.1054}{k} = \frac{2.2877}{k'}$$

$$\Rightarrow \frac{k'}{k} = 2.7296$$

Using Arrhenius equation, we get

$$\Rightarrow \log\frac{k'}{k} = \frac{E_a}{2.303\,R}\left(\frac{T'-T}{TT'}\right)$$

$$\log(2.7296) = \frac{E_a}{2.303\times8.314}\left(\frac{308-298}{298\times308}\right)$$

$$E_a = \frac{2.303\times8.314\times298\times308\times\log(2.7296)}{305-298}$$
$$= 76{,}640.096 \text{ J mol}^{-1}$$
$$= 76.64 \text{ kJ mol}^{-1}$$

Now, calculating k at 318 K,

It is given that, $A = 4 \times 10^{10} \text{ s}^{-1}$, T = 318 K

From Arrhenius equation, we get:

$$\log k = \log A - \frac{E_a}{2.303RT}$$
$$= \log(4\times10^{10}) - \frac{76.64\times10^3}{2.303\times8.314\times318}$$
$$= (0.6021 + 10) - 12.5876$$
$$= -1.9855$$
$$k = \text{Antilog}(-1.9855)$$
$$= 1.034 \times 10^{-2} \text{ s}^{-1}$$

Q. 30. The rate of a reaction quadruples when the temperature changes from 293 K to 313 K. Calculate the energy of activation of the reaction assuming that it does not change with temperature. [NCERT Ex. Q. 3.30, Page 88]

Ans. $$\log\frac{k_2}{k_1} = \frac{E_a}{2.303R}\left(\frac{T_2-T_1}{T_1T_2}\right)$$

It is given that,

$k_2 = 4k_1$
$T_1 = 293$ K
$T_2 = 313$ K

$$\therefore \log\frac{4k_1}{k_2} = \frac{E_a}{2.303\times8.314}\left(\frac{313-293}{293\times313}\right)$$

$$\therefore 0.6021 = \frac{20\times E_a}{2.303\times8.314\times293\times313}$$

$$\therefore E_a = \frac{0.6021\times2.303\times8.314\times293\times313}{20}$$
$$= 52863.33 \text{ J mol}^{-1}$$
$$= 52.86 \text{ kJ mol}^{-1}$$

Therefore, activation energy = 52.86 kJ mol^{-1}

□□

d- AND *f*-BLOCK ELEMENTS

- Iron, copper, silver and gold are among the transition elements that have played important roles in the development of human civilisation. The inner transition elements such as Th, Pa and U are proving excellent sources of nuclear energy in modern times.

Scan to know more about this topic

d- and *f*-block elements Part I

The Transition Elements (*d*-Block)

- ***d*-block elements:** The elements in which last electron enters in the *d* - sub-shell, i.e., penultimate shell and lies in the middle of the periodic table belonging to groups 3-12.
- **Transition elements:** The elements of *d*-block are known as transition elements as they possess properties that are transitional between the *s*-block and *p*-block elements. Transition elements are defined as elements which have incompletely filled *d*-orbitals in their ground states or in its most common oxidation state. Transition elements have four series:
  - **(i) First transition series:** These elements have incomplete 3*d*-orbitals, and they are from Sc (21) to Zn (30).
  - **(ii) Second transition series:** These elements have incomplete 4*d*-orbitals, and they are from Y (39) to Cd (48).
  - **(iii) Third transition series:** These elements have incomplete 5*d*-orbitals, and they are La (57) and then from Hf (72) to Hg (80).
  - **(iv) Fourth transition series:** These elements have incomplete 6*d*-orbitals.

    Known elements of this series are: actinium (89) and then from Rf (104) to Cn (112).
- **General electronic configuration of transition elements:** Valence shell electronic configuration is $(n-1)d^{1-10}ns^{1-2}$, where *n* is the outermost shell.

Electronic Configuration of *d*-Block Elements

Series	Group 3	Group 4	Group 5	Group 6	Group 7	Group 8	Group 9	Group 10	Group 11	Group 12
3*d* series	Sc (21) $3d^14s^2$	Ti (22) $3d^24s^2$	V (23) $3d^34s^2$	Cr (24) $3d^54s^1$	Mn (25) $3d^54s^2$	Fe (26) $3d^64s^2$	Co (27) $3d^74s^2$	Ni (28) $3d^84s^2$	Cu (29) $3d^{10}4s^1$	Zn (30) $3d^{10}4s^2$
4*d* series	Y (39) $4d^15s^2$	Zr (40) $4d^25s^2$	Nb (41) $4d^45s^1$	Mo (42) $4d^55s^1$	Tc (43) $4d^65s^1$	Ru (44) $4d^75s^1$	Rh (45) $4d^85s^1$	Pd (46) $4d^{10}5s^0$	Ag (47) $4d^{10}5s^1$	Cd (48) $4d^{10}5s^2$
5*d* series	La (57) $4f^0 5d^1 6s^2$	Hf (72) $4f^{14}5d^26s^2$	Ta (73) $4f^{14}5d^36s^2$	W (74) $4f^{14}5d^46s^2$	Re (75) $4f^{14}5d^56s^2$	Os (76) $4f^{14}5d^66s^2$	Ir (77) $4f^{14}5d^76s^2$	Pt (78) $4f^{14}5d^96s^1$	Au (79) $4f^{14}5d^{10}6s^1$	Hg (80) $4f^{14}5d^{10}6s^2$
6*d* series	Ac (89) $5f^06d^17s^2$	Rf (104) $5f^{14}6d^27s^2$	Db (105) $5f^{14}6d^37s^2$	Sg (106) $5f^{14}6d^47s^2$	Bh (107) $5f^{14}6d^57s^2$	Hs (108) $5f^{14}6d^67s^2$	Mt (109) $5f^{14}6d^77s^2$	Ds (110) $5f^{14}6d^87s^2$	Rg (111) $5f^{14}6d^{10}7s^1$	Cn (112) $5f^{14}6d^{10}7s^2$

Mnemonics

3-*d* series

Concept: First Row Transition Elements-3-*d* series

Mnemonics: **S**cary **T**iny **V**icious **C**reatures **M**ingle (with) **F**ellow **C**ow **N**ilgai **C**ougar **Z**ebra.

Interpretations: Scandium(**Sc**), Titanium(**Ti**), Vanadium(**V**), Chromium(**Cr**), Manganese(**Mn**), Iron(**Fe**), Cobalt(**Co**), Nickel(**Ni**), Copper(**Cu**), Zinc(**Zn**)

4-*d* series

Concept: Second Row Transition Elements-4-*d* series

Mnemonics: **Y**esterday **Z**ora **N**abbed a **M**onkey **T**Ricking her **Rh**eumatic **Pad**osan **Ag**nes **Cad**illac.

Interpretations: Y, Zr, Nb > Mo, Tc, Ru, Rh, Pd, Ag, Cd

5-*d* series

Concept: Third Row Transition Elements-5-d series

Mnemonics: **L**ate **H**arry **T**ook **W**alk, **R**eached **O**ffice **I**n **P**ajamas **A**fter an **H**our.

Interpretations: La......, Hf, Ta, W, Re, OS, Ir, Pt, Au, Hg

General Characteristics of Transition Elements

Physical Properties:

(i) All are metals.

(ii) These are malleable and ductile except mercury which is liquid.

d- and f-Block Elements

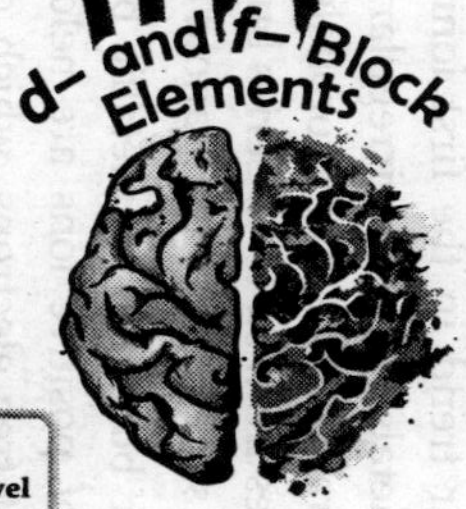

d–Block transition elements groups 3–12

- **Position :** Between *s*- and *p*–blocks.
- **Electronic configuration :** $(n-1)d^{1-10}ns^{1-2}$
- **Physical properties :** Show typical metallic properties, melting and boiling point are high; High enthalpies of atomization.
- Decrease in radius with increasing atomic number. 'Lanthanoid contraction is due to filling of *4f* before *5d* orbitals, hence 2nd, 3rd d-series exhibit similar radii. Also due to imperfect shielding of one e^- by another in the same set of orbitals in same set of orbitals.'
- **Ionisation enthalpies :** Increases from left to right.
- **Oxidation states :** Variable; higher oxidation state is stable.
- Trends in $E_o M_2^+/M$: E_o for Mn, Ni and Zn are more negative than expected.
- Trends in $E_o M_{3+}/M_{2+}$: Variable.
- **Chemical reactivity and E° values :** Variable; Ti^{2+}, V^{2+} and Cr^{2+} are strong reducing agents.
- **Magnetic properties :** Diamagnetism and paramagnetism. Magnetic moment increases with increasing atomic number.
- **Formation of coloured ions :** Form coloured compounds due to *d-d* transitions.
- **Formation of complex compounds :** Form a large number of complex compounds.
- **Catalytic properties :** Due to variable oxidation states and ability to form complexes.
- **Forms interstitial compounds :** Non-stoichiometric and are neither ionic nor covalent.
- **Alloy formation :** Due to similar atomic sizes.

Uses

- Helps in production of iron and steels.
- TiO in pigment industry.
- MnO_2 in dry battery cells.
- As catalysts in industry.
- Ni complexes useful in the polymerization of alkynes and other organic compounds such as benzene.
- AgBr in photographic industry.

Oxides and oxoanions of metals

- Potassium dichromate $K_2Cr_2O_7$

Preparation : $4FeCr_2O_4 + 8Na_2CO_3 + 7O_2 \rightarrow 8Na_2CrO_4 + 2Fe_2O_3 + 8CO_2$

$2Na_2CrO_4 + 2H^+ \rightarrow Na_2Cr_2O_7 + 2Na^+ + H_2O$

$Na_2Cr_2O_7 + 2KCl \rightarrow K_2Cr_2O_7 + 2NaCl$

Properties : $Cr_2O_7^{2-} + 14H^+ + 6e^- \rightarrow 2Cr^{3+} + 7H_2O$

Oxidises iodides to iodine, H_2S to S, SO_3^{2-} to SO_4^{2-}, NO_2^- to NO_3^-

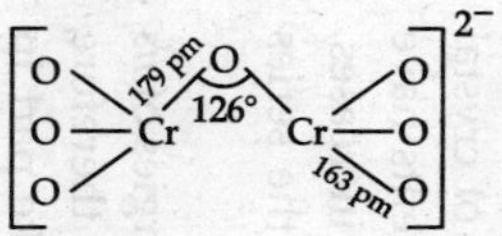

- Potassium permanganate $KMnO_4$

Preparation : $2MnO_2 + 4KOH + O_2 \rightarrow 2K_2MnO_4 + 2H_2O$

$3MnO_4^{2-} + 4H^+ \rightarrow 2MnO_4^- + MnO_2 + 2H_2O$

$2Mn^{2+} + 5S_2O_8^{2-} + 8H_2O \rightarrow 2MnO_4^- + 10SO_4^{2-} + 16H^+$

Properties : Intense colour, weak temperature dependent paramagnetism

$MnO_4^- + 8H^+ + 5e^- \rightarrow Mn^{2+} + 4H_2O$

Oxidizes I^- to I_2, Fe^{2+} to Fe^{3+}, $C_2O_4^{2-}$ to CO_2, S^{2-} to S, SO_3^{2-} to SO_4^{2-}, NO_2^- to NO_3^-

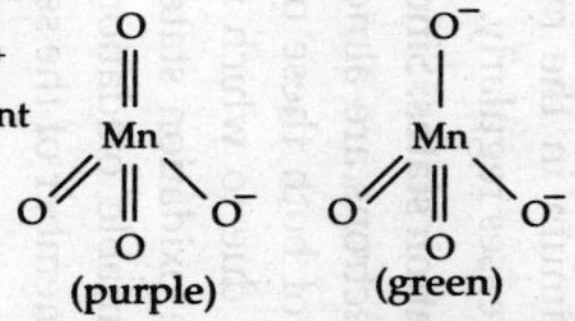

f– Block transition Elements

Lanthanoid contraction is progressive decrease in atomic/ionic radii from La^{3+} to Lu^{3+}

Actinoids

- Electronic configuration: $[Rn]5f^{1-14}6d^{0-1}7s^2$
- Ionic sizes : Gradual decrease along the series.
- Oxidation states : Most common is +3. They show oxidation number of +4, +5, +6 and +7.
- **General characteristics :**
  - –Silvery in appearance.
  - –Display variety of structures.
  - –Highly reactive metals.
  - –Irregularities in metallic radii, greater than in lanthanoids.
  - –Magnetic properties more complex than lanthanoids.

Lanthanoids

- **Electronic configuration :** $4f^{1-14}5d^{0-1}6s^2$
- **Atomic and ionic sizes :** Decrease from La to Lu
- **Oxidation states :** Most common is +3. Some elements exhibit +2 and +4.
- **General characteristics :**
  - Silvery white soft metals and tarnish rapidly in air.
  - Hardness increases with increasing atomic number.
  - Metallic structure and good conductors of heat and electricity.
- Variable density.
- Trivalent lanthanoid ions are coloured.
- **Ionisation Enthalpies :** Low third ionisation enthalpies.
- Good reducing agents.

Chemical Properties

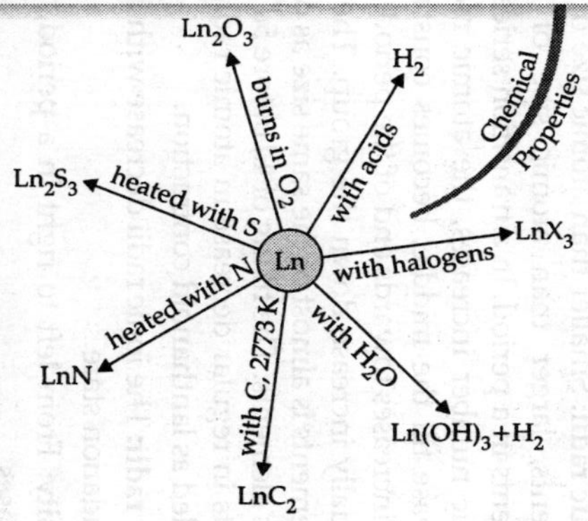

Trace the Mind Map
- First Level
- Second Level
- Third Level

(iii) High thermal and electrical conductivity.

(iv) Metallic luster and sonorous.

(v) **Atomic radii:** Smaller than atomic size of *s*-block elements, larger than atomic size of *p*-block elements in a period. In a transition series, as the atomic number increases, the atomic radii first decrease till the middle, becomes constant and then increases towards end of the period.
It usually increase down the group. The size of 4*d* elements is almost of the same size as of the 5*d* series elements. The filling of 4*d* before 5*d* orbitals results in regular decrease in atomic radii which is called as lanthanoid contraction.

(vi) **Ionic radii:** The ionic radii decrease with increase in oxidation state.

(vii) **Density:** From left to right in a period, density increases.

(viii) **Ionisation enthalpy:** Along the series from left to right, there is an increase in ionisation enthalpy. Irregular trend in the first ionisation enthalpy of 3*d* metals is due to irregularity in electronic configuration of 4*s* and 3*d* orbitals. In a group, I.E. decreases from 3*d* to 4*d* series but increases from 4*d* to 5*d* series due to lanthanoid contraction.

(ix) **Metallic bonding:** In metallic bonding, regular lattice of positive ions are held together by a cloud of free electrons, which can move freely through the lattice. Transition metal atoms are held together by strong metallic bonds.

(x) **Enthalpy of atomisation:** Enthalpy of atomisation is the heat required to convert 1 mole of crystal lattice into free atoms. Transition elements have high enthalpy of atomisation. It first increases, becomes maximum in the middle of the series and then decreases regularly.

(xi) **Variable oxidation states:** Since the energies of *ns* and $(n-1)d$ electrons are almost equal, therefore the electrons of both these orbitals take part in the reactions, due to which transition elements show variable oxidation states. Transition metal ions show variable oxidation states except the first and last member of the series.

(xii) **Electrode potential:** The electrode potential develops on a metal electrode when it is in equilibrium with a solution of its ions, leaving electrons from the electrode. Transition metals have lower value of reduction potential. Variation in $E^{\ominus}$ value is irregular due to the regular variation in ionisation enthalpies ($I.E._1 + I.E._2$), sublimation and hydration enthalpies.

(xiii) **Catalytic properties:** Many of the transition metals and their compounds, particularly oxides act as catalysts for a number of chemical reactions. Iron, cobalt, nickel, platinum, chromium, manganese and their compounds are the commonly used catalysts.
All transitional metals show multiple oxidation states and have large surface area so, all metals work as a catalyst.

(xiv) **Magnetic properties:** On the basis of the behaviour of substances in magnetic field, they are of two types:

(a) Diamagnetic, and

(b) Paramagnetic.

Diamagnetic substances have paired electrons only. e.g., Zn has no (zero) unpaired electrons.

In paramagnetic substances, it is necessary to have at least one unpaired electron. Paramagnetism increases with the increase in number of unpaired electrons. Paramagnetism may be measured by magnetic moment.
Magnetic moment,

$$\mu = \sqrt{n(n+2)} \text{ B.M.},$$

where, n = number of unpaired electrons in atom or ion and B.M. = Bohr magneton (unit of magnetic moment). Diamagnetic and paramagnetic substances are repelled and attracted in the magnetic field respectively.

(xv) **Melting and boiling points:** Except zinc, cadmium and mercury, all other transition elements have high melting and boiling points. This is due to strong metallic bonds and presence of partially filled *d*-orbitals in the shell of the atom of element.

(xvi) **Complex formation:** They have tendency to form complex ions due to high charge on the transition metal ions and the availability of *d*-orbitals for accommodating electrons donated by the ligand atoms.

(xvii) **Formation of coloured compounds:** Transition metals form-coloured ions due to the presence of unpaired *d*-electrons. As a result, light is absorbed in the visible region to cause excitation of unpaired *d*-electrons ($d-d$ transition) and colour observed corresponds to the complementary colour of the light absorbed. Cu^+, Zn^{2+} and Cd^{2+} are colourless due to the absence of unpaired *d*-electrons (d^{10}).

(xviii) **Formation of alloys:** Alloy formation is due to almost similar size of the metal ions, their high ionic charges and the availability of *d*-orbitals for bond formation. Therefore, these metals can mutually substitute their position in their crystal lattice to form alloys. e.g., steel, brass.

(xix) **Formation of interstitial compounds:** Interstitial compounds are known for transition metals as small-sized atoms of H, B, C, N, etc., can easily occupy positions in the voids present in the crystal lattices of transition metals. Characteristics of interstitial compounds:

- High melting points.
- Hard.
- Chemically inert.
- Retain metallic conductivity.
- Non-stoichiometric.

- **Oxides of Transition metals:** They form oxides of the general composition MO, M_2O_3, MO_2, M_2O_5 and MO_6. Oxides in the lower oxidation states are generally basic while those in the higher oxidation states are amphoteric or acidic. For example,

+2	+3	+2, +3	+4	+7
MnO	Mn_2O_3	Mn_3O_4	MnO_2	Mn_2O_7
Basic	Amphoteric	Amphoteric	Amphoteric	Acidic

- **Important Compounds of Transition Elements:**
  - **Potassium Dichromate ($K_2Cr_2O_7$)**

Preparation: It is prepared from chromate ore in the following steps:

(i) Chromate ore is fused with sodium carbonate in the presence of air to give sodium chromate.

$$4FeCr_2O_4 + 8Na_2CO_3 + 7O_2 \rightarrow 2Fe_2O_3 + \underset{\text{Sodium chromate}}{8Na_2CrO_4} + 8CO_2$$

(ii) Na_2CrO_4 is filtered and acidified with conc. H_2SO_4 to give $Na_2Cr_2O_7$.

$$2Na_2CrO_4 + 2H^+ \rightarrow Na_2Cr_2O_7 + 2Na^+ + H_2O_2$$

(iii) Sodium dichromate solution is treated with KCl to give $K_2Cr_2O_7$.

$$Na_2Cr_2O_7 + 2KCl \rightarrow K_2Cr_2O_7 + 2NaCl$$

Properties:

(a) It is an orange, crystalline solid.

(b) Reaction with alkali:

$$Cr_2O_7^{2-} + 2OH^- \rightarrow \underset{\substack{\text{Chromate ion} \\ \text{(Yellow)}}}{2CrO_4^{2-}} + H_2O$$

(c) Reaction with acid:

$$2CrO_4^{2-} + 2H^+ \rightarrow \underset{\substack{\text{Dichromate ion} \\ \text{(orange red)}}}{Cr_2O_7^{2-}} + H_2O$$

In acidic solutions, oxidising action is

$$Cr_2O_7^{2-} + 14H^+ + 6e^- \rightarrow 2Cr^{3+} + 7H_2O$$

(d) It is a powerful oxidising agent. For example,

(i) It oxidises ferrous to ferric.

$$Cr_2O_7^{2-} + 14H^+ + 6e^- \rightarrow 2Cr^{3+} + 7H_2O$$
$$[Fe^{2+} \rightarrow Fe^{3+} + e^-] \times 6$$
$$\overline{Cr_2O_7^{2-} + 6Fe^{2+} + 14H^+ \rightarrow 2Cr^{3+} + 6Fe^{3+} + 7H_2O}$$

(ii) It oxidises stannous to stannic.

$$Cr_2O_7^{2-} + 14H^+ + 6e^- \rightarrow 2Cr^{3+} + 7H_2O$$
$$[Sn^{2+} \rightarrow Sn^{4+} + 2e^-] \times 3$$
$$\overline{Cr_2O_7^{2-} + 3Sn^{2+} + 14H^+ \rightarrow 2Cr^{3+} + 7H_2O + 3Sn^{4+}}$$

(iii) It oxidises sulphur dioxide to sulphate.

$$Cr_2O_7^{2-} + 14H^+ + 6e^- \rightarrow 2Cr^{3+} + 7H_2O$$
$$[SO_2 + 2H_2O \rightarrow SO_4^{2-} + 4H^+ + 2e^-] \times 3$$
$$\overline{Cr_2O_7^{2-} + 3SO_2 + 2H^+ \rightarrow 2Cr^{3+} + 3SO_4^{2-} + H_2O}$$

(iv) It oxidises hydrogen sulphide to sulphur.

$$Cr_2O_7^{2-} + 14H^+ + 6e^- \rightarrow 2Cr^{3+} + 7H_2O$$
$$[H_2S \rightarrow 2H^+ + S + 2e^-] \times 3$$
$$\overline{Cr_2O_7^{2-} + 3H_2S + 8H^+ \rightarrow 2Cr^{3+} + 3S + 7H_2O}$$

(v) It oxidises iodides to iodine.

$$Cr_2O_7^{2-} + 14H^+ + 6e^- \rightarrow 2Cr^{3+} + 7H_2O$$
$$[2I^- \rightarrow I_2 + 2e^-] \times 3$$
$$\overline{Cr_2O_7^{2-} + 6I^- + 14H^+ \rightarrow 2Cr^{3+} + 3I_2 + 7H_2O}$$

Uses:

(i) In leather industry for chrome tanning.

(ii) Preparation of azo compounds.

(iii) As a primary standard in volumetric analysis for the estimation of reducing agent.

Scan to know more about this topic

d- and f- block elements part-II

Structure:

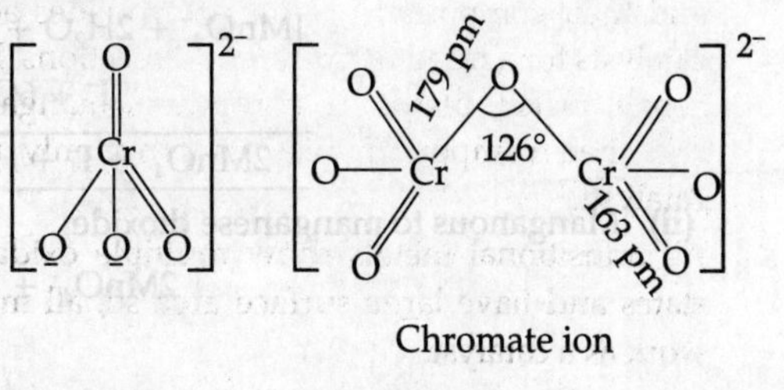

Chromate ion

Dichromate ion

- **Potassium permanganate ($KMnO_4$)**

Preparation:

(i) It is prepared from pyrolusite ore with KOH in the presence of oxidising agent like KNO_3. The dark green potassium manganate undergoes electrolytic oxidation to produce potassium permanganate.

$$2MnO_2 + 4KOH + O_2 \rightarrow 2K_2MnO_4 + 2H_2O$$
$$3MnO_4^{2-} + 4H^+ \rightarrow 2MnO_4^- + MnO_2 + 2H_2O$$

(ii) Commercially, it is prepared by alkaline oxidative fusion of MnO_2 followed by electrolytic oxidation of manganate (VI)

$$MnO_2 + 2e^- \xrightarrow[\text{Oxidised with air/}KNO_3]{\text{Fused with KOH}} \underset{\text{Manganate ion}}{MnO_4^{2-}}$$

$$MnO_4^{2-} \xrightarrow[\text{in alkaline solution}]{\text{Electrolytic oxidation}} \underset{\text{Permanganate ion}}{MnO_4^-} + 1e^-$$

(iii) In laboratory, by oxidation of manganese (II) ion salt by peroxodisulphate to permanganate.

$$2Mn^{2+} + \underset{\text{Peroxodisulphate}}{5S_2O_8^{2-}} + 8H_2O \rightarrow \underset{\text{Permanganate}}{2MnO_4^-} + 10SO_4^{2-} + 16H^+$$

Properties:

(i) Dark purple crystalline solid.

(ii) Sparingly soluble in water.

(iii) Decomposes on heating at 513 K.

$$2KMnO_4 \rightarrow K_2MnO_4 + MnO_2 + O_2$$

(iv) Acts as a powerful oxidising agent in acidic, alkaline and neutral medium. For example:

1. In acidic medium oxidises:

(i) Iodide to iodine:

$$[MnO_4^- + 8H^+ + 5e^- \rightarrow Mn^{2+} + 4H_2O] \times 2$$
$$[2I^- \rightarrow I_2 + 2e^-] \times 5$$
$$2MnO_4^- + 10I^- + 16H^+ \rightarrow 2Mn^{2+} + 5I_2 + 8H_2O$$

(ii) Ferrous to ferric:

$$MnO_4^- + 8H^+ + 5e^- \rightarrow Mn^{2+} + 4H_2O$$
$$[Fe^{2+} \rightarrow Fe^{3+} + e^-] \times 5$$
$$MnO_4^- + 5Fe^{2+} + 8H^+ \rightarrow Mn^{2+} + 5Fe^{3+} + 4H_2O$$

(iii) Oxalate to carbon dioxide:

$$[MnO_4^- + 8H + 5e^- \rightarrow Mn^{2+} + 4H_2O] \times 2$$
$$[C_2O_4^{2-} \rightarrow 2CO_2 + 2e^-] \times 5$$
$$2MnO_4^- + 5C_2O_4^{2-} + 16H^+ \rightarrow 2Mn^{2+} + 10CO_2 + 8H_2O$$

(iv) Hydrogen sulphide to sulphur:

$$[MnO_4^- + 8H^+ + 5e^- \rightarrow Mn^{2+} + 4H_2O] \times 2$$
$$[S^{2-} \rightarrow S + 2e^-] \times 5$$
$$2MnO_4^- + 5S^{2-} + 16H^+ \rightarrow 2Mn^{2+} + 5S + 8H_2O$$

(v) Sulphite to sulphate:

$$[MnO_4^- + 8H^+ + 5e^- \rightarrow Mn^{2+} + 4H_2O] \times 2$$
$$[SO_3^{2-} + H_2O \rightarrow SO_4^{2-} + 2H^+ + 2e^-] \times 5$$
$$5SO_3^{2-} + 2MnO_4^- + 6H^+ \rightarrow 2Mn^{2+} + 5SO_4^{2-} + 3H_2O$$

(vi) Nitrite to nitrate:

$$[MnO_4^- + 8H^+ + 5e^- \rightarrow Mn^{2+} + 4H_2O] \times 2$$
$$[NO_2^- + H_2O \rightarrow NO_3^- + 2H^+ + 2e^-] \times 5$$
$$2MnO_4^- + 5NO_2^- + 6H^+ \rightarrow 2Mn^{2+} + 5NO_3^- + 3H_2O$$

2. In neutral alkaline medium:

(i) Iodide to iodate:

$$[MnO_4^- + 2H_2O + 3e^- \rightarrow MnO_2 + 4OH^-] \times 2$$
$$I^- + 6OH^- \rightarrow IO_3^- + 3H_2O + 6e^-$$
$$2MnO_4^- + I^- + H_2O \rightarrow IO_3^- + 2MnO_2 + 2OH^-$$

(ii) Manganous to manganese dioxide:

$$2MnO_4^- + 3Mn^{2+} + 2H_2O \rightarrow 5MnO_2 + 4H^+$$

Uses:

(i) Bleaching of wool, silk, cotton and other textile fibres.

(ii) Decolourisation of oils.

(iii) In analytical chemistry (titration).

(iv) In organic synthesis.

Structure:

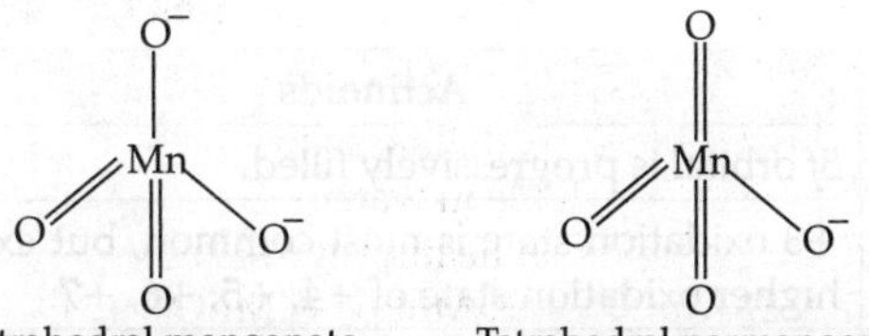

Tetrahedral manganate ion (Green) Tetrahedral permanganate ion (Purple)

The Inner Transition Elements (*f*-Block)

- ***f*-block elements:** The elements in which filling of electrons takes place in (*n*–2) *f*-subshell which belongs to anti-penultimate (third to the outermost) energy shell. This block consists of two series of elements known as Lanthanoids and Actinoids. These elements are also known as inner transition elements. The general electronic configuration of the *f*- block elements is

$$(n-2)f^{1-14}\,(n-1)d^{0-1}\,ns^2$$

For lanthanoids, n is 6 while its value is 7, for actinoids. There are many exceptions in the electronic configuration.

Lanthanoids

- The series involves the filling of 4*f*-orbitals following lanthanum La (Z = 57) is called the lanthanoid series. There are 14 elements in this series starting with Ce (Z = 58) to Lu (Z = 71).

Electronic configuration: [Xe] $4f^{1-14}\,5d^{0-1}\,6s^2$

Physical properties:

(i) Highly dense metals, soft, malleable and ductile.

(ii) High melting point.

(iii) Forms alloys easily with other metals.

(iv) Magnetic properties: Among lanthanoids, La^{3+} and Lu^{3+} which have $4f^0$ or $4f^{14}$ electronic configurations are diamagnetic and all other trivalent lanthanoid ions are paramagnetic due to the presence of unpaired electrons.

(v) Atomic and ionic sizes: With increasing atomic number, the atomic and ionic radii decrease from one element to the other, but the decrease is very small.

A steady decrease in the size of lanthanoids with increase in atomic number is known as lanthanoid contraction.

Consequences of Lanthanoid contraction:

(a) It leads to similar physical and chemical properties among lanthanoids.

(b) Zr and Hf have same properties, due to similar atomic radii.

(c) Chemical separation of lanthanoids become difficult.

(vi) Oxidation state: They mainly give +3 oxidation state. Some elements show +2 and +4 oxidation states.

(vii) Colour: Some of the trivalent ions are coloured. This happens due to the absorption in visible region of the spectrum resulting in *f-f* transitions.

Chemical properties: All lanthanoids are highly electropositive metals and have almost similar chemical reactivity.

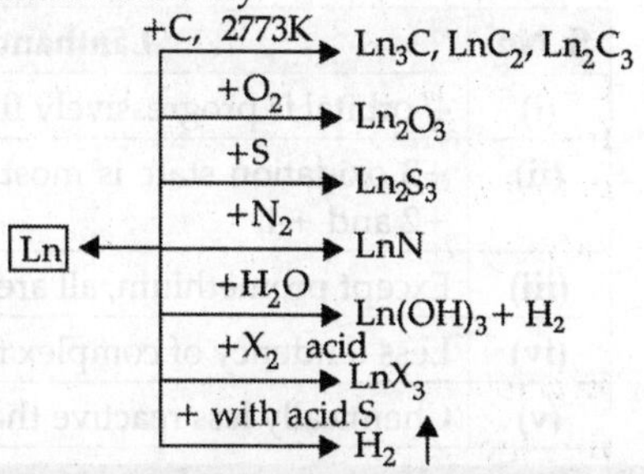

Mnemonics

Lanthanides

Concept: Lanthanides Series

Mnemonics: **Late CEO Promoted Nadia Palmer Smart to Europe so she said Goodbye to Toby a Day before Hoarding Eroding Timber in Yard of Lu.**

Interpretations: La, Ce, Pr, Nd, Pm, Sm, Eu, Gd, Tb, Dy, Ho, Er, Tm, Yb, Lu

Uses:

(i) Misch metal is the alloy of cerium (about 55%) and various other Lanthanoid elements (40-43%). It also contains iron up to 5% and traces of sulphur, carbon, silicon calcium and aluminium. It is a pyrophoric material; hence it is used in lighter flints.

(ii) Lanthanoid oxides are used for polishing glass.

(iii) Cerium salts are used in dyeing cotton and also as catalysts.

(iv) Lanthanoid compounds are used as catalyst for hydrogenated dehydrogenation and petroleum cracking.

(v) Pyrophoric alloys are used for making tracer bullets and shells.

- **Actinoids:** The series involving the filling of 5*f* orbitals from actinium, Ac (Z = 89) up to lawrencium, Lr (Z = 103) comprises of actinoids.
- **Electronic configuration:** [Rn] $5f^{1-14}\,6d^{0-1}\,7s^2$
- **Physical properties:**

(i) Highly dense metals and form alloys with other metals.

(ii) Silvery white metals.

(iii) Highly electropositive.

(iv) High melting point.

(v) Ionic and atomic radii: The atomic and ionic size decreases with an increase in atomic number due to actinoid contraction. The electrons are added to 5*f* shell resulting in an increase in the nuclear charge causing the shell to shrink inwards. This is known as actinoid contraction.

(vi) Colour: Many actinoid ions are coloured.

(vii) **Magnetic properties:** Many actinoid ions are paramagnetic.

(viii) **Oxidation State:** The common oxidation state exhibited is +3. They also exhibit oxidation state of +4, +5, +6 and +7.

(ix) Many elements are radioactive.

Chemical reactivity: Less reactive towards acids.

Uses:

(i) Thorium is used in the treatment of cancer and in incandescent gas mantles.

(ii) Uranium is used in the glass industry, in medicines and as nuclear fuel.

(iii) Plutonium is used in atomic reactors and in atomic bombs.

- **Difference between Lanthanoids and Actinoids:**

S. No.	Lanthanoids	Actinoids
(i)	4*f* orbital is progressively filled.	5*f* orbital is progressively filled.
(ii)	+3 oxidation state is most common along with +2 and +4.	+3 oxidation state is most common, but exhibit higher oxidation state of +4, +5, +6, +7.
(iii)	Except promethium, all are non-radioactive.	All are radioactive.
(iv)	Less tendency of complex formation.	Strong tendency of complex formation.
(v)	Chemically less reactive than actinoids.	More reactive than lanthanoids.

Some Applications of *d*- and *f*- Block Elements

- Iron and steels are the most important construction materials. Their production is based on the reduction of iron oxides, the removal of impurities and the addition of carbon and alloying metals such as Cr, Mn and Ni.
- Some compounds are manufactured for special purposes such as TiO for the pigment industry and MnO_2 for use in dry battery cells. The battery industry also requires Zn and Ni/Cd.
- The elements of Group 11 are still worthy of being called the coinage metals, although Ag and Au are restricted to collection items and the contemporary UK 'copper' coins are copper-coated steel. The 'silver' UK coins are a Cu/Ni alloy.
- Many of the metals and/or their compounds are essential catalysts in the chemical industry. V_2O_5 catalyses the oxidation of SO_2 in the manufacture of sulphuric acid.
- $TiCl_4$ with Al(CH3)$_3$ forms the basis of the Ziegler catalysts used to manufacture polyethylene (polythene).
- Iron catalysts are used in the Haber process for the production of ammonia from N2/H2 mixtures.
- Nickel catalysts enable the hydrogenation of fats to proceed.
- In the Wacker process, the oxidation of ethyne to ethanal is catalysed by $PdCl_2$.
- Nickel complexes are useful in the polymerisation of alkynes and other organic compounds such as benzene.
- The photographic industry relies on the special light-sensitive properties of AgBr.

Mnemonics

Actinides

Concept: Actinide Series

Mnemonics: Active Thor Paid Ur Nephew for Pumpkins.

- **Amy Came Back from California.**
- **Einstein and Fermi Made No. of Laws.**

Interpretations: Ac, Th, Pa, U, Np, Pu, Am, Cm, Bk, Cf, Es, Fm, Md, No, Lr

NCERT CORNER

Intext Questions

Page - 92

Q. 4.1. Silver atom has completely filled *d* orbitals ($4d^{10}$) in its ground state. How can you say that it is a transition element?

Ans. Those elements which have partially filled *d* or *f* subshell in any oxidation state are called transition elements. Silver (Ag) has a completely filled 4*d* orbital ($4d^{10}5s^1$) in its ground state. Now, silver displays two oxidation states (+1 and +2). In the +1 oxidation state, an electron is removed from the *s*-orbital. However, in the +2-oxidation state, an electron is removed from the *d*-orbital. Thus, the *d*-orbital now becomes incomplete ($4d^9$). Hence, it is a transition element.

Page - 95

Q. 4.2. In the series Sc (Z = 21) to Zn (Z = 30), the enthalpy of atomization of zinc is the lowest, i.e., 126 kJ mol^{-1}. Why?

Ans. In the series Sc (Z = 21) to Zn (Z = 30), the enthalpy of atomization of Zn is the lowest, that is 126 kJ mol^{-1} because the extent of metallic bonding an element undergoes decides the enthalpy of atomization. The more extensive the metallic bonding of an element, the more will be its enthalpy of atomization. In all transition metals (except Zn, electronic configuration: $3d^{10}4s^2$), there are some unpaired electrons that account for their stronger metallic bonding. Due to the absence of these unpaired electrons, the inter-atomic electronic bonding is the weakest in Zn and as a result, it has the least enthalpy of atomization.

Page - 97

Q. 4.3. Which of the 3*d* series of the transition metals exhibits the largest number of oxidation states and why?

Ans. Mn (Z = 25) = $3d^5 4s^2$.

Mn has the maximum number of unpaired electrons present in the *d*-subshell. Compounds of manganese therefore range from Mn(0) as Mn(s), Mn(II) as MnO, Mn(II, III) as Mn_3O_4, Mn(IV) as MnO_2, or manganese dioxide, Mn(VII) in the permanganate ion MnO_4^-, and so on. Hence, Mn exhibits the largest number of oxidation states, ranging from +2 to +7.

Page - 98

Q. 4.4. The $E^0_{(M^{2+}/M)}$ value for copper is positive (+0.34 V). What is possible reason for this? (Hint: consider its high $\Delta_a H^\ominus$ and low $\Delta_{hyd}H^\ominus$).

Ans. The $E^\ominus_{(M^{2+}/M)}$ value of a metal depends on the energy changes involved in the following:

(i) Sublimation: The energy required for converting one mole of an atom from the solid state to the gaseous state.

$$M(s) \rightarrow M(g) \qquad \Delta_a H$$

(ii) Ionization: The energy required to take out electrons from one mole of atoms in the gaseous state.

$$M(s) \rightarrow M(g) \qquad \Delta_i H$$

(iii) Hydration: The energy released when one mole of ions is hydrated.

$$M^{2+}(g) \rightarrow M^{2+}(aq) \qquad \Delta_{hyd} H$$

Now, copper has a high energy of atomization and low hydration energy. Hence, the $E^\ominus_{(M^{2+}/M)}$ value for copper is positive.

Page - 100

Q. 4.5. How would you account for the irregular variation of ionization enthalpies (first and second) in the first series of the transition elements?

Ans. Ionization enthalpies are found to increase in the given series. This occurs due to a continuous filling of the inner *d*-orbitals. The irregular variations of ionization enthalpies can be attributed to the extra stability of configurations such as d^0, d^5, d^{10}. Since these states are exceptionally stable, their ionization enthalpies are very high. In case of first ionization energy, chromium (Cr) has low ionization energy. This is because after losing one electron, it attains the stable configuration ($3d^5$). On the other hand, zinc (Zn) has exceptionally high first ionization energy as an electron has to be removed from stable and fully filled orbitals ($3d^{10}4s^2$). Second ionization energies are higher than the first since it becomes difficult to remove an electron when an electron has already been taken out. Also, elements like Cr and Cu have exceptionally high second ionization energies as after losing the first electron, they have attained the stable configuration (Cr^+: $3d^5$ and Cu^+: $3d^{10}$). Hence, taking out one electron more from this stable configuration will require a lot of energy.

Page - 101

Q. 4.6. Why is the highest oxidation state of a metal exhibited in its oxide or fluoride only?

Ans. The highest oxidation state of a metal exhibited in its oxide or fluoride only because both oxide and fluoride ions are highly electronegative and have a very small size. So, due to these properties, they are able to oxidize the metal to its highest oxidation state.

Q. 4.7. Which is a stronger reducing agent Cr^{2+} or Fe^{2+} and why ?

Ans. Cr^{2+} is a better reducing agent than Fe^{3+}. The following reactions are involved when Cr^{2+} and Fe^{2+} act as reducing agents:

$$Cr^{2+} \rightarrow Cr^{3+}$$
$$Fe^{2+} \rightarrow Fe^{3+}$$

The $E^\ominus_{Cr^{2+}/Cr^{3+}}$ value is - 0.41 V and $E^\ominus_{Fe^{3+}/Fe^{2+}}$ is +0.77 V. This means that Cr^{2+} can be easily oxidized to Cr^{3+}, but Fe^{2+} does not get oxidized to Fe^{3+} easily.

Page - 103

Q. 4.8. Calculate the 'spin only' magnetic moment of $M^{2+}_{(aq)}$ ion (Z = 27)

Ans. Z = 27

So electronic configuration is [Ar] $3d^7 4s^2$

Therefore, M^{2+} = [Ar] $3d^7$

$3d^7$ =

↑↓	↑↓	↑	↑	↑

That is 3 unpaired electrons

Therefore, $n = 3$

$$\sqrt{n(n+2)} = \mu$$
$$\sqrt{3(3+2)} = \mu$$
$$\sqrt{15} = \mu$$
$$\mu \approx 4 \text{ BM}$$

Q. 4.9. Explain why Cu^+ ion is not stable in aqueous solutions?

Ans. Cu^{2+} is more stable than Cu^+ in an aqueous medium. As energy is required to remove one electron from Cu^+ to Cu^{2+}, high hydration energy of Cu^{2+} compensates for it. Therefore, Cu^+ ion in an aqueous solution is unstable. It disproportionate to give Cu^{2+} and Cu.

$$2Cu^+(aq) \rightarrow Cu^{2+}(aq) + Cu(s)$$

Page - 113

Q. 4.10. Actinoid contraction is greater from element to element than lanthanoid contraction. Why?

Ans. In actinoids, 5*f* orbitals are filled. These 5*f* orbitals have a poorer shielding effect than 4*f* orbitals (in lanthanoids). Thus, the effective nuclear charge experienced by electrons in valence shells in case of actinoids is much more that that experienced by lanthanoids. Hence, the size contraction in actinoids is greater as compared to that in lanthanoids.

Exercise Questions

Q. 1. Write down the electronic configuration of:
(i) Cr^{3+} (iii) Cu^{+} (v) Co^{2+} (vii) Mn^{2+}
(ii) Pm^{3+} (iv) Ce^{4+} (vi) Lu^{2+} (viii) Th^{4+}
[NCERT Ex. Q. 4.1, Page 115]

Ans. (i) $Cr^{3+} = [Ar]^{18}3d^3$
(ii) $Pm^{3+} = [Xe]^{54}4f^4$
(iii) $Cu^{+} = [Ar]^{18}3d^{10}$
(iv) $Ce^{4+} = [Xe]^{54}$
(v) $Co^{2+} = [Ar]^{18}3d^7$
(vi) $Lu^{2+} = [Xe]^{54}4f^{14}5d^1$
(vii) $Mn^{2+} = [Ar]^{18}3d^5$
(viii) $Th^{4+} = [Rn]^{86}$

Q. 2. Why are Mn^{2+} compounds more stable than Fe^{2+} towards oxidation to their +3 state?
[NCERT Ex. Q. 4.2, Page 115]

Ans. Electronic configuration of Mn^{2+} is $[Ar]^{18}3d^5$. Electronic configuration of Fe^{2+} is $[Ar]^{18}3d^6$. It is known that half-filled and fully filled orbitals are more stable. Therefore, Mn in (+2) state has a stable d^5 configuration. This is the reason Mn^{2+} shows resistance to oxidation to Mn^{3+}. Also, Fe^{2+} has $3d^6$ configuration and by losing one electron, its configuration changes to a more stable $3d^5$ configuration. Therefore, Fe^{2+} easily gets oxidized to Fe^{3+} oxidation state.

Q. 3. Explain briefly how +2 state becomes more and more stable in the first half of the first-row transition elements with increasing atomic number?
[NCERT Ex. Q. 4.3, Page 115]

Ans. The oxidation states present in the first half of the first row of transition metals are given in the Following table:

	Sc	Ti	V	Cr	Mn
Oxidation state		+2	+2	+2	+2
	+3	+3	+3	+3	+3
		+4	+4	+4	+4
			+5	+5	+5
				+6	+6
					+7

In the first row of transition series, it is observed that except Sc, all other metals displays +2 oxidation state. On moving from Sc to Mn, the atomic number increases. Thus, the number of electrons in the *3d*-orbital also increases.

Sc (+2) = d^1
Ti (+2) = d^2
V (+2) = d^3
Cr (+2) = d^4
Mn (+2) = d^5

Elements attains +2 oxidation state by the loss of the two 4*s* electrons. The stability of +2 in the first series increases till first half as by losing 2 electrons, these elements acquire stable oxidation state.

Q. 4. To what extent do the electronic configurations decide the stability of oxidation states in the first series of the transition elements? Illustrate your answer with examples. [NCERT Ex. Q. 4.4, Page 115]

Ans. Transition elements show many oxidation states like manganese (Mn) exhibits maximum number of oxidation states (+2 to +7). The stability of +2 oxidation state increases with the increase in atomic number because more electrons are getting filled in the *d*-orbitals. Scandium, does not show +2 oxidation state. Its electronic configuration is (Ar) $4s^23d^1$. By losing all three electrons, it attains noble gas configuration and become more stable. In the similar way, Ti (+4) and V (+5) are very stable.

Q. 5. What may be the stable oxidation state of the transition element with the following *d* electron configurations in the ground state of their atoms: $3d^3$, $3d^5$, $3d^8$ and $3d^4$? [NCERT Ex. Q. 4.5, Page 115]

Ans.

Electronic configuration in ground state	Stable oxidation state
$3d^3$ (Vanadium)	+2, +3, +4 and +5
$3d^5$ (Chromium)	+3, +4, +6
$3d^5$ (Manganese)	+2, +4, +6, +7
$3d^8$ (Cobalt)	+2, +3
$3d^4$	There is no $3d^4$ configuration in ground state.

Q. 6. Name the oxo metal anions of the first series of the transition metals in which the metal exhibits the oxidation state equal to its group number.
[NCERT Ex. Q. 4.6, Page 115]

Ans. (i) Vanadate, VO_3^- Oxidation state of V is + 5.
(ii) Chromate, CrO_4^{2-} Oxidation state of Cr is +6.
(iii) Permanganate, MnO_4^- Oxidation state of Mn is +7.

Q. 7. What is lanthanoid contraction? What are the consequences of lanthanoid contraction?
[NCERT Ex. Q. 4.7, Page 115]

Ans. As we move along the lanthanoid series, the atomic number increases gradually by one. This means that the number of electrons and protons present in an atom also increases by one. As electrons are being added to the same shell, the effective nuclear charge increases. This happens because the increase in nuclear attraction due to the addition of proton is more pronounced than the increase in the interelectronic repulsions due to the addition of electron. Also, with the increase in atomic number, the number of electrons in the 4 *f* orbital also increases. The 4 *f* electrons have poor shielding effect. Therefore, the effective nuclear charge experienced by the outer electrons increases. Consequently, the attraction of the nucleus for the outermost electrons increases. This results in a steady decrease in the size of lanthanoids with the increase in the atomic number. This is termed as lanthanoid contraction.

Consequences of lanthanoid contraction

(i) There is similarity in the properties of second and third transition series.

(ii) Separation of lanthanoids is possible due to lanthanoid contraction.

(iii) It is due to lanthanoid contraction that there is variation in the basic strength of lanthanoid hydroxides. (Basic strength decreases from $La(OH)_3$ to $Lu(OH)_3$.

Q. 8. What are the characteristics of the transition elements and why are they called transition elements? Which of the *d*-block elements may not be regarded as the transition elements? [NCERT Ex. Q. 4.8, Page 115]

Ans. Those elements in which the atoms or ions (in stable oxidation state) contain partially filled *d*-orbital are called transition elements. These elements lie in the *d*-block and show a transition of properties between *s*-block and *p*-block. That is why these elements are called as transition elements. Elements such as Zn, Cd, and Hg cannot be classified as transition elements because these have completely filled *d*-subshell.

Q. 9. In what way is the electronic configuration of the transition elements different from that of the non-transition elements? [NCERT Ex. Q. 4.9, Page 115]

Ans. Electronic configuration of transition elements $= (n-1)d^{1\text{-}10}\, ns^{0\text{-}2}$.

Electronic configuration of non-transition elements$= ns^{1\text{-}2}$ or $ns^2np^{1\text{-}6}$.

Transition metals have a partially filled *d*-orbital whereas the non-transition elements do not have *d*-orbitals.

Q. 10. What are the different oxidation states exhibited by the lanthanoids? [NCERT Ex. Q. 4.10, Page 115]

Ans. In the lanthanoid series, +3 oxidation state is most common that is Ln(III) compounds are predominant. However, +2 and +4 oxidation states can also be found in the solution or in solid compounds.

Q. 11. Explain giving reasons:

(i) Transition metals and many of their compounds show paramagnetic behaviour.

(ii) The enthalpies of atomisation of the transition metals are high.

(iii) The transition metals generally form coloured compounds.

(iv) Transition metals and their many compounds act as good catalyst. [NCERT Ex. Q. 4.11, Page 115]

Ans. (i) Transition metals show paramagnetic behaviour. Paramagnetism arises due to the presence of unpaired electrons with each electron having a magnetic moment associated with its spin angular momentum and orbital angular momentum. However, in the first transition series, the orbital angular momentum is quenched. Therefore, the resulting paramagnetism is only because of the unpaired electrons.

(ii) Transition elements have high effective nuclear charge and a large number of valence electrons. Therefore, they form very strong metallic bonds. As a result, the enthalpy of atomization of transition metals is high.

(iii) It is due to the presence of unpaired electrons, due to which they undergo *d-d* transitions by absorbing light from visible region and radiate complementary colour.

(iv) It is due to variable oxidation states. They have large surface and can form intermediate with reactants which readily change into products.

Q. 12. What are interstitial compounds? Why are such compounds well known for transition metals? [NCERT Ex. 4.12, Page 115]

Ans. Interstitial sites are present in transition metals because of its larger size. Transition metals can trap atoms of other elements of smaller size, such as H, C, N, in the interstitial sites of their crystal lattices. The resulting compounds are called interstitial compounds.

Q. 13. How is the variability in oxidation states of transition metals different from that of the non-transition metals? Illustrate with examples. [NCERT Ex. 4.13, Page 115]

Ans. Due to the presence of *d*-orbital electrons, transition elements show multiple oxidation states as compared to non-transition elements. The oxidation state can vary from +1 to the highest oxidation state by removing all its valence electrons. In transition elements, the oxidation states differ by 1 (Fe^{2+} and Fe^{3+}; Cu^+ and Cu^{2+}). In non-transition elements, the oxidation states differ by 2, for example, +2 and +4 or +3 and +5, etc.

Q. 14. Describe the preparation of potassium dichromate from iron chromite ore. What is the effect of increasing pH on a solution of potassium dichromate? [NCERT Ex. 4.14, Page 115]

Ans. Potassium dichromate is prepared from chromate, which in turn is obtained by the fusion of chromite ore ($FeCr_2O_4$) with sodium or potassium carbonate in free excess of air. The reaction with sodium carbonate occurs as follows:

$$4FeCr_2O_4 + 8Na_2CO_3 + 7O_2 \rightarrow 8Na_2CrO_4 + 2Fe_2O_3 + 8CO_2$$

The yellow solution of sodium chromate is filtered and orange sodium dichromate, $Na_2Cr_2O_7.\ H_2O$ can be crystallized.

Sodium dichromate is more soluble than potassium dichromate. The latter is therefore, prepared by treating the solution of sodium dichromate with potassium chloride.

$$Na_2Cr_2O_7 + 2KCl \rightarrow K_2Cr_2O_7 + 2NaCl$$

Orange crystals of potassium dichromate crystallise out. The chromates and dichromate are interconvertible in aqueous solution depending upon pH of the solution. If pH of potassium dichromate is increased, it is converted to yellow potassium chromate.

$$2CrO_4^{2-} + 2H^+ \rightarrow Cr_2O_7^{2-} + H_2O$$

$$Cr_2O_7^{2-} + 2OH^- \rightarrow 2CrO_4^{2-} + H_2O$$

Q. 15. Describe the oxidising action of potassium dichromate and write the ionic equations for its reaction with:

(i) iodide, (ii) iron(II) solution and (iii) H_2S

[NCERT Ex. 4.15, Page 115]

Ans. $K_2Cr_2O_7$ is a powerful oxidizing agent. In dilute sulphuric acid medium, the oxidation state of Cr changes from +6 to +3. The oxidizing action can be represented as follows:

$$Cr_2O_7^{2-} + 14H^+ + 6e^- \rightarrow 2Cr^{3+} + 7H_2O$$

(i) Iodide: Iodide ion is oxidized to iodine by the acidified solution of $K_2Cr_2O_7$.

Reaction:

$$Cr_2O_7^{2-} + 14H^+ + 6e^- \rightarrow 2Cr^{3+} + 7H_2O$$
$$6I^- \rightarrow 3I_2 + 6e^-$$
$$Cr_2O_7^{2-} + 14H^+ + 6I^- \rightarrow 3I_2 + 2Cr^{3+} + 7H_2O$$

(ii) Iron (II) solution: Ferrous salts (Fe^{2+}) are oxidized to ferric (Fe^{3+}) salts when they are treated with acidified $K_2Cr_2O_7$.

$$Cr_2O_7^{2-} + 14H^+ + 6e^- \rightarrow 2Cr^{3+} + 7H_2O$$
$$6Fe^{2+} \rightarrow 6Fe^{3+} + 6e^-$$
$$Cr_2O_7^{2-} + 6Fe^{2+} + 14H^+ \rightarrow 2Cr^{3+} + 6Fe^{3+} + 7H_2O$$

(iii) H_2S is oxidized to Sulphur:

$$Cr_2O_7^{2-} + 3H_2S + 8H^+ \rightarrow 2Cr^{3+} + 7H_2O + 3S$$

Q. 16. Describe the preparation of potassium permanganate. How does the acidified permanganate solution react with
(i) iron(II) ions, (ii) SO_2 and (iii) oxalic acid? Write the ionic equations for the reactions.
[NCERT Ex. Q. 4.16, Page 116]

Ans. Potassium permanganate can be prepared from pyrolusite (MnO_2).

The ore is fused with potassium hydroxide (KOH) in the presence of either atmospheric oxygen or an oxidising agent, such as KNO_3 or $KClO_4$, to give K_2MnO_4.

$$2MnO_2 + 4KOH + O_2 \xrightarrow{\text{heat}} \underset{\text{(green)}}{2K_2MnO_4} + 2H_2O$$

The green mass can be extracted with water and then oxidized either electrolytically or by-passing chlorine/ozone into the solution.

Electrolytic oxidation:

$$K_2MnO_4 \rightarrow 2K^+ + MnO_4^{2-}$$
$$H_2O \rightarrow H^+ + OH^-$$

At anode:

$$\underset{\text{(Green)}}{MnO_4^{2-}} \rightarrow \underset{\text{(Purple)}}{MnO_4^-} + e^-$$

Manganate ions are oxidized to permanganate ions.

Oxidation by chlorine:

$$2K_2MnO_4 + Cl_2 \rightarrow 2KMnO_4 + 2KCl$$
$$2MnO_4^{2-} \rightarrow 2MnO_4^- + 2Cl^-$$

Oxidation by ozone:

$$2K_2MnO_4 + O_3 + H_2O \rightarrow 2KMnO_4 + 2KOH + O_2$$
$$2MnO_4^{2-} + O_3 + H_2O \rightarrow 2MnO_4^{2-} + 2OH^- + O_2$$

(i) Acidified $KMnO_4$ solution oxidizes Fe (II) ions to Fe (III) ions, that is, ferrous ions to ferric ions.

$$MnO_4^- + 8H^+ + 5e^- \rightarrow Mn^{2+} + 4H_2O$$
$$Fe^{2+} \rightarrow Fe^{3+} + e^-] \times 5$$
$$MnO_4^- + 5Fe^{2+} + 8H^+ \rightarrow Mn^{2+} + 5Fe^{3+} + 4H_2O$$

(ii) Acidified potassium permanganate oxidizes SO_2 to sulphuric acid.

$$MnO_4^- + 6H^+ + 5e^- \rightarrow Mn^{2+} + 3H_2O] \times 2$$
$$2H_2O + 2SO_2 + O_2 \rightarrow 4H^+ + 2SO_4^{2-} + 2e^-] \times 5$$
$$2MnO_4^- + 10SO_2 + 5O_2 + 4H_2O \rightarrow 2Mn^{2+} + 10SO_4^{2-} + 8H^+$$

(iii) Acidified potassium permanganate oxidized oxalic acid to carbon dioxide.

$$MnO_4^- + 8H^+ + 5e^- \rightarrow Mn^{2+} + 4H_2O] \times 2$$
$$C_2O_4^{2-} \rightarrow 2CO_2 + 2e^-] \times 5$$

$$2MnO_4^- + 5C_2O_4^{2-} + 16H^+ \rightarrow 2Mn^{2+} + 10CO_2 + 8H_2O$$

Q. 17. For M^{2+}/M and M^{3+}/M^{2+} systems the $E^\ominus$ values for some metals are as follows:

Cr^{2+}/Cr	–0.9 V	Cr^{3}/Cr^{2+}	–0.4 V
Mn^{2+}/Mn	–1.2 V	Mn^{3+}/Mn^{2+}	+1.5 V
Fe^{2+}/Fe	–0.4 V	Fe^{3+}/Fe^{2+}	+0.8 V

Use this data to comment upon:
(i) the stability of Fe^{3+} in acid solution as compared to that of Cr^{3+} or Mn^{3+} and
(ii) the ease with which iron can be oxidised as compared to a similar process for either chromium or manganese metal. [NCERT Ex. 4.17, Page 116]

Ans. (i) The $E^\ominus$ value for Fe^{3+}/Fe^{2+} is higher than that for Cr^{3+}/Cr^{2+} and lower than that for Mn^{3+}/Mn^{2+}. These metal ions can be arranged in the increasing order of their stability as:

$$Mn^{3+} < Fe^{3+} < Cr^{3+}$$

So, the reduction of Fe^{3+} to Fe^{2+} is easier than the reduction of Mn^{3+} to Mn^{2+}, but not as easy as the reduction of Cr^{3+} to Cr^{2+}. Hence, Fe^{3+} is more stable than Mn^{3+}, but less stable than Cr^{3+}.

(ii) The reduction potentials order increases in the following order:

$$Mn^{2+}/Mn < Cr^{2+}/Cr < Fe^{2+}/Fe$$

Thus, the oxidation of Fe to Fe^{2+} is not as easy as the oxidation of Cr to Cr^{2+} and the oxidation of Mn to Mn^{2+}.

Q. 18. Predict which of the following will be coloured in aqueous solution? Ti^{3+}, V^{3+}, Cu^+, Sc^{3+}, Mn^{2+}, Fe^{3+} and Co^{2+}. Give reasons for each. [NCERT Ex. 4.18, Page 116]

Ans. Ti^{3+}, V^{3+}, Mn^{2+}, Fe^{3+}, Co^{2+} are coloured. These ions are coloured due to presence of unpaired electrons, they can undergo d-d transitions.

Q. 19. Compare the stability of +2 oxidation state for the elements of the first transition series.
[NCERT Ex. Q. 4.19, Page 116]

Ans. It is clearly seen from the table that the maximum number of oxidation states is shown by Mn, varying from +2 to +7. The number of oxidation states increases on moving from Sc to Mn. On moving from Mn to Zn, the number of oxidation states decreases due to a decrease in the number of available unpaired electrons. The relative stability of the +2 oxidation state increases on moving from top to bottom. This is because on moving from top to bottom, it becomes more and more difficult to remove the third electron from the *d*-orbital.

Sc			+3				
Ti	+1	+2	+3	+4			
V	+1	+2	+3	+4	+5		
Cr	+1	+2	+3	+4	+5	+6	
Mn	+1	+2	+3	+4	+5	+6	+7
Fe	+1	+2	+3	+4	+5	+6	
Co	+1	+2	+3	+4	+5		
Ni	+1	+2	+3	+4			
Cu	+1	+2	+3				
Zn		+2					

Q. 20. Compare the chemistry of actinoids with that of the lanthanoids with special reference to:
(i) electronic configuration

(ii) atomic and ionic sizes
(iii) oxidation state and
(iv) chemical reactivity. [NCERT Ex. Q. 4.20, Page 116]

Ans. (i) Electronic configuration: The general electronic configuration for lanthanoids is $[Xe]^{54}4f^{0-14}5d^{0-1}6s^2$ and that for actinoids is $[Rn]^{86}5f^{1-14}6d^{0-1}7s^2$. Unlike $4f$ orbitals, $5f$ orbitals are not deeply buried and participate in bonding to a greater extent.

(ii) Atomic and Ionic sizes: Similar to lanthanoids, actinoids also exhibit actinoid contraction (overall decrease in atomic and ionic radii). The contraction is greater due to the poor shielding effect of $5f$ orbitals.

(iii) Oxidation states: The principal oxidation state of lanthanoids is (+3). However, sometimes we also encounter oxidation states of + 2 and + 4. This is because of extra stability of fully filled and half-filled orbitals. Actinoids exhibit a greater range of oxidation states. This is because the $5f$, $6d$, and $7s$ levels are of comparable energies. Again, (+3) is the principal oxidation state for actinoids. Actinoids such as lanthanoids have more compounds in +3 state than in +4 state.

(iv) Chemical reactivity: In the lanthanoid series, the earlier members of the series are more reactive. They have reactivity that is comparable to Ca. With an increase in the atomic number, the lanthanoid start behaving similar to Al. Actinoids, on the other hand, are highly reactive metals, especially when they are finely divided. When they are added to boiling water, they give a mixture of oxide and hydride. Actinoids combine with most of the non-metals at moderate temperatures. Alkalies have no action on these actinoids. In case of acids, they are slightly affected by nitric acid (because of the formation of a protective oxide layer).

Q. 21. How would you account for the following:
(i) Of the d^4 species, Cr^{2+} is strongly reducing while manganese(III) is strongly oxidising.
(ii) Cobalt(II) is stable in aqueous solution but in the presence of complexing reagents it is easily oxidised.
(iii) The d^1 configuration is very unstable in ions.
[NCERT Ex. Q. 4.21, Page 116]

Ans. (i) Cr^{2+} is strongly reducing in nature. It has a d^4 configuration. While acting as a reducing agent, it gets oxidized to Cr^{3+} (electronic configuration, d^3). This d^3 configuration can be written as t^3_{2g} configuration, which is a more stable configuration. In the case of $Mn^{3+}(d^4)$, it acts as an oxidizing agent and gets reduced to $Mn^{2+}(d^5)$. This has an exactly half-filled d-orbital and is highly stable.

(ii) Co(II) is stable in aqueous solutions. However, in the presence of strong field complexing reagents, it is oxidized to Co (III). Although the third ionization energy for Co is high, but the higher amount of crystal field stabilization energy (CFSE) released in the presence of strong field ligands overcomes this ionization energy.

(iii) The ions in d^1 configuration tend to lose one more electron to get into stable d^0 configuration. Also, the hydration or lattice energy is more than sufficient to remove the only electron present in the d-orbital of these ions. Therefore, they act as reducing agents.

Q. 22. What is meant by 'disproportionation'? Give two examples of disproportionation reaction in aqueous solution. [NCERT Ex. Q. 4.22, Page 116]

Ans. Those reactions in which the same substance undergoes oxidation as well as reduction that is oxidation number of an element increases as well as decreases to form two different products.

For example,

$$3\overset{+5}{Cr}O_4^{3-} + 8H^+ \rightarrow 2\overset{+6}{Cr}O_4^{2-} + \overset{+3}{Cr^{3+}} + 4H_2O$$

Cr(V) is oxidized to Cr(VI) and reduced to Cr(III).

$$3\overset{+6}{Mn}O_4^{2-} + 4H^+ \rightarrow 2\overset{+7}{Mn}O_4^- + \overset{+4}{Mn}O_2 + 2H_2O$$

Mn (VI) is oxidized to Mn(VII) and reduced to Mn(IV).

Q. 23. Which metal in the first series of transition metals exhibits +1 oxidation state most frequently and why? [NCERT Ex. Q. 4.23, Page 116]

Ans. In the first transition series, copper (Cu) exhibit +1 oxidation state very often. This occurs because Cu (+1) has an electronic configuration of $[Ar]d^{10}$. The completely filled d-orbital makes it highly stable.

Q. 24. Calculate the number of unpaired electrons in the following gaseous ions: Mn^{3+}, Cr^{3+}, V^{3+} and Ti^{3+}. Which one of these is the most stable in aqueous solution? [NCERT Ex. Q. 24, Page 116]

Ans. $Mn^{3+} = [Ar]3d^4$ = 4 unpaired electrons
$Cr^{3+} = [Ar]3d^3$ = 3 unpaired electrons
$V^{3+} = [Ar]3d^2$ = 2 unpaired electrons
$Ti^{3+} = [Ar]3d^1$ = 1 unpaired electron

Cr^{3+} is the most stable in aqueous solutions owing because of half-filled t^3_{2g} level.

Q. 25. Give examples and suggest reasons for the following features of the transition metal chemistry:
(i) The lowest oxide of transition metal is basic, the highest is amphoteric/acidic.
(ii) A transition metal exhibits highest oxidation state in oxides and fluorides.
(iii) The highest oxidation state is exhibited in oxoanions of a metal. [NCERT Ex. Q. 4.25, Page 116]

Ans. (i) The lower oxide of transition metal is basic because the metal atom has low oxidation state whereas higher one is acidic due to high oxidation state. For example: MnO is basic whereas Mn_2O_7 is acidic. Oxides in lower oxidation states are ionic hence basic. Oxides in higher oxidation state are covalent hence acidic.

(ii) A transition metal exhibits higher oxidation states in oxides and fluorides because oxygen and fluorine are highly electronegative elements, small in size and strongest oxidizing agents. For example : Osmium shows an oxidation state of +6 in OsF_6 and vanadium shows an oxidation state of +5 in V_2O_5.

(iii) Oxo metal anions have highest oxidation state, example Cr in $Cr_2O_7^{2-}$ has an oxidation state of +6 whereas Mn in MnO_4^- has an oxidation state of +7. This is again due to the combination of the metal with oxygen, which is highly electronegative and oxidizing agent.

Q. 26. Indicate the steps in the preparation of:
(i) $K_2Cr_2O_7$ from chromite ore.
(ii) $KMnO_4$ from pyrolusite ore.
[NCERT Ex. Q. 4.26, Page 116]

Ans. (i) Potassium dichromate ($K_2Cr_2O_7$) is prepared from chromite ore ($FeCr_2O_4$) in the following steps:

Step (1): Preparation of sodium chromate

$$4FeCr_2O_4 + 16NaOH + 7O_2 \rightarrow 8Na_2CrO_4 + 2Fe_2O_3 + 8H_2O$$

Step (2): Conversion of sodium chromate into sodium dichromate

$$2Na_2CrO_4 + \text{conc. } H_2SO_4 \rightarrow Na_2Cr_2O_7 + Na_2SO_4 + H_2O$$

Step (3): Conversion of sodium dichromate to potassium dichromate

$$Na_2Cr_2O_7 + 2KCl \rightarrow K_2Cr_2O_7 + 2NaCl$$

Potassium chloride being less soluble than sodium chloride is obtained in the form of orange-coloured crystals and can be removed by filtration. The dichromate ($Cr_2O_7^{2-}$) ion exists in equilibrium with chromate (CrO_4^{2-}) ion at pH= 4. However, by changing the pH, they can be interconverted.

$$\underset{\text{(Yellow)}}{\underset{\text{Chromate}}{2CrO_7^{2-}}} \underset{\text{Alkali}}{\xrightarrow{\text{Acid}}} \underset{\text{chromate}}{\underset{\text{Hydrogen}}{2HCrO_4^-}} \underset{\text{Akali}}{\xrightarrow{\text{Acid}}} \underset{\text{(Orange)}}{\underset{\text{Dichromate}}{Cr_2O_7^{2-}}}$$

(ii) Potassium permanganate ($KMnO_4$) is prepared from pyrolusite (MnO_2). The ore is fused with potassium hydroxide (KOH) in the presence of either atmospheric oxygen or an oxidising agent, such as KNO_3 or $KClO_4$, to give K_2MnO_4.

$$2MnO_2 + 4KOH + O_2 \xrightarrow{\text{heat}} \underset{\text{(Green)}}{2K_2MnO_4} + 2H_2O$$

The green mass obtained is extracted with water. After that, it is oxidized electrolytically or by-passing chlorine or ozone into the solution.

Electrolytic oxidation

$$K_2MnO_4 \rightarrow 2K^+ + MnO_4^{2-}$$
$$H_2O \rightarrow H^+ + OH^-$$

At anode, manganate ions are oxidized to permanganate ions.

$$\underset{\text{Green}}{MnO_4^{2-}} \rightarrow \underset{\text{Purple}}{MnO_4^-} + e^-$$

Oxidation by chlorine:

$$2K_2MnO_4 + Cl_2 \rightarrow 2KMnO_4 + 2KCl$$
$$2MnO_4^{2-} + Cl_2 \rightarrow 2MnO_4^- + 2Cl^-$$

Oxidation by ozone:

$$2K_2MnO_4 + O_3 + H_2O \rightarrow 2KMnO_4 + 2KOH + O_2$$
$$2MnO_4^{2-} + O_3 + H_2O \rightarrow 2MNO_4^{2-} + 2OH^- + O_2$$

Q. 27. What are alloys? Name an important alloy which contains some of the lanthanoid metals. Mention its uses. [NCERT Ex. Q. 4.27, Page 116]

Ans. Alloys are homogenous mixture of two or more metals. It can either be a partial solid solution or a complete solid solution. Alloys are usually found to possess different physical properties than those of the component elements. An important alloy of lanthanoids is Mischmetal. It contains lanthanoids (94–95%), iron (5%), and traces of S, C, Si, Ca, and Al.

Uses:

(i) Mischmetal is used in cigarettes and gas lighters.
(ii) It is used in flame throwing tanks.
(iii) It is used in tracer bullets and shells.

Q. 28. What are inner transition elements? Decide which of the following atomic numbers are the atomic numbers of the inner transition elements: 29, 59, 74, 95, 102, 104. [NCERT Ex. Q. 4.28, Page 116]

Ans. Inner transition metals are those elements in which the last electron enters in the *f*-orbital. The elements in which the 4*f* and the 5*f* orbitals are progressively filled are called *f*-block elements. Among the given atomic numbers, the atomic numbers of the inner transition elements are 59, 95, and 102.

Q. 29. The chemistry of the actinoid elements is not so smooth as that of the lanthanoids. Justify this statement by giving some examples from the oxidation state of these elements. [NCERT Ex. Q. 4.29, Page 116]

Ans. All the actinoids are radioactive. Although the naturally occurring elements and the earlier members have relatively long half-lives, the man-made elements have half lifes from days to 3 minutes for lawrencium (Z=103). This high radioactivity makes their study more difficult. There is a greater range of oxidation states which is in part attributed to the fact that 5*f*, 6*d*, and 7*s* orbitals are comparable energies.

Actinoids, in general, show + 3 oxidation state. They also show +4, +5, +6 and +7 oxidation states.

Q. 30. Which is the last element in the series of the actinoids? Write the electronic configuration of this element. Comment on the possible oxidation state of this element. [NCERT Ex. Q. 4.30, Page 116]

Ans. Lawrencium (atomic number = 103) is the last element in the series of actinoids.

Its electronic configuration is $[Rn]5f^{14}6d^17s^2$.

The possible oxidation state of Lr is +3 due to stable electronic configuration after losing 3 electrons.

Q. 31. Use Hund's rule to derive the electronic configuration of Ce^{3+} ion and calculate its magnetic moment on the basis of 'spin-only' formula. [NCERT Ex. 4.31, Page 117]

Ans. Ce^{3+} has electronic configuration $[Xe]4f^1$

Here magnetic moment is calculated on the basis of 'spin only' formula:

$$\mu = \sqrt{n(n+2)}$$

where, n = number of unpaired electrons

Here $n = 1$

Therefore, magnetic moment of Ce^{3+}

$$\mu = \sqrt{1(1+2)}\ \text{B.M.}$$
$$= \sqrt{3}\ \text{B.M.}$$
$$= 1.732\ \text{B.M.}$$

Q. 32. Name the members of the lanthanoid series which exhibit +4 oxidation states and those which exhibit +2 oxidation states. Try to correlate this type of behaviour with the electronic configurations of these elements. [NCERT Ex. Q. 4.32, Page 117]

Ans. The lanthanoids that exhibit +2 and +4 oxidation states are shown in the given table.

+2 Oxidation state	+4 Oxidation state
Nd (Atomic number = 60)	Ce (Atomic number = 58)
Sm (Atomic number = 62)	Pr (Atomic number = 59)
Eu (Atomic number = 63)	Nd (Atomic number = 60)
Tm (Atomic number = 69)	Tb (Atomic number = 65)
Yb (Atomic number = 70)	Dy (Atomic number = 66)

Ce after forming Ce^{4+} attains a stable electronic configuration of [Xe].

Tb after forming Tb^{4+} attains a stable electronic configuration of $[Xe]\ 4f^7$.

Eu after forming Eu^{2+} attains a stable electronic configuration of $[Xe]\ 4f^7$.

Yb after forming Yb^{2+} attains a stable electronic configuration of $[Xe]\ 4f^{14}$.

Q. 33. Compare the chemistry of the actinoids with that of lanthanoids with reference to:

(i) electronic configuration, (ii) oxidation states and (iii) chemical reactivity. [NCERT Ex. Q. 4.33, Page 117]

Ans. Refer Q. 20. (i), (iii) & (iv).

Q. 34. Write the electronic configurations of the elements with the atomic numbers 61, 91, 101, and 109. [NCERT Ex. Q. 4.34, Page 117]

Ans.

Atomic number	Electronic configuration
61	$[Xe]^{54}\ 4f^5\ 5d^0\ 6s^2$
91	$[Rn]^{86}\ 5f^2\ 6d^1\ 7s^2$
101	$[Rn]^{86}\ 5f^{13}\ 5d^0\ 7s^2$
109	$[Rn]^{86}\ 5f^{14}\ 6d^7\ 7s^2$

Q. 35. Compare the general characteristics of the first series of the transition metals with those of the second and third series metals in the respective vertical columns. Give special emphasis on the following points:

(i) electronic configurations
(ii) oxidation states
(iii) ionisation enthalpies and
(iv) atomic sizes. [NCERT Ex. Q. 4.35, Page 117]

Ans. The properties of the elements of the first transition series differ from those of the heavier transition elements in many ways.

(i) Electronic configuration: Electrons enter into the 3*d* orbital in the first transition series while the electrons enter into the 4*d* and 5*d* orbitals in the second and third transition series.

(ii) +2and +3oxidation states are common for elements in the first transition series, while higher oxidation states are more common for the heavier elements.

In first transition series, lower oxidation state is more stable, whereas in heavier transition elements, higher oxidation states are more stable, Example: Ni^+ is more stable than Pt^{2+} but Pt^{4+} is more stable than Ni^{4+}.

(iii) Ionization enthalpies: 3*d* and 4*d* series elements have lower ionisation enthalpies than 5*d* series elements. The reason for while 5*d* series elements have higher ionisation enthalpy is that these elements have poor shielding effect and valence electrons experience higher effective nuclear charge which results in comparably higher ionisation enthalpies than 3*d* and 4*d* elements.

(iv) Atomic sizes: Since, on moving down the group atomic size increases. So, 3*d* series elements have lower atomic size than 4*d* series elements. But because of the lanthanoid contractions, the atomic size of the elements of 4*d* and 5*d* series are almost same.

Q. 36. Write down the number of 3*d* electrons in each of the following ions: Ti^{2+}, V^{2+}, Cr^{3+}, Mn^{2+}, Fe^{2+}, Fe^{3+}, Co^{2+}, Ni^{2+} and Cu^{2+}. Indicate how would you expect the five 3*d* orbitals to be occupied for these hydrated ions (octahedral). [NCERT Ex. Q. 4.36, Page 117]

Ans.

Metal ion	Number of *d*-electrons	Filling of *d*-orbitals
Ti^{2+}	2	t_{2g}^2
V^{2+}	3	t_{2g}^3
Cr^{3+}	3	t_{2g}^3
Mn^{2+}	5	$t_{2g}^3e_g^2$
Fe^{2+}	6	$t_{2g}^4e_g^2$
Fe^{3+}	5	$t_{2g}^3e_g^2$
CO^{2+}	7	$t_{2g}^5e_g^2$
Ni^{2+}	8	$t_{2g}^6eg^2$
Cu^{2+}	9	$t_{2g}^6eg^3$

Q. 37. Comment on the statement that elements of the first transition series possess many properties different from those of heavier transition elements. [NCERT Ex. Q. 4.37, Page 117]

Ans. The properties of the elements of the first transition series differ from those of the heavier transition elements in many ways

(i) The atomic sizes of the elements of the first transition series are smaller than those of the heavier elements (elements of 2nd and 3rd transition series).

However, the atomic sizes of the elements in the third transition series are virtually the same as those of the corresponding members in the second transition series. This is due to lanthanoid contraction.

(ii) +2 and +3 oxidation states are more common for elements in the first transition series, while higher oxidation states are more common for the heavier elements.

(iii) The enthalpies of atomisation of the elements in the first transition series are lower than those of the corresponding elements in the second and third transition series.

(iv) The melting and boiling points of the first transition series are lower than those of the heavier transition elements. This is because of the occurrence of stronger metallic bonding (M–M bonding).

(v) The elements of the first transition series form low-spin or high-spin complexes depending upon the strength of the ligand field. However, the heavier transition elements form only low-spin complexes, irrespective of the strength of the ligand field.

Q. 38. What can be inferred from the magnetic moment values of the following complex species ?

Example:	Magnetic Moment (BM)
$K_4[Mn(CN)_6]$	2.2
$[Fe(H_2O)_6]^{2+}$	5.3
$K_2[MnCl_4]$	5.9

[NCERT Ex. Q. 4.38, Page 117]

Ans. Magnetic moment $\mu = \sqrt{n(n+2)}$.

For $n = 1$, $\mu = \sqrt{1(1+2)} = \sqrt{3} = 1.732$.

For $n = 2$, $\mu = \sqrt{2(2+2)} = \sqrt{8} = 2.83$.

For $n = 4$, $\mu = \sqrt{4(4+2)} = \sqrt{24} = 4.899$.

For $n = 5$, $\mu = \sqrt{5(5+2)} = \sqrt{35} = 5.92$.

(a) $K_4[Mn(CN)_6]^-$: In this complex, Mn is in +2 oxidation state and μ = 2.2 BM. It means that it has only one unpaired electron. When CN^- ligands approach Mn^{2+} ion, the electron in 3*d*-orbital pair up. Thus, CN^- is a strong ligand. The hybridization is d^2sp^3 forming inner-orbital octahedral complex.

(b) $[Fe(H_2O)_6]^{2+}$: In this complex, Fe is in +2 oxidation state and μ = 5.3. It means that there are four unpaired electrons in 3*d*. Also, the 3*d* electrons do not pair up when the H_2O molecules approach. Thus, H_2O is a weak ligand. The hybridisation involved in sp^3d^2, forming an outer orbital complex.

(c) $K_2[MnCl_4]$: In this complex, Mn is in +2 oxidation state and μ = 5.92. It means that there are five unpaired electrons. The hybridization involved is sp^3 forming a tetrahedral complex Cl is a weak ligand.

CHAPTER 5

COORDINATION COMPOUNDS

Scan to know more about this topic

Coordination compounds

- Coordination compounds are the backbone of modern inorganic and bio-inorganic chemistry and chemical industry.
- **Coordination Compound:** A coordination compound contains a central metal atom or ion surrounded by a number of oppositely charged ions or neutral molecules. There is a coordinate bond between metal atom and these ions or molecules, e.g., $[Cu(NH_3)_4]^{2+}$.
- **Double Salt:** When two or more salts are added to form a stable compound and breaks into constituent ions when dissolved in water or any solvent, e.g., $FeSO_4(NH_4)_2SO_4.6H_2O$ (Mohr's salt).
- **Properties of double salts:**
  - **(i)** They give simple ions in aqueous solution because they are ionic compounds.
  - **(ii)** They do not contain coordinate bonds.
  - **(iii)** They exist only in solid state as double salt.
  - **(iv)** They are soluble in water.
- **Coordinate bonds:** A type of covalent bond in which one of the atoms supplies both the electrons. It can be considered as a combination of transfer and sharing of electrons. Coordinate bonds are also called semi-polar bonds.
- **Central metal atom or ion:** The metal atom or ion surrounded by a fixed number of ions or molecules is called central metal atom or ion, e.g., in $K_4[Fe(CN)_6]$, Fe^{2+} is a central metal ion. These central atoms/ions are also called as Lewis acids.
- **Ligand:** The neutral molecules or ions (usually anions) which are attached with the central metal atom or ion in complex compound. e.g., Cl^-, OH^-, CN^-, CO, NH_3, H_2O, etc. A ligand may be neutral or charged species.
- **Types of ligands:**
  - **(i) On the basis of number of donor sites:**
  - **(a) Unidentate ligands:** Contain one donor atom. e.g., $\ddot{N}H_3$, $H_2\ddot{O}$:
  - **(b) Bidentate ligands:** Contain two donor atoms. e.g., $(COO^-)_2$, $CH_2-\ddot{N}H_2$ | $CH_2-\ddot{N}H_2$
  - **(c) Polydentate ligands:** Contain several donor atoms. e.g., EDTA it can bind through two nitrogen and four oxygen atoms.
  - **(ii) On the basis of charge:**
  - **(a) Cationic ligands:** Carry positive charge. *e.g.*, NO_2^+, $N_2H_5^+$.
  - **(b) Anionic ligands:** Carry negative charge. e.g., X^- (halo), CN^-(cyano).
  - **(c) Neutral ligands:** Do not carry any charge. e.g., $\ddot{N}H_3$ (ammine), $H_2\ddot{O}$: (aqua).
  - **(iii) On the basis of affinity of donor atom:**
  - **(a) Chelate ligands:** A bidentate or polydentate uses its two or more donor atoms to bind a single metal ion, then a ring like structure is obtained. It is called as chelate and the ligand is known as chelate ligand.

e.g., 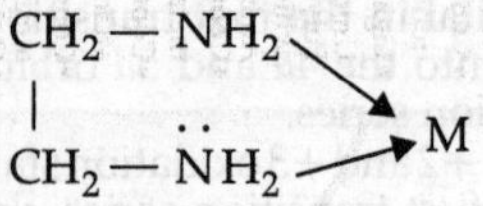

  - **(b) Ambidentate ligands:** A ligand which contains two donor atoms but only one of them forms a coordinate bond at a time with central metal/ion is called ambidentate ligand.

e.g., 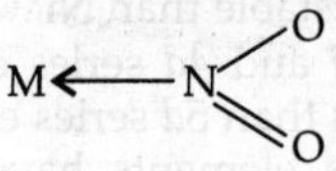

Nitrito— N (N donor atom)

M ← SCN
Thiocyanato (S donor atom)

M ← NCS
Isothiocynato (N donor atom)

M ← O — N = O
nitrito-O (O donor atom)

  - **(c) Bridging ligands:** It is the ligand which can bound to more than one metal atom, e.g.: B_2H_6 in which H^- is a hydride ion that act as inorganic bridging ligand.
- **Coordination number:** The coordination number (CN) of a metal ion in a complex is defined as the number of ligand donor atoms to which the metal is directly bonded. It is determined by the number of sigma bonds formed by the ligand with the central atom/ion (pi bonds are not counted). Eg. In the complex ions, $[PtCl_6]^{2-}$ and $[Ni(NH_3)_4]^{2+}$, the coordination number of Pt and Ni are 6 and 4 respectively.
- **Coordination polyhedron:** The spatial arrangement of the ligand atoms which are directly attached to the central atoms or ions define a coordination polyhedron about the central atom *e.g.*, $[Pt\ Cl_4]^{2-}$ is square planar.
- **Charge on the complex ion:** The charge on the complex ion is equal to the algebraic sum of the charges on all the ligands coordinated to the central metal ion.
- **Donor atom:** An atom in the Lewis base that forms the bond with the central atom/ion is called donor atom because it donates the pair of electrons.
- **Denticity:** The number of ligating groups or coordinating atoms in a ligand is called denticity e.g., unidentate, bidentate, etc.
- **Applications of chelates:**
  - **(i)** In the softening of hard water.
  - **(ii)** In the separation of lanthanoids and actinoids.
  - **(iii)** In the detection as well as estimation of some metal ions such as nickel (II) ion.

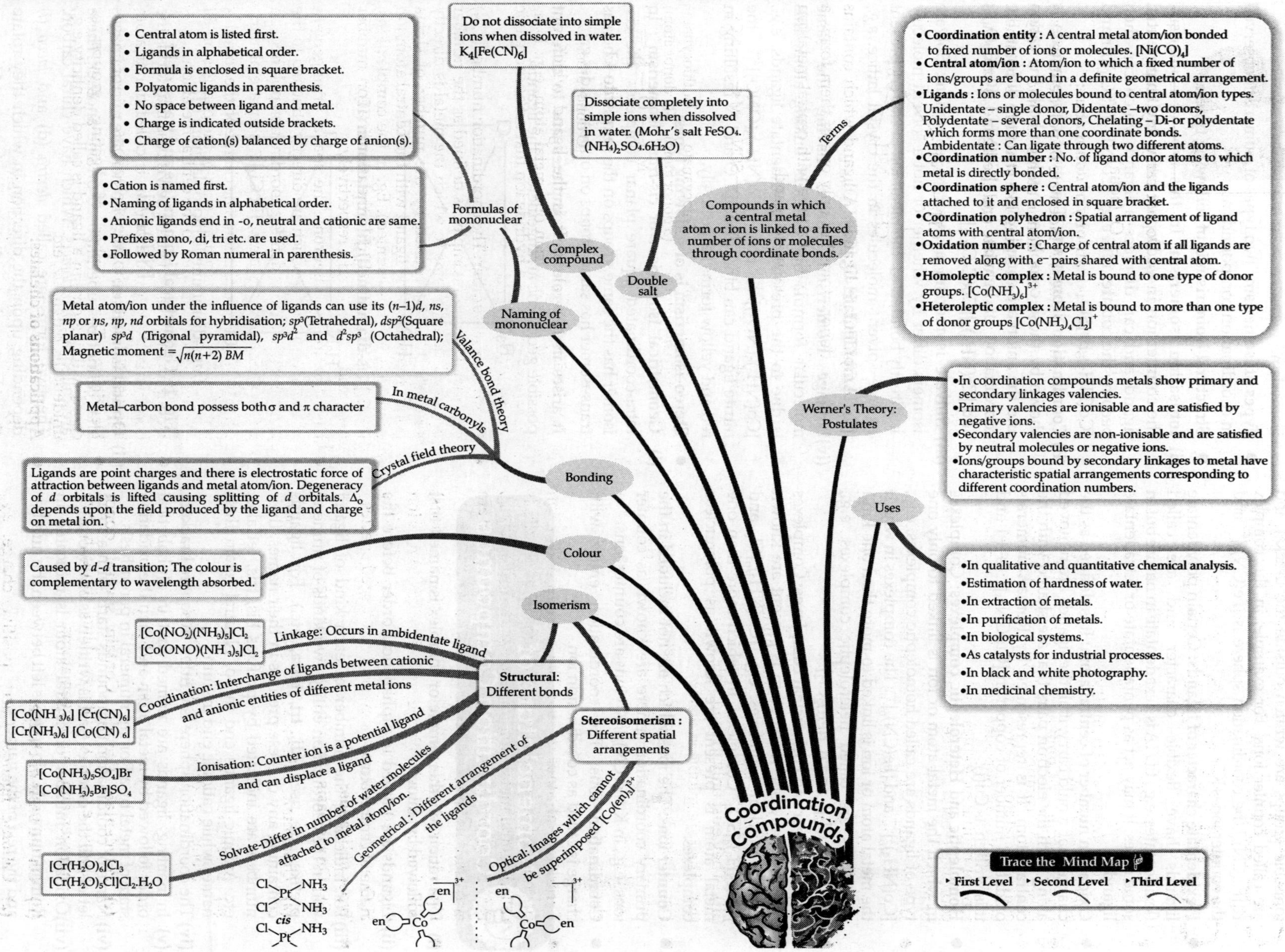
Coordination Compounds
Terms
• Coordination entity : A central metal atom/ion bonded to fixed number of ions or molecules. [Ni(CO)4]
• Central atom/ion : Atom/ion to which a fixed number of ions/groups are bound in a definite geometrical arrangement.
• Ligands : Ions or molecules bound to central atom/ion types. Unidentate – single donor, Didentate –two donors, Polydentate – several donors, Chelating – Di-or polydentate which forms more than one coordinate bonds. Ambidentate : Can ligate through two different atoms.
• Coordination number : No. of ligand donor atoms to which metal is directly bonded.
• Coordination sphere : Central atom/ion and the ligands attached to it and enclosed in square bracket.
• Coordination polyhedron : Spatial arrangement of ligand atoms with central atom/ion.
• Oxidation number : Charge of central atom if all ligands are removed along with e⁻ pairs shared with central atom.
• Homoleptic complex : Metal is bound to one type of donor groups. [Co(NH3)6]3+
• Heteroleptic complex : Metal is bound to more than one type of donor groups [Co(NH3)4Cl2]+
Compounds in which a central metal atom or ion is linked to a fixed number of ions or molecules through coordinate bonds.
Werner's Theory: Postulates
• In coordination compounds metals show primary and secondary linkages valencies.
• Primary valencies are ionisable and are satisfied by negative ions.
• Secondary valencies are non-ionisable and are satisfied by neutral molecules or negative ions.
• Ions/groups bound by secondary linkages to metal have characteristic spatial arrangements corresponding to different coordination numbers.
Uses
• In qualitative and quantitative chemical analysis.
• Estimation of hardness of water.
• In extraction of metals.
• In purification of metals.
• In biological systems.
• As catalysts for industrial processes.
• In black and white photography.
• In medicinal chemistry.
Double salt
Dissociate completely into simple ions when dissolved in water. (Mohr's salt FeSO4.(NH4)2SO4.6H2O)
Complex compound
Do not dissociate into simple ions when dissolved in water. K4[Fe(CN)6]
Naming of mononuclear
Formulas of mononuclear
• Central atom is listed first.
• Ligands in alphabetical order.
• Formula is enclosed in square bracket.
• Polyatomic ligands in parenthesis.
• No space between ligand and metal.
• Charge is indicated outside brackets.
• Charge of cation(s) balanced by charge of anion(s).
• Cation is named first.
• Naming of ligands in alphabetical order.
• Anionic ligands end in -o, neutral and cationic are same.
• Prefixes mono, di, tri etc. are used.
• Followed by Roman numeral in parenthesis.
Bonding
Valance bond theory
Metal atom/ion under the influence of ligands can use its (n–1)d, ns, np or ns, np, nd orbitals for hybridisation; sp3(Tetrahedral), dsp2(Square planar) sp3d (Trigonal pyramidal), sp3d2 and d2sp3 (Octahedral); Magnetic moment = √n(n+2) BM
In metal carbonyls
Metal–carbon bond possess both σ and π character
Crystal field theory
Ligands are point charges and there is electrostatic force of attraction between ligands and metal atom/ion. Degeneracy of d orbitals is lifted causing splitting of d orbitals. Δo depends upon the field produced by the ligand and charge on metal ion.
Colour
Caused by d-d transition; The colour is complementary to wavelength absorbed.
Isomerism
Structural: Different bonds
Linkage: Occurs in ambidentate ligand
[Co(NO2)(NH3)5]Cl2
[Co(ONO)(NH3)5]Cl2
Coordination: Interchange of ligands between cationic and anionic entities of different metal ions
[Co(NH3)6] [Cr(CN)6]
[Cr(NH3)6] [Co(CN)6]
Ionisation: Counter ion is a potential ligand and can displace a ligand
[Co(NH3)5SO4]Br
[Co(NH3)5Br]SO4
Solvate-Differ in number of water molecules attached to metal atom/ion.
[Cr(H2O)6]Cl3
[Cr(H2O)5Cl]Cl2.H2O
Stereoisomerism : Different spatial arrangements
Geometrical : Different arrangement of the ligands
Optical: Images which cannot be superimposed [Co(en)3]3+
cis
Trace the Mind Map
First Level
Second Level
Third Level

- **Coordination sphere:** The central atom/ion and the ligands attached to it are enclosed in square bracket and is collectively termed as coordination sphere. The ionisable groups are written outside the bracket and are called counter ions. For example, in the complex $K_4[Fe(CN)_6]$,the coordination sphere is $[Fe(CN)_6]^{4-}$ and the counter ion is K^+.
- **Flexidentate character of ligands:** Certain polydentate ligands have flexible character and are called flexidentates. e.g., EDTA is hexadentate in nature but in some cases, it may act as pentadentate or tetradentate ligand.
- **Oxidation number of central atom:** It is defined as the charge that would carry, if all the ligands are removed along with the electron pairs that are shared with the central atom. It is represented by Roman numerals oxidation number of copper in $[Cu(CN)_4]^{3-}$ is +1 and it is written as Cu(I).
- **Homoleptic and Heteroleptic complexes:** Complexes in which the metal atom or ion is linked to only one type of ligands are called homoleptic complexes, e.g., $[Co(NH_3)_6]^{3+}$ and $[Fe(CN)_6]^{4-}$. The complexes in which the metal atom or ion is linked to more than one kind of ligands are called heteroleptic complexes. e.g., $[Co(NH_3)_4Cl_2]^+$ and $[Cr(en)_2Cl_2]^+$.
- **Homonuclear and Polynuclear complexes:** Complexes in which only one metal atom is present are known as homonuclear complexes. e.g., $[Co(NH_3)_6]Cl_3$ and $[Cu(NH_3)_4]SO_4$. Complexes in which more than one metal atom is present are known as polynuclear complexes.
- **Counter ions:** The ions which are not included in the primary coordination sphere are known as counter ions. e.g., in $K_4[Fe(CN)_6]$, K^+ ions are counter ions.
- **Coordination ions:** The coordination entity with charge is called as coordination ion.

Nomenclature of Coordination Compounds

(i) The cation whether simple or complex is named first followed by anion.

(ii) Ligands are named in alphabetical order before the name of central atom.

(iii) For indicating the number of each kind of ligand within the coordination entity, two kinds of numeral prefixes are used (**di, tri, tetra**, etc.). For ligands containing any of these prefixes in their names, their numbers are indicated by prefixes bis, tris, tetrakis, etc. Anionic ligands end in –o. Neutral retain their names while cationic end in -ium.

(iv) The coordination sphere is written in square bracket.

(v) In naming, ligands are named first in alphabetical order followed by metal atom and then the oxidation state of metal by a Roman numeral in parenthesis.

(vi) Name of coordination compounds starts with a small letter and the complex part is written as one word.

(vii) Oxidation number of central atom is indicated in Roman numerals. No space is left between the number and the rest of the name.

- **Isomers:** Two or more coordination compounds which have the same molecular formula but have their ligands attached to the isomers metal atom or ion in different ways are known as isomers and hence, they differ in their physical and chemical properties. The phenomenon of different isomers is known as isomerism.
- **Types of isomerism:** Two types of isomerism observed in coordination compounds are:
- **Structural isomerism is of following types:**

(i) Ionisation isomerism: In this type of isomerism, the counter ion in a complex salt is itself a potential ligand and can displace a ligand which can then become the counter ion. e.g., $[Co(NH_3)_5(SO_4)]Br$ and $[Co(NH_3)_5Br]SO_4$.

(ii) Coordination isomerism: This type of isomerism is shown by those complexes in which both the cation and the anion are complex ions and they differ in the coordination of ligands. e.g., $[Co(NH_3)_6][Cr(C_2O_4)_3]$ and $[Cr(NH_3)_6][Co(C_2O_4)_3]$.

(iii) Solvate isomerism or hydrate isomerism: Solvate isomers differ by whether or not a solvent molecule is directly bonded to the metal ion or merely present as free solvent molecules in the crystal lattice. *e.g.*, $[Cr(H_2O)_5Cl]Cl_2.H_2O$, $[Cr(H_2O)_6]Cl_3$.

(iv) Linkage isomerism: Isomers having the same molecular formula but different linking atom, this is due to the presence of ambidentate ligands. e.g., $[Co(NH_3)_5(NO_2)]^{2+}$ and $[Co(NH_3)_5(ONO)]^{2+}$ the nitrite ligand can bind through O and N resulting in red and yellow forms respectively.

- **Stereo-isomerism is of following types:**

(i) Geometrical isomerism or *cis-trans* isomerism : In tetra-coordinated square planar complexes, the cis-isomer has the same groups on the same side whereas trans-isomer has same groups on opposite sides e.g.,

It arises in heteroleptic complexes due to different possible geometric arrangement of the ligands.

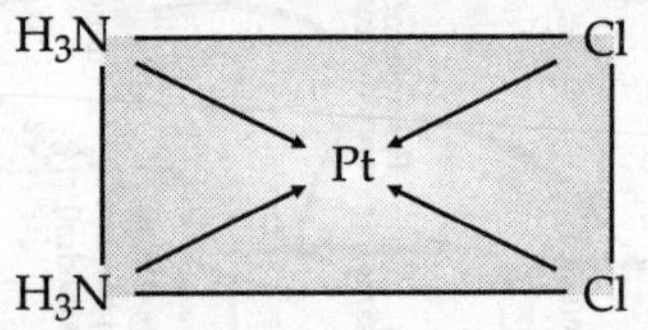

cis-**diamminedichloroplatinum (II)**

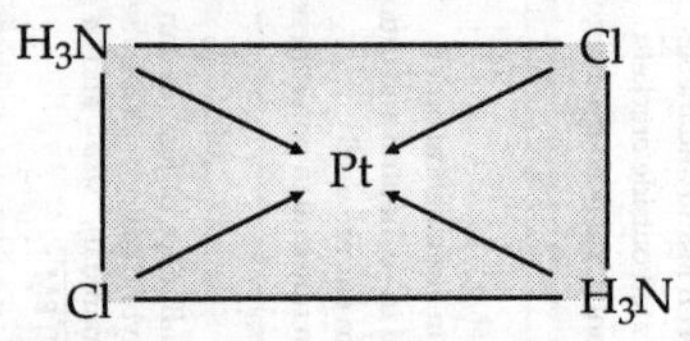

trans-diamminedichloroplatinum (II)

Fig. 1: Geometrical isomers (cis and trans) of Pt $[NH_3)_2Cl_2]$

(ii) Optical isomerism: Optical isomers are mirror images that cannot be superimposed on one another. These are called as *enantiomers*. Which have chiral carbon. The two forms are called *dextro* **(d)** and *laevo (l)* depending upon the direction in which they rotate the plane of polarised light in a polarimeter (*d* rotates to the right, *l* to the left). Optical isomerism is common in octahedral complexes involving didentate ligands.

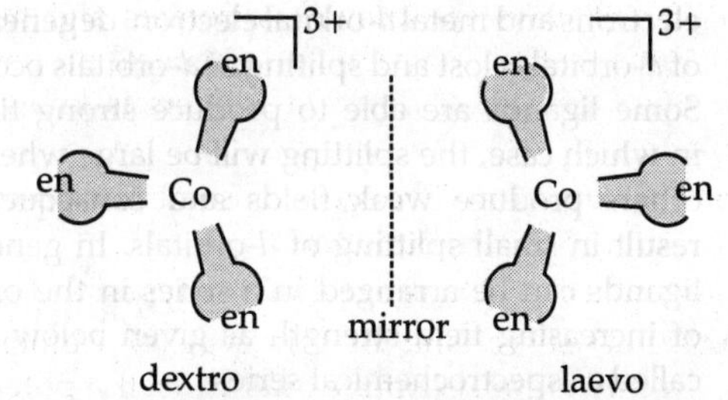

Fig. 2: Optical isomers (*d* and *l*) of $[Co(en)_3]^{3+}$

Werner's Theory of Coordination Compounds

Different postulates of Werner's Coordination theory are given below:

(i) Metal ions possess two types of valency (a) primary or ionisable valency and (b) Secondary or non ionisable valency.

(ii) Every metal ion has a fixed number of secondary valency and this is known as coordination number.

(iii) **Primary valencies** are satisfied by charged ions while secondary valencies are satisfied by ligands or neutral molecules with lone pair of electrons.

(iv) Secondary valencies are directed in space towards internal positions.

(v) He stated that octahedral, tetrahedral and square planar geometrical shapes are more common in coordination compounds of transition metals.

- **Limitation of Werner's theory:** This theory does not explain the following queries:

(i) Why is the complex forming tendency limited to a few elements only?

(ii) Why do bonds in the coordination complexes are of directional nature?

(iii) Why are certain complexes of magnetic nature show geometrical and optical isomerism ?

Scan to know more about this topic

Werner's theory

Bonding in Coordination Compounds

- It was developed by Pauling. The brief points are:

(i) A suitable number of vacant orbitals must be present in the central metal atom or ion for the formation of coordinate bond with the ligands.

(ii) Central metal ion can use appropriate number of *s*, *p* or *d*-orbitals for hybridisation depending upon total number of ligands.

(iii) The hybridised orbitals are allowed to overlap with those ligand orbitals that can donate an electron pair for bonding.

(iv) The outer orbitals (high spin) or inner orbitals (low spin) complexes are formed depending upon whether outer *d*-orbitals or inner *d*-orbitals are used.

Valence Bond Theory:

In the diamagnetic octahedral complex, $[Co(NH_3)_6]^{3+}$, the cobalt ion is in +3 oxidation state and has the electronic configuration 3d^6. The hybridisation scheme is as shown in diagram.

	3*d*	4*s*	4*p*
Orbitals of Co^{3+} ion	⇅ ↿ ↿ ↿ ↿	☐	☐ ☐ ☐
d^2sp^3 hybridised orbitals of Co^{3+}.	⇅ ⇅ ⇅	d^2sp^3 hybrid	☐ ☐ ☐ ☐ ☐ ☐
$[Co(NH_3)_6]^{3+}$ (inner orbital or low spin complex)	⇅ ⇅ ⇅	Six pairs of electrons from six NH_3 molecules	⇅ ⇅ ⇅ ⇅ ⇅ ⇅

Six pairs of electrons, one from each NH_3 molecule, occupy the six hybrid orbitals. Thus, the complex has octahedral geometry and is diamagnetic because of the absence of unpaired electron. In the formation of this complex, since the inner *d* orbital (3*d*) is used in hybridisation, the complex, $[Co(NH_3)_6]^{3+}$ is called an inner orbital or low spin or spin paired complex. The paramagnetic octahedral complex, $[CoF_6]^{3-}$ uses outer orbital (4*d*) in hybridisation (sp^3d^2). It is thus called outer orbital or high spin or spin free complex. Thus,

	3*d*	4*s*	4*p*	4*d*
Orbitals of Co^{3+} ion	⇅ ↿ ↿ ↿ ↿	☐	☐ ☐ ☐	☐ ☐ ☐ ☐ ☐
sp^3d^3 hybridised orbitals of Co^{3+}	⇅ ↿ ↿ ↿ ↿	sp^3d^3 hybrid	☐ ☐ ☐ ☐ ☐ ☐	☐ ☐ ☐
$[CoF_6]^{3-}$ (outer orbital or high spin complex)	⇅ ↿ ↿ ↿ ↿	Six pairs of electrons from six F^- ions	⇅ ⇅ ⇅ ⇅ ⇅ ⇅	☐ ☐ ☐

- **Limitation of Valence Bond Theory:**
  - **(i)** It cannot explain the detailed magnetic properties of complex compounds.
  - **(ii)** It cannot explain the optical absorption spectra of coordination compounds.
  - **(iii)** It cannot predict property whether a particular 4-coordinate complex is square planar or tetrahedral in nature.
  - **(iv)** It fails to make distinction between strong and weak ligands.
  - **(v)** It does not explain thermodynamic or kinetic stabilities of coordination compounds.
- **Crystal Field Theory (CFT):**

Scan to know more about this topic

Crystal field theory

In an octahedral coordination entity with six ligands surrounding the metal atom/ion, there will be repulsion between the electrons in metal d orbitals and the electrons (or negative charges) of the ligands. Such a repulsion is more when the metal d orbital is directed towards the ligand than when it is away from the ligand. Thus, the $d_{x^2-y^2}$ and d_{z^2} orbitals which point towards the axes along the direction of the ligand will experience more repulsion and will be raised in energy; and the d_{xy}, d_{yz} and d_{xz} orbitals which are directed between the axes will be lowered in energy relative to the average energy in the spherical crystal field. Thus, the degeneracy of the d orbitals has been removed due to ligand electron-metal electron repulsions in the octahedral complex to yield three orbitals of lower energy, t_{2g} set and two orbitals of higher energy, e_g set. This splitting of the coordination compounds degenerate levels due to the presence of ligands in a definite geometry is termed as crystal field splitting and the energy separation is denoted by Δo (the subscript o is for octahedral) (Fig. 3). Thus, the energy of the two eg orbitals will increase by (3/5) Δo and that of the three t^2_g will decrease by (2/5)Δo. The crystal field splitting, Δ_o, depends upon the field produced by the ligand and charge on the metal ion. Some ligands are able to produce strong fields in which case, the splitting will be large whereas others produce weak fields and consequently result in small splitting of d orbitals.

(1) If Δo < P, the fourth electron enters one of the eg orbitals giving the configuration $t^3_{2g}e_g$. Ligands for which Δo < P are known as weak field ligands and form high spin complexes.

(2) If Δ_o > P, it becomes more energetically favourable for the fourth electron to occupy a t_{2g} orbital with configuration $t^4_{2g}\, e_g^0$. Ligands which produce this effect are known as strong field ligands and form low spin complexes.

(i) The ligands is considered as point charge or point dipole.

(ii) Interaction between metal ion and ligand is considered as electrostatic in nature.

(iii) Metal ion is supposed to be present at the origin of the axis. Ligands approach to metal ion along the axis of octahedral complex between the axis of tetrahedral complex and in the case of square planar complex four ligand approach to metal ion along *x*, *y* plane.

(iv) Due to the approach of the ligand hence due to the electrostatic interaction between ligands electrons and metal *d*-orbital electron, degeneracy of *d*-orbital is lost and spliting of *d*-orbitals occurs.

(v) Some ligands are able to produce strong fields in which case, the splitting will be large whereas others produce weak fields and consequently result in small splitting of *d*-orbitals. In general, ligands can be arranged in a series in the order of increasing field strength as given below and called as spectrochemical series:

$$I^- < Br^- < SCN^- < Cl^- < S^{2-} < F^- < OH^- < C_2O_4^{2-} < H_2O < NCS^- < EDTA^{4-} < NH_3 < en < CN^- < CO$$

Mnemonics

Concept: Spectro Chemical Series

Mnemonics: I Bought Some Copies to Study Fundamental of Chemistry. He Nurtured Excellence in Necessary Coordination Compounds

Interpretations: $I^- < Br^- < SCN^- < Cl^- < S^{2-} < OH^- < C_2O_4^{2-} < H_2O < NCS- < EDTA^{4-} < NH_3 < CN^- < CO$

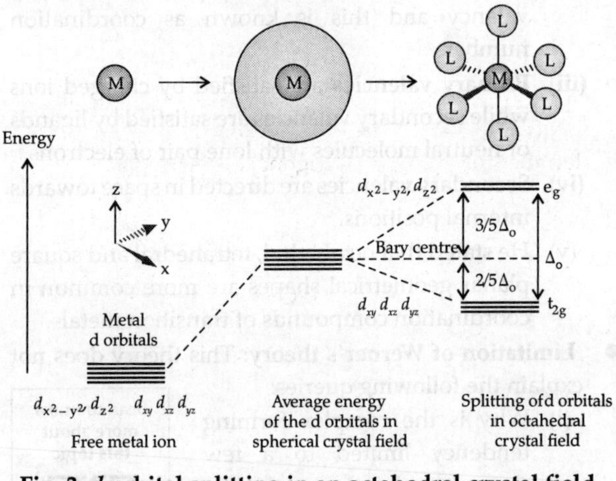

Fig. 3: *d*-orbital splitting in an octahedral crystal field

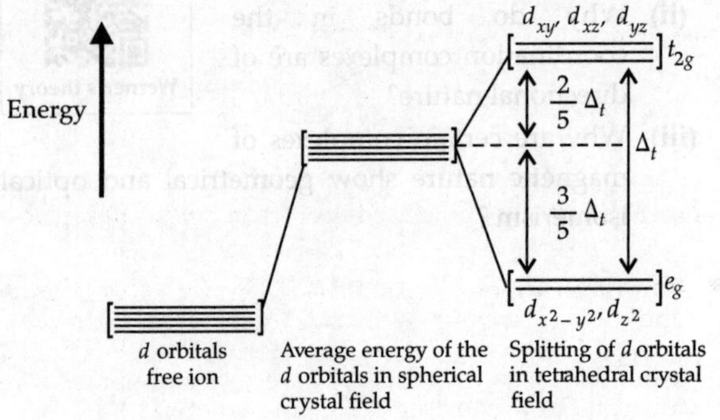

Fig. 4: *d*-orbital splitting in a tetrahedral crystal field

(vi) Explanation of colour and magnetic behaviour in complexes is possible by crystal field theory.

(v) Nature of the ligands.

- **Factors influencing the magnitude of orbital splitting energy (Δ):**
  - (i) Oxidation state of the metal ion.
  - (ii) Position of the metal ion.
  - (iii) Geometry of the complex.

Bonding in Metal Carbonyls

- **Metal carbonyls:** Homoleptic carbonyls are formed by *d*-block elements and contain carbonyl ligands only. *e.g.*, $[V(CO)_6]$, $[Cr(CO)_6]$, $[Mo(CO)_6]$, $[W(CO)_6]$, $[Mn_2(CO)_{10}]$, $[Fe(CO)_5]$, $[Fe_2(CO)_9]$, $[Co_2(CO)_8]$, $[Co_4(CO)_{12}]$, $[Ni(CO)_4]$, etc. Metal carbonyls of outside the central part of *d*-block are unstable.

Properties of metal carbonyls:

(i) Metal carbonyls are mostly solids at room temperature. Exceptions being iron and nickel carbonyls which are liquids.

(ii) The mononuclear carbonyls are volatile and toxic.

(iii) Most of metal carbonyls are soluble in hydrocarbon solvents except $[Fe_2(CO)_9]$.

(iv) Mononuclear carbonyls are either colourless or light coloured.

(v) They are highly reactive due to metal centre and the CO ligands.

(vi) Metal carbonyls are used as industrial catalyst and as precursor in organic synthesis.

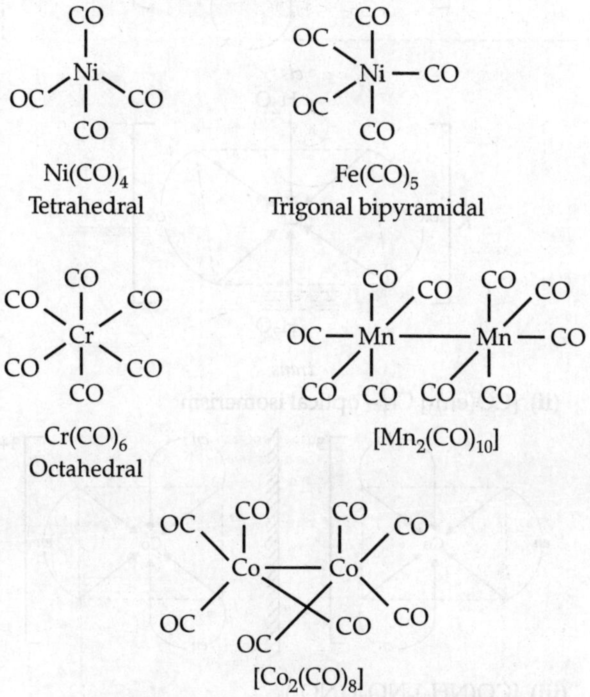

Fig. 5: Structures of some representative homoleptic metal carbonyls

- **Bonding in metal carbonyls:** It also involves both σ- and π-bond. σ-bond is formed by overlapping of lone pair on CO to the vacant d^- orbitals of metal whereas π-bond is formed by back donation of pair of electrons to vacant anti-bonding orbital of carbonyl.
- **Factors affecting the stability of 'coordination' complexes:**

(i) **Nature of the central ion:** Greater the charge density on the central metal ion, greater is the stability of the complex.

(ii) **Nature of the ligand:** More basic ligands have a tendency to donate the electron pairs to central metal ion more easily resulting in a stable complex.

(iii) **Chelate effect:** Entropy increases when chelation occurs and so the formation of the complex becomes more favourable.

- **Application of complex compounds:**

(i) They are used in photography, *i.e.*, AgBr forms soluble complex with sodium thiosulphate in photography.

(ii) $K[Ag(CN)_2]$ is used for electroplating of silver, $K[Au(CN)_2]$ is used for gold plating.

(iii) Some of ligands oxidise Co^{2+} to Co^{3+} ion.

(iv) EDTA is used for estimation of Ca^{2+} and Mg^{2+} in hard water.

(v) Silver and gold are extracted by treating Zn with their cyanide complexes.

(vi) Ni^{2+} is tested and estimated by DMG (dimethyl glyoxime).

(vii) *cis*-platin $[Pt(NH_3)_2Cl_2]$ is used as antitumor agent in the treatment of cancer.

(viii) EDTA is used to remove Pb by forming Pb-EDTA complex which is eliminated in urine.

(ix) Haemoglobin contains Fe, chlorophyll contains Mg and vitamin B_{12} contain Co^{2+} 'which are all coordination compounds'.

(x) Bauxite is purified by forming complex with NaOH.

(xi) Coordination compounds are used as catalysts for many industrial processes.

- **Magnetic properties of coordination compounds**

For metal ions with upto three electrons in the d orbitals, like Ti^{3+} (d^1); V^{3+} (d^2); Cr^{3+} (d^3); two vacant d orbitals are available for octahedral hybridisation with 4s and 4p orbitals. The magnetic behaviour of these free ions and their coordination entities is similar. When more than three 3d electrons are present, the required pair of 3d orbitals for octahedral hybridisation is not directly available (as a consequence of Hund's rule). Thus, for d^4 (Cr^{2+}, Mn^{3+}), d^5 (Mn^{2+}, Fe^{3+}), d^6 (Fe^{2+}, Co^{3+}) cases, a vacant pair of d orbitals results only by pairing of 3*d* electrons which leaves two, one and zero unpaired electrons, respectively. The magnetic data agree with maximum spin pairing in many cases, especially with coordination compounds containing d^6 ions. However, with species containing d^4 and d^5 ions there are complications. $[Mn(CN)_6]^{3-}$ has magnetic moment of two unpaired electrons while $[MnCl_6]^{3-}$ has a paramagnetic moment of four unpaired electrons. $[Fe(CN)_6]^{3-}$ has magnetic moment of a single unpaired electron while $[FeF_6]^{3-}$ has a paramagnetic moment of five unpaired electrons. $[CoF_6]^{3-}$ is paramagnetic with four unpaired electrons while $[Co(C_2O_4)_3]^{3-}$ is diamagnetic. This apparent anomaly is explained by valence bond theory in terms of formation of inner orbital and outer orbital coordination entities. $[Mn(CN)_6]^{3-}$, $[Fe(CN)_6]^{3-}$ and $[Co(C_2O_4)_3]^{3-}$ are inner orbital complexes involving d^2sp^3 hybridisation, the former two complexes are paramagnetic and the latter diamagnetic. On the other hand, $[MnCl_6]^{3-}$, $[FeF_6]^{3-}$ and $[CoF^{6-}]^{3-}$ are outer orbital complexes involving sp^3d^2 hybridisation and are paramagnetic corresponding to four, five and four unpaired electrons.

Colour in coordination compounds

The most distinctive properties of transition metal complexes is their wide range of colours.

The colour in the coordination compounds is explained by crystal field theory. For example, the complex $[Ti(H_2O)^6]^{3+}$, is violet in colour and an octahedral complex where the single electron (Ti^{3+} is a $3d^1$ system) in the metal *d* orbital is in the t_{2g} level in the ground state of the complex. The next higher state available for the electron is the empty eg level. If light corresponding to the energy of blue-green region is absorbed by the complex, it would excite the electron from t^{o}_{2g} level to the eg level ($t^1_{2g}\ e^o_g \rightarrow t^o_{2g}\ e_g{}^1$). Consequently, the complex appears violet in colour (Fig. 9.10). The crystal field theory attributes the colour of the coordination compounds to *d-d* transition of the electron.

Please notice that in the absence of ligand, crystal field splitting does not occur and hence the substance is colourless. For example, removal of water from $[Ti(H_2O)_6]Cl_3$ on heating renders it colourless. Similarly, anhydrous $CuSO_4$ is white, but $CuSO_4.5H_2O$ is blue in colour.

NCERT CORNER

Intext Questions

Page - 125

Q. 5.1. Write the formulas for the following coordination compounds:

(i) Tetraamminediaquacobalt(III) chloride

(ii) Potassium tetracyanonickelate(II)

(iii) Tris(ethane-1, 2-diamine) chromium(III)chloride

(iv) Amminebromidochloridonitrito-N-platinate(II)

(v) Dichloridobis(ethane-1,2-diamine) platinum(IV) nitrate

(vi) Iron(III) hexacyanoferrate(II).

Ans. (i) $\left[CO(H_2O)_2(NH_3)_4\right]Cl_3$

(ii) $K_2\left[Ni(CN)_4\right]$

(iii) $\left[Cr(en)_3\right]Cl_3$

(iv) $\left[Pt(NH)_3BrCl(NO_2)\right]$

(v) $\left[PtCl_2(en)_2\right](NO_3)_2$

(vi) $Fe_4\left[Fe(CN)_6\right]_3$

Q. 5.2. Write the IUPAC names of the following coordination compounds:

(i) $[Co(NH_3)_6]Cl_3$

(ii) $[Co(NH_3)_5Cl]Cl_2$

(iii) $K_3[Fe(CN)_6]$

(iv) $K_3[Fe(C_2O_4)_3]$

(v) $K_2[PdCl_4]$

(vi) $[Pt(NH_3)_2Cl(NH_2CH_3)]Cl$

Ans. (i) Hexaamminecobalt(III) chloride

(ii) Pentaamminechloridocobalt(III) chloride

(iii) Potassium hexacyanoferrate(III)

(iv) Potassium trioxalatoferrate(III)

(v) Potassium tetrachloridopalladate(II)

(vi) Diamminechlorido(methylamine) platinum (II) chloride

Page - 128

Q. 5.3. Indicate the type of isomerism exhibited by the following complexes and draw the structure for these isomers:

(i) $K[Cr(H_2O)_2(C_2O_4)_2]$

(ii) $[CO(en)_3]Cl_3$

(iii) $[CO(NH_3)_5(NO_2)](NO_3)_2$

(iv) $[Pt(NH_3)(H_2O)Cl_2]$

Ans. (i) Geometrical isomerism (cis and trans)

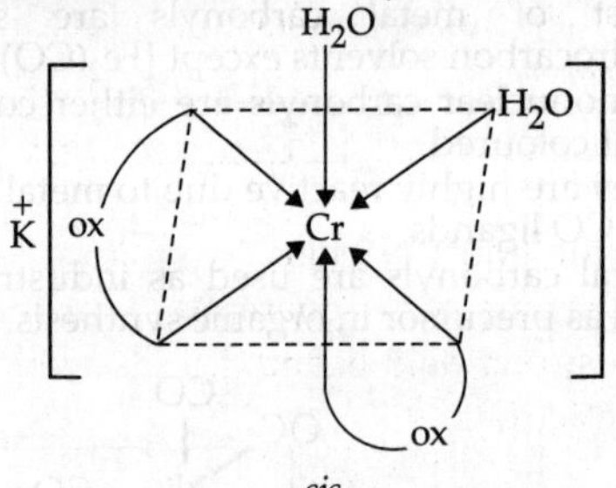

cis

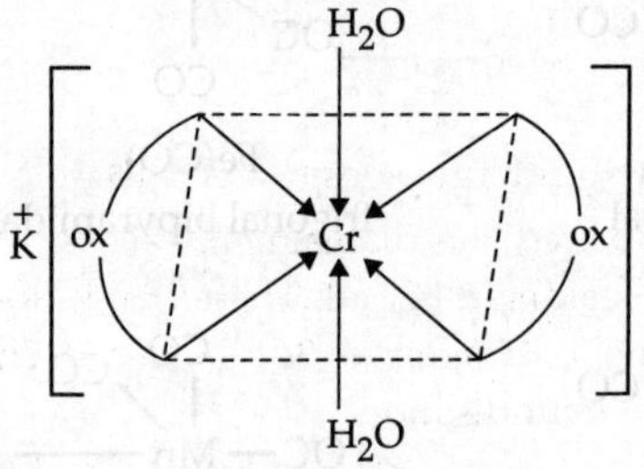

trans

(ii) $[CO(en)_3]\ Cl_3$ – optical isomerism

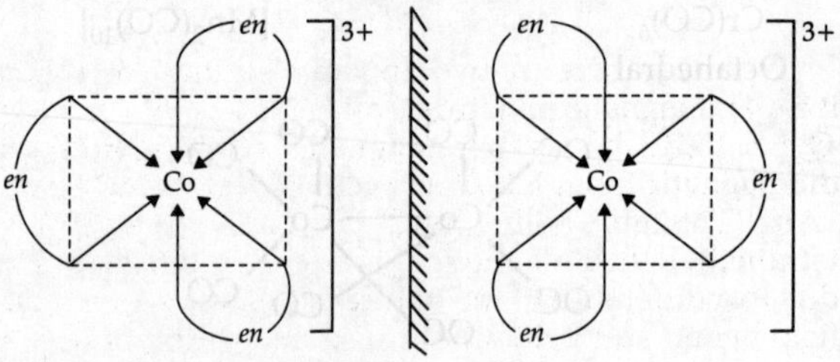

(iii) $[CO(NH_3)_5NO_2]\ (NO_3)_2$

(a) Ionisation isomerism

$[CO(NH_3)_5(NO_2)]\ (NO_3)_2$ & $[CO(NH_3)_5\ (NO_3)]\ (NO_2)\ (NO_3)$

(b) Linkage isomerism

$[CO(NH_3)_5\ (NO_2)]\ (NO_3)_2$ & $[CO(NH_3)_5(ONO)]\ (NO_3)_2$

(iv) $[Pt(NH_3)\ (H_2O)Cl_2]$ – Geometrical isomerism

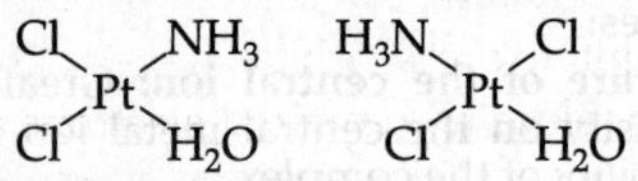

Q. 5.4. Give evidence that $[Co(NH_3)_5Cl]SO_4$ and $[Co(NH_3)_5SO_4]Cl$ are ionisation isomers.

Ans. When ionisation isomers are dissolved in water, they ionise to give different ions. These ions then react differently with different reagents to give different products.

$[CO(NH_3)_5Cl]SO_4 + Ba^{2+} \longrightarrow BaSO_4 \downarrow$
White precipitate

$[CO(NH_3)_5Cl]SO_4 + Ag^+ \longrightarrow$ No reaction

$[CO(NH_3)_5SO_4]Cl + Ba^{2+} \longrightarrow$ No reaction

$[CO(NH_3)_5SO_4]Cl + Ag^+ \longrightarrow AgCl \downarrow$
White precipitate

Page - 135

Q. 5.5. Explain on the basis of Valence Bond Theory that $[Ni(CN)_4]^{2-}$ ion with square planar structure is diamagnetic and the $[NiCl_4]^{2-}$ ion with tetrahedral geometry is paramagnetic.

Ans. Ni is in the +2 oxidation state, *i.e.*, in d^8 configuration.

d^8 configuration:

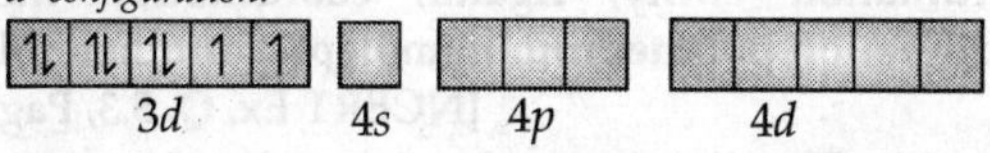

There are four CN^- ions. Thus, it can either have a tetrahedral geometry or square planar geometry. Since CN^- ion is a strong-field ligand, it causes the pairing of unpaired 3*d* electrons.

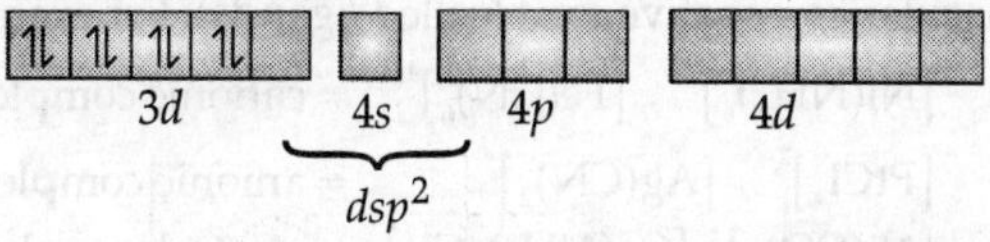

It now undergoes dsp^2 hybridisation. Since all electrons are paired, it is diamagnetic. In case of $[NiCl_4]^{2-}$, Cl^- ion is a weak-field ligand. Therefore, it does not lead to the pairing of unpaired 3*d* electrons. Therefore, it undergoes sp^3 hybridisation.

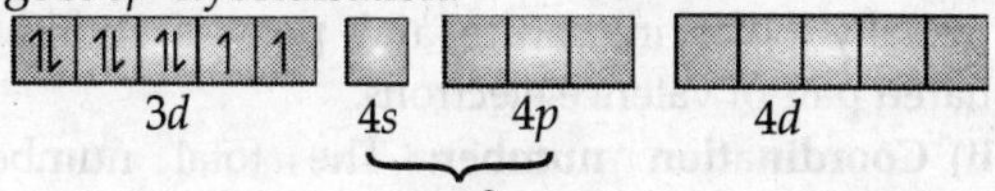

Since, there are two unpaired electrons in this case, it is paramagnetic in nature.

Q. 5.6. $[NiCl_4]^{2-}$ is paramagnetic while $[Ni(CO)_4]$ is diamagnetic though both are tetrahedral. Why?

Ans. Though both $[NiCl_4]^{2-}$ and $[Ni(CO)_4]$ are tetrahedral, their magnetic characters are different. This is due to a difference in the nature of ligands. Cl^- is a weak-field ligand and it does not cause the pairing of unpaired 3*d* electrons. Hence, $[NiCl_4]^{2-}$ is paramagnetic.

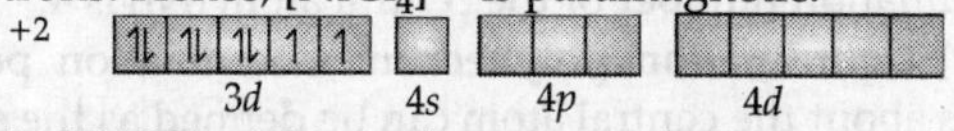

In $Ni(CO)_4$, Ni is in the zero oxidation state, that is, it has a configuration of $3d^8 4s^2$.

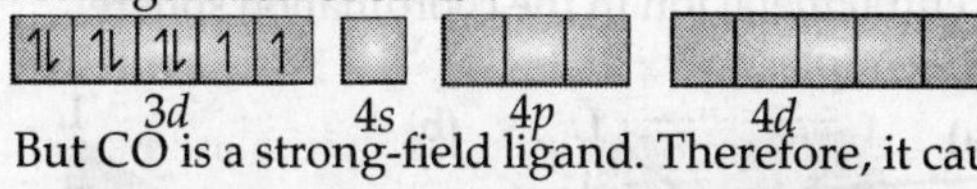

But CO is a strong-field ligand. Therefore, it causes the pairing of unpaired 3*d* electrons. Also, it causes the 4*s* electrons to shift to the 3*d* orbital, thereby giving rise to sp^3 hybridisation. Since no unpaired electrons are present in this case, $[Ni(CO)_4]$ is diamagnetic.

Q. 5.7. $[Fe(H_2O)_6]^{3+}$ is strongly paramagnetic whereas $[Fe(CN)6]^{3-}$ is a weakly paramagnetic. Explain.

Ans. $[Fe(H_2O)_6]^{3+}$

Fe(26): $3d^6\ 4s^2$

Fe^{3+}: $3d^5\ 4s^{\circ}$

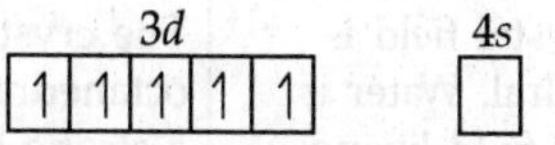

H_2O being a weak ligand does not pair up and hence, the complex is strongly paramagnetic.

$[Fe(CN)_6]^{3-}$

Fe(26): $3d^6\ 4s^2$

Fe^{3+}: $3d^5\ 4s^{\circ}$

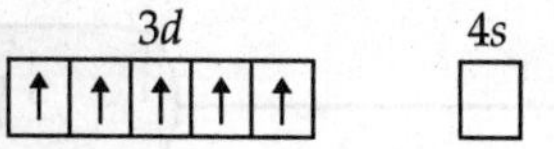

CN^- being a strong field ligand pairs up the e^- so that we have,

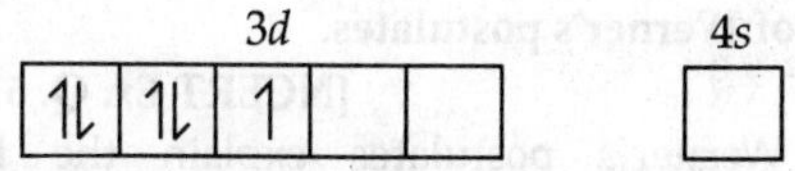

Due to only one unpaired e^-, the complex is weakly paramagnetic.

Q. 5.8. Explain $[Co(NH_3)_6]^{3+}$ is an inner orbital complex whereas $[Ni(NH_3)_6]^{2+}$ is an outer orbital complex.

Ans.

$[Co(NH_3)_6]^{3+}$	$[Ni(NH_3)_6]^{2+}$
Oxidation state of cobalt = +3.	Oxidation state of Ni = +2.
Electronic configuration of cobalt = d^6.	Electronic configuration of nickel = d^8.
NH_3 is a strong field ligand therefore it causes the pairing. Hence, Co can undergo d^2sp^3 hybridization. Therefore, it is an inner orbital complex.	If NH_3 causes the pairing, then only one 3d orbital is empty. Thus, it cannot undergo d^2sp^3 hybridisation. Therefore, it undergoes sp^3d^2 hybridisation. Hence, it forms an outer orbital complex.

Q. 5.9. Predict the number of unpaired electrons in the square planar $[Pt(CN)_4]^{2-}$ ion.

Ans. $[Pt(CN)_4]^{2-}$

In this complex, Pt is in the +2 state. It forms a square planar structure. This means that it undergoes dsp^2 hybridisation. Now, the electronic configuration of Pt(+2) is $5d^8$.

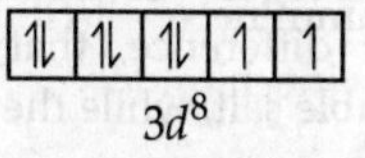

CN^- being a strong-field ligand causes the pairing of unpaired electrons. Hence, there are no unpaired electrons in $[Pt(CN)_4]^{2-}$.

Q. 5.10. The hexaquamanganese(II) ion contains five unpaired electrons, while the hexacyano ion contains only one unpaired electron. Explain using Crystal Field Theory.

Ans.

$[Mn(H_2O)_6]^{2+}$	$[Mn(CN)_6]^{4-}$
Mn is in the +2 oxidation state.	Mn is in the +2 oxidation state.
The electronic configuration is d^5.	The electronic configuration is d^5.

The crystal field is octahedral. Water is a weak field ligand. Therefore, the arrangement of the electrons in $[Mn(H_2O)_6]^{2+}$ is $t_{2g}^3 e_g^2$.	The crystal field is octahedral. Cyanide is a strong field ligand. Therefore, the arrangement of the electrons in $[Mn(CN)_6]^{4-}$ is $t_{2g}^5 e_g^0$.

Hexa aquo manganese (II) ion has five unpaired electrons.	Hexacyano ion has only one unpaired electron.

Exercise Questions

Q. 1. Explain the bonding in coordination compounds in terms of Werner's postulates.

[NCERT Ex. Q. 5.1, Page 138]

Ans. Werner's postulates explain the bonding in coordination compounds as follows:

(a) A metal exhibits two types of valencies namely, primary and secondary valencies. Primary valencies are satisfied by negative ions while secondary valencies are satisfied by both negative and neutral ions.

(In modern terminology, the primary valency corresponds to the oxidation number of the metal ion, whereas the secondary valency refers to the coordination number of the metal ion).

(b) A metal ion has a definite number of secondary valencies around the central atom. Also, these valencies project in a specific direction in the space assigned to the definite geometry of the coordination compound.

(c) Primary valencies are usually ionisable, while secondary valencies are non-ionisable.

Q. 2. $FeSO_4$ solution mixed with $(NH_4)_2SO_4$ solution in 1: 1 molar ratio gives the test of Fe^{2+} ion but $CuSO_4$ solution mixed with aqueous ammonia in 1: 4 molar ratio does not give the test of Cu^{2+} ion. Explain why?

[NCERT Ex. Q. 5.2, Page 138]

Ans. $$(NH_4)_2SO_4 + FeSO_4 + 6H_2O \rightarrow \underset{\text{Mohr's salt}}{FeSO_4(NH_4)_2SO_4 \cdot 6H_2O}$$

$$CuSO_4 + 4NH_3 + 5H_2O \rightarrow \underset{\text{tetraamminecopper(II)sulphate}}{[Cu(NH_3)_4]SO_4 \cdot 5H_2O}$$

Both the compounds, *i.e.*, $FeSO_4 \cdot (NH_4)_2SO_4 \cdot 6H_2O$ and $[Cu(NH_3)_4]SO_4 \cdot 5H_2O$ fall under the category of addition compounds with only one major difference, that is, the former is an example of a double salt, while the latter is a coordination compound.

A double salt is an addition compound that is stable in the solid state but that which breaks up into its constituent ions in the dissolved state. These compounds exhibit individual properties of their constituents. For example, $FeSO_4 \cdot (NH_4)_2SO_4 \cdot 6H_2O$ breaks into Fe^{2+}, NH_4^+, and SO_4^{2-} ions. Hence, it gives a positive test for Fe^{2+} ions.

A coordination compound is an addition compound which retains its identity in the solid as well as in the dissolved state. However, the individual properties of the constituents are lost. This happens because $[Cu(NH_3)_4]SO_4 \cdot 5H_2O$ does not show the test for Cu^{2+}. The ions present in the solution of $[Cu(NH_3)_4]SO_4 \cdot 5H_2O$ are $[Cu(NH_3)_4]^{2+}$ and SO_4^{2-}.

Q. 3. Explain with two examples each of the following: coordination entity, ligand, coordination number, coordination polyhedron, homoleptic and heteroleptic.

[NCERT Ex. Q. 5.3, Page 138]

Ans. (i) Coordination entity: A coordination entity is an electrically charged radical or species carrying a positive or negative charge. In a coordination entity, the central atom or ion is surrounded by a suitable number of neutral molecules or negative ions (called ligands). For example:

$[Ni(NH_3)_6]^{2+}$, $[Fe(CN)_6]^{4+}$ = cationic complex

$[PtCl_4]^{2-}$, $[Ag(CN)_2]^-$ = anionic complex

$[Ni(CO)_4]$, $[Co(NH_3)_4Cl_2]$ = neutral complex

(ii) Ligands: The neutral molecules or negatively charged ions that surround the metal atom in a coordination entity or a coordination complex are known as ligands. For example, $\ddot{N}H_3$, $H_2\ddot{O}$, Cl^-, ^-OH. Ligands are usually polar in nature and possess at least one unshared pair of valence electrons.

(iii) Coordination number: The total number of ligands (either neutral molecules or negative ions) that get attached to the central metal atom in the coordination sphere is called the coordination number of the central metal atom. It is also referred to as its ligancy. For example:

(a) In the complex, $K_2[PtCl_6]$, there are six chloride ions attached to Pt in the coordinate sphere. Therefore, the coordination number of Pt is 6.

(b) Similarly, in the complex $[Ni(NH_3)_4]Cl_2$, the coordination number of the central atom (Ni) is 4.

(iv) Coordination polyhedron: Coordination polyhedrons about the central atom can be defined as the spatial arrangement of the ligands that are directly attached to the central metal ion in the coordination sphere. For example:

(a) 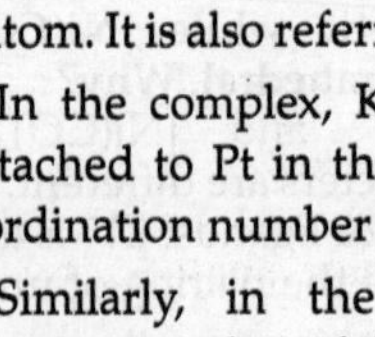

Square planar

(b) 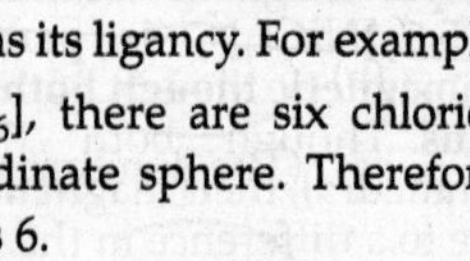

Tetrahedral

(v) Homoleptic complexes: These are those complexes in which the metal ion is bound to only one kind of a donor group. For example: $[Co(NH_3)_6]^{3+}$, $[PtCl_4]^{2-}$, etc.

(vi) Heteroleptic complexes: Heteroleptic complexes are those complexes where the central metal ion is bound to more than one type of a donor group. For example: $[Co(NH_3)_4Cl_2]^+$, $[Co(NH_3)_5Cl]^{2+}$

Q. 4. What is meant by unidentate, bidentate and ambidentate ligands? Give two examples for each.

[NCERT Ex. Q. 5.4, Page 138]

Ans. A ligand may contain one or more unshared pairs of electrons which are called the donor sites of ligands. Now, depending on the number of these donor sites, ligands can be classified as follows:

(i) Unidentate ligands: Ligands with only one donor sites are called unidentate ligands. For example, $\ddot{N}H_3$, Cl^-, etc.

(ii) Bidentate ligands: Ligands that have two donor sites are called bidentate ligands. For example,

(a) Ethane-1,2-diamine

$H_2\ddot{N}—CH_2$
|
$H_2\ddot{N}—CH_2$

(b) Oxalate ion

$(C_2O_4^{2-})$ or COO^- | COO^-

(iii) Ambidentate ligands: Ligands that can attach themselves to the central metal atom through two different atoms are called ambidentate ligands. For example,

(a) 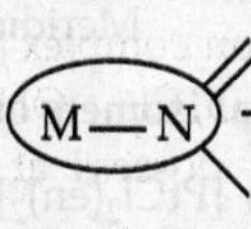 ⟶ Nitro group

(The donor atom is N)

M—O—N=O ⟶ Nitrito group

(The donor atom is oxygen)

(b) M—SCN ⟶ Thiocyanate

(The donor atom is S)

M—NCS ⟶ Isothiocyanate

(The donor atom is N).

Q. 5. Specify the oxidation numbers of the metals in the following coordination entities:

(i) $[Co(H_2O)(CN)(en)_2]^{2+}$

(ii) $[CoBr_2(en)_2]^+$

(iii) $[PtCl_4]^{2-}$

(iv) $K_3[Fe(CN)_6]$

(v) $[Cr(NH_3)_3Cl_3]$ **[NCERT Ex. Q. 5.5, Page 138]**

Ans. (i) $[Co(H_2O)(CN)(en)_2]^{2+}$

Let the oxidation number of Co be x. The charge on the complex is +2.

[Co (H₂O) (CN) (en)₂]²⁺ → $x + 0 + (-1) + 2(0) = +2$

$x - 1 = +2$

$x = +3$

(ii) $[Co\ (Br)_2\ (en)_2]^{2+}$ → $x\ \ +2(-1)\ \ +2(0) = +1$

$x - 2 = +1$

$x = +3$

(iii) $[PtCl_4]^{2-}$

Let the oxidation number of Pt be x. The charge on the complex is –2.

$[Pt\ (Cl)_4]^{2-}$ → $x + 4(-1) = -2$

$x - 4 = -2$

$x = +2$

(iv) $K_3[Fe(CN)_6]$

i.e., $[Fe\ (CN)_6]^{3-}$ → $x\ \ +6(-1) = -3$

$x = +3$

(v) $[Cr\ (NH_3)_3\ Cl_3]$ → $x + 3(0) + 3(-1) = 0$

$x - 3 = 0$

$x = +3$

Q. 6. Using IUPAC norms write the formulas for the following:

(i) Tetrahydroxozincate(II)

(ii) Potassium tetrachloridopalladate(II)

(iii) Diamminedichloridoplatinum(II)

(iv) Potassium tetracyanonickelate(II)

(v) Pentaamminenitrito-O-cobalt(III)

(vi) Hexaamminecobalt(III) sulphate

(vii) Potassium tri(oxalato)chromate(III)

(viii) Hexaammineplatinum(IV)

(ix) Tetrabromidocuprate(II)

(x) Pentaamminenitrito-N-cobalt(III)

[NCERT Ex. Q. 5.6, Page 138]

Ans. (i) $[Zn(OH)_4]^{2-}$

(ii) $K_2[PdCl_4]$

(iii) $[Pt(NH_3)_2Cl_2]$

(iv) $K_2[Ni(CN)_4]$

(v) $[Co(ONO)(NH_3)_5]^{2+}$

(vi) $[Co(NH_3)_6]_2(SO_4)_3$

(vii) $K_3[Cr(C_2O_4)_3]$

(viii) $[Pt(NH_3)_6]^{4+}$

(ix) $[Cu(Br)_4]^{2-}$

(x) $[Co(NH_3)_5NO_2]^{2+}$

Q. 7. Using IUPAC norms write the systematic names of the following:

(i) $[Co(NH_3)_6]Cl_3$

(ii) $[Pt(NH_3)_2Cl(NH_2CH_3)]Cl$

(iii) $[Ti(H_2O)_6]^{3+}$
(iv) $[Co(NH_3)_4Cl(NO_2)]Cl$
(v) $[Mn(H_2O)_6]^{2+}$
(vi) $[NiCl_4]^{2-}$
(vii) $[Ni(NH_3)_6]Cl_2$
(viii) $[Co(en)_3]^{3+}$
(ix) $[Ni(CO)_4]$ **[NCERT Ex. Q. 5.7, Page 138]**

Ans. (i) Hexaamminecobalt(III)chloride
(ii) Diamminechlorido(methylamine) platinum(II) chloride
(iii) Hexaquatitanium(III)ion
(iv) Tetraamminichloridonitrito-N-Cobalt(III)chloride
(v) Hexaquamanganese(II)ion
(vi) Tetrachloridonickelate(II)ion
(vii) Hexaamminenickelate(II)chloride
(viii) Tris(ethane-1, 2-diammine) cobalt(III)ion
(ix) Tetracarbonylnickel(0)

Q. 8. List various types of isomerism possible for coordination compounds, giving an example of each. [NCERT Ex. Q. 5.8, Page 138]

Ans.

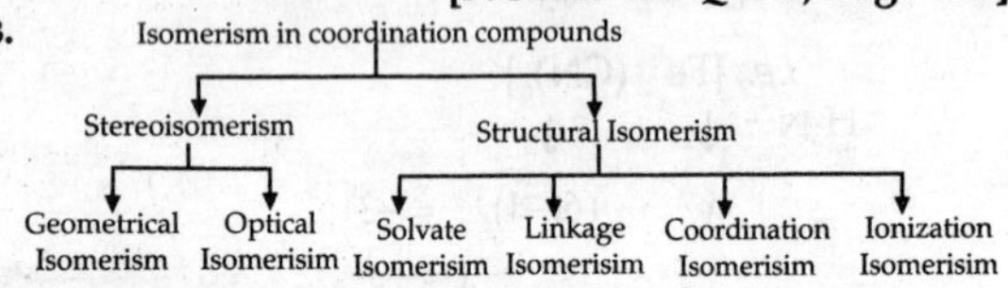

(i) Geometrical isomerism: This type of isomerism is common in heteroleptic complexes. It arises due to the different possible geometric arrangements of the ligands. For example:

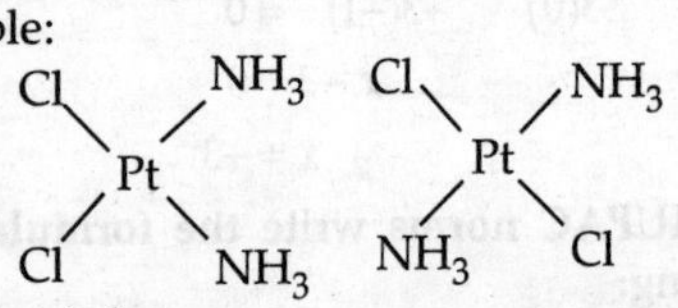

cis-isomer *trans*-isomer

(ii) Optical isomerism: This type of isomerism arises in chiral molecules. Isomers are mirror images of each other and are non-superimposable.

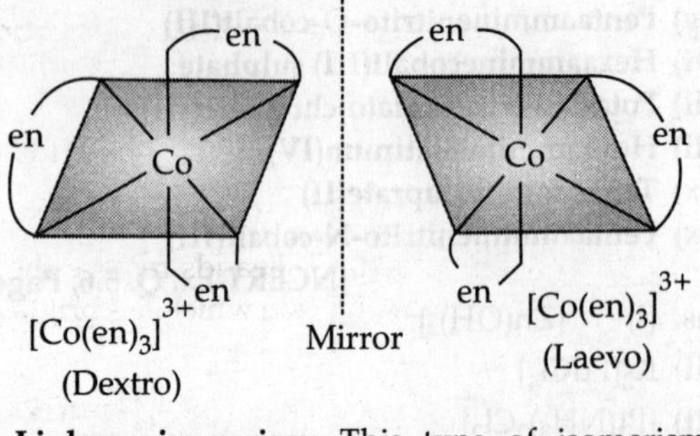

(iii) Linkage isomerism: This type of isomerism is found in complexes that contain ambidentate ligands. e.g., $[Co(NH_3)_5(NO_2)]Cl_2$ and $[Co(NH_3)_5(ONO)Cl_2$.

(iv) Coordination isomerism: This type of isomerism arises when the ligands are interchanged between cationic and anionic entities of different metal ions present in the complex. $[Co(NH_3)_6][Cr(CN)_6]$ and $[Cr(NH_3)_6][Co(CN)_6]$.

(v) Ionisation isomerism: This type of isomerism arises when a counter ion replaces a ligand within the coordination sphere. Thus, complexes that have the same composition, but furnish different ions when dissolved in water are called ionization isomers. e.g., $[Co(NH_3)_5SO_4]Br$ and $[Co(NH_3)_5Br]SO_4$.

(vi) Solvate isomerism: Solvate isomers differ by whether or not the solvent molecule is directly bonded to the metal ion or merely present as a free solvent molecule in the crystal lattice. e.g., $[Cr(H_2O)_6]Cl_3$ $[Cr(H_2O)_5Cl]Cl_2.H_2O$, $[Cr(H_2O)_5Cl_2]Cl.2H_2O$

Q. 9. How many geometrical isomers are possible in the following coordination entities?
(i) $[Cr(C_2O_4)_3]^{3-}$ **(ii)** $[Co(NH_3)_3Cl_3]$ **[NCERT Ex. Q. 5.9, Page 138]**

Ans. (i) $[Cr(C_2O_4)_3]^{3-}$: No geometric isomer is possible as it is a bidentate ligand.

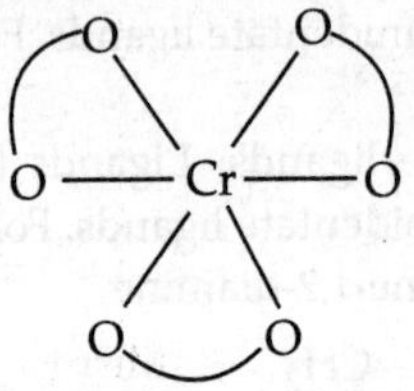

(ii) $[Co(NH_3)_3Cl_3]$: Two geometrical isomers are possible.

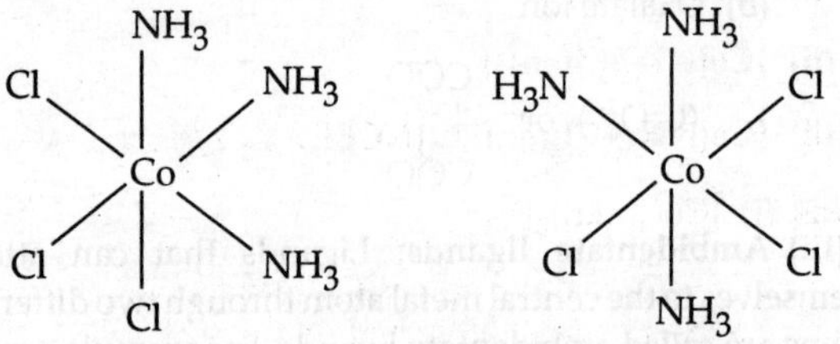

Facial Meridional

Q. 10. Draw the structures of optical isomers of:
(a) $[Cr(C_2O_4)_3]^{3-}$. **(b)** $[PtCl_2(en)_2]^{2+}$.
(c) $[Cr(NH_3)_2Cl_2(en)]^+$ **[NCERT Ex. Q. 5.10, Page 138]**

Ans. (a) $[Cr(C_2O_4)_3]^{3-}$:

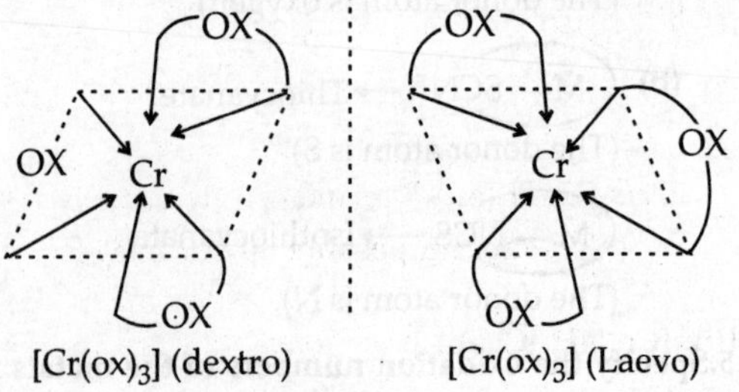

$[Cr(ox)_3]$ (dextro) $[Cr(ox)_3]$ (Laevo)

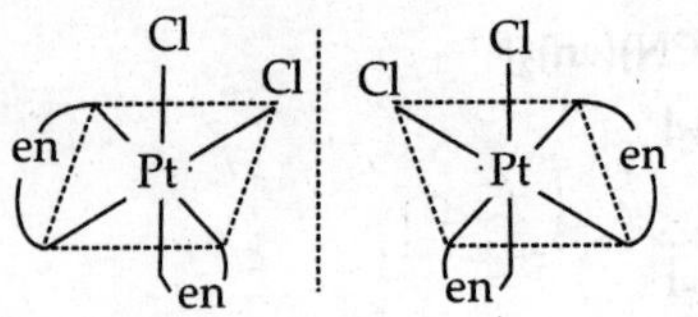

(b) (*cis*-isomer only) *cis*-$[PtCl_2(en)_2]^{2+}$:

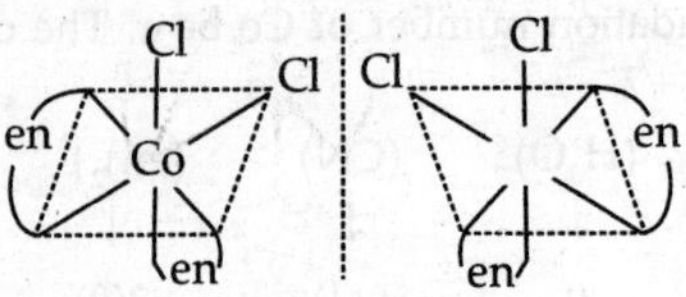

Mirror

(c) (*cis*-isomer only) *cis*-$[Cr(NH_3)_2Cl_2(en)]^+$

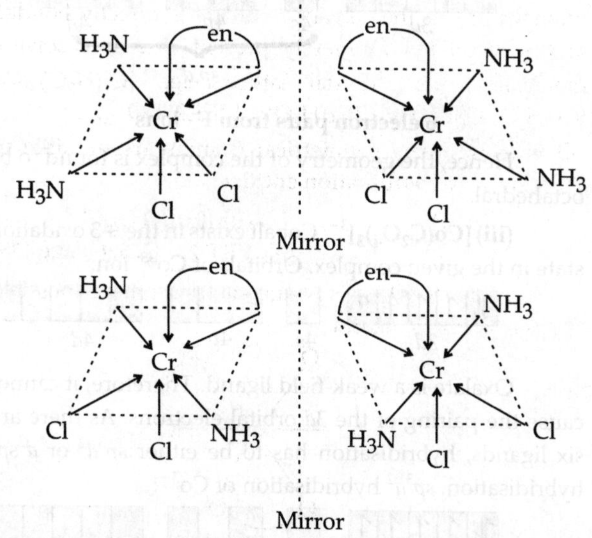

Q. 11. Draw all the isomers (geometrical and optical) of:

(i) $[CoCl_2(en)_2]^+$.

(ii) $[Co(NH_3)Cl(en)_2]^{2+}$.

(iii) $[Co(NH_3)_2Cl_2(en)]^+$. [NCERT Ex. Q. 5.11, Page 139]

Ans. (i) $[CoCl_2(en)_2]^+$:

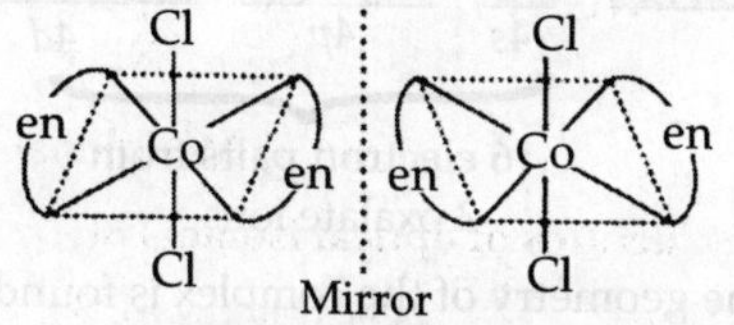

***trans*-$[CoCl_2(en)_2]^+$ isomer-optically inactive (Superimposable mirror images)**

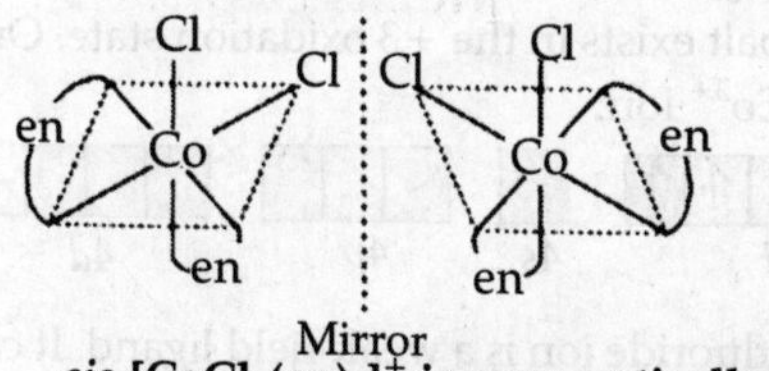

***cis*-$[CoCl_2(en)_2]^+$ isomer-optically active (Non-superimposable mirror images)**

(ii) $[Co(NH_3)Cl(en)_2]^{2+}$: *Trans*-isomers are optically inactive. *Cis*-isomers are optically active.

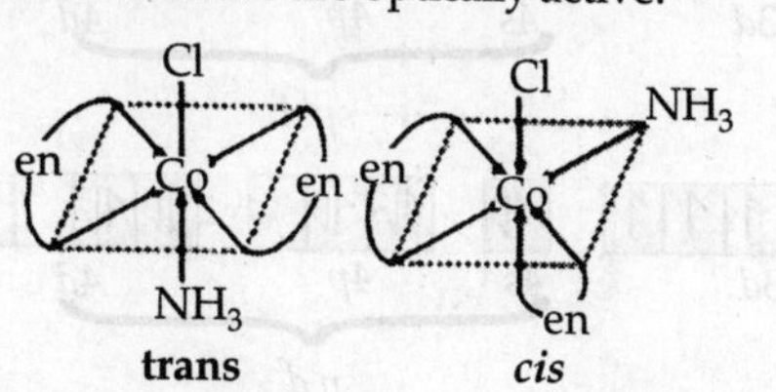

trans **cis**

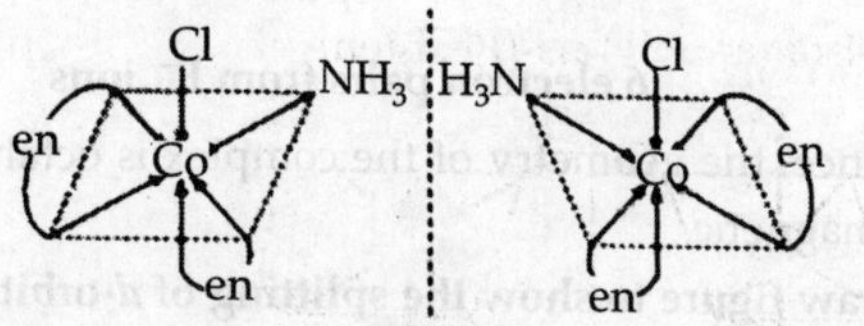

Mirror

***cis*-isomer**

(iii) $[Co(NH_3)_2Cl_2(en)]^+$:

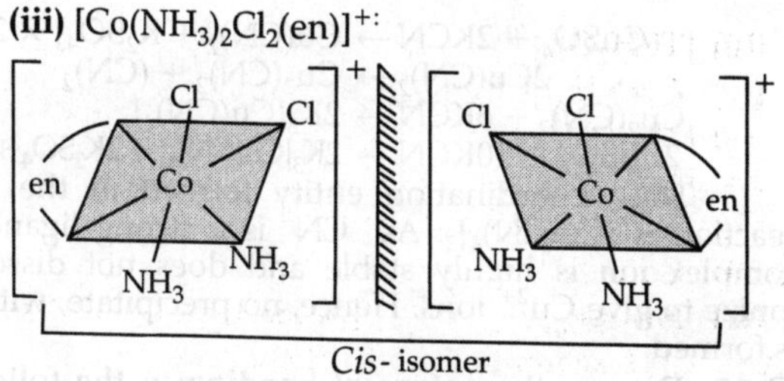

Cis- isomer

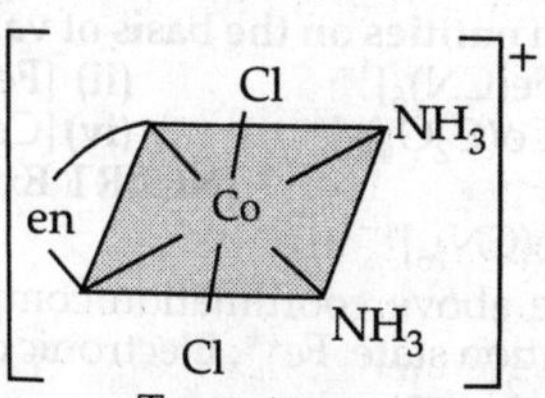

Trans- isomer

Q. 12. Write all the geometrical isomers of $[Pt(NH_3)(Br)(Cl)(py)]$ and how many of these will exhibit optical isomers? [NCERT Ex. Q. 5.12, Page 139]

Ans. $[Pt(NH_3)(Br)(Cl)(py)$:

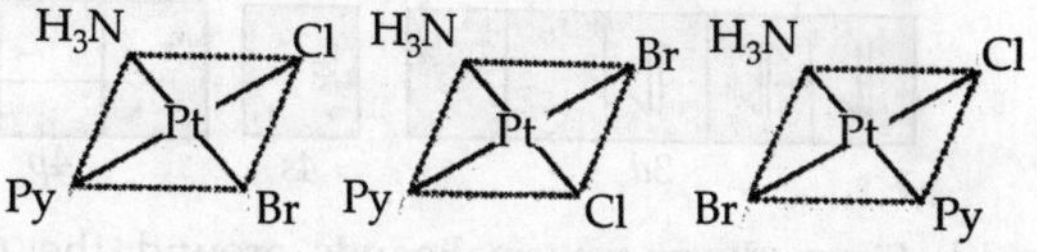

From the above isomers, none will exhibit optical isomers. Tetrahedral complexes rarely show optical isomerisation. They do so only in the presence of unsymmetrical chelating agents.

Q. 13. Aqueous copper sulphate solution (blue in colour) gives:

(i) a green precipitate with aqueous potassium fluoride, and

(ii) a bright green solution with aqueous potassium chloride

Explain these experimental results. [NCERT Ex. Q. 5.13, Page 139]

Ans. Aqueous $CuSO_4$ exists as $[Cu(H_2O)_4]SO_4$ which has blue colour due to $[Cu[H_2O)_4]^{2+}$ ions.

(i) When KF is added, the weak H_2O ligands are replaced by F ligands forming $[CuF_4]^{2-}$ ion which is a green precipitate.

$$\left[Cu(H_2O)_4\right]^{2+} + 4F^- \rightarrow \left[Cu(F)_4\right]^{2-} + 4H_2O$$

(Green)

(ii) When KCl is added, Cl^- ligands replace the weak H_2O ligands forming $[CuCl_4]^{2-}$ ion which has bright green colour.

$$\left[Cu(H_2O)_4\right]^{2+} + 4Cl^- \rightarrow \left[CuCl_4\right]^{2-} + 4H_2O$$

(Bright green)

In both these cases, the weak-field ligand water is replaced by the F^- and Cl^- ions.

Q. 14. What is the coordination entity formed when excess of aqueous KCN is added to an aqueous solution of copper sulphate? Why is it that no precipitate of copper sulphide is obtained when $H_2S(g)$ is passed through this solution? [NCERT Ex. Q. 5.14, Page 139]

Ans. First cupric cyanide is formed which decomposes to give cuprous cyanide and cyanogen gas. Cuprous cyanide dissolves in excess of potassium cyanide to form the complex, $K_3[Cu(CN)_4]$.

$$CuSO_4 + 2KCN \rightarrow Cu(CN)_2 + K_2SO_4] \times 2$$
$$2Cu(CN)_2 \rightarrow Cu_2(CN)_2 + (CN)_2$$
$$Cu_2(CN)_2 + 6KCN \rightarrow 2K_3[Cu(CN)_4]$$
$$2CuSO_4 + 10KCN \rightarrow 2K_3[Cu(CN)_4] + 2K_2SO_4 + (CN)_2$$

Thus, coordination entity formed in the above reaction is $[Cu(CN)_4]_3$. As CN^- is a strong ligand, the complex ion is highly stable and does not dissociate/ionize to give Cu^{2+} ions. Hence, no precipitate, with H_2S is formed.

Q. 15. Discuss the nature of bonding in the following coordination entities on the basis of valence bond theory:

(i) $[Fe(CN)_6]^{4-}$ **(ii)** $[FeF_6]^{3-}$
(iii) $[Co(C_2O_4)_3]^{3-}$ **(iv)** $[CoF_6]^{3-}$

[NCERT Ex. Q. 5.15, Page 139]

Ans. (i) $[Fe(CN)_6]^{4-}$:

In the above coordination complex, iron exists in the +2 oxidation state. Fe^{2+}: Electronic configuration is $3d^6$

Orbitals of Fe^{2+} ion:

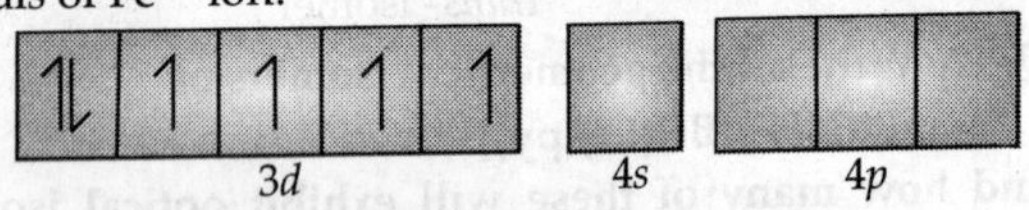

As CN^- is a strong-field ligand, it causes the pairing of the unpaired 3*d* electrons.

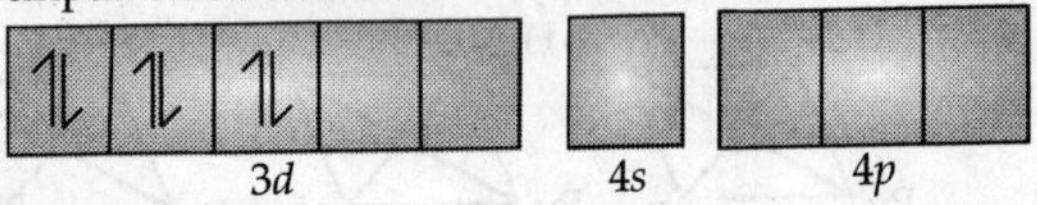

Since there are six ligands around the central metal ion, the most feasible hybridisation is d^2sp^3. d^2sp^3 hybridised orbitals of Fe^{2+} are:

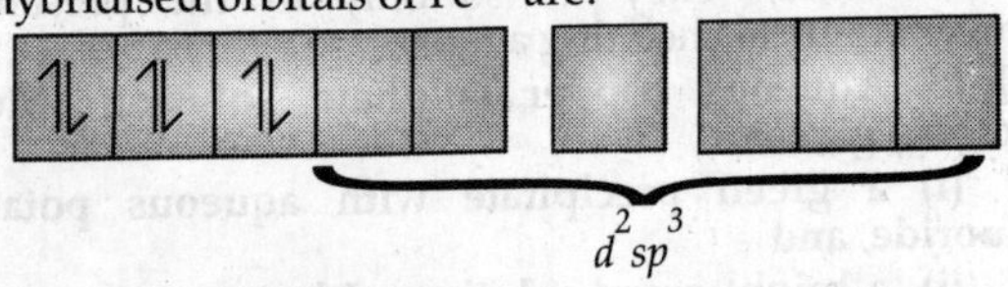

Six electron pairs from CN^- ions occupy the six hybrid d^2sp^3 orbitals.

Then,

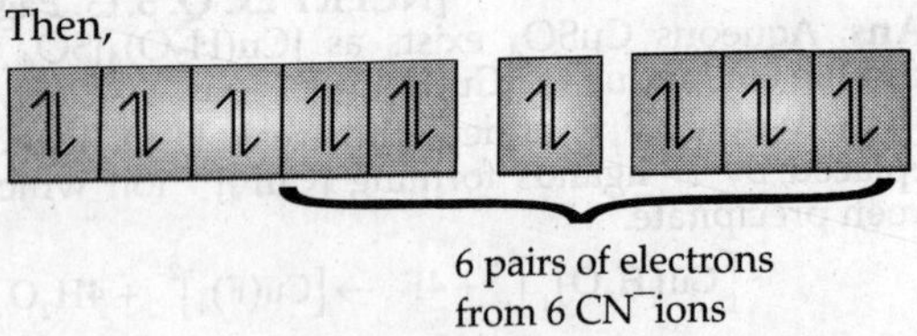

Hence, the geometry of the complex is octahedral and the complex is diamagnetic (as there are no unpaired electrons).

(ii) $[FeF_6]^{3-}$:

In this complex, the oxidation state of Fe is +3.

Orbitals of Fe^{3+} ion:

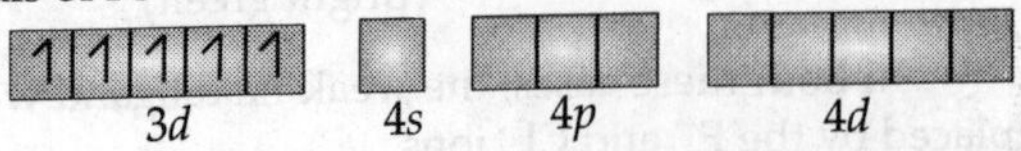

There are six F^- ions. Thus, it will undergo d^2sp^3 or sp^3d^2 hybridisation. As F^- is a weak-field ligand, it does not cause the pairing of the electrons in the 3*d* orbital. Hence, the most feasible hybridisation is sp^3d^2.

sp^3d^2 hybridised orbitals of Fe are:

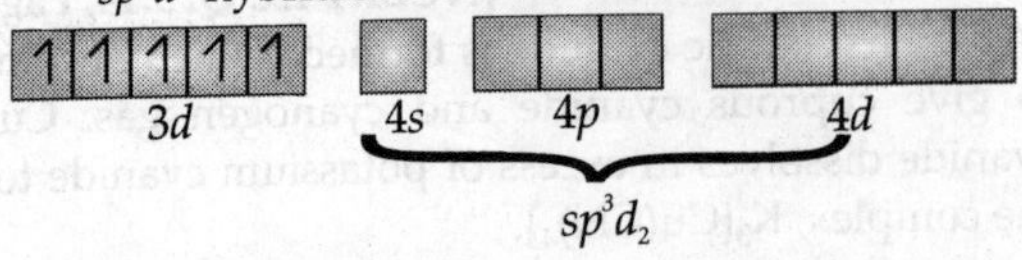

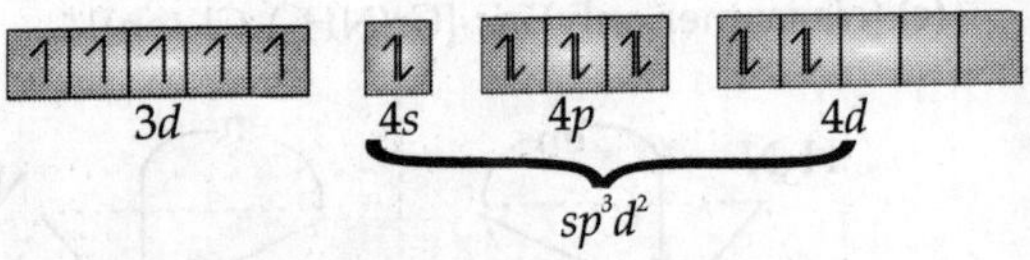

6 electron pairs from F^- ions

Hence, the geometry of the complex is found to be octahedral.

(iii) $[Co(C_2O_4)_3]^{3-}$: Cobalt exists in the +3 oxidation state in the given complex. Orbitals of Co^{3+} ion:

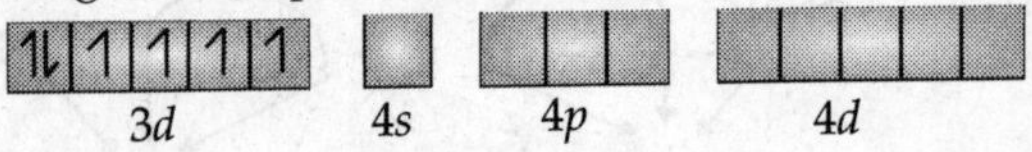

Oxalate is a weak-field ligand. Therefore, it cannot cause the pairing of the 3*d* orbital electrons. As there are six ligands, hybridisation has to be either sp^3d^2 or d^2sp^3 hybridisation. sp^3d^2 hybridisation of Co^{3+}:

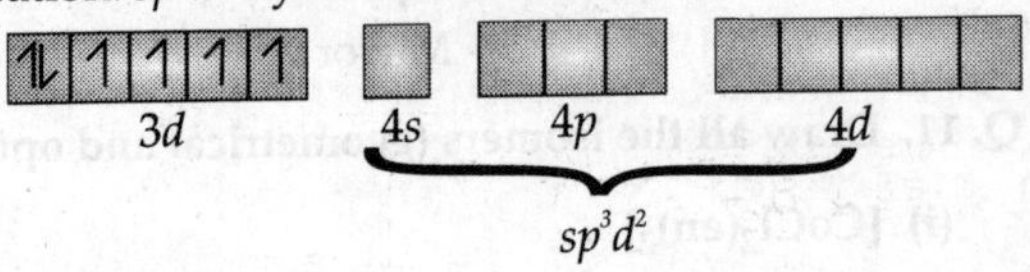

The six electron pairs from the three oxalate ions (oxalate anion is a bidentate ligand) occupy these sp^3d^2 orbitals.

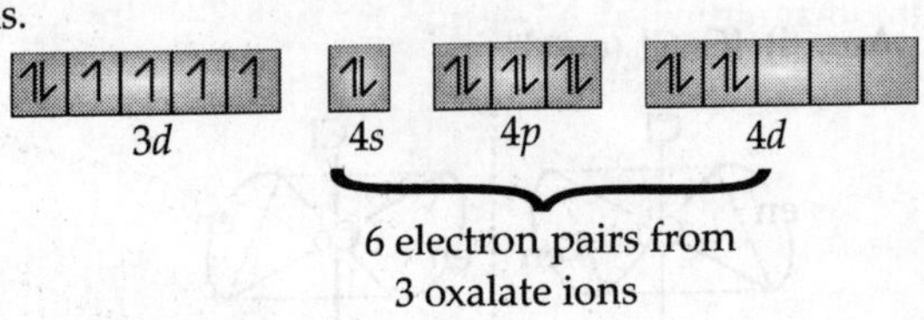

Hence, the geometry of the complex is found to be octahedral.

(iv) $[CoF_6]^{3-}$:

Cobalt exists in the +3 oxidation state. Orbitals of Co^{3+} ion:

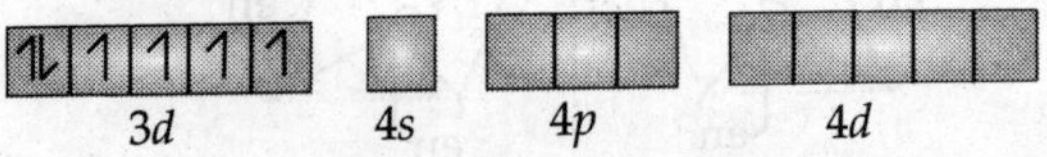

Again, fluoride ion is a weak-field ligand. It cannot cause the pairing of the 3*d* electrons. As a result, the Co^{3+} ion will undergo sp^3d^2 hybridisation. sp^3d^2 hybridised orbitals of Co^{3+} ion are:

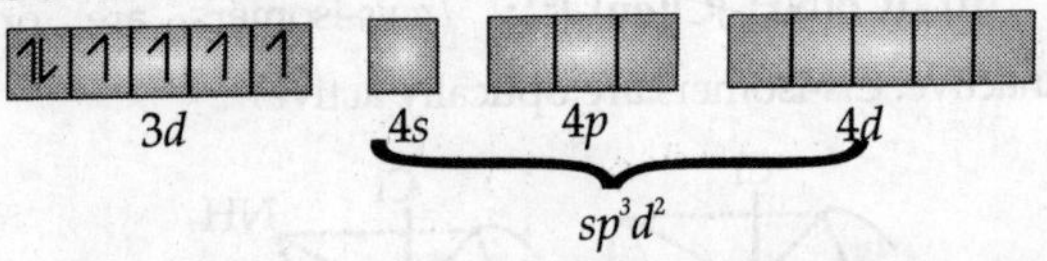

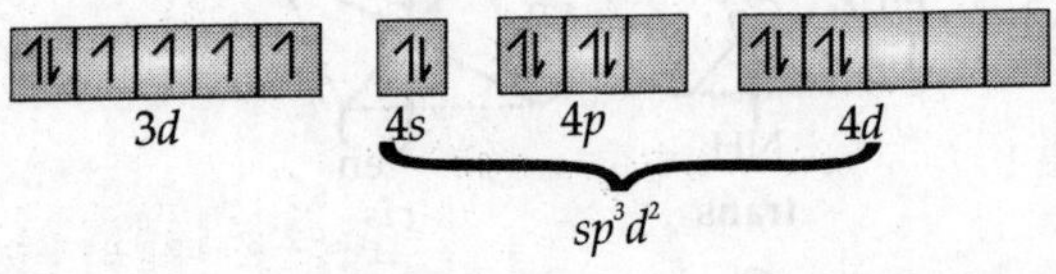

6 electron pairs from F^- ions

Hence, the geometry of the complex is octahedral and paramagnetic.

Q. 16. Draw figure to show the splitting of *d*-orbitals in an octahedral crystal field.

[NCERT Ex. Q. 5.16, Page 139]

Ans.

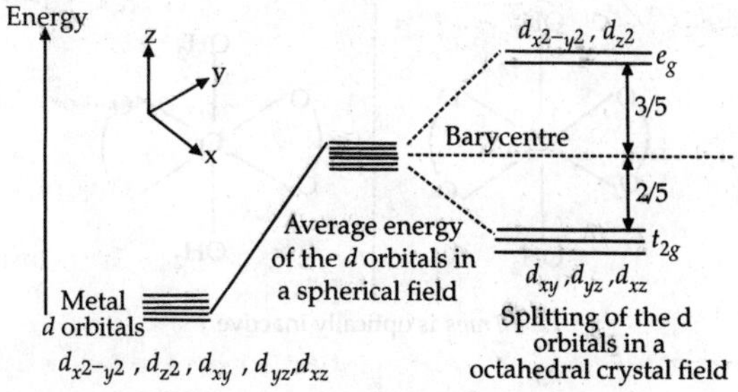

Q. 17. What is spectrochemical series? Explain the difference between a weak-field ligand and a strong-field ligand. [NCERT Ex. Q. 5.17, Page 139]

Ans. Spectrochemical series is the arrangement of ligands in the ascending order of crystal field splitting. Weak field ligands have smaller value of crystal field splitting energy. They form high spin complexes. Whereas strong field ligands have larger value of crystal field splitting energy. They form low spin complexes. In general, ligands can be arranged in a series in the order of increasing field strength as given below:

$I^- < Br^- < SCN^- < Cl^- < S^{2-} < F^- < OH^- < C_2O_4^{2-} < H_2O < NCS^- < edta^{4-} < NH_3 < en < CN^- <$ CO.

Q. 18. What is crystal field splitting energy? How does the magnitude of Δ_0 decide the actual configuration of *d*-orbitals in a coordination entity? [NCERT Ex. Q. 5.18, Page 139]

Ans. When the ligands approach a transition metal ion, the d-orbitals split, into two sets, one with lower energy and the other with higher energy. The difference of energy between the two sets of orbitals is called crystal field splitting energy (Δ_0 for octahedral field). If $\Delta_0 < P$ (pairing energy), the fourth electron enters one of the e.g., orbitals giving the configuration $t^3_{2g}e^1_g$, thus forming high spin complexes. Such ligands for which $\Delta_0 < P$ are called weak field ligands. If $\Delta_0 > P$, the fourth electron pairs up in one of the t_{2g} orbitals giving the configuration $t^4_{2g}e^1_g$ thereby forming low spin complexes. Such ligands for which $\Delta_0 > P$ are called strong field ligands.

Q. 19. $[Cr(NH_3)_6]^{3+}$ is paramagnetic while $[Ni(CN)_4]^{2-}$ is diamagnetic. Explain why? [NCERT Ex. Q. 5.19, Page 139]

Ans. The presence of three unpaired electrons in $[Cr(NH_3)_6]^{3+}$ explains its paramagnetic character

Cr^{3+}

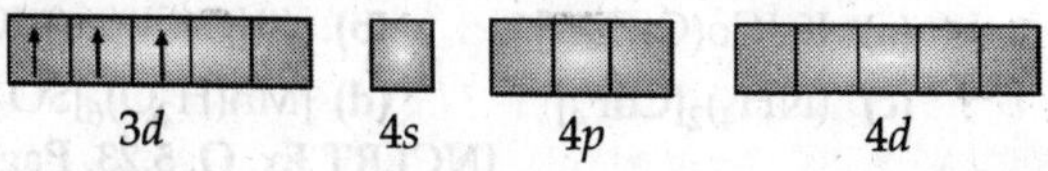

As NH_3 is a weak ligand does not lead to pairing of electrons

Ni^{2+}:

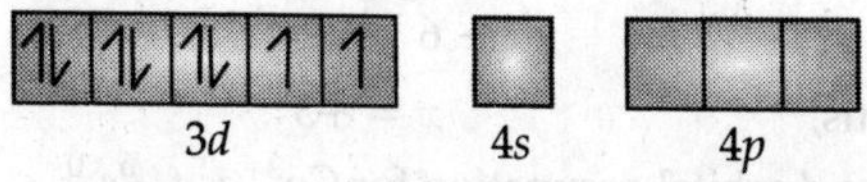

$[Ni(CN)_4]^{2-}$ is diamagnetic, since there is no unpaired electrons.

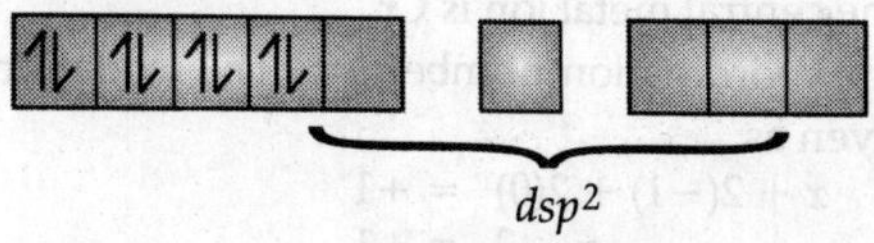

Pairing of electrons occurs due to strong CN^- ligand

Q. 20. A solution of $[Ni(H_2O)_6]^{2+}$ is green but a solution of $[Ni(CN)_4]^{2-}$ is colourless. Explain. [NCERT Ex. Q. 5.20, Page 139]

Ans. In $[Ni(H_2O)_6]^{2+}$, $H_2\ddot{O}$ is a weak-field ligand. Therefore, there are unpaired electrons in Ni^{2+}. In this complex, the *d* electrons from the lower energy level can be excited to the higher energy level, *i.e.*, the possibility of *d*–*d* transition is present. Hence, $Ni(H_2O)_6]^{2+}$ is green coloured.

In $[Ni(CN)_4]^{2-}$, the electrons are all paired as CN is a strong-field ligand. Therefore, *d*–*d* transition is not possible in $[Ni(CN)_4]^{2-}$. Hence, it is colourless.

Q. 21. $[Fe(CN)_6]^{4-}$ and $[Fe(H_2O)_6]^{2+}$ are of different colours in dilute solutions. Why? [NCERT Ex. Q. 5.21, Page 139]

Ans. The colour of a particular coordination compound depends on the magnitude of the crystal-field splitting energy, Δ_0. This CFSE in turn depends on the nature of the ligand. In case of $[Fe(CN)_6]^{4-}$ and $[Fe(H_2O)_6]^{2+}$, the colour differs because there is a difference in the CFSE.

Now, CN^- is a strong-field ligand having a higher CFSE value as compared to the CFSE value of water. This means that the absorption of energy for the intra *d*–*d* transition also differs. Hence, the transmitted colour also differs.

Q. 22. Discuss the nature of bonding in metal carbonyls. [NCERT Ex. Q. 5.22, Page 139]

Ans. In metal carbonyl, the metal carbon bond (M – C) possess both the σ and π-bond character. The bond are formed by overlap of atomic orbital of metal with that of C-atom of carbon monoxide in following sequence:

(a) σ-bond is first formed between metal and carbon when a vacant d-orbital of metal atom overlaps with an orbital containing lone pair of electrons on C-atom of carbon monoxide (: C ≡ O).

(b) In addition to σ-bond in metal carbonyl, the electrons from filled d-orbitals of a transition metal atom/ion are back donated into anti bonding π-orbitals of carbon monoxide. This stabilises the metal ligand bonding. The above two concepts are shown in following figure:

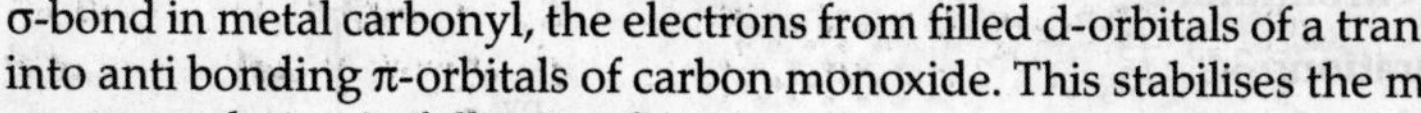

σ-overlap: Donation of lone pair of electrons on carbon into a vacant orbital on the metals

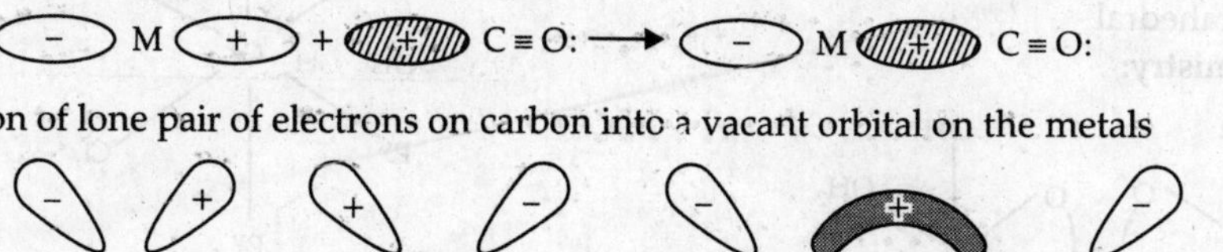

π-overlap: Donation of electrons from a filled metal d-orbital into a vacant antibonding π-orbital of CO.

Q. 23. Give the oxidation state, *d*-orbital occupation and coordination number of the central metal ion in the following complexes:

(a) $K_3[Co(C_2O_4)_3]$ **(b)** *cis*-$[CrCl_2(en)_2]Cl$

(c) $(NH_4)_2[CoF_4]$ **(d)** $[Mn(H_2O)_6]SO_4$

[NCERT Ex. Q. 5.23, Page 139]

Ans. (a) $K_3[Co(C_2O_4)_3]$:

The central metal ion is Co. Its coordination number is 6. The oxidation state can be given as:

$$x - 6 = -3$$

Thus, $x = +3$

The *d* orbital occupation for Co^{3+} is $t_{2g}^{6}e_g^{0}$.

(b) *cis*-$[CrCl_2(en)_2]Cl$

The central metal ion is Cr.

The coordination number is 6. The oxidation state can be given as:

$$x + 2(-1) + 2(0) = +1$$
$$x - 2 = +1$$

Thus, $x = +3$

The *d* orbital occupation for Cr^{3+} is t_{2g}^{3}.

(c) $(NH_4)_2[CoF_4]$:

The central metal ion is Co. The coordination number is 4.

The oxidation state can be given as:

$$x - 4 = -2$$

Thus, $x = +2$

The *d* orbital occupation for Co^{2+} is $e_g^{4}t_{2g}^{3}$.

(d) $[Mn(H_2O)_6]SO_4$

The central metal ion is Mn. The coordination number is 6. The oxidation state can be given as:

Thus, $x + 0 = +2.$

$x = +2$

The *d* orbital occupation for Mn is $t_{2g}^{3}e_g^{2}$.

Q. 24. Write down the IUPAC name for each of the following complexes and indicate the oxidation state, electronic configuration and coordination number. Also give stereochemistry and magnetic moment of the complex:

(i) $K[Cr(H_2O)_2(C_2O_4)_2].3H_2O$

(ii) $[Co(NH_3)_5Cl]Cl_2$

(iii) $[CrCl_3(py)_3]$

(iv) $Cs[FeCl_4]$

(v) $K_4[Mn(CN)_6]$ **[NCERT Ex. Q. 5.24, Page 139]**

Ans. (i) $K[Cr(H_2O)_2(C_2O_4)_2].3H_2O$:

IUPAC name:

Potassiumdiaquadioxalatochromate(III)trihydrate.

Oxidation state of chromium: 3

Electronic configuration: $3d^3 : t_{2g}^3$

Coordination number: 6

Shape: Octahedral

Stereochemistry:

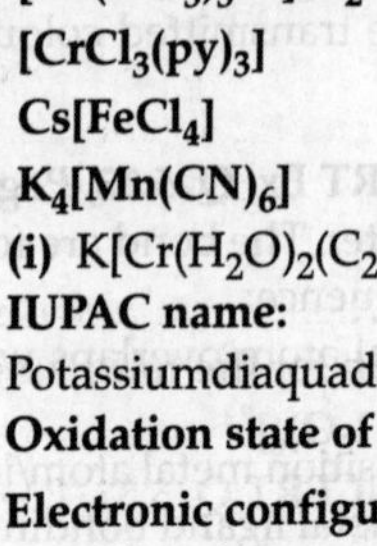

Trans

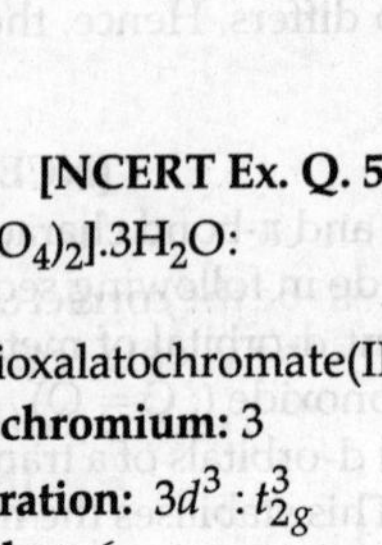

Cis

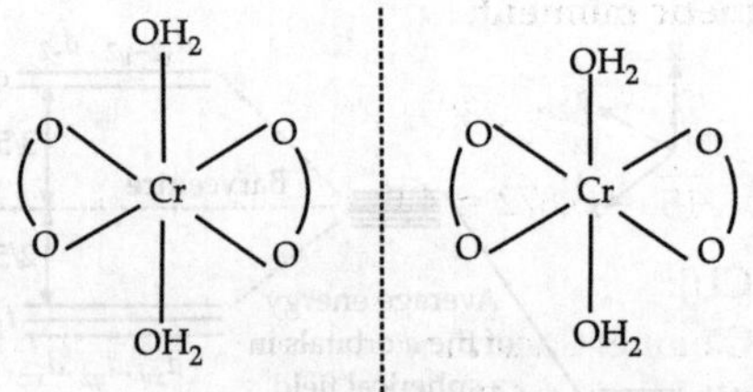

Trans **is optically inactive**

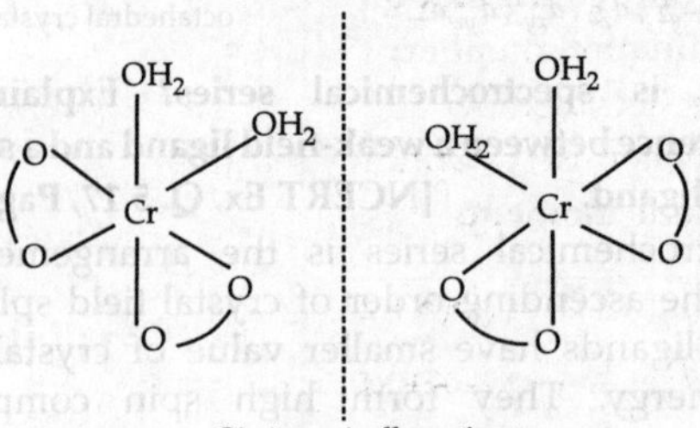

Cis **is optically active**

Magnetic moment, m $= \sqrt{n(n+2)} = \sqrt{3(3+2)}$

$= \sqrt{15} = 3.872 \approx 4$ BM

(ii) $[Co(NH_3)_5Cl]Cl_2$

IUPAC name:

Pentaamminechloridocobalt(III)chloride

Oxidation state of Co: +3

Coordination number: 6

Shape: Octahedral

Electronic configuration: d^6: t_{2g}^{6}

Stereochemistry:

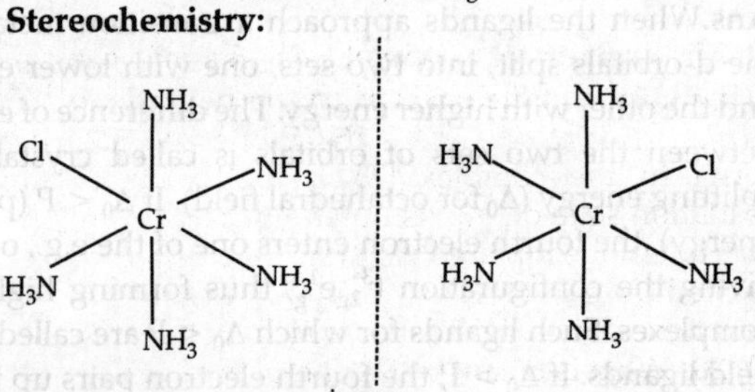

isomers

Magnetic moment = 0

(iii) $CrCl_3(py)_3$:

IUPAC name:

Trichloridotripyridinechromium (III)

Oxidation state of chromium: +3

Electronic configuration for d^3: t_{2g}^{3}

Coordination number: 6

Shape: Octahedral

Stereochemistry:

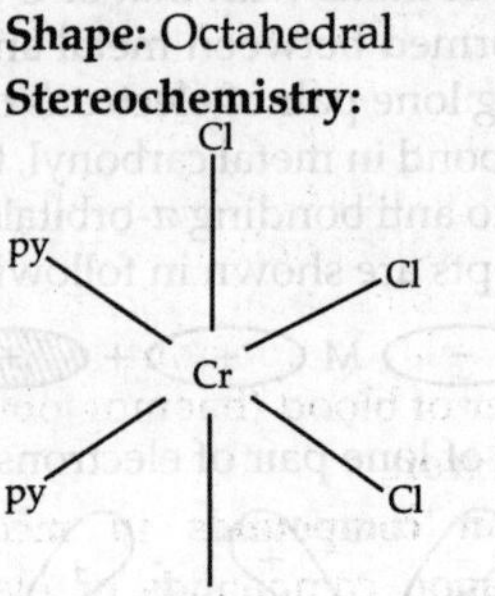

Facial isomer

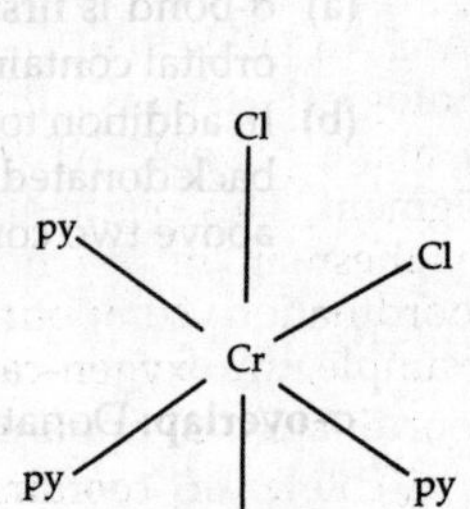

Meridional isomer

Both isomers are optically active. Therefore, a total of four isomers exist.

Magnetic moment:

$$m = \sqrt{n(n+2)} = \sqrt{3(3+2)}$$

$$= \sqrt{15} = 3.872 \approx 4 \text{ BM}$$

(iv) $Cs[FeCl_4]$:

IUPAC name: Caesiumtetrachloridoferrate (III)

Oxidation state of Fe: +3

Electronic configuration of d^6: $e_g^{\,2}t_{2g}^{\,3}$

Coordination number: 4

Shape: Tetrahedral

Stereochemistry: Optically inactive

Magnetic moment:

$$m = \sqrt{n(n+2)} = \sqrt{5(5+2)}$$

$$= \sqrt{35} = 5.92 \approx 6 \text{ BM}$$

(v) $K_4[Mn(CN)_6]$

IUPAC name: Potassium hexacyanomanganate(II)

Oxidation state of manganese: +2

Electronic configuration: d^5: t_{2g}^5

Coordination number: 6

Shape: Octahedral.

Stereochemistry: Optically inactive

Magnetic moment:

$$m = \sqrt{n(n+2)} = \sqrt{1(1+2)}$$

$$= \sqrt{3} = 1.732 \text{ BM}$$

Q. 25. Explain the violet colour of the complex $[Ti(_H2O)_6]^{3+}$ on the basis of crystal field theory. **[NCERT Ex. Q. 5.25, Page 139]**

Ans. In the complex $[Ti(H_2O)_6]^{3+}$, the Ti atom has oxidation state of +3. Its outer electronic configuration is $3d^2$. It has one inpaired electron. This unpaired electron is excited from t_{2g} level to $3g$ level by absorbing yellow light and hence appears violet coloured.

Q. 26. What is meant by *Chelate effect* ? Give an example. **[NCERT Ex. Q. 5.26, Page 139]**

Ans. Formation of stable complex with a polydentate ligand due to stronger bonding is known as chelate effect.

E.g. ethylenediamine-cadmium.

Q. 27. Discuss briefly giving an example in each case the role of coordination compounds in:

(i) Biological system.
(ii) Medicinal chemistry.
(iii) Analytical chemistry.
(iv) Extraction/metallurgy of metals.

[NCERT Ex. Q. 5.27, Page 139]

Ans. (i) Role of coordination compounds in biological systems: We know that photosynthesis is made possible by the presence of the chlorophyll pigment. This pigment is a coordination compound of magnesium. In the human biological system, several coordination compounds play important roles. For example, the oxygen-carrier of blood (haemoglobin) is a coordination compound of iron.

(ii) Role of coordination compounds in medicinal chemistry: Certain coordination compounds of platinum (*e.g.*, *cis*-platin) are used for inhibiting the growth of tumors.

(iii) Role of coordination compounds in analytical chemistry: During salt analysis, a number of basic radicals are detected with the help of the colour changes they exhibit with different reagents. These colour changes are a result of the coordination compounds or complexes that the basic radicals form with different ligands.

(iv) Role of coordination compounds in extraction or metallurgy of metals: The process of extraction of some of the metals from their ores involves the formation of complexes. For example, in aqueous solution, gold combines with cyanide ions to form $[Au(CN)_2]$. From this solution, gold is later extracted by the addition of zinc metal.

Q. 28. How many ions are produced from the complex $Co(NH_3)_6Cl_2$ in solution? [NCERT Ex. Q. 5.28, Page 139]

(i) 6 (ii) 4 (iii) 3 (iv) 2

Ans. Coordination number of cobalt = 6

Hence, the complex is $[Co(NH_3)_6]Cl_2$. it ionizes in the solution as follows:

$$[Co(NH_3)_6]Cl_2 \xrightarrow{+aq} [Co(NH_3)_6]^{2+} + 2Cl^-$$

Thus, three ions are produced. Hence, the correct option is (iii).

Q. 29. Amongst the following ions which one has the highest magnetic moment value?

(i) $[Cr(H_2O)_6]^{3+}$ **(ii)** $[Fe(H_2O)_6]^{2+}$

(iii) $[Zn(H_2O)_6]^{2+}$ **[NCERT Ex. Q. 5.29, Page 140]**

Ans. (i) No. of unpaired electrons in $[Cr(H_2O)_6]^{3+} = 3$

Then, $\mu = \sqrt{n(n+2)}$

$$= \sqrt{3(3+2)} = \sqrt{15} = 3.87 \text{ BM}$$

(ii) No. of unpaired electrons in $[Fe(H_2O)_6]^{2+} = 4$

Then, $\mu = \sqrt{4(4+2)}$

$$= \sqrt{24} = 4.89 \text{ BM}$$

(iii) No. of unpaired electrons in $[Zn(H_2O)_6]^{2+} = 0$

Hence, $[Fe(H_2O)_6]^{2+}$ has the highest magnetic moment value.

Q. 30. Amongst the following, the most stable complex is **[NCERT Ex. Q. 5.30, Page 140]**

(i) $[Fe(H_2O)_6]^{3+}$ **(ii)** $[Fe(NH_3)_6]^{3+}$

(iii) $[Fe(C_2O_4)_3]^{3-}$ **(iv)** $[FeCl_6]^{3-}$

Ans. In each of the given complex, Fe is in + 3 oxidation state. As $C_2O_4^{\,2-}$ is bidentate chelating ligand, it forms chelate rings and hence (iii) out of complexes given above is the most stable complex

Q. 31. What will be the correct order for the wave lengths of absorption in the visible region for the following. $[Ni(NO_2)_6]^{4-}$, $[Ni(NH_3)_6]^{2+}$, $[Ni(H_2O)_6]^{2+}$ **[NCERT Q. 5.31, Page 140]**

Ans. The order of the ligand in the spectro chemical series is: $H_2O < NH_3 < NO_2^-$

So, the wavelength of the light observed will be in the following order:

$$[Ni(H_2O)_6]^{2+} > [Ni(NH_3)_6]^{2+} > [Ni(NO_2)_6]^{4-}$$

Thus, the wave lengths observed [$E = hc/\lambda$] will be in the opposite order.

□□

CHAPTER 6

HALOALKANES AND HALOARENES

- Halogenated compunds persist in the environment due to their resistance to breakdown by soil bacteria.
- Haloalkanes are aliphatic hydrocarbons where a hydrogen atom is replaced by halogen, while haloarenes are aromatic hydrocarbons where hydrogen in the benzene ring is replaced with a halogen atom.
- Halogen atom is attached to sp^3 hybridized carbon atom in haloalkanes while in haloarenes it is attached to sp^2 hybridized carbon atom of the aryl group.

Classification

- **On the basis of the number of halogen atom:** These may be classified as mono, di or polyhalogen compounds depending on whether they contain one, two or more halogen atoms in their structures. For example,

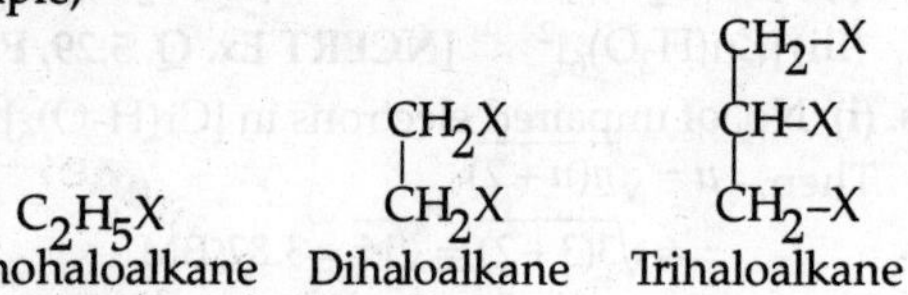

Monohaloalkane Dihaloalkane Trihaloalkane

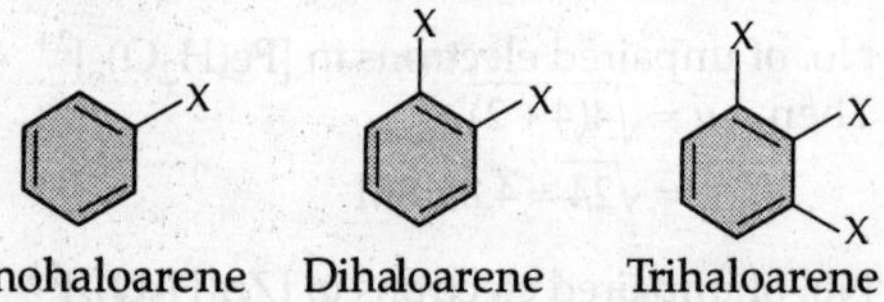

Monohaloarene Dihaloarene Trihaloarene

Dihalogen compounds may be further classified as:

(i) Geminal dihalides: Two halogen atoms are attached to the same carbon atom. For example,

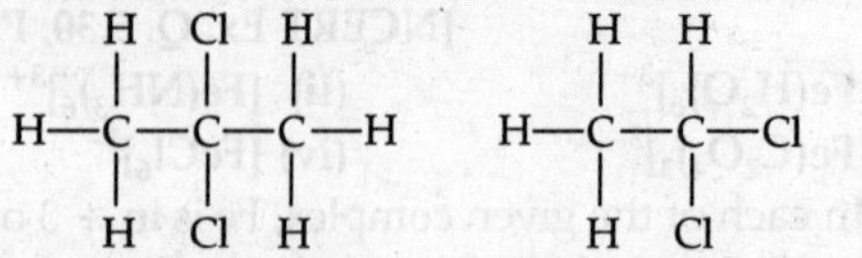

Isopropylidene chloride (2, 2–Dichloropropane) Ethylidene chloride (1, 1–Dichloroethane)

(ii) Vicinal dihalides: Two halogen atoms are attached to adjacent carbon atoms. For example,

$Cl-CH_2-CH_2-Cl$ Ethylene dichloride (1, 2-Dichloroethane)

$CH_3-CH(Cl)-CH_2-Cl$ Propylene dichloride (1, 2-Dichloropropane)

- **On the basis of sp^3 hybridisation:**

(i) Haloalkanes or alkyl halides (R—X): General formula is C_nH_{2n+1} X. They are further classified as primary, secondary and tertiary haloalkanes.

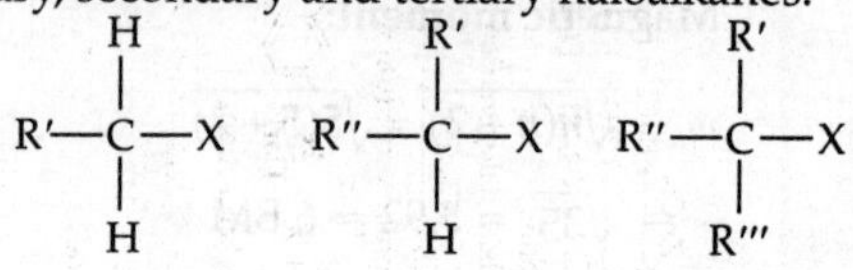

Primary haloalkane Secondary haloalkane Tertiary haloalkane

(ii) Allylic halides: Halogen is bonded to allylic carbon.

$CH_2=CH-CH-X$ Allyl halide (3-Halo–1–propene)

3-Halocylohex–1–ene

(iii) Benzylic halides: Halogen atom is bonded to an sp^3 hybridized carbon atom next to an aromatic ring.

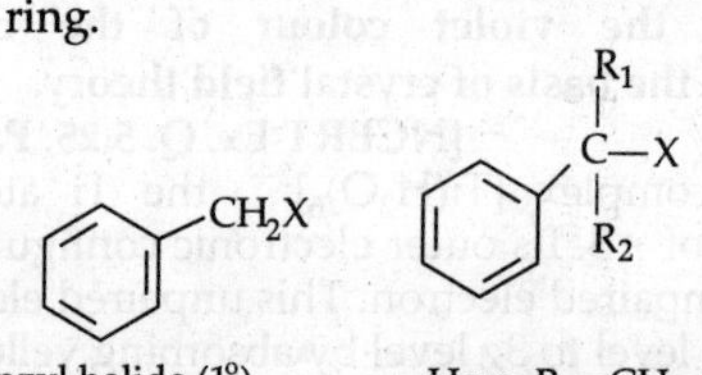

Benzyl halide (1°) Here, $R_1=CH_3$, $R_2=H$ (2°) or $R_1=R_2=CH_3$ (3°)

- **On the basis of sp^2 hybridization:**

(i) Vinylic halides: Halogen is bonded to one of the carbon atoms of a vinylic carbon.

$CH_2=CH-X$ Vinyl halide

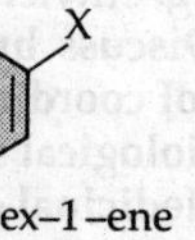

1–Halocylohex–1–ene

(ii) Aryl halides: Halogen atom is directly bonded to sp^2 hybridized carbon atom of an aromatic ring.

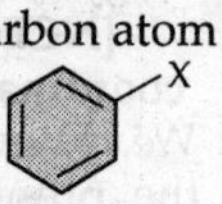

Halobenzene

Nomenclature

- **Common and IUPAC name of some halides:**

Table 1

Structure	IUPAC Name	Common names
CH_3Cl	Chloromethane	Methyl chloride
CH_3CH_2Cl	Chloroethane	Ethyl chloride

- Reactions :
  - (a) Nucleophilic substitution
    - (i) Resonance effect

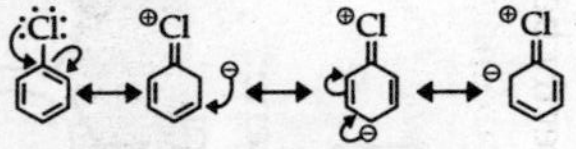

    - (ii) Hybridisation of C in C-X bond : Haloalkane –sp³; Haloarence –sp²
    - (iii) Phenyl cation unstabilised by resonance

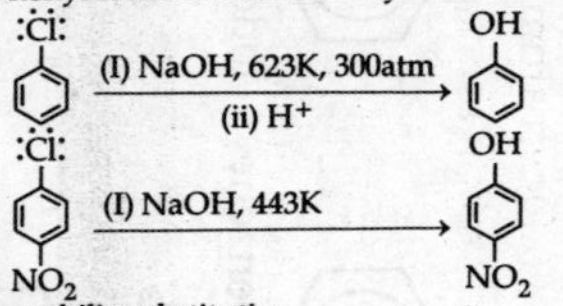

  - (b) Electrophilic substitution

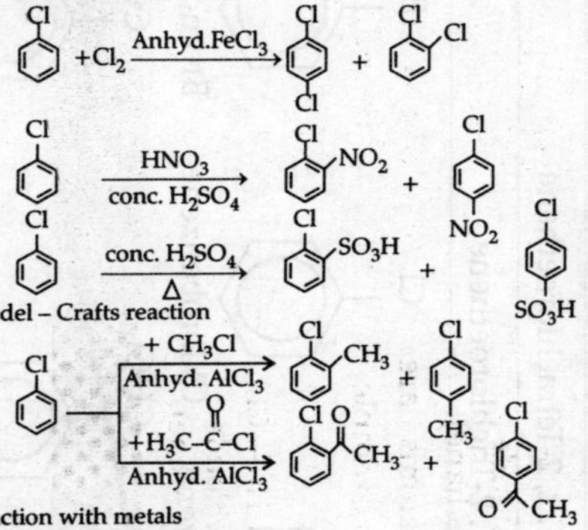

  - (c) Reaction with metals
    - Wurtz – Fitting reaction
    - Fittig reaction

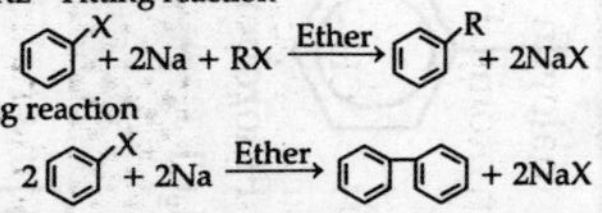

- No. of halogen atoms

C_2H_5X Monohaloalkane; $CH_2X–CH_2X$ Dihaloalkane

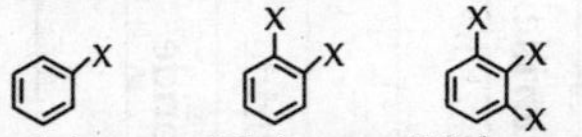

- Compounds containing sp^3 C–X bond
  - (a) Alkyl halides

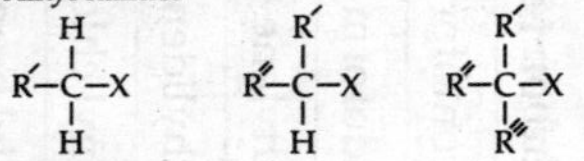

  - (b) Allylic halides

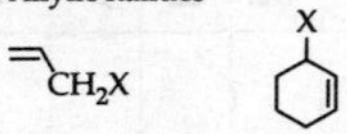

  - (c) Benzylic halides

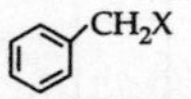

- Compounds containing sp^2 C–X bond
  - (a) Vinylic halides
  - (b) Aryl halides

- Nomenclature
  - Common name : Alkyl group followed by halides. Dihalogen derivatives, prefixes o–, m–, p– are used.
  - IUPAC name : Numerals are used.
- Nature of C –X bond
  - : Carbon –halogen bond is polarised.

$$>\overset{\delta+}{C}–\overset{\delta-}{X}$$

=>Preparation

- From alcohol :

$$R–OH + HCl \xrightarrow{ZnCl_2} R–Cl + H_2O$$
$$3R–OH + PX_3 \longrightarrow 3R–X + H_3PO_3$$
$$ROH + PCl_5 \longrightarrow R–Cl + POCl_3 + HCl$$

- From hydrocarbons :
  - (a) By free radical halogenation

$$CH_3CH_2CH_2CH_3 \xrightarrow{Cl_2/UV} CH_3CH_2CH_2CH_2Cl + CH_3CH_2CHClCH_3$$

  - (b) By electrophilic substitution

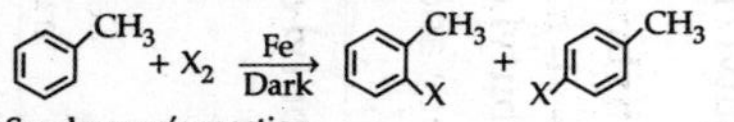

  - (c) Sandmeyer's reaction

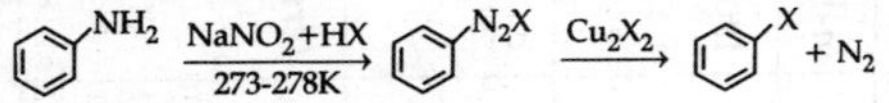

  - (d) From alkenes

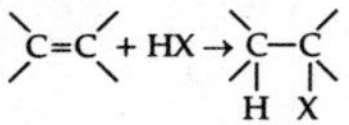

$$H_2C=CH_2 + Br_2 \xrightarrow{CCl_4} BrCH_2–CH_2Br$$

- Halogen exchange :

$$R–X + NaI \rightarrow R – I + NaX$$

=>Properties

- Physical : Colourless, volatile, sweet smell.
  - Lower members are gases at room temperature while higher are solids.
  - B.P : RI > RBr > RCl > RF.
  - M.P : Para isomers have high m.p. than ortho and meta – isomers.
  - Density : Increases with increase in number of C/X atoms and atomic masses of the X atoms.
  - Solubility : Very slightly soluble in water.
- Chemical :
  - (a) Nucleophilic substitution

$$\bar{Nu} + >\overset{\delta+}{C}–\overset{\delta-}{X} \longrightarrow >C – Nu + X^-$$

For S_N2 reaction →
Tertiary, Secondary, Primary
← For S_N1 reaction

  - (b) Elimination reaction

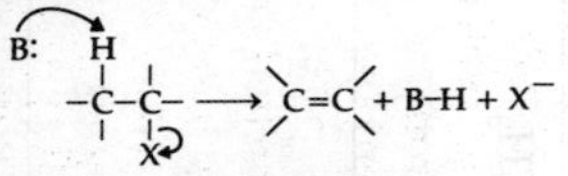

B = Base; X = Leaving group

  - (c) Reaction with metals

$$CH_3CH_2Br + Mg \longrightarrow CH_3CH_2MgBr$$

Wurtz reaction :

$$2RX + 2Na \xrightarrow{Dry\ ether} RR + 2NaX$$

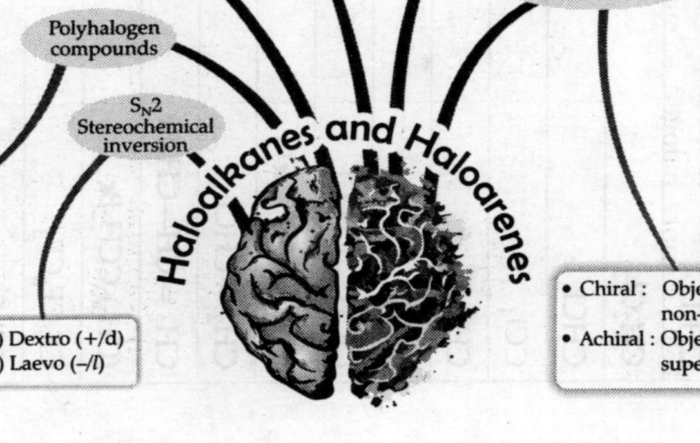

- Manufacture of refrigerants and propellants.
- Cleaning fluid.

- Solvent for fats, alkaloids, I etc.
- Production of freon.

For aerosol propellants, refrigeration and air conditioning purposes.

- Paint remover.
- Propellant in aerosols.
- Metal cleaning and finishing solvent.

(a) Dextro (+/d)
(b) Laevo (–/l)

- Chiral : Objects which are non-superimposable.
- Achiral : Objects which are superimposable.

Trace the Mind Map
- First Level
- Second Level
- Third Level

$CH_3-CH_2-CH_2Cl$	1-Chloropropane	*n*-Propyl chloride
$CH_3-\underset{\underset{Cl}{\vert}}{CH}-CH_3$	2-Chloropropane	Isopropyl chloride
$CH_3-CH_2-CH_2-CH_2Cl$	1-Chlorobutane	*n*-Butyl chloride
$CH_3-\underset{\underset{CH_3}{\vert}}{CH}-CH_2Cl$	1-Chloro-2-methyl propane	Isobutyl chloride
$CH_3-CH_2-\underset{\underset{Cl}{\vert}}{CH}-CH_3$	2-Chlorobutane	*Sec.* butyl chloride
$CH_3-\overset{\overset{CH_3}{\vert}}{\underset{\underset{Cl}{\vert}}{C}}-CH_3$	2-Chloro-2-methyl propane	*tert* butyl chloride
CH_3F	Fluoromethane	Methyl fluoride
CH_3Br	Bromomethane	Methyl bromide
CH_3I	Iodomethane	Methyl iodide
CH_2Cl_2	Dichloromethane	Methylene dichloride
$CHCl_3$	Trichloromethane	Chloroform
CCl_4	Tetrachloromethane	Carbon tetrachloride
$CHBr_3$	Tribromomethane	Bromoform
CHI_3	Triiodomethane	Iodoform
$ClCH_2-CH_2Cl$	1, 2-Dichloroethane	Ethylene dichloride
CH_3CHCl_2	1, 1-Dichloroethane	Ethylidene chloride
$CH_2=CHCl$	Chloroethene	Vinyl chloride
$CH_2=CH-CH_2Br$	3-Bromopropene	Allyl bromide
$(CH_3)_3CCH_2Br$	1-Bromo-2, 2-dimethylpropane	neo-pentylbromide
$CF_3CF_2CF_3$	Octafluoropropane	Perfluoropropane
CCl_2F_2	Dichlorodifluoromethane	Freon
$CHCl_2-CHCl_2$	1, 1, 2, 2-Tetrachloroethane	Acetylene tetrachloride
$CHCl=CCl_2$	1, 1, 2-Trichloroethene	Acetylene trichloride

Benzene

Fluorobenzene

Chlorobenzene

Bromobenzene

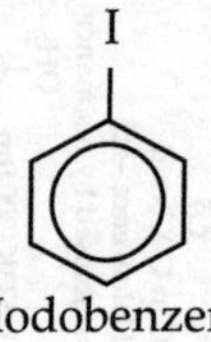
Iodobenzene

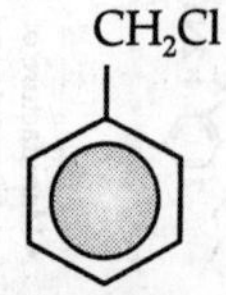

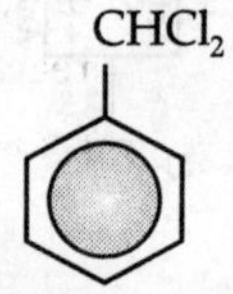

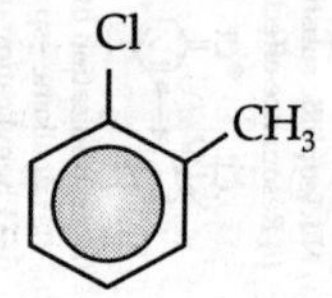

IUPAC name	1-Chloro –1 – phenylmethane	Dichlorophenyl methane	Trichlorophenyl methane	1– Chloro – 2 – methyl benzene
Common name	(Benzyl chloride)	(Benzyldene chloride) (Benzal chloride)	(Benzotrichloride)	(2 – Chlorotoluene)

Methods of Preparation of Haloalkenes

(a) From alcohols: Alkyl halides are prepared from alcohols, which are easily accessible. This method cannot be used to obtain aryl halides as the carbon-oxygen bond in phenols has a partial double bond character and it is difficult to break that bond.

$$R - OH + HX \xrightarrow{\text{anhydrous } ZnCl_2/HCl} R - X + H_2O$$
$(X = Cl, Br, I)$

$$R - OH + NaBr + H_2SO_4 \longrightarrow R - Br + NaHSO_4 + H_2O$$

$$3R - OH + PX_3 \longrightarrow 3R - X + H_3PO_3 \ (X = Cl, Br)$$

$$R - OH + PCl_5 \longrightarrow R - Cl + POCl_3 + HCl$$

$$R - OH \xrightarrow[X_2 = Br_2, I_2]{\text{Red } P/X_2} R - X$$

$$R - OH + SOCl_2 \longrightarrow R - Cl + SO_2\uparrow + HCl\uparrow$$

The reactions of primary and secondary alcohols with HX requires the presence of the anhydrous $ZnCl_2$.

(b) From hydrocarbons: By free radical halogenation.

$$\underset{\text{n-Butane}}{CH_3CH_2CH_2CH_3} \xrightarrow[\text{Or heat}]{Cl_2/\text{UV Light}} \underset{n\text{-Butyl chloride}}{CH_3CH_2CH_2CH_2Cl} + \underset{\text{Sec.-Butyl chloride}}{CH_3CH_2CHClCH_3} \text{ (Major Product)}$$

(c) From alkenes:

(i) Addition of hydrogen halide:

$$>C = C< + H - X \longrightarrow >\underset{X}{C} - \underset{H}{C}< \quad (X = Cl, Br, I)$$

$$R - CH = CH_2 + \overset{\delta+}{H} - \overset{\delta-}{X} \xrightarrow{\text{Markovnikov's Rule}} R - \underset{X}{CH} - CH_3$$

$$R - CH = CH_2 + H - Br \xrightarrow[\text{Anti Markovnikov's addition}]{\text{Benzoyl peroxide}} R - CH_2 - CH_2 - Br$$

(ii) Addition of Halogens:

$$\underset{H}{\overset{H}{>}}C = C\underset{H}{\overset{H}{<}} + Br_2 \xrightarrow{CCl_4} \underset{\text{vic-Dibromide}}{BrCH_2 - CH_2Br}$$

(d) Halide Exchange:

(i) Finkelstein Reaction: Alkyl iodides are often prepared by the reaction of alkyl chlorides/ bromides with NaI in dry acetone is prepared by this reaction.

$$R - X + NaI \xrightarrow{\text{Dry acetone}} R - I + NaX\downarrow \ (X = Cl, Br)$$

(ii) Swarts Reaction: The synthesis of alkyl fluorides is best accomplished by heating an alkyl chloride/ bromide in the presence of a metallic fluoride such as AgF, Hg_2F_2, CoF_2 or SbF_3 by this reaction.

$$R - X \xrightarrow{AgF,\ Hg_2F_2,\ CoF_2 \text{ or } SbF_3} R - F$$

- **Nature of C-X bond in haloalkanes:** The carbon-halogen bond is polarised. Carbon atom holds partial positive charge and halogen atom holds partial negative charge. This occurs due to difference in electronegativity. Halogens are more electronegative than carbon. Size of the halogen atoms increases down the group from fluorine to iodine. Carbon-halogen bond length also increases from C-F to C-I.
- **Physical properties of haloalkanes:** Haloalkanes are colourless when pure but compounds of bromine and iodine are coloured.

(i) Melting and boiling points: Due to polar and strong dipole-dipole interactions between the molecules of halogen derivatives have high B.P. and M.P. This increase in B.P. and M.P. than their parent hydrocarbon depends on increasing size, mass of halogens and magnitude of Van Der Waals forces of attractions. The increasing order is RF< RCl < RBr < RI. With respect to isomeric alkyl halides, B.P. decreases with increase in branching due to less surface area and weak intermolecular forces.

(ii) Density: It increases with increase in carbon atoms, halogen atoms and atomic mass of the halogen atoms.

(iii) Solubility: Haloalkanes are insoluble in water but are soluble in organic solvents.

- **Chemical properties of haloalkanes:** Reactivity of haloalkanes, depends on the C-X bond cleavage. Higher the bond dissociation energy of C-X bond, lesser will be the reactivity. Dissociation energy of C-X bond decreases with increase in the halogen size, *i.e.,* C–Cl > C–Br > C–I. Reactivity order of haloalkanes would be:

Chlorides < Bromides < Iodides

There are three types of chemical reactions with haloalkanes:

(a) Nucleophilic substitution reactions: When an atom or group of atoms is replaced by a nucleophile the reaction is called as nucleophilic substitution reaction, *e.g.,*

$$>\overset{\delta+}{C} - \overset{\delta-}{X} + \underset{\text{Nucleophile}}{:\overset{\ominus}{Z}} \longrightarrow \underset{\text{Product}}{>\overset{\delta+}{C} - \overset{\delta-}{Z}} + \underset{\text{Leaving group}}{:\overset{\ominus}{X}}$$

The following is the order of reactivity RCl < RBr < RI

$RCH_2X < R_2CHX < R_3CX$

$R-X$ (Alkyl halide) reacts as follows:

$$R-X \xrightarrow{KOH(aq)} R-OH + KX \quad \text{(Alcohol)}$$

$$R-X \xrightarrow{\overset{+}{Na}\overset{-}{OR}} R-O-R' + NaX \quad \text{(Ether)}$$

$$R-X \xrightarrow{KCN(alc.)} R-CN + KX \quad \text{(Alkyl cyanide)}$$

$$R-X \xrightarrow{AgCN} R-NC + AgX \quad \text{(Alkyl isocyanide)}$$

$$R-X \xrightarrow{KNO_2} R-O-N=O \quad \text{(Alkyl nitrite)}$$

$$R-X \xrightarrow{AgNO_2} R-NO_2 \quad \text{(Nitroalkane)}$$

$$R-X \xrightarrow{R'-\overset{O}{\overset{\|}{C}}-O-Ag} R-\overset{O}{\overset{\|}{C}}-O-R' + AgX \quad \text{(Ester)}$$

$$R-X \xrightarrow{LiAlH_4} R-H \quad \text{(Alkane)}$$

$$R-X \xrightarrow{NH_3} R-NH_2 + H-X \quad \text{(Amine)}$$

$$R-X \xrightarrow{NaSH} R-SH + NaX \quad \text{(Thioalcohol)}$$

$$R-X \xrightarrow{\overset{+}{Na}\overset{-}{C}\equiv CH} R-C\equiv CH + NaX \quad \text{(Higher alkyne)}$$

(b) Reaction with metals: Most organic chlorides, bromides and iodides react with certain metals to give compounds containing carbon-metal bonds. Such compounds are known as organo-metallic compounds. The most important class of organo-metallic compounds is alkyl magnesium halide, RMgX, referred as Grignard Reagent which is prepared as below:

(1) Reaction with magnesium:

$$\underset{\text{Alkyl halide}}{R-X} + Mg \xrightarrow{\text{Dry ether}} \underset{\text{Alkyl magnesium halide (Grignard reagent)}}{RMgX}$$

$$CH_3-CH_2-Br + Mg \xrightarrow{\text{Dry ether}} \underset{\text{Ethyl magnesium bromide}}{CH_3-CH_2-MgBr}$$

(2) Reduction with sodium (Wurtz reaction): Alkyl halides react with sodium in dry ether to give hydrocarbons containing double the number of carbon atoms present in the halide.

$$R-X + 2Na + X-R \xrightarrow{\text{Dry ether}} R-R + 2NaX$$

$$CH_3-CH_2-Cl + 2Na + Cl-CH_2-CH_3 \xrightarrow{\text{Dry ether}} \underset{n\text{-Butane}}{CH_3-CH_2-CH_2-CH_3} + 2NaCl$$

(3) Reduction:

$$R-X + 2(H) \xrightarrow{Zn/HCl(conc.)} R-H + H-X$$

$$CH_3-CH_2-Cl + 2(H) \xrightarrow{Zn/HCl(conc.)} CH_3-CH_3 + HCl$$

(4) Elimination reaction: Alkyl halides undergo β-elimination of hydrogen atom from β-carbon atom and halogen atom to form alkenes on being heated with KOH (alc.) or KNH_2, *e.g.*,

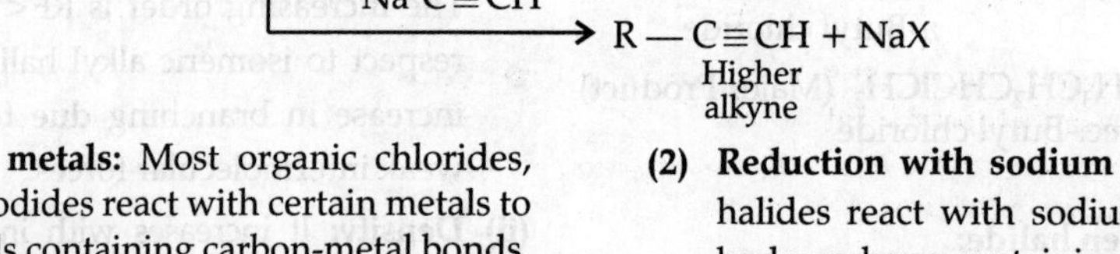

2-Chloro-2-methylpropane → 2-methylpropene

The reaction is called *dehydrohalogenation.*

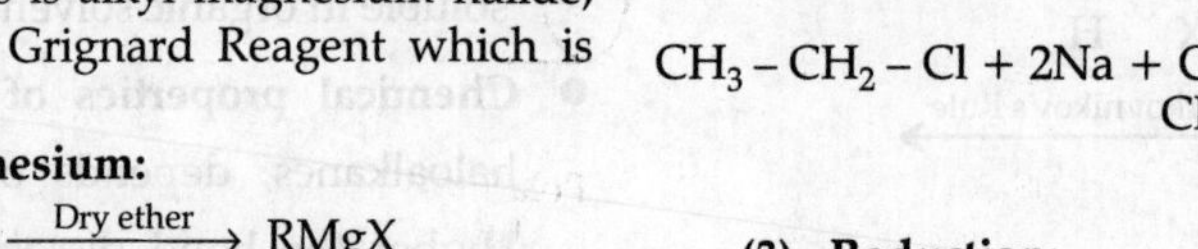

Ethene

- **Reactivity of S_N1 and S_N2 mechanisms:** S = Substitution, N = Nucleophilic, 2 = Bimolecular, 1 = Unimolecular. Nucleophilic substitution seldom occurs exclusively by one mechanism only. With a given halogen, primary, secondary and tertiary halides shows opposite order of reactivity in the two mechanisms.

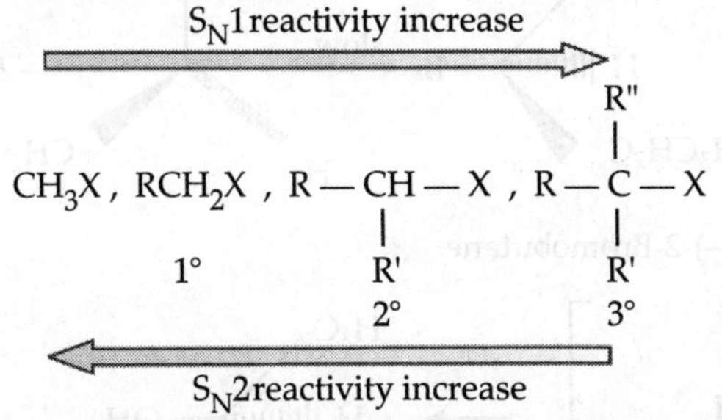

- **Stereoisomerism:** Isomerism exhibited by two or more compounds with the same molecular and structural formula, but different spatial arrangements of atoms or groups in space is called stereoisomerism.
- **Plane-polarised light:** The beam of light whose oscillations or vibrations are confined to one plane only is called plane-polarised light. It is obtained by passing a monochromatic light (light of single wavelength) through a nicol prism.
- **Nicol prism:** A nicol prism is a special type of prism made from calcite, a special crystalline form of calcium carbonate. It is a device for producing plane polarised light.
- **Optical rotation:** Property of rotating the plane of polarisation either towards left or right.
- **Dextrorotatory:** Those substances which rotate the plane of polarisation of light towards right, *i.e.*, in clockwise direction are called dextrorotatory. It is conventionally given a positive sign. It is denoted by '*d*' and a positive (+) sign is placed before the degree of rotation.
- **Laevorotatory:** Those substances which rotate the plane of polarisation of light towards the left, *i.e.*, in anticlockwise direction are called laevorotatory. It is denoted by '*l*' and a negative (–) sign is placed before the degree of rotation.
- **Specific rotation:** The extent of experimentally observed angle of rotation (optical rotation, represented by α_{obs}) of a substance depends upon the following factors:
  (i) nature of substance,
  (ii) wavelength of the light used,
  (iii) the number of optically active molecules in the path of light beam (which depends upon concentration of sample),
  (iv) length of polarimeter tube,
  (v) solvent used.

Specific rotation $[\alpha]_D^{t^oC}$

$$= \frac{\text{observed rotation } (\alpha_{obs})}{\text{length of tube } (d_m) \times \text{concentration of solution (g mol}^{-1})}$$

- **Optically active substances:** Those substances which rotate the plane of polarisation of plane-polarised light when it is passed through their solutions are called optically active substances. This phenomenon is called optical activity.
- **Polarimeter:** The angle of rotation by which the plane-polarised light is rotated, can be measured by using an instrument called polarimeter. A schematic diagram of a polarimeter is shown in the figure below:

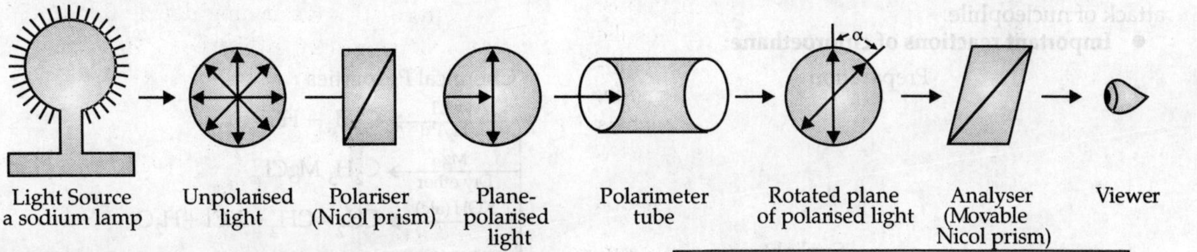

- **Enantiomers:** Those stereoisomers which are mirror images of each other but non-superimposable are called enantiomers, e.g., *d*(+) glucose and *l*(–) glucose are enantiomers.
- **Asymmetric molecule:** If all the four substituents attached to carbon are different, the resulting molecule will lack symmetry. Such a molecule is called asymmetric molecule. Asymmetry of molecule is responsible for optical activity in such organic compounds.
- **Symmetrical objects:** Those objects whose projections are superimposable on their mirror images are symmetrical objects, e.g., a sphere, a cube, a cone, a tetrahedron are all identical to their mirror images and can thus be superimposed.
- **Chiral:** An object which is non-superimposable on its mirror image is said to be chiral. The property of being chiral is known as chirality. A chiral object is also called dissymmetric. e.g.,

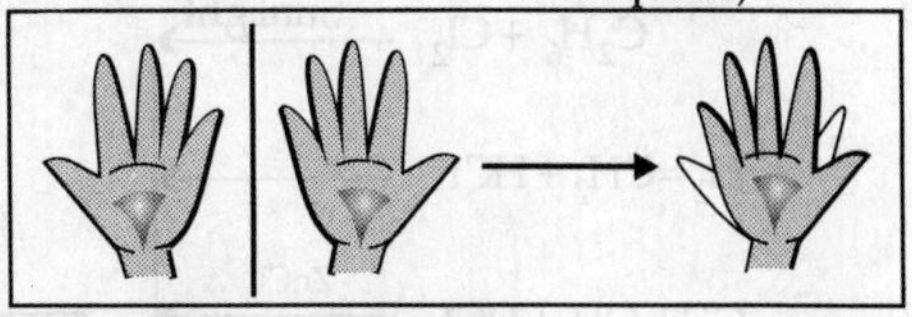

Non-superimposable hands

- **Achiral:** Achiral objects are those objects which are superimposable on their mirror images.
- **Asymmetric carbon (Chiral carbon):** The carbon atom which is attached with four different groups of atoms is called asymmetric or chiral carbon atom.
- **Racemic mixture:** A mixture containing equal amounts of enantiomers which does not show any optical activity. It is optically inactive due to external compensation.
- **Racemisation:** The process of conversion of an enantiomer into racemic mixture is known as racemisation.
- **Absolute configuration:** The three dimensional structure of a molecule that has one or more centres of chirality is referred to its absolute configuration.

- **Diastereoisomers:** Those pairs of stereoisomers which are not mirror images of each other and are non-superimposable.
  - (i) Diastereoisomers have different physical properties.
  - (ii) Diastereoisomers differ in magnitude of specific rotation.
  - (iii) A compound with two chiral centres does not always have four stereoisomers.
- **Example of racemisation in S_N1 mechanism:** When optically active alkyl halide undergoes S_N1 mechanism, it is accompanied by racemisation because intermediate carbocation formed is sp^2-hybridized and polar. Nucleophile (OH^-) has equal probability of attacking it from either side leading to formation of equal amount of dextro and laevo-rotatory alcohols. As the products of S_N1 mechanism has both inversion as well as rotation, the products formed by this reaction would be racemic mixture of alcohols.

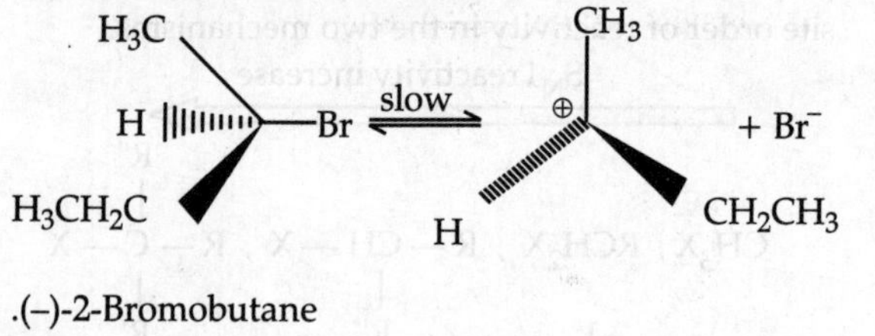

.(–)-2-Bromobutane

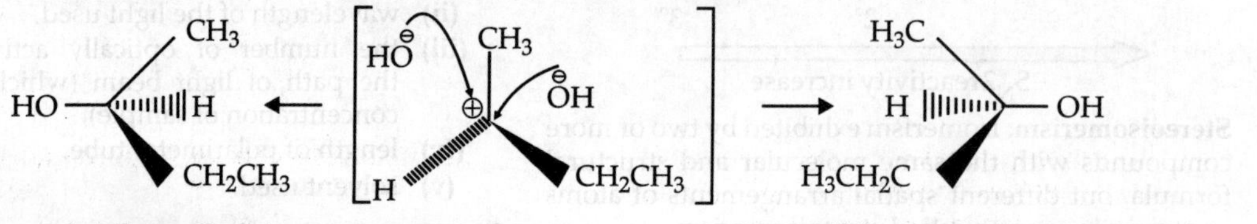

(+)-Butan-2-ol (-)-Butan-2-ol

- **Meso compounds:** Those compounds which have two or more (even number) chiral carbon atoms and have an internal plane of symmetry are called meso compounds. They are optically inactive due to internal compensation.
- **Example of inversion in S_N2 mechanism:** When optically active *d* (+) alkyl halide is treated with OH^-, we get optically active *l* (–) alcohol due to back side attack of nucleophile.

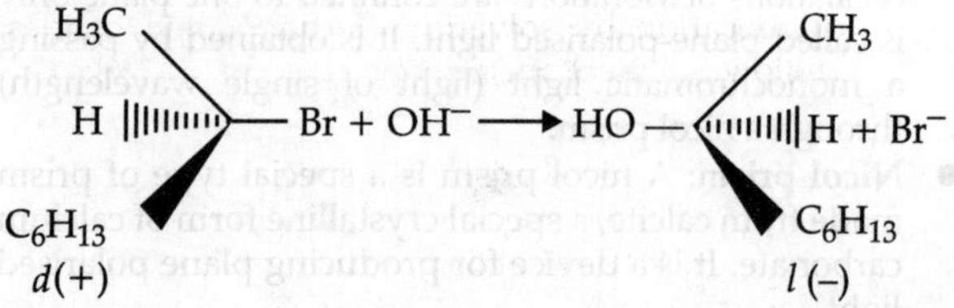

When *d*(+)-2-bromooctane is reacted with NaOH, *l*(–)-2-octanol is formed. Thus, S_N2 mechanism leads to inversion of configuration. This inversion is called Walden's inversion.

- **Important reactions of chloroethane:**

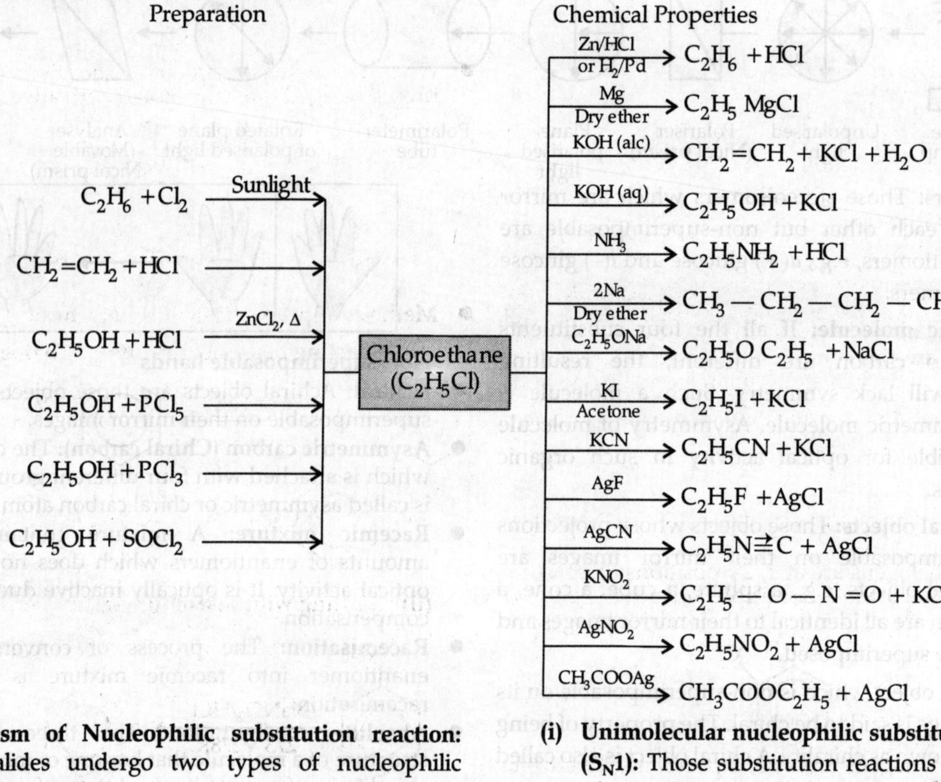

- **Mechanism of Nucleophilic substitution reaction:** Alkyl halides undergo two types of nucleophilic substitution reactions.

(i) **Unimolecular nucleophilic substitution reaction (S_N1):** Those substitution reactions in which rate of reaction depends upon the concentration of only one of the reactants, i.e., alkyl halides are called S_N1 reactions, e.g., hydrolysis of tertiary butyl chloride follows S_N1 reaction. This reaction takes place in two steps:

STEP I:

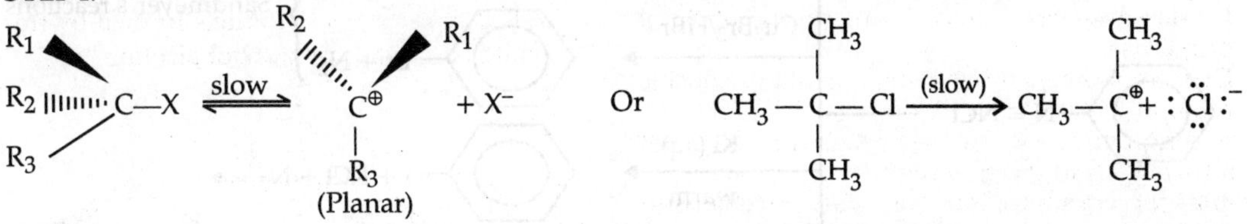

STEP II:

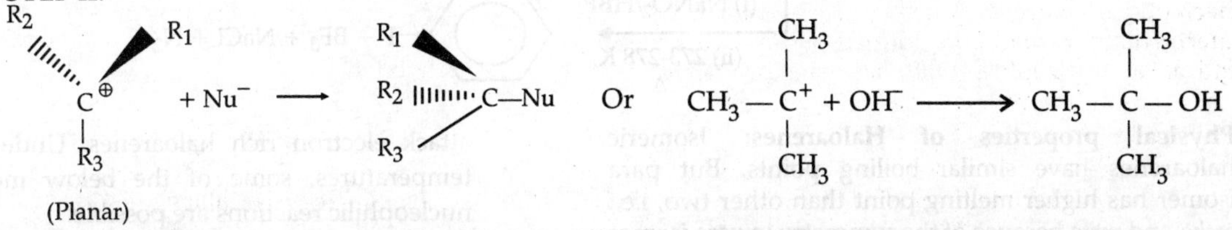

The slowest step is the rate determining step which involves one species only. Therefore, rate of reaction depends only on the concentration of tertiary butyl chloride. Polar protic solvents like water, alcohol favours S_N1 because they stabilize carbocation by solvation. Tertiary alkyl halides follow S_N1 mechanism.

(ii) Biomolecular nucleophilic substitution reaction (S_N2): The reaction whose rate depends on the concentration of two species, alkyl halide and nucleophile. They involve one step mechanism. Back side attack of nucleophile and departing of leaving group takes place simultaneously.

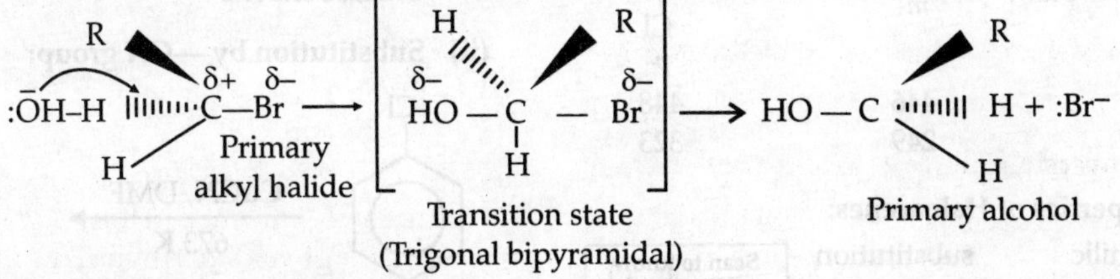

Non-polar solvents favour S_N2 mechanism.
Primary halides follow S_N2 mechanism.

Mnemonics

Concept: S_N1 reaction
Mnemonics: Curt - 1
Interpretations: Carbocation intermediate
- Unimolecular Reaction.
- Racemic mixture is obtained.
- Two steps process.
- Ist order kinetics.

Haloarenes

- Haloarenes are the compounds formed by replacing one or more hydrogen atoms in an aromatic ring with halogen atoms. For example, monohalogen derivative

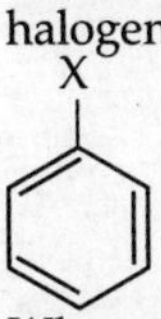

(X = F, Cl, Br, or I).

- When two halogens are at 1, 2- positions of benzene ring, it is called ortho-substituted derivative. e.g.,

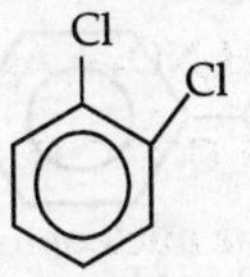

- When two halogens are at 1, 3-positions of benzene ring, it is called *meta*-substituted derivative e.g.,

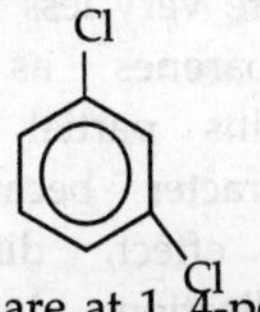

- When two halogens are at 1, 4-positions of benzene ring, it is called *para*-substituted derivative. e.g.,

- **Methods of preparation of Haloarenes:**

(i) Reacting benzene directly with halogen:

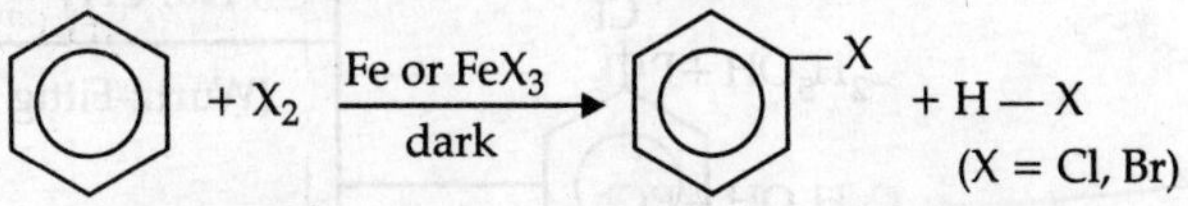

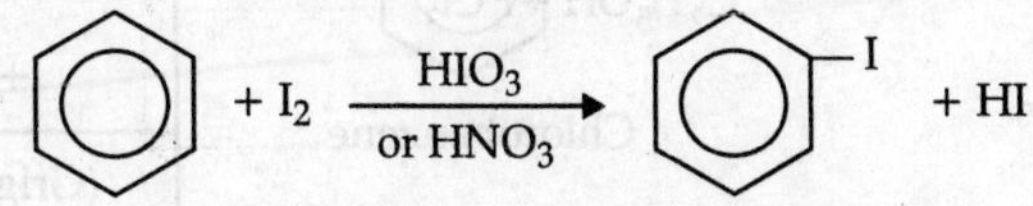

(ii) Starting with diazonium salts:

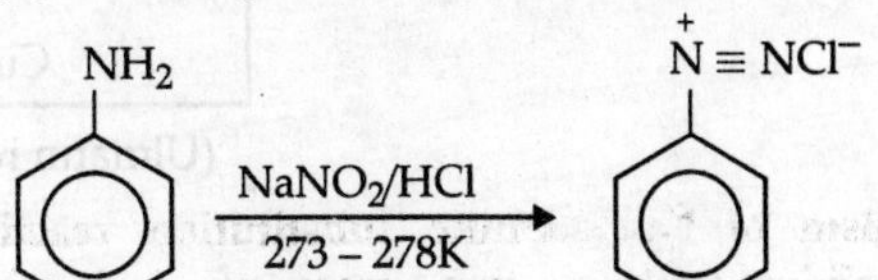

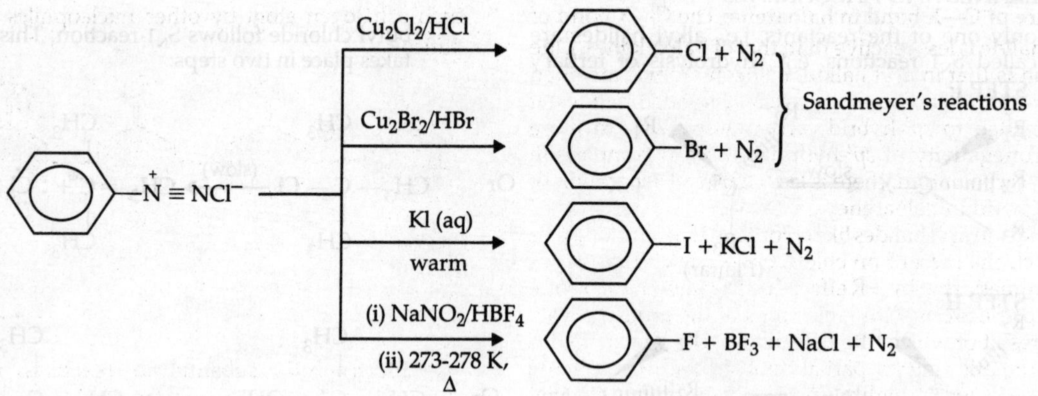

- **Physical properties of Haloarenes:** Isomeric haloarenes have similar boiling points. But para isomer has higher melting point than other two, i.e., *ortho*-and *meta*-because of the symmetry in *para*-isomer which occupies the crystal lattice better than *ortho* and *meta* isomers.

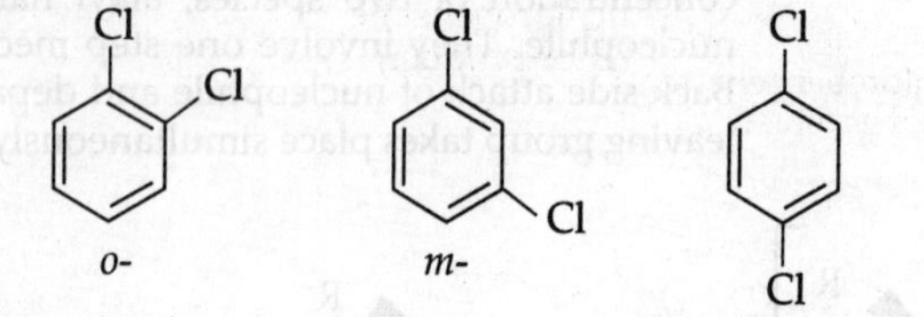

	o-	m-	p-
b.p. (K)	453	446	448
m.p. (K)	256	249	323

- **Chemical properties of Haloarenes:**

(a) Nucleophilic substitution reactions are very less possible with haloarenes as C—X bond attains partial double bond character because of resonance effect, difference in hybridization, instability of the formed phenyl cation. Due to these repulsions, it makes difficult for electron rich nucleophile to attack electron rich haloarenes. Under higher temperatures, some of the below mentioned nucleophilic reactions are possible.

Scan to know more about this topic

Haloalkanes and Haloarenes

(i) Substitution by —OH group (Dow's process):

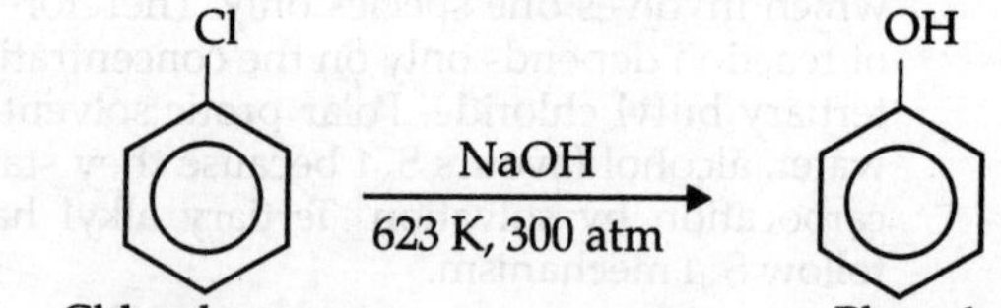

(ii) Substitution by —CN group:

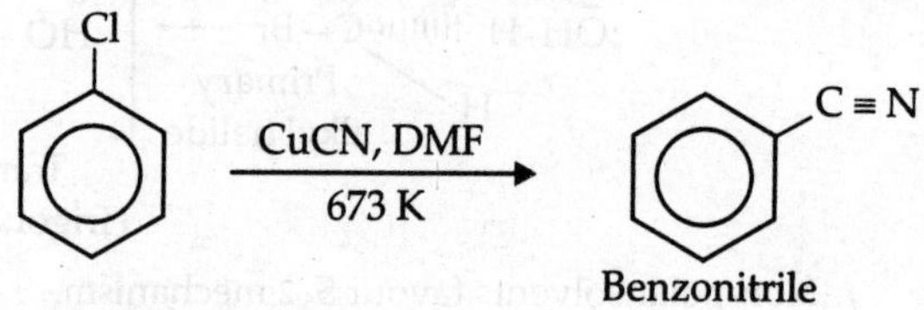

(iii) Substitution by —NH_2 group:

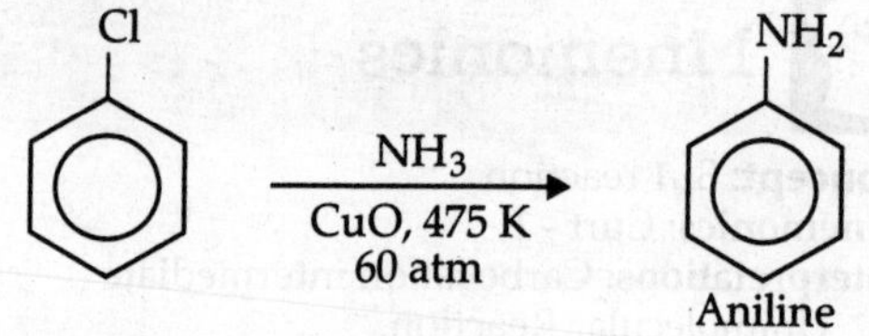

(iv) Reaction with metals:

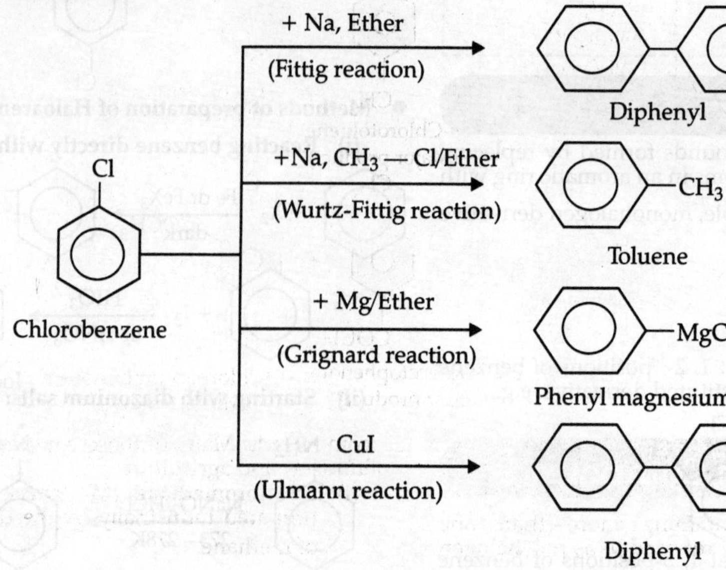

- **Nature of C—X bond in haloarene**: The C—X bond of aryl halide is less reactive than that of haloalkanes. One reason is that in aryl halide, halogen atom is attached to sp^2-hybrid carbon atom whereas in alkyl halides, it is attached to sp^3-hybrid carbon atom. Due to more electronegativity of sp^2-hybrid carbon in comparison to sp^3-carbon atom, there is less charge in separation of C—X bond in haloarene.
Secondly in aryl halides like chlorobenzene, the lone pair of electrons present on chlorine atom migrate towards the aromatic ring by +R effect due to conjugation of lone pair of electrons with π-electrons of the aromatic ring. As a result of which, the halogen atom is attached with the aromatic ring by partial double bond. The phenyl cation formed is highly unstable. The replacement of such a halogen atom by other nucleophiles becomes difficult.

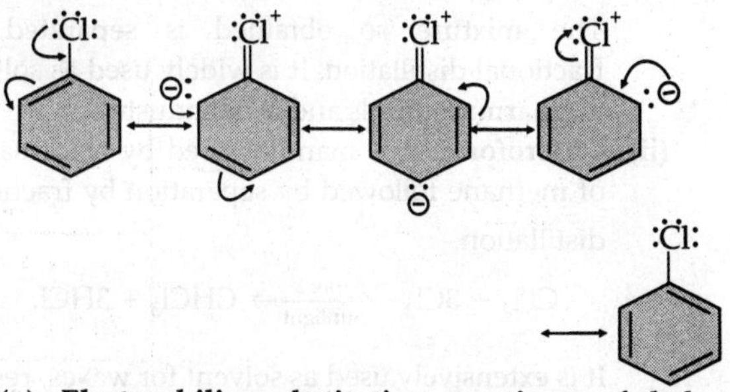

(v) Electrophilic substitution reactions of haloarenes: It takes place at ortho and para positions:

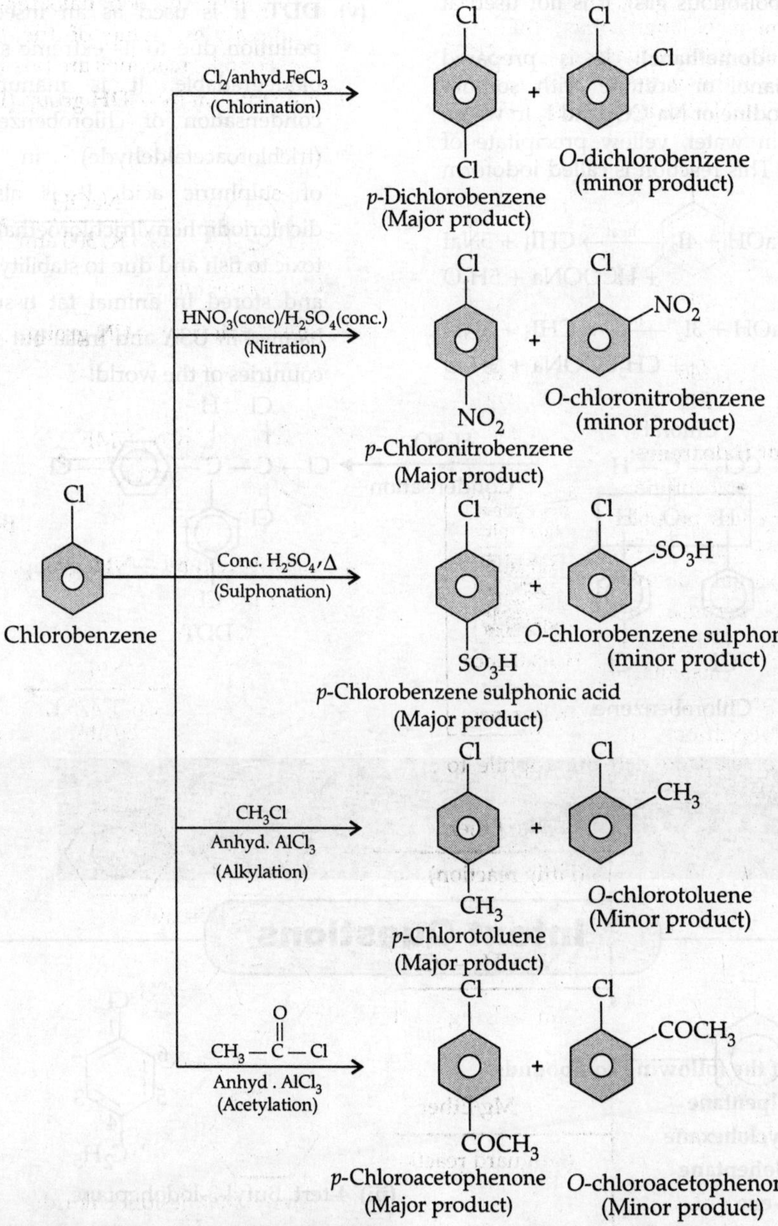

Polyhalogen Compounds

- Carbon compounds containing more than one halogen atoms are usually referred to as polyhalogen compounds. Many of those compounds are useful in industry and agriculture.

(i) Dichloromethane (Methylene chloride): It is prepared industrially by the direct chlorination of methane.

$$CH_4 + 2Cl_2 \xrightarrow{hv} CH_2Cl_2 + 2HCl$$

The mixture so obtained is separated by fractional distillation. It is widely used as solvent in pharmaceuticals and food industry.

(ii) Chloroform: It is manufactured by chlorination of methane followed by separation by fractional distillation.

$$CH_4 + 3Cl_2 \xrightarrow[\text{Sunlight}]{hv} CHCl_3 + 3HCl.$$

It is extensively used as solvent for waxes, resins, rubber, fats, etc. It was earlier used as anaesthetic and swallowing agent, but due to formation of phosgene gas (poisonous gas), it is not used at present.

(iii) Iodoform (Triiodomethane): It is prepared by heating ethanol or acetone with sodium hydroxide and iodine or Na_2CO_3 and I_2 in water. It is insoluble in water, yellow precipitate of CHI_3 is formed. This reaction is called iodoform reaction.

$$CH_3CH_2OH + 6NaOH + 4I_2 \xrightarrow{\text{heat}} CHI_3 + 5NaI + HCOONa + 5H_2O$$

$$CH_3COCH_3 + 4NaOH + 3I_2 \xrightarrow{\text{heat}} CHI_3 + 3NaI + CH_3COONa + 3H_2O$$

It is used as an antiseptic for dressing wounds.

(iv) Carbon tetrachloride (Tetrachloromethane): It is prepared by chlorination of methane or by action of chlorine on CS_2 in the presence of $AlCl_3$ as catalyst.

$$CS_2 + 3Cl_2 \xrightarrow[\Delta]{AlCl_3} CCl_4 + SCl_2$$
(Sulphur dichloride)

$$CH_4 + 4Cl_2 \xrightarrow{hv} CCl_4 + 4HCl$$

It is highly used as a solvent for fats, resins, etc. It is used in fire extinguisher.

(v) DDT: It is used as an insecticide. It creates pollution due to its extreme stability. It is non-biodegradable. It is manufactured by the condensation of chlorobenzene with chloral (trichloroacetaldehyde) in the presence of sulphuric acid. It is also called *p, p'*-dichloriodiphenyltrichloroethane. It is highly toxic to fish and due to stability, it gets deposited and stored in animal fat tissues. Thus it was banned in USA and India but still used in other countries of the world.

Chloral

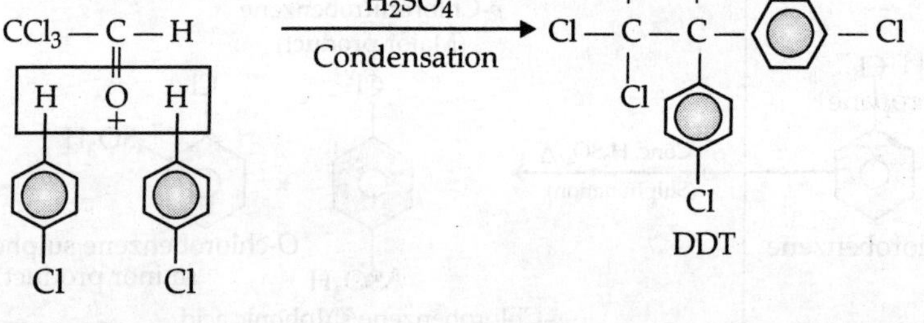

DDT

Chlorobenzene

NCERT CORNER

Intext Questions

Page - 163

Q. 6.1. Write structures of the following compounds:

(i) 2-Chloro-3-methylpentane
(ii) 1-Chloro-4-ethylcyclohexane
(iii) 4-tert. -butyl-3-iodoheptane
(iv) 1,4-Dibromobut-2-ene
(v) 1-Bromo-4-sec. butyl-2-methylbenzene

Ans. (i) 2-Chloro-3-methylpentane

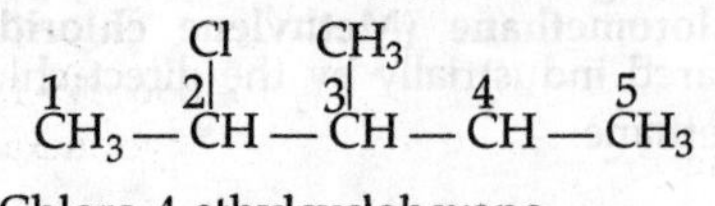

(ii) 1-Chloro-4-ethylcyclohexane

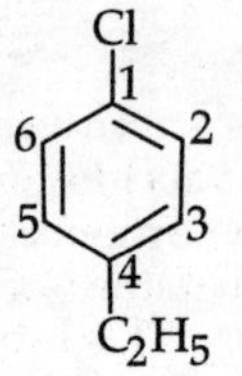

(iii) 4-tert. Butyl-3-iodoheptane

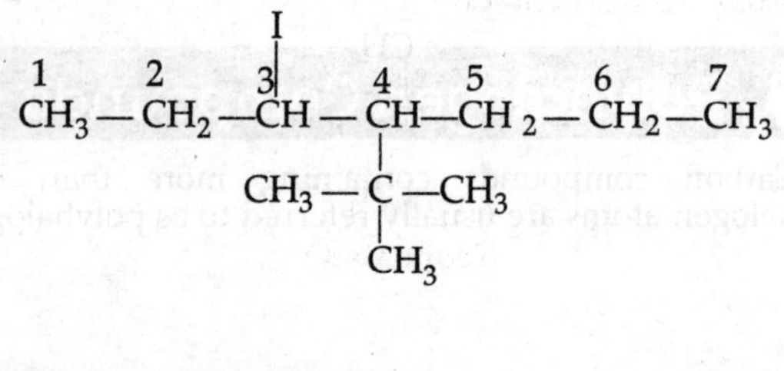

(iv) 1, 4-Dibromobut-2-ene

$$\overset{1}{Br-CH_2}-\overset{2}{CH}=\overset{3}{CH}-\overset{4}{CH_2}-Br$$

(v) 1-Bromo-4-sec. butyl-2-methylbenzene

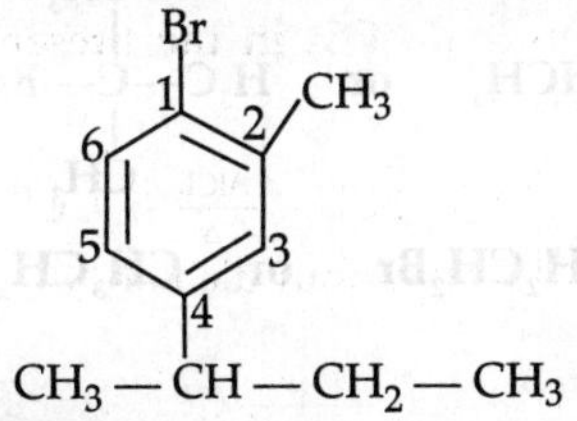

Page - 167

Q. 6.2. Why is sulphuric acid not used during the reaction of alcohols with KI?

Ans. $2KI + H_2SO_4 \rightarrow 2KHSO_4 + 2HI$

$$2HI + H_2SO_4 \rightarrow I_2 + SO_2 + H_2O$$

In the presence of sulphuric acid (H_2SO_4), KI produces HI which is an oxidizing agent, it oxidizes HI (produced in the reaction to I_2).

As a result, the reaction between alcohol and HI to produce alkyl iodide cannot occur. Therefore, sulphuric acid is not used during the reaction of alcohols with KI. Instead, a non-oxidizing acid such as H_3PO_4 is used.

Q. 6.3. Write structures of different dihalogen derivatives of propane.

Ans. There are four different dihalogen derivatives of propane. The structures of these derivatives are shown below.

(i) $Br-\underset{\substack{|\\Br}}{CH}-CH_2-CH_3$ ... as printed: Br on C-1

$$\overset{\displaystyle Br}{\overset{|}{Br-CH_2}}-CH_2-CH_3$$

1, 1-Dibromopropane

(ii) $$CH_3-\underset{\substack{|\\Br}}{\overset{\substack{Br\\|}}{C}}-CH_3$$

2, 2-Dibromopropane

(iii) $$Br-CH_2-\underset{\substack{|\\Br}}{CH}-CH_3$$

1, 2-Dibromopropane

(iv) $$Br-CH_2-CH_2-CH_2-Br$$

1, 3-Dibromopropane

Q. 6.4. Among the isomeric alkanes of molecular formula C_5H_{12}, identify the one that on photochemical chlorination yields

(i) A single monochloride.

(ii) Three isomeric monochlorides.

(iii) Four isomeric monochlorides.

Ans. (i) To have a single monochloride, there should be only one type of H-atom in the isomer of the alkane of the molecular formula C_5H_{12}. This is because, replacement of any H-atom leads to the formation of the same product. The isomer is neopentane.

$$CH_3-\underset{\substack{|\\CH_3}}{\overset{\substack{CH_3\\|}}{C}}-CH_3$$

Neopentane

(ii) To have three isomeric monochlorides, the isomer of the alkane of themolecular formula

$$\overset{1}{CH_3}-\overset{2}{CH_2}-\overset{3}{CH_2}-\overset{4}{CH_2}-\overset{5}{CH_3}$$

n-Pentane

C_5H_{12} should contain three different types of H-atoms.

Therefore, the isomer is *n*-pentane. It can be observed that there are three types of H-atoms labelled as *a, b* and *c* in *n*-pentane.

(iii) To have four isomeric monochlorides, the isomer of the alkane of the molecular formula C_5H_{12} should contain four different types of H-atoms. Therefore, the isomer is 2-methylbutane. It can be observed that there are four types of H-atoms labelled as *a, b, c,* and *d* in 2-methylbutane.

$$\overset{a}{CH_3}-\overset{b}{\underset{}{CH}}(\overset{a}{CH_3})-\overset{c}{CH_2}-\overset{d}{CH_3}$$

Q. 6.5. Draw the structures of major monohalo products in each of the following reactions:

(i) 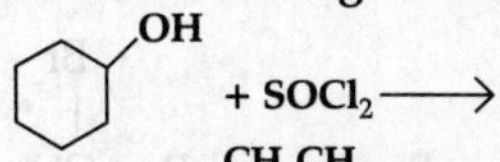

(ii) 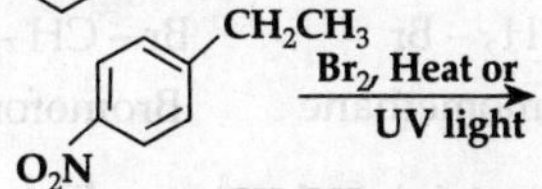

(iii) 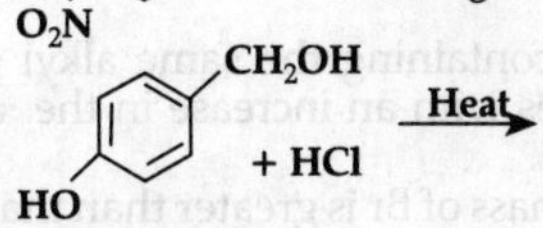

(iv) 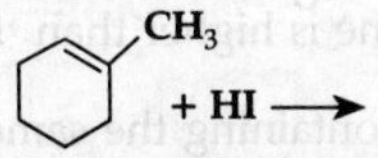

(v) $CH_3CH_2Br + NaI \longrightarrow$

(vi) 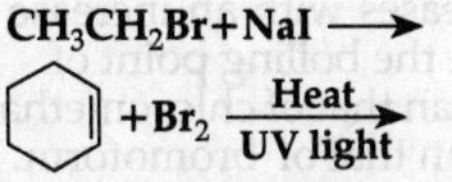

Ans.

(i) 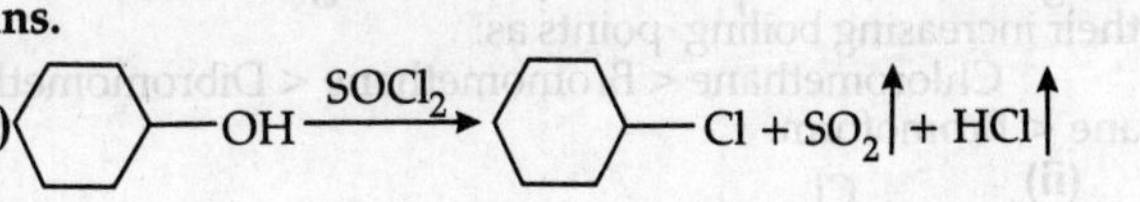

(ii) 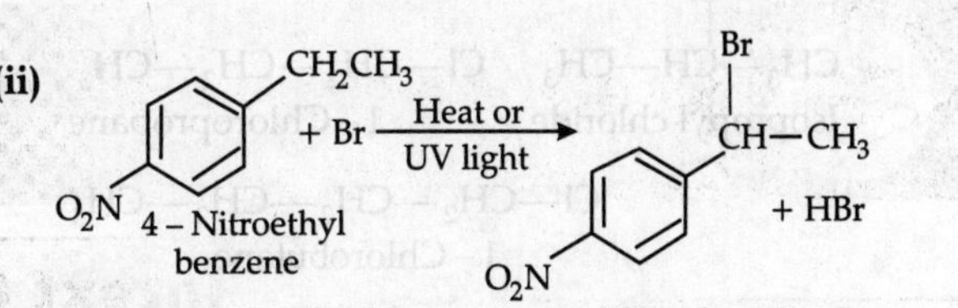

1 – Bromo – 1 – (4 – Nitrophenyl) ethane

(iii) 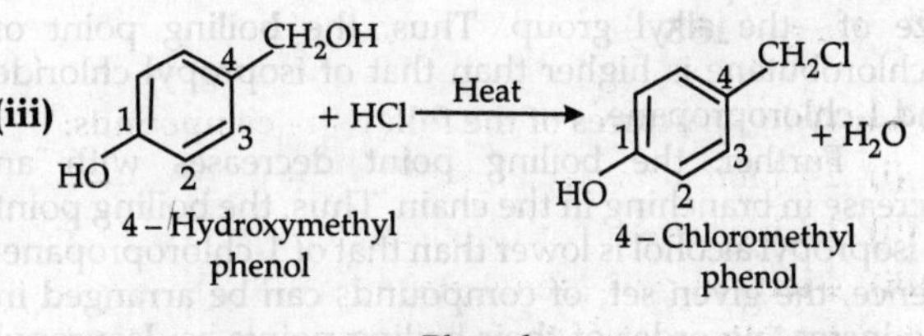

(iv) 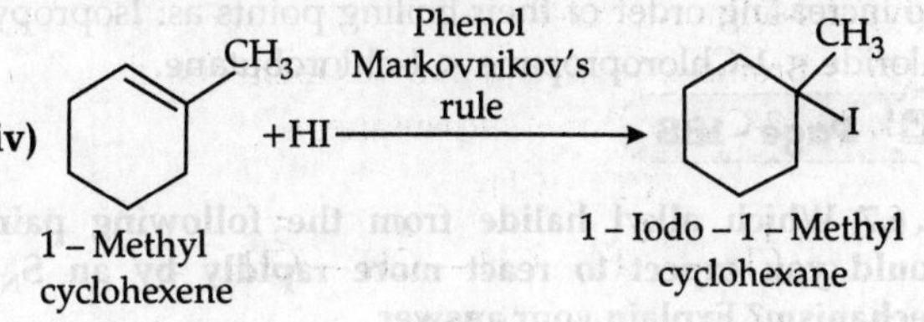

(v) $CH_3CH_2Br + NaI \rightarrow CH_3CH_2I + NaBr$

Bromoethane   Iodoethane

(vi) 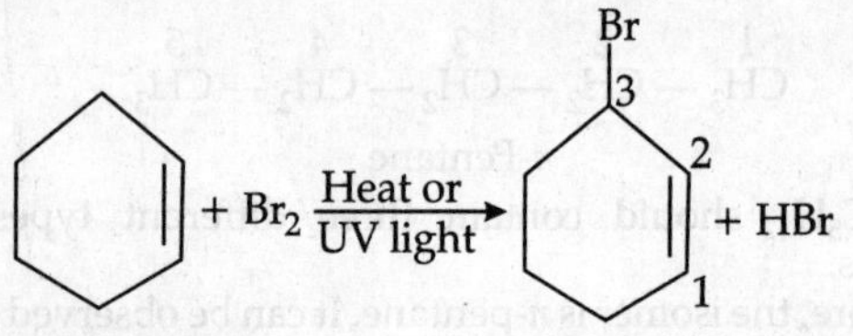

Cyclohexene   3 – Bromocyclohexene

Page - 169

Q. 6.6. Arrange each set of compounds in order of increasing boiling points.
(i) Bromomethane, Bromoform, Chloromethane, Dibromomethane.
(ii) 1-Chloropropane, Isopropyl chloride, 1-Chlorobutane.

Ans.(i)

CH_3-Cl (Chloromethane) CH_3-Br (Bromomethane)

$Br-CH_2-Br$ (Dibromomethane) $Br-CH(Br)-Br$ (Bromoform)

For alkyl halides containing the same alkyl group, the boiling point increases with an increase in the atomic mass of the halogen atom.

Since, the atomic mass of Br is greater than that of Cl, the boiling point of bromomethane is higher than that of chloromethane.

Further, for alkyl halides containing the same alkyl group, the boiling point increases with an increase in the number of halides. Therefore, the boiling point of Dibromomethane is higher than that of chloromethane and bromomethane, but lower than that of bromoform. Hence, the given set of compounds can be arranged in the order of their increasing boiling points as:

Chloromethane < Bromomethane < Dibromomethane < Bromoform.

(ii)

$CH_3-CH(Cl)-CH_3$ (Isopropyl chloride) $Cl-CH_2-CH_2-CH_3$ (1 – Chloropropane)

$Cl-CH_2-CH_2-CH_2-CH_3$ (1 – Chlorobutane)

For alkyl halides containing the same halide, the boiling point increases with an increase in the size of the alkyl group. Thus, the boiling point of 1-chlorobutane is higher than that of isopropyl chloride and 1-chloropropane.

Further, the boiling point decreases with an increase in branching in the chain. Thus, the boiling point of isopropyl alcohol is lower than that of 1-chloropropane. Hence, the given set of compounds can be arranged in the increasing order of their boiling points as: Isopropyl chloride < 1-Chloropropane < 1-chlorobutane.

Page - 186

Q. 6.7. Which alkyl halide from the following pairs would you expect to react more rapidly by an S_N2 mechanism? Explain your answer.

(i) $CH_3CH_2CH_2CH_2Br$ **or** $CH_3CH_2CH(Br)CH_3$

(ii) $CH_3CH_2CH(Br)CH_3$ **or** $H_3C-C(CH_3)_2-Br$

(iii) $CH_3CH(CH_3)CH_2CH_2Br$ **or** $CH_3CH_2CH(CH_3)CH_2Br$

Ans. (i) $CH_3CH_2CH_2CH_2Br$ $CH_3CH_2CH(Br)-CH_3$

1 - Bromobutane(1°)   **2 - Bromobutane(2°)**

2-Bromobutane is a 2° alkylhalide whereas 1-bromobutane is a 1° alkyl halide. The approaching of nucleophile is more hindered in 2-bromobutane than in 1-bromobutane. Therefore, 1-bromobutane reacts more rapidly than 2-bromobutane by an S_N2 mechanism.

(ii) $CH_3-CH_2-CH(Br)-CH_3$ (2 - Bromobutane(2°)) $CH_3-C(CH_3)_2-Br$ (2 - Bromo - 2 - methylpropane(3°))

2-Bromobutane is 2° alkylhalide whereas 2-bromo-2-methylpropane is 3° alkyl halide. Therefore, greater numbers of substituents are present in 3° alkyl halide than in 2° alkyl halide to hinder the approaching nucleophile. Hence, 2-bromobutane reacts more rapidly than 2-bromo-2-methylpropane by an S_N2 mechanism.

(iii) $CH_3-CH(CH_3)-CH_2-CH_2-Br$

1 - Bromo - 3 - methylbutane(1°)

$CH_3-CH_2-CH(CH_3)-CH_2-Br$

1 - Bromo - 2 - methylpropane(1°)

Both the alkyl halides are primary. However, the substituent $-CH_3$ is at a greater distance to the carbon atom linked to Br in 1-bromo-3-methylbutane than in 1-bromo- 2-methylbutane. Therefore, the approaching nucleophile is less hindered in case of the former than in case of the latter. Hence, the former reacts faster than the latter by S_N2 mechanism.

Q. 6.8. In the following pairs of halogen compounds, which compound undergoes faster S_N1 reaction?

(i) 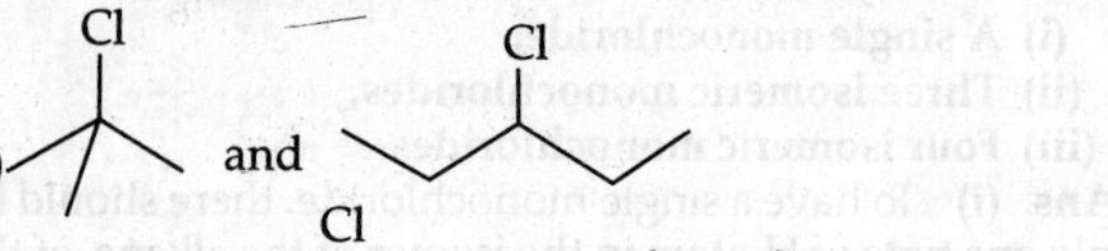

(ii) 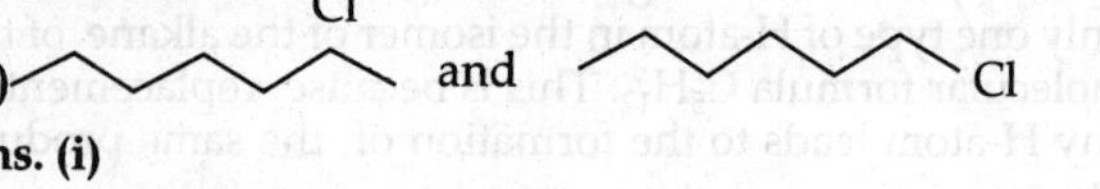

Ans. (i)

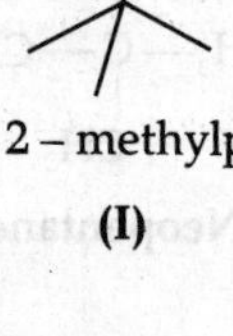

2 – Chloro – 2 – methylpropane (3°)

(I)

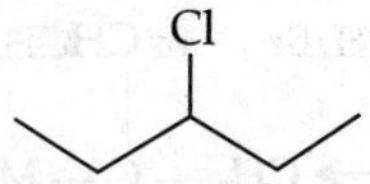

3 – Chloropentane (2°)
(II)

S_N1 reaction proceeds via the formation of carbocation. The alkyl halide (I) is 3° while (II) is 2°. Therefore, (I) forms 3° carbocation while (II) forms 2° carbocation. Greater the stability of the carbocation, faster is the rate of S_N1 reaction. Since, 3° carbocation is more stable than 2° carbocation. (I), i.e., 2–chloro-2-methylpropane, undergoes faster S_N1 reaction than (II), i.e., 3- chloropentane.

(ii)

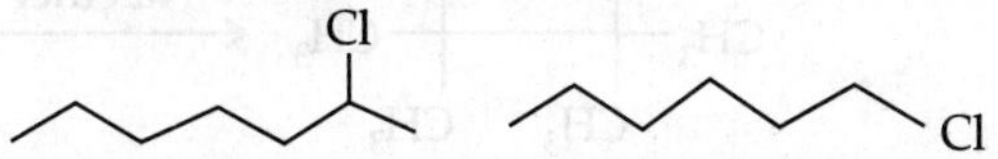

2 – Chloroheptane (2°) **(I)** 1 –Chlorohexane (1°) **(II)**

The alkyl halide (I) is 2° while (II) is 1°. 2° carbocation is more stable than 1° carbocation. Therefore, (I), 2–chloroheptane, undergoes faster S_N1 reaction than (II), 1-chlorohexane.

Q. 6.9. Identify A, B, C, D, E, R and R_1 in the following:

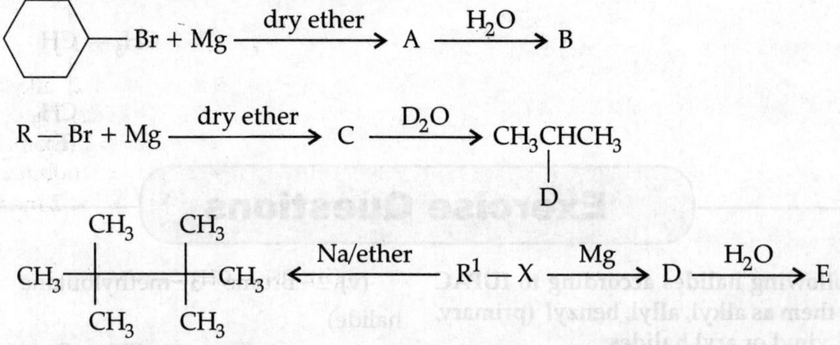

Ans.

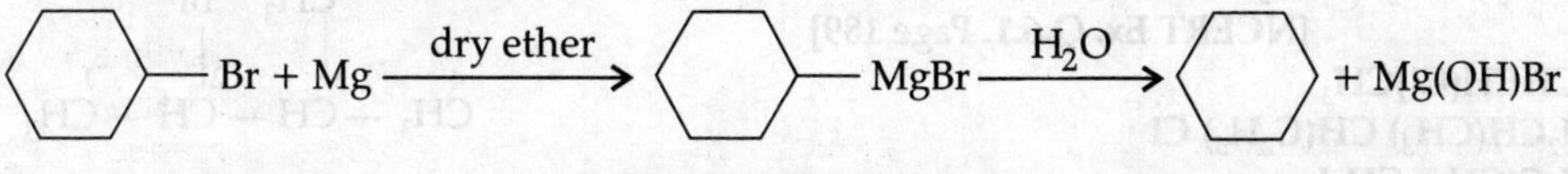

Bromocyclohexane — Cyclohexylmagnesium bromide (A) — Cyclohexane (B)

Since D of D_2O gets attached to the carbon atom to which MgBr is attached, C is

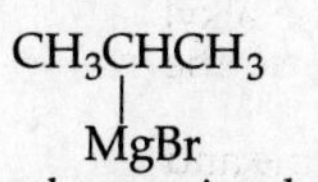

Isopropylmagnesium bromide

Therefore, the compound R – Br is

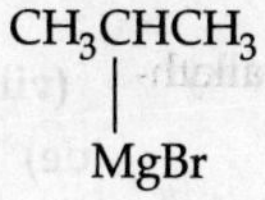

2 – Bromopropane

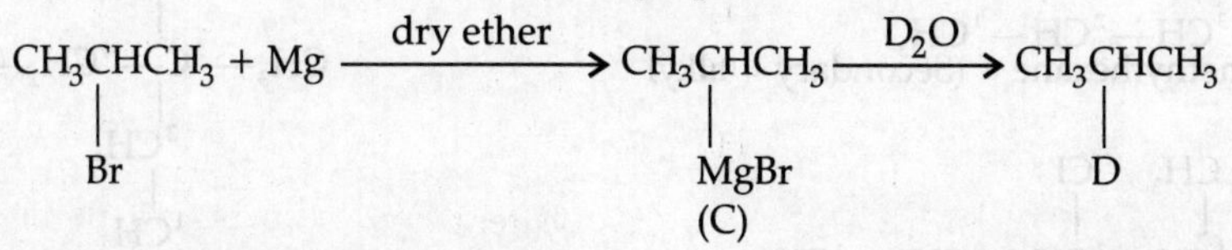

(C)

When an alkyl halide is treated with Na in the presence of ether, a hydrocarbon containing double the number of carbon atoms as present in the original halide is obtained as product. This is known as Wurtz reaction. Therefore, the halide, R^1–X, is

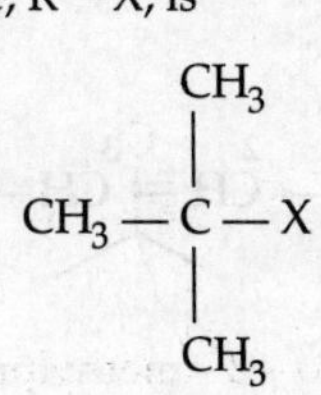

tert-Butylhalide

Therefore, compound D is

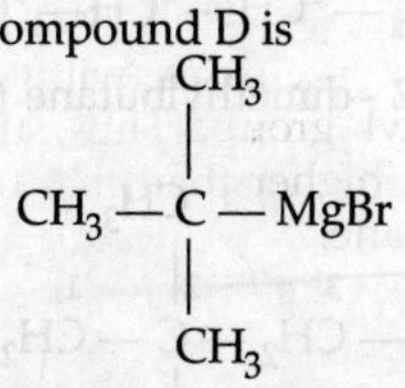

tert-Butylhalide

And, compound E is

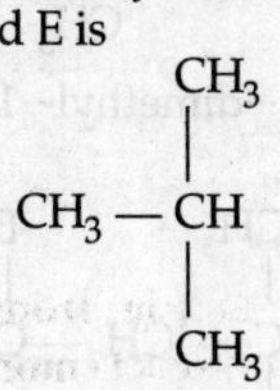

2-Methylpropane

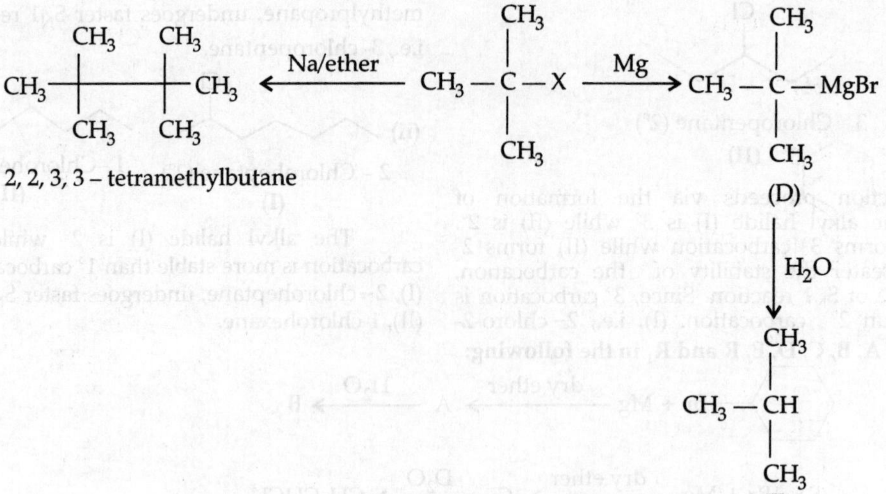

2, 2, 3, 3 – tetramethylbutane

(D)

(E)

Exercise Questions

Q. 1. Name the following halides according to IUPAC system and classify them as alkyl, allyl, benzyl (primary, secondary, tertiary), vinyl or aryl halides:

[NCERT Ex. Q.6.1, Page 189]

(i) $(CH_3)_2CHCH(Cl)CH_3$

(ii) $CH_3CH_2CH(CH_3)\ CH(C_2H_5)\ Cl$

(iii) $CH_3CH_2C(CH_3)_2CH_2I$

(iv) $(CH_3)_3CCH_2CH(Br)C_6H_5$

(v) $CH_3CH(CH_3)\ CH(Br)CH_3$

(vi) $CH_3C(C_2H_5)_2CH_2Br$

(vii) $CH_3C(Cl)(C_2H_5)\ CH_2CH_3$

(viii) $CH_3CH{=}C(Cl)CH_2CH(CH_3)_2$

(ix) $CH_3CH{=}CHC(Br)(CH_3)_2$

(x) *p*-$ClC_6H_4CH_2CH(CH_3)_2$

(xi) *m*-$ClCH_2C_6H_4CH_2C(CH_3)_3$

(xii) *o*-Br-$C_6H_4CH(CH_3)\ CH_2CH_3$

Ans. (i) 2–Chloro–3–methylbutane (Secondary alkyl halide)

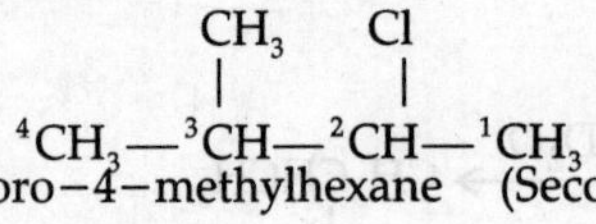

(ii) 3–Chloro–4–methylhexane (Secondary alkyl halide)

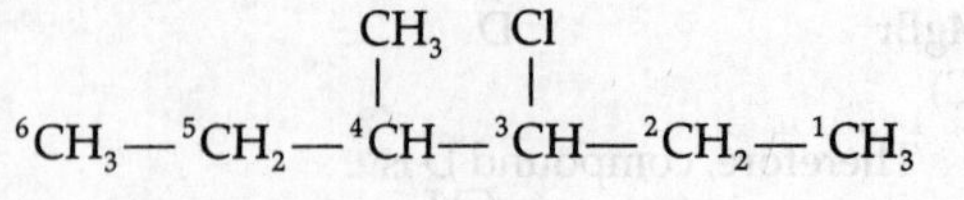

(iii) 1–Iodo–2, 2 –dimethylbutane (Primary alkyl halide)

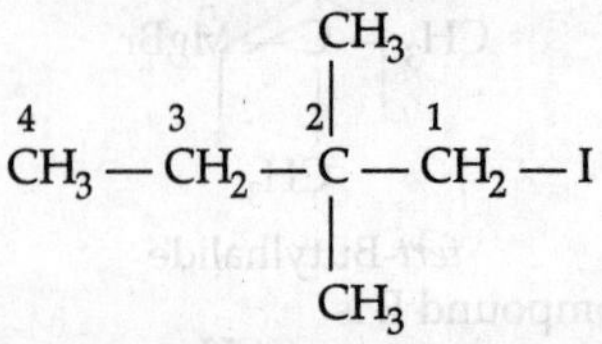

(iv) 1–Bromo–3, 3–dimethyl–1–phenylbutane (Secondary benzyl halide)

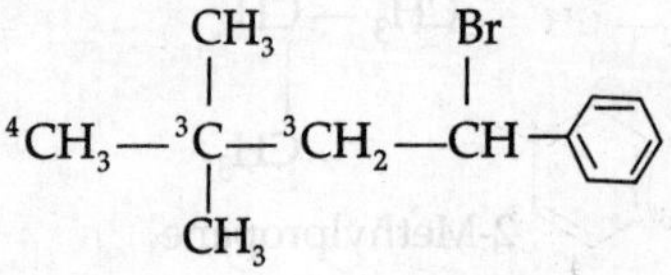

(v) 2–Bromo–3–methylbutane (Secondary alkyl halide)

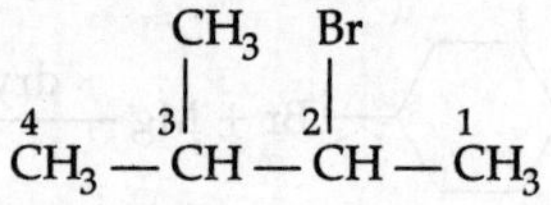

(vi) 1–Bromo–2–ethyl–2–methylbutane (Primary alkyl halide)

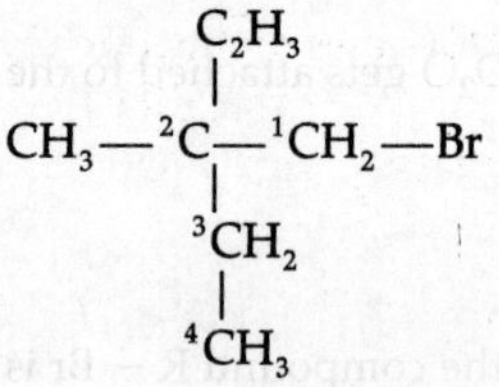

(vii) 3–Chloro–3–methylpentane (Tertiary alkyl halide)

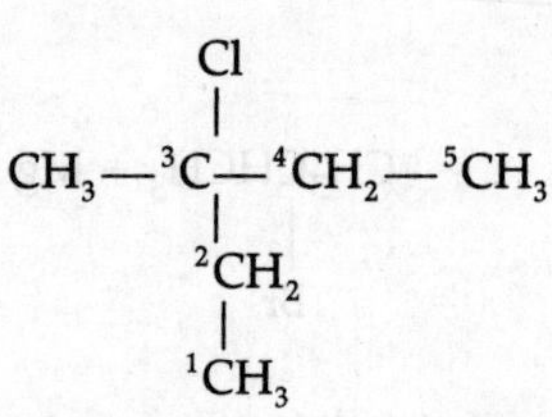

(viii) 3–Chloro–5–methylhex–2–ene(Vinyl halide)

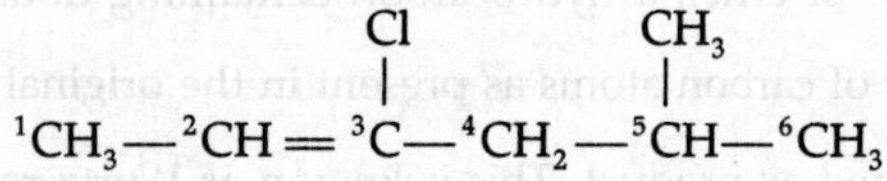

(ix) 4–Bromo–4–methylpent–2–ene (Allyl halide)

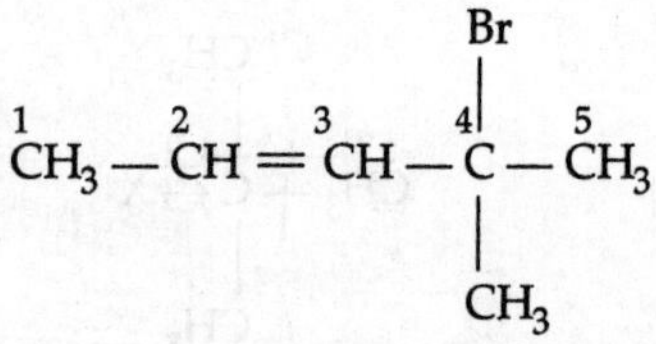

(x) 1–Chloro–4–(2–methylpropyl) benzene (Aryl halide)

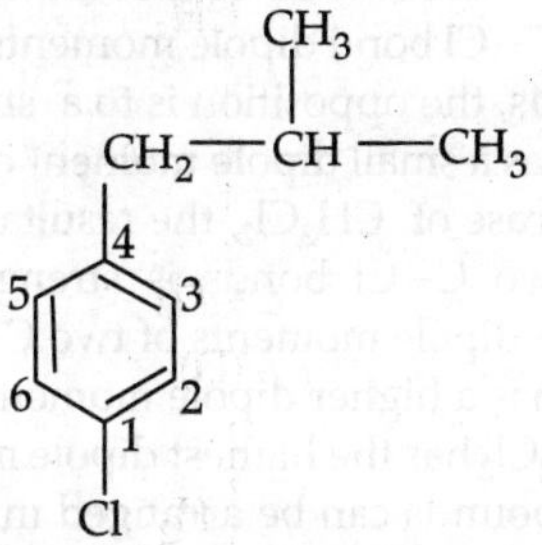

(xi) 1−Chloromethyl−3−(2, 2−dimethylpropyl) benzene (Primary benzyl halide)

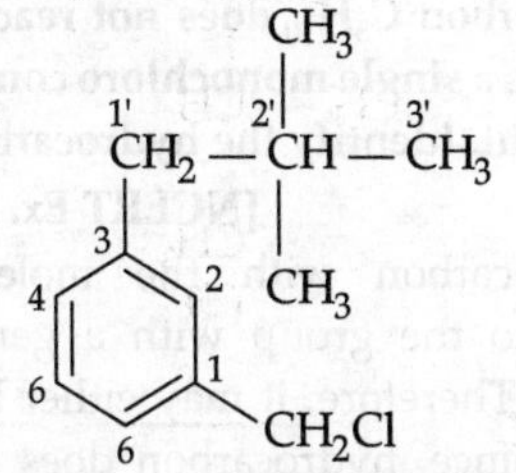

(xii) 1−Bromo−2−(1−methylpropyl) benzene (Aryl halide)

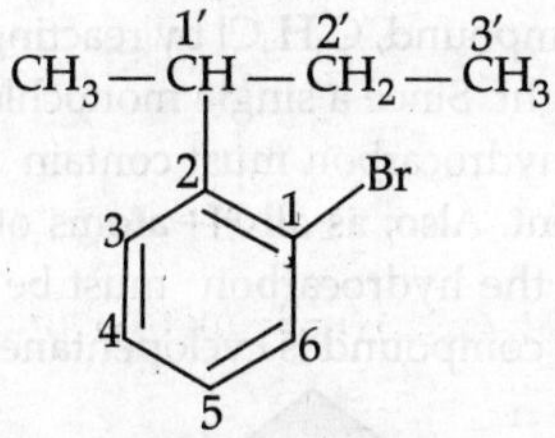

Q. 2. Give the IUPAC names of the following compounds: [NCERT Ex. Q.6.2, Page 189]

(i) $CH_3CH(Cl)CH(Br)CH_3$

(ii) $CHF_2CBrClF$

(iii) $ClCH_2C \rightarrow CCH_2Br$

(iv) $(CCl_3)_3CCl$

(v) $CH_3C(p\text{-}ClC_6H_4)_2CH(Br)CH_3$

(vi) $(CH_3)_3CCH{=}CClC_6H_4I\text{-}p$

Ans. (i) 2−Bromo−3−chlorobutane

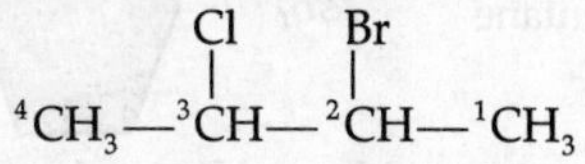

(ii) 1−Bromo−1−chloro−1, 1, 2−trifluoroethane

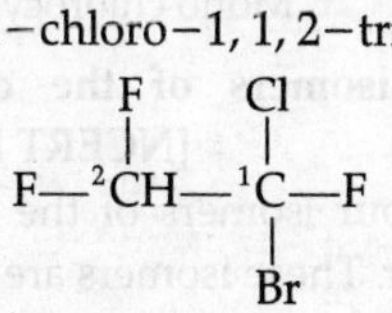

(iii) 1−Bromo−4−chlorobut−2−yne

$$Cl-\overset{4}{C}H_2-\overset{3}{C}\equiv\overset{2}{C}-\overset{1}{C}H_2-Br$$

(iv) 2−(Trichloromethyl) −1,1,1,2,3,3,3−heptachloropropane

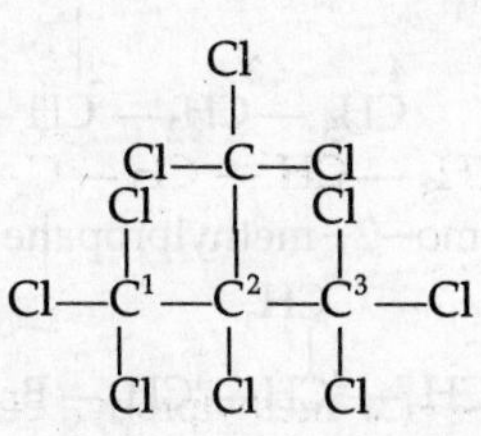

(v) 2−Bromo−3, 3−bis-(4−chlorophenyl) butane

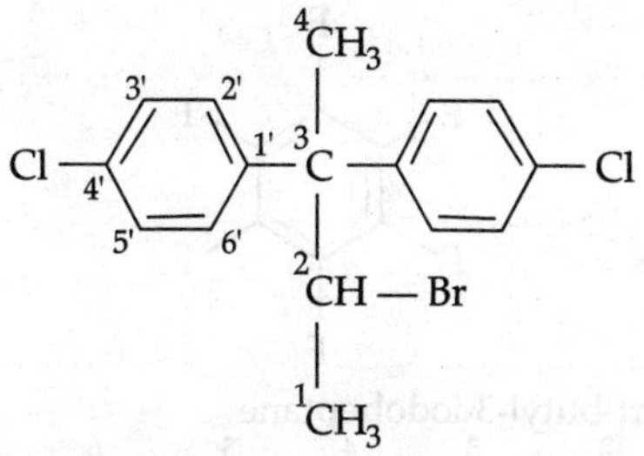

(vi) 1−chloro−1−(4−iodophenyl)−3, 3−dimethylbut−1−ene

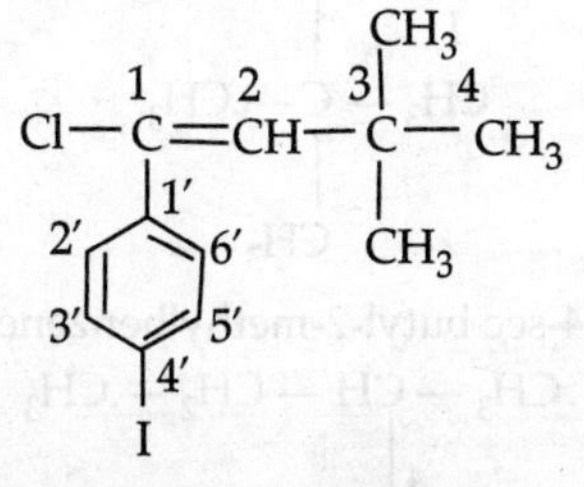

Q. 3. Write the structures of the following organic halogen compounds. [NCERT Ex. Q.6.3, Page 189]

(i) 2-Chloro-3-methylpentane

(ii) *p*-Bromochlorobenzene

(iii) 1-Chloro-4-ethylcyclohexane

(iv) 2-(2-Chlorophenyl)-1-iodooctane

(v) Perfluorobenzene

(vi) 4-tert-butyl-3-iodoheptane

(vii) 1-Bromo-4-sec-butyl-2-methylbenzene

(viii) 1,4-Dibromobut-2-ene

Ans. (i) 2-Chloro-3-methylpentane

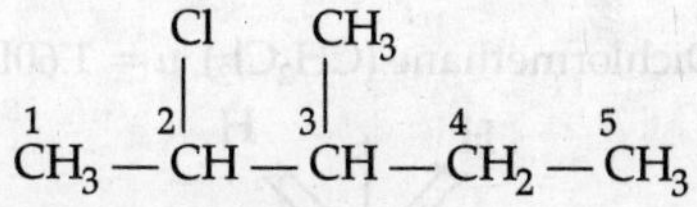

(ii) *p*-Bromochlorobenzene

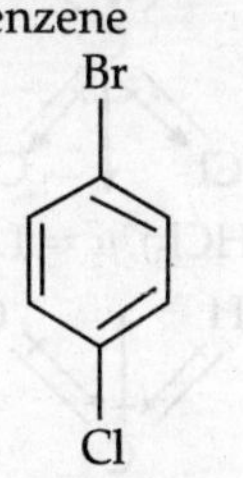

(iii) 1-Chloro-4-ethylcyclohexane

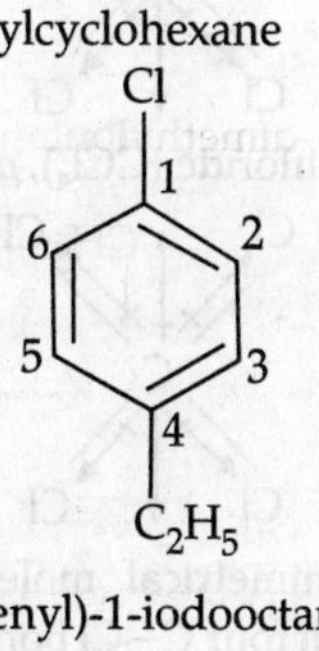

(iv) 2-(2-Chlorophenyl)-1-iodooctane

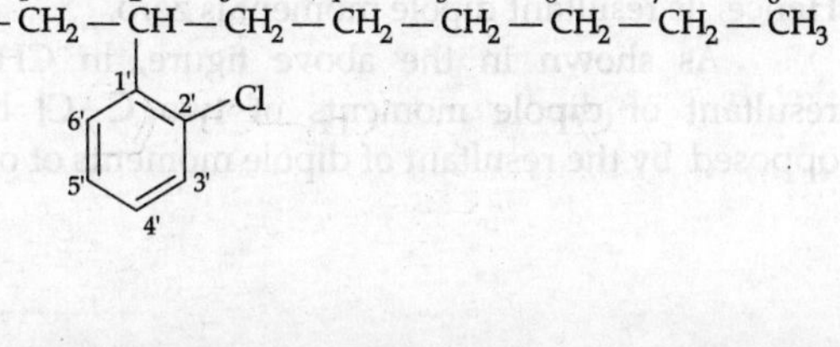

(v) Perfluorobenzene

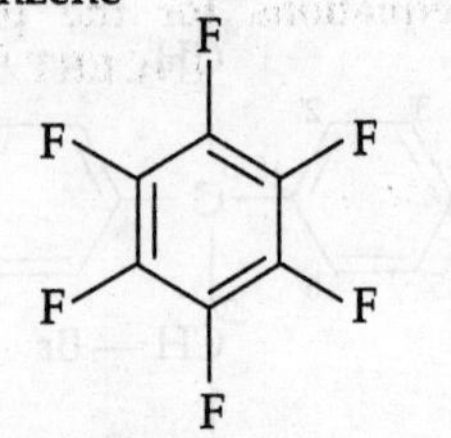

(vi) 4-tert-butyl-3-iodoheptane

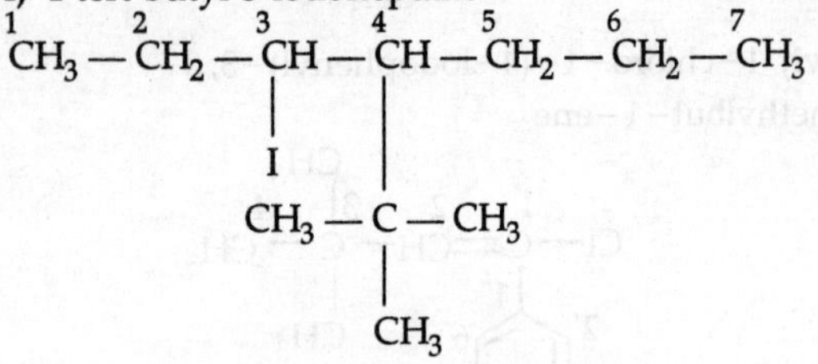

(vii) Bromo-4-sec-butyl-2-methylbenzene

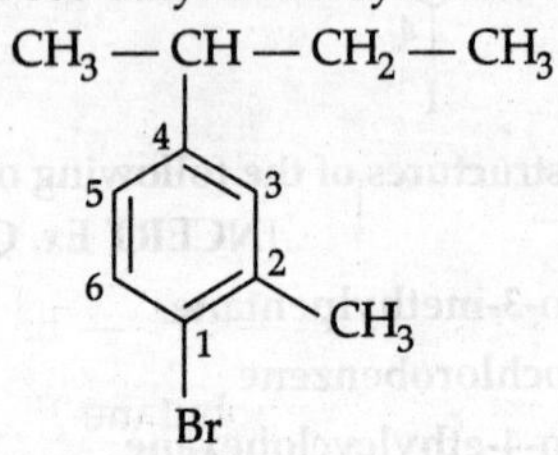

(viii) 1, 4-Dibromobut-2-ene

$$Br-\overset{1}{C}H_2-\overset{2}{C}H=\overset{3}{C}H-\overset{4}{C}H_2-Br$$

Q. 4. Which one of the following has the highest dipole moment? **[NCERT Ex. Q.6.4, Page 189]**

(i) CH_2Cl_2

(ii) $CHCl_3$

(iii) CCl_4

Ans. (i) Dichlormethane (CH_2Cl_2), $\mu = 1.60D$

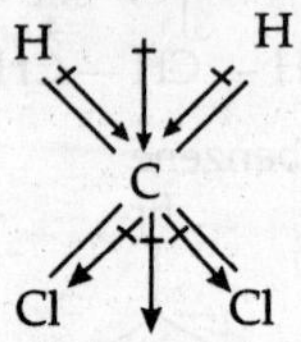

(ii) Chloroform ($CHCl_3$), $\mu = 1.08D$

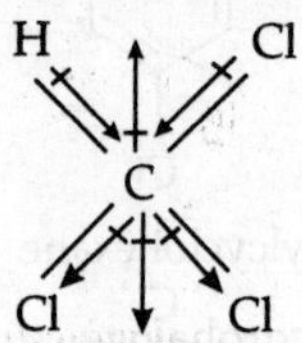

(iii) Carbon tetrachloride (CCl_4), $\mu = 0D$

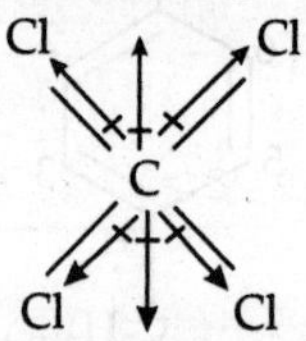

CCl_4 is a symmetrical molecule. Therefore, the dipole moments of all four C–Cl bonds cancel each other. Hence, its resultant dipole moment is zero.

As shown in the above figure, in $CHCl_3$, the resultant of dipole moments of two C–Cl bonds is opposed by the resultant of dipole moments of one C–H bond and one C–Cl bond. Since the resultant of one C–H bond and one C–Cl bond dipole moments is smaller than two C–Cl bonds, the opposition is to a small extent. As a result, $CHCl_3$ has a small dipole moment of 1.08 D.On the other hand, in case of CH_2Cl_2, the resultant of the dipole moments of two C–Cl bonds is strengthened by the resultant of the dipole moments of two C–H bonds. As a result, CH_2Cl_2 has a higher dipole moment of 1.60 D than $CHCl_3$, i.e., CH_2Cl_2 has the highest dipole moment. Hence, the given compounds can be arranged in the increasing order of their dipole moments as:

$$CCl_4 < CHCl_3 < CH_2Cl_2$$

Q. 5. A hydrocarbon C_5H_{10} does not react with chlorine in dark but gives a single monochloro compound C_5H_9Cl in bright sunlight. Identify the hydrocarbon.

[NCERT Ex. Q.6.5, Page 189]

Ans. A hydrocarbon with the molecular formula, C_5H_{10} belongs to the group with a general molecular formula C_nH_{2n}. Therefore, it may either be an alkene or a cycloalkane. Since, hydrocarbon does not react with chlorine in the dark, it cannot be an alkene. Thus, it should be a cycloalkane. Further, the hydrocarbon gives a single monochloro compound, C_5H_9Cl by reacting with chlorine in bright sunlight. Since a single monochloro compound is formed, the hydrocarbon must contain H–atoms that are all equivalent. Also, as all H–atoms of a cycloalkane are equivalent, the hydrocarbon must be a cycloalkane. Hence, the said compound is cyclopentane.

Cyclopentane (C_5H_{10})

The reactions involved in the question are:

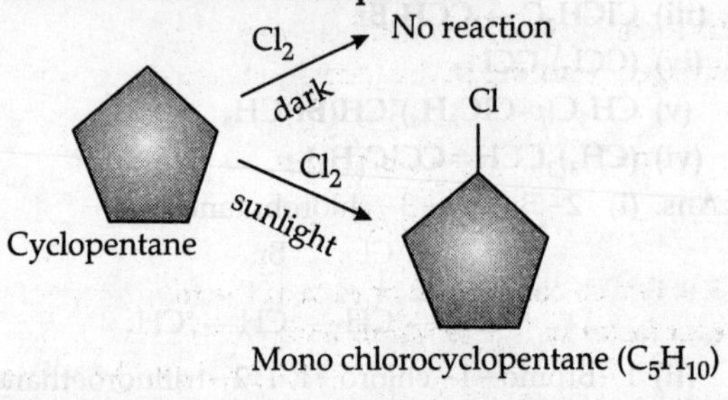

Q. 6. Write the isomers of the compound having formula C_4H_9Br. **[NCERT Ex. Q.6.6, Page 189]**

Ans. There are four isomers of the compound having the formula C_4H_9Br. These isomers are given below.

(a) 1–Bromobutane

$$\overset{4}{C}H_3-\overset{3}{C}H_2-\overset{2}{C}H_2-\overset{1}{C}H_2-Br$$

(b) 2–Bromobutane

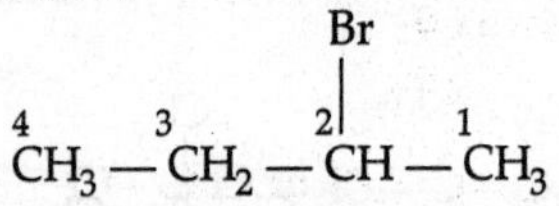

(c) 1–Bromo–2–methylpropane

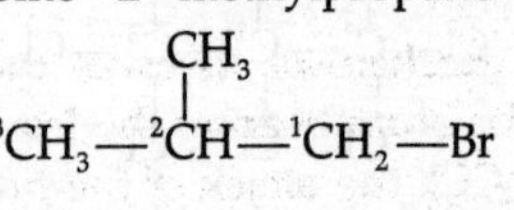

(d) 2–Bromo–2–methylpropane

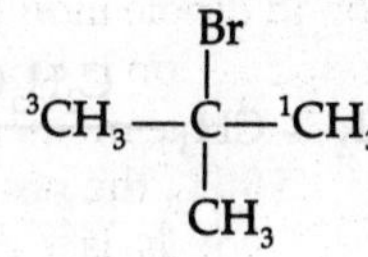

Ans.

(i) $CH_3—CH_2—CH_2—CH_2—OH + HI \xrightarrow{ZnCl_2} CH_3—CH_2—CH_2—CH_2—I + H_2O$

I - Butanol → I- Iodobutane

(ii) $CH_3 — CH_2 — CH_2 — CH_2 — Cl + NaI \xrightarrow[\text{(Finkelstein reaction)}]{\text{dry acetone}} NaCl + CH_3 — CH_2 — CH_2 — CH_2 — I$

I – Chlorobutane → 1– Iodobutane

(iii) $CH_3 — CH_2 — CH{=}CH_2 + HBr \xrightarrow[\text{(Anti-Markovnikov's addition)}]{\text{Peroxide}} CH_3 — CH_2 — CH_2 — CH_2 — Br$ (I – Bromobutane)

$CH_3 — CH_2 — CH_2 — CH_2 — Br \xrightarrow{\text{NaI/dry acetone}} NaBr + CH_3 — CH_2 — CH_2 — CH_2 — I$ (1– Iodobutane)

Q. 8.What are ambident nucleophiles? Explain with an example. [NCERT Ex. Q.6.8, Page 189]

Ans. Ambident nucleophiles are nucleophiles having two nucleophilic sites. Thus, ambident nucleophiles have two sites through which they can attack. For example, nitrite ion is an ambident nucleophile.

$$[^{-}O—\ddot{N}{=}O]$$

Nitrite ion can attack through oxygen resulting in the formation of alkyl nitrites. Also, it can attack through nitrogen resulting in the formation of nitroalkanes.

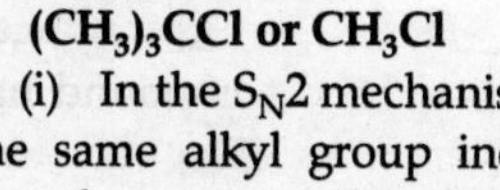

Alkylnitrite

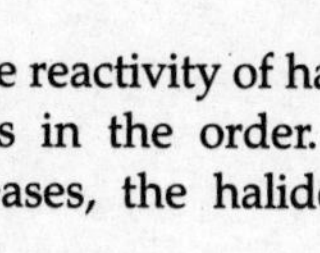

Nitroalkane

Q. 9.Which compound in each of the following pairs will react faster in S_N2 reaction with –OH? [NCERT Ex. Q.6.9, Page 190]

(i) CH_3Br or CH_3I

(ii) $(CH_3)_3CCl$ or CH_3Cl

Ans. (i) In the S_N2 mechanism, the reactivity of halides for the same alkyl group increases in the order. This happens because as the size increases, the halide ion becomes a better leaving group.

$$R–F << R–Cl < R–Br < R–I$$

Therefore, CH_3I will react faster than CH_3Br in S_N2 reactions with OH^-.

(ii)

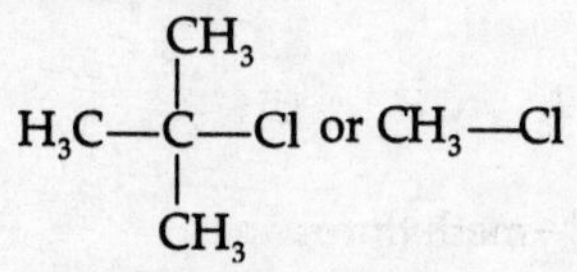

The S_N2 mechanism involves the attack of the nucleophile at the atom bearing the leaving group. But, in case of $(CH_3)_3CCl$, the attack of the nucleophile at the carbon atom is hindered because of the presence of bulky substituents on that carbon atom bearing the leaving group. On the other hand, there are no bulky substituents on the carbon atom bearing the leaving group in CH_3Cl. Hence, CH_3Cl reacts faster than $(CH_3)_3CCl$ in S_N2 reaction with –OH.

Q. 7.Write the equations for the preparation of 1–iodobutane from [NCERT Ex. Q.6.7, Page 189]

(i) 1-butanol

(ii) 1-chlorobutane

(iii) but-1-ene.

Q. 10. Predict all the alkenes that would be formed by dehydrohalogenation of the following halides with sodium ethoxide in ethanol and identify the major alkene: [NCERT Ex. Q.6.10, Page 190]

(i) 1-Bromo-1-methylcyclohexane

(ii) 2-Chloro-2-methylbutane

(iii) 2,2,3-Trimethyl-3-bromopentane.

Ans. (i) 1–bromo–1–methylcyclohexane

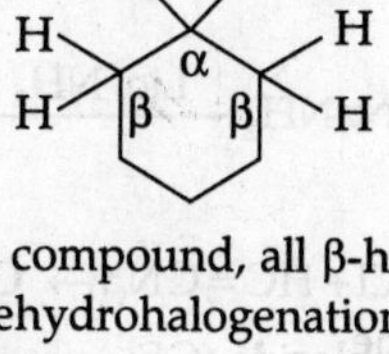

In the given compound, all β-hydrogen atoms are equivalent. Thus, dehydrohalogenation of this compound gives only one alkene.

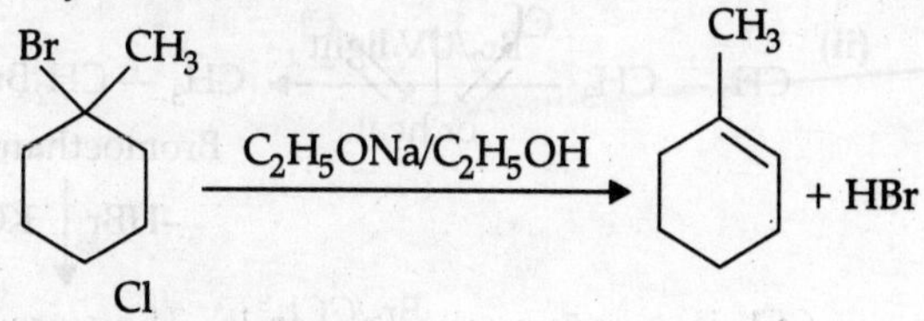

(ii)

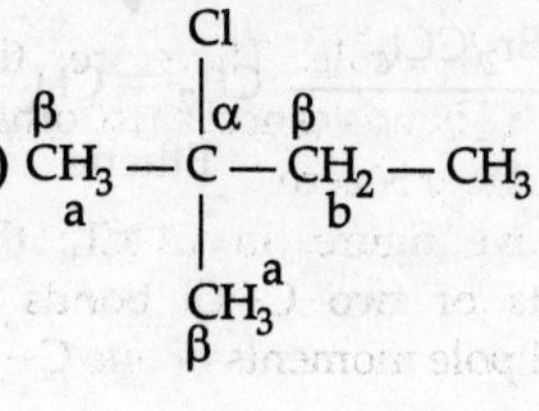

In the given compound, there are two different sets of equivalent β-hydrogen atoms labelled as *a* and *b*. Thus, dehydrohalogenation of the compound yields two alkenes.

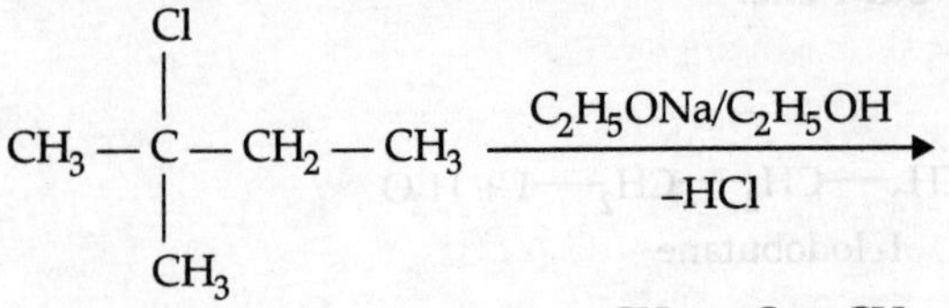

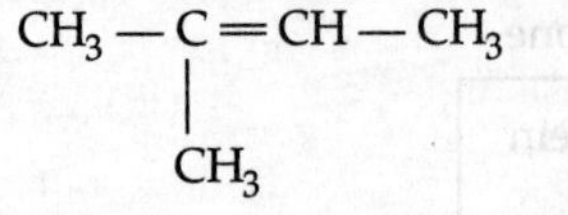

2–Methylbut –2–ene (I)

+

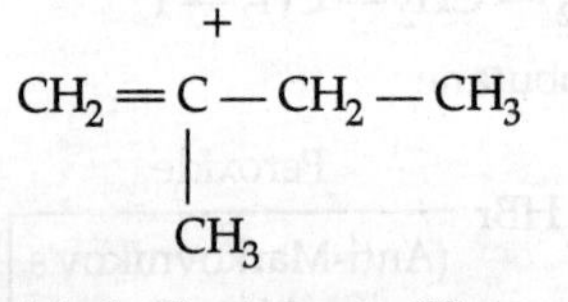

2–Methylbut –1–ene (II)

Saytzeff's rule implies that in dehydrohalogenation reactions, the alkene having a greater number of alkyl groups attached to a doubly bonded carbon atoms is preferably produced. Therefore, alkene (I) i.e., 2-methylbut-2-ene is the major product in this reaction.

(iii)

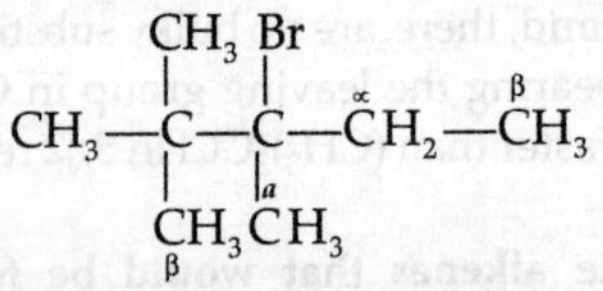

2, 2, 3-trimethyl-3-bromopentane

In the given compound, there are two different sets of equivalent β-hydrogen atoms labelled as *a* and *b*. Thus, dehydrohalogenation of the compound yields two alkenes.

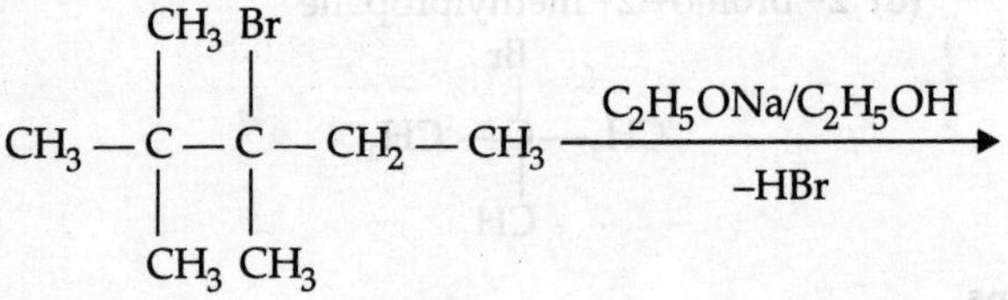

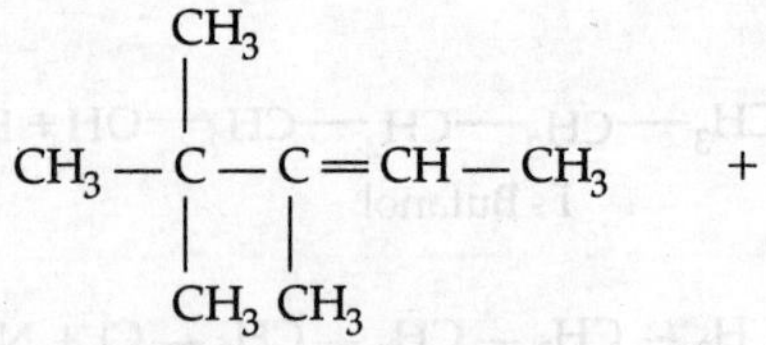

3, 4, 4–Trimethylpent – 2–ene (I)

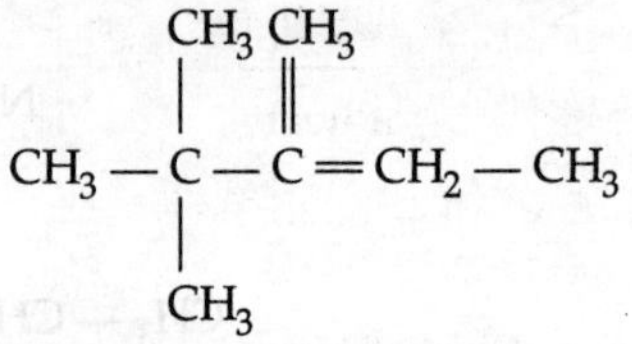

2–Ethyl – 3, 3–dimethylbut – 1 – ene (II)

According to Saytzeff's rule, in dehydrohalogenation reactions, the alkene having a greater number of alkyl groups attached to the doubly bonded carbon atom is preferably formed. Hence, alkene (I), i.e., 3,4,4-trimethylpent-2-ene is the major product in this reaction.

Q. 11. How will you bring about the following conversions?

(i) Ethanol to but-1-yne
(ii) Ethane to bromoethene
(iii) Propene to 1-nitropropane
(iv) Toluene to benzyl alcohol
(v) Propene to propyne
(vi) Ethanol to ethyl fluoride
(vii) Bromomethane to propanone
(viii) But-1-ene to but-2-ene
(ix) 1-Chlorobutane to *n*-octane
(x) Benzene to biphenyl.

[NCERT Ex. Q.6.11, Page 190]

Ans.

(i)

$$\underset{\text{Ethanol}}{CH_3CH_2OH} \xrightarrow{SOCl_2,\ Pyridine} \underset{\text{Chloroethane}}{CH_3CH_2Cl} + SO_2\uparrow + HCl$$

$$\underset{\text{Ethyne}}{HC\equiv CH} + NaNH_2 \xrightarrow{Liq.\ NH_3} \underset{\text{Sodium acetylide}}{HC\equiv \overset{-}{C}\overset{+}{N}a}$$

$$\underset{\text{Chloroethane}}{CH_3CH_2-Cl} + HC\equiv\overset{-}{C}\overset{+}{N}a \rightarrow \underset{\text{But - 1 - yne}}{CH_3CH_2C\equiv CH} + NaCl$$

(ii)

$$CH_3-CH_3 \xrightarrow[\text{or heat}]{Br_2/UV\ light} \underset{\text{Bromoethane}}{CH_3-CH_2Br} + HBr$$

$$CH_3-CH_2Br \xrightarrow[-HBr]{KOH(alc),\ \Delta} \underset{\text{Ethene}}{CH_2=CH_2}$$

$$CH_2=CH_2 \xrightarrow{Br_2/CCl_4} \underset{\text{vic-Dibromide}}{BrCH_2-BrCH_2}$$

$$BrCH_2-BrCH_2 \xrightarrow{\Delta,\ KOH(alc)} \underset{\text{Bromoethene}}{CH_2=CHBr}$$

(iii)

$$CH_3 - CH_3 = CH_2 + HBr \xrightarrow{\text{Peroxide}} CH_3 - CH_2 - CH_2Br$$

Propene → 1–Bromopropane

$$CH_3 - CH_2 - CH_2Br \xrightarrow{AgNO_2} AgBr + CH_3 - CH_2 - CH_2NO_2$$

1–Nitropropane

(iv)

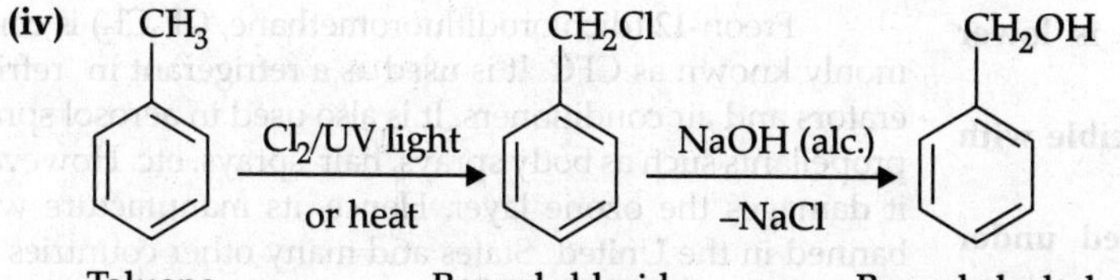

Toluene → Benzyl chloride → Benzyl alcohol

(v)

$$CH_3 - CH = CH_2 \xrightarrow{Br_2/CCl_4} CH_3 - \underset{Br}{\underset{|}{CH}} - \underset{Br}{\underset{|}{CH_2}} \xrightarrow[\text{Liq.}NH_3]{NaNH_2} CH_3 - C \equiv CH$$

Propene → 1,2-Dibromopropane → Propyne

(vi)

$$CH_3 - CH_2 - OH \xrightarrow[-POCl_3,\ -HCl]{PCl_5} CH_3 - CH_2 - Cl$$

Ethanol → Chloroethane

$$CH_3 - CH_2 - Cl \xrightarrow{AgF} CH_3 - CH_2 - F$$

Ethyl fluoride

(vii)

$$CH_3 - Br \xrightarrow{KCN\ (alc.)} CH_3 - CN \xrightarrow{CH_3-MgBr} CH_3 - \underset{CH_3}{\underset{|}{C}} = NMgBr$$

Bromethane → Acetonitrile

$$CH_3 - \underset{CH_3}{\underset{|}{C}} = NMgBr \xrightarrow{\text{Hydrolysis}\ H_3O^+} CH_3 - \underset{CH_3}{\underset{|}{C}} = O$$

Propanone

(viii)

$$CH_3CH_2CH = CH_2 \xrightarrow[\text{(Markovnikov addition)}]{HBr} CH_3CH_2\overset{Br}{\overset{|}{C}}HCH_3$$

But-l-ene → 2–Bromobutane

$$CH_3CH_2\overset{Br}{\overset{|}{C}}HCH_3 \xrightarrow[-HBr]{KOH(alc),\ \Delta} CH_3CH = CHCH_3$$

But-2-ene

(ix) $2CH_3CH_2CH_2CH_2Cl + 2Na \xrightarrow[\text{Wurtz reaction}]{\text{Dry ether}} CH_3CH_2CH_2CH_2CH_2CH_2CH_2CH_3 + 2NaCl$

1-chlorobutane (n-octane)

(x)

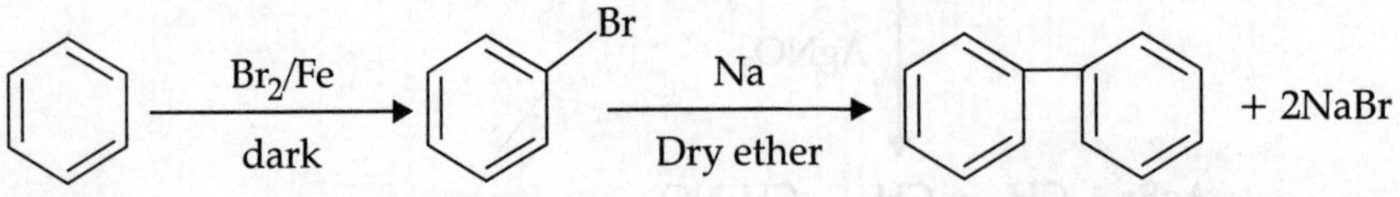

Benzene Bromobenzene Diphenyl

Q. 12. Explain why:

(i) the dipole moment of chlorobenzene is lower than that of cyclohexyl chloride?

(ii) alkyl halides, though polar, are immiscible with water?

(iii) Grignard reagents should be prepared under anhydrous conditions?

[NCERT Ex. Q.6.12, Page 190]

Ans. (i)

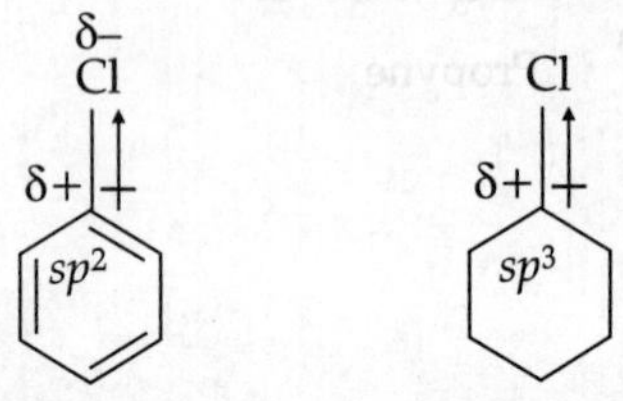

Chlorobenzene Cyclohexyl chloride

In chlorobenzene, the Cl-atom is linked to a sp^2 hybridized carbon atom. In cyclohexyl chloride, the Cl-atom is linked to a sp^3 hybridized carbon atom. Now, sp^2 hybridized carbon has more s-character than sp^3 hybridized carbon atom. Therefore, the former is more electronegative than the latter.

Therefore, the density of electrons of C–Cl bond near the Cl-atom is less in chlorobenzene than in cyclohexyl chloride.Moreover, the –R effect of the benzene ring of chlorobenzene decreases the electron density of the C–Cl bond near the Cl-atom. As a result, the polarity of the C–Cl bond in chlorobenzene decreases. Hence, the dipole moment of chlorobenzene is lower than that of cyclohexyl chloride.

(ii) To be miscible with water, the solute-water force of attraction must be stronger than the solute solute and water-water forces of attraction. Alkyl halides are polar molecules and so held together by dipole-dipole interactions. Similarly, strong H-bonds exist between the water molecules. The new force of attraction between the alkyl halides and water molecules is weaker than the alkyl halide-alkyl halide and water-water forces of attraction. Hence, alkyl halides (though polar) are immiscible with water.

(iii) Grignard reagents are very reactive. In the presence of moisture, they react to give alkanes.Therefore, grignard reagents should be prepared under anhydrous conditions.

$$\overset{\delta-}{R}\overset{\delta+}{Mg}\overset{\delta-}{X} + H_2O \longrightarrow R-H + Mg(OH)X$$

Grigrard reagent Alkane

Q. 13. Give the uses of Freon-12, DDT, carbon tetrachloride and iodoform. [NCERT Ex. Q.6.13, Page 190]

Ans.Uses of Freon–12

Freon-12 (dichlorodifluoromethane, CF_2Cl_2) is commonly known as CFC. It is used as a refrigerant in refrigerators and air conditioners. It is also used in aerosol spray propellants such as body sprays, hair sprays, etc. However, it damages the ozone layer. Hence, its manufacture was banned in the United States and many other countries in 1994.

Uses of DDT

DDT (*p, p*–dichlorodiphenyltrichloroethane) is one of the best-known insecticides. It is very effective against mosquitoes and lice. But due its harmful effects, it was banned in the United States in 1973.

Uses of carbontetrachloride (CCl_4)

(i) It is used for manufacturing refrigerants and propellants for aerosol cans.

(ii) It is used as feedstock in the synthesis of chlorofluorocarbons and other chemicals.

(iii) It is used as a solvent in the manufacture of pharmaceutical products.

(iv) Until the mid-1960's, carbon tetrachloride was widely used as a cleaning fluid, a degreasing agent in industries, a spot reamer in homes, and a fire extinguisher.

Uses of iodoform (CHI_3)

Iodoform was used earlier as an antiseptic, but now it has been replaced by other formulations containing iodine-due to its objectionable smell. The antiseptic property of iodoform is only due to the liberation of free iodine when it comes in contact with the skin.

Q. 14. Write the structure of the major organic product in each of the following reactions:

[NCERT Ex. Q.6.14, Page 190]

(i) $CH_3CH_2CH_2Cl + NaI \xrightarrow[\text{heat}]{\text{acetone}}$

(ii) $(CH_3)_3CBr + KOH \xrightarrow[\text{heat}]{\text{ethanol}}$

(iii) $CH_3CH(Br)CH_2CH_3 + NaOH \xrightarrow{\text{water}}$

(iv) $CH_3CH_2Br + KCN \xrightarrow{\text{aq. ethanol}}$

(v) $C_6H_5ONa + C_2H_5Cl \rightarrow$

(vi) $CH_3CH_2CH_2OH + SOCl_2 \rightarrow$

(vii) $CH_3CH_2CH{=}CH_2 + HBr \xrightarrow{\text{peroxide}}$

(viii) $CH_3CH{=}C(CH_3)_2 + HBr \rightarrow$

Ans.

(i) $CH_3CH_2CH_2Cl + NaI \xrightarrow[\text{heat}]{\text{acetone}} CH_3CH_2CH_2I + NaCl$

1 – Chloropropane (Finkelstein reaction) 1 – Iodopropane

(ii) $(CH_3)_3CBr + KOH \xrightarrow[\text{heat}]{\text{ethanol}} CH_3 - C(CH_3) = CH_2 + KBr + H_2O$

2-Bromo-2-methylpropane (Dehydrohalogenation) 2-Methylpropene

(iii) $CH_3CH(Br)CH_2CH_3 + NaOH \xrightarrow{\text{Water}} CH_3CH(OH)CH_2CH_3 + NaBr$

2 – Bromobutane Butan– 2 – ol

(iv) $CH_3CH_2Br + KCN \xrightarrow[\text{(Nucleophilic substitution)}]{\text{aq. ethanol}} CH_3H_2CN + KBr$

Bromobutane Cyanoethane

(v) $C_6H_5ONa + C_2H_5Cl \xrightarrow{\text{(Williamson synthesis)}} C_6H_5 - O - C_2H_5 + NaCl$

Sodium phenoxide Chloroethane Phenetole

(vi) $CH_3CH_2CH_2OH + SOCl_2 \rightarrow CH_3CH_2CH_2Cl + SO_2\uparrow + HCl$

1 – Propanol 1 – Chloropropane

(vii) $CH_3CH_2CH = CH_2 + HBr \xrightarrow[\text{(Anti–Markovnikov's addition)}]{\text{Peroxide}} CH_3CH_2CH_2CH_2 - Br$

But – 1 – ene 1 – Bromobutane

(viii) $CH_3CH = C(CH_3)_2 + HBr \xrightarrow{\text{(Markovnikov addition)}} CH_3 - CH_2 - C(Br)(CH_3) - CH_3$

2-Methylbut-2-ene 2-Bromo-2-methylbutane

Q. 15. Write the mechanism of the following reaction: [NCERT Ex. Q.6.15, Page 190]

$$nBuBr + KCN \xrightarrow{EtOH-H_2O} nBuCN$$

Ans. The given reaction is:

$$nBuBr + KCN \xrightarrow{EtOH-H_2O} nBuCN$$

The given reaction is an S_N2 reaction. In this reaction, CN^- acts as the nucleophile and attacks the carbon atom to which Br is attached. CN^- ion is an ambident nucleophile and can attack through both C and N. In this case, it attacks through the C-atom.

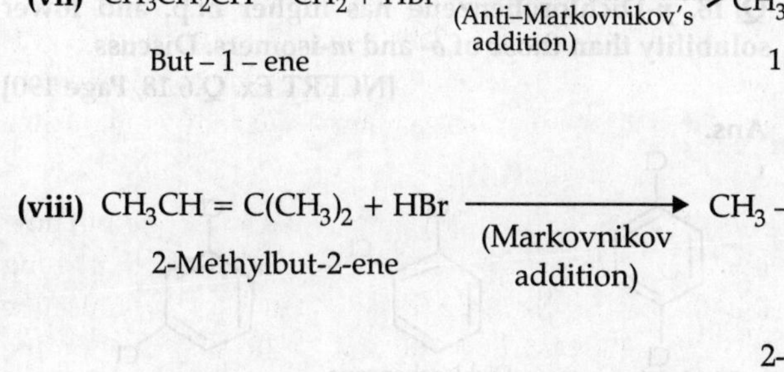

Q. 16. Arrange the compounds of each set-in order of reactivity towards S_N2 displacement:

(i) 1-Bromo-2-methylbutane, 1-Bromopentane, 2-Bromo-pentane

(ii) 1-Bromo-3-methylbutane, 2-Bromo-2-methylbutane, 3-Bromo-2- methylbutane

(iii) 1-Bromobutane, 1-Bromo-2,2-dimethylpropane, 1-Bromo-2-methylbutane, 1Bromo-3- methylbutane.

[NCERT Ex. Q.6.16, Page 190]

Ans. (i)

$CH_3CH_2CH_2CH_2CH_2—Br$

1 – Bromopentane (1°)

$CH_3CH_2CH_2CH(Br)CH_3$ 2 - Bromopentane (2°)

$CH_3CH_2C(Br)(CH_3)CH_3$ 2 - Bromo - 2 – methylbutane (3°)

An S_N2 reaction involves the approaching of the nucleophile to the carbon atom to which the leaving group is attached. When the nucleophile is sterically hindered, then the reactivity towards S_N2 displacement decreases. Due to the presence of substituent, hindrance to the approaching nucleophile increases in the following order.

1- Bromopentane < 2-bromopentane < 2-Bromo-2-methylbutane

Hence, the increasing order of reactivity towards S_N2 displacement is: 2-Bromo-2- methylbutane < 2-Bromopentane < 1-Bromopentane

(ii)

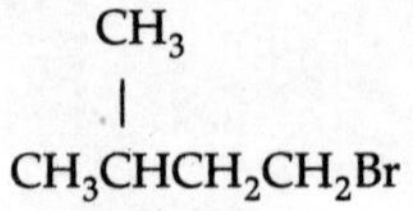

1 - Bromo - 3 - methylbutane(1°)

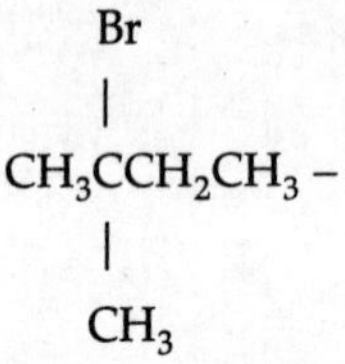

2 - Bromo - 2 methylbutane(3°)

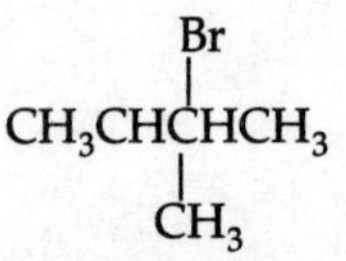

2 - Bromo - 3 methylbutane(2°)

Since steric hindrance in alkyl halides increases in the order of 1° < 2° < 3°, the increasing order of reactivity towards S_N2 displacement is 3° < 2° < 1°.

Hence, the given set of compounds can be arranged in the increasing order of their reactivity towards S_N2 displacement as:

2-Bromo-2-methylbutane < 2-Bromo-3-methylbutane < 1-Bromo-3-methylbutane.

[2- Bromo-3-methylbutane is incorrectly given in NCERT]

(iii)

$CH_3-CH_2-CH_2-CH_2-Br$

1– Bromobutane

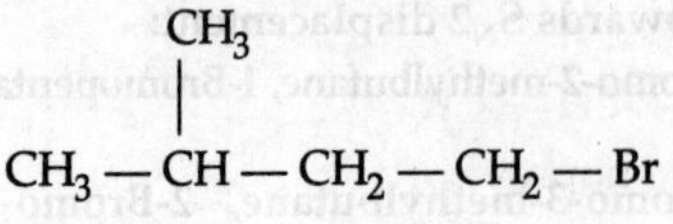

1– Bromo – 3 – methylbutane

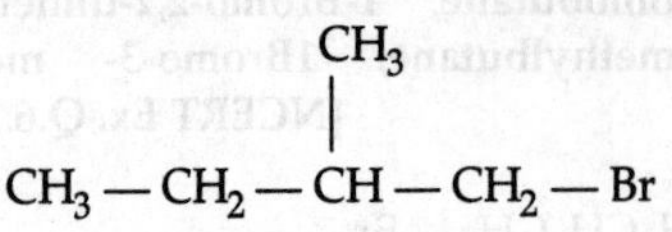

1– Bromo – 2 – methylbutane

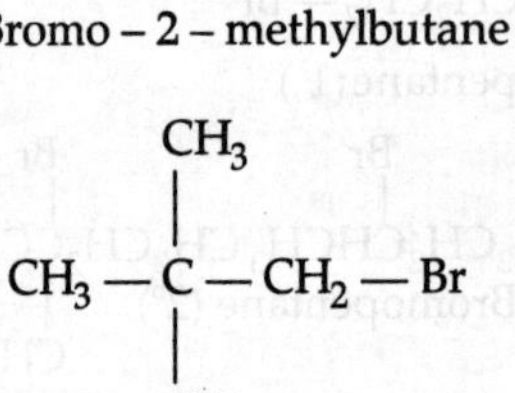

1–Bromo – 2, 2 – dimethylpropar

The steric hindrance to the nucleophile in the S_N2 mechanism increases with a decrease in the distance of the substituents from the atom containing the leaving group. Further, the steric hindrance increases with an increase in the number of substituents. Therefore, the increasing order of steric hindrances in the given compounds is as below:

1-Bromobutane < 1-Bromo-3-methylbutane < 1-Bromo-2-methylbutane < 1-Bromo-2, 2-dimethylpropane

Hence, the increasing order of reactivity of the given compounds towards S_N2 displacement is:

1-Bromo-2, 2-dimethylpropane < 1-Bromo-2-methylbutane < 1-Bromo-3- ethylbutane < 1- Bromobutane

Q. 17. Out of $C_6H_5CH_2Cl$ and $C_6H_5CHClC_6H_5$, which is more easily hydrolysed by aqueous KOH?

[NCERT Ex. Q.6.17, Page 190]

Ans.

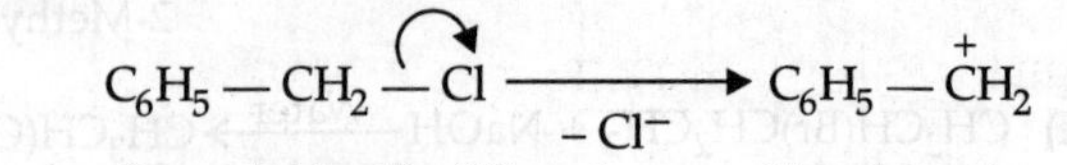

Benzyl chloride (1°) 1° carbocation

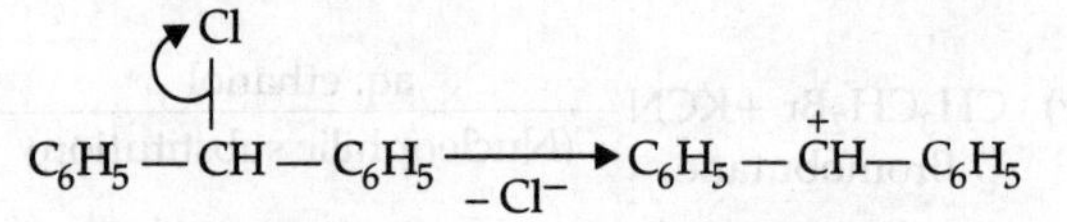

Chlorodiphenylmethane 2° carbocation

Hydrolysis by aqueous KOH proceeds through the formation of carbocation. If carbocation is stable, then the compound is easily hydrolyzed by aqueous KOH. Now, $C_6H_5CH_2Cl$ forms 1°-carbocation, while $C_6H_5CHClC_6H_5$ forms 2°-carbocation, which is more stable than 1°-carbocation. Hence, $C_6H_5CHClC_6H_5$ is hydrolyzed more $C_6H_5CH_2Cl$ easily than by aqueous KOH.

Q. 18. *p*-Dichlorobenzene has higher m.p. and lower solubility than those of *o*- and *m*-isomers. Discuss.

[NCERT Ex. Q.6.18, Page 190]

Ans.

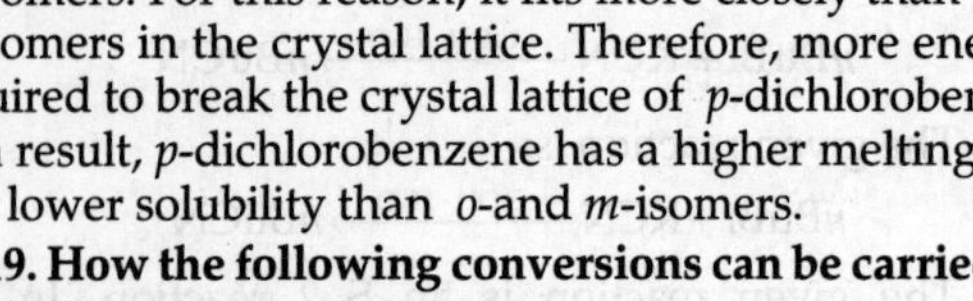

p- Dichlorobenzene *o*- Dichlorobenzene *m*- Dichlorobenzene

p-Dichlorobenzene is more symmetrical than *o*-and *m*-isomers. For this reason, it fits more closely than *o*-and *m*-isomers in the crystal lattice. Therefore, more energy is required to break the crystal lattice of *p*-dichlorobenzene. As a result, *p*-dichlorobenzene has a higher melting point and lower solubility than *o*-and *m*-isomers.

Q. 19. How the following conversions can be carried out?

(i) Propene to propan-1-ol

(ii) Ethanol to but-1-yne

(iii) 1-Bromopropane to 2-bromopropane

(iv) Toluene to benzyl alcohol

(v) Benzene to 4-bromonitrobenzene

(vi) Benzyl alcohol to 2-phenylethanoic acid

(vii) Ethanol to propanenitrile

(viii) Aniline to chlorobenzene

(ix) 2-Chlorobutane to 3, 4-dimethylhexane

(x) 2-Methyl-1-propene to 2-chloro-2-methylpropane

(xi) Ethyl chloride to propanoic acid

(xii) But-1-ene to n-butyliodide

(xiii) **2-Chloropropane to 1-propanol**
(xiv) **Isopropyl alcohol to iodoform**
(xv) **Chlorobenzene to *p*-nitrophenol**
(xvi) **2-Bromopropane to 1-bromopropane**
(xvii) **Chloroethane to butane**
(xviii) **Benzene to diphenyl**
(xix) ***tert*-Butyl bromide to isobutyl bromide**
(xx) **Aniline to phenylisocyanide**

[NCERT Ex. Q.6.19, Page 190-191]

Ans.

(i)

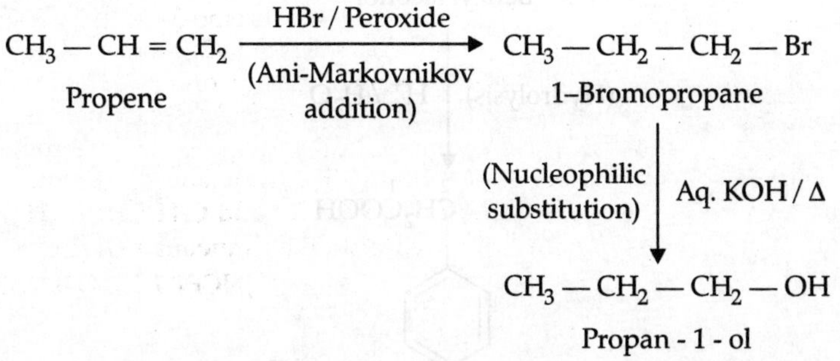

(ii)

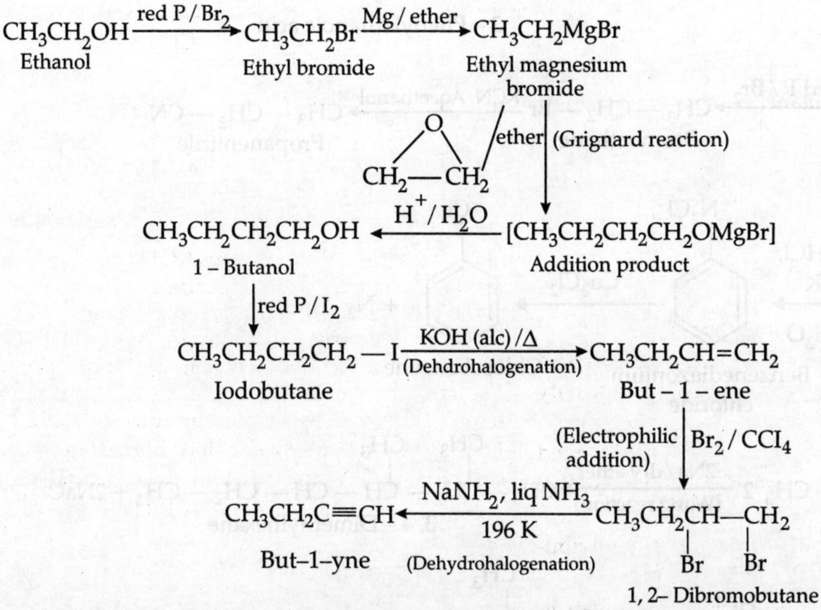

(iii)

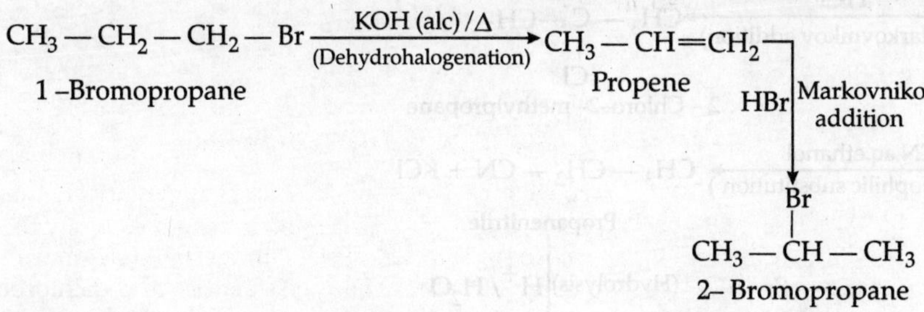

(iv)

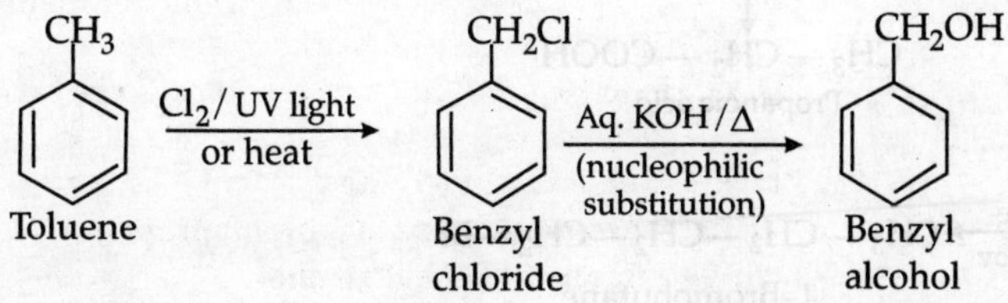

(v)

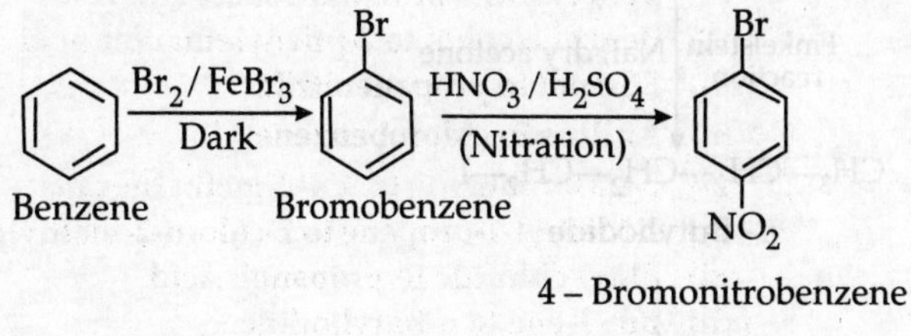

(vi)

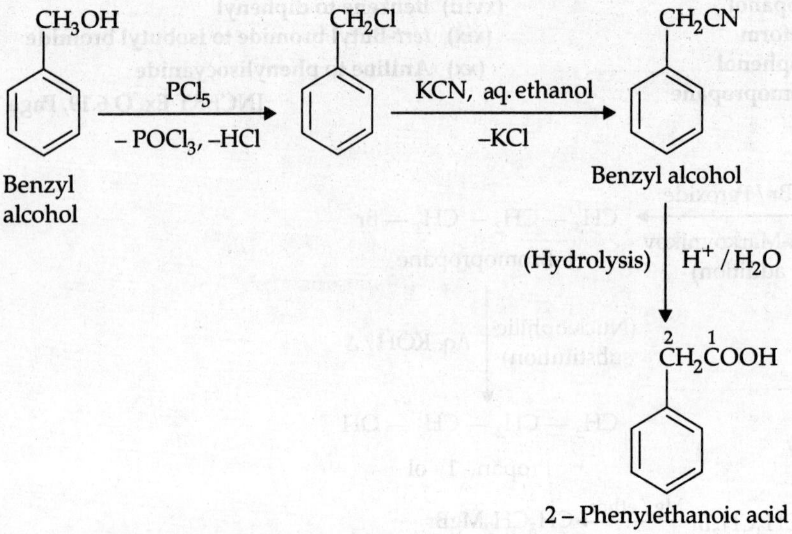

(vii) $CH_3-CH_2-OH \xrightarrow{\text{red P / Br}_2} CH_3-CH_2-Br \xrightarrow{\text{KCN, Aq. ethanol}} CH_3-CH_2-CN$

Ethanol → Bromoethane → Propanenitrile

(viii)

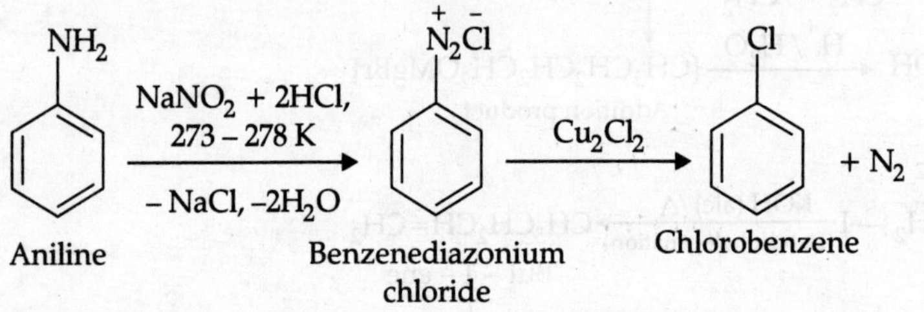

(ix)

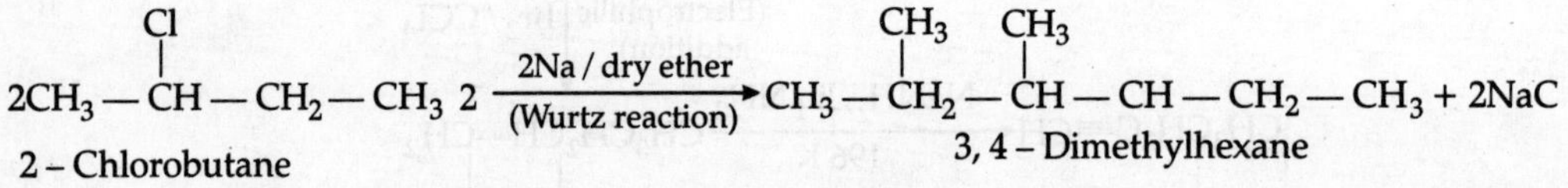

(x)

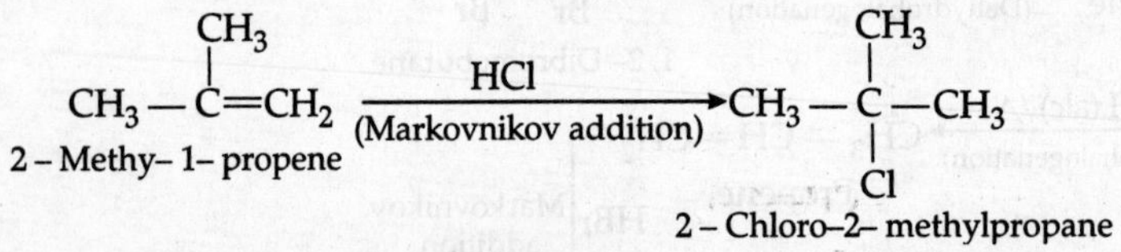

(xi) $CH_3-CH_2-Cl \xrightarrow[\text{(Nucleophilic substitution)}]{\text{KCN,aq.ethanol}} CH_3-CH_2-CN + KCl$

Ethylchloride → Propanenitrile

$\xrightarrow[\text{(Hydrolysis)}]{H^+/H_2O} CH_3-CH_2-COOH$

Propanoic acid

(xii) $CH_3-CH_2-CH{=}CH_2 \xrightarrow[\text{(Anti–Markovnikov addition)}]{\text{HBr / Peroxide}} CH_3-CH_2-CH_2-CH_2-Br$

But–1– ene → 1–Bromobutane

$\xrightarrow[\text{Finkelstein reaction}]{\text{NaI, dry acetone}} CH_3-CH_2-CH_2-CH_2-I$

n– Butyliodide

(xiii)

$$CH_3-\underset{\underset{\text{2–Chloropropane}}{}}{\overset{Cl}{\overset{|}{C}H}}-CH_3 \xrightarrow[\text{(Dehydrohalogenation)}]{\text{KOH (alc) / }\Delta} \underset{\text{Propene}}{CH_3-CH=CH_2} + HCl$$

$$\underset{\text{Propene}}{CH_3-CH=CH_2} \xrightarrow[\text{(Anti– Markovnikov addition)}]{\text{HBr / Peroxide}} \underset{\text{1–Bromopropane}}{CH_3-CH_2-CH_2\,Br}$$

$$\underset{\text{1–Bromopropane}}{CH_3-CH_2-CH_2\,Br} \xrightarrow[\text{(Nuclcophilic substitution)}]{\text{aq.KOH}/\Delta} \underset{\text{1– Propanol}}{CH_3-CH_2-CH_2-OH}$$

(xiv)

$$\underset{\text{Isoproyl alcohol}}{CH_3-\overset{OH}{\overset{|}{C}H}-CH_3} \xrightarrow[\text{(Oxidation)}]{CrO_3} \underset{\text{Propanone}}{CH_3-\overset{O}{\overset{\|}{C}}-CH_3}$$

$$\underset{\text{Propanone}}{CH_3-\overset{O}{\overset{\|}{C}}-CH_3} \xrightarrow[\text{(Iodoform reaction)}]{NaOI} CH_3-\overset{O}{\overset{\|}{C}}-ONa + \underset{\text{Iodoform}}{CHI_3}$$

(xv)

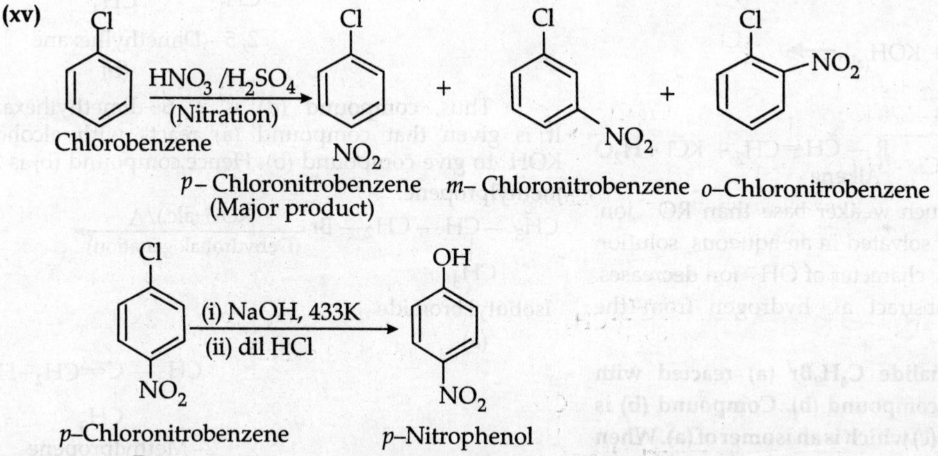

(xvi)

$$\underset{\text{2– Bromopropane}}{CH_3-\overset{Br}{\overset{|}{C}H}-CH_3} \xrightarrow[\text{Dehydrohalogenation}]{\text{KOH(alc.)}/\Delta} \underset{\text{Propene}}{CH_3-CH=CH_2} + HBr$$

$$\underset{\text{Propene}}{CH_3-CH=CH_2} \xrightarrow[\text{(Anti – Markovnikov addition)}]{\text{HBr/ Peroxide}} \underset{\text{1–Bromopropane}}{CH_3-CH_2-CH_2-Br}$$

(xvii)

$$\underset{\text{Chloroethane}}{CH_3-CH_2-Cl} \xrightarrow[\text{(Wurtz reaction)}]{\text{2Na/ dry ether}} \underset{\text{Butane}}{CH_3-CH_2-CH_2-CH_3} + 2NaCl$$

(xviii)

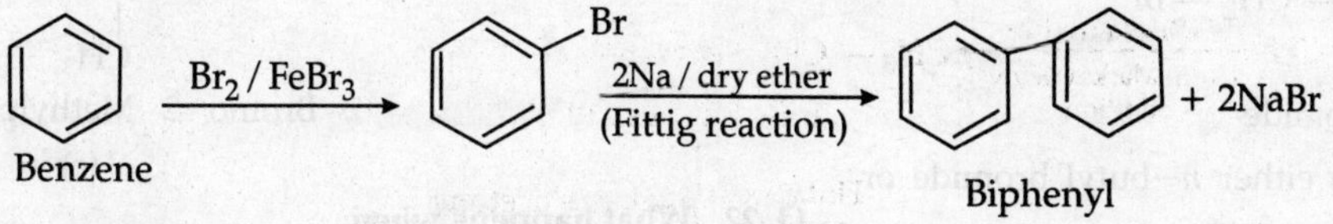

(xix)

$$\underset{\text{Tert – butylbromide}}{CH_3-\overset{Br}{\overset{|}{\underset{\underset{CH_3}{|}}{C}}}-CH_3} \xrightarrow[\text{(Dehydrohalogenation)}]{\text{KOH (alc) }/\Delta} \underset{\text{2–Methylpropene}}{CH_3-\underset{\underset{CH_3}{|}}{C}=CH_2} \xrightarrow[\text{(Anti / Markovnikov addition)}]{\text{HBr / Peroxide}} \underset{\text{Isobutylbromide}}{CH_3-\underset{\underset{CH_3}{|}}{CH}-CH_2-Br}$$

(xx)

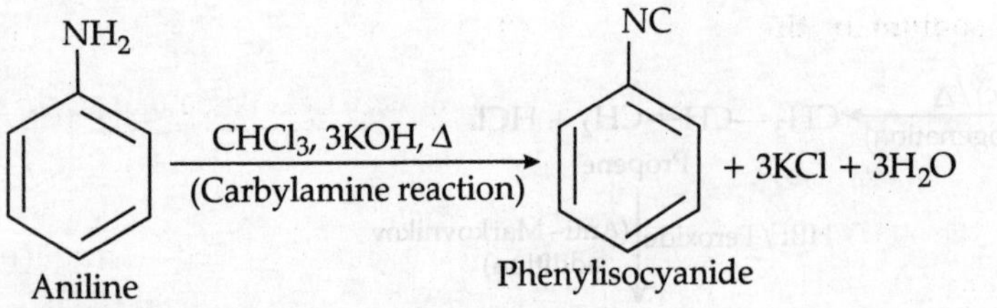

Q. 20. The treatment of alkyl chlorides with aqueous KOH leads to the formation of alcohols but in the presence of alcoholic KOH, alkenes are major products. Explain. **[NCERT Ex. Q.6.20, Page 191]**

Ans. In an aqueous solution, KOH almost completely ionizes to give OH^- ions. OH^- ion is a strong nucleophile, which leads the alkyl chloride to undergo a substitution reaction to form alcohol.

$$\underset{\text{Alkyl chloride}}{R-Cl} + KOH_{(aq)} \longrightarrow \underset{\text{Alcohol}}{R-OH} + KCl$$

On the other hand, an alcoholic solution of KOH contains alkoxide (RO^-) ion, which is a strong base. Thus, it can abstract a hydrogen from the β-carbon of the alkyl chloride and form an alkene by eliminating a molecule of HCl.

$$\underset{\text{Alkyl chloride}}{R-\underset{\beta}{CH_2}-\underset{\alpha}{CH_2}-Cl} + KOH_{(alc)} \longrightarrow \underset{\text{Alkene}}{R-CH{=}CH_2} + KCl + H_2O$$

OH^- ion is a much weaker base than RO^- ion. Also, OH^- ion is highly solvated in an aqueous solution and as a result, the basic character of OH^- ion decreases. Therefore, it cannot abstract a hydrogen from the β-carbon.

Q. 21. Primary alkyl halide C_4H_9Br (a) reacted with alcoholic KOH to give compound (b). Compound (b) is reacted with HBr to give (c) which is an isomer of (a). When (a) is reacted with sodium metal it gives compound (d), C_8H_{18} which is different from the compound formed when *n*-butyl bromide is reacted with sodium. Give the structural formula of (a) and write the equations for all the reactions. **[NCERT Ex. Q.6.21, Page 191]**

Ans. There are two primary alkyl halides having the formula, C_4H_9Br. They are *n*-bulyl bromide and isobutyl bromide.

$$\underset{n\text{-Butylbromide}}{CH_3-CH_2-CH_2-CH_2-Br}$$

$$\underset{\text{Isobutyl bromide}}{CH_3-\underset{\underset{CH_3}{|}}{CH}-CH_2-Br}$$

Therefore, compound (a) is either *n*−butyl bromide or isobutyl bromide.

Now, compound (a) reacts with Na metal to give compound (b) of molecular formula, C_8H_{18}, which is different from the compound formed when *n*−butyl bromide reacts with Na metal. Hence, compound (a) must be isobutyl bromide.

$$\underset{n\text{-Butyl bromide}}{2CH_3CH_2CH_2CH_2Br} \xrightarrow[\text{(Wurtz reaction)}]{\text{2Na/ dry ether}} \underset{n\text{-Octane}}{CH_3CH_2CH_2CH_2CH_2CH_2CH_2CH_3} + 2NaBr$$

$$\underset{\substack{\text{Isobutyl bromide} \\ \text{(a)}}}{CH_3\underset{\underset{CH_3}{|}}{CH}CH_2Br} \xrightarrow[\text{(Wurtz reaction)}]{\text{2Na / dry ether}} \underset{\substack{\text{2, 5 – Dimethylhexane} \\ \text{(b)}}}{CH_3\underset{\underset{CH_3}{|}}{CH}CH_2CH_2\underset{\underset{CH_3}{|}}{CH}CH_3} + 2NaBr$$

Thus, compound (d) is 2, 5−dimethylhexane. It is given that compound (a) reacts with alcoholic KOH to give compound (b). Hence,compound (b) is 2−methylpropene.

$$\underset{\substack{\text{Isobutyl bromide} \\ \text{(a)}}}{CH_3-\underset{\underset{CH_3}{|}}{CH}-CH_2-Br} \xrightarrow[\text{(Dehydrohalogenation)}]{\text{KOH (alc.)/}\Delta} \underset{\substack{\text{2- Methylpropene} \\ \text{(b)}}}{CH_3-\underset{\underset{CH_3}{|}}{C}{=}CH_2} + HBr$$

Also, compound (b) reacts with HBr to give compound (c) which is an isomer of (a). Hence, compound (c) is 2−bromo−2−methylpropane.

$$\underset{\substack{\text{2- Methylpropene} \\ \text{(b)}}}{CH_3-\underset{\underset{CH_3}{|}}{CH}{=}CH_2} \xrightarrow[\text{(Markovnikov addition)}]{\text{HBr}} \underset{\substack{\text{2- Bromo -2- Methylpropane} \\ \text{(c)}}}{CH_3-\overset{\overset{Br}{|}}{\underset{\underset{CH_3}{|}}{CH}}-CH_3}$$

Q. 22. What happens when

(i) *n*-butyl chloride is treated with alcoholic KOH,

(ii) bromobenzene is treated with Mg in the presence of dry ether,

(iii) chlorobenzene is subjected to hydrolysis,

(iv) ethyl chloride is treated with aqueous KOH,

(v) methyl bromide is treated with sodium in the presence of dry ether,

(vi) methyl chloride is treated with KCN.

[NCERT Ex. Q.6.22, Page 191]

Ans. (i) When $n-$butyl chloride is treated with alcoholic KOH, the formation of but$-1-$ene takes place. This reaction is a dehydrohalogenation reaction.

$$CH_3-CH_2-CH_2-CH_2-Cl \xrightarrow[\text{Dehydrohalogenation}]{\text{KOH (alc.)}/\Delta} CH_3-CH_2-CH{=}CH_2+KCl+H_2O$$

$n-$ Butyl chloride → But–1–ene

(ii) When bromobenzene is treated with Mg in the presence of dry ether, phenylmagnesium bromide is formed.

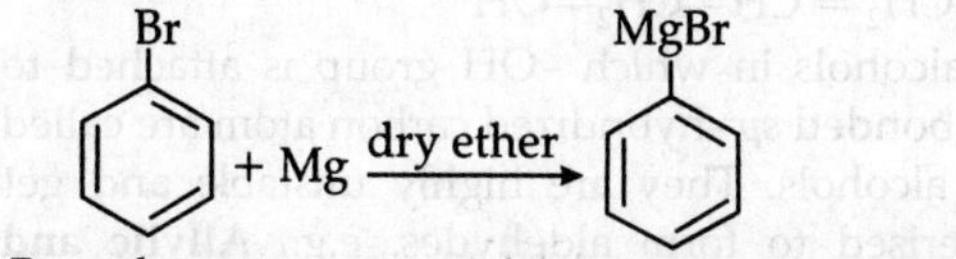

Bromobenzene Phenylmagnesium bromide

(iii) Chlorobenzene does not undergo hydrolysis under normal conditions. However, it undergoes hydrolysis when heated in an aqueous sodium hydroxide solution at a temperature of 623 K and a pressure of 300 atm to form phenol.

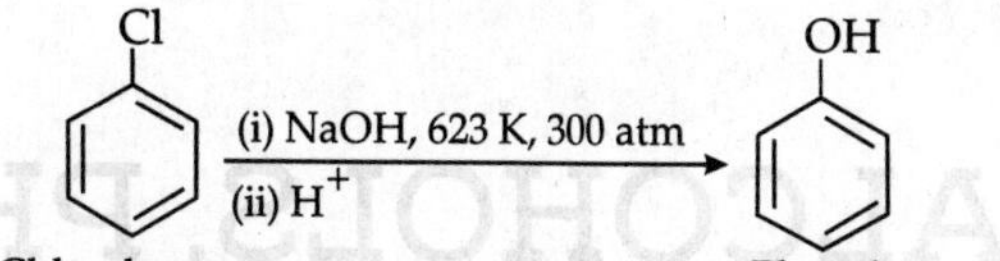

Chlorobenzene Phenol

(iv) When ethyl chloride is treated with aqueous KOH, it undergoes hydrolysis to form ethanol.

$$CH_3-CH_2-Cl \xrightarrow[\text{(Hydrolysis)}]{\text{KOH}} CH_3-CH_2-OH+KCl$$

Ethyl chloride → Ethanol

(v) When methyl bromide is treated with sodium in the presence of dry ether, ethane is formed. This reaction is known as the Wurtz reaction.

$$2CH_3-Br + 2Na \xrightarrow[\text{(Wurtz reaction)}]{\text{Dry ether}} CH_3-CH_3+2NaBr$$

Methyl bromide → Ethane

(vi) When methyl chloride is treated with KCN, it undergoes a substitution reaction to give methyl cyanide.

$$CH_3-Cl + KCN \xrightarrow[\text{substitution}]{\text{Nucleophilic}} CH_3-CN+KCl$$

Methy chloride → Methyl cyanide

□□

CHAPTER 7

ALCOHOLS, PHENOLS AND ETHERS

- Alcohols, phenols and ethers are the basic compounds for the formation of detergents, antiseptics and fragrance respectively.
- **Alcohol:** When one hydrogen atom of an alkane is replaced by –OH group, the compounds obtained are called alcohols having general formula $C_nH_{2n+1}OH$.

Scan to know more about this topic

Nomenclature of alcohols

Classification of Alcohols

(a) Mono, di, tri and polyhydric alcohols:

(i) Those alcohols which contain one –OH group, e.g., CH_3OH, C_2H_5OH, etc., are called monohydric alcohols.

(ii) Those alcohols which contain two –OH groups, are called dihydric alcohols. Their general formula is $C_nH_{2n}(OH)_2$. They are called diols. e.g., CH_2OH–CH_2OH Ethane-1, 2-diol.

(iii) Those alcohols which contain three hydroxyl (–OH) groups, are called trihydric alcohols. They are also called triols.

Their general formula is $C_nH_{2n-1}(OH)_3$.

e.g., CH_2OH–$CHOH$–CH_2OH Propane-1, 2, 3-triol.

(iv) Those alcohols which have more than one –OH groups are called polyhydric alcohols. e.g., CH_2OH–CH_2OH Glycol.

(b) 1°, 2° and 3° alcohols:

(i) The alcohol in which –OH group is attached to primary (1°) carbon atom is called primary alcohol, e.g., CH_3OH, C_2H_5OH, etc.

(ii) The alcohol in which –OH group is attached to secondary (2°) carbon atom is called secondary alcohol. e.g., CH_3—$CH(OH)$—CH_3 (2-propanol).

(iii) The alcohol in which —OH group is attached to tertiary (3°) carbon atom is called tertiary alcohol.

e.g., CH_3—$C(CH_3)_2$—OH or $(CH_3)_3COH$ (2-methylpropan-2-ol).

(c) Allylic and vinylic alcohols:

(i) Those alcohols in which –OH group is attached to single bonded sp^3-hybridized carbon next to carbon-carbon double bond, that is to an allylic carbon are called allylic alcohols. e.g.,

$$CH_2 = CH—CH_2—OH$$

(ii) Those alcohols in which –OH group is attached to double bonded sp^2-hybridized carbon atom are called vinylic alcohols. They are highly unstable and get tautomerised to form aldehydes. e.g., **Allylic and benzylic alcohols may be primary, secondary or tertiary.**

$$\underset{\text{(Vinyl alcohol)}}{CH_2{=}CHOH} \rightleftharpoons \underset{\text{(Acetaldehyde)}}{CH_3-\overset{O}{\overset{\|}{C}}-H}$$

(d) Benzyl alcohol: The alcohol in which –OH group is attached to single bonded sp^3-hybridised carbon atom attached to aromatic ring is called benzyl alcohol. e.g.,

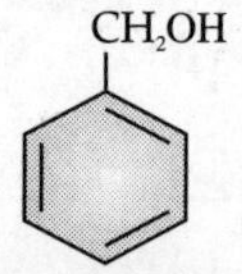

Benzyl alcohol
(Phenyl methanol)

- **Common and IUPAC Names of Some Alcohols**

Table 1

Formula	Common Name	IUPAC Name
CH_3OH	Methyl alcohol	Methanol
CH_3CH_2OH	Ethyl alcohol	Ethanol
$CH_3CH_2CH_2OH$	*n*-Propyl alcohol	Propan-1-ol
$CH_3CHOHCH_3$	*iso*-Propyl alcohol	Propan-2-ol
$(CH_3)_2CH—CH_2OH$	*iso*-Butyl alcohol	2-Methylpropan-1-ol
$CH_3CH_2CHOHCH_3$	*sec*- Butyl alcohol	Butan-2-ol
$(CH_3)_3C—OH$	*tert*- Butyl alcohol	2-Methylpropan-2-ol
$CH_2(OH) — CH_2(OH)$	Ethylene glycol	Ethane-1, 2-diol
$CH_2(OH) — CH(OH) — CH_2(OH)$	Glycerol or Glycerine	Propane-1, 2, 3-triol

- **IUPAC names of some Phenols:**

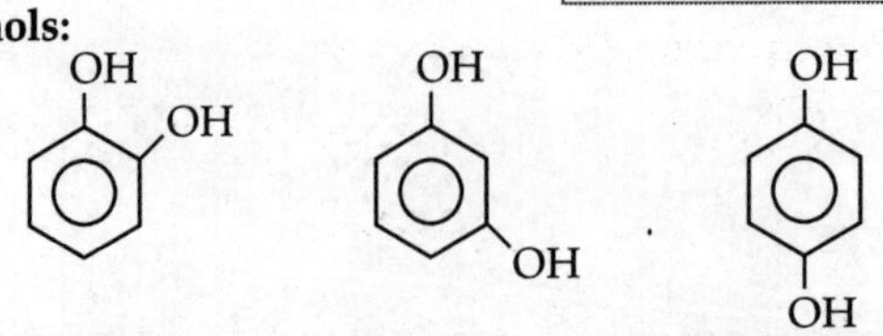

Common name	Catechol	Resorcinol	Hydroquinoneor quinol
IUPAC name	Benzene-1,2-diol	Benzene-1,3-diol	Benzene-1,4-diol

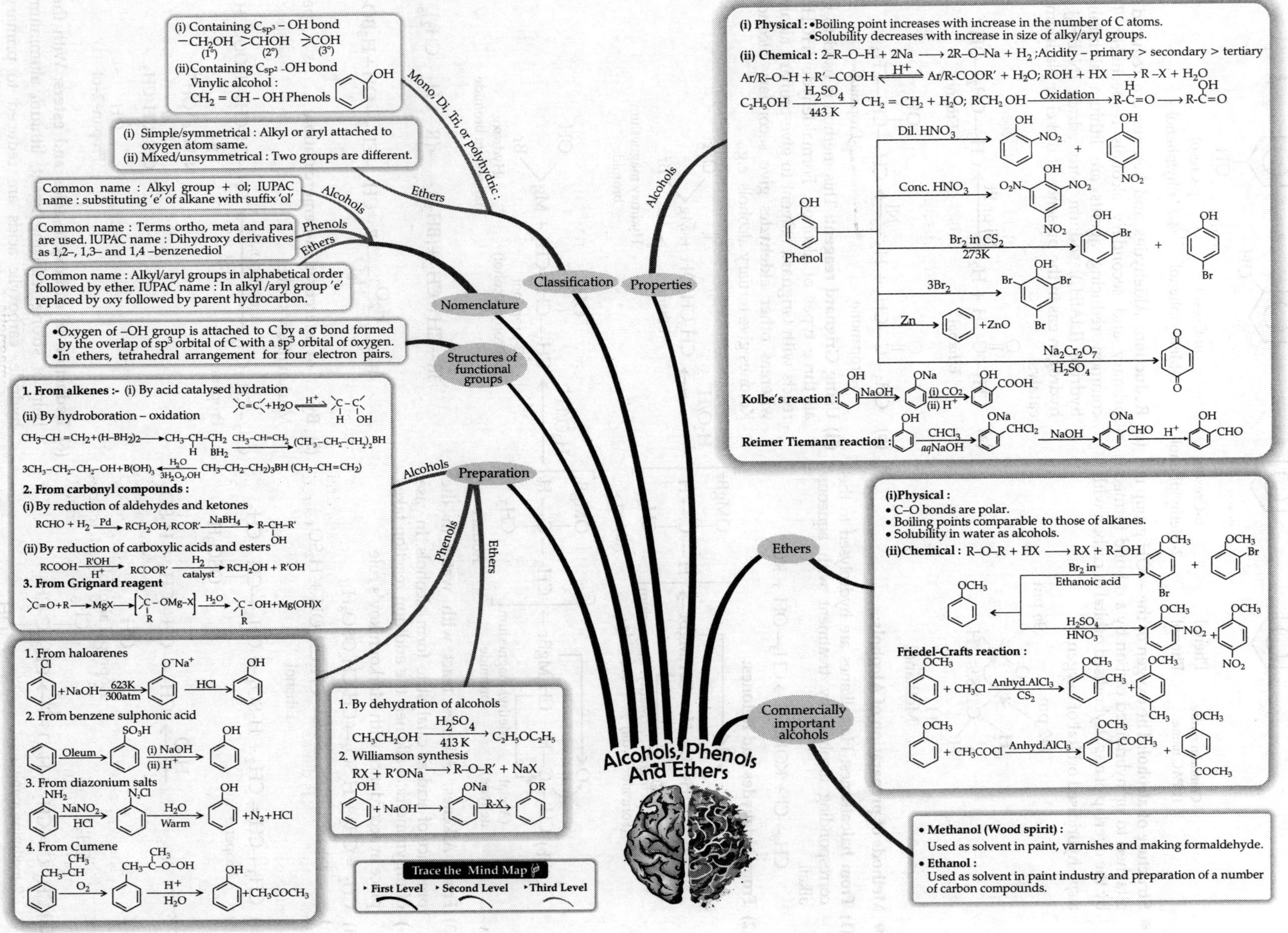
Alcohols, Phenols And Ethers
Classification
Mono, Di, Tri, or polyhydric :
(i) Containing C_{sp^3} – OH bond
$-CH_2OH$ (1°) >CHOH (2°) ≥COH (3°)
(ii) Containing C_{sp^2} -OH bond
Vinylic alcohol :
$CH_2 = CH - OH$ Phenols
Ethers
(i) Simple/symmetrical : Alkyl or aryl attached to oxygen atom same.
(ii) Mixed/unsymmetrical : Two groups are different.
Nomenclature
Alcohols
Common name : Alkyl group + ol; IUPAC name : substituting 'e' of alkane with suffix 'ol'
Phenols
Common name : Terms ortho, meta and para are used. IUPAC name : Dihydroxy derivatives as 1,2–, 1,3– and 1,4 –benzenediol
Ethers
Common name : Alkyl/aryl groups in alphabetical order followed by ether. IUPAC name : In alkyl /aryl group 'e' replaced by oxy followed by parent hydrocarbon.
Structures of functional groups
•Oxygen of –OH group is attached to C by a σ bond formed by the overlap of sp^3 orbital of C with a sp^3 orbital of oxygen.
•In ethers, tetrahedral arrangement for four electron pairs.
Preparation
Alcohols
1. From alkenes :- (i) By acid catalysed hydration
(ii) By hydroboration – oxidation
2. From carbonyl compounds :
(i) By reduction of aldehydes and ketones
$RCHO + H_2 \xrightarrow{Pd} RCH_2OH$, $RCOR' \xrightarrow{NaBH_4} R-CH(OH)-R'$
(ii) By reduction of carboxylic acids and esters
$RCOOH \xrightarrow[H^+]{R'OH} RCOOR' \xrightarrow[catalyst]{H_2} RCH_2OH + R'OH$
3. From Grignard reagent
Phenols
1. From haloarenes
+NaOH 623K 300atm HCl
2. From benzene sulphonic acid
Oleum (i) NaOH (ii) H^+
3. From diazonium salts
$NaNO_2$ HCl H_2O Warm $+N_2+HCl$
4. From Cumene
O_2 H^+ H_2O $+CH_3COCH_3$
Ethers
1. By dehydration of alcohols
$CH_3CH_2OH \xrightarrow[413\ K]{H_2SO_4} C_2H_5OC_2H_5$
2. Williamson synthesis
$RX + R'ONa \longrightarrow R-O-R' + NaX$
+ NaOH R-X
Properties
Alcohols
(i) Physical : •Boiling point increases with increase in the number of C atoms.
•Solubility decreases with increase in size of alky/aryl groups.
(ii) Chemical : $2R-O-H + 2Na \longrightarrow 2R-O-Na + H_2$;Acidity – primary > secondary > tertiary
$Ar/R-O-H + R'-COOH \rightleftharpoons^{H^+} Ar/R-COOR' + H_2O$; $ROH + HX \longrightarrow R-X + H_2O$
$C_2H_5OH \xrightarrow[443\ K]{H_2SO_4} CH_2 = CH_2 + H_2O$; $RCH_2OH \xrightarrow{Oxidation} R-CHO \longrightarrow R-COOH$
Phenol
Dil. HNO_3
Conc. HNO_3
Br_2 in CS_2 273K
$3Br_2$
Zn +ZnO
$Na_2Cr_2O_7$ H_2SO_4
Kolbe's reaction : NaOH (i) CO_2 (ii) H^+
Reimer Tiemann reaction : $CHCl_3$ aqNaOH NaOH H^+
Ethers
(i)Physical :
• C–O bonds are polar.
• Boiling points comparable to those of alkanes.
• Solubility in water as alcohols.
(ii)Chemical : $R-O-R + HX \longrightarrow RX + R-OH$
Br_2 in Ethanoic acid
H_2SO_4 HNO_3
Friedel-Crafts reaction :
$+ CH_3Cl$ Anhyd.$AlCl_3$ CS_2
$+ CH_3COCl$ Anhyd.$AlCl_3$
Commercially important alcohols
• Methanol (Wood spirit) :
Used as solvent in paint, varnishes and making formaldehyde.
• Ethanol :
Used as solvent in paint industry and preparation of a number of carbon compounds.
Trace the Mind Map
First Level Second Level Third Level

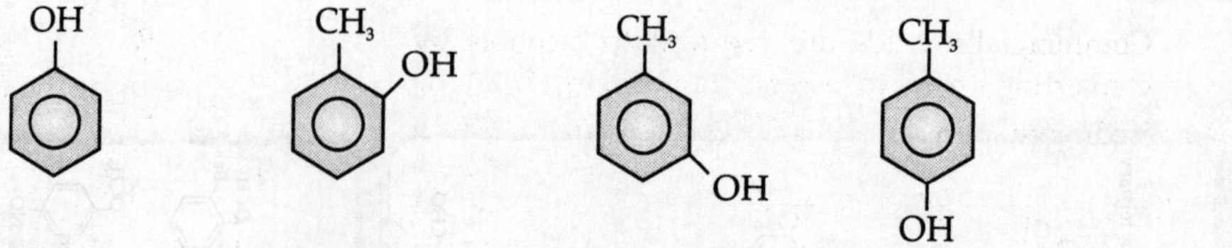

Common name	Phenol	*o*-Cresol	*m*-Cresol	*p*-Cresol
IUPAC name	Phenol	2-Methylphenol	3-Methylphenol	4-Methylphenol

- **Structure of alcohol:** The oxygen of the —OH group is attached to sp^3 hybridized carbon by a σ bond formed by the overlap of a sp^3 hybridised orbital of carbon with a sp^3 hybridised orbital of oxygen.

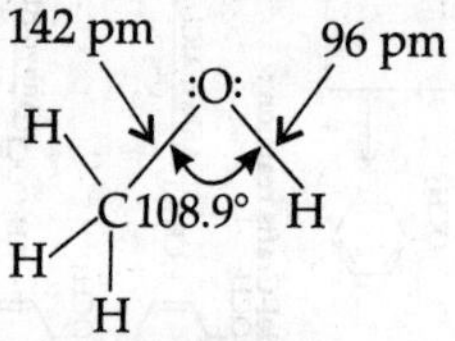

Methanol

- **Methods of preparation of Alcohols:**

(1) From haloalkanes: Haloalkanes are hydrolysed to the corresponding alcohols by treatment with aqueous alkali.

$$CH_3—Cl + KOH(aq) \rightarrow CH_3—OH + KCl$$

(2) From Aldehydes and Ketones:

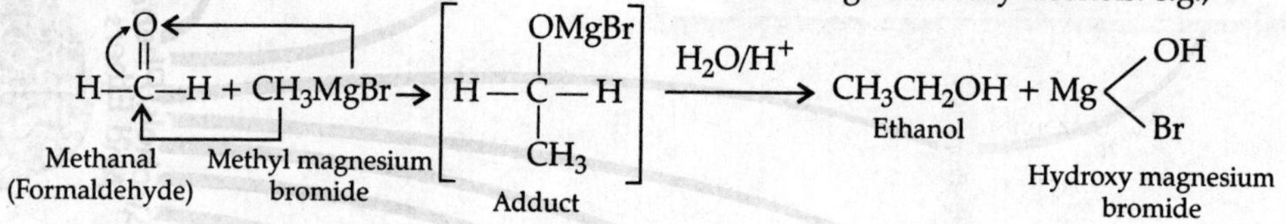

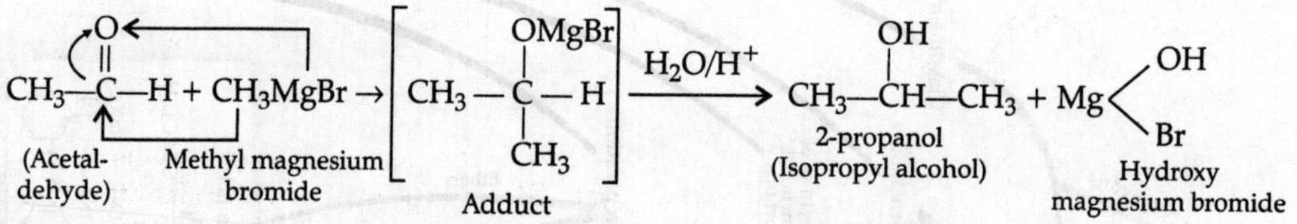

(3) From Alkenes: Alkenes react with water in the presence of acid as catalyst to form alcohols. In case of unsymmetrical alkenes, the addition reaction takes place in accordance with Markovnikov's rule

(i) $\underset{\text{Ethene}}{CH_2 = CH_2} + H_2SO_4 \rightarrow CH_3CH_2OSO_3H \xrightarrow{H_2O} \underset{\text{Ethanol}}{CH_3CH_2OH} + H_2SO_4$

(ii) $\underset{\text{Propene}}{CH_3—CH = CH_2} + H_2SO_4 \rightarrow CH_3—\underset{OSO_3H}{CH}-CH_3 \xrightarrow{H_2O} \underset{\text{Isopropyl alcohol}}{CH_3 - \underset{OH}{CH} - CH_3} + H_2SO_4$

(iii) $\underset{\text{2-methylpropene}}{CH_3-\overset{CH_3}{C} = CH_2} + H_2O \xrightarrow{H^+} \underset{\text{2-methylpropan-2-ol}}{CH_3-\overset{CH_3}{\underset{OH}{C}}-CH_3}$

(4) By hydroboration-oxidation: As per anti Markovnikov's rule -

$$3R-CH=CH_2+(BH_3)_2 \longrightarrow (R-CH_2-CH_2)_3B \xrightarrow[OH^-,H_2O]{H_2O_2} R-CH_2-CH_2-OH+H_3BO_3$$

(5) By oxymercuration-demercuration: As per Markovnikov's rule:

$$\underset{\text{Propene}}{CH_3-CH=CH_2} \xrightarrow[H_2O]{(CH_3COO)_2Hg} CH_3-\underset{OH}{CH}-CH_2-HgOOCCH_3 \xrightarrow{NaBH_4 \mid OH^-} \underset{\text{Propan-2-ol}}{CH_3-\underset{OH}{CH}-CH_3}$$

(6) Reduction of carboxylic acids and esters: With the help of strong reducing agent, lithium aluminium hydride, carboxylic acids are reduced to primary alcohols.

$$RCOOH \xrightarrow[\text{(ii) } H_2O]{\text{(i) } LiAlH_4} RCH_2OH$$

(i) **Reduction:** Aldehydes and ketones are reduced to primary and secondary alcohols respectively. The common reducing agents are lithium aluminium hydride ($LiAlH_4$), sodium borohydride ($NaBH_4$) or hydrogen gas in the presence of nickel or platinum as catalyst.

(a) $\underset{\text{Ethanal}}{CH_3—\overset{O}{\overset{\|}{C}}—H} + H_2 \xrightarrow{\text{Ni or Pt}} \underset{\text{Ethanol}}{CH_3—CH_2—OH}$

(b) $\underset{\text{2-Propanone}}{CH_3—\overset{O}{\overset{\|}{C}}—CH_3} + H_2 \xrightarrow{Ni} \underset{\text{2-Propanol}}{CH_3—\overset{OH}{CH}—CH_3}$

(ii) **Using Grignard reagent:** This method is used to get all three types of alcohols. Formaldehyde (HCHO) reacts with Grignard reagent to give primary alcohol whereas other aldehydes give secondary alcohols. Ketones give tertiary alcohols. e.g.,

Commercially, acids are reduced to alcohols by converting them to esters, followed by catalytic hydrogenation.

$$RCOOH \xrightarrow[H^+]{R'OH} RCOOR' \xrightarrow[Catalyst]{H_2} RCH_2OH + R'OH$$

- **Preparation of Phenols:**

(i) From aryl halides

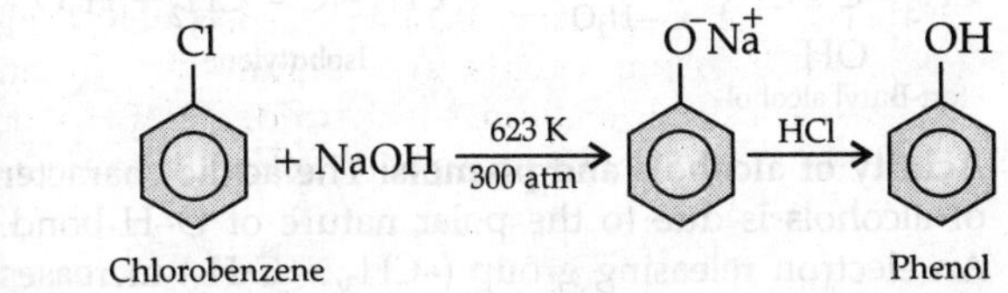

(ii) From benzenesulphonic acid

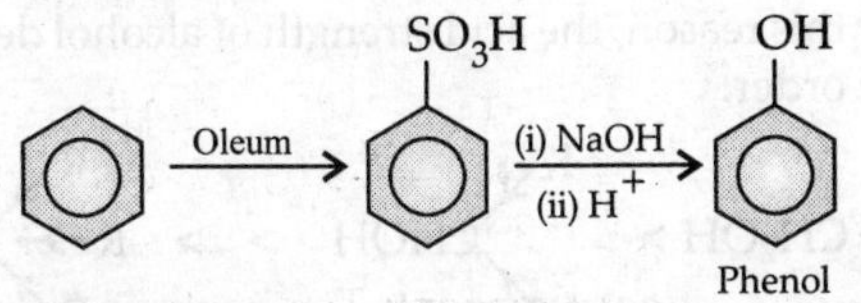

(iii) From diazonium salts

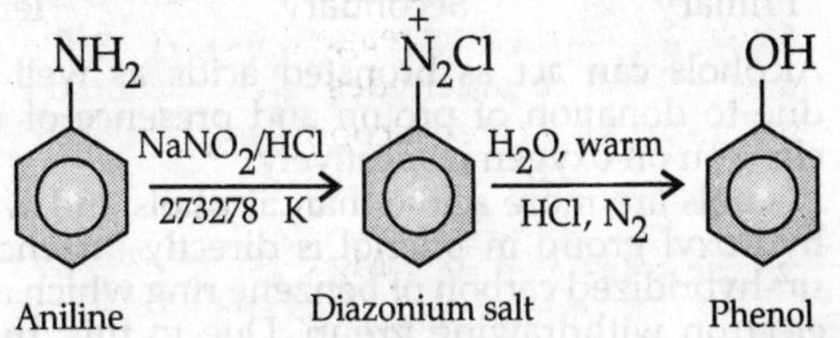

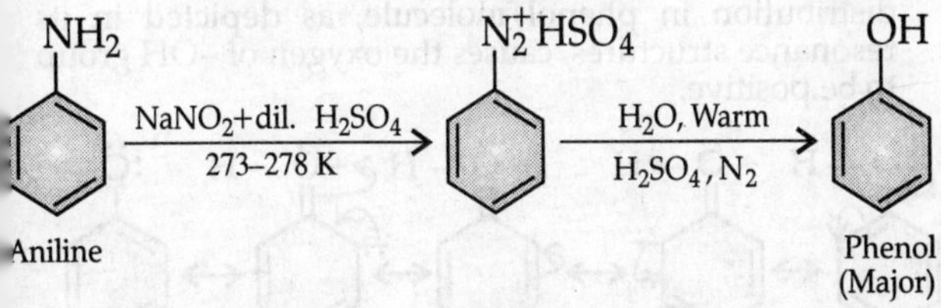

(iv) From Cumene:

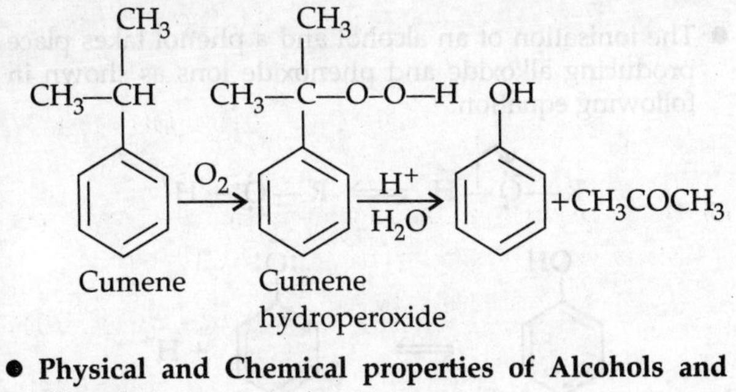

- **Physical and Chemical properties of Alcohols and Phenols:**

(1) Physical properties:

(i) Boiling points: The boiling points of alcohols and phenols increase with increase in the number of carbon atoms (increase in Van der Waals forces). In alcohols, the boiling points decrease with increase of branching in carbon chain (because of decrease in Van der Waals forces with decrease in surface area).

The –OH group in alcohols and phenols is involved in intermolecular hydrogen bonding **resulting in** high boiling point, which is lacking in ethers and hydrocarbons.

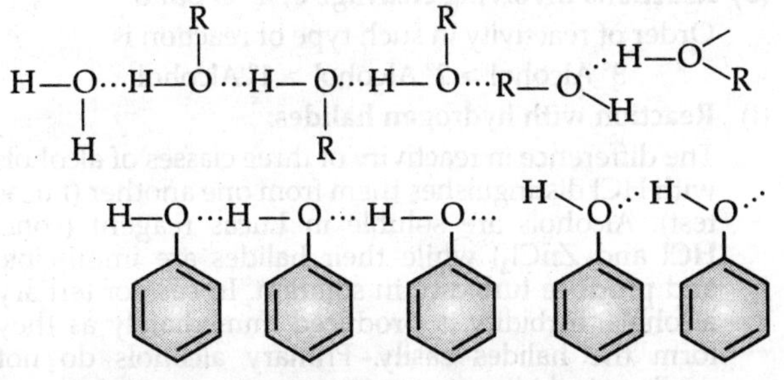

(ii) Solubility: Solubility of alcohols and phenols in water is due to their ability to form hydrogen bonds with water molecules. The solubility decreases with increase in size of alkyl/aryl (hydrophobic) groups.

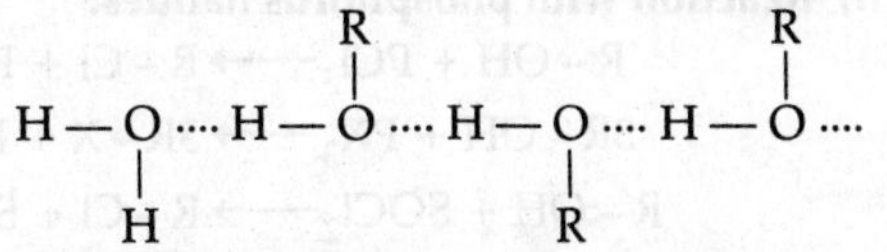

(2) Chemical properties: Alcohols and phenols react both as nucleophiles and electrophiles. The bond between O–H is broken when alcohols react as *nucleophiles.*

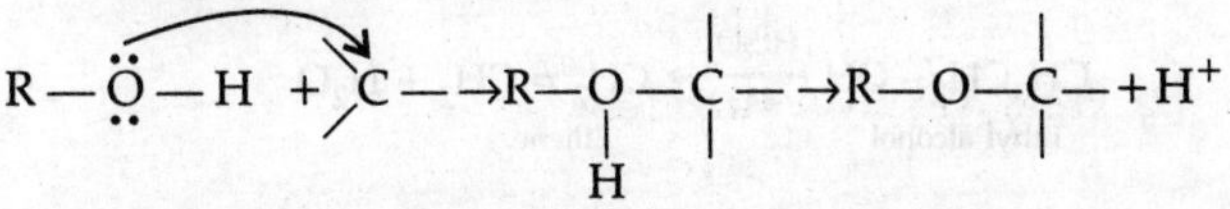

The bond between C–O is broken when they react as *electrophiles.*

$$R—CH_2OH + H^+ \longrightarrow RCH_2\overset{+}{O}H_2$$

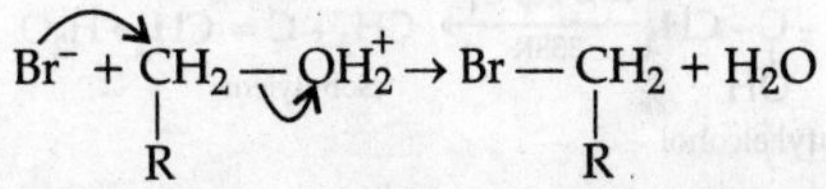

The reactions of alcohols can be classified into:

(a) Reactions involving the cleavage of O–H bond:

(i) Reaction with metals:

$$2R–O–H + 2Na \longrightarrow 2R–\bar{O}\overset{+}{Na} + H_2$$

Sodium alkoxide

$$CH_3–CH_2–OH + Na \longrightarrow CH_3–CH_2–\bar{O}\overset{+}{Na} + \frac{1}{2}H_2$$

Sodium ethoxide

$$6(CH_3)_3C–OH + 2Al \longrightarrow 2((CH_3)_3C–O)_3Al + 3H_2$$

3° Butyl alcohol — Aluminium tert-butoxide

The above reactions show that alcohols and phenols are acidic in nature. In fact, alcohols and phenols are Bronsted acids, i.e., they can donate a proton to a stronger base (B:).

(ii) Esterification:

$$R–COOH + R'–OH \overset{H^+}{\rightleftharpoons} R–COOR' + H_2O$$

Carboxylic acid, Alcohol, Ester

$$(R–CO)_2O + R'–OH \overset{H^+}{\rightleftharpoons} R–COOR' + R–COOH$$

Acid anhydride, Ester

$$R–COCl + R'–OH \xrightarrow{Pyridine} R–COOR' + HCl$$

Acid chloride, Ester

(b) Reactions involving cleavage of C–O bond:

Order of reactivity in such type of reaction is

3° Alcohol > 2° Alcohol > 1° Alcohol

(i) Reaction with hydrogen halides:

The difference in reactivity of three classes of alcohols with HCl distinguishes them from one another (Lucas test). Alcohols are soluble in Lucas reagent (conc. HCl and $ZnCl_2$) while their halides are immiscible and produce turbidity in solution. In case of tertiary alcohols, turbidity is produced immediately as they form the halides easily. Primary alcohols do not produce turbidity at room temperature.

$$\underset{\text{Alcohol}}{R-OH} + \underset{\text{Hydrogen halide}}{H-X} \xrightarrow{\text{anhyd. } ZnCl_2} \underset{\text{Alkyl halide}}{R-X} + H_2O$$

(ii) Reaction with phosphorus halides:

$$R-OH + PCl_5 \longrightarrow R-Cl + POCl_3 + HCl$$
$$3R-OH + PX_3 \longrightarrow 3R-X + H_3PO_3$$
$$R-OH + SOCl_2 \longrightarrow R-Cl + SO_2\uparrow + HCl$$

(c) Reactions involving both the alkyl and hydroxyl group:

(i) Dehydration: 3° Alcohol > 2° Alcohol > 1° Alcohol

$$\underset{\text{Ethyl alcohol}}{CH_3CH_2-OH} \xrightarrow[443\text{ K}]{H_2SO_4} \underset{\text{Ethene}}{CH_2=CH_2} + H_2O$$

$$\underset{\text{Isopropyl alcohol}}{CH_3-CH(OH)-CH_3} \xrightarrow[440K]{85\%\ H_3PO_4} \underset{\text{Propylene}}{CH_3-CH=CH_2} + H_2O$$

$$\underset{tert\text{.butyl alcohol}}{CH_3-C(CH_3)(OH)-CH_3} \xrightarrow[358K]{20\%\ H_3PO_4} \underset{\text{Isobutylene}}{CH_3-C(CH_3)=CH_2} + H_2O$$

(ii) Oxidation:

$$\underset{1°\text{ Alcohol}}{R-CH_2-OH} + [O] \xrightarrow[\text{or alk.}KMnO_4,\ -H_2O]{K_2Cr_2O_7/H_2SO_4} R-CHO \xrightarrow{[O]} \underset{\text{Carboxylic acid}}{R-COOH}$$

$$\underset{2°\text{ Alcohol}}{RR'CH-OH} \xrightarrow{CrO_3} \underset{\text{Ketone}}{RR'C=O}$$

$$\underset{3°\text{ Butyl alcohol}}{CH_3-C(CH_3)(OH)-CH_3} \xrightarrow[{[O]},\ -H_2O]{\text{Hot conc. } HNO_3} CH_3-C(CH_3)=CH_2 \xrightarrow[{[O]}]{-H_2O,\ -CO_2} \underset{\text{Acetone}}{(CH_3)_2C=O} \xrightarrow[-H_2O,\ -CO_2]{[O]} \underset{\text{Acetic acid}}{CH_3COOH}$$

(iii) Dehydrogenation:

$$\underset{1°\text{Alcohol}}{R-CH_2-OH} \xrightarrow[573K]{Cu} \underset{\text{Aldehyde}}{R-CHO} + H_2$$

$$\underset{2°\text{Alcohol}}{RR'CH-O-H} \xrightarrow[573K]{Cu} \underset{\text{Ketone}}{RR'C=O} + H_2$$

$$\underset{\text{tert-Butyl alcohol}}{CH_3-C(CH_3)(OH)-CH_3} \xrightarrow[-H_2O]{\text{Hot conc. } HNO_3} \underset{\text{Isobutylene}}{CH_3-C(CH_3)=CH_2} + H_2O$$

- **Acidity of alcohols and phenols:** The acidic character of alcohols is due to the polar nature of O-H bond. An electron releasing group ($-CH_3$, $-C_2H_5$) increases electron density on oxygen tending to decrease the polarity of O–H bond. This decreases the acid strength. For this reason, the acid strength of alcohol decreases in the order:

$$\underset{\text{Primary}}{R\rightarrow CH_2OH} > \underset{\text{Secondary}}{R_2 \rightarrow CHOH} > \underset{\text{Tertiary}}{R_3 \rightarrow C-OH}$$

- Alcohols can act as bronsted acids as well as bases due to donation of proton and presence of unpaired electron on oxygen respectively.
- Phenols are more acidic than alcohols and water. The hydroxyl group in phenol is directly attached to the sp^2-hybridized carbon of benzene ring which acts as an electron withdrawing group. Due to this, the charge distribution in phenol molecule, as depicted in its resonance structures, causes the oxygen of –OH group to be positive.

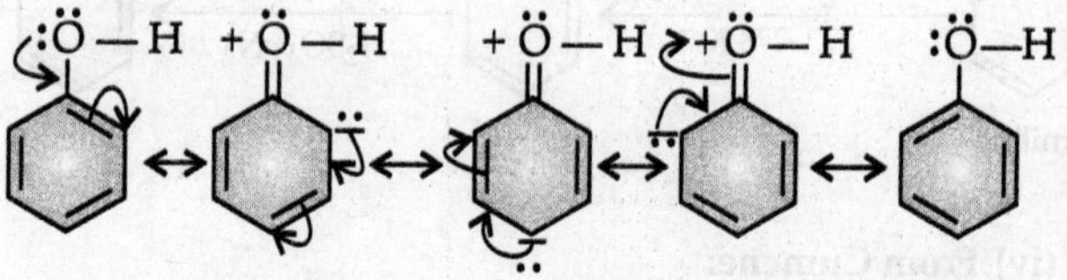

- The ionisation of an alcohol and a phenol takes place producing alkoxide and phenoxide ions as shown in following equation:

$$R-\ddot{O}-H \rightleftharpoons R-\ddot{O}:^- + H^+$$

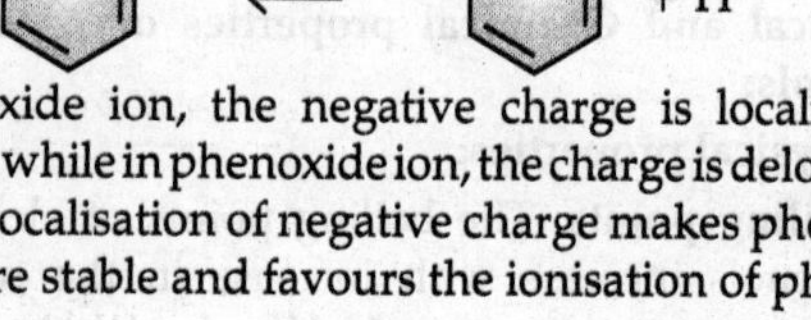

- In alkoxide ion, the negative charge is localised on oxygen while in phenoxide ion, the charge is delocalised. The delocalisation of negative charge makes phenoxide ion more stable and favours the ionisation of phenol.

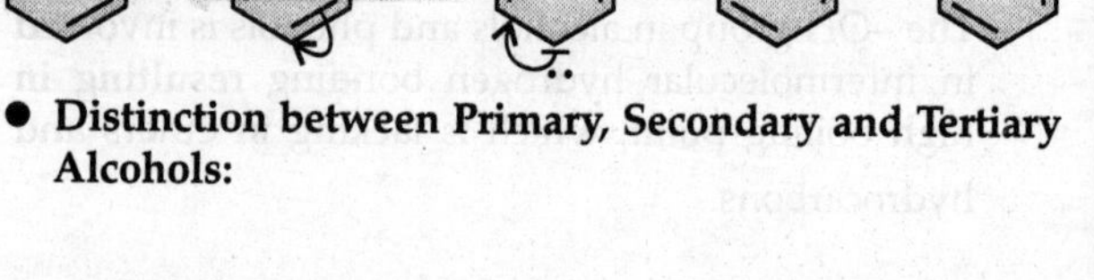

- **Distinction between Primary, Secondary and Tertiary Alcohols:**

(i) Lucas Test: Alcohol on treating with Lucas reagent forms a clear solution. Alkyl chlorides are formed on reaction which being insoluble results in the turbidity in the solution.

$$\text{Alcohol} \xrightarrow[ZnCl_2]{HCl} \text{Alkyl chloride} + H_2O$$

Tertiary alcohol is indicated, if turbidity appears immediately. Secondary alcohol is indicated, if turbidity appears within five minutes. Primary alcohol is indicated, if turbidity appears on heating.

(ii) Iodoform test: When ethanol or any alcohol containing the group $CH_3-CH(OH)-$ is heated with iodine and aqueous NaOH or Na_2CO_3 solution at 333 – 343 K, a yellow precipitate of iodoform is obtained.

$$CH_3OH + I_2 + NaOH \xrightarrow{\Delta} \text{No reaction}$$

$$CH_3CH_2CH_2CH(OH)CH_3 + 4I_2 + 6NaOH \xrightarrow{\Delta}$$

$$\underset{\text{Iodoform}}{CHI_3} + CH_3CH_2CH_2COONa + 5NaI + 5H_2O$$

(iii) Ferric chloride test of phenols: Phenol gives a violet coloured water soluble complex with ferric chloride.

$$6C_6H_5OH + FeCl_3 \longrightarrow \underset{\text{Violet complex}}{[Fe(OC_6H_5)_6]^{3-}} + 3H^+ + 3HCl$$

- **Reactions of Ethanol:**

$$C_2H_5OH \xrightarrow[\text{anhyd. } ZnCl_2 \text{ (Lucas reagent)}]{HCl} C_2H_5Cl + HCl$$

$$C_2H_5OH \xrightarrow{HI + \text{Red P}} C_2H_6 + I_2 + H_2O$$

$$C_2H_5OH \xrightarrow{NH_3/ThO_2, 630K} C_2H_5NH_2 + \text{Secondary and tertiary amine}$$

$$C_2H_5OH \xrightarrow{PCl_5} C_2H_5Cl + POCl_3 + HCl$$

$$C_2H_5OH \xrightarrow{SOCl_2} C_2H_5Cl + SO_2\uparrow + HCl$$

$$C_2H_5OH \xrightarrow{Na} C_2H_5\overset{\ominus}{O}\overset{\oplus}{Na}$$

$$C_2H_5OH \xrightarrow[\text{or } (CH_3CO)_2O]{CH_3COOH \text{ or } CH_3COCl} C_2H_5OOCCH_3 + CH_3COOH$$

$$C_2H_5OH \xrightarrow[520K]{Al_2O_3} C_2H_5OC_2H_5 + H_2O$$

$$C_2H_5OH \xrightarrow[620 K]{Al_2O_3} CH_2=CH_2 + H_2O$$

$$C_2H_5OH \xrightarrow{[O]} CH_3CHO \xrightarrow{[O]} CH_3COOH$$

$$C_2H_5OH \xrightarrow[410K]{\text{Heat with } H_2SO_4,\ C_2H_5OH \text{ in excess}} C_2H_5-O-C_2H_5$$

$$C_2H_5OH \xrightarrow[440K]{H_2SO_4 \text{ in excess}} CH_2=CH_2$$

$$C_2H_5OH \xrightarrow{Cu, 573K} CH_3CHO + H_2$$

$$C_2H_5OH \xrightarrow{Cl_2} CH_3CHO \xrightarrow{Cl_2} CCl_3CHO$$

$$C_2H_5OH \xrightarrow{I_2 + NaOH} CHI_3$$

$$C_2H_5OH \xrightarrow{CH_3MgI} CH_4 + Mg\begin{matrix} I \\ OC_2H_5 \end{matrix}$$

- **Differences between or identification of Methyl Alcohol and Ethyl Alcohol:**

Table 2

S. No.	Test	Methyl alcohol	Ethyl alcohol
(i)	Boiling point	338K	351.2K
(ii)	On heating with I_2 and NaOH.	No reaction.	Iodoform is obtained.
(iii)	On heating with anhydrous sodium acetate and conc. sulphuric acid.	A specific odour of methyl acetate is produced.	Ethyl acetate is formed which has a sweet fruity odour.
(iv)	On heating with salicylic acid and conc. H_2SO_4.	Methyl salicylate (oil of winter green) is formed which has a characteristic odour.	No specific smell.
(v)	On heating with bleaching powder.	No reaction.	Chloroform with sweet smell is formed.

- **Methods of preparation of Glycol:**

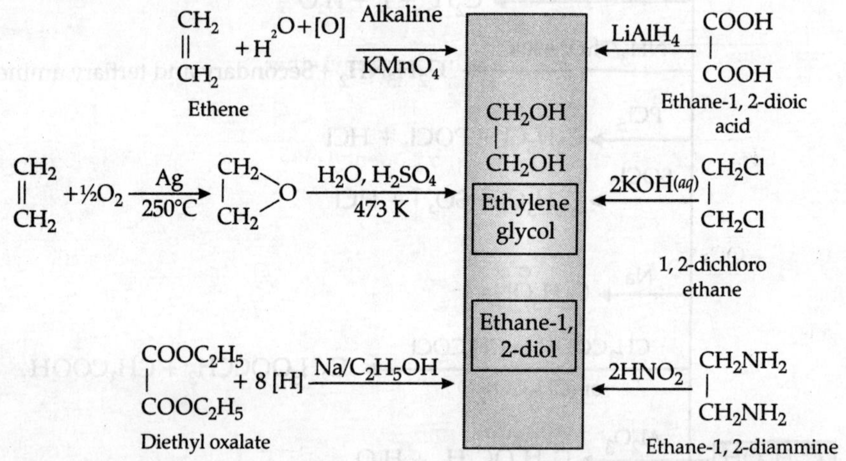

- **Methods of preparation of Glycerol:**

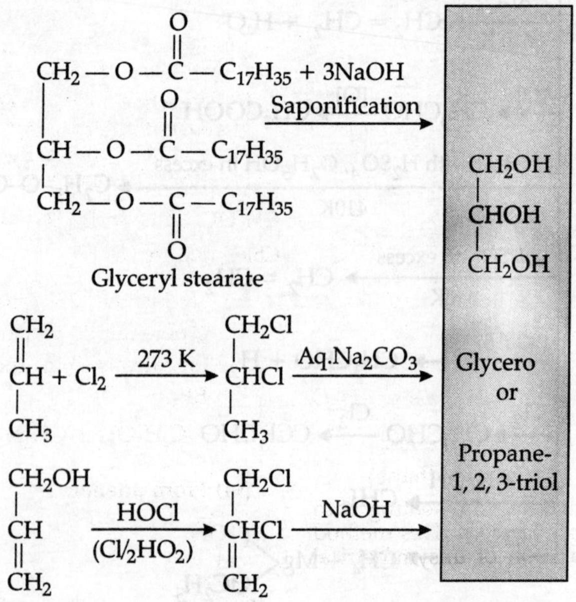

- **Ethers:** Compounds with general formula $C_nH_{2n+2}O$. They are represented by the general structure, R–O–R'.
- **Nomenclature of Ethers:** Ethers are named from names of alkyl/aryl/ groups written as separate words in alphabetical order and adding the word 'ether' at the end. If both the alkyl groups are the same, the prefix '*di*' is added before the alkyl group. For example, $C_2H_5OC_2H_5$ is diethyl ether. These types of ethers are called symmetrical ethers. If both the alkyl groups are different, for example, $CH_3OC_2H_5$ is ethylmethyl ether. These types of ethers are called unsymmetrical ethers. During naming ethers, the larger alkyl group is chosen as the parent hydrocarbon.

Scan to know more about this topic

Alcohols, phenols and ethers

- **Common and IUPAC names of some Ethers are:**

Table 2

Compound	Common name	IUPAC name
CH_3OCH_3	Dimethyl ether	Methoxymethane
$C_2H_5OC_2H_5$	Diethyl ether	Ethoxyethane
$CH_3OCH_2CH_2CH_2CH_3$	Methyl *n*-butyl ether	1-Methoxybutane
$C_6H_5OCH_3$	Methyl phenyl ether (Anisole)	Methoxybenzene
$C_2H_5—O—C_6H_5$	Ethyl phenyl ether (Phenetole)	Ethoxybenzene
$C_6H_5O(CH_2)_6—CH_3$	Heptyl phenyl ether	1-Phenoxyheptane
$CH_3O—CH(CH_3)—CH_3$	Methyl isopropyl ether	2-Methoxypropane
$C_6H_5—O—CH_2—CH_2—CH(CH_3)—CH_2$	Phenyl isopentyl ether	3-Methylbutoxybenzene
$CH_3O—CH_2—CH_2—OCH_3$	—	1, 2-Dimethoxyethane
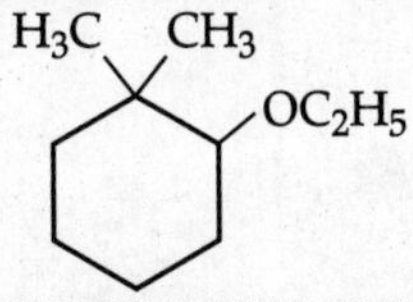		2-Ethoxy-1, 1-dimethylcyclohexane

- **Methods of Preparation of Ethers:**

(i) Williamson's synthesis: When alkyl halide reacts with sodium alkoxide, ethers are formed. *e.g.*,

$$R-X + \overset{+}{Na}-\bar{O}-R' \longrightarrow R-O-R' + NaX$$

Alkyl halide; Sodium alkoxide; Ether

$$C_2H_5Br + CH_3-C(CH_3)_2-ONa \longrightarrow CH_3-C(CH_3)_2-OC_2H_5 + NaBr$$

2-ethoxy-2-methylpropane

(ii) Dehydration of alcohols: Alcohols are dehydrated to ethers in presence of concentrated sulphuric acid at 413 K. The reaction involves the removal of one molecule of water from two moles of alcohols.

$$C_2H_5\boxed{OH + H}OC_2H_5 \xrightarrow[413\ K]{conc.\ H_2SO_4} C_2H_5OC_2H_5 + H_2O$$

Ethyl alcohol; Diethyl ether (Ethoxy ethane)

Alcohols can also be dehydrated by heating with alumina at 523 K and high pressure. This method is not suitable for preparation of unsymmetrical ethers.

(iii) Heating alkyl halides with dry silver oxide: Ethers can be prepared by heating alkyl halides with dry silver oxide (Ag_2O).

$$2C_2H_5Cl + Ag_2O \xrightarrow{heat} C_2H_5—O—C_2H_5 + 2AgCl$$

$$CH_3Cl + Ag_2O + C_2H_5Cl \rightarrow CH_3—O—C_2H_5 + 2AgCl$$

Mixed ethers or unsymmetrical ethers can be prepared by this method.

(iv) Reaction of lower halogenated ethers with Grignard reagent: Higher homologous ethers can be prepared by action of Grignard reagent on lower halogenated ethers.

$$CH_3OCH_2Cl + BrMgC_2H_5 \rightarrow CH_3\text{–}O\text{–}CH_2\text{–}C_2H_5 + Mg\langle^{Br}_{Cl}$$

Chlorodimethyl ether; Methyl propyl ether

(v) Action of diazomethane on alcohols: Methyl ethers can be prepared by action of diazomethane on alcohols in the presence of catalysts like BF_3.

$$C_2H_5OH + CH_2N_2 \xrightarrow{BF_3} C_2H_5OCH_3 + N_2$$

Methyl ethyl ether

(vi) From phenol:

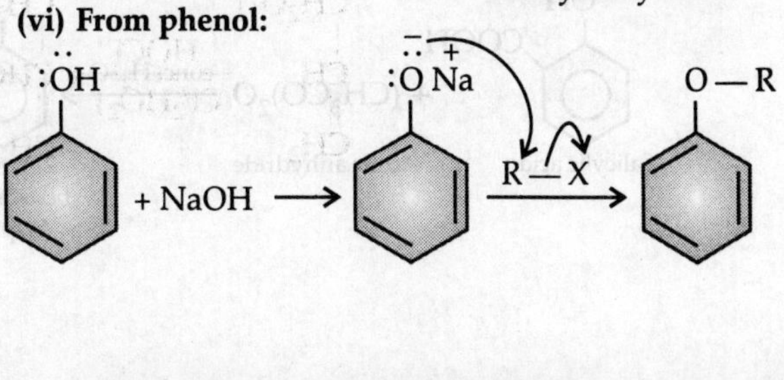

- **Physical Properties:**

(i) Colourless, pleasant smelling and volatile liquids.

(ii) Lower boiling points than alcohols.

(iii) Solubility is comparable to those of corresponding alcohols due to the ability of their molecules to form hydrogen bond with water molecules.

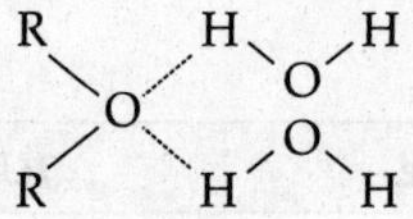

- **Chemical properties:**

(i) Cleavage with halogen acid:

$$\underset{\text{Ether}}{R-O-R} + HX \xrightarrow{373\ K} \underset{\text{Alcohol}}{ROH} + \underset{\text{Alkyl halide}}{RX} \ (X = Br, I)$$

$$C_2H_5OC_2H_5 + HI \xrightarrow{373\ K} C_2H_5OH + C_2H_5I$$

$$C_2H_5OC_2H_5 + \underset{\text{(Excess)}}{2HI} \xrightarrow{373\ K} 2C_2H_5I + H_2O$$

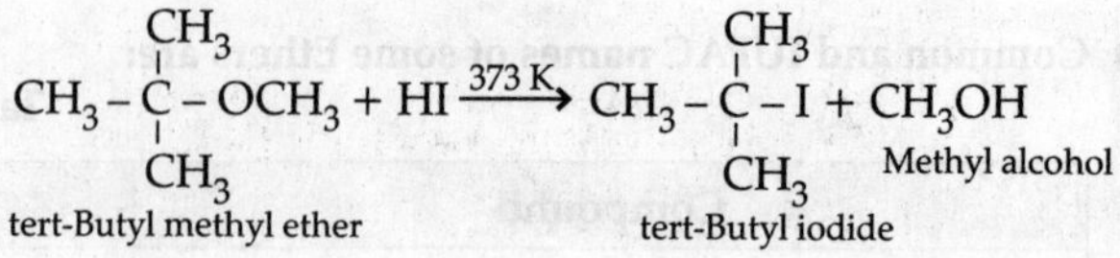

(ii) Ring substitution in aromatic ethers:

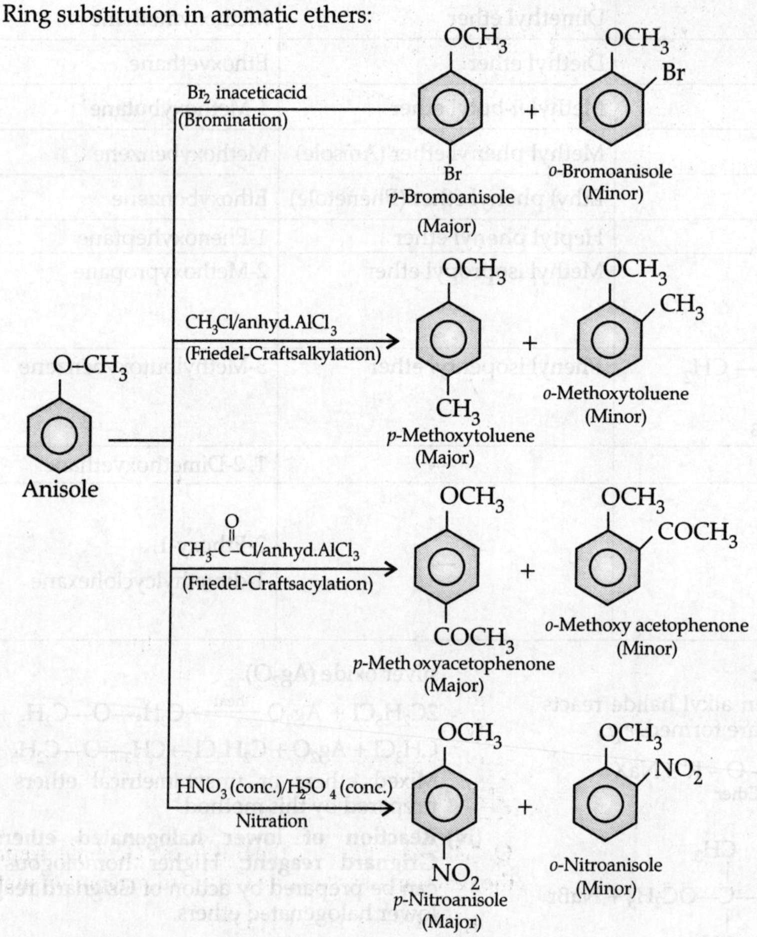

- **Some important name reactions:**

(i) Kolbe's reaction:

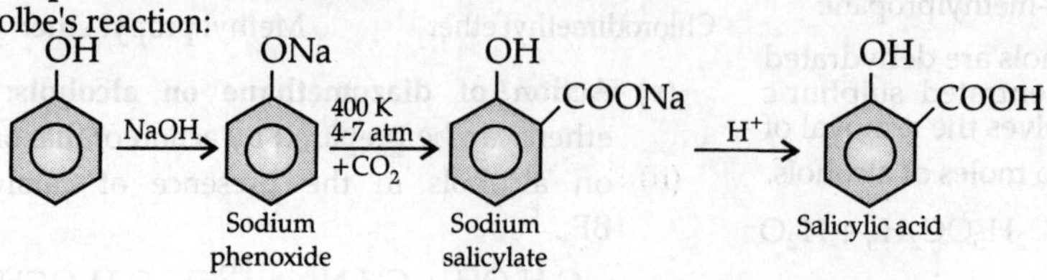

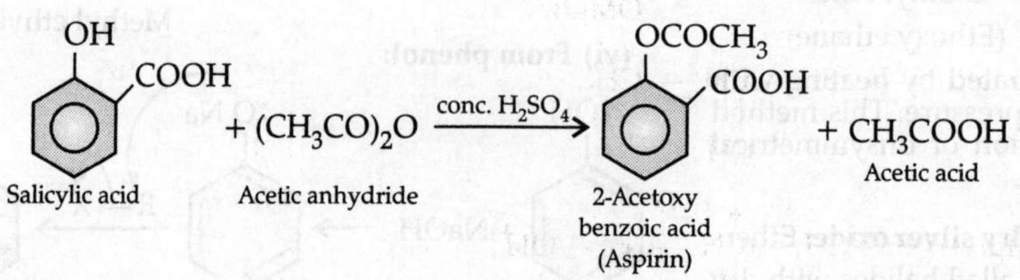

(ii) Fries Rearrangement:

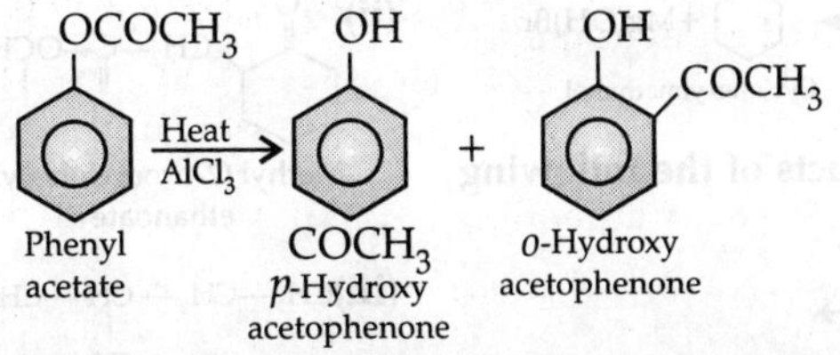

NCERT CORNER

Intext Questions

Page - 195

Q. 7.1. Classify the following as primary, secondary and tertiary alcohols:

(i) 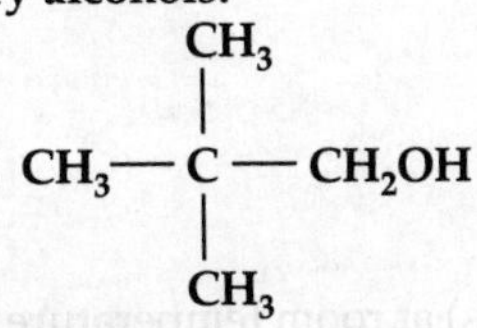

(ii) $H_2C = CH—CH_2OH$

(iii) $CH_3—CH_2—CH_2—OH$

(iv) 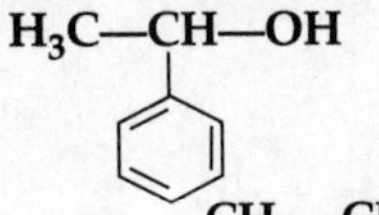

(v) 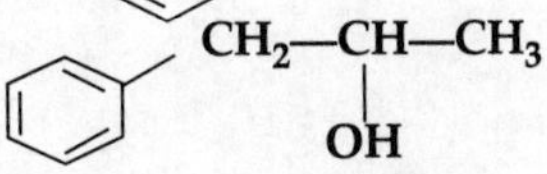

(vi) 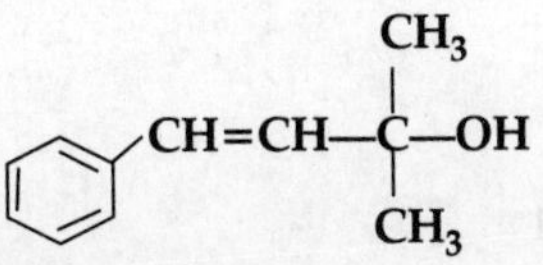

Ans. Primary alcohols: (i), (ii) and (iii)
Secondary alcohols: (iv) and (v)
Tertiary alcohols: (vi)

Q. 7.2. Identify allylic alcohols in the above examples.

Ans. Allylic alcohols: (ii) and (vi).

Q. 7.3. Name the following compounds according to IUPAC system.

(i) 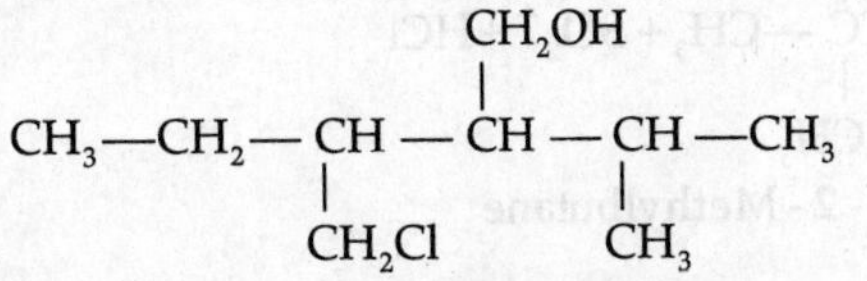

(ii) 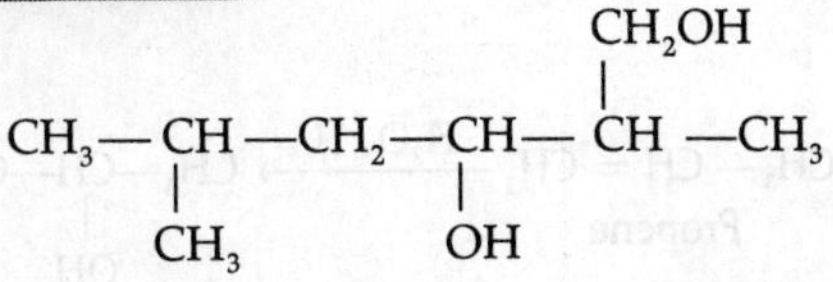

(iii) 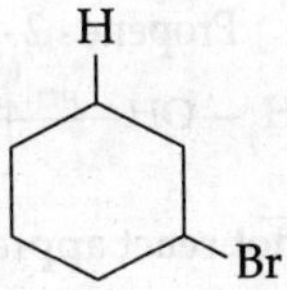

(iv) 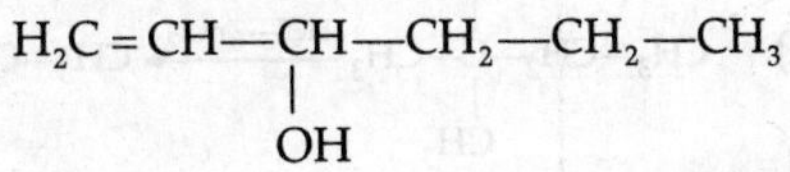

(v) 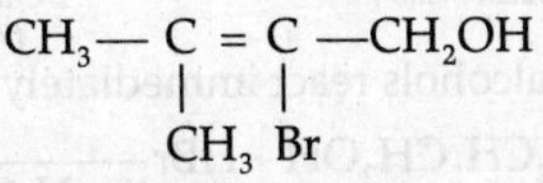

Ans. (i) 3-Chloromethyl-2-isopropylpentan-l-ol
(ii) 2, 5-Dimethylhexane-1,3-diol
(iii) 3-Bromocyclohexanol
(iv) Hex-l-en-3-ol
(v) 2-Bromo-3-methyl-but-2-en-1 -ol

Page - 203

Q. 7.4. Show how are the following alcohols prepared by the reaction of a suitable Grignard reagent on methanal.

(i) 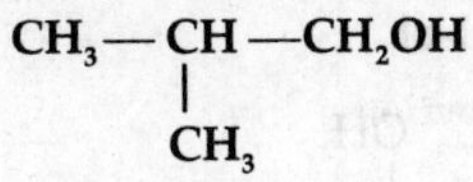

(ii) 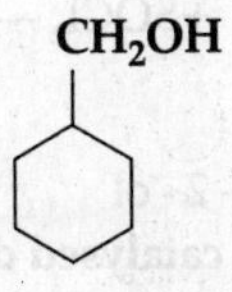

Ans. (i) 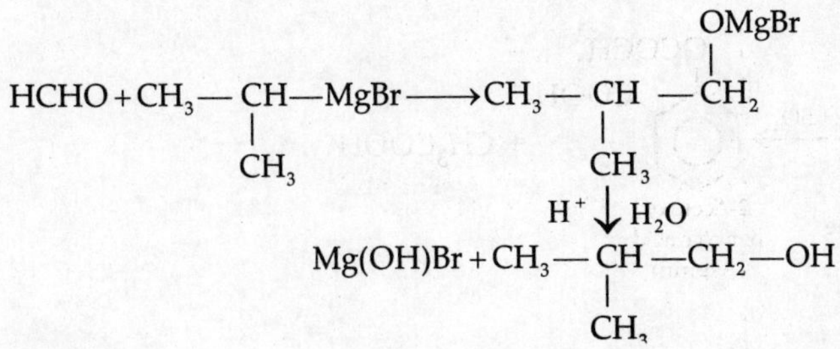

(ii) 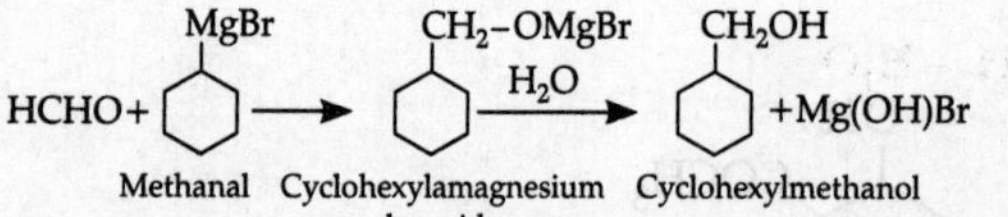

Methanal Cyclohexylamagnesium bromide Cyclohexylmethanol

Q. 7.5. Write structures of the products of the following reactions:

(i) $CH_3-CH=CH_2 \xrightarrow{H_2O/H^+}$

(ii) 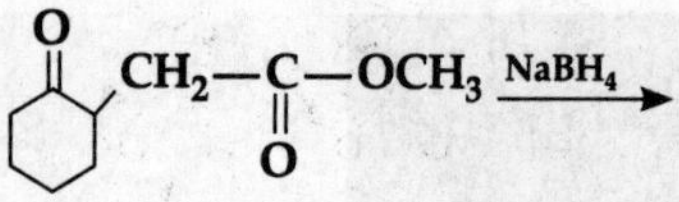

(iii) $CH_3-CH_2-\underset{\displaystyle CH_3}{\underset{|}{CH}}-CHO \xrightarrow{NaBH_4}$

Ans. (i) $CH_3-CH=CH_2 \xrightarrow{H_2O/H^+} CH_3-\underset{\displaystyle OH}{\underset{|}{CH}}-CH_3$

Propene → Propene - 2 - ol

(ii) 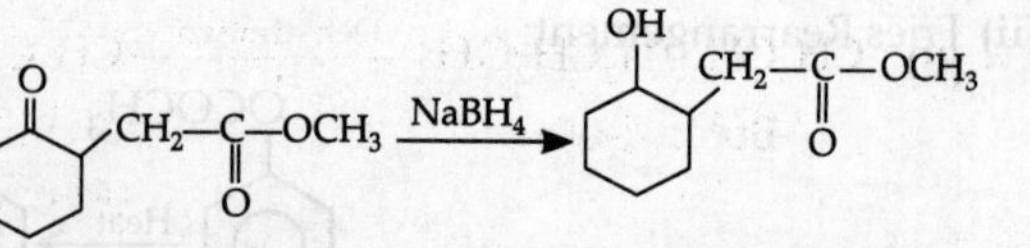

Methyl (2-oxocyclohexyl) ethanoate → Methyl (2-hydroxycyclohexyl) ethanoate

(iii) $CH_3-CH_2-\underset{\displaystyle CH_3}{\underset{|}{CH}}-CHO \xrightarrow{NaBH_4} CH_3-CH_2-\underset{\displaystyle CH_3}{\underset{|}{CH}}-CH_2OH$

2 - Methylbutanal → 2 - Methylbutanal - 1 -ol

Page - 213

Q. 7.6. Give structures of the products you would expect when each of the following alcohol reacts with

(a) $HCl-ZnCl_2$
(b) HBr and
(c) $SOCl_2$.
(i) Butan-1-ol
(ii) 2-Methylbutan-2-ol

Ans. (a) (i) $CH_3-CH_2-CH_2-CH_2-OH \xrightarrow{HCl-ZnCl_2}$ No reaction

Butan - 1 - ol

Primary alcohols do not react appreciably with Lucas' reagent ($HCl-ZnCl_2$) at room temperature.

(ii) $CH_3-CH_2-\underset{\displaystyle CH_3}{\overset{\displaystyle OH}{\overset{|}{\underset{|}{C}}}}-CH_3 \xrightarrow{HCl-ZnCl_2} CH_3-CH_2-\underset{\displaystyle CH_3}{\underset{|}{C}}-CH_3+H_2O$

2-Methylbutan-2-ol(3°) → 2-Chloro-2-Methylbutan (White tuirbidity)

Tertiary alcohols react immediately with Lucas' reagent.

(b) (i) $CH_3CH_2CH_2CH_2OH + HBr \xrightarrow[-H_2O]{} CH_3CH_2CH_2CH_2Br$

Butan-1- ol → 1 - Bromobutane

(ii) $CH_3-CH_2-\underset{\displaystyle CH_3}{\overset{\displaystyle OH}{\overset{|}{\underset{|}{C}}}}-CH_3 + HBr \longrightarrow CH_3-CH_2-\underset{\displaystyle CH_3}{\overset{\displaystyle Br}{\overset{|}{\underset{|}{C}}}}-CH_3 + SO_2\uparrow + HCl$

2 - Methylbutan - 2 - ol → 2 - bromo - 2 - Methylbutane

(c) (i) $CH_3CH_2CH_2CH_2OH + SOCl_2 \longrightarrow CH_3CH_2CH_2CH_2Cl + SO_2 + HCl$

Butan-1-ol → **1 - chlorobutane**

(ii) $CH_3-CH_2-\underset{\displaystyle CH_3}{\overset{\displaystyle OH}{\overset{|}{\underset{|}{C}}}}-CH_3 + SOCl_2 \longrightarrow CH_3-CH_2-\underset{\displaystyle CH_3}{\overset{\displaystyle Cl}{\overset{|}{\underset{|}{C}}}}-CH_3 + SO_2\uparrow + HCl$

2-Methylbutan - 2 - ol → 2 - Chloro - 2 - Methylbutane

Q. 7.7. Predict the major product of acid catalysed dehydration of

1. 1-methylcyclohexanol and
2. Butan-1-ol

Ans. (i) 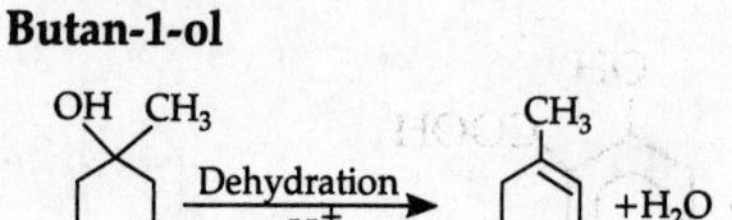

1-Methylcyclohexanol → 1-Methylcyclohexene (Major product)

(ii) $CH_3CH_2CH_2CH_2OH \xrightarrow[H^+]{\text{Dehydration}} CH_3CH = CHCH_3 + H_2O$

Butan-1-ol — But-2-ene (Major product)

Q. 7.8. *Ortho*-and *para*-nitrophenols are more acidic than phenol. Draw the resonance structures of the corresponding phenoxide ions.

Ans. The attachment of the $-NO_2$ group to the phenol molecule at *O*– and *p*-positions decreases the electron density on oxygen atom. This causes the oxygen atom to pull the bond pair of electrons of the O–H bond towards itself thereby facilitating the release of H as H^+.

The resonance structures of the phenoxide ions are:

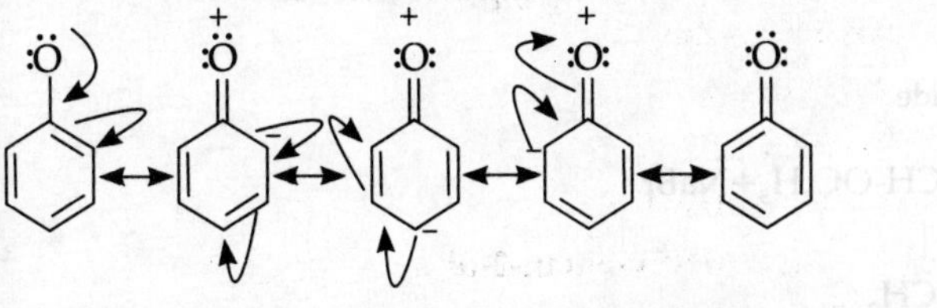

Resonance structure of the phenoxide ion

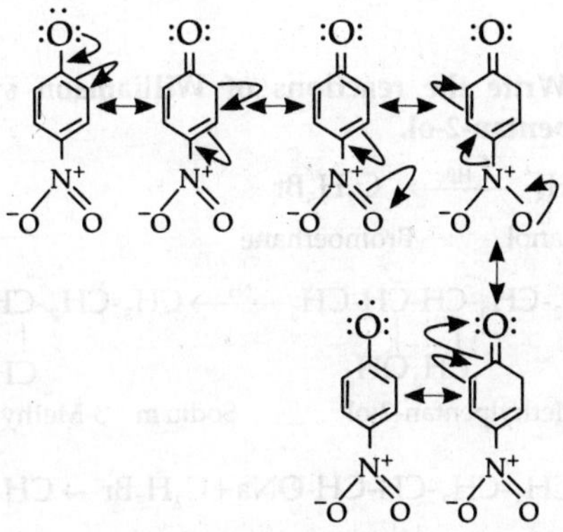

Resonance structures of *o*-nitrophenoxide ion

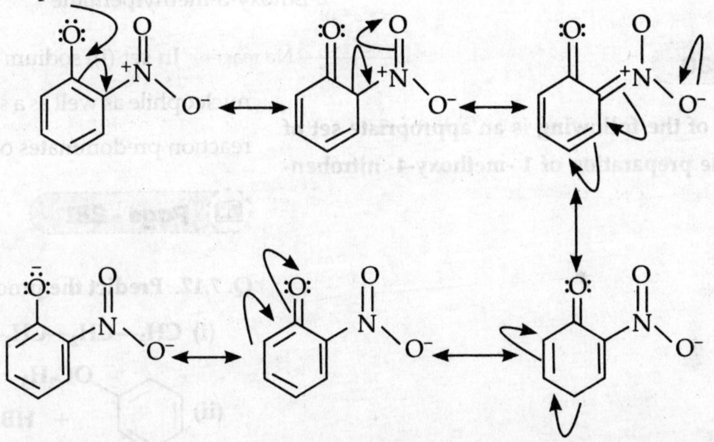

Resonance structures of *m*-nitrophenoxide ion

It can be observed that the presence of nitro groups increases the stability of phenoxide ion.

Q. 7.9. Write the equations involved in the following reactions:
(i) Reimer-Tiemann reaction
(ii) Kolbe's reaction

Ans. (i) Reimer-Tiemann reaction:

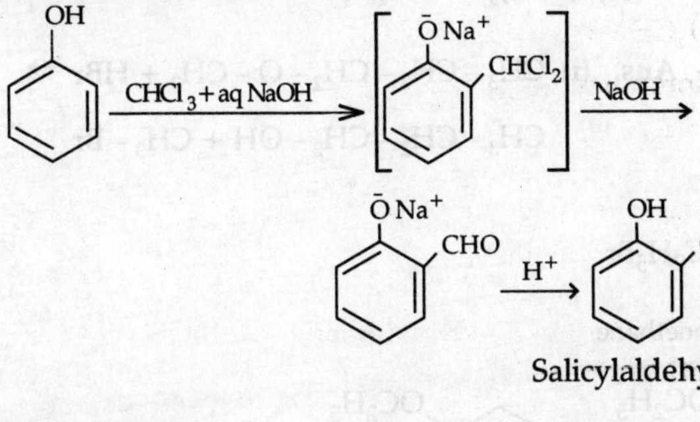

Salicylaldehyde

(ii) Kolbe's reaction:

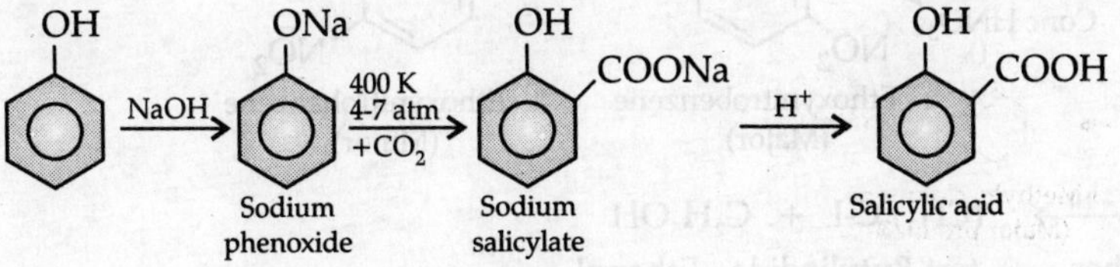

Sodium phenoxide — Sodium salicylate — Salicylic acid

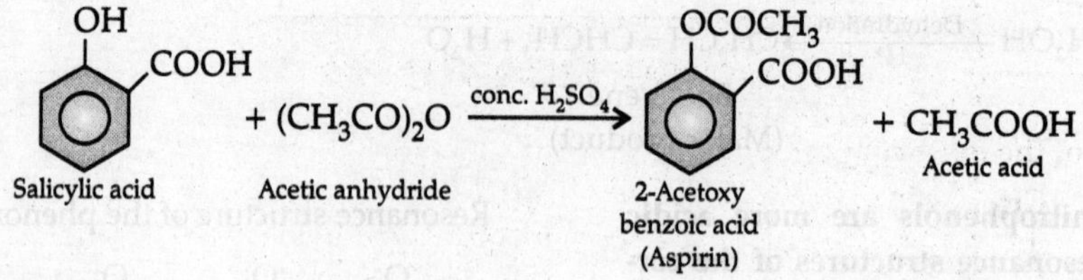

Q. 7.10. Write the reactions of Williamson synthesis of 2-ethoxy-3-methylpentane starting from ethanol and 3-methylpentan-2-ol.

Ans. $C_2H_5 \xrightarrow{HBr} C_2H_5Br$

Ethanol Bromoethane

$$CH_3\text{-}CH_2\text{-}\underset{CH_3}{\underset{|}{CH}}\text{-}\underset{OH}{\underset{|}{CH}}\text{-}CH_3 \xrightarrow{Na} CH_3\text{-}CH_2\text{-}\underset{CH_3}{\underset{|}{CH}}\text{-}\underset{CH_3}{\underset{|}{CH}}\text{-}ONa$$

3-Methylpentan-2-ol Sodium 3-Methylpentan-2-oxide

$$CH_3\text{-}CH_2\text{-}\underset{CH_3}{\underset{|}{CH}}\text{-}\underset{CH_3}{\underset{|}{CH}}\text{-}ONa + C_2H_5Br \rightarrow CH_3\text{-}CH_2\text{-}\underset{CH_3}{\underset{|}{CH}}\text{-}\underset{CH_3}{\underset{|}{CH}}\text{-}OC_2H_5 + NaBr$$

2-Ethoxy-3-methylpentane

Page - 220

Q. 7.11. Which of the following is an appropriate set of reactants for the preparation of 1 -methoxy-4- nitrobenzene and why?

(i)

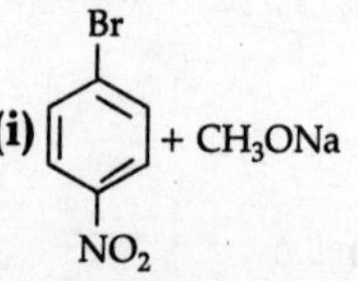

(ii)

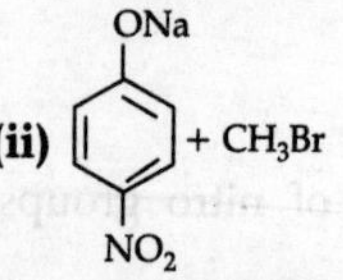

Ans. Set (ii) is an appropriate set of reactants for the preparation of 1-methoxy-4-nitrobenzene.

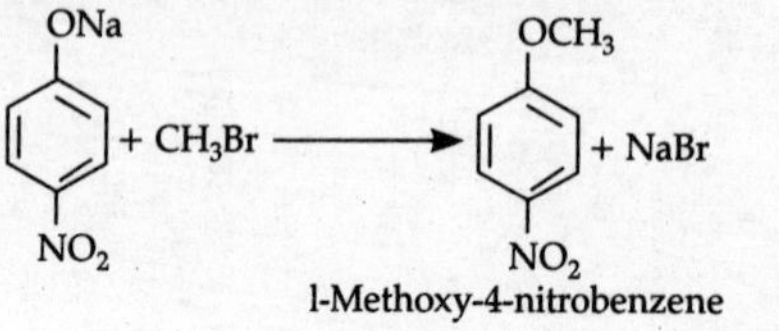

In set (i), sodium methoxide (CH_3ONa) is a strong nucleophile as well as a strong base. Hence, an elimination reaction predominates over a substitution reaction.

Page - 221

Q. 7.12. Predict the products of the following reactions:

(i) $CH_3—CH_2—CH_2—O—CH_3 + HBr \rightarrow$

(ii)

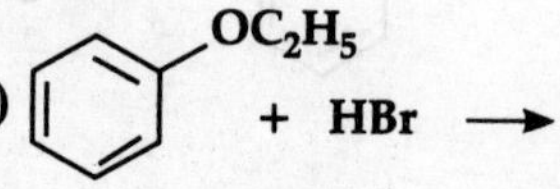

(iii)

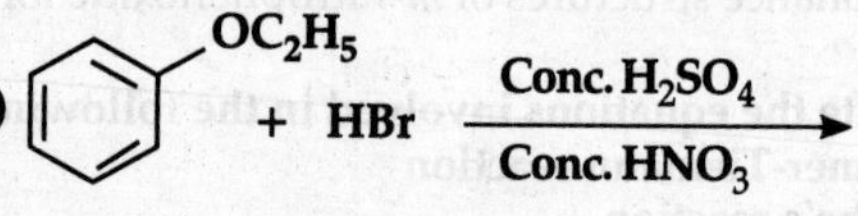

(iv) $(CH_3)_3C-OC_2H_5 \xrightarrow{HI}$

Ans. (i) $CH_3-CH_2-CH_2-O-CH_3 + HBr \rightarrow$

$CH_3-CH_2-CH_2-OH + CH_3-Br$

(ii)

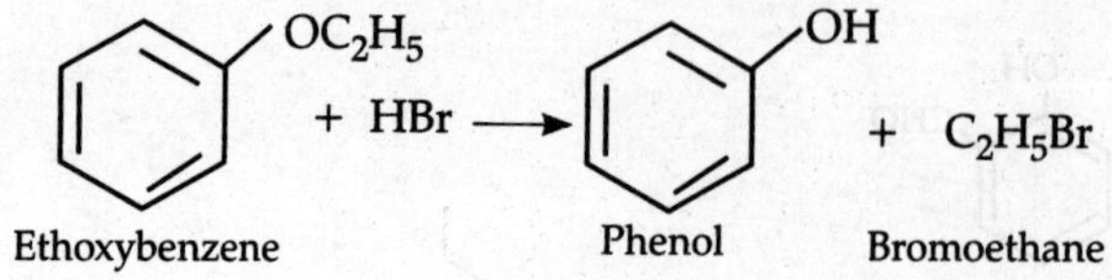

(iii)

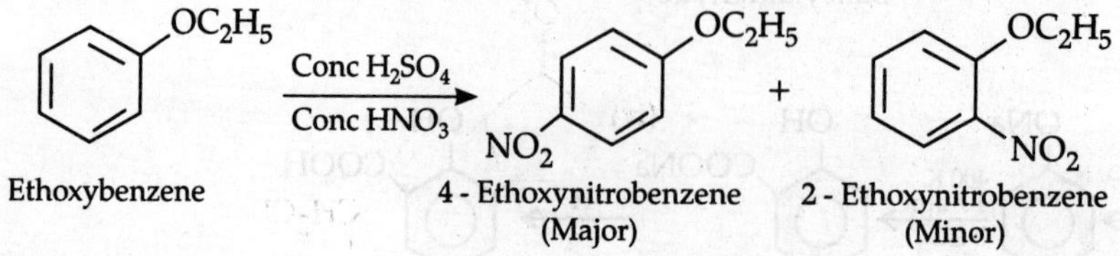

(iv) $(CH_3)_3\ C\text{-}OC_2H_5 \xrightarrow{HI} (CH_3)_3C\text{-}I + C_2H_5OH$

tert-Butyl ethyl ether tert-Butyliodide Ethanol

Exercise Questions

Q. 1. Write IUPAC names of the following compounds:

(i) 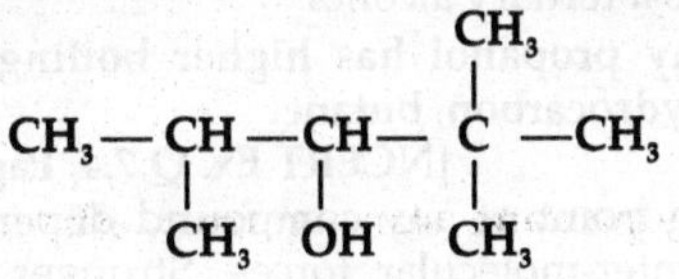

(ii) 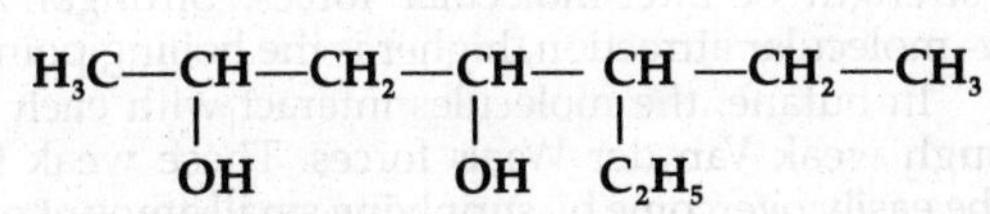

(iii) 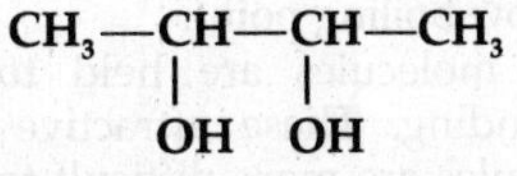

(iv) 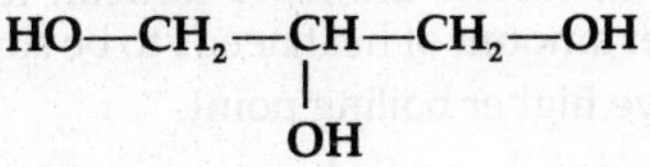

(v) 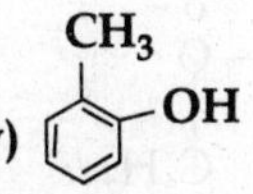

(vi) 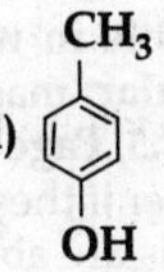

(vii) 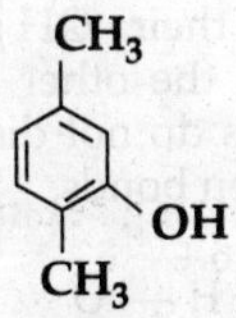

(viii) 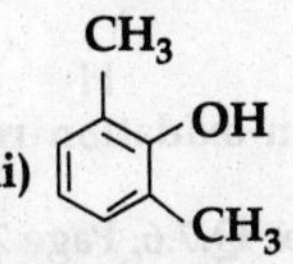

(ix) 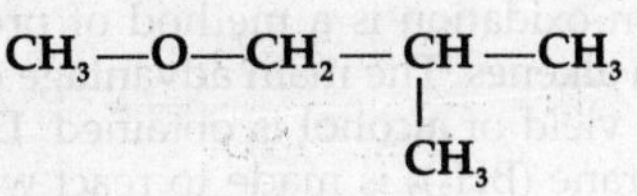

(x) $C_6H_5-O-C_2H_5$

(xi) $C_6H_5-O-C_7H_{15}(n-)$

(xii) 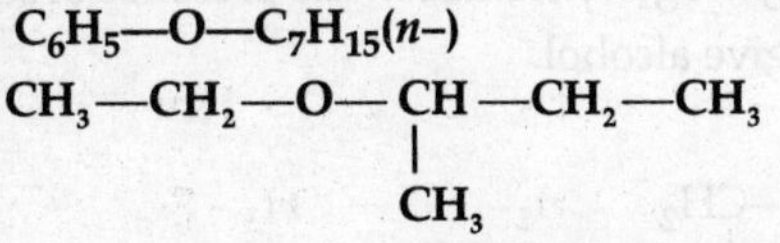

[NCERT Ex. Q.7.1, Page 222]

Ans. (i) 2,2,4-Trimethylpentan-3-ol
(ii) 5-Ethylheptane-2,4-diol
(iii) Butane-2,3-diol
(iv) Propane-1,2,3-triol
(v) 2-Methylphenol
(vi) 4-Methylphenol
(vii) 2,5-Dimethylphenol
(viii) 2,6-Dimethylphenol
(ix) l-Methoxy-2-methylpropane
(x) Ethoxybenzene
(xi) 1-Phenoxyheptane
(xii) 2-Ethoxybutane

Q. 2. Write structures of the compounds whose IUPAC names are as follows:

(i) 2-Methylbutan-2-ol
(ii) 1-Phenylpropan-2-ol
(iii) 3,5-Dimethylhexane-1,3,5-triol
(iv) 2,3-Diethylphenol
(v) 1-Ethoxypropane
(vi) 2-Ethoxy-3-methylpentane
(vii) Cyclohexylmethanol
(viii) 3-Cydohexylpentan-3-ol
(ix) Cyclopent-3-en-1 -ol
(x) 3-Chloromethylpentan-1-ol

[NCERT Ex. Q.7.2, Page 222]

Ans.

(i) 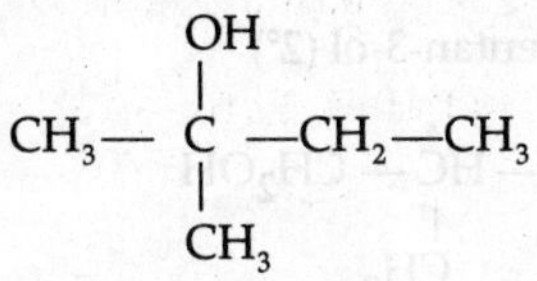

(ii) 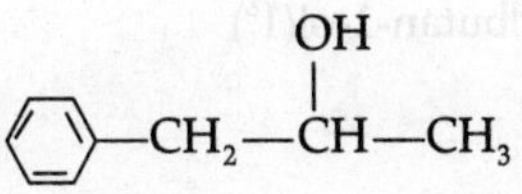

(iii) 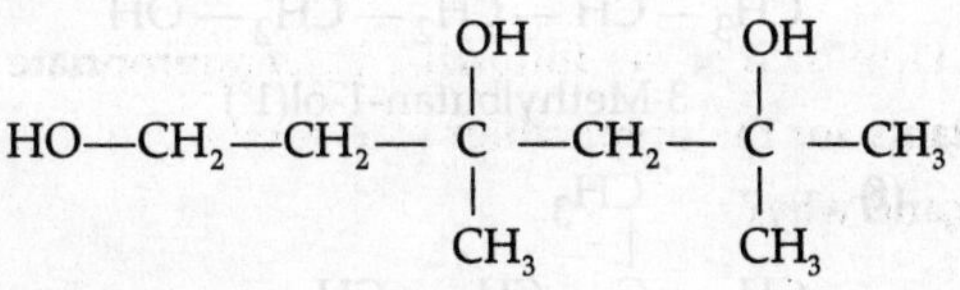

(iv) 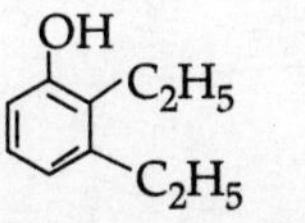

(v) $CH_3CH_2OCH_2CH_2CH_3$

(vi) 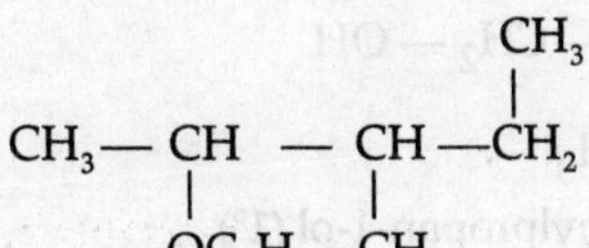

(vii) 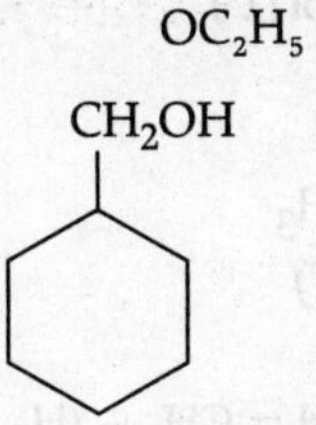

(viii) 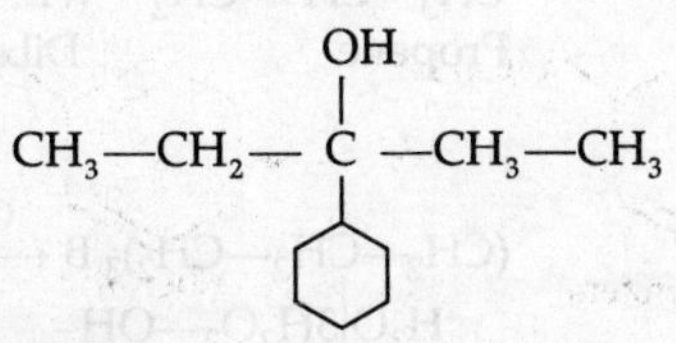

(ix) 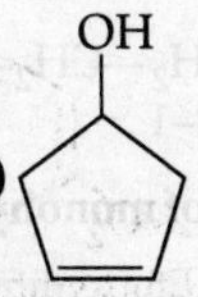

(x) 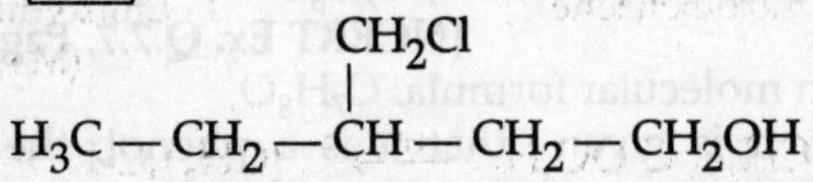

Q. 3. (i) Draw the structures of all isomeric alcohols of molecular formula $C_5H_{12}O$ and give their IUPAC names.

(ii) Classify the isomers of alcohols in question 3 (i) as primary, secondary and tertiary alcohols.
[NCERT Ex. Q.7.3, Page 222]

Ans. (i) The isomeric alcohols with molecular formula $C_5H_{12}O$ are:

(a) $CH_3-CH_2-CH_2-CH_2-CH_2-OH$

Pentanol (1°)

(b)
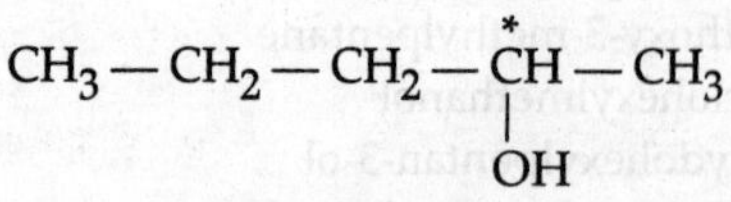

Pentan-2-ol (2°)

(c)
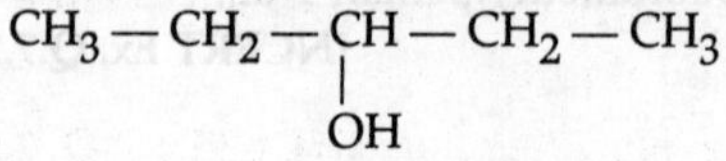

Pentan-3-ol (2°)

(d)
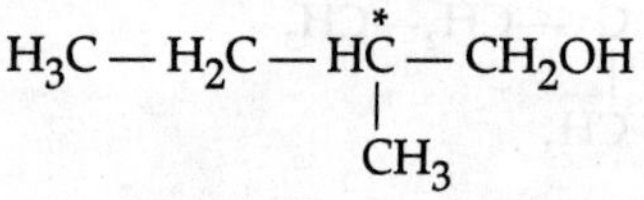

2-Methylbutan-1-ol(1°)

(e)
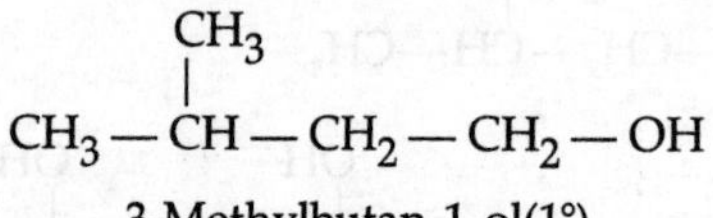

3-Methylbutan-1-ol(1°)

(f)
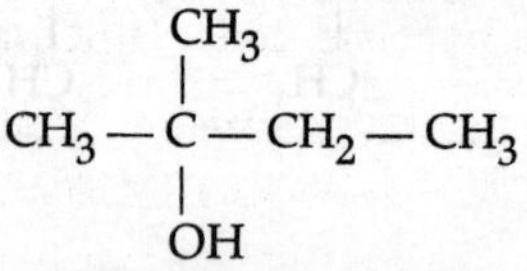

2-Methylbutan-2-ol(3°)

(g)
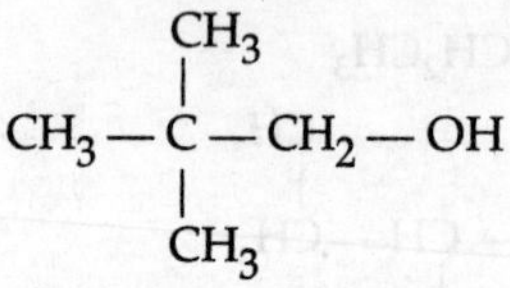

2,2-Dimethylpropan-1-ol (1°)

(h)
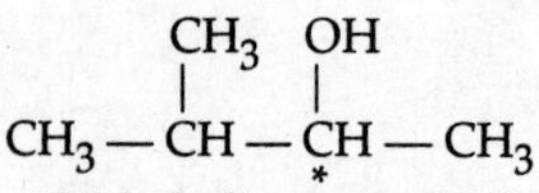

3-Methylbutan-2-ol(2°)

Isomers (b), (d) and (h) contain chiral carbon atoms thus, they exhibit enantiomerism.

(ii) Isomers (a), (d), (e) and (g) are primary alcohols. Isomers (b), (c) and (h) are secondary alcohols. Isomer (f) is a tertiary alcohol.

Q. 4. Explain why propanol has higher boiling point than that of the hydrocarbon, butane.
[NCERT Ex. Q.7.4, Page 222]

Ans. The boiling point of any compound depends on the strength of inter-molecular forces. Stronger is the inter- molecular attraction, higher is the boiling point.

In butane, the molecules interact with each other through weak Van der Waals forces. These weak forces can be easily overcome by supplying small amount of heat energy. Thus, they have low boiling point.

In propanol, the molecules are held together by strong hydrogen bonding. These attractive forces operating between molecules are more difficult to break and therefore higher amount of heat needs to be supplied, hence propanol have higher boiling point.

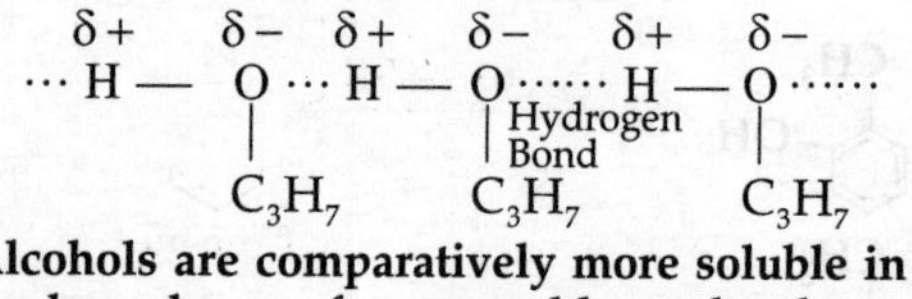

Q. 5. Alcohols are comparatively more soluble in water than hydrocarbons of comparable molecular masses. Explain this fact. **[NCERT Ex. Q.7.5, Page 222]**

Ans. Organic compounds are soluble in water if they are able to form hydrogen bonds with it. Alcohols are able to establish this interaction by the virtue of their –OH group and are therefore soluble in water. On the other hand, other hydrocarbons of comparable mass do not dissolve in water since they cannot form hydrogen bonds.

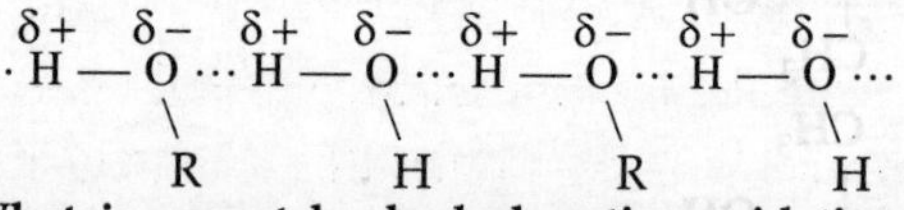

Q. 6. What is meant by hydroboration-oxidation reaction? Illustrate it with an example.
[NCERT Ex. Q.7.6, Page 222]

Ans. Hydroboration-oxidation is a method of preparation of alcohols from alkenes. The main advantage of this method is that high yield of alcohol is obtained. During hydroboration, diborane $(BH_3)_2$ is made to react with an alkene to form an addition product. This product is then treated with hydrogen peroxide in the presence of sodium hydroxide to give alcohol.

For example,

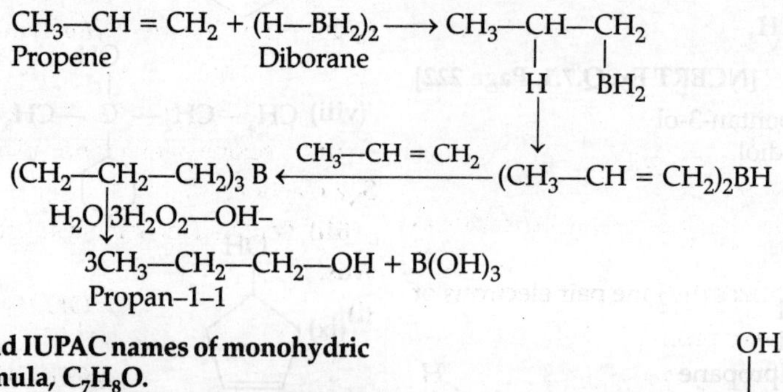

Q. 7. Give the structure and IUPAC names of monohydric phenols of molecular formula, C_7H_8O.
[NCERT Ex. Q.7.7, Page 222]

Ans. Given molecular formula: C_7H_8O

Since, it is given that it is a phenol, the basic skeleton will be

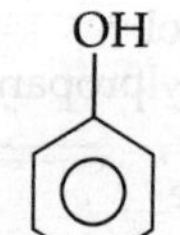

This structure accounts for C_6H_6O. Remaining CH_2 when added to the phenol gives following structures:

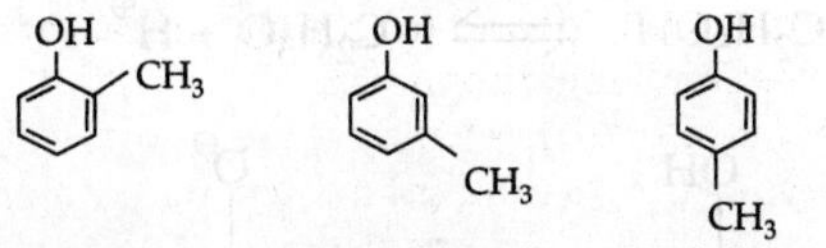

2-Methylphenol (o-cresol) | 3-Methylphenol (m-cresol) | 4-Methylphenol (p-cresol)

Q. 8. While separating a mixture of *ortho* and *para* nitrophenols by steam distillation, name the isomer which will be steam volatile. Give reason. **[NCERT Ex. Q.7.8, Page 222]**

Ans. During steam distillation, it is the lower boiling compound which distills out first. Between *ortho*- and *para*-nitrophenol it is the *ortho*-isomer which will be steam volatile since it has a lower boiling point.

The difference in boiling point between the two isomers can be understood based on the structural difference. In *ortho*-isomer intramolecular hydrogen bonding takes place while in the *para*-isomer, inter-molecular hydrogen bonding takes place.

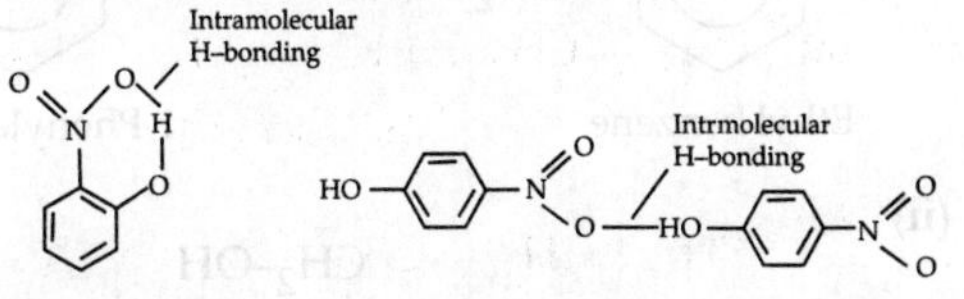

o-nitrophenol | p-Nitrophenol

As a result of the strong forces operating between the molecules of *p*-isomer, the boiling point is higher and it is not steam volatile.

Q. 9. Give the equations of reactions for the preparation of phenol from cumene. **[NCERT Ex. Q. 7.9, Page 222]**

Ans.

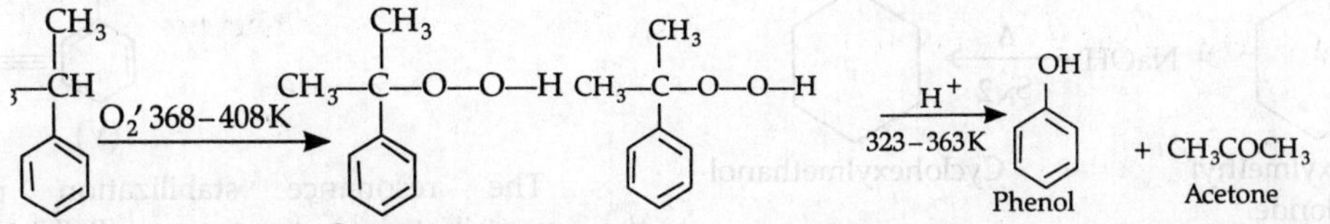

Cumene | Cumene

Q. 10. Write chemical reaction for the preparation of phenol from chlorobenzene. **[NCERT Ex. Q.7.10, Page 222]**

Ans.

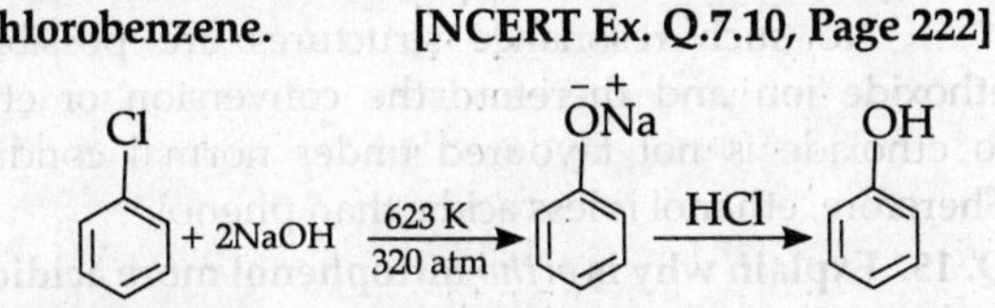

Chlorobenzene | Sodium phenoxide | Phenol

Q. 11. Write the mechanism of hydration of ethene to yield ethanol. **[NCERT Ex. Q.7.11, Page 222]**

Ans. The acid catalysed hydration of ethene may be represented as:

$$H_2C=CH_2 \xrightarrow{H_3O^+/\Delta} H_3C-CH_2-OH$$

Ethene → Ethanol

The mechanism followed by the above reaction may be depicted as

Step 1: Generation of carbocation: Protonation of ethene yields a carbocation as

$$H_2\ddot{O}: + H^{\oplus} \longrightarrow H_3O^+$$

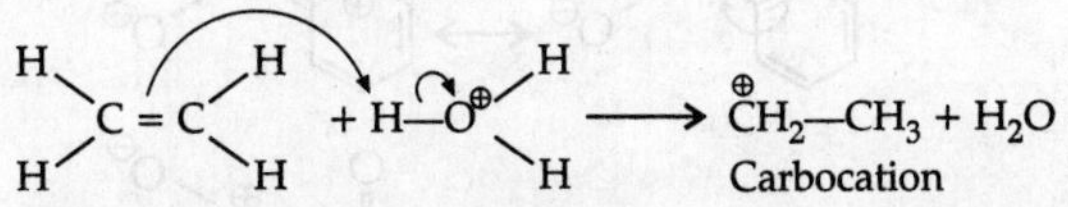

Step 2: Nucleophilic attack of water on carbocation:

The carbocation polarizes the lone pair electrons of O of water and hydration takes place.

$$H_3C-\overset{\oplus}{C}H_2 + H_2\ddot{O}: \rightleftharpoons H_3C-CH_2-\overset{\oplus}{O}H_2$$

Step 3: Formation of product, Regeneration of the proton:

$$H_3C-CH_2-\overset{\oplus}{O}H_2 \longrightarrow CH_3-CH_2-OH + H^{\oplus}$$

Ethanol

Q. 12. You are given benzene, conc. H_2SO_4 and NaOH. Write the equations for the preparation of phenol using these reagents. **[NCERT Ex. Q.7.12, Page 222]**

Ans. Using the given reagents, phenol may be prepared as:

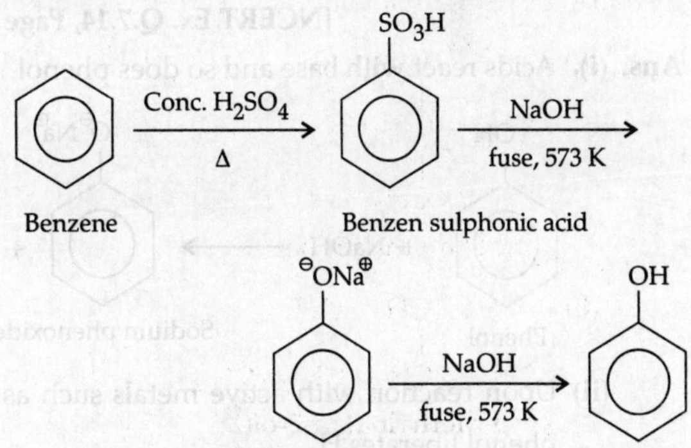

Q. 13. Show how will you synthesise: **[NCERT Ex. Q.7.13, Page 223]**

(i) 1 -Phenylethanol from a suitable alkene.

(ii) Cyclohexylmethanol using an alkyl halide by an S_N2 reaction.

(iii) Pentan-1-ol using a suitable alkyl halide.

Ans.

(i)

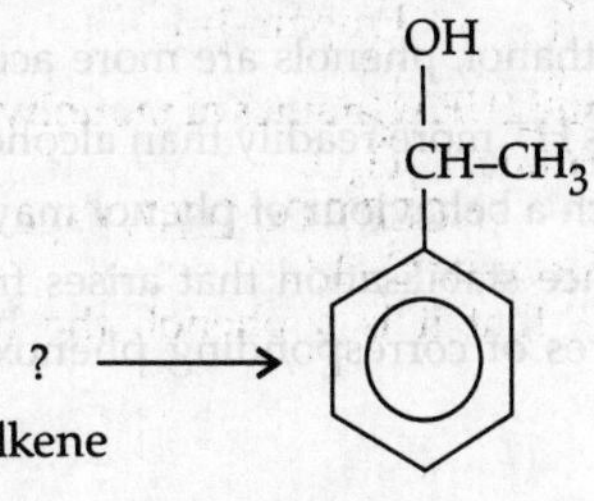

Alkene

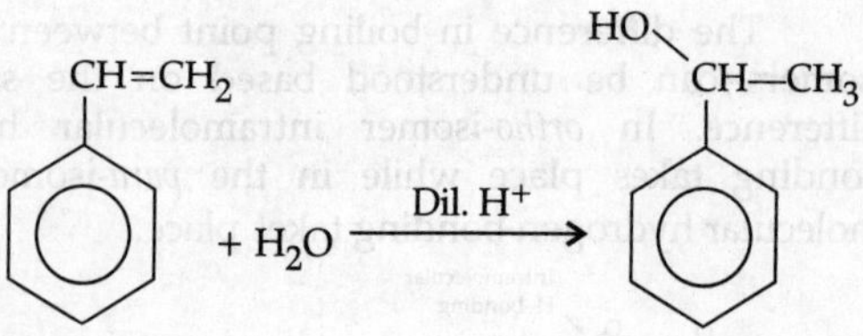

Ethyl benzene 1-Phenylethanol

(ii)

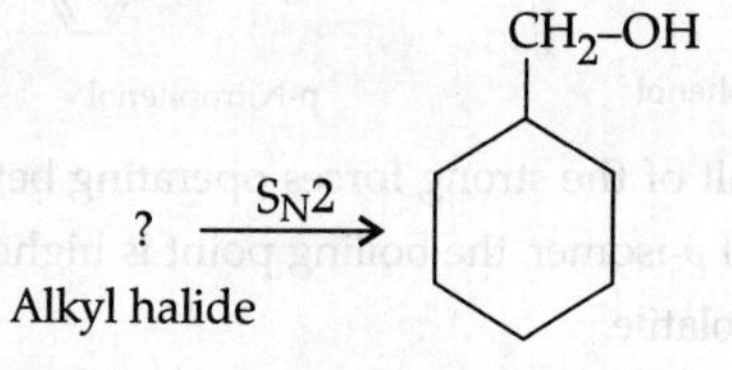

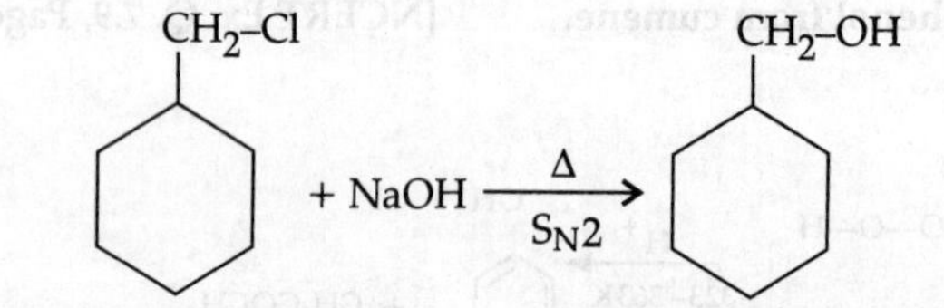

Cyclohexylmethyl choloride Cyclohexylmethanol

(iii)

$$\underset{\text{Alkyl halide}}{?} \longrightarrow CH_3-(CH_2)_3-CH_2OH$$

$$CH_3-(CH_2)_3-CH_2-Cl + NaOH \xrightarrow[\Delta]{S_N2,\text{hydrolysis}} \underset{\text{Pentan-1-ol}}{CH_3-(CH_2)_3-CH_2-OH}$$

Q. 14. Give two reactions that show the acidic nature of phenol. Compare acidity of phenol with that of ethanol. [NCERT Ex. Q.7.14, Page 223]

Ans. (i) Acids react with base and so does phenol.

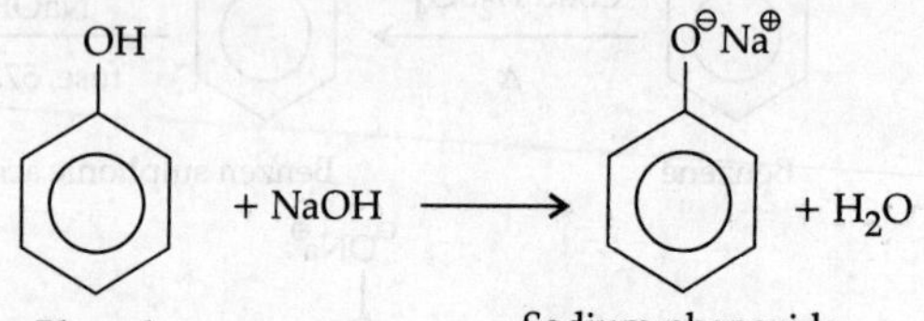

Phenol Sodium phenoxide

(ii) Upon reaction with active metals such as Na, phenol liberates H_2.

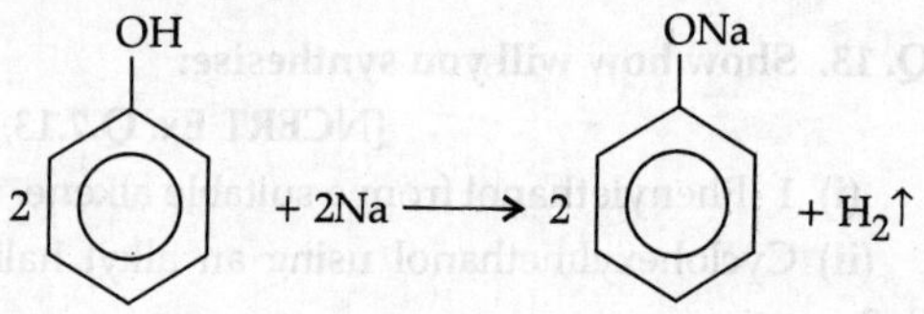

These two reactions demonstrate the acidic nature of phenol.

As compared to ethanol, phenols are more acidic. They lose their H atom as H^+ more readily than alcohols.

The reason for such a behaviour of phenol may be attributed to the resonance stabilisation that arises from the contributing structures of corresponding phenoxide ion.

$$C_2H_5OH \rightleftharpoons C_2H_5O^{\ominus} + H^{\oplus}$$

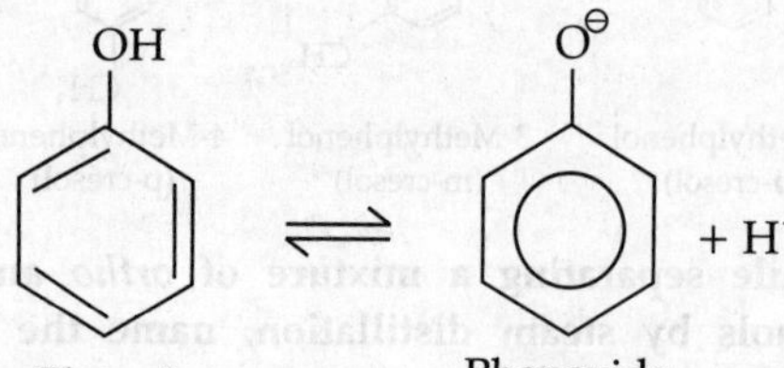

Phenol Phenoxide

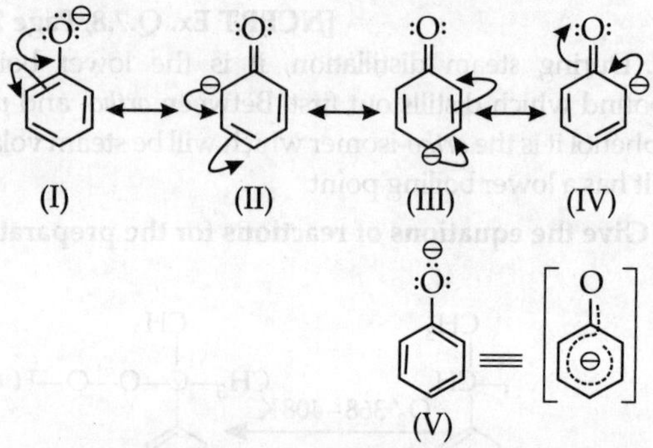

The resonance stabilization provided by the contributing structures (I)-(V) more than compensates for the bond breakage energy of O–H bond and thus causes phenol to be acidic in nature.

No such resonance structures are possible for ethoxide ion and therefore the conversion of ethanol to ethoxide is not favoured under normal conditions. Therefore, ethanol is less acidic than phenol.

Q. 15. Explain why is *ortho* nitrophenol more acidic than *ortho* methoxyphenol? [NCERT Ex. Q.7.15, Page 223]

Ans.

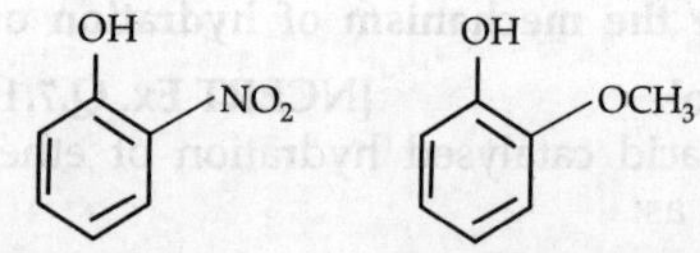

o–Nitrophenol *o*–Methoxyphenol

The acidity of phenol arises from the loss of H of O–H group as H^+. This loss is facilitated if the polarity of the O–H bond increases and H carries substantial δ^+ charge.

In (I), the presence of the highly electron withdrawing $-NO_2$ group at the *ortho*-position increases the polarity of the O–H bond.

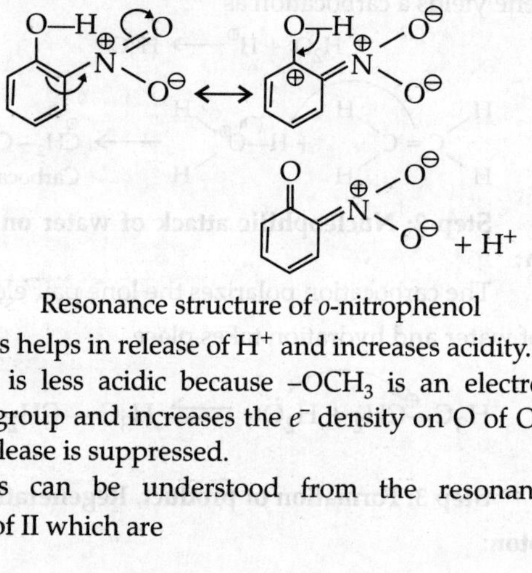

Resonance structure of *o*-nitrophenol

This helps in release of H^+ and increases acidity.

(II) is less acidic because $-OCH_3$ is an electron releasing group and increases the e^- density on O of OH and H^+ release is suppressed.

This can be understood from the resonance structure of II which are

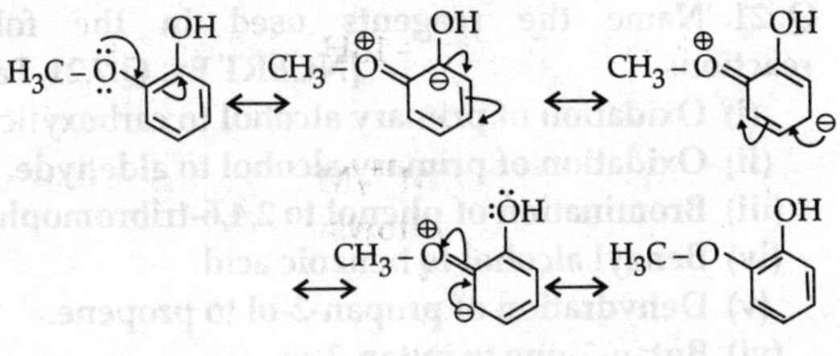

Resonance structure of *o*-methoxyphenol

Q. 16. Explain how does the -OH group attached to a carbon of benzene ring activates it towards electrophilic substitution. [NCERT Ex. Q.7.16, Page 223]

Ans. In an electrophilic substitution reaction, an electron deficient species attacks the benzene ring which is e^- rich.

When an -OH group is attached to the benzene ring, by the virtue of its electron releasing nature increases the e^- density of the ring and thus activates it, i.e., makes it a welcome site for electrophiles.

The increase in electron density can be visualised as:

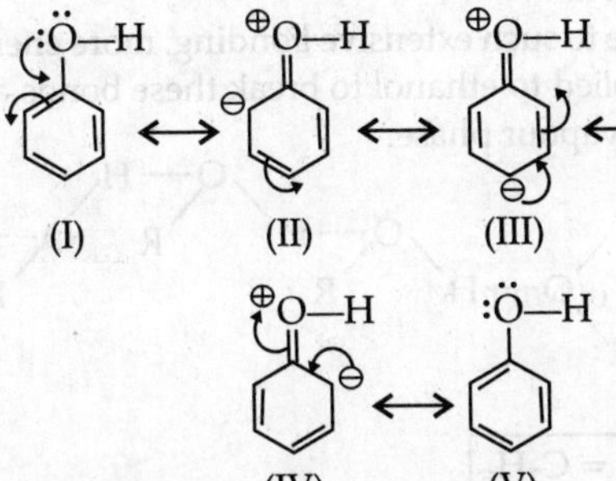

From structures (I)–(V), we find that the attachment of hydroxyl group to benzene has increased the electron density (-ve charge) on the ring carbon atoms (especially C-2, C-4 and C-6). It is therefore said to have activated the ring towards electrophiles which are attracted to the increased electron density.

Q. 17. Give equations of the following reactions:

(i) Oxidation of propan-1 -ol with alkaline KMnO$_4$ solution.

(ii) Bromine in CS$_2$ with phenol.

(iii) Dilute HNO$_3$ with phenol.

(iv) Treating phenol with chloroform in presence of aqueous NaOH. [NCERT Ex. Q.7.17, Page 223]

Ans.

(i)

$$\underset{\text{Propan-1-ol}}{CH_3-CH_2-CH_2OH} \xrightarrow{\text{alk. KMnO}_4} \underset{\text{Propanoic acid}}{CH_3CH_2COOH + H_2O}$$

(ii)

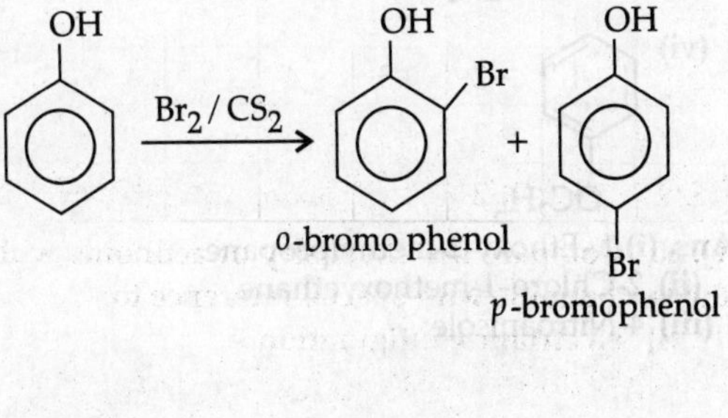

o-bromo phenol, *p*-bromophenol

(iii)

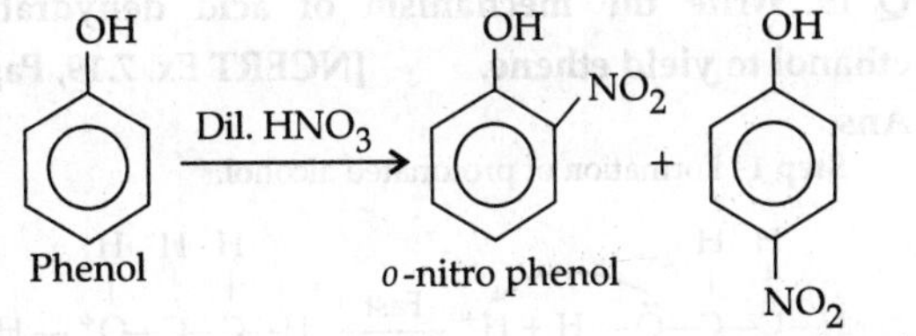

Phenol, *o*-nitro phenol, *p*-nitrophenol

(iv)

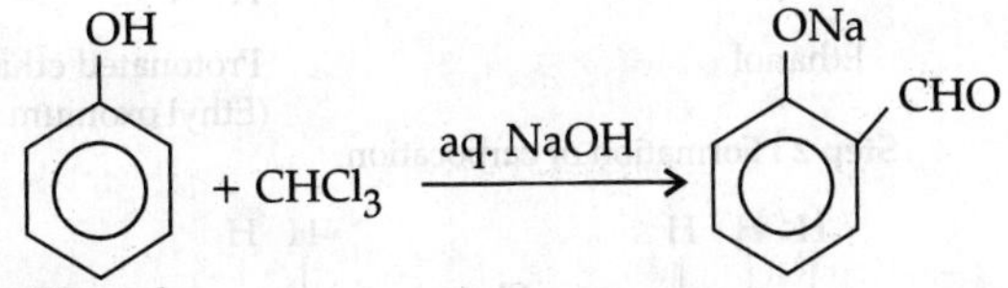

Phenol

Q. 18. Explain the following with an example.

(i) Kolbe's reaction

(ii) Reimer-Tiemann reaction

(iii) Williamson ether synthesis

(iv) Unsymmetrical ether.

[NCERT Ex. Q.7.18, Page 223]

Ans. (i) Kolbe's reaction: Sodium phenoxide is heated with CO_2 at 400 K under a pressure of 4-7 atm which on acidification results in salicylic acid.

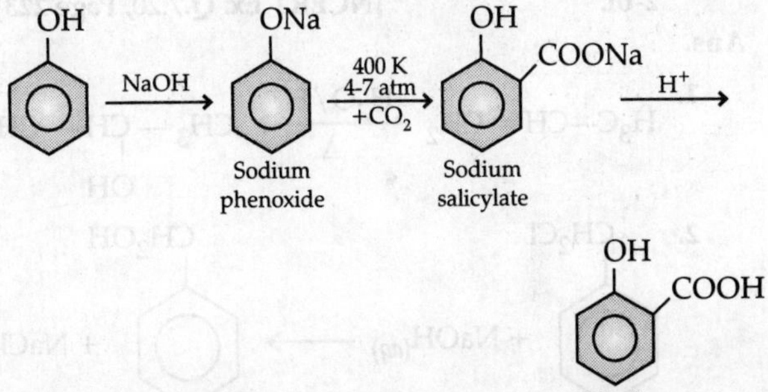

Sodium phenoxide, Sodium salicylate, Salicylic acid

(ii) Reimer-Tiemann reaction:

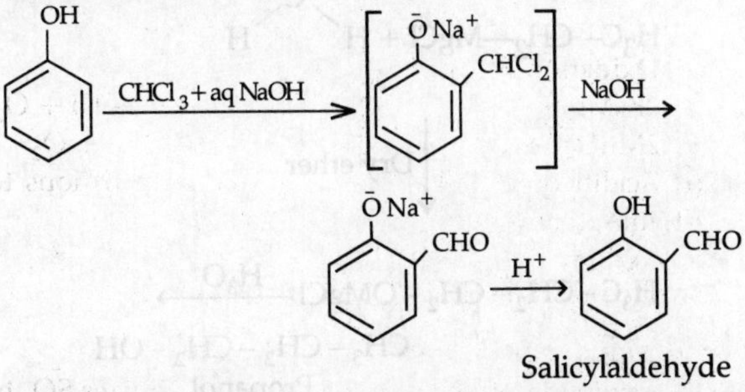

Salicylaldehyde

(iii) Williamson ether synthesis: An alkyl halide reacts with sodium alkoxide or sodium phenoxide to form ether.

$$\underset{\text{Alkyl halide}}{R-X} + \underset{\text{Sodium alkoxide}}{\overset{+}{Na}-\overset{-}{O}-R'} \longrightarrow \underset{\text{Ether}}{R-O-R'} + NaX$$

(iv) Unsymmetrical ethers: Unsymmetrical ethers are organic compounds where the ethereal oxygen atom is attached to two different alkyl or aryl groups, e.g.,

$C_2H_5-O-CH_3$, $C_6H_5O-C_2H_5$, etc.

Q. 19. Write the mechanism of acid dehydration of ethanol to yield ethene. **[NCERT Ex. 7.19, Page 223]**

Ans.

Step 1 : Formation of protonated alcohol.

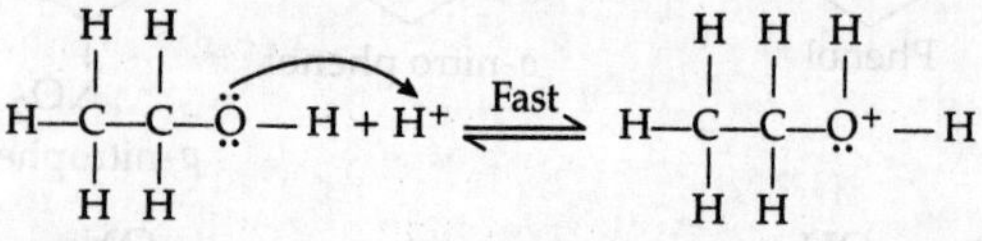

Ethanol — Protonated ethanol (Ethyl oxonium ion)

Step 2 : Formation of carbocation.

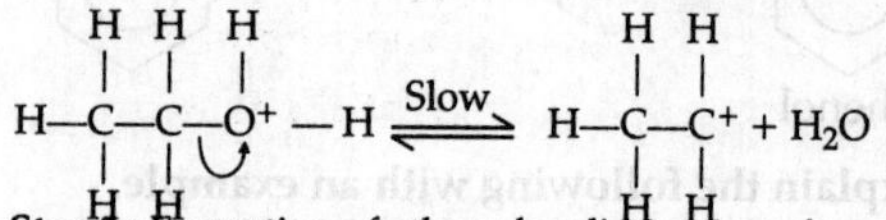

Step 3 : Formation of ethene by elimination of a proton.

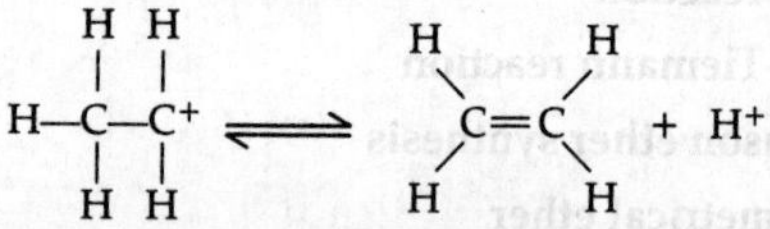

Ethene

Q. 20. How are the following conversions carried out?

1. **Propene → Propan-2-ol**
2. **Benzyl chloride → Benzyl alcohol**
3. **Ethyl magnesium chloride → Propan-1-ol**
4. **Methyl magnesium bromide → 2-Methylpropan-2-ol.** **[NCERT Ex. Q.7.20, Page 223]**

Ans.

1\.

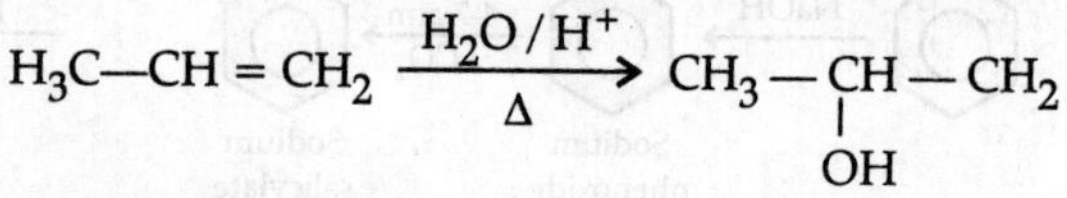

2\.

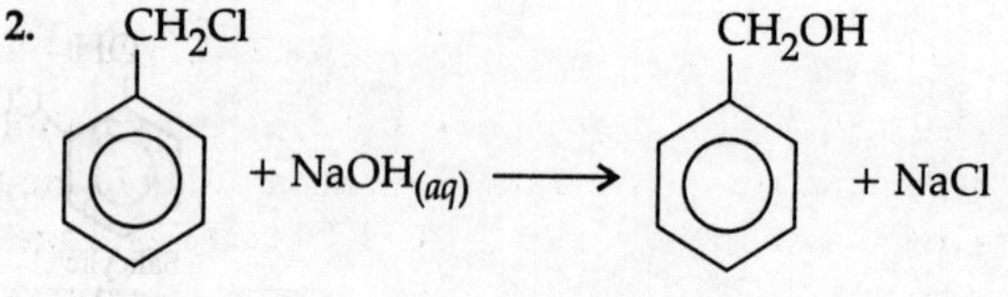

3\.

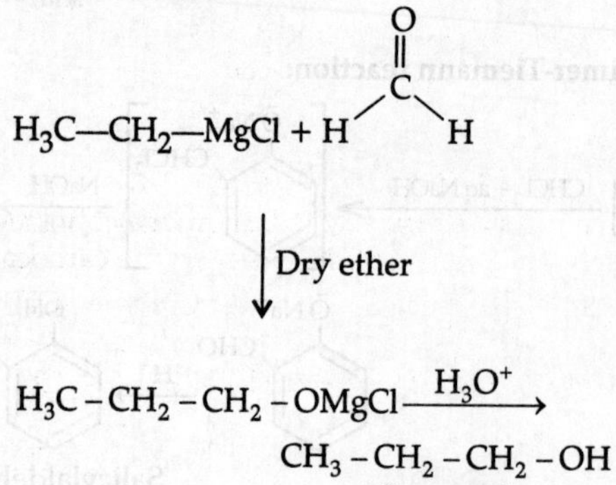

Propanol

4\.

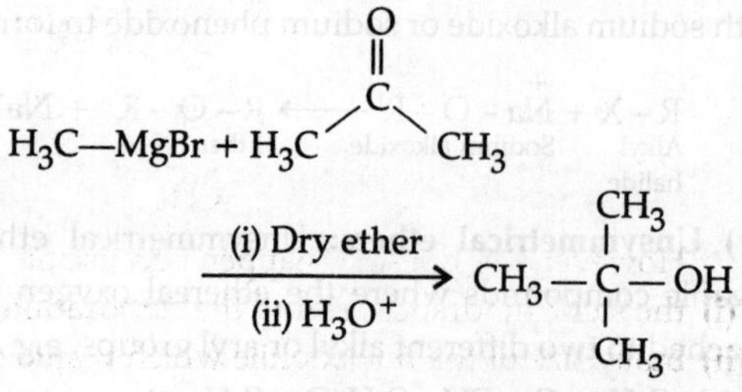

2-methyl propan-2-ol

Q. 21. Name the reagents used in the following reactions : **[NCERT Ex. Q.7.21, Page 223]**

(i) Oxidation of primary alcohol to carboxylic acid.
(ii) Oxidation of primary alcohol to aldehyde.
(iii) Bromination of phenol to 2,4,6-tribromophenol.
(iv) Benzyl alcohol to benzoic acid.
(v) Dehydration of propan-2-ol to propene.
(vi) Butan-2-one to butan-2-ol.

Ans. (i) Alkaline $KMnO_4$
(ii) Pyridinium chlorochromate (PCC) in chloromethane (CH_2Cl_2)
(iii) Br_2/H_2O
(iv) Alkaline $KMnO_4$
(v) Conc. H_2SO_4 or H_3PO_4 at 433-443K
(vi) H_2/Ni or $NaBH_4$ or $LiAlH_4$

Q. 22. Give reason for the higher boiling point of ethanol in comparison to methoxymethane. **[NCERT Ex. Q.7.22, Page 223]**

Ans. The higher boiling point of ethanol may be attributed to the presence of intermolecular hydrogen bonding in it.

Due to such extensive bonding, more energy needs to be supplied to ethanol to break these bonds and move it into the vapour phase.

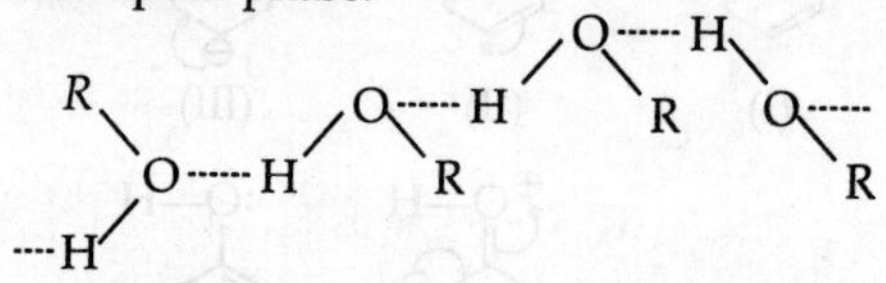

$R = C_2H_5$

Methoxymethane, an ether, lacks such hydrogen bonding and is therefore a low boiling liquid.

$$CH_3-O-CH_3$$

Methoxymethane
(lacks H-bonding between molecules)

Q. 23. Give IUPAC names of the following ethers: **[NCERT Ex. Q.7.23, Page 224]**

(i) 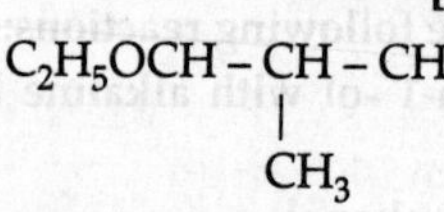

(ii) $CH_3OCH_2CH_2Cl$

(iii) $O_2N-C_6H_4-OCH_3(p)$

(iv) $CH_3CH_2CH_2OCH_3$

(v) 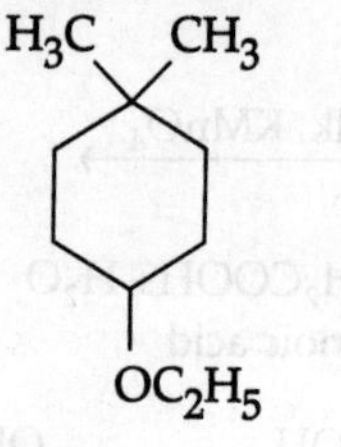

(vi) 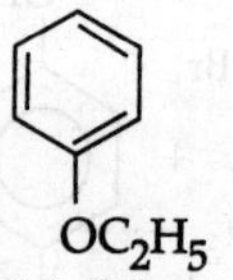

Ans. (i) 1 -Ethoxy-2-methylpropane
(ii) 2-Chloro-1-methoxyethane
(iii) 4-Nitroanisole

(iv) 1-Methoxypropane
(v) 1-Ethoxy-4,4-dimethylcyclohexane
(vi) Ethoxybenzene

Q. 24. Write the names of reagents and equations for the preparation of the following ethers by Williamson's synthesis:
(i) 1-Propoxypropane
(ii) Ethoxybenzene
(iii) 2-Methyl-2-methoxypropane
(iv) 1-Methoxyethane **[NCERT Ex. Q.7.24, Page 223]**

Ans.

(i)
$$\underset{\text{Sodium propoxide}}{CH_3CH_2CH_2\overset{\ominus}{O}\overset{\oplus}{Na}} + \underset{\text{1-bromo propane}}{CH_3CH_2CH_2-Br} \xrightarrow{\text{Heat}}$$
$$\underset{\text{1–Propoxypropane}}{CH_3CH_2CH_2-O-CH_2CH_2CH_3} + NaBr$$

(ii)
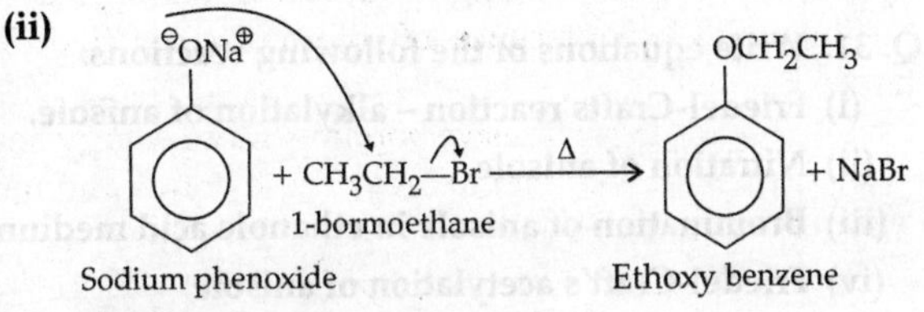

(iii)
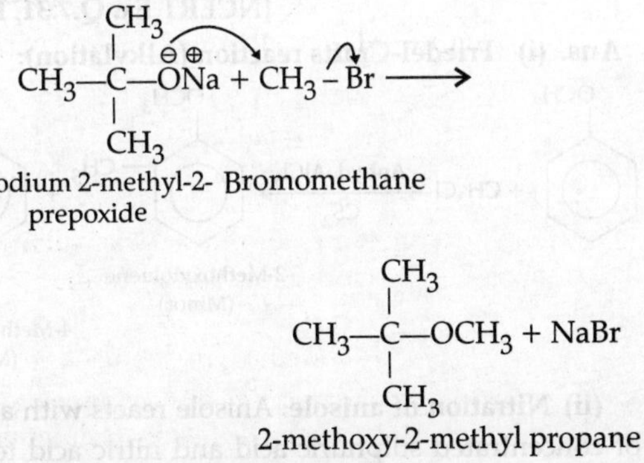

(iv)
$$\underset{\text{Sodium ethoxide}}{CH_3CH_3\overset{\ominus}{O}\overset{\oplus}{Na}} + \underset{\text{Bromo methane}}{CH_3-Br} \xrightarrow{\text{Heat}}$$
$$\underset{\text{1-methoxy ethane}}{CH_3CH_3-O-CH_3} + NaBr$$

Q. 25. Illustrate with examples the limitations of Williamson synthesis for the preparation of certain types of ethers. **[NCERT Ex. Q.7.25, Page 224]**

Ans. The main limitation of Williamson's ether synthesis lies in its unemployability for preparation of unsymmetrical ethers where the compound contains secondary or tertiary alkyl groups. e.g., reaction between *tert*-butyl bromide and sodium methoxide yields an alkene.

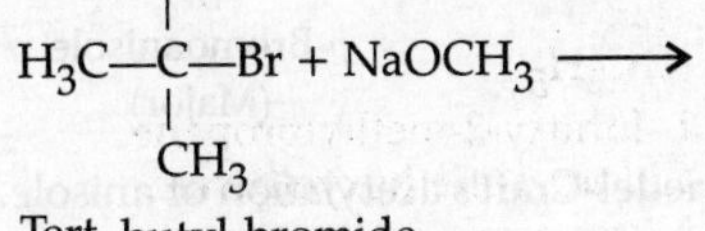

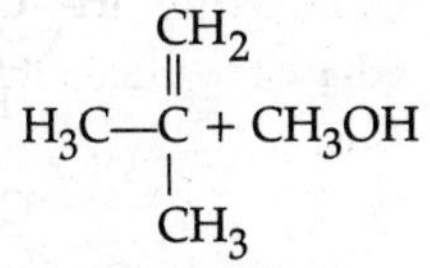

This is because the competing elimination reaction predominates over S_N2 and alkene is formed.

Q. 26. How is 1-propoxypropane synthesised from propan-1 -ol? Write mechanism of this reaction. **[NCERT Ex. Q.7.26, Page 224]**

Ans. $\underset{\text{Propanol}}{CH_3CH_2CH_2OH} \xrightarrow{?} \underset{\text{Propoxypropane}}{(CH_3CH_2CH_2)_2O}$

This reaction can be brought about as:

$$\underset{\text{Propanol}}{CH_3CH_2CH_2OH} + SOCl_2 \longrightarrow CH_3CH_2CH_2Cl + SO_2\uparrow + HCl$$

$$2CH_3CH_2CH_2OH + \underset{\text{metal}}{2Na} \longrightarrow CH_3CH_2CH_2\overset{-}{O}\overset{\oplus}{Na} + H_2$$

$$\underset{\text{1 – Chloroporpane}}{CH_3CH_2CH_2Cl} + \underset{\text{Sodium propoxide}}{CH_3CH_2CH_2\overset{-}{O}\overset{\oplus}{Na}} \longrightarrow \underset{\text{Propoxypropane}}{(CH_3CH_2CH_2)_2O}$$

Mechanism: S_N2 attack of propoxide on the halide

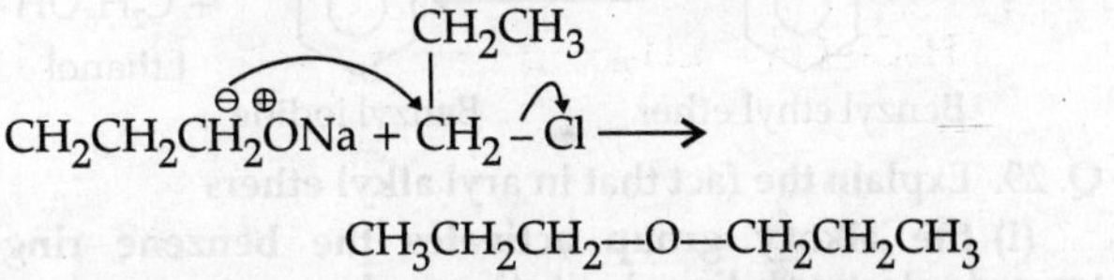

Q. 27. Preparation of ethers by acid dehydration of secondary or tertiary alcohols is not a suitable method. Give reason. **[NCERT Ex. Q.7.27, Page 224]**

Ans. Consider the reaction between propan-2-ol molecules in the presence of acid.

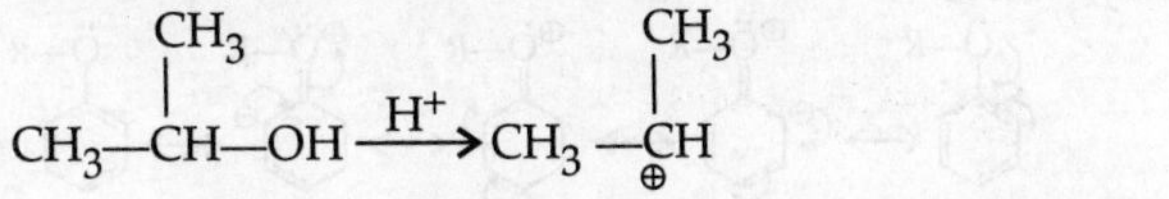

If an ether is to be formed, another alcohol molecule must carry out a nucleophilic attack on the carbocation as

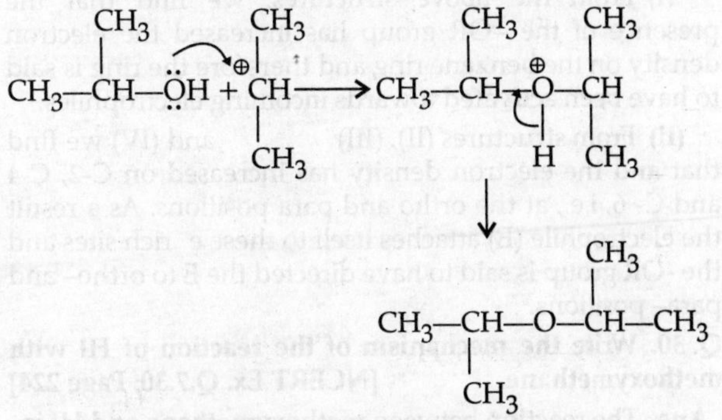

However, this does not happen because of

(i) the steric hindrance around the carbocation, and

(ii) bulky size of the nucleophile which would further cause crowding. As a result, the carbocation prefers to lose a proton and forms an alkene.

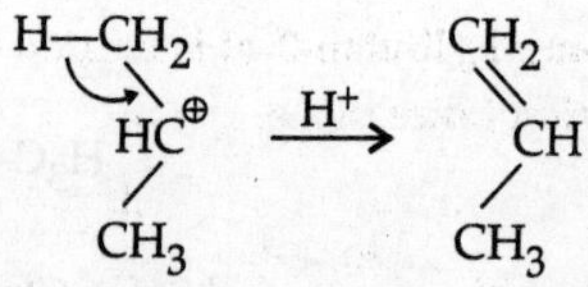

For the same reason 3° alcohols in the presence of acid do not form ethers since 3° alcohols are even more sterically hindered than 2° alcohols.

Q. 28. Write the equation of the reaction of hydrogen iodide with:

(i) 1-propoxypropane

(ii) methoxybenzene; and

(iii) benzyl ethyl ether. [NCERT Ex. Q.7.28, Page 224]

Ans.

(i)

$$\underset{\text{1-propoxy propane}}{CH_3CH_2CH_3-O-CH_2CH_2CH_3} \xrightarrow[373\,K]{HI} \underset{\text{Propan-1-ol}}{CH_3CH_2CH_2-OH} + \underset{\text{Iodopropane}}{CH_3CH_2CH_2-I}$$

(ii)

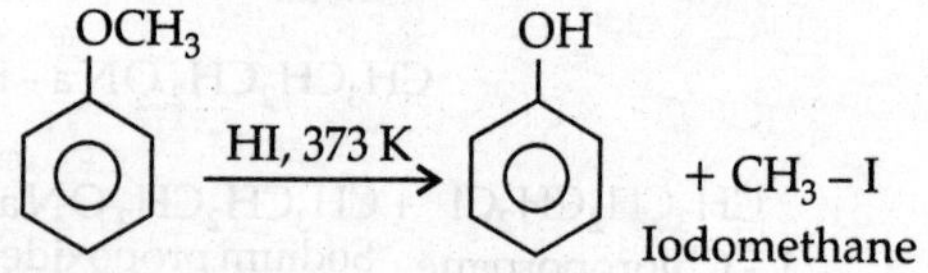

Methoxybenzene → Phenol + Iodomethane

(iii)

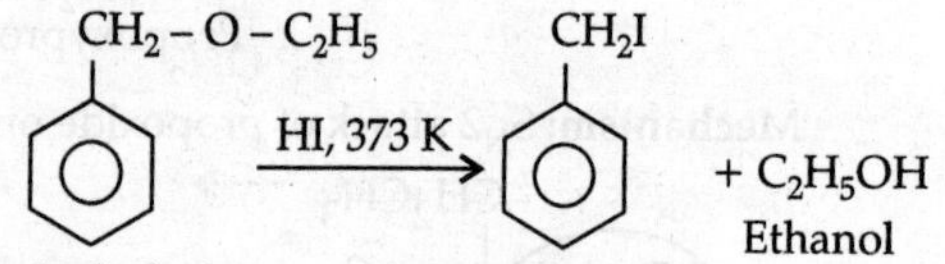

Benzyl ethyl ether → Benzyl iodide + Ethanol

Q. 29. Explain the fact that in aryl alkyl ethers

(i) the alkoxy group activates the benzene ring towards electrophilic substitution and

(ii) it directs the incoming substituents to ortho– and para– positions in benzene ring.

[NCERT Ex. Q.7.29, Page 224]

Ans. Consider the following resonance structures of aryl alkyl ethers:

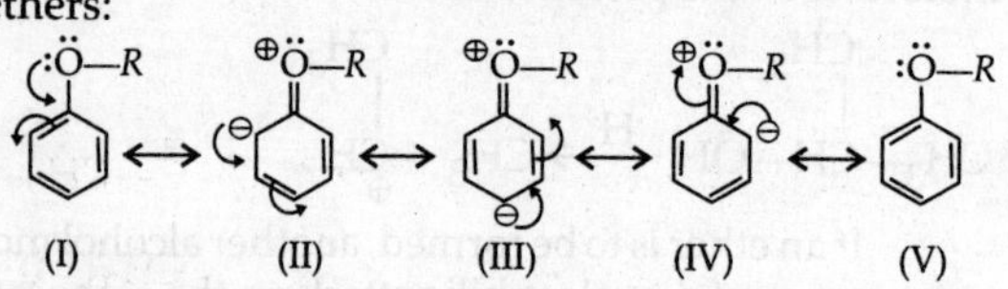

(I) (II) (III) (IV) (V)

(i) From the above structures, we find that the presence of the –OR group has increased the electron density on the benzene ring and therefore the ring is said to have been activated towards incoming electrophiles.

(ii) From structures (II), (III) and (IV) we find that and the electron density has increased on C-2, C-4 and C- 6, i.e., at the ortho and para positions. As a result the electrophile (E) attaches itself to these e^- rich sites and the -OR group is said to have directed the E to ortho– and para– positions.

Q. 30. Write the mechanism of the reaction of HI with methoxymethane. [NCERT Ex. Q.7.30, Page 224]

Ans. The reaction between methoxymethane and HI is:

$$CH_3-O-CH_3 + HI \longrightarrow CH_3I + CH_3OH$$

Step I: Generation of oxonium ion: Protonation of ether molecule

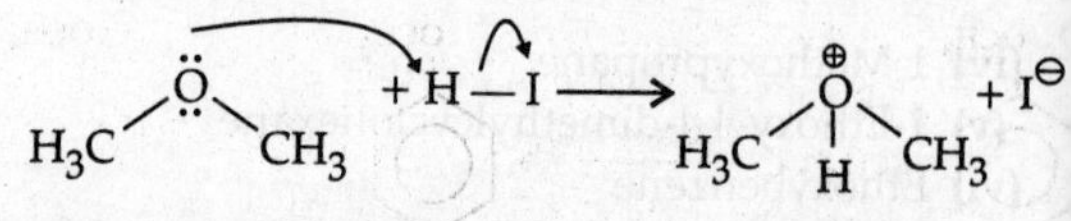

Step II: Nucleophilic attack on oxonium ion:

$$CH_3-\overset{\oplus}{\underset{H}{O}}-CH_3 + I^{\ominus} \xrightarrow{S_N2} \underset{\text{Methanol}}{CH_3-O-H} + \underset{\text{Methyl iodide}}{CH_3I}$$

If excess HI is used, metanol formed above reacts with HI to form methyl iodide.

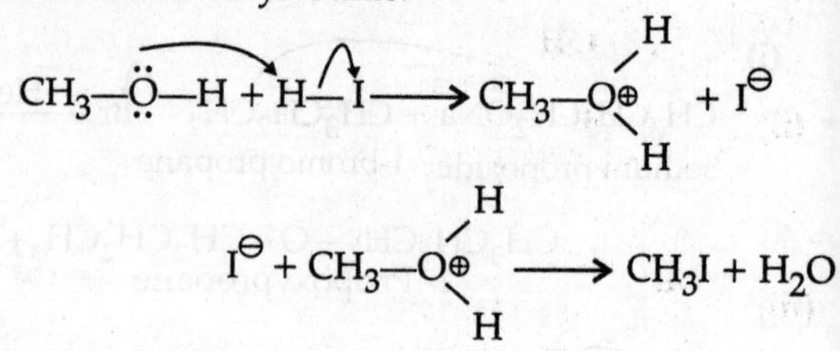

Q. 31. Write equations of the following reactions:

(i) Friedel-Crafts reaction – alkylation of anisole.

(ii) Nitration of anisole.

(iii) Bromination of anisole in ethanoic acid medium.

(iv) Friedel-Craft's acetylation of anisole.

[NCERT Ex. Q.7.31, Page 224]

Ans. (i) Friedel-Crafts reaction (Alkylation):

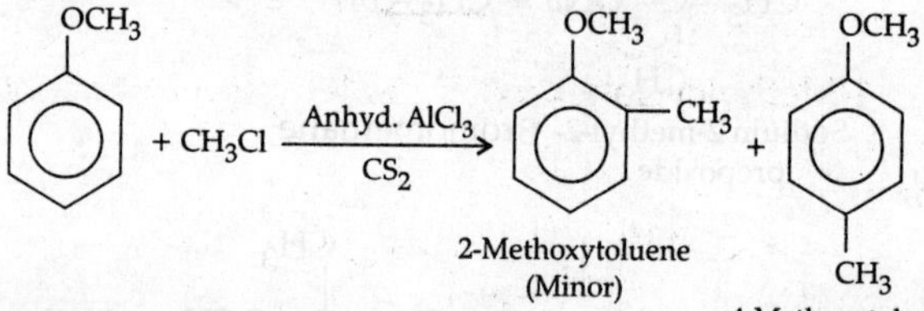

2-Methoxytoluene (Minor) + 4-Methoxytoluene (Major)

(ii) Nitration of anisole: Anisole reacts with a mixture of concentrated sulphuric acid and nitric acid to yield a mixture of *ortho* and *para* nitroanisole.

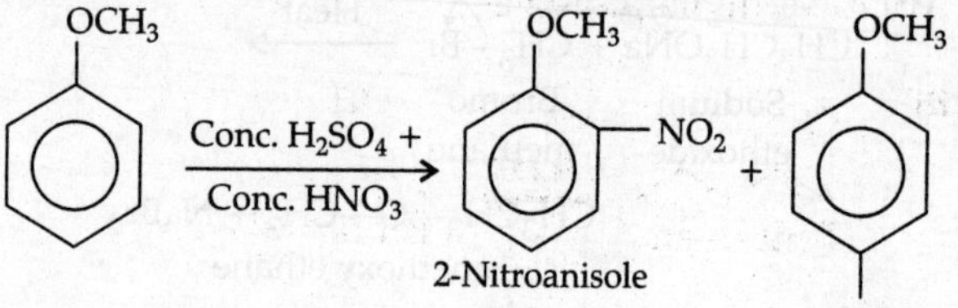

2-Nitroanisole (Minor) + 4-Nitroanisole (Major)

(iii) Bromination

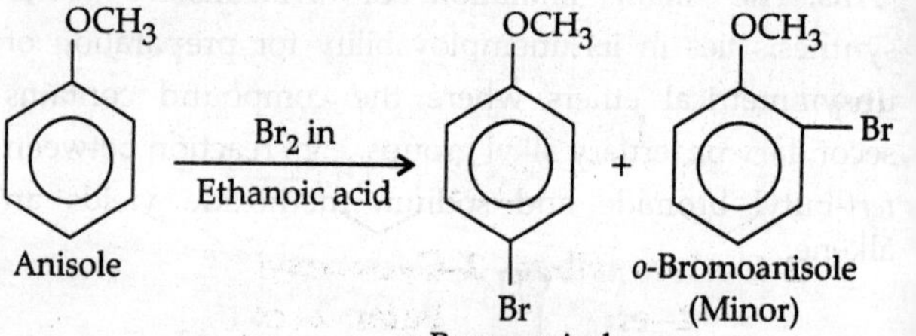

Anisole → *p*-Bromoanisole (Major) + *o*-Bromoanisole (Minor)

(iv) Friedel-Craft's acetylation of anisole.

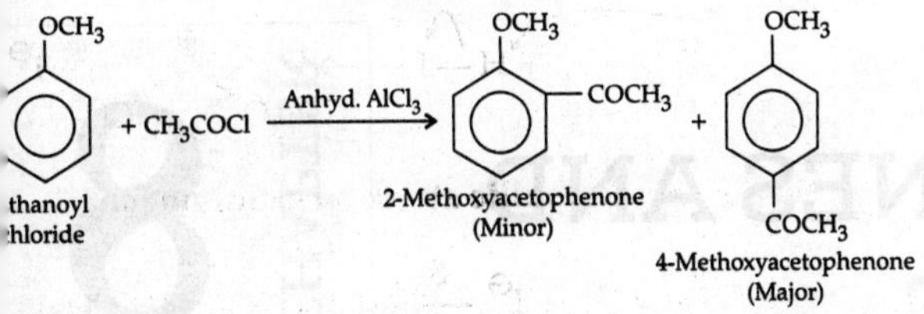

Q. 32. Show how would you synthesise the following alcohols from appropriate alkenes.

(i)
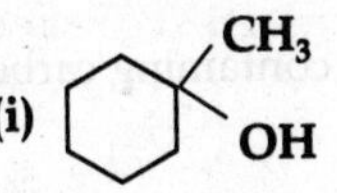

(ii)
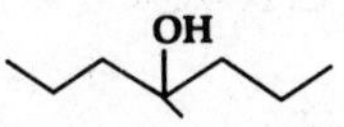

(iii)
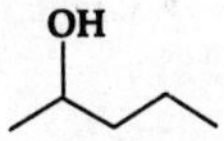

(iv)
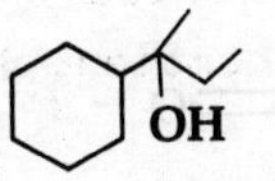

[NCERT Ex. Q.7.32, Page 224]

Ans.

(i)
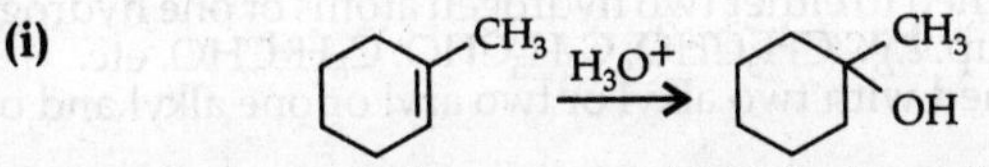

1-Methylcyclohexone 1-Methylcyclohexanol

or – 1– ol

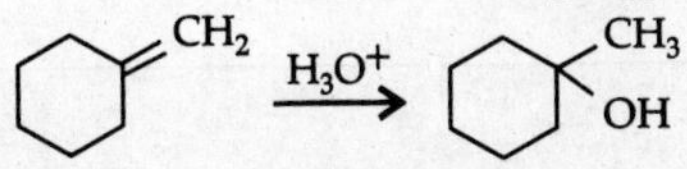

(ii)
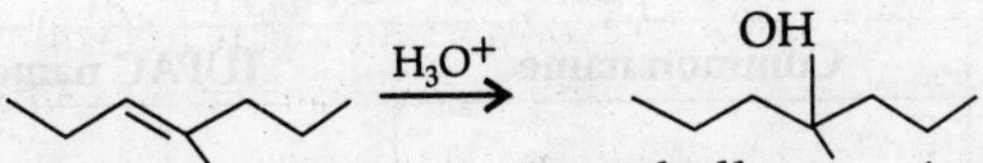

4–Methylhept-3-ene 4–methylheptan-4-ol

(iii)
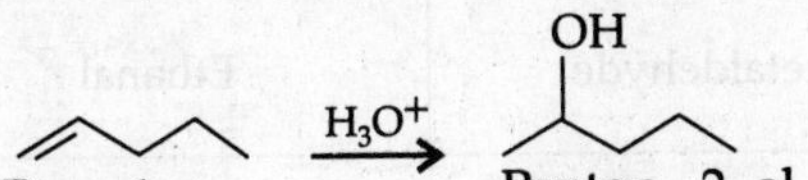

Pent–1–en Pentan –2–ol

or

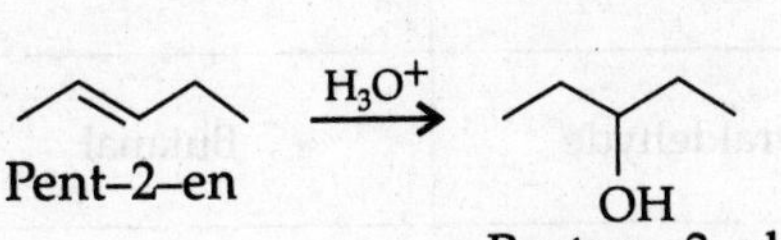

Pent–2–en Penton –3–ol

(iv)
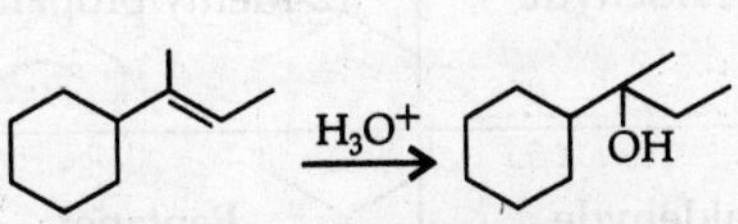

2–Cyclohexylbut –2– en 2–Cyclohexyl- butan-2– ol

Q. 33. When 3-methylbutan-2-ol is treated with HBr, the following reaction takes place:

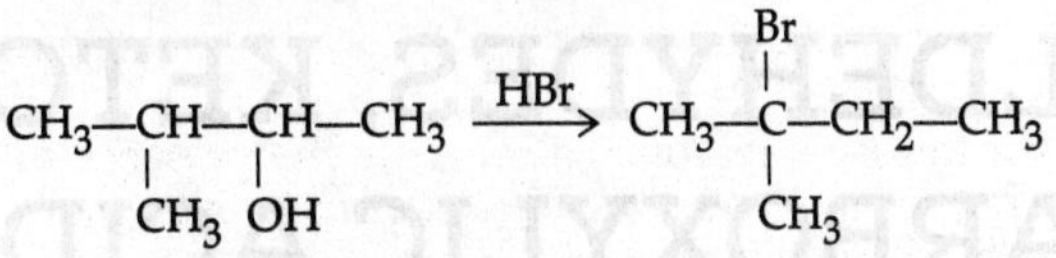

Give a mechanism for this reaction.

[Hint: The secondary carbocation formed in step II rearranges to a more stable tertiary carbocation by a hydride ion shift from 3rd carbon atom.]

[NCERT Ex. Q.7.33, Page 224]

Ans. The given reaction is an example of carbocation rearrangment which takes place by hydride shift. The mechanism for it is:

Step 1: Formation of carbocation: Protonation of alcohol.

$$HBr \longrightarrow H^+ + Br^\ominus$$

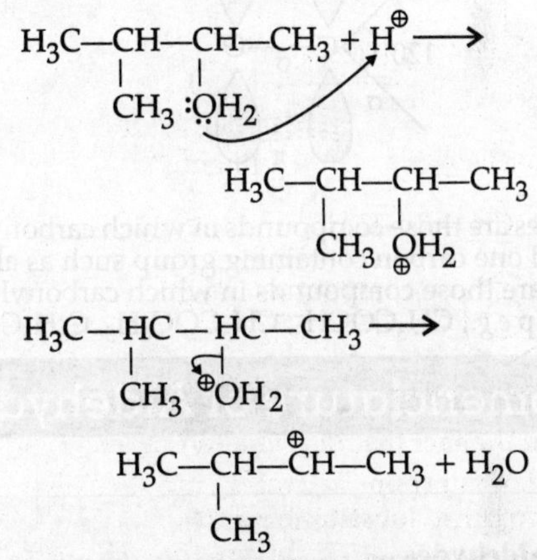

2° Carbocation

Step 2: 1, 2-hydride shift: formation of a more stable, 3° carbocation.

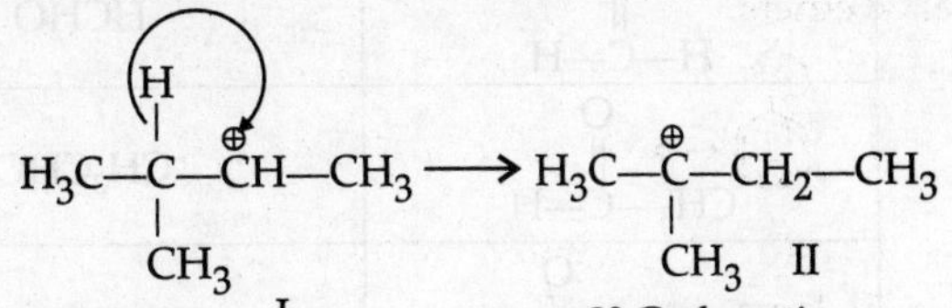

Initially, a 2° carbocation (I) was formed. But, due to the higher stability of its 3° counter part, the hydride shift takes place and the more stable carbocation (II) is formed.

Step 3 Attack of nucleophile: Generation of product

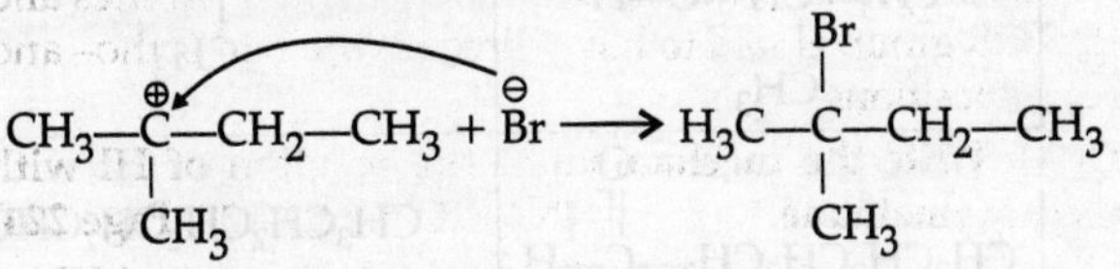

□□

CHAPTER 8

ALDEHYDES, KETONES AND CARBOXYLIC ACIDS

- Carbonyl compounds are of utmost importance to carbonic chemistry. They are constitutents of fabrics, flavourings, plastics and drugs.
- **Carbonyl group:** The functional group >C=O is called carbonyl group. Organic compounds containing carbonyl group are aldehydes and ketones. The general formulae of these compounds are

$$R-\overset{\overset{O}{\|}}{C}-H \qquad\qquad R-\overset{\overset{O}{\|}}{C}-R'$$

Aldehyde (where R=H or any alkyl, aryl group) — Ketone (where R and R' may be same or different alkyl or aryl group)

Structure of Carbonyl Group:

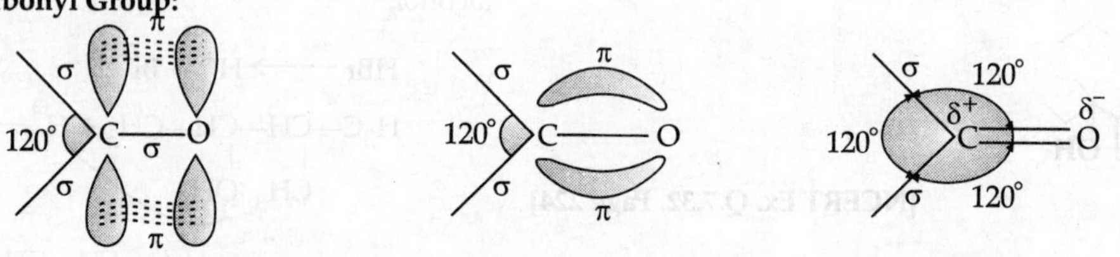

Fig. 1

- Aldehydes are those compounds in which carbonyl group is attached to either two hydrogen atoms or one hydrogen atom and one carbon containing group such as alkyl or aryl group. *e.g.*, CH_3CHO, C_2H_5CHO, C_6H_5CHO, etc.
- Ketones are those compounds in which carbonyl group is attached with two alkyl or two aryl or one alkyl and one aryl group *e.g.*, CH_3COCH_3, $CH_3COC_6H_5$, $C_6H_5COC_6H_5$, etc.

Nomenclature of Aldehydes and Ketones

Table 1

Aldehydes	**General formula:** $R-\overset{\overset{O}{\|}}{C}-H$, where $R = C_nH_{2n+1}$		
Structural formula	**Condensed formula**	**Common name**	**IUPAC name**
$H-\overset{\overset{O}{\|}}{C}-H$	HCHO	Formaldehyde	Methanal
$CH_3-\overset{\overset{O}{\|}}{C}-H$	CH_3CHO	Acetaldehyde	Ethanal
$CH_3CH_2-\overset{\overset{O}{\|}}{C}-H$	CH_3CH_2CHO	Propionaldehyde	Propanal
$CH_3CH_2CH_2-\overset{\overset{O}{\|}}{C}-H$	$CH_3CH_2CH_2CHO$	Butyraldehyde	Butanal
$CH_3-\underset{\underset{CH_3}{\vert}}{CH}-\overset{\overset{O}{\|}}{C}-H$	$CH_3-\underset{\underset{CH_3}{\vert}}{CH}-CHO$	Isobutyraldehyde	2-Methylpropanal
$CH_3CH_2CH_2CH_2-\overset{\overset{O}{\|}}{C}-H$	$CH_3CH_2CH_2CH_2CHO$	Valeraldehyde	Pentanal
$CH_3-\underset{\underset{CH_3}{\vert}}{CH}-CH_2-\overset{\overset{O}{\|}}{C}-H$	$CH_3-\underset{\underset{CH_3}{\vert}}{CH}-CH_2CHO$	Isovaleraldehyde	3-Methylbutanal

ALDEHYDES AND KETONES:

(i) Physical:

Boiling points are higher than hydrocarbons and ethers of comparable molecular masses and lower than alcohols of similar molecular masses due to absence of intermolecular hydrogen bonding.

(ii)Chemical :Nucleophilic addition reactions :

Aldehydes are more reactive than ketones due to steric and electronic reasons.

$HCN + OH^- \rightleftharpoons :CN^- + H_2O;\ \overset{\delta+}{C}=\overset{\delta-}{O} + :CN^- \rightleftharpoons \left[>C(O^-)(CN) \right] \xrightleftharpoons{H^+} >C(CN)(OH)$ Cyanohydrin

$R_2C=O + \begin{matrix} CH_2OH \\ CH_2OH \end{matrix} \xrightleftharpoons[\text{Dil. HCl}]{\text{HCl gas}} R_2C\begin{matrix} O-CH_2 \\ O-CH_2 \end{matrix} + H_2O$

Reduction : (a) To alcohols – aldehydes and ketones reduce to primary and secondary alcohols respectively by $NaBH_4$ or $LiAlH_4$.

(b) To hydrocarbons –

$>C=O \xrightarrow[\text{HCl}]{\text{Zn-Hg}} >CH_2 + H_2O$ (Clemmensen Reduction)

$>C=O \xrightarrow[-H_2O]{NH_2NH_2} >C=NNH_2 \xrightarrow[\text{Heat}]{\text{KOH/Ethylene glycol}} >CH_2 + N_2$ (Wolff-Kishner Reduction)

Oxidation: $RCHO \xrightarrow{[O]} R\text{-}COOH$

Tollen's test : $RCHO + 2[Ag(NH_3)_2]^+ + 3OH^- \longrightarrow RCOO^- + 2Ag\downarrow + 2H_2O + 4NH_3$ (Silver mirror)

Fehling's test : $RCHO + 2Cu^{2+} + 5OH^- \longrightarrow RCOO^- + Cu_2O\downarrow + 3H_2O$ (Red brown ppt)

Haloform reaction:

$R\text{-}\overset{O}{\overset{\|}{C}}\text{-}CH_3 \xrightarrow{NaOX} R\text{-}\overset{O}{\overset{\|}{C}}\text{-}ONa + CHX_3$ (X = Cl, Br, I)

Reactions due to α - hydrogen:

$2CH_3CHO \xrightleftharpoons{\text{dil.NaOH}} H_3C\text{-}\overset{OH}{\overset{|}{C}H}\text{-}CH_2\text{-}\overset{O}{\overset{\|}{C}}\text{-}H \xrightarrow[-H_2O]{\Delta} CH_3\text{-}CH=CH\text{-}CHO$

$2CH_3COCH_3 \xrightleftharpoons{Ba(OH)_2} (CH_3)_2C(OH)\text{-}CH_2\text{-}CO\text{-}CH_3 \xrightarrow[-H_2O]{\Delta} CH_3\text{-}\overset{CH_3}{\overset{|}{C}}=CH\text{-}CO\text{-}CH_3$

$CH_3CHO + CH_3CH_2CHO \xrightarrow[\Delta]{NaOH} CH_3\text{-}CH=CH\text{-}CHO + CH_3\text{-}CH_2\text{-}CH=\underset{CH_3}{\underset{|}{C}}\text{-}CHO$

Cannizzaro reaction : $2HCHO + \text{conc } KOH \xrightarrow{\Delta} CH_3OH + HCOOK$

Electrophilic substitution reaction:

$C_6H_5CHO \xrightarrow[\text{273-283 K}]{HNO_3/H_2SO_4}$ m-$NO_2C_6H_4CHO$

Carboxylic acids:

(i) Physical: Higher boiling points than aldehydes, ketones or alcohols. Solubility decreases with increasing number of C atoms.

(ii)Chemical : $2RCOOH + 2Na \longrightarrow 2RCOONa + H_2$

Forms corresponding anhydride on heating with mineral acids

$RCOOH + R'OH \xrightleftharpoons{H^+} RCOOR' + H_2O$

$RCOOH + PCl_5 \longrightarrow RCOCl + POCl_3 + HCl$

$CH_3COOH + NH_3 \rightleftharpoons CH_3COO^-\overset{+}{N}H_4 \xrightarrow[-H_2O]{\Delta} CH_3CONH_2$

$RCOOH \xrightarrow[H_3O^+]{B_2H_6} RCH_2OH$

$RCOONa \xrightarrow[\text{NaOH \& CaO}]{\text{Heat}} R\text{-}H + Na_2CO_3$

$RCH_2COOH \xrightarrow[H_2O]{X_2/\text{Red P}} R\text{-}\underset{X}{\underset{|}{C}H}\text{-}COOH$ (HVZ reaction) (X=Cl, Br)

1. Aldehydes and Ketones

Common names :

- Replace corresponding carboxylic acids with aldehyde.
- Alkyl phenyl ketones by adding acyl group as prefix to phenone.
- IUPAC names :
- Replacing –e with –al and –one as required.

Structure of Carbonyl group

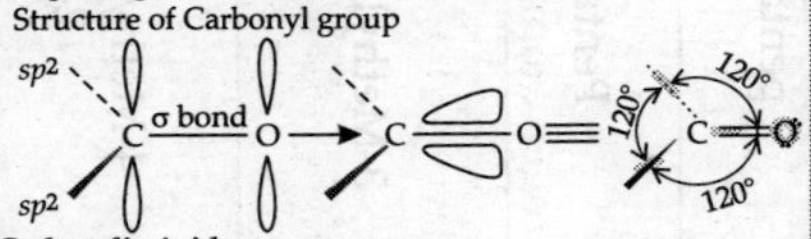

2. Carboxylic Acids

Common names : end with –ic

- IUPAC names : replace –e in the corresponding alkane with –oic acid.
- Structure of Carboxyl Group

$-C(=O)\text{-}\ddot{O}\text{-}H \longleftrightarrow -\overset{+}{C}(O^-)\text{-}\ddot{O}\text{-}H \longleftrightarrow -C(O^-)=\overset{+}{\ddot{O}}\text{-}H$

3. USES

(a) Carboxylic acids

- Methanoic acid in rubber, textile, dyeing, leather industries.
- Ethanoic acid as solvent.
- Higher fatty acids in manufacture of soaps and detergents.

(b) Aldehydes of ketones

- As solvents.
- Starting materials and reagents for synthesis of products.

ALDEHYDES:

1. From acyl chloride

$C_6H_5COCl \xrightarrow[\text{Pd-BaSO}_4]{H_2} C_6H_5CHO$

2. From nitriles and esters : Stephen reaction

$RCN + SnCl_2 + HCl \longrightarrow RCH=NH \xrightarrow{H_3O^+} RCHO$

3. From hydrocarbons : Etard reaction

$C_6H_5CH_3 + CrO_2Cl_2 \xrightarrow{CS_2} C_6H_5CH(OCrOHCl_2)_2 \xrightarrow{H_3O^+} C_6H_5CHO$

$C_6H_5CH_3 \xrightarrow{Cl_2/hv} C_6H_5CHCl_2 \xrightarrow[373K]{H_2O} C_6H_5CHO$

Gattermann – Koch reaction $C_6H_6 \xrightarrow[\text{Anhyd.AlCl}_3]{\text{CO, HCl}} C_6H_5CHO$

KETONES:

1.From acyl chloride

$2R\text{–}Mg\text{–}X + CdCl_2 \longrightarrow R_2Cd + 2Mg(X)Cl$

$R_2Cd + 2R'\text{-}\overset{O}{\overset{\|}{C}}\text{-}Cl \longrightarrow 2R'\text{-}\overset{O}{\overset{\|}{C}}\text{-}R + CdCl_2$

2.From nitriles

$CH_3CH_2CN + C_6H_5MgBr \xrightarrow{\text{Ether}} CH_3CH_2\text{-}\overset{NMgBr}{\overset{\|}{C}}\text{-}C_6H_5 \xrightarrow{H_3O^+} C_2H_5\text{-}\overset{O}{\overset{\|}{C}}\text{-}C_6H_5$

3.From benzene or substituted benzenes

$C_6H_6 + Ar/R\text{-}\overset{O}{\overset{\|}{C}}\text{-}Cl \xrightarrow{\text{Anhyd.AlCl}_3} C_6H_5\text{-}\overset{O}{\overset{\|}{C}}\text{-}Ar/R$

Carboxylic Acids:

1.From primary alcohols and aldehydes $RCH_2OH \xrightarrow[H_3O^+]{\text{alk. }KMnO_4} RCOOH$

2.From alkylbenzenes $C_6H_5CH_3 \xrightarrow{KMnO_4\text{-}KOH} C_6H_5COOK \xrightarrow{H_3O^+} C_6H_5COOH$

3.From nitriles and amides $R\text{–}CN \xrightarrow[H_2O]{H^+ \text{ or } OH^-} R\text{-}\overset{O}{\overset{\|}{C}}\text{-}NH_2 \xrightarrow[\Delta]{H^+ \text{ or } OH^-} RCOOH$

4.From Grignard reagents $R\text{–}Mg\text{–}X + CO_2 \longrightarrow R\text{-}\overset{O}{\overset{\|}{C}}\text{-}O^-MgX^+ \xrightarrow{H_3O^+} RCOOH$

5.From acyl halides and anhydrides

$RCOCl \xrightarrow{OH^-/H_2O} RCOO^- + Cl^- \xrightarrow{H_3O^+} RCOOH$

$C_6H_5COOCOCH_3 \xrightarrow{H_2O} C_6H_5COOH + CH_3COOH$

6.From esters

$C_6H_5COOC_2H_5 \xrightleftharpoons{H_3O^+} C_6H_5COOH + C_2H_5OH$

$CH_3CH_2CH_2COOC_2H_5 \xrightleftharpoons{NaOH} CH_3CH_2CH_2COONa + C_2H_5OH \xrightarrow{H_3O^+} CH_3CH_2CH_2COOH$

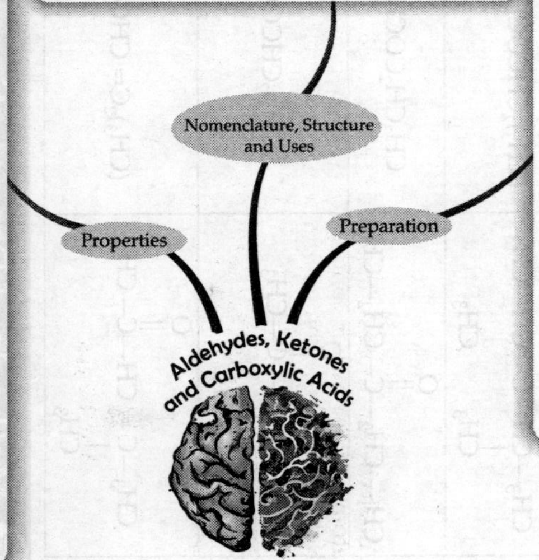

Trace the Mind Map
- First Level
- Second Level
- Third Level

$CH_3-CH_2-CH(CH_3)-C(=O)-H$	$CH_3-CH_2-CH(CH_3)-CHO$	α-Methylbutyraldehyde	2-Methylbutanal

Table 2

Ketones	General formula: $R-\overset{O}{\overset{\parallel}{C}}-R'$ and $R' = C_{n'}H_{2n'+1}$ $(n = n', n \neq 0)$		
Structural Formula	**Condensed formula**	**Common name**	**IUPAC name**
$CH_3-C(=O)-CH_3$	CH_3COCH_3	Acetone	Propanone
$CH_3-C(=O)-CH_2-CH_3$	$CH_3COCH_2CH_3$	Ethyl methyl ketone	Butan-2-one or Butanone
$CH_3-C(=O)-CH_2-CH_2-CH_3$	$CH_3COCH_2CH_2CH_3$	Methyl *n*-Propyl ketone	Pentan-2-one
$CH_3-CH(CH_3)-C(=O)-CH(CH_3)-CH_3$	$(CH_3)_2CHCOCH(CH_3)_2$	Diisopropyl ketone	2, 4-Dimethyl pentan-3-one
$CH_3-CH_2-C(=O)-CH_2-CH_3$	$CH_3CH_2COCH_2CH_3$	Diethyl ketone	Pentan-3-one
$CH_3-CH(CH_3)-C(=O)-CH_3$	$(CH_3)_2CHCOCH_3$	Isopropyl methyl ketone	3-Methylbutan-2-one
$CH_3-C(CH_3)=CH-C(=O)-CH_3$	$(CH_3)_2C= CHCOCH_3$	Mesityl oxide	4-Methylpent-3-en-2-one

Methods of Preparation of Aldehydes and Ketones

(a) Preparation of Aldehydes:

(i) By oxidation of primary alcohols: Aldehydes can be prepared by the oxidation of primary alcohols.

$$\underset{1^\circ \text{ Alcohol}}{RCH_2OH} + [O] \xrightarrow[\text{or } KMnO_4]{K_2Cr_2O_7/H_2SO_4} \underset{\text{Aldehyde}}{R-CHO} + H_2O$$

$$\underset{1^\circ \text{ Alcohol}}{R-CH_2-OH} \xrightarrow{PCC} \underset{\text{Aldehyde}}{R-CHO}$$

Scan to know more about this topic

Nomenclature of aldehyde, ketones and carboxylic acids

(ii) By dehydrogenation of alcohols:

$$\underset{1^\circ \text{ Alcohol}}{R-CH_2-OH} \xrightarrow[573K]{Cu} \underset{\text{Aldehyde}}{RCHO} + H_2$$

(iii) From hydrocarbons: From hydrocarbons, aldehydes can be prepared either by ozonolysis of alkenes or by hydration of alkynes.

(a) By ozonolysis of alkenes:

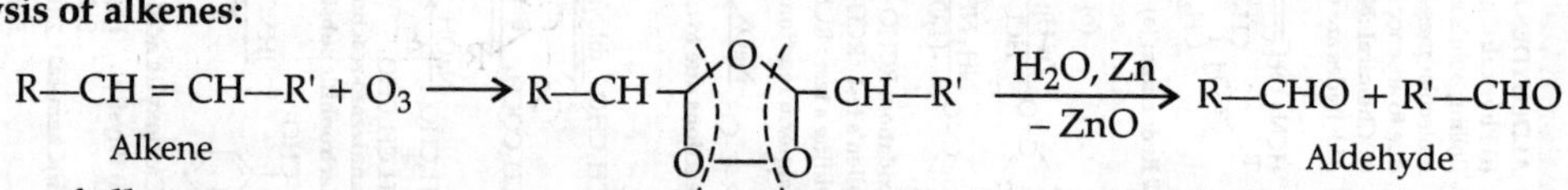

(b) By hydration of alkynes:

$$\underset{\substack{\text{Ethyne}\\\text{(Acetylene)}}}{CH \equiv CH} + H_2O \xrightarrow[333K]{H_2SO_4/HgSO_4} \underset{\text{Unstable}}{\left[CH_2 = \overset{OH}{\overset{|}{CH}}\right]} \rightarrow \underset{\substack{\text{Ethanal}\\\text{(Acetaldehyde)}}}{CH_3-CHO}$$

(iv) From acyl chloride:

$$R-\overset{O}{\overset{\|}{C}}-Cl + H_2 \xrightarrow[\text{Rosenmund Reduction}]{Pd\text{-}BaSO_4,S} R-\overset{O}{\overset{\|}{C}}-H + HCl$$

Acyl chloride → Aldehyde

$$CH_3-\overset{O}{\overset{\|}{C}}-Cl + H_2 \xrightarrow{Pd\text{-}BaSO_4,S} CH_3-\overset{O}{\overset{\|}{C}}-H + HCl$$

Acetyl chloride → Acetaldehyde

(v) From nitriles and esters:

$$SnCl_2 + 2HCl \rightarrow SnCl_4 + 2[H]$$

$$R-C\equiv N + HCl + 2[H] \rightarrow R-CH=NH.HCl \xrightarrow[\cdot NH_4Cl]{+H_2O} RCHO$$

Aldehyde

This reaction is called Stephen reaction.

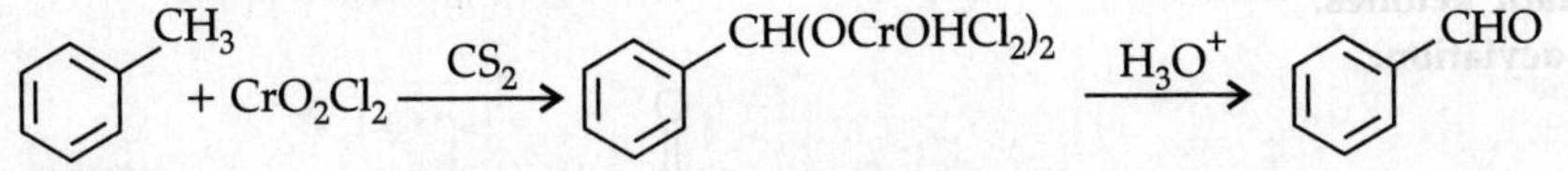

Toluene Chromium complex Benzaldehyde

This is called Etard reaction.

(ii) By side chain chlorination followed by hydrolysis:

It is the commercial method of preparation of benzaldehyde

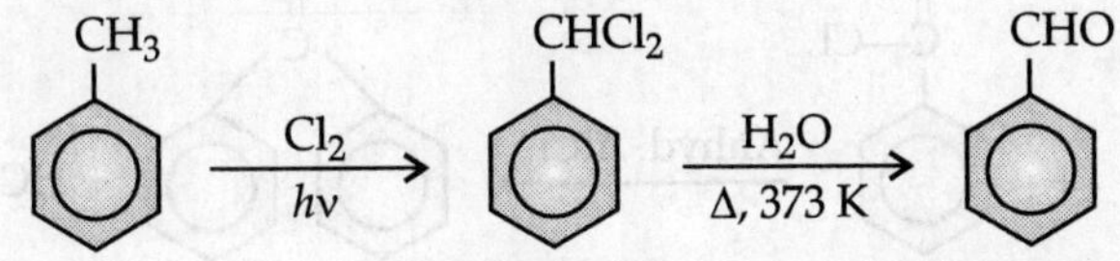

Toluene Benzal chloride Benzaldehyde

(iii) By Gattermann - Koch reaction:

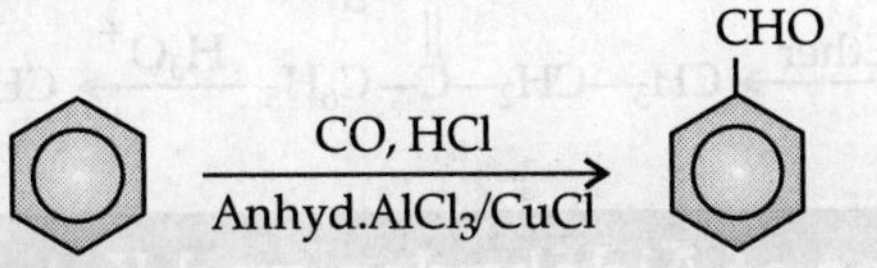

Benzene Benzaldehyde

(c) Preparation of Ketones:

(i) By oxidation of secondary alcohols:

$$\begin{matrix}R\\R'\end{matrix}\!\!>CH-OH + [O] \xrightarrow[\text{or } CrO_3]{K_2Cr_2O_7/H_2SO_4} \begin{matrix}R\\R'\end{matrix}\!\!>C=O + H_2O$$

2° Alcohol → Ketone

(ii) By dehydrogenation of secondary alcohols:

$$\begin{matrix}R\\R'\end{matrix}\!\!>CH-OH \xrightarrow[573K]{Cu} \begin{matrix}R\\R'\end{matrix}\!\!>C=O + H_2$$

2° Alcohol → Ketone

(iii) By ozonolysis of alkenes:

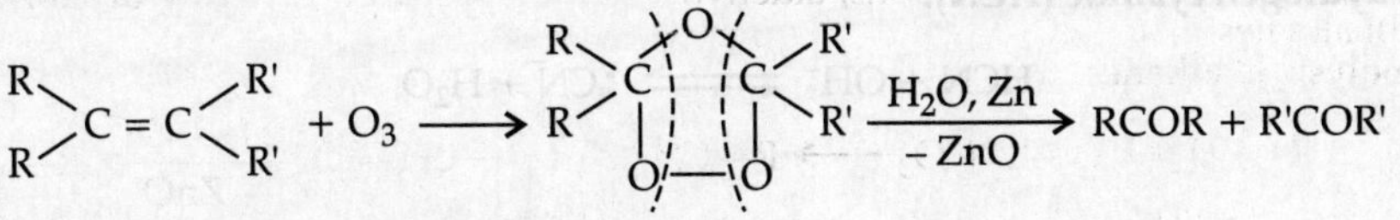

(iv) By hydration of alkynes: (By Kucherov's reaction)

$$CH_3-C\equiv CH + \xrightarrow[\text{at } 60°-80°\,C]{20\%\,H_2SO_4/HgSO_4} \left[CH_3-\overset{OH}{\overset{|}{C}}=CH_2\right] \xrightleftharpoons{\text{Tautomeric change}} CH_3-\overset{O}{\overset{\|}{C}}-CH_3$$

Unstable Acetone

$$HC \equiv CH \xrightarrow[\text{at } 50° - 60° C]{1\%\ Ag^+,\ 20\%\ H_2SO_4} [H_2C = \overset{OH}{\overset{|}{C}}H] \xrightleftharpoons{\text{Tautomeric change}} CH_3 - CHO$$

(v) From acyl chlorides:

$$2R - MgX + CdCl_2 \rightarrow R_2Cd + 2MgXCl$$

$$\underset{\text{Acyl chloride}}{2R'-\overset{O}{\overset{||}{C}}-Cl} + \underset{\text{Bialkyl cadmium}}{R_2Cd} \longrightarrow \underset{\text{Ketone}}{2R'-\overset{O}{\overset{||}{C}}-R} + CdCl_2$$

(vi) From nitriles:

$$\underset{\text{Ethyl magnesium bromide}}{CH_3-\overset{\delta^-}{C}H_2-\overset{\delta^+}{Mg}Br} + CH_3-\overset{\delta^+}{C}\equiv\overset{\delta^-}{N} \xrightarrow{\text{ether}} CH_3-\underset{CH_2-CH_3}{\underset{|}{C}} = NMgBr \xrightarrow{H_3O^+} \underset{\text{Ethylmethyl ketone}}{H_3C-\overset{O}{\overset{||}{C}}-CH_2-CH_3} + Mg\begin{matrix} NH_2 \\ Br \end{matrix}$$

(d) Preparation of Aromatic ketones:

(i) By Friedel-Crafts acylation:

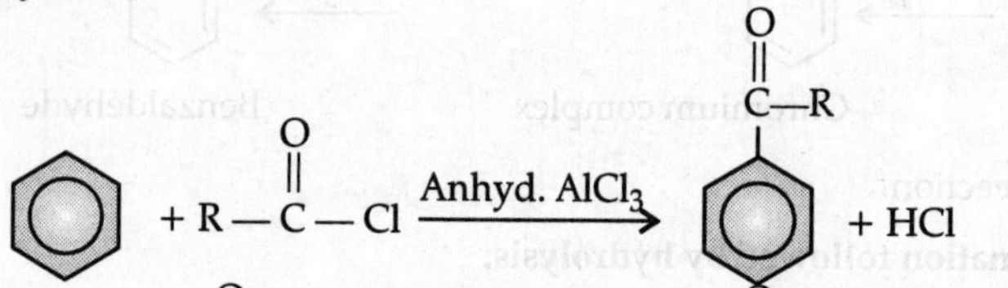

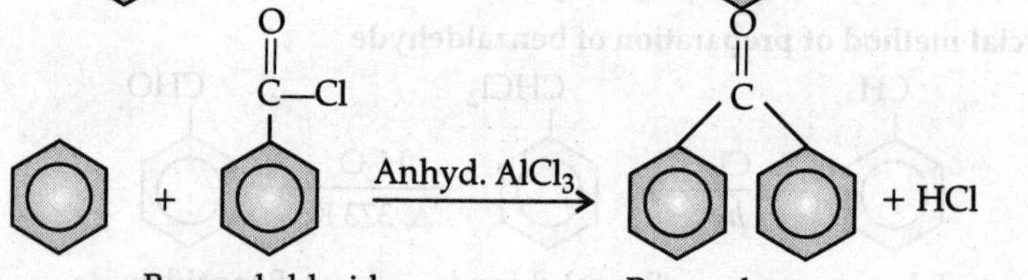

Benzoyl chloride Benzophenone

(ii) From nitriles:

$$\underset{\text{Ethyl cyanide}}{CH_3-CH_2-C\equiv N} + C_6H_5MgBr \xrightarrow{\text{Ether}} CH_3-CH_2-\overset{NMgBr}{\overset{||}{C}}-C_6H_5 \xrightarrow{H_3O^+} \underset{\text{Propiophenone}}{CH_3-CH_2-\overset{O}{\overset{||}{C}}-C_6H_5} + Mg\begin{matrix} NH_2 \\ Br \end{matrix}$$

Physical Properties of Aldehydes and Ketones

(i) Most of the aldehydes (except formaldehyde which is a gas) are liquids at room temperature. The lower ketones are colourless liquids and have a pleasant smell.

(ii) Both of these have relatively high boiling point as compared to hydrocarbons of comparable molecular masses due to presence of polar carbonyl group. But they have lower b.p. than alcohols of comparable molecular masses.

(iii) The lower members of aldehydes and ketones (up to four carbon atoms) are soluble in water due to hydrogen bonding.

Chemical Properties of Aldehydes and Ketones

- Aldehydes and ketones are highly reactive compounds. Both undergo nucleophilic addition reaction.

Some important nucleophilic addition reactions:

(i) Addition of hydrogen cyanide (HCN):

$$HCN + OH^- \rightleftharpoons :\bar{C}N + H_2O$$

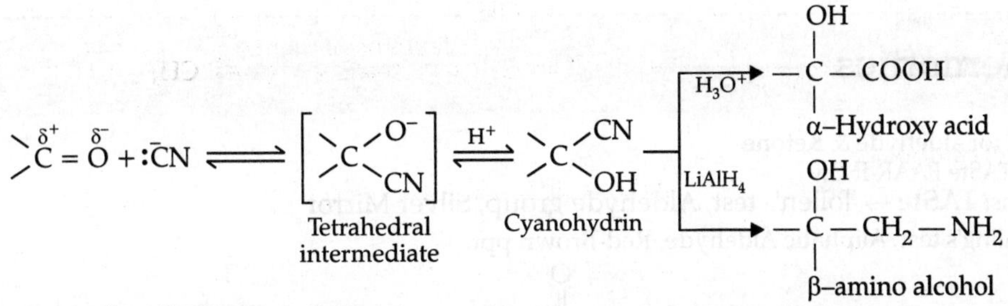

(ii) Addition to sodium hydrogen sulphite:

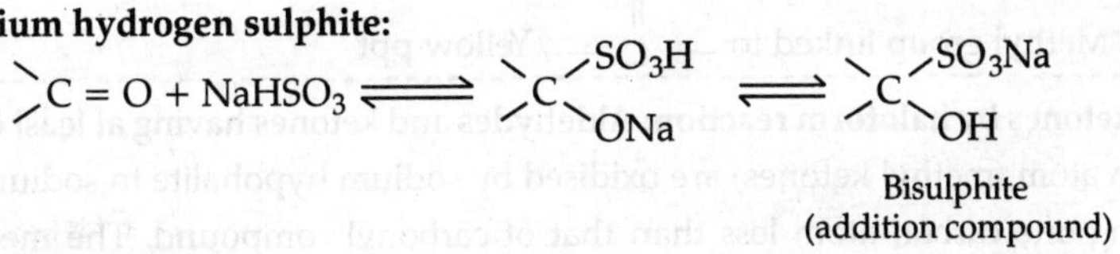

(iii) Addition of Grignard reagent:

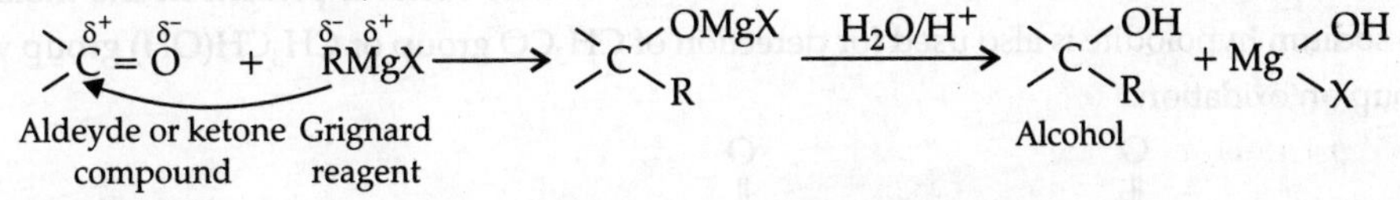

(iv) Addition of alcohols:

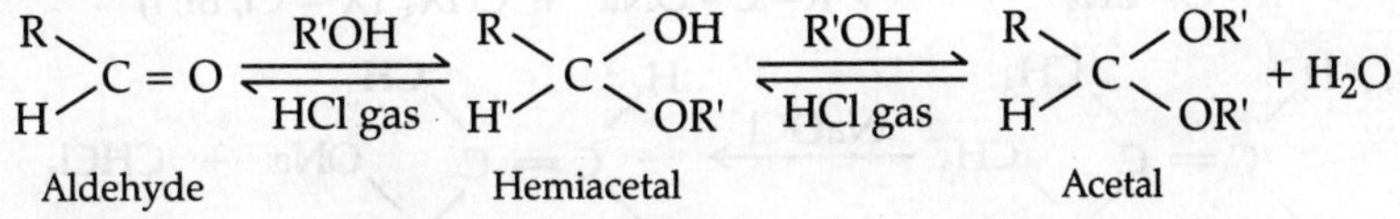

Ketones react with dihydric alcohols to give ketals.

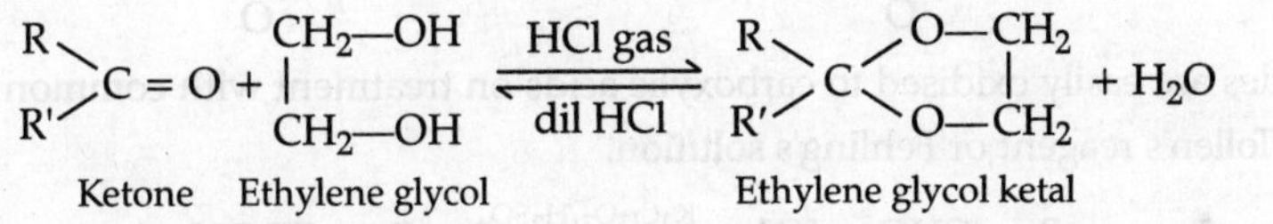

(v) Addition of ammonia and its derivatives:

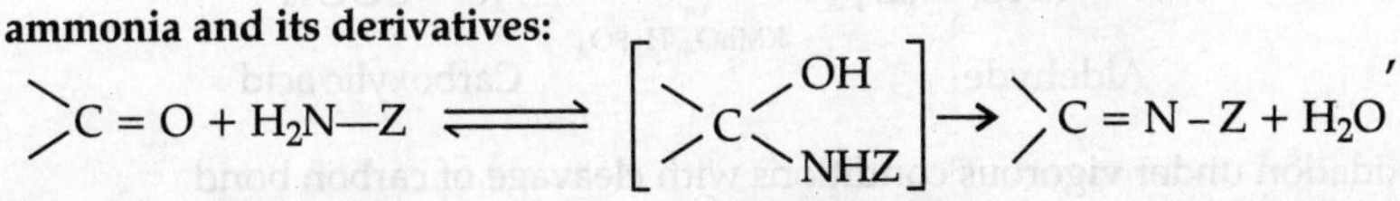

where Z = Alkyl, aryl, –OH, $–NH_2$, $C_6H_5NH–$, $–NHCONH_2$, etc.

- **Reduction:**

(i) Reduction to alcohols:

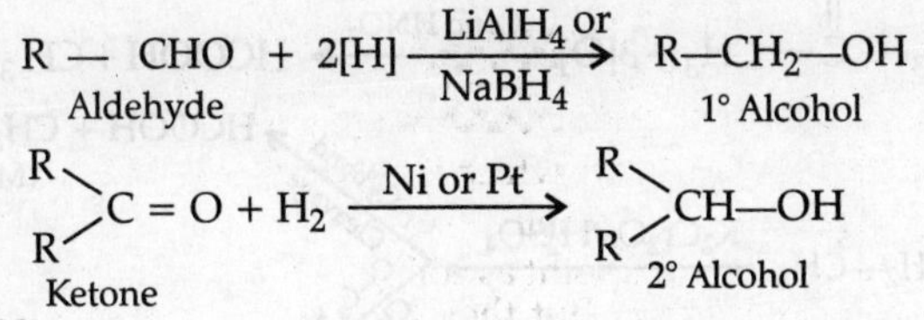

(ii) Reduction to hydrocarbons:

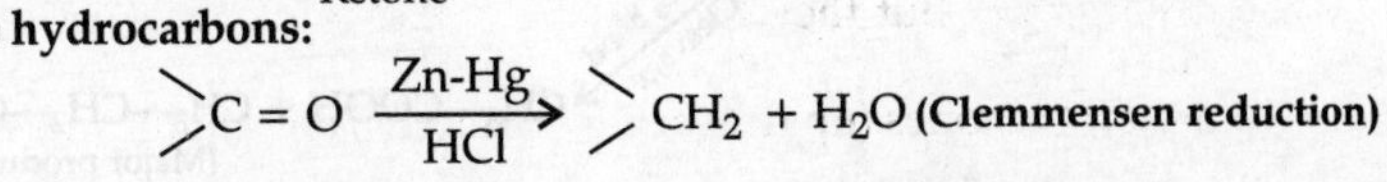

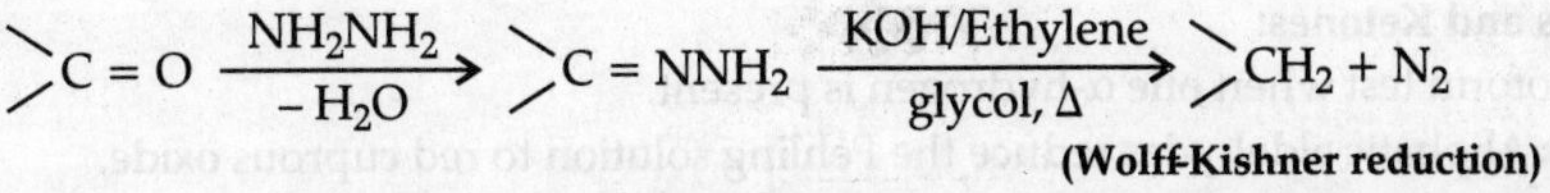

- **Tollens' test:** On warming an aldehyde with freshly prepared ammoniacal silver nitrate solution (Tollens' reagent), a bright silver mirror is produced due to the formation of silver metal. The aldehydes are oxidised to corresponding carboxylate anion. The reaction occurs in alkaline medium.

$$RCHO + 2[Ag(NH_3)_2]^+ + 3\bar{O}H \longrightarrow RCO\bar{O} + 2Ag + 2H_2O + 4NH_3$$

- **Fehling's test:** Fehling reagent comprises of two solutions, Fehling solution A and Fehling solution B. Fehling solution A is aqueous copper sulphate and Fehling solution B is alkaline sodium potassium tartarate (Rochelle salt). These two solutions are mixed in equal amounts before test. On heating an aldehyde with Fehling's reagent, a reddish brown precipitate is obtained. Aldehydes are oxidised to corresponding carboxylate anion. Aromatic aldehydes do not respond to this test.

$$R\text{-}CHO + 2Cu^{2+} + 5\bar{O}H \longrightarrow RCO\bar{O} + \underset{\text{Red-brown ppt}}{Cu_2O\downarrow} + CH_2O$$

Mnemonics

Concept: Test for aldehyde & Ketone
Mnemonics: TASte FAAR IMLy
Interpretations: TASte → Tollen's test, Aldehyde group, Silver Mirror
FAAR → Fehling's test, Aliphatic Aldehyde, Red-Brown ppt.

IMLY → Iodoform test, Methyl group linked to $-\overset{O}{\overset{\|}{C}}-$, Yellow ppt

- **Oxidation of methyl ketones by haloform reaction:** Aldehydes and ketones having at least one methyl group linked to the carbonyl carbon atom (methyl ketones) are oxidised by sodium hypohalite to sodium salts of corresponding carboxylic acids having one carbon atom less than that of carbonyl compound. The methyl group is converted to haloform. This oxidation does not affect a carbon-carbon double bond, if present in the molecule. Iodoform reaction with sodium hypoiodite is also used for detection of CH_3CO group or $CH_3CH(OH)$ group which produces CH_3CHO group on oxidation.

$$R-\overset{O}{\overset{\|}{C}}-CH_3 \xrightarrow{NaOX} R-\overset{O}{\overset{\|}{C}}-ONa + CHX_3 \quad (X = Cl, Br, I)$$

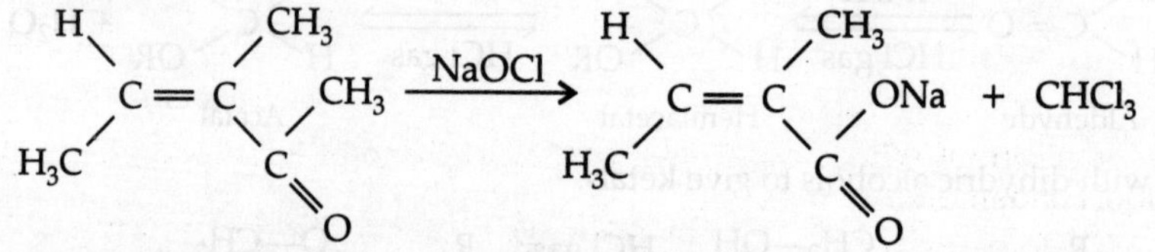

- **Oxidation:** Aldehydes are easily oxidised to carboxylic acids on treatment with common oxidizing agents or mild oxidising agent like Tollen's reagent or Fehling's solution.

$$\underset{\text{Aldehyde}}{R-CHO} + [O] \xrightarrow[\text{KMnO}_4/\text{H}_2\text{SO}_4]{\text{K}_2\text{Cr}_2\text{O}_7/\text{H}_2\text{SO}_4 \text{ or}} \underset{\text{Carboxylic acid}}{R-COOH}$$

Ketones undergo oxidation under vigorous conditions with cleavage of carbon bond.

$$CH_3-\overset{O}{\overset{\|}{C}}-CH_3 + 3[O] \xrightarrow{\text{Conc. HNO}_3} HCOOH + CH_3-COOH$$

$$\overset{1}{C}H_3-\overset{2}{\overset{O}{\overset{\|}{C}}}-\overset{3}{C}H_2-\overset{4}{C}H_2-\overset{5}{C}H_3 \xrightarrow{K_2Cr_2O_7/H_2SO_4}$$

$$\xrightarrow{C_1-C_2 \text{ bond Cleavage}} HCOOH + CH_3CH_2CH_2COOH \text{ (Minor product)}$$

$$\xrightarrow{C_2-C_3 \text{ bond Cleavage}} CH_3-COOH + CH_3-CH_2-COOH \text{ (Major product)}$$

- **Test for Aldehydes and Ketones:**
  - **(i)** Both give iodoform test when one α-hydrogen is present.
  - **(ii) Fehling's test:** Aliphatic aldehydes reduce the Fehling solution to red cuprous oxide.

$$R-CHO + 2CuO + 5OH^- \rightarrow R-COOH + \underset{\text{(red ppt.)}}{Cu_2O\downarrow} + 3H_2O$$

  Aromatic aldehydes do not respond to this test.
  - **(iii)** Ketones are not oxidised by Tollen's reagent.
  Aldehydes form silver mirror with ammonical silver nitrate (Tollen's reagent) solution.

$$R-CHO + 2[Ag(NH_3)_2]^+ \xrightarrow{OH^-} R-COOH + \underset{\text{(Silver mirror)}}{2Ag\downarrow} + H_2O + 4NH_3$$

- **Reaction due to α-hydrogen:**
α-hydrogen in aldehydes and ketones is acidic in nature due to strong electron withdrawing effect of carbonyl group. As a result, aldehydes and ketones undergo a number of reactions.

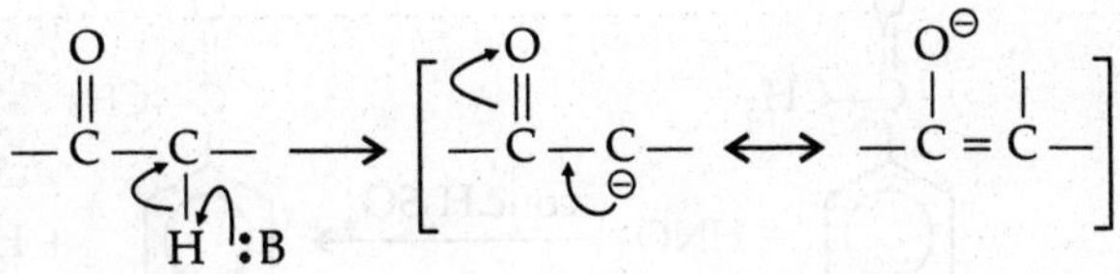

(i) Aldol condensation: Aldehydes and ketones having at least one α-hydrogen react in presence of dilute alkali to form β-hydroxy aldehydes (aldol) or β-hydroxy ketones (ketol).

$$2CH_3-CHO \underset{}{\overset{\text{dil. NaOH}}{\rightleftharpoons}} \underset{\substack{\text{3-Hydroxybutanal}\\ \text{(Aldol)}}}{CH_3-\underset{OH}{\underset{|}{CH}}-CH_2-CHO} \xrightarrow[-H_2O]{\Delta} \underset{\text{But-2-enal}}{CH_3-CH=CH-CHO}$$

$$2CH_3-CO-CH_3 \overset{Ba(OH)_2}{\rightleftharpoons} \underset{\text{Ketol}}{CH_3-\overset{CH_3}{\overset{|}{\underset{OH}{\underset{|}{C}}}}-CH_2CO-CH_3} \xrightarrow[-H_2O]{\Delta} \underset{\text{4-Methylpent-3-en-2-one}}{CH_3-\overset{CH_3}{\overset{|}{C}}=CH-CO-CH_3}$$

(ii) Cross aldol condensation: When two different aldehydes and/or ketones undergo aldol condensation, it is called cross aldol condensation.

$$CH_3CHO + CH_3CH_2CHO \xrightarrow[2.\ \Delta,\ -H_2O]{1.\ \text{dil. NaOH}}$$

$CH_3-CH=CH-CHO$ + $CH_3CH_2-CH=\underset{CH_3}{\underset{|}{C}}-CHO$

Simple or self aldol products

$CH_3-CH=\underset{CH_3}{\underset{|}{C}}-CHO$ + $CH_3-CH_2-CH=CHCHO$

Cross aldol products

(iii) Cannizzaro Reaction: Aldehydes undergo self oxidation and reduction on heating with conc. alkali. The aldehydes which do not have α-hydrogen undergo this reaction.

$$\underset{\text{Formaldehyde}}{H_2C=O + H_2C=O} + \text{conc. KOH} \xrightarrow{\Delta} \underset{\text{Methyl alcohol}}{H-\overset{H}{\overset{|}{\underset{H}{\underset{|}{C}}}}-OH} + \underset{\text{Potassium formate}}{H-C(=O)-OK}$$

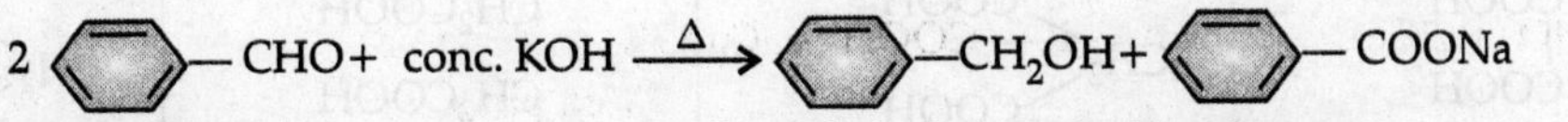

Benzaldehyde Benzyl alcohol Sodium benzoate

(iv) Electrophilic substitution reaction:

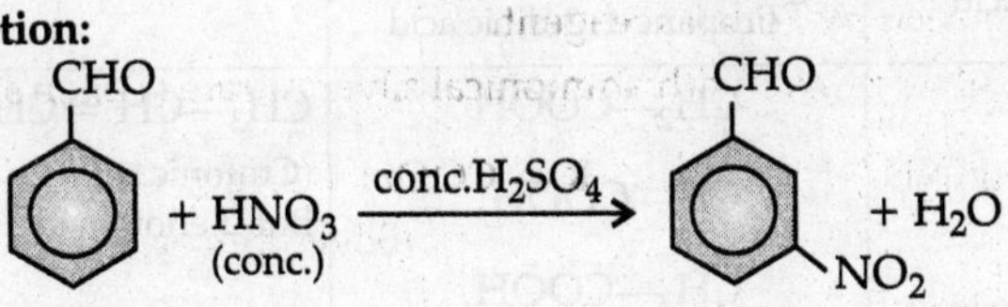

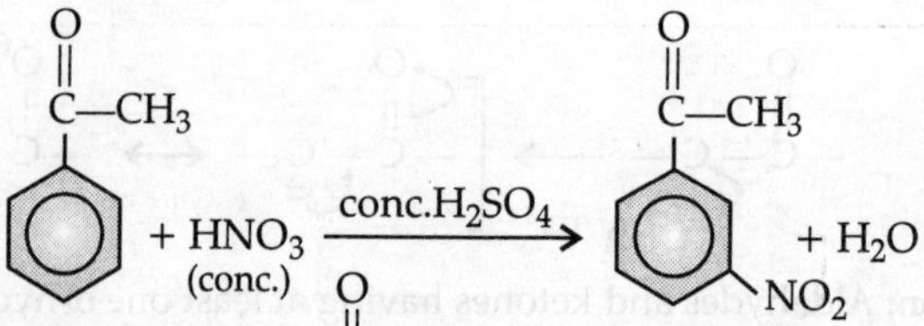

- Carboxylic acids are those compounds which have —C(=O)—OH group. The carboxyl group is made up of carboxyl, >C=O and hydroxyl, –OH group, hence, its name is carboxyl group.

Structure of Carboxyl Group

- The bonds to the carboxyl carbon lie in one plane separated by about 120°. The carboxylic carbon is less electrophilic than carbonyl carbon due to possible resonance structures.

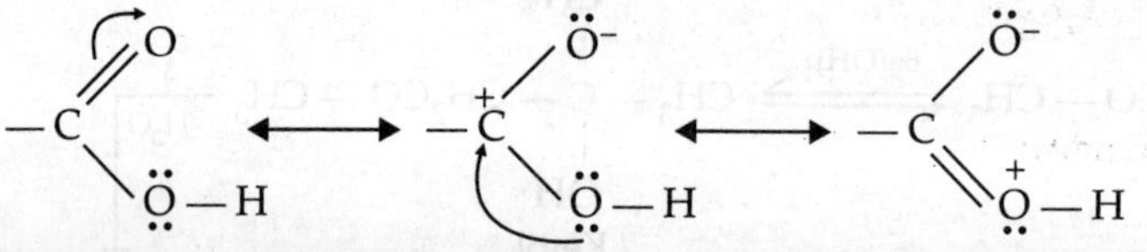

Nomenclature of Carboxylic Acids

- Derived by replacing terminal 'e' of the alkane with 'oic acid'.

Table 3

Carboxylic acids	**General formula:** R—C(=O)—OH, where R = C_nH_{2n+1}		
Structural formula	**Condensed formula**	**Common name**	**IUPAC name**
R—C(=O)—OH	HCOOH	Formic acid	Methanoic acid
CH_3—C(=O)—OH	CH_3COOH	Acetic acid	Ethanoic acid
CH_3CH_2—C(=O)—OH	CH_3CH_2COOH	Propionic acid	Propanoic acid
$CH_3CH_2CH_2$—C(=O)—OH	$CH_3CH_2CH_2COOH$	Butyric acid	Butanoic acid
CH_3—CH(CH_3)—C(=O)—OH	$(CH_3)_2CHCOOH$	Isobutyric acid	2-Methylpropanoic acid

Dicarboxylic Acids

COOH—COOH (Oxalic acid) Ethane-1, 2-dioic acid	CH_2(COOH)(COOH) (Malonic acid) Propane-1, 3-dioic acid	CH_2COOH—CH_2COOH Butane-1, 4-dioic acid	CH_2(CH_2COOH)(CH_2COOH) (Glutaric acid) Pentane-1, 5-dioic acid
CH_2CH_2COOH—CH_2CH_2COOH (Adipic acid) Hexane-1, 6-dioic acid	CH_2—COOH CH—COOH CH_2—COOH Propane-1, 2- 3-tricarboxylic acid	CH_3—CH = CH—COOH (Crotonic acid) But-2-enoic acid	CH_3—CH(OH)—COOH (Lactic acid) 2-Hydroxypropanoic acid

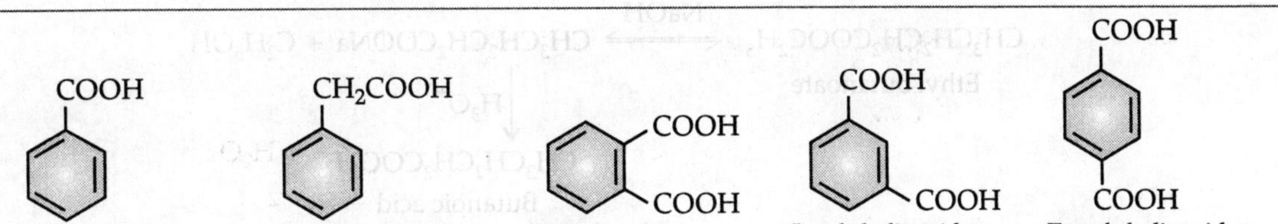

Benzoic acid or Benzene carboxylic acid | Phenylacetic acid or 2-Phenylethanoic acid | Phthalic acid or Benzene-1, 2-dicarboxylic acid | Isophthalic acid or Benzene-1, 3-dicarboxylic acid | Terephthalic acid or Benzene-1, 4-dicarboxylic acid

Methods of preparation of Carboxylic acids:

(i) By oxidation of primary alcohols and aldehydes:

$$\underset{1^\circ \text{ Alcohol}}{R-CH_2-OH} \xrightarrow[\text{(ii) } H_3O^+]{\text{(i) Alk.}KMnO_4} \underset{\text{Carboxylic acid}}{R-COOH}$$

$$\underset{\text{Aldehyde}}{R-CHO} + [O] \xrightarrow{K_2Cr_2O_7/H_2SO_4} \underset{\text{Carboxylic acid}}{R-COOH}$$

(ii) From nitriles and amides:

$$R-C\equiv N \xrightarrow[H_2O]{H_3O^+} \underset{\text{acid amide}}{R-\overset{O}{\overset{\|}{C}}-NH_2} \xrightarrow[H_2O]{H_3O^+} \underset{\text{Carboxylic acid}}{R-\overset{O}{\overset{\|}{C}}-OH}$$

(iii) From Grignard reagent:

$$\overset{\delta^-}{R}-\overset{\delta^+}{Mg}-X + \underset{\text{(dry ice)}}{\overset{O}{\overset{\|}{C}}=O} \xrightarrow[\text{Ether}]{\text{Dry}} R-\overset{O}{\overset{\|}{C}}-OMgX \xrightarrow{H_3O^+} \underset{\text{Carboxylic acid}}{R-\overset{O}{\overset{\|}{C}}-OH}$$

(iv) From hydrolysis of acyl halide and acid anhydrides:

$$\underset{\text{Acyl chloride}}{R-\overset{O}{\overset{\|}{C}}-Cl} \xrightarrow{H_2O} R-COOH + Cl^-$$

$$\underset{\text{Acyl chloride}}{R-\overset{O}{\overset{\|}{C}}-Cl} \xrightarrow{OH^-/H_2O} R-\overset{O}{\overset{\|}{C}}-O^- \xrightarrow{H_3O^+} \underset{\text{Carboxylic acid}}{R-\overset{O}{\overset{\|}{C}}-OH}$$

$$\underset{\text{Benzoic anhydride}}{(C_6H_5CO)_2O} \xrightarrow{H_2O} \underset{\text{Benzoic acid}}{2C_6H_5-COOH}$$

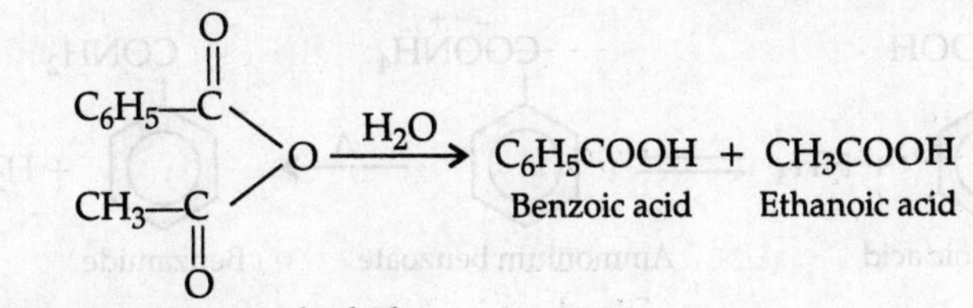

Benzoic ethanoic anhydride

- **From esters:** Acidic hydrolysis of esters gives directly carboxylic acids while basic hydrolysis gives carboxylates, which on acidification give corresponding carboxylic acids.

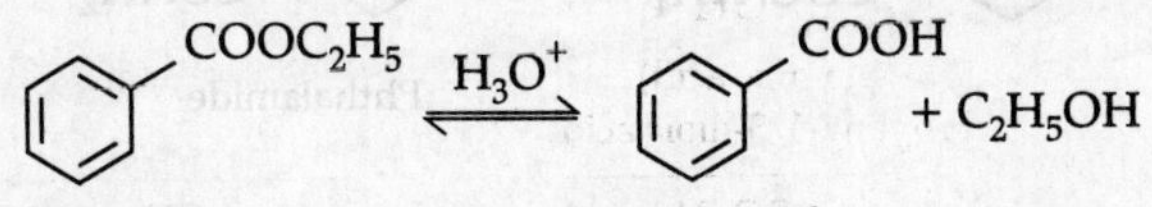

Ethyl benzoate | Benzoic acid

$$CH_3CH_2CH_2COOC_2H_5 \xrightleftharpoons{NaOH} CH_3CH_2CH_2COONa + C_2H_5OH$$

Ethyl butanoate

$$\downarrow H_3O^+$$

$$CH_3CH_2CH_2COOH$$

Butanoic acid

- **Physical properties of Carboxylic acids:**
  (i) Lower members are colourless liquid with pungent smell, while higher members are odourless waxy solid. Benzoic acid is a crystalline solid.
  (ii) First four members are water miscible due to tendency to form hydrogen bond. Higher acids are insoluble.
  (iii) Carboxylic acids have higher boiling point due to their ability to form intermolecular hydrogen bonding.
  (iv) Carboxylic acid with even number of carbon atoms have higher melting points than those with odd number of carbon atoms above or below it.
- **Chemical Properties:** Chemical properties of carboxylic acids are classified as follows:
  (i) Reaction involving cleavage of O — H bond: Reactions with metals and alkalies.

$$2R-COOH + 2Na \rightarrow 2R-COONa + H_2$$

Sodium carboxylate

$$R-COOH + NaOH \rightarrow R-COONa + H_2O$$

$$R-COOH + NaHCO_3 \rightarrow R-COONa + H_2O + CO_2\uparrow$$

(ii) Reactions involving cleavage of C — OH Bond:

(a) Formation of anhydride:

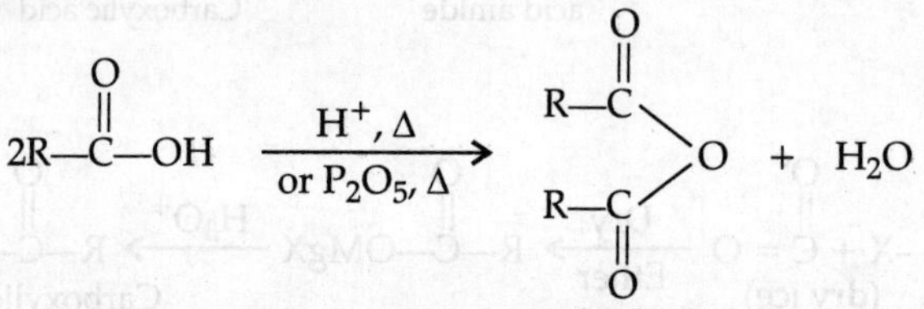

Acid anhydride

(b) Esterification:

$$R-COOH + R'-OH \xrightleftharpoons{H^+} R-COOR' + H_2O$$

(c) Reaction with PCl_5, PCl_3 and $SOCl_2$

$$R-COOH + PCl_5 \rightarrow RCOCl + POCl_3 + HCl$$

acyl chloride

$$R-COOH + SOCl_2 \rightarrow RCOCl + SO_2\uparrow + HCl\uparrow$$

(d) Reaction with ammonia:

$$R-COOH + NH_3 \rightleftharpoons R-COO^- - \overset{+}{N}H_4 \xrightarrow[-H_2O]{\Delta} R-CONH_2$$

Carboxylic acid — Amide

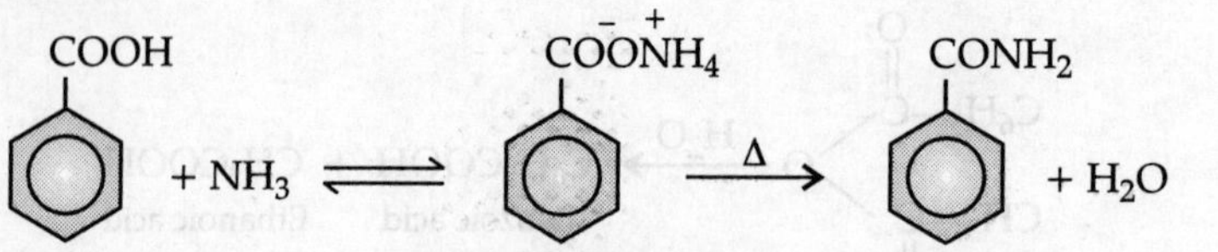

Benzoic acid — Ammonium benzoate — Benzamide

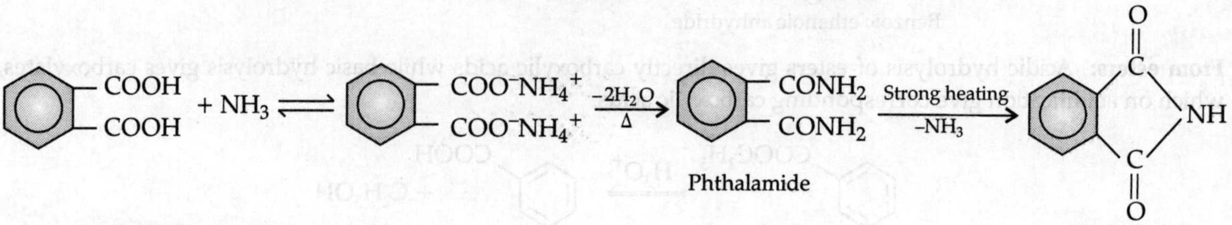

Phthalamide — Phthalimide

(iii) Reduction involving –COOH group:

(a) Reduction:

$$R-COOH \xrightarrow[(ii)\ H_3O^+]{(i)\ LiAlH_4\ /\ Ether\ or\ B_2H_6} R-CH_2-OH$$

1° – Alcohol

(b) Decarboxylation:

$$\underset{\text{Sodium carboxylate}}{R-COONa} \xrightarrow[\Delta]{\text{NaOH and CaO}} R-H + Na_2CO_3$$

(c) Halogenation:

$$R-CH_2-COOH \xrightarrow[\text{(ii) } H_2O]{\text{(i) } X_2/\text{Red P}} R-\underset{}{\overset{X}{\overset{|}{C}}}H-COOH$$

(X = Cl, Br)

This reaction is known as Hell-Volhard-Zelinsky reaction.

(iv) Ring Substitution Reaction:

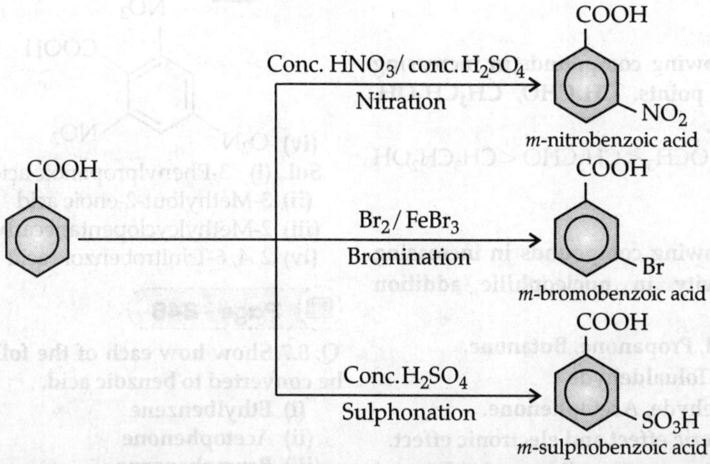

NCERT CORNER

Intext Questions

Page - 231

Q. 8.1. Write the structures of the following compounds.
(i)α-Methoxypropionaldehyde
(ii)3-Hydroxybutanal
(iii)2-Hydroxycyclopentanecarbaldehyde
(iv)4-Oxopentanal
(v)Di-sec.butyl ketone
(vi)4-Fluoroacetophenone

Ans. (i) $H_3C-\overset{CH_3O}{\overset{|}{C}}H-\overset{O}{\overset{||}{C}}-H$

(ii) $H_3C-\overset{OH}{\overset{|}{C}}H-CH_2-\overset{O}{\overset{||}{C}}-H$

(iii)

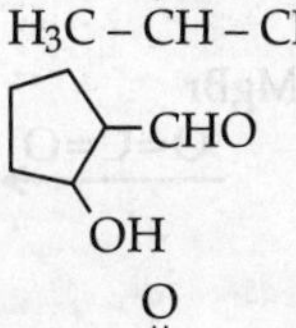

(iv) $CH_3-\overset{O}{\overset{||}{C}}-CH_2-CH_2-CHO$

(v) $CH_3CH_2\overset{H_3C}{\overset{|}{C}}H-\overset{O}{\overset{||}{C}}-\overset{CH_3}{\overset{|}{C}}H-CH_2CH_3$

(vi)

Page - 234

Q. 2.2. Write the structures of the products of the following reactions:

(i)

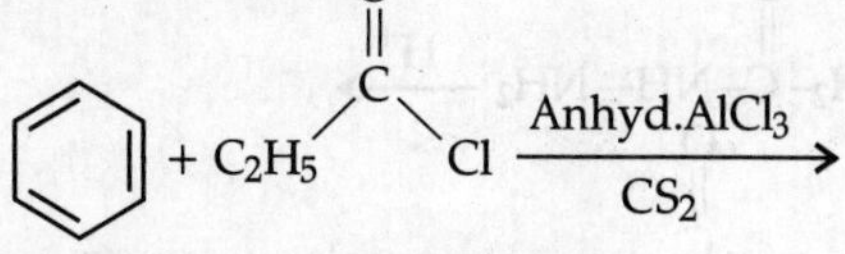

(ii) $(C_6H_5CH_2)_2Cd + 2CH_3COCl \rightarrow$

(iii) $H_3C-C\equiv C-H \xrightarrow{Hg^{2+},\ H_2SO_4}$

(iv)

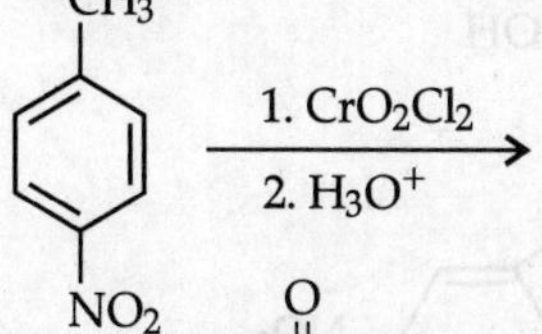

Sol. (i)

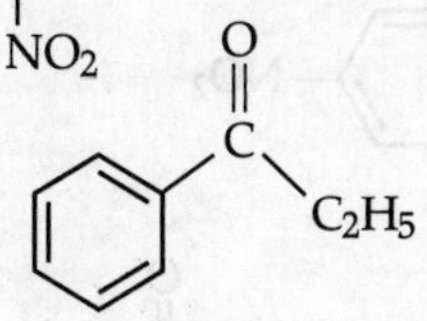

(ii)

(iii) 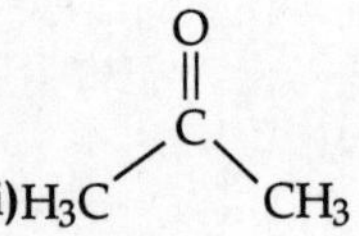

(iv) 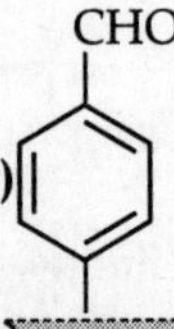

Page - 236

Q. 8.3. Arrange the following compounds in increasing order of their boiling points. CH_3CHO, CH_3CH_2OH, CH_3OCH_3, $CH_3CH_2CH_3$.

Ans. $CH_3CH_2CH_3 < CH_3OCH_3 < CH_3CHO < CH_3CH_2OH$

Page - 243

Q. 8.4. Arrange the following compounds in increasing order of their reactivity in nucleophilic addition reactions.

(i) Ethanal, Propanal, Propanone, Butanone.

(ii) Benzaldehyde, p-Tolualdehyde, p – Nitrobenzaldehyde, Acetophenone.

Hint: Consider steric effect and electronic effect.

Ans. (i) Butanone < Propanone < Propanal < Ethanal

(ii) Acetophenone < p-Tolualdehyde, Benzaldehyde < p-Nitrobenzaldehyde

Q. 8.5. Predict the products of the following reactions:

(i) 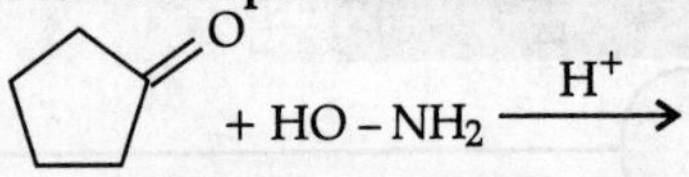

(ii) 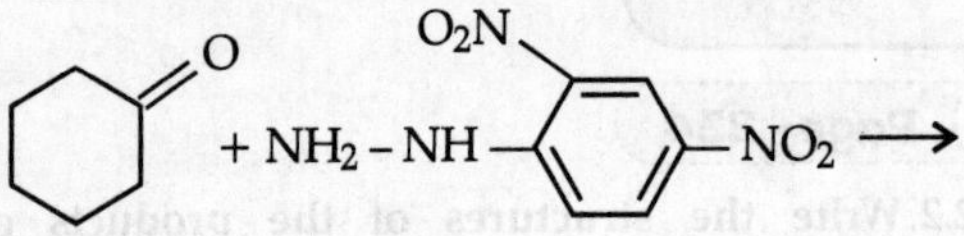

(iii) R – CH = CH – CHO +

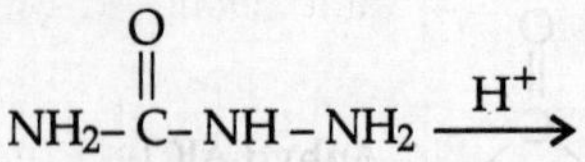

(iv) 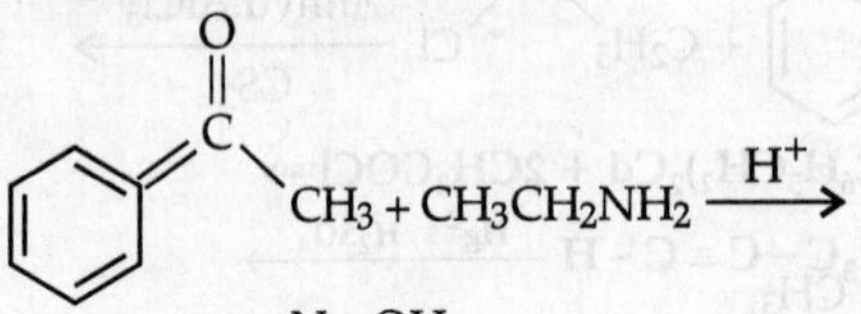

Sol. (i) 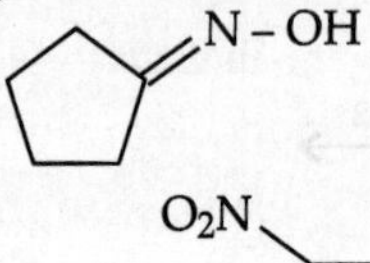

(ii) 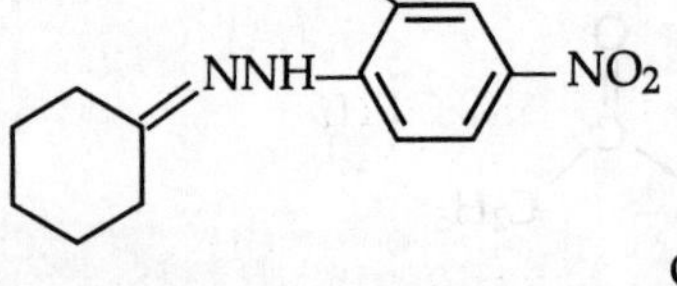

(iii) 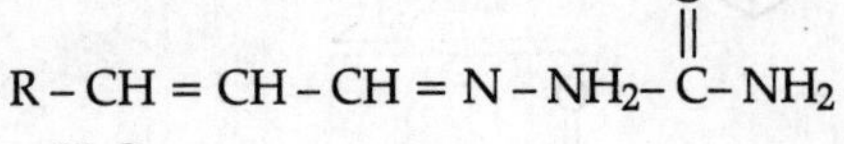

(iv) 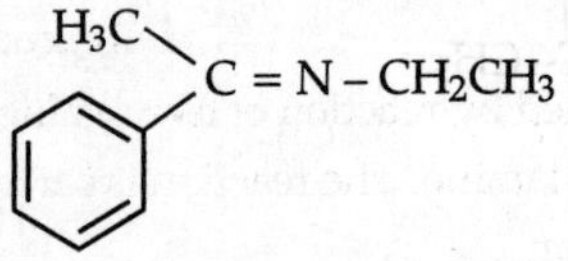

Page - 245

Q. 8.6. Give the IUPAC names of the following compounds:

(i) $PhCH_2CH_2COOH$

(ii) $(CH_3)_2C = CHCOOH$

(iii) 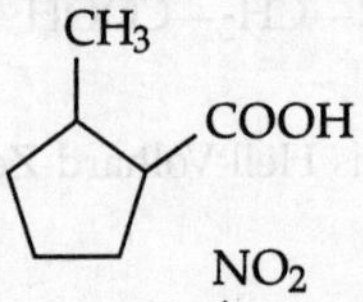

(iv) 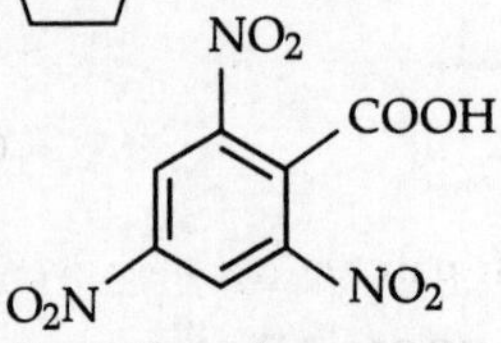

Sol. (i) 3-Phenylpropanoic acid

(ii) 3-Methylbut-2-enoic acid

(iii) 2-Methylcyclopentanecarboxylic acid

(iv) 2, 4, 6-Trinitrobenzoic acid

Page - 248

Q. 8.7. Show how each of the following compounds can be converted to benzoic acid.

(i) Ethylbenzene

(ii) Acetophenone

(iii) Bromobenzene

(iv) Phenylethene (Styrene)

Sol. (i) 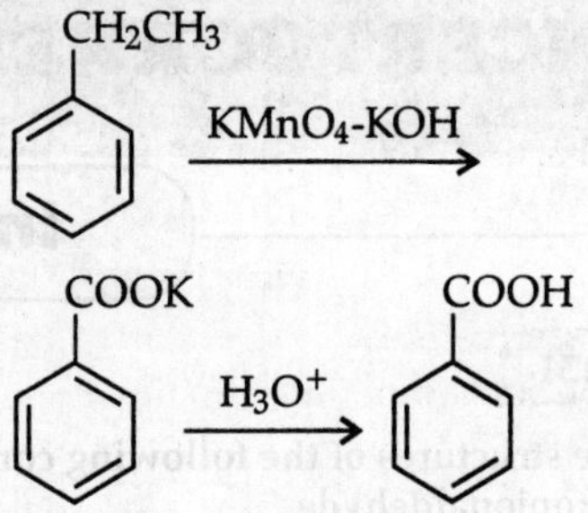

(ii) 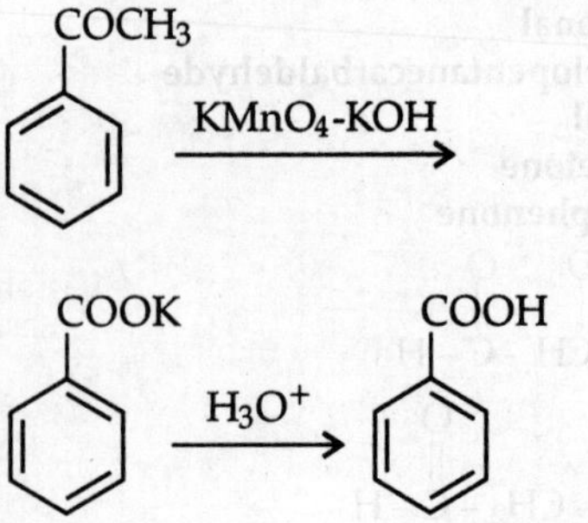

(iii) 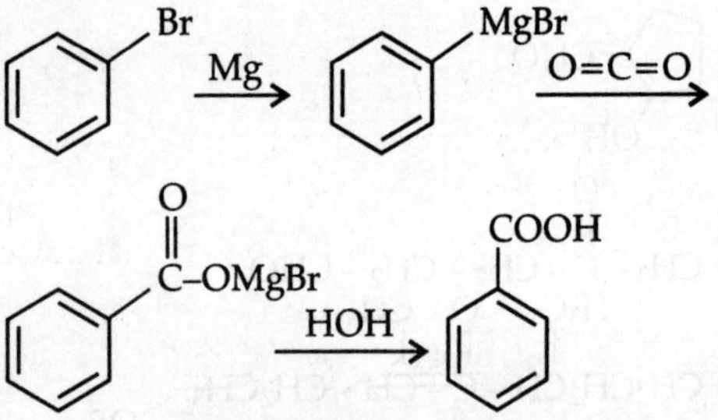

(iv) 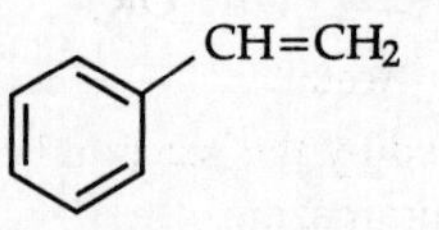

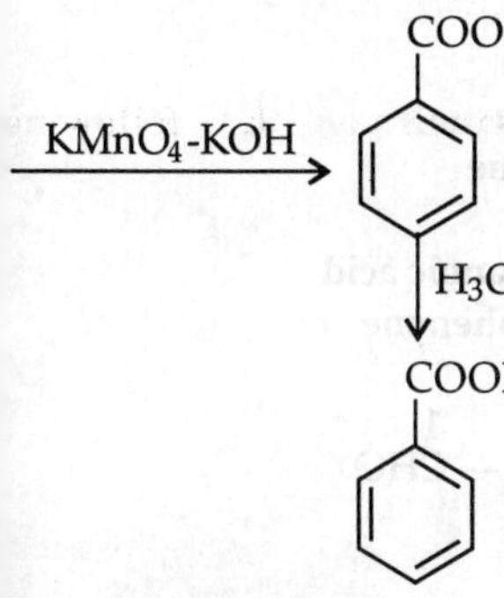

or 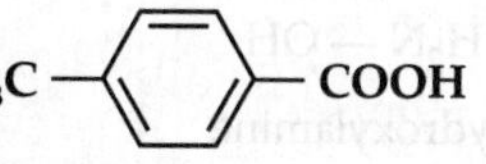

Page - 254

Q. 8.8. Which acid of each pair shown here would you expect to be stronger ?

(i) CH_3CO_2H or CH_2FCO_2H

(ii) CH_2FCO_2H or CH_2ClCO_2H

(iii) $CH_2FCH_2CH_2CO_2H$ or $CH_3CHFCH_2CO_2H$

(iv) 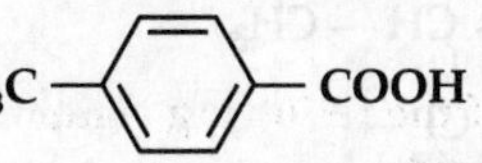

Ans. (i) $H_2CFCOOH$ will be stronger of the two. The presence of electronegative F atom at the α-C causes electron withdrawal from the COOH and facilitates the release of H^+.

(ii) CH_2FCO_2H is a stronger acid for the same reason as stated above. F is more electronegative than Cl, so it withdraws electrons from the carboxyl group to a greater extent.

(iii) CH_3CHFCH_2COOH is stronger. Although both the given acids have F atom in them, it is the proximity of F in CH_3CHFCH_2COOH to the COOH group which makes it more acidic.

(iv) 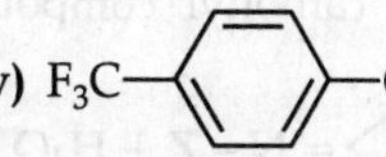

is more acidic due to the presence of electron withdrawing CF_3 group in it.

Exercise Questions

Q. 1. What is meant by the following terms? Give an example of the reaction in each case.

[NCERT Q. 8.1, Page 255]

(i) Cyanohydrin	**(ii) Acetal**
(iii) Semicarbazone	**(iv) Aldol**
(v) Hemiacetal	**(vi) Oxime**
(vii) Ketal	**(viii) Imine**
(ix) 2,4-DNP derivative	**(x) Schiff's base**

Ans. (i) Carbonyl compounds in the presence of an alkali, react with HCN to form an addition product called cyanohydrin.

$$HCN + \bar{O}H \rightleftharpoons H_2O + \bar{C}N$$

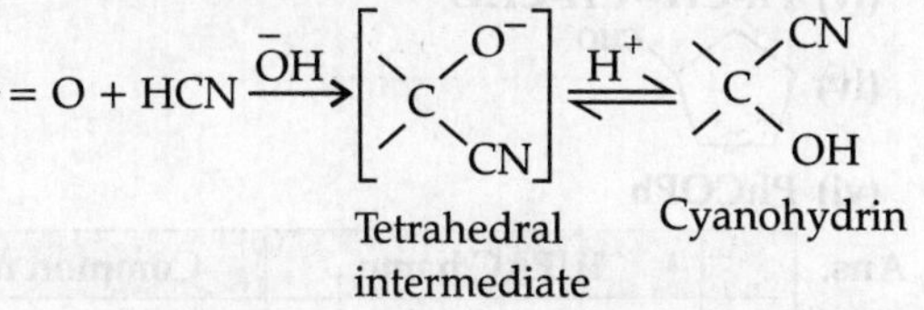

(ii) Acetals are gem-dialkoxy compounds formed when aldehydes react with monohydric alcohols in the presence of dry HCl gas.

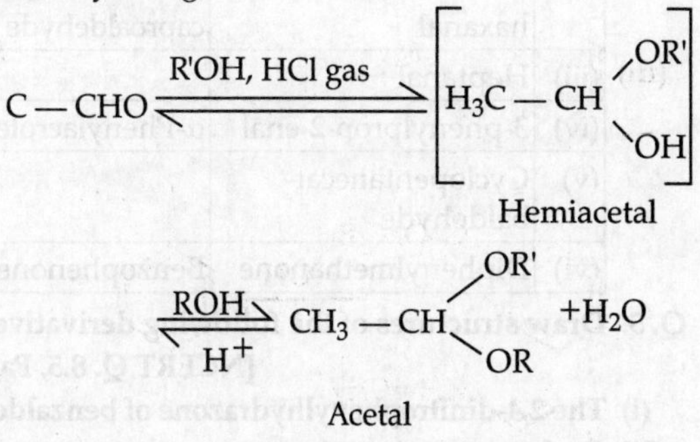

(iii) Semicarbazone is formed by the reaction between carbonyl compounds and semicarbazide.

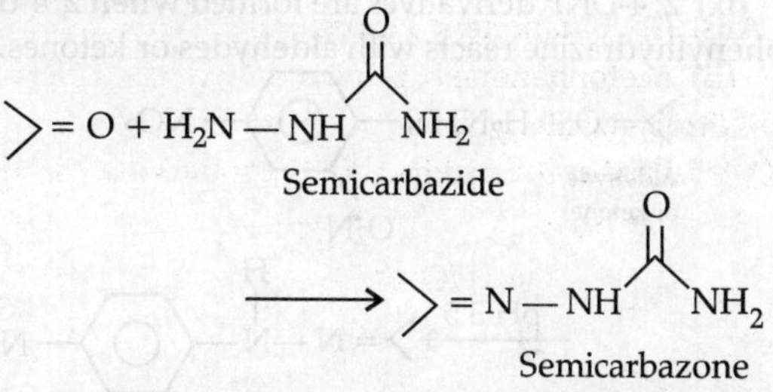

(iv) β-Hydroxy aldehydes are called aldol. Aldehydes and ketones containing at least one α-H atom undergo a reaction in the presence of dilute alkali to form aldol compounds e.g.,

$$2CH_3CHO \xrightleftharpoons{\text{dil } \bar{O}H} CH_3\underset{\substack{|\\ OH}}{CH}-CH_2CHO$$

3–hydroxybutanal (aldol)

$$\xrightarrow[-H_2O]{\Delta} CH_3CH=CHCHO$$

But–2–enal

(v) Hemiacetals are gem-alkoxyalcohols which are produced from the addition of one molecule of monohydric alcohol to an aldehyde in the presence of HCl gas.

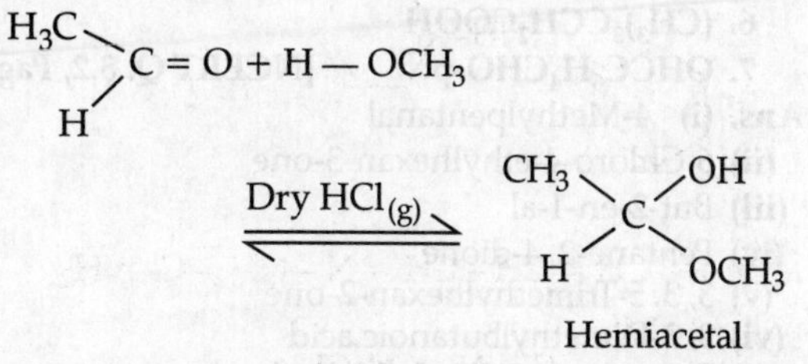

(vi) Oximes are formed by reaction between aldehydes or ketones and hydroxylamine. The reaction is carried out in mildly acidic condition.

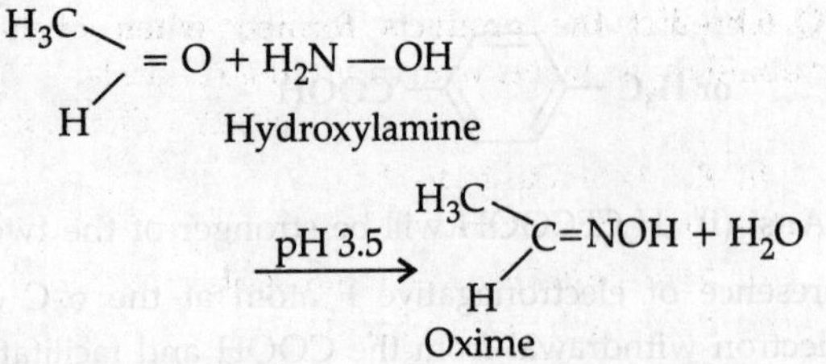

(vii) Ketals are cyclic products formed by the reaction of ketones with ethylene glycol in the presence of dry HCl gas.

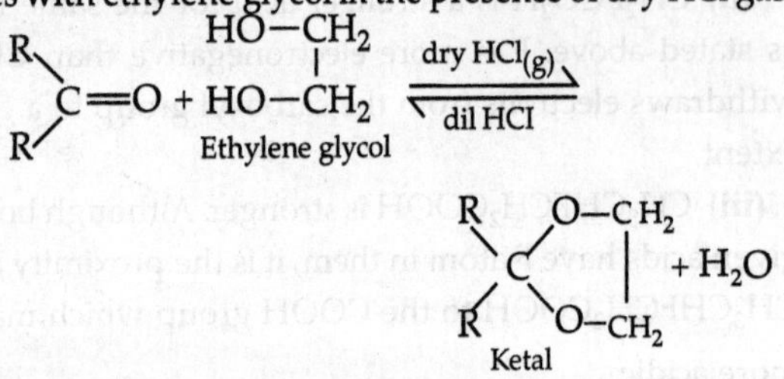

(viii) Imines are formed when carbonyl compounds react with ammonia derivative.

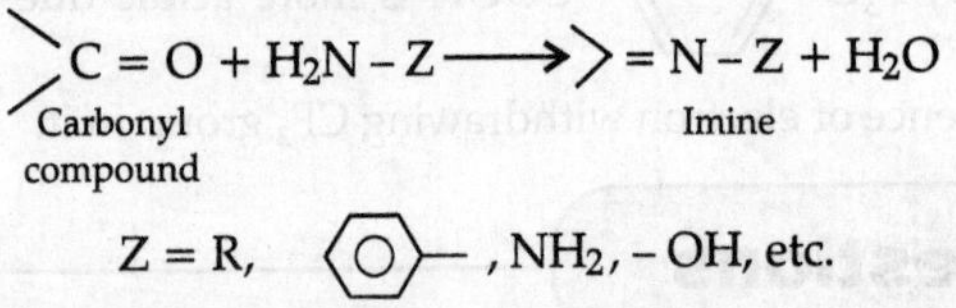

(ix) 2, 4-DNP derivatives are formed when 2, 4-dinitrophenylhydrazine reacts with aldehydes or ketones.

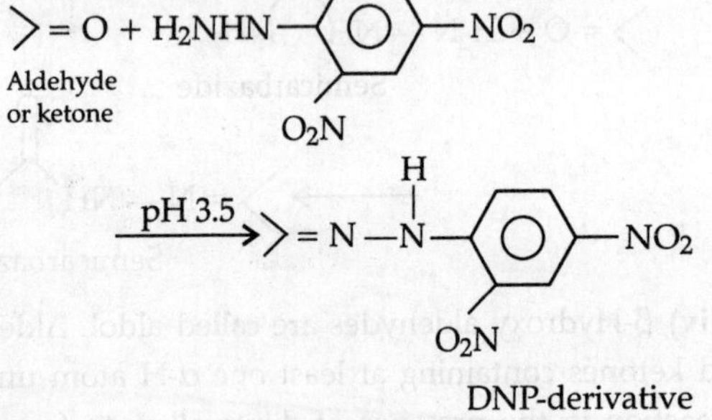

(x) Reaction between aldehydes or ketones with 1° aliphatic or aromatic amines yields a Schiff's base.

$$R-CHO + H_2N-R' \xrightarrow{\text{very dil } H^+} RCH=N-R' + H_2O$$

(Schiff's base)

Q. 2 Name the following compounds according to IUPAC system of nomenclature:

1. $CH_3CH(CH_3)CH_2CH_2CHO$
2. $CH_3CH_2COCH(C_2H_5)CH_2CH_2Cl$
3. $CH_3CH{=}CHCHO$
4. $CH_3COCH_2COCH_3$
5. $CH_3CH(CH_3)CH_2C(CH_3)_2COCH_3$
6. $(CH_3)_3CCH_2COOH$
7. $OHCC_6H_4CHO$-p **[NCERT Q. 8.2, Page 255]**

Ans. (i) 4-Methylpentanal
(ii) 6-Chloro-4-ethylhexan-3-one
(iii) But-2-en-1-al
(iv) Pentane-2, 4-dione
(v) 3, 3, 5-Trimethylhexan-2-one
(vi) 3, 3-Dimethylbutanoic acid
(vii) Benzene-1, 4-dicarbaldehyde

Q. 3. Draw the structures of the following compounds. [NCERT Q. 8.3, Page 255]

(i) 3-Methylbutanal
(ii) p-Nitropropiophenone
(iii) p-Methylbenzaldehyde
(iv) 4-Methylpent-3-en-2-one
(v) 4-Chloropentan-2-one
(vi) 3-Bromo-4-phenylpentanoic acid
(vii) p, p′-Dihydroxybenzophenone
(viii) Hex-2-en-4-ynoic acid

Sol. (i) 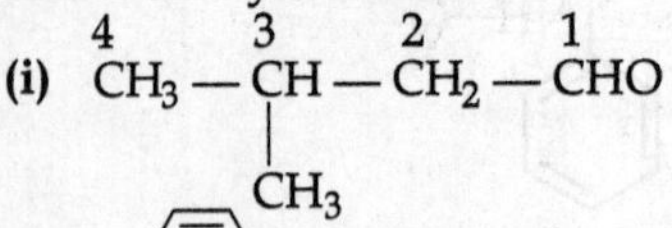

(ii) 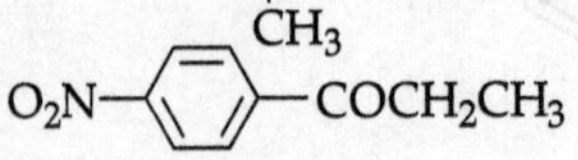

(iii) 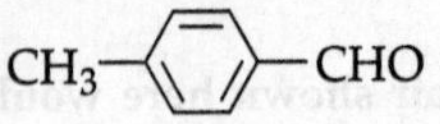

(iv) 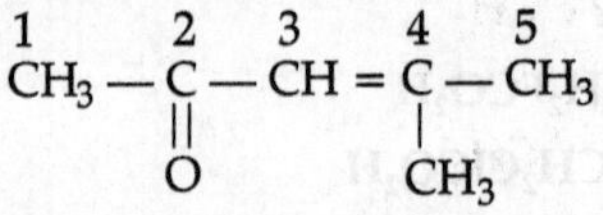

(v) 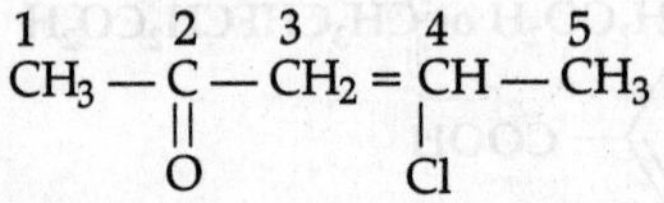

(vi) 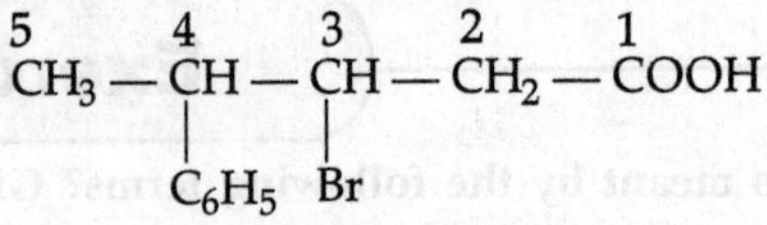

(vii) 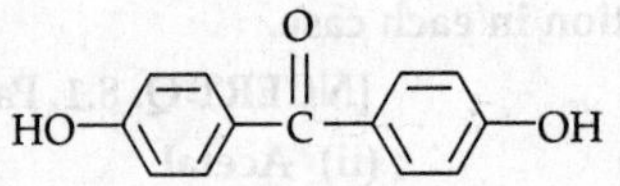

(viii) 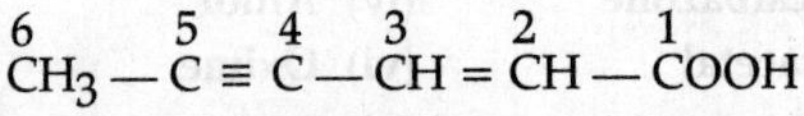

Q. 4. Write the IUPAC names of the following ketones and aldehydes. Wherever possible, give also common names. [NCERT Q. 8.4, Page 255]

(i) $CH_3CO(CH_2)_4CH_3$
(ii) $CH_3CH_2CHBrCH_2CH(CH_3)CHO$
(iii) $CH_3(CH_2)_5CHO$
(iv) Ph-CH=CH-CHO
(iv) 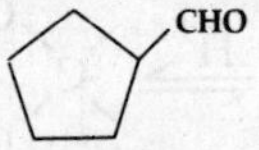
(vi) PhCOPh

Ans.

	IUPAC name	Common name
(i)	Heptan-2-one	Methyl n-propyl ketone
(ii)	4-Bromo-2-methyl-haxanal	γ-Bromo-α-methyl-caproaldehyde
(iii)	Heptanal	
(iv)	3-phenylprop-2-enal	α-Phenylacrolein
(v)	Cyclopentanecar-baldehyde	
(vi)	Diphenylmethanone	Benzophenone

Q.5. Draw structures of the following derivatives: [NCERT Q. 8.5, Page 255]

(i) The 2,4-dinitrophenylhydrazone of benzaldehyde
(ii) Cyclopropanone oxime

(iii) Acetaldehydedimethylacetal
(iv) The semicarbazone of cyclobutanone
(v) The ethylene ketal of hexan-3-one
(vi) The methyl hemiacetal of formaldehyde

Ans.

(i) 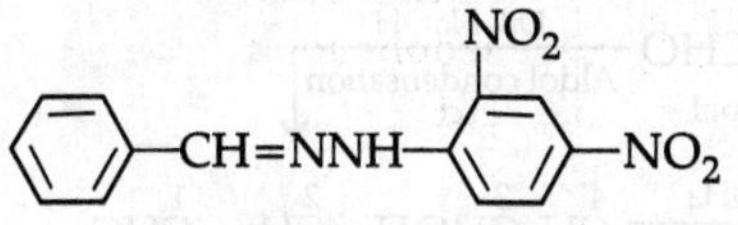

(ii) 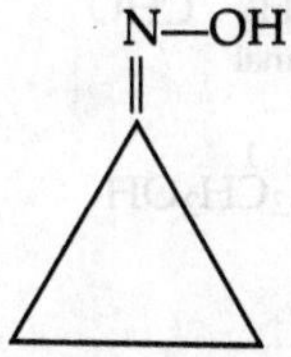

(iii) 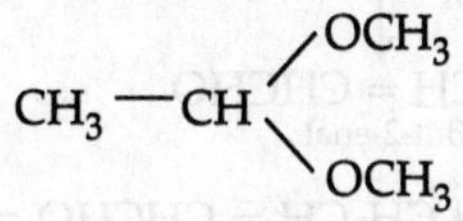

(iv) 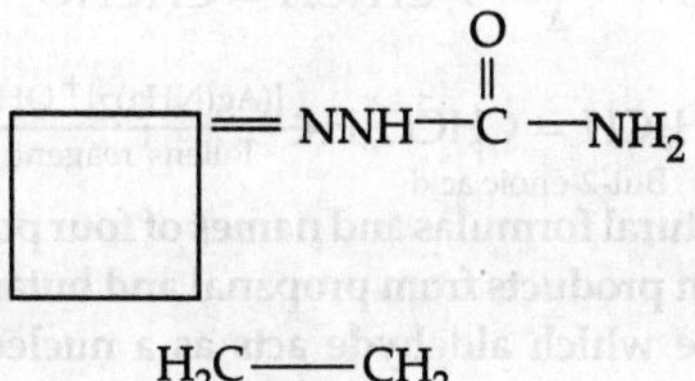

(v) 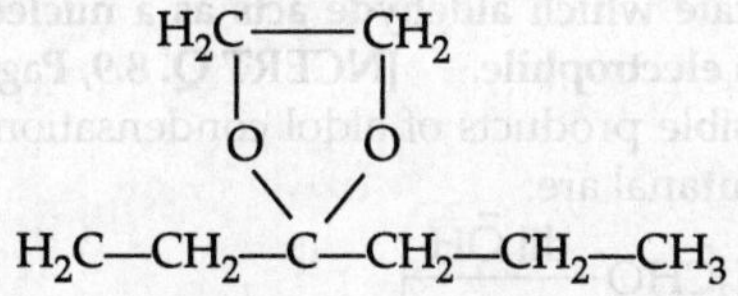

(vi) 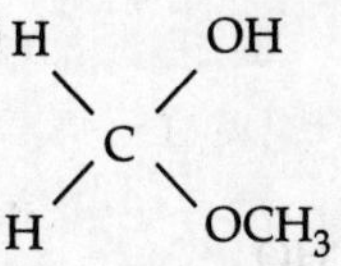

Q. 6.Predict the products formed when cyclohexane carbaldehyde reacts with following reagents: **[NCERT Q. 8.6, Page 256]**

(i) PhMgBr and then H_3O^+
(ii) Tollens' reagent
(iii) Semicarbazide and weak acid
(iv) Excess ethanol and acid
(v) Zinc amalgam and dilute hydrochloric acid

Ans.

(i) 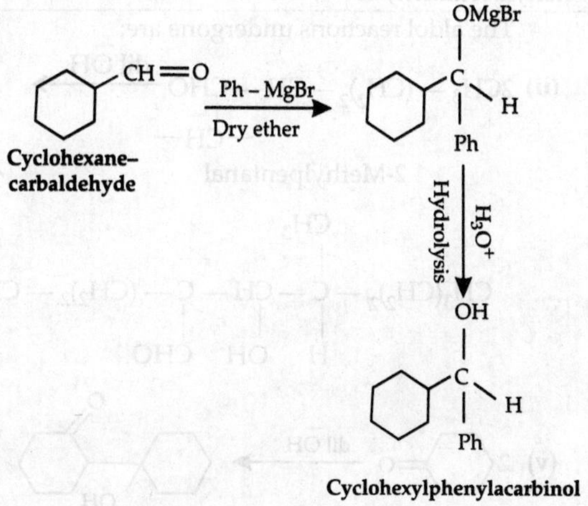

(ii) 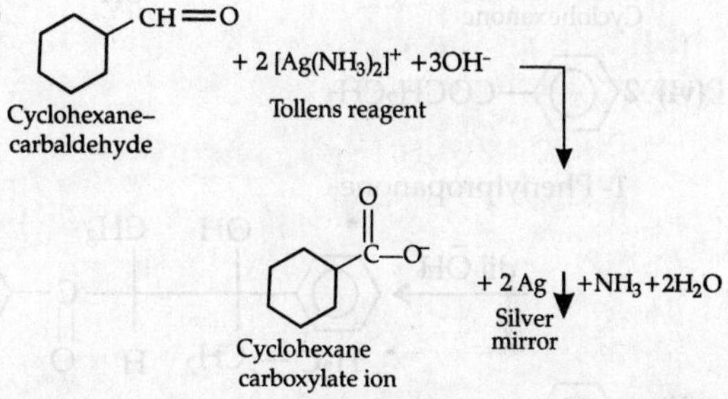

(iii) 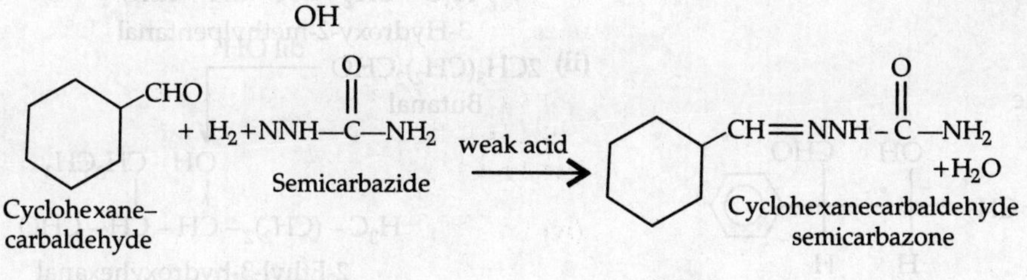

(iv) 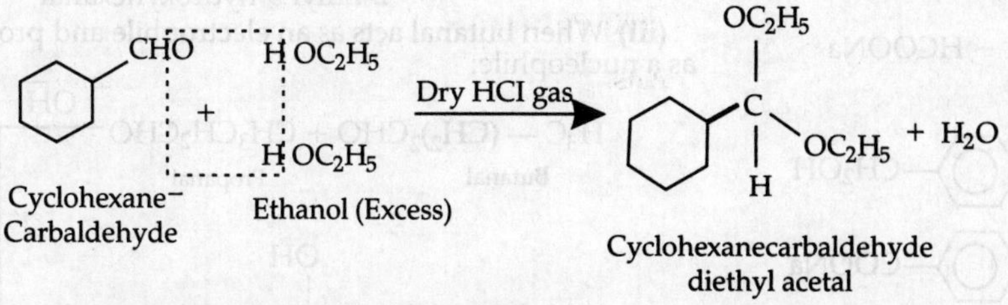

(v) 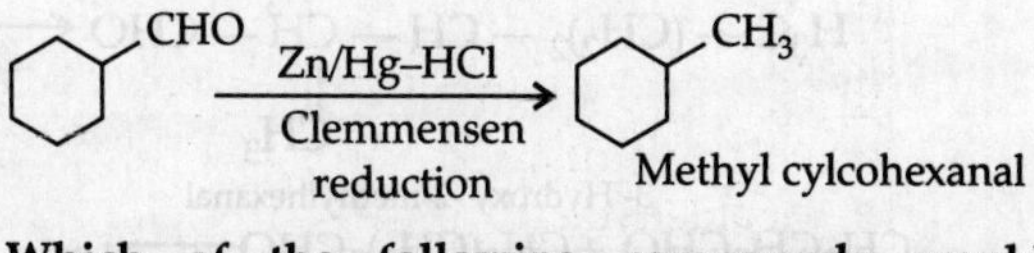

Q. 7. Which of the following compounds would undergo aldol condensation, which the Cannizzaro reaction and which neither? Write the structures of the expected products of aldol condensation and Cannizzaro reaction. **[NCERT Q. 8.7, Page 256]**
(i) Methanal, (ii) 2-Methylpentanal, (iii) Benzaldehyde, (iv) Benzophenone, (v) Cyclohexanone, (vi) 1-Phenylpropanone, (vii) Phenylacetaldehyde, (viii) Butan-1-ol, (ix) 2, 2-Dimethylbutanal

Sol. Aldol condensation is shown by those aldehydes or ketones which have at least one α-H atom while Cannizzaro reaction is undergone by aldehydes that have no α-H atom.

Therefore, the given compounds can be classified as:

Aldol Condensation	Cannizzaro Condensation	Neither
2-Methylpentanal	Methanal	Butan-1-ol
Cyclohexanone	Benzaldehyde	Benzophenone
1-Phenylpropanone	2, 2-Dimelthylbutanal	
Phenylacetaldehyde		

The aldol reactions undergone are:

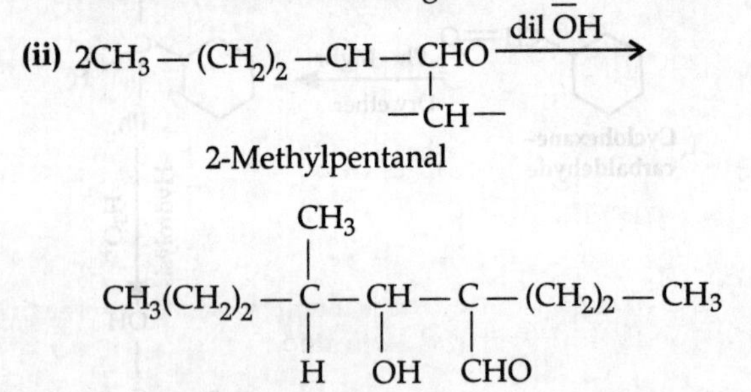

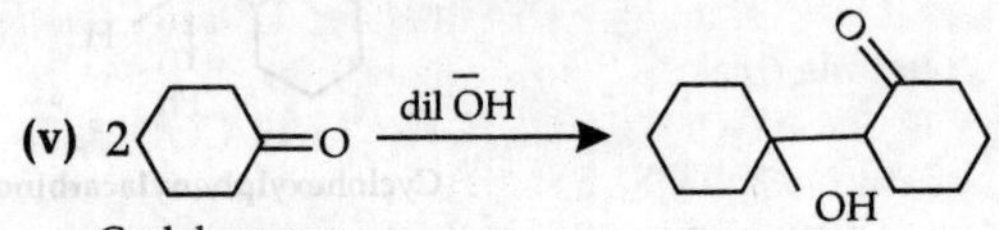

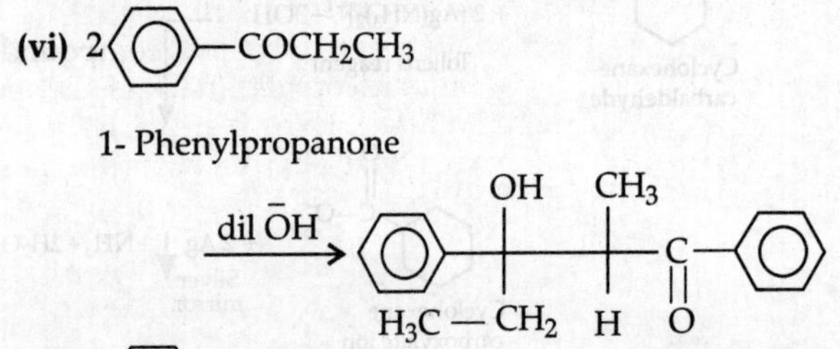

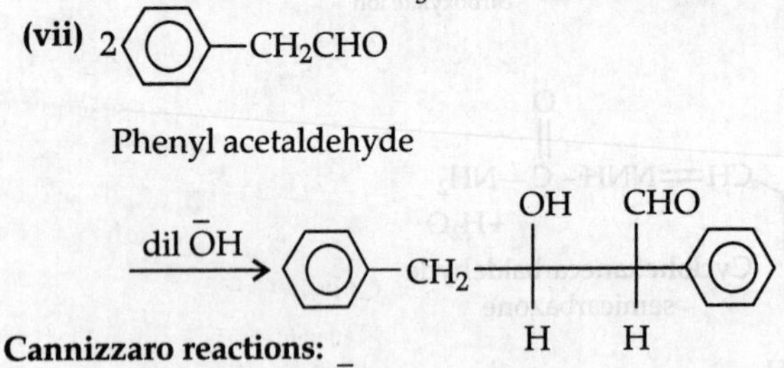

Cannizzaro reactions:

(i) $2HCHO \xrightarrow{\text{Conc. } \bar{O}H} H_3COH + HCOONa$

Methanal

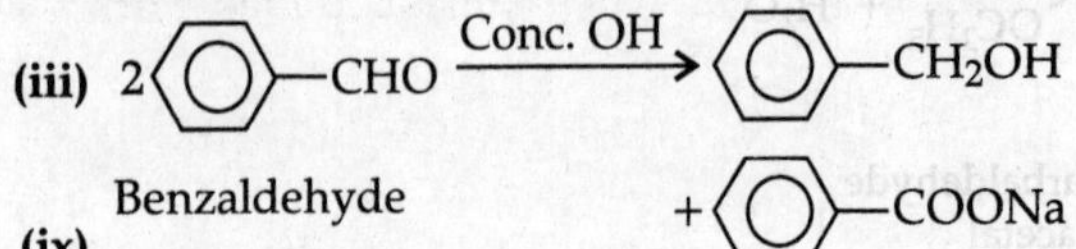

(ix)

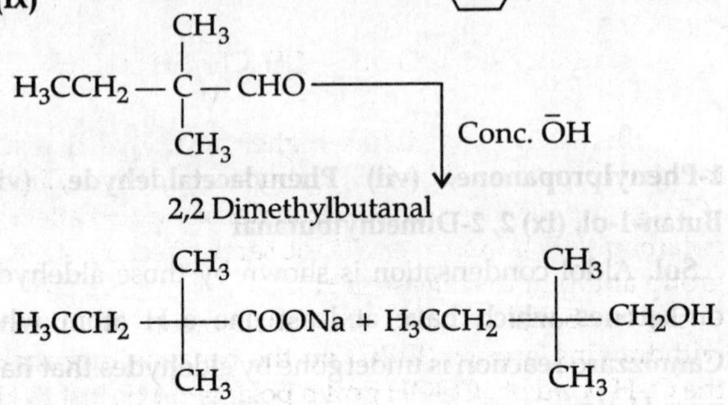

Q. 8. How will you convert ethanal into the following compounds? **[NCERT Q. 8.8, Page 256]**

(i) Butane-1, 3-diol
(ii) But-2-enal
(iii) But-2-enoic acid

Ans. (i)

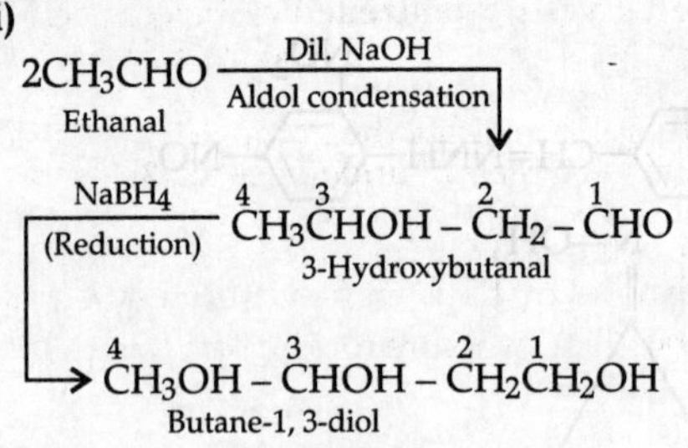

(ii)

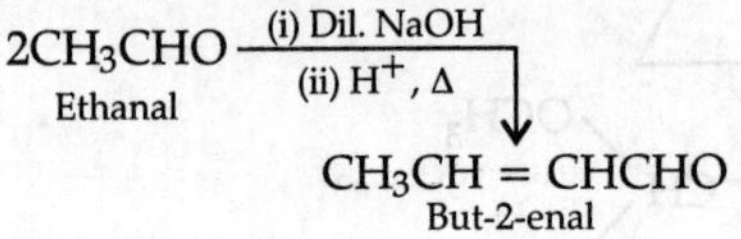

(iii)

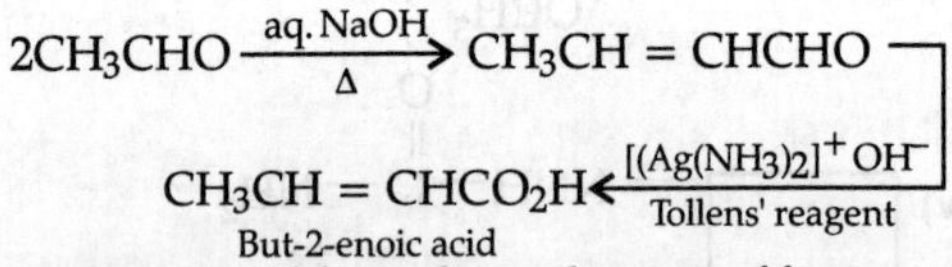

Q. 9. Write structural formulas and names of four possible aldol condensation products from propanal and butanal. In each case, indicate which aldehyde acts as a nucleophile and which as an electrophile. **[NCERT Q. 8.9, Page 256]**

Sol. The possible products of aldol condensation from propanal and butanal are:

(i)

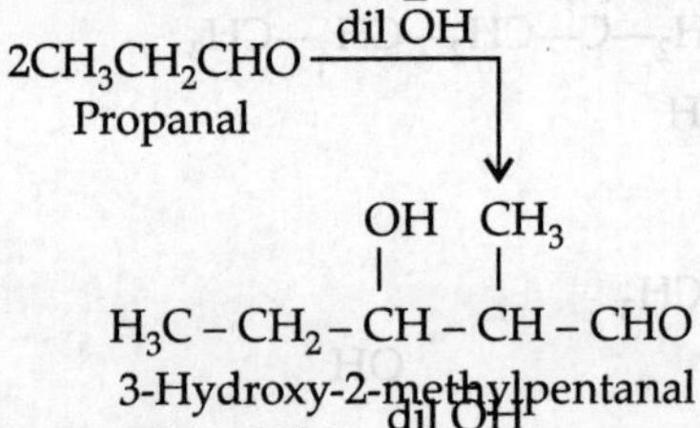

(ii)

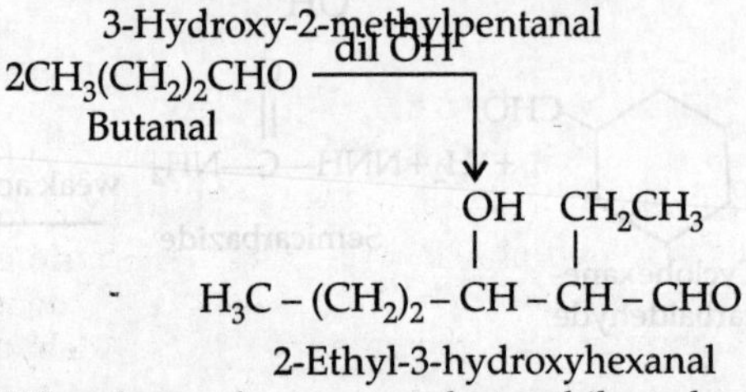

(iii) When butanal acts as an electrophile and propanal as a nucleophile:

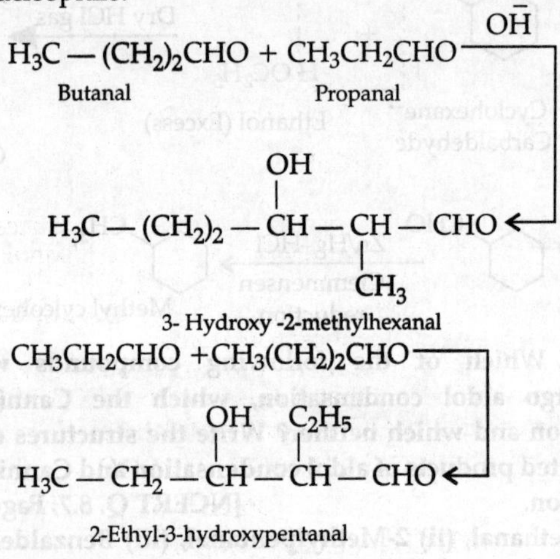

(iv) When propanal serves as an electrophile and butanal as nucleophile:

Q. 10. An organic compound with the molecular formula $C_9H_{10}O$ forms 2, 4-DNP derivative, reduces Tollens' reagent and undergoes Cannizzaro reaction. On vigorous oxidation, it gives 1, 2-benzenedicarboxylic acid. Identify the compound. [NCERT Q. 8.10, Page 256]

Ans. (i) It is given that the compound reduces Tollens' reagent. This proves that the compound is an aldehyde. Further, the fact that it undergoes Cannizzaro reaction shows that it lacks an α-H atom.

(ii) On oxidation it yields 1,2-benzenedicarboxylic acid. This shows that it is an o-substituted benzaldehyde. The only possible structure for the compound is:

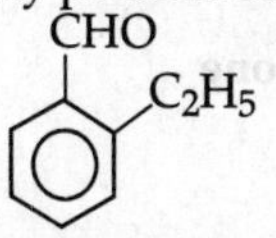

The reactions undergone are:

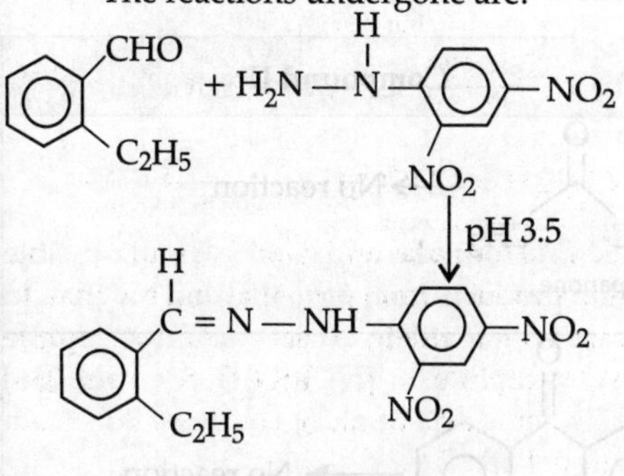

2,4-DNP derivative

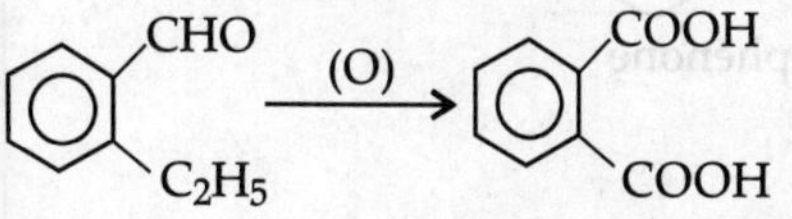

Benzene-1,2-dicarboxylic acid

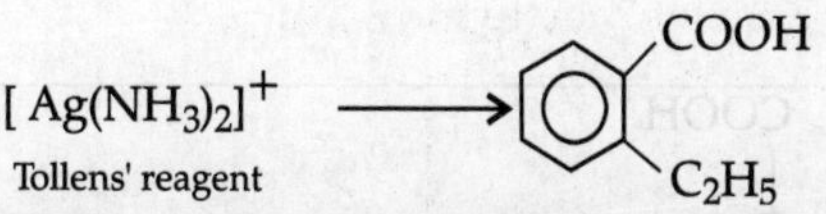

Q. 11. An organic compound (A) (molecular formula $C_8H_{16}O_2$) was hydrolysed with dilute sulphuric acid to give a carboxylic acid (B) and an alcohol (C). Oxidation of (C) with chromic acid produced (B). (C) on dehydration gives but-1-ene. Write equations for the reactions involved. [NCERT Q. 8.11, Page 256]

Ans. Given

$$\underset{(C_8H_{16}O_2)}{A} \xrightarrow[H_3O^+]{\text{dilute}} \underset{\text{Carboxylic acid}}{B} + \underset{\text{Alcohol}}{C} \xrightarrow{CrO_3/H^+} B$$

$$C \xrightarrow{-H_2O} \underset{\text{But-1-ene}}{CH_3-CH_2-HC=CH_2}$$

(i) Compound (A) upon hydrolysis produces one molecule each of a carboxylic acid and alcohol. This indicates that (A) is an ester.

(ii) (C) upon oxidation produces (B) proving that (C) and (B) have same no. of carbon atoms.

(iii) (C) on dehydration produces but-1-ene. This, coupled with the fact that it gives a carboxylic acid (B) on oxidation shows that (C) is a primary alchohol

∴ (C) is $CH_3-CH_2-CH_2-CH_2OH$

Butan-1-ol

(B) is $CH_3-(CH_2)_2-COOH$

Butanoic acid

and (A) is $H_3C(CH_2)_2-\overset{O}{\overset{\|}{C}}-O-(CH_2)_3CH_3$

Butyl butanaote

The reactions involved may be summarised as:

$$\underset{(A)}{CH_3(CH_2)_2-\overset{O}{\overset{\|}{C}}-O-(CH_2)_3CH_3} \xrightarrow{\text{dil } H^+} \underset{(C)}{CH_3(CH_2)_2CH_2OH} + \underset{(B)}{CH_3(CH_2)_2COOH}$$

$$(C) \xrightarrow{CrO_3/H^+} (B)$$

$$(C) \xrightarrow{H^+/\Delta} \underset{\text{But-1-ene}}{CH_3CH_2CH=CH_2}$$

Q. 12. Arrange the following compounds in increasing order of their property as indicated : [NCERT Q. 8.12, Page 256]

(i) Acetaldehyde, Acetone, Di-tert-butyl ketone, Methyl tert-butyl ketone (reactivity towards HCN)

(ii) $CH_3CH_2CH(Br)COOH$, $CH_3CH(Br)CH_2COOH$, $(CH_3)_2CHCOOH$, $CH_3CH_2CH_2COOH$ (acid strength)

(iii) Benzoic acid, 4-Nitrobenzoic acid, 3,4-Dinitrobenzoic acid, 4-Methoxybenzoic acid (acid strength).

Sol. (i) The reaction between carbonyl compounds and HCN proceeds via the nucleophilic attack of CN^- on carbonyl carbon. Such an attack takes place faster if the carbonyl carbon is not attached to large alkyl groups. Less is the steric hindrance, more reactive is the compound.

∴ The order is:

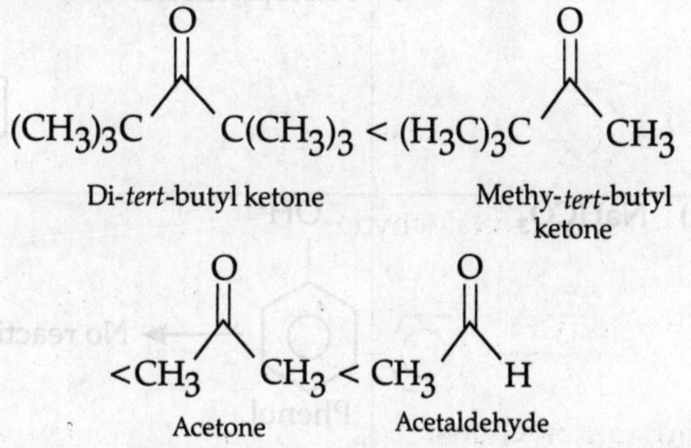

(ii) The presence of any electron withdrawing group or electronegative atom in carboxylic acid molecule increases the acidic strength of the acid. Moreover, the acidity decreases if the atom/group is bounded further off the α-carbon.

$$\underset{I}{(CH_3)_2CHCOOH} < \underset{II}{CH_3(CH_2)_2COOH} < \underset{III}{CH_3\overset{Br}{\overset{|}{C}}HCH_2COOH} < \underset{IV}{CH_3CH_2\overset{Br}{\overset{|}{C}}HCOOH}$$

Between I and II the higher acidity of II is due to lesser number of $-CH_3$ groups on the α-carbon. $-CH_3$ group increases the electron density by +I effect on α-carbon which in turn exerts the same effect on –COOH group and hinders release of H^+.

(iii) In benzoic acid, the attachment of electron withdrawing groups (EWG) on the benzene ring makes the O–H bond of –COOH group polar and H is lost as H^+. Therefore, the order is

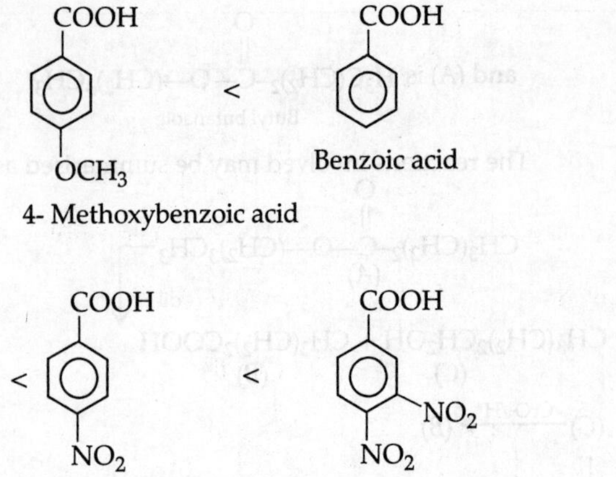

4- Methoxybenzoic acid < Benzoic acid < 4- Nitronbenzoic acid < 3, 4- Dinitrobenzoic acid

Q. 13. Give simple chemical tests to distinguish between the following pairs of compounds.

[NCERT Q. 8.13, Page 256]

(i) Propanal and Propanone

(ii) Acetophenone and Benzophenone

(iii) Phenol and Benzoic acid

(iv) Benzoic acid and Ethyl benzoate

(v) Pentan-2-one and Pentan-3-one

(vi) Benzaldehyde and Acetophenone

(vii) Ethanal and Propanal

Ans. The given set of compounds may be distinguish by the following reaction.

Reagent / Compound	Compound I	Compound II
(i) Ammoniacal silver nitrate $2[Ag(NH_3)_2]^+$ (Tollen's reagent)	CH_3-CH_2-CHO Propanal → $CH_3CH_2COO^- + 2Ag^+ + 2H_2O + 4NH_3$ Silver mirror	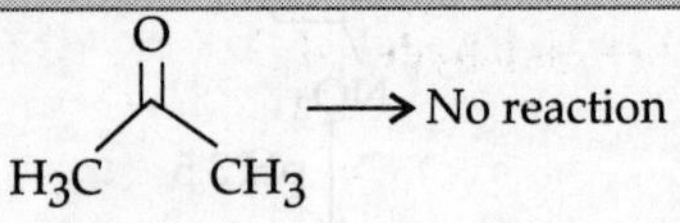 → No reaction
(ii) NaOI	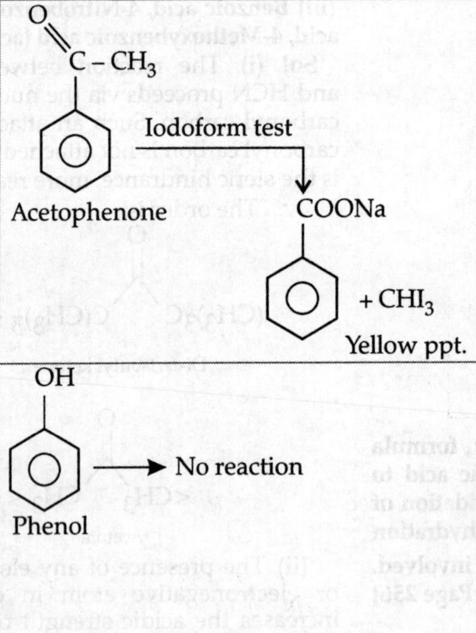	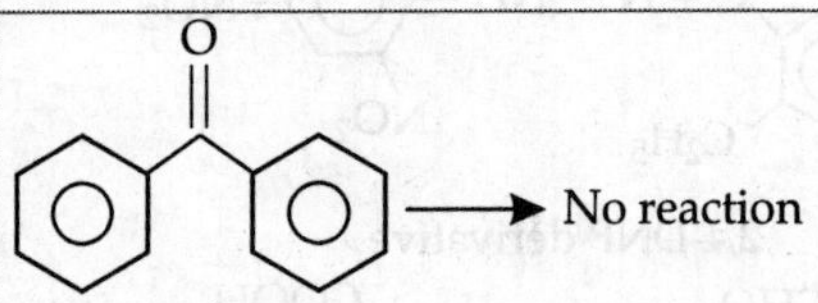
(iii) $NaHCO_3$	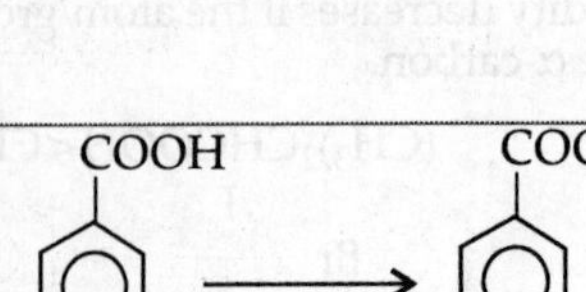	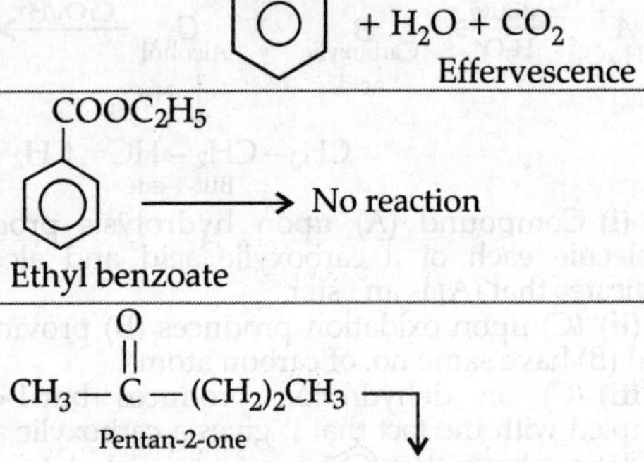
(iv) $NaHCO_3$	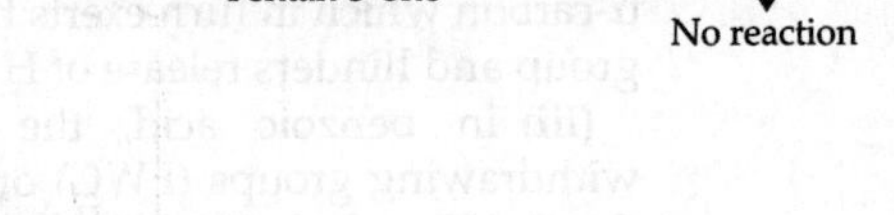	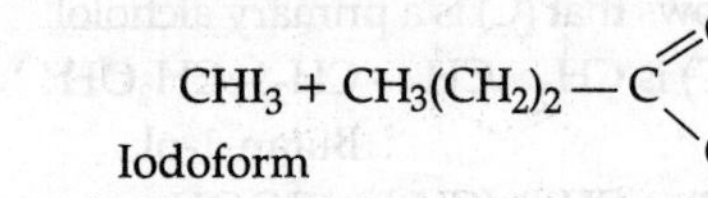
(v) NaOI	$CH_3-CH_2-\overset{O}{\overset{\|\|}{C}}-CH_2-CH_3$ Pentan-3-one → No reaction	$CH_3-\overset{O}{\overset{\|\|}{C}}-(CH_2)_2CH_3$ Pentan-2-one → $CHI_3 + CH_3(CH_2)_2-C(=O)O^-$ Iodoform (yellow ppt.)

(vi) NaOI	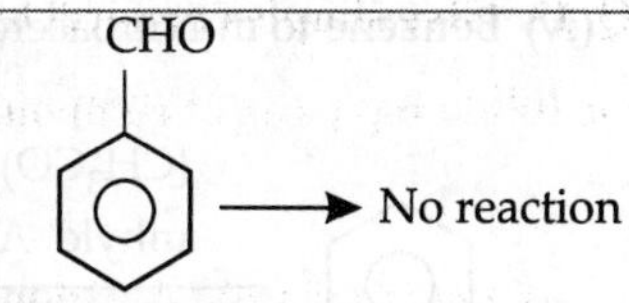 Benzaldehyde	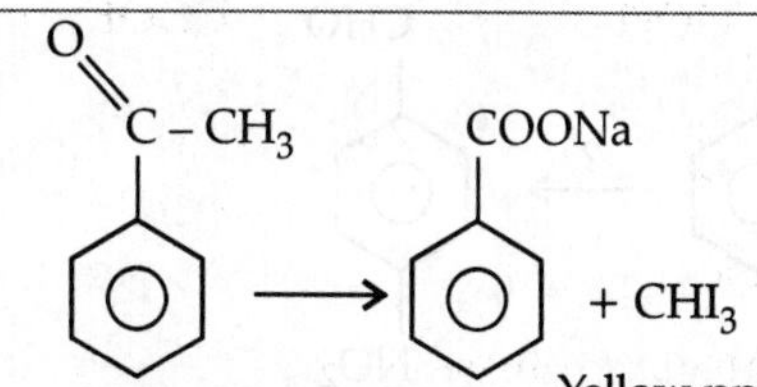 Acetophenone Yellow ppt.
(vii) NaOI	$CH_3CHO \longrightarrow 2CHI_3 + HCOONa$ Ethanal Yellow ppt.	$CH_3CH_2CHO \longrightarrow$ No reaction Propanal

Q. 14. How will you prepare the following compounds from benzene? You may use any inorganic reagent and any organic reagent having not more than one carbon atom: [NCERT Q. 8.14, Page 256]

(i) **Methyl benzoate**
(ii) ***m*-Nitrobenzoic acid**
(iii) ***p*-Nitrobenzoic acid**
(iv) **Phenylacetic acid**
(v) ***p*-Nitrobenzaldehyde.**

Ans.

(i) 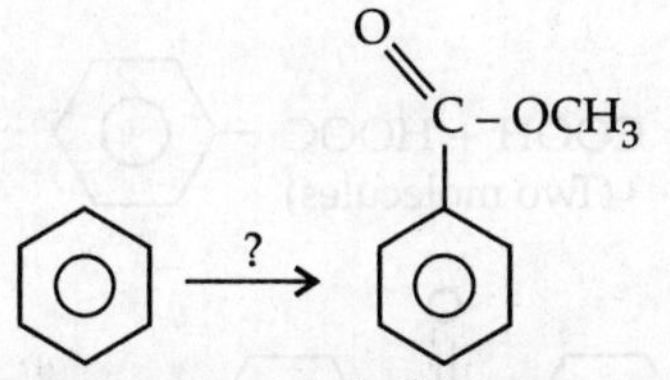

Benzoate Methyl benzoate

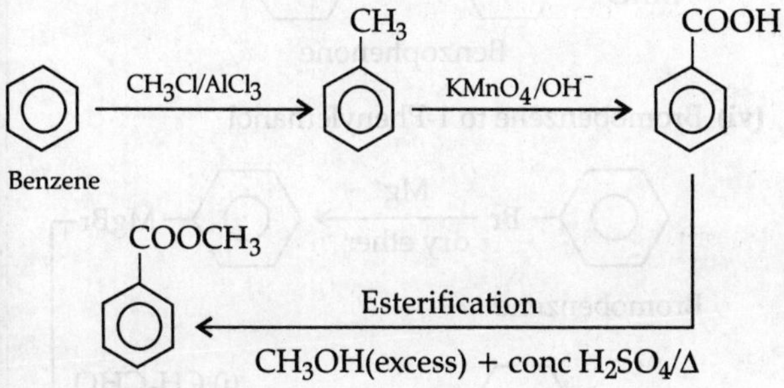

Methyl benzoate

(ii) 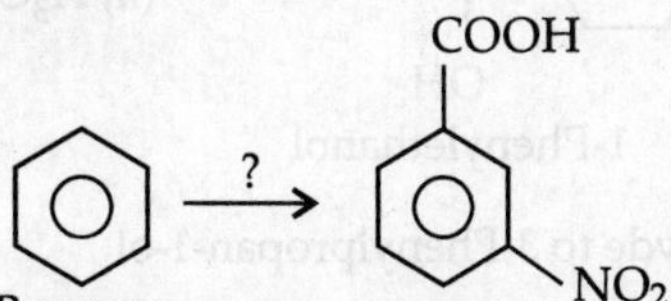

Benzene *p*-Nitrobenzoic acid

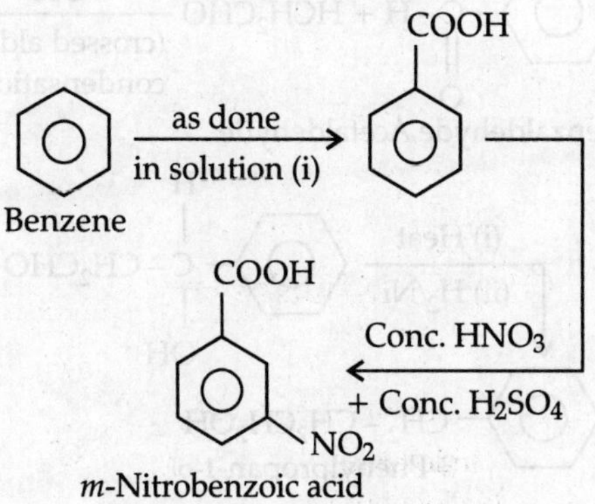

m-Nitrobenzoic acid

(iii) 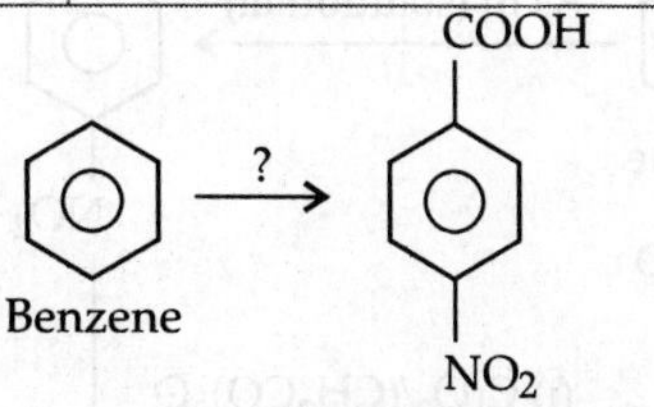

Benzene *p*-Nitrobenzoic acid

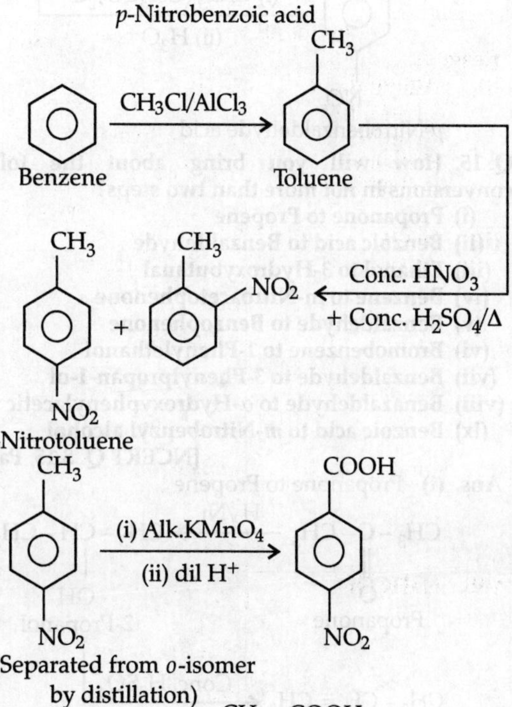

(Separated from *o*-isomer by distillation)

(iv) 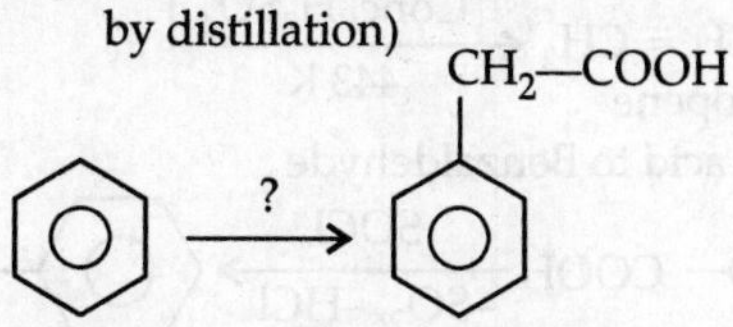

Benzene Phenylacetic acid

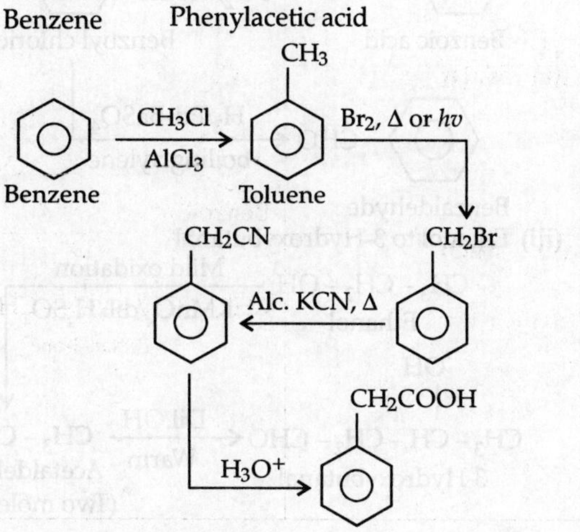

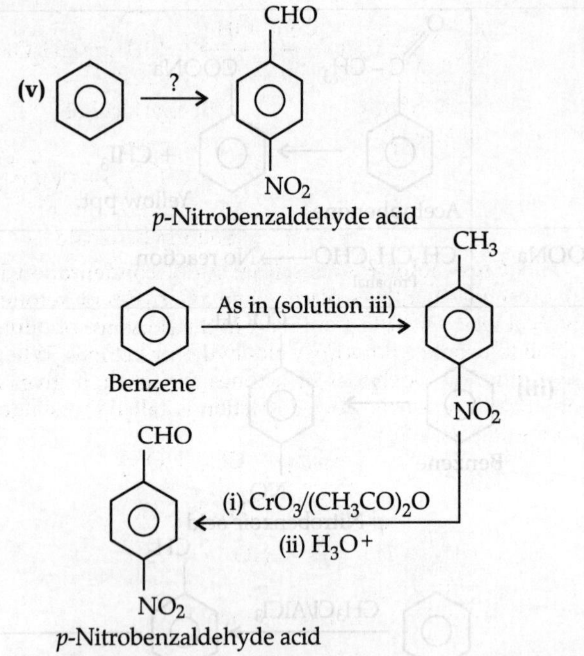

Q. 15. How will you bring about the following conversions in not more than two steps?

(i) Propanone to Propene
(ii) Benzoic acid to Benzaldehyde
(iii) Ethanol to 3-Hydroxybutanal
(iv) Benzene to m-Nitroacetophenone
(v) Benzaldehyde to Benzophenone
(vi) Bromobenzene to 1-Phenylethanol
(vii) Benzaldehyde to 3-Phenylpropan-1-ol
(viii) Benazaldehyde to α-Hydroxyphenylacetic acid
(ix) Benzoic acid to *m*-Nitrobenzyl alcohol

[NCERT Q. 8.15, Page 256]

Ans. (i) Propanone to Propene

$$CH_3-\underset{\underset{O}{\|}}{C}-CH_3 \xrightarrow{H_2/Ni} CH_3-\underset{\underset{OH}{|}}{CH}-CH_3$$

Propanone 2-Propanol

$$CH_3-CH=CH_2 \xleftarrow[443\text{ K}]{\text{Conc. }H_2SO_4}$$

Propene

(ii) Benzoic acid to Benzaldehyde

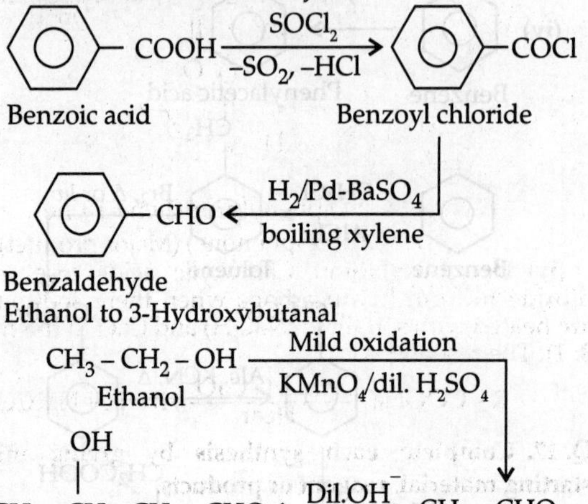

(iii) Ethanol to 3-Hydroxybutanal

$$\underset{\text{Ethanol}}{CH_3-CH_2-OH} \xrightarrow[\text{KMnO}_4/\text{dil. }H_2SO_4]{\text{Mild oxidation}}$$

$$\underset{\text{3-Hydroxybutanal}}{CH_3-\overset{\overset{OH}{|}}{CH}-CH_2-CHO} \xleftarrow[\text{Warm}]{\text{Dil.}OH^-} \underset{\text{Acetaldehyde (Two molecules)}}{CH_3-CHO}$$

(iv) Benzene to m-Nitroacetophenone

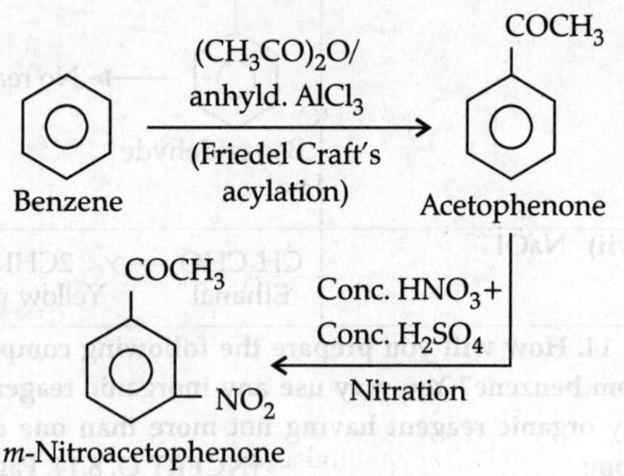

(v) Benzaldehyde to Benzophenone

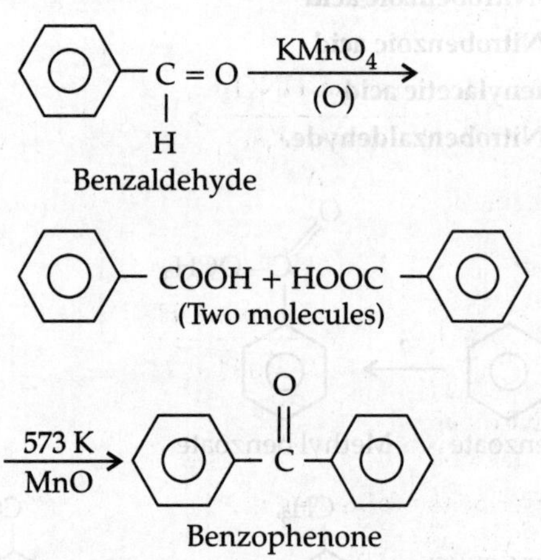

(vi) Bromobenzene to 1-Phenylethanol

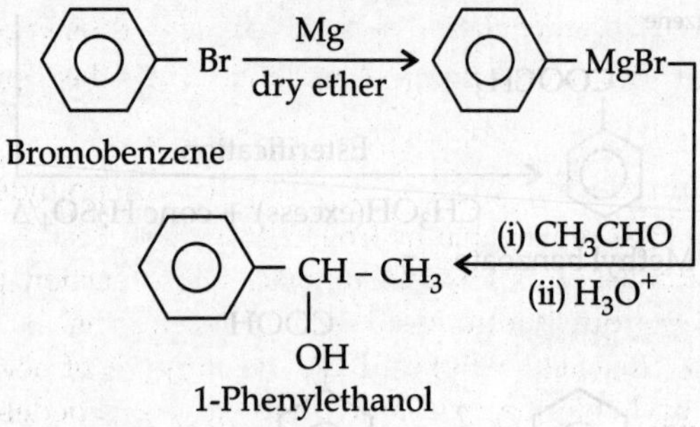

(vii) Benzaldehyde to 3-Phenylpropan-1-ol

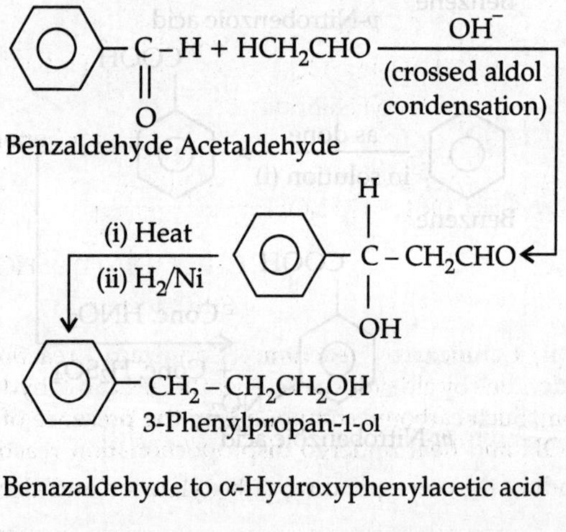

(viii) Benazaldehyde to α-Hydroxyphenylacetic acid

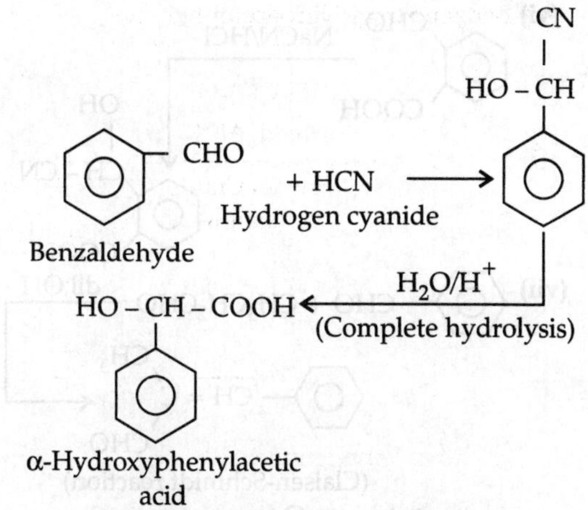

(ix) Benzoic acid to *m*-Nitrobenzyl alcohol

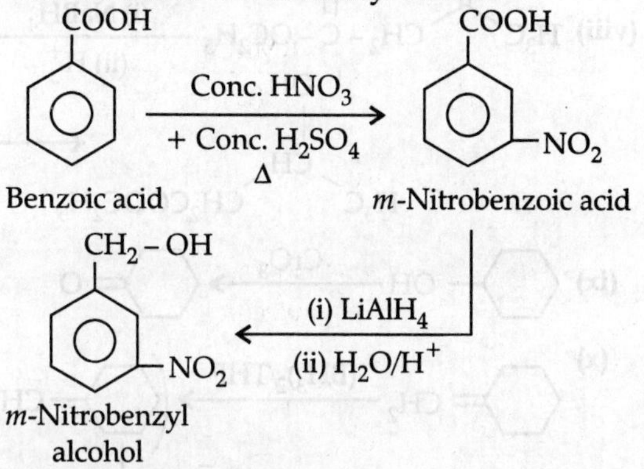

Q. 16. Describe the following :

(i) Acetylation

(ii) Cannizzaro reaction

(iii) Cross aldol condensation

(iv) Decarboxylation **[NCERT Q. 8.16, Page 256]**

Ans. (i) Acetylation: Acetylation is the process of introducing an $R-\overset{O}{\overset{||}{C}}-$ group in compounds that contain a replaceable hydrogen atom. The best example of acetylation is Friedel-Crafts aclyation reaction where RCO– group is introduced on the benzene ring.

Reagents employed for the purpose of acylation are acyl chloride, acid anhydride etc. e.g., Friedel-crafts acylation:

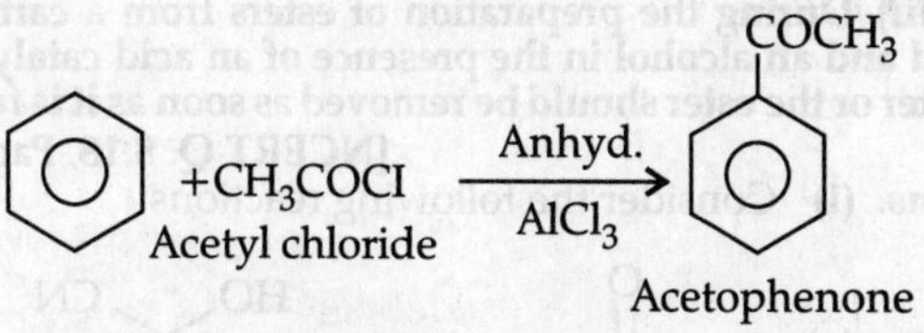

$$CH_3COCl + C_2H_5OH \xrightarrow{\text{Pyridine}} CH_3COOC_2H_5 + HCl$$

Ethyl acetate

(ii) Cannizzaro reaction: Cannizaro reaction is undergone by aldeydes or ketones that lack an α-hydrogen atom. Such carbonyl compounds in the presence of conc. NaOH and heat undergo disproportionation reaction to produce the corresponding carboxylate ion and alcohol.

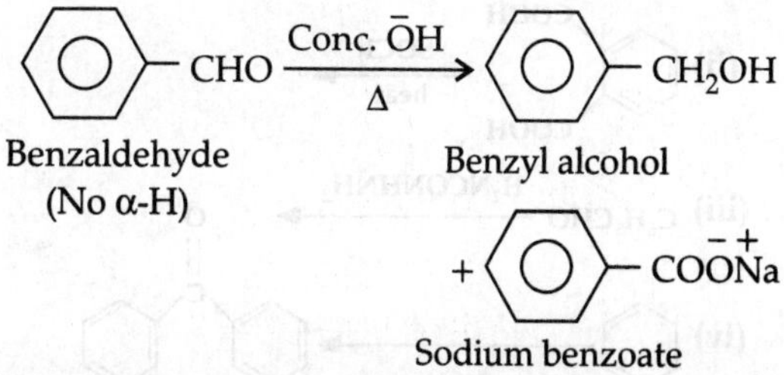

(iii) Cross-aldol condensation: Aldol condensation is the reaction that takes place, when aldehydes or ketones with at least one α-H atom react in the presence of dilute alkali to produce β-hydroxy aldehydes or ketones. When two different aldehydes or ketones are taken, it gives a mixture of products. Such a reaction is called cross-aldol condensation.

$$CH_3CHO + CH_3CH_2CHO \xrightarrow{\text{1. NaOH, 2. Heat}}$$

$CH_3-CH=CH-CHO$
But-2-enal
From two molecules of ethanal

$+CH_3CH_2-CH=\underset{CH_3}{\underset{|}{C}}-CHO$
2-Methylpent-2-enal
From two molecules of propanal

Simple or self aldol product

Ketones can also be used as one component in the cross aldol reactions.

$CH_3-CH=\underset{CH_3}{\underset{|}{C}}-CHO + CH_3CH_2-CH=CHCHO$

2-Methylbut-2-enal Pent-2-enal

From one molecule of ethanal and one molecule of propanal

Cross aldol products

Ketones can also be used as one component in the cross aldol reactions

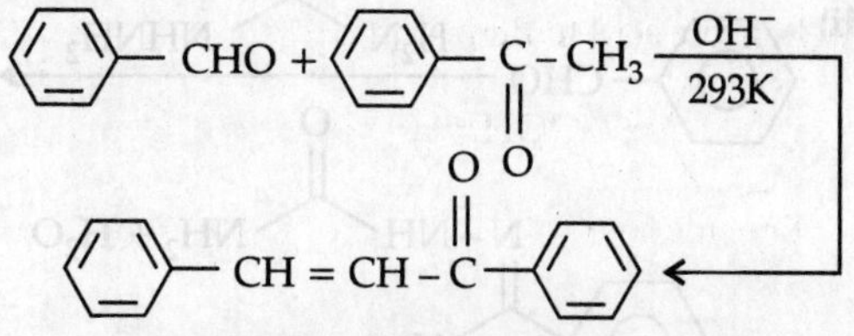

1, 3-Diphenylprop-2-ene-1-one

(Benzalacetophenone) (Major product)

(iv) Decarboxylation: Carboxylic acids lose carbon dioxide to form hydrocarbons when there sodium salts are heated with sodalime (NaOH) and CaO in the ratio of 3: 1). The reaction is

$$R-COONa \xrightarrow[\text{Heat}]{NaOH+CaO} R-H + Na_2CO_3$$

Q. 17. Complete each synthesis by giving missing starting material, reagent or products.

(i) 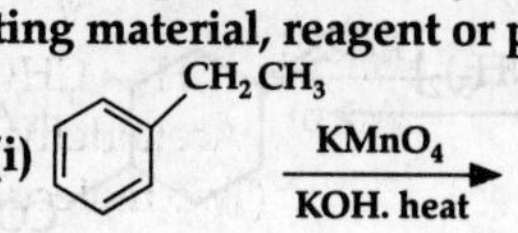

(ii) 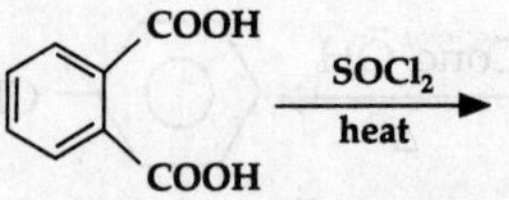

(iii) $C_6H_5CHO \xrightarrow{H_2NCONHNH_2}$

(iv) 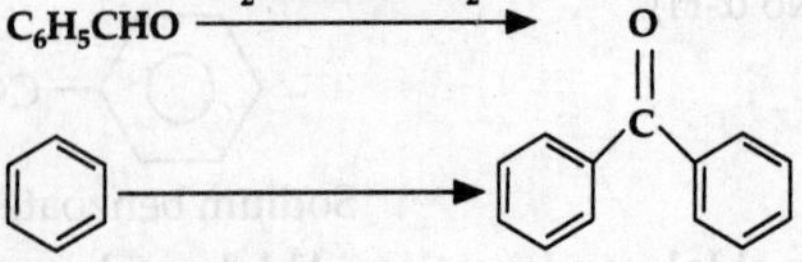

(v) 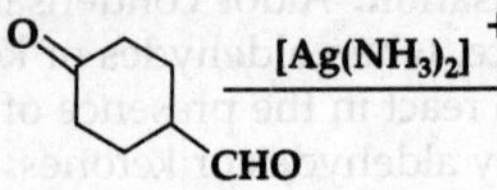

(vi) 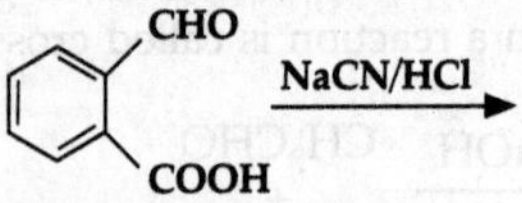

(vii) $C_6H_5CHO + CH_3CH_2CHO \xrightarrow{\text{dil NaOH}}$

(viii) $CH_3COCH_2COOC_2H_5 \xrightarrow[\text{(ii) } H^+]{\text{(i) } NaBH_4}$

(ix) 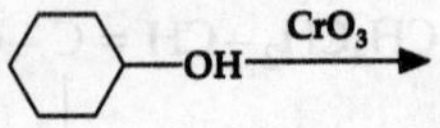

(x) 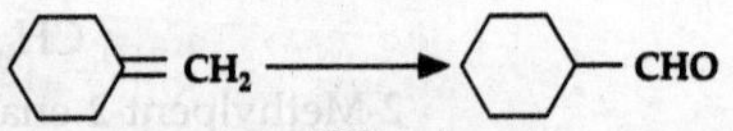

(xi) 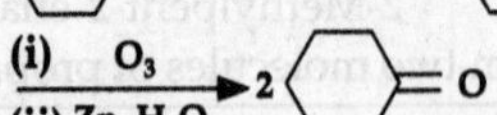

[NCERT Q. 8.17, Page 257]

Ans.

(i) 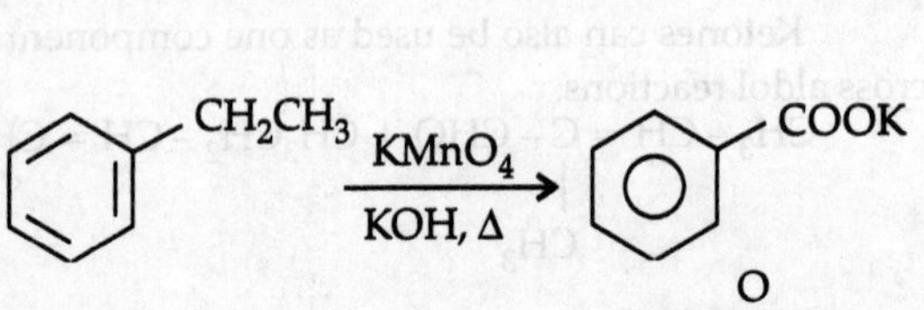

(ii) 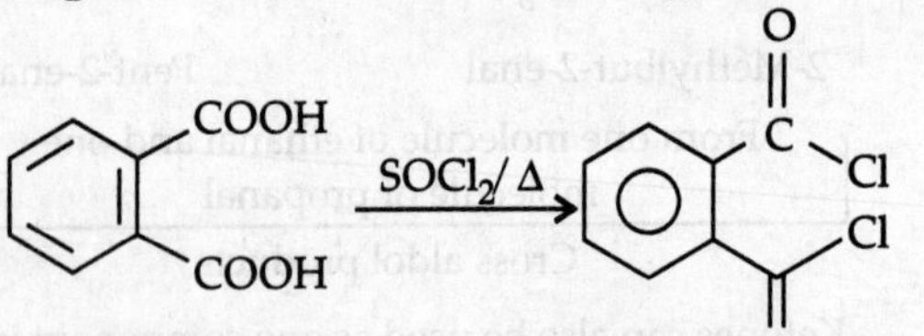

(iii) 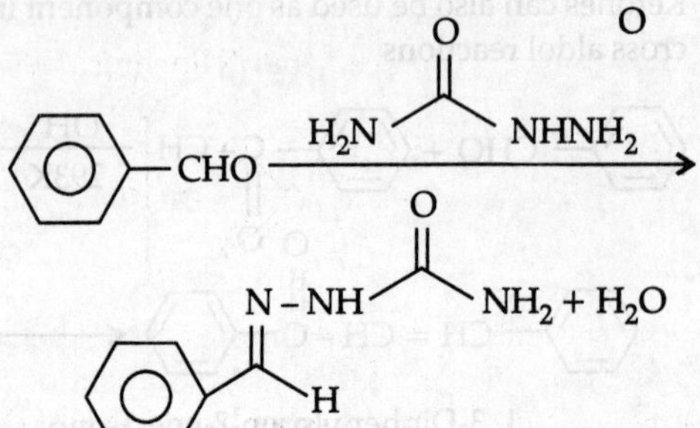

(iv) 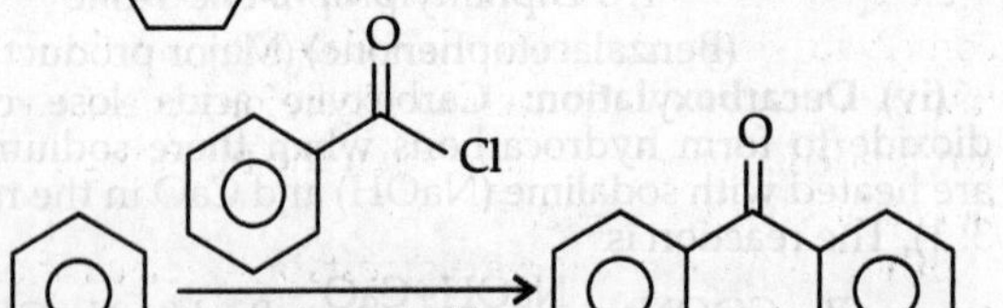

(v) 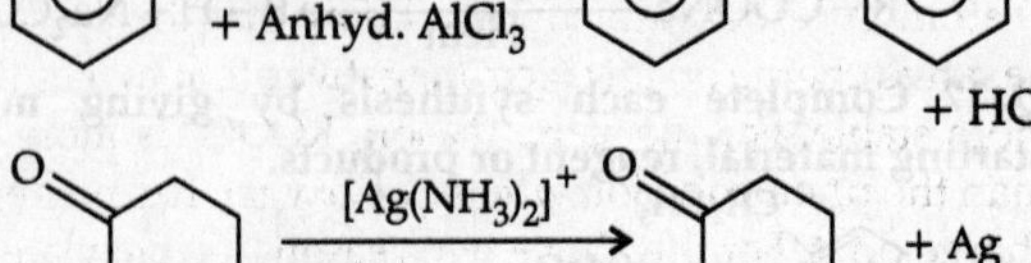

(vi) 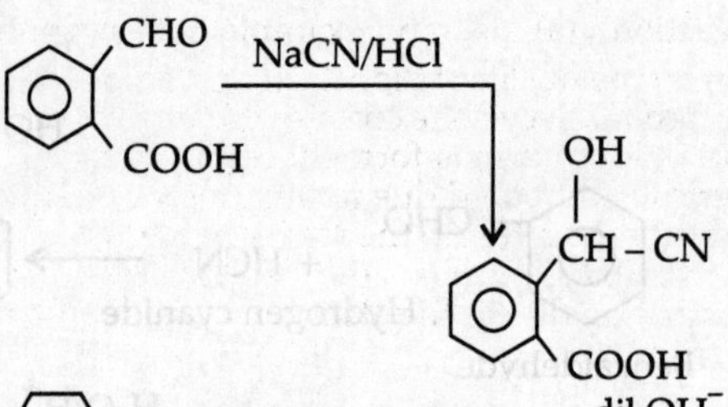

(vii) 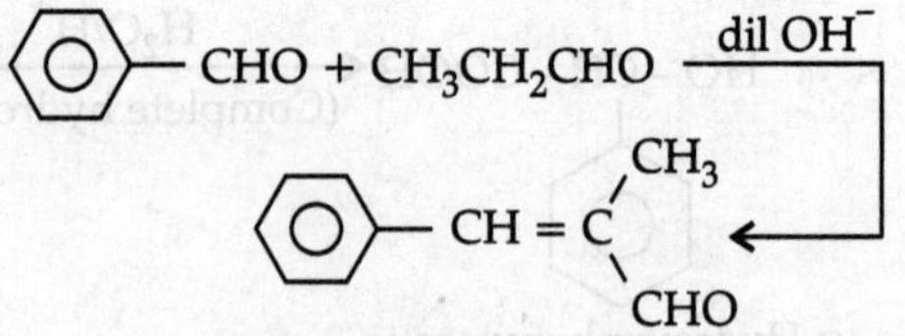

(Claisen-Schmidt reaction)

(viii) 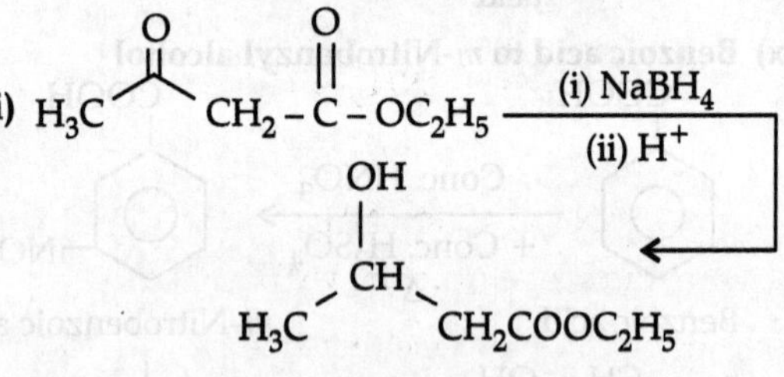

(ix) 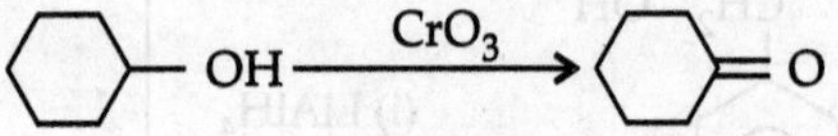

(x) 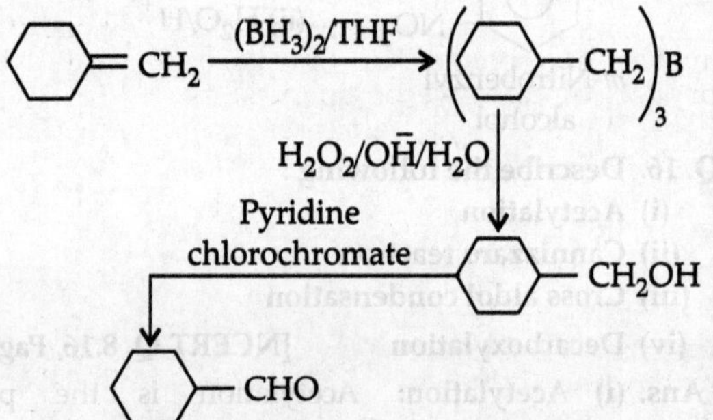

(xi) 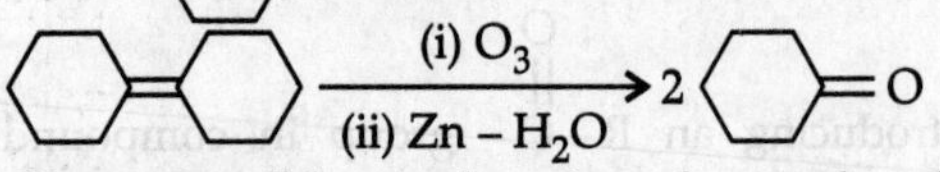

Q. 18. Give plausible explanation for each of the following:

(i) Cyclohexanone forms cyanohydrin in good yield but 2, 2, 6 trimethylcyclohexanone does not.

(ii) There are two $-NH_2$ groups in semicarbazide. However, only one is involved in the formation of semicarbazones.

(iii) During the preparation of esters from a carboxylic acid and an alcohol in the presence of an acid catalyst, the water or the ester should be removed as soon as it is formed.

[NCERT Q. 8.18, Page 257]

Ans. (i) Consider the following reactions:

(a) 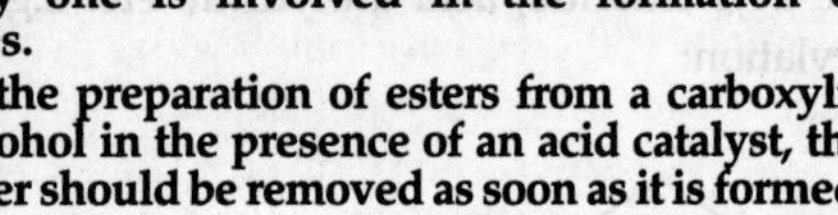

(I)

Cyclohexanone

(b) 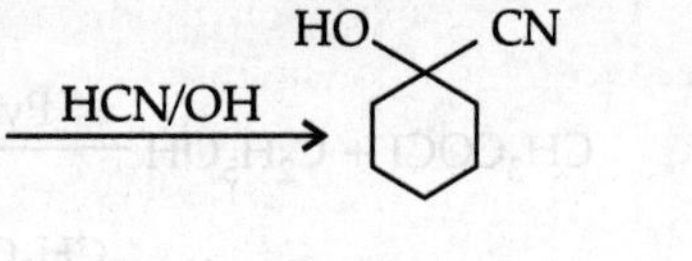

(II)

Reaction (a) is an example of cyanohydrin formation by the nucleophilic attack of cyanide ion on the carbonyl carbon. In cyclohexanone, this attack takes place easily and cyanohydrin is formed. But in II, attack of the Nu^- is sterically hindered due to the presence of the three methyl groups. As a result, the reaction does not occur.

(ii) Semicarbazide has the following resonance structures arising due to the electron withdrawing nature of the O atom.

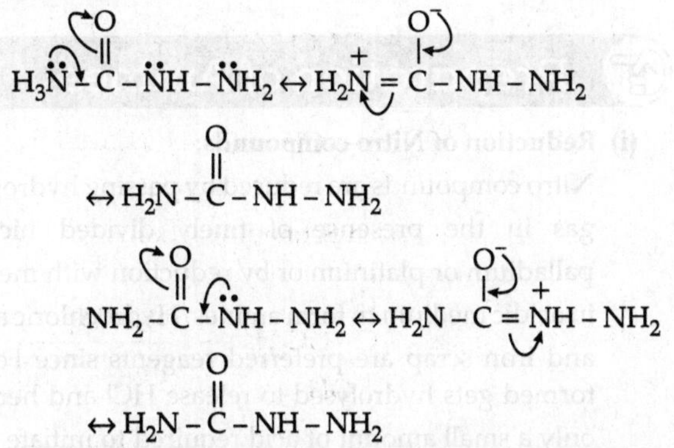

From the above structure we find that the lone pair of electrons on N atoms on either side of >C = O group are delocalized, involved in resonance. Therefore, they are not available for carrying out the nucleophilic attack on the aldehyde or ketone.

But, the $-NH_2$ (terminal one) is intact, i.e., it is not involved in resonance and thus its, lone pair is available for attack on carbonyl compounds.

This is why the semicarbazone is formed through this N atom only.

(iii) $\underset{\text{acid}}{RCOOH} + \underset{\text{alcohol}}{R'OH} \overset{H^+}{\rightleftharpoons} \underset{\text{ester}}{RCOOR'} + H_2O$

The esterification reaction is a reversible reaction. If water and the ester are allowed to remain in the reaction mixture the hydrolysis of the ester would take place. Hence, water or ester should be removed as soon as it is formed.

Q. 19. An organic compound contains 69.77% carbon, 11.63% hydrogen and rest oxygen. The molecular mass of the compound is 86. It does not reduce Tollens' reagent but forms an addition compound with sodium hydrogensulphite and give positive iodoform test. On vigorous oxidation, it gives ethanoic and propanoic acid. Write the possible structure of the compound.

[NCERT Q. 8.19, Page 257]

Ans. (a) The given compound does not reduce Tollens' reagent which implies that it is not an aldehyde.

(b) Positive iodoform test proves that it has a $CH_3-\overset{O}{\overset{\|}{C}}-$ group.

(c) The oxidation products are indicative of the presence of 5 carbon atoms.

To find the exact molecular formula

%C = 69.77%, %H = 11.63%

%O = 100 – (69.77 + 11.63) = 18.6%

$$C : H : O = \frac{69.77}{12} : \frac{11.63}{1} : \frac{18.6}{16}$$

The structure based on inferences a, b and c is

$$H_3C-\overset{O}{\overset{\|}{C}}-CH_2CH_2CH_3$$

Reactions involved are:

$$H_3C-\overset{O}{\overset{\|}{C}}(CH_2)_2CH_3 + NaHSO_3 \longrightarrow \underset{CH_3\quad\quad (CH_2)_2CH_3}{\overset{OH\quad\quad \overset{-}{S}O_3\overset{+}{Na}}{C}}$$

Addition compound

$$CH_3-\overset{O}{\overset{\|}{C}}-(CH_2)_2CH_3 + 3I_2 + 4NaOH \xrightarrow{\text{Iodoform reaction}} \underset{\text{Yellow}}{CHI_3}\downarrow + CH_3CH_2CH_2COONa + 3NaI + 3H_2O$$

$$CH_3-\overset{O}{\overset{\|}{C}}-(CH_2)_2CH_3 \xrightarrow{(O)} \underset{\text{Ethanoic acid}}{CH_3COOH} + \underset{\text{Propionic acid}}{CH_3CH_2COOH}$$

Q. 20. Although phenoxide ion has more number of resonating structures than carboxylate ion, carboxylic acid is a stronger acid than phenol. Why?

[NCERT Q. 8.20, Page 257]

Ans. (i) Phenoxide ion has the following resonating structures:

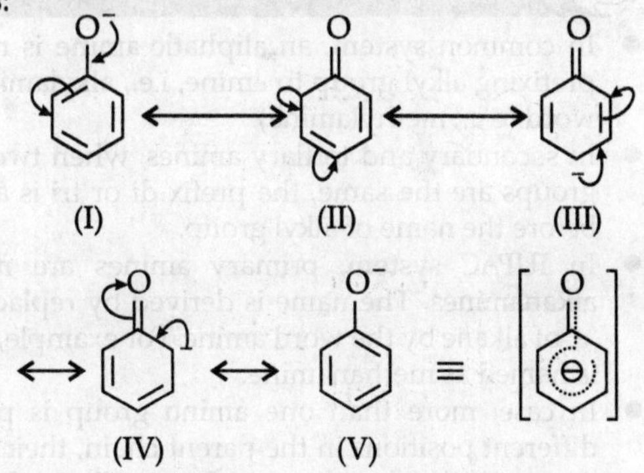

(I) (II) (III) (IV) (V)

Carboxylate ion has the following resonance structures.

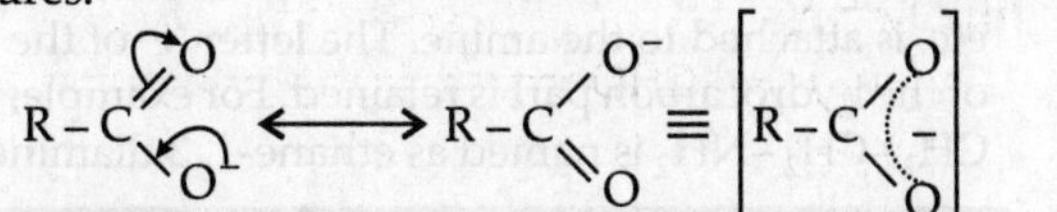

A B

(ii) Phenoxide ion is a resonance hybrid of structures I to V, where each structure has a contribution of 20% in the resonance hybrid. On the other hand, each of the two contributing structures of carboxylate ion contribution 50% towards the resonance hybrid. Therefore, the carboxylate ion tends to the more stable than the phenoxide ion and hence has higher acidity.

(iii) The negative charge that rests on the electronegative O atom in carboxylate ion. We know that the presence of negative charge on an electronegative atom makes the ion more stable. For the same reason, $RCOO^-$ is more stable than the phenoxide ion where the oxygen has no negative charge on it. For the above two reasons, carboxylate ion is more stable and has higher acidity than phenol.

CHAPTER 9

AMINES

- The chief commercial use of amines is as intermediates in the synthesis of medicines and fibres.
- **Amines:** Amines are considered as amino derivatives of hydrocarbons or alkyl derivatives of ammonia. In these compounds, one, two or three hydrogen atoms are replaced by alkyl or aryl groups. Aliphatic amino compounds are called amino alkanes and aromatic amines are called amino arenes. *e.g.*, CH_3NH_2, $C_2H_5NH_2$, $C_6H_5NH_2$, etc.

Scan to know more about this topic

Names of Amines

Classification of Amines

—NH_2	—NH—	—N—
Primary (1°)	Secondary (2°)	Tertiary (3°)

Nomenclature

- In common system, an aliphatic amine is named by prefixing alkyl group to amine, i.e., alkylamine as one word (e.g., methylamine).
- In secondary and tertiary amines, when two or more groups are the same, the prefix di or tri is appended before the name of alkyl group.
- In IUPAC system, primary amines are named as alkanamines. The name is derived by replacement of 'e' of alkane by the word amine. For example, CH_3NH_2 is named as methanamine.
- In case, more than one amino group is present at different positions in the parent chain, their positions are specified by giving numbers to the carbon atoms bearing –NH_2 groups and suitable prefix such as di, tri, etc. is attached to the amine. The letter 'e' of the suffix of the hydrocarbon part is retained. For example, $H_2N–CH_2–CH_2–NH_2$ is named as ethane-1, 2-diamine.

Structure of Amine

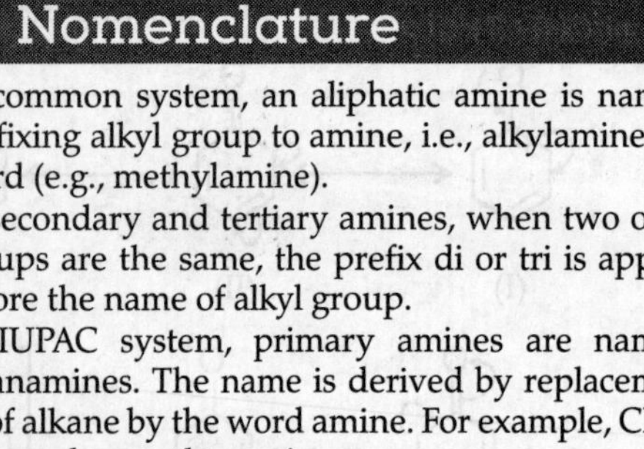

Fig. 1: Pyramidal shape of trimethylamine

Preparation of Amines

(i) Reduction of Nitro compounds:

Nitro compounds are reduced by passing hydrogen gas in the presence of finely divided nickel, palladium or platinum or by reduction with metals in acidic medium to form amines. Hydrochloric acid and iron scrap are preferred reagents since $FeCl_2$ formed gets hydrolysed to release HCl and hence, only a small amount of acid required to initiate the reaction.

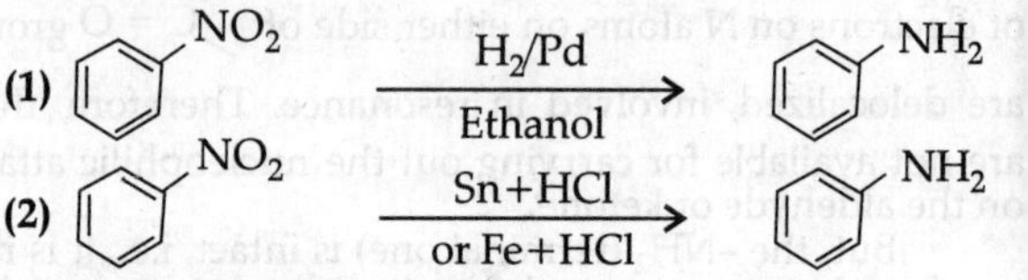

(ii) By ammonolysis of alkyl halides:

$$R–X + NH^3 \rightarrow \underset{(1°)}{RNH_2} \xrightarrow{RX} \underset{(2°)}{R_2NH} \xrightarrow{RX}$$

$$\underset{(3°)}{R_3N} \xrightarrow{RX} R_4\overset{+}{N}\overset{-}{X}$$

Quaternary ammonium salt

The free amine can be obtained from the ammonium salt by treatment with a strong base:

$$R — \overset{+}{N}H_3 \overset{-}{X} + NaOH \rightarrow R — NH_2 + H_2O + \overset{+}{Na}\overset{-}{X}$$

(1) It gives a mixtures of amines and quaternary ammonium salts.

(2) It is not suitable to prepare aniline and other aromatic amines.

(iii) By reduction of nitriles:

$$2H_2 + R — C \equiv N \xrightarrow{Ni} R — CH_2 — NH_2$$

$$R — C \equiv N + 4\,[H] \xrightarrow[\text{or } LiAlH_4]{Na(Hg) / C_2H_5OH} R — CH_2 — NH_2$$

1° amine

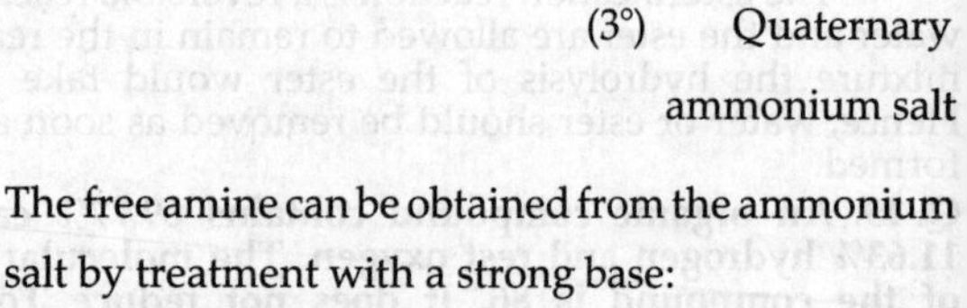

Benzylamine

Amines

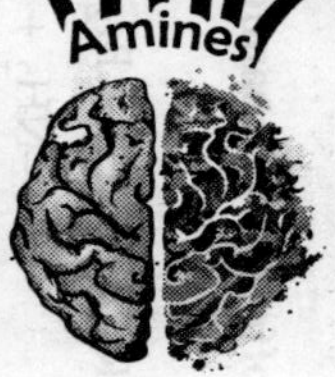

Preparation

1. Reduction of nitro compounds

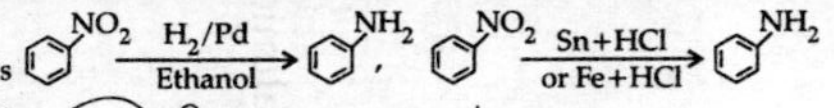

2. Ammonolysis of alkyl halides: $NH_3 + R-X \longrightarrow R-\overset{+}{N}H_3\overset{-}{X}$

3. Reduction of nitriles: $R-C\equiv N \xrightarrow[Na(Hg)/C_2H_5OH]{H_2/Ni} R-CH_2NH_2$

4. Reduction of amides: $R-\overset{O}{\overset{\|}{C}}-NH_2 \xrightarrow[H_2O]{LiAlH_4} R-CH_2-NH_2$

5. Gabriel phthalimide synthesis

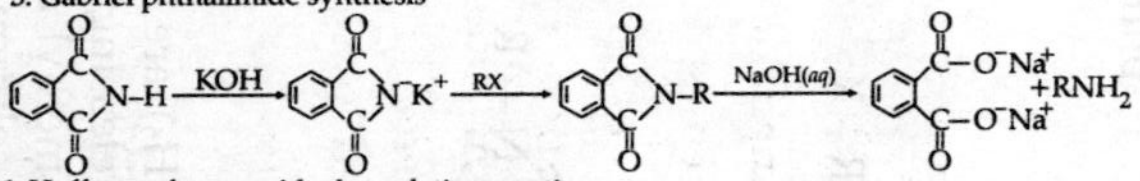

6. Hoffmann bromamide degradation reaction

$R-\overset{O}{\overset{\|}{C}}-NH_2+Br_2+4NaOH \longrightarrow R-NH_2 + Na_2CO_3+2NaBr+2H_2O$

Physical properties

- Lower aliphatic amines are gases. Primary amines with three or more C atoms are liquid and higher ones are solid.
- Arylamines are colourless but get coloured on storage.
- Lower aliphatic amines are soluble in water, while higher are insoluble.
- Primary and secondary amines form intermolecular association.
- Boiling point : primary > secondary > tertiary

Derivatives of ammonia, obtained by replacement of one, two or all the three H-atoms by alkyl and/or aryl groups

Structure

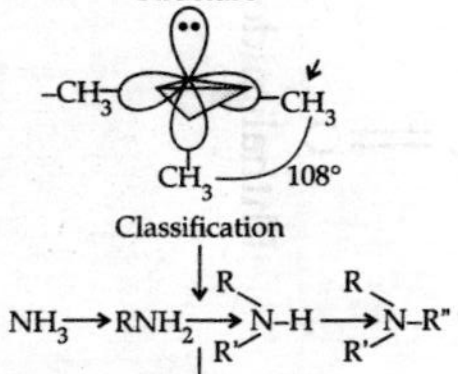

Nomenclature

Common name : Aliphatic amine is named by prefixing alkyl group to amine. In secondary and tertiary amines prefix di or tri is put before name of alkyl group. **IUPAC name :** replacement of 'e' of alkane by the word amine. Suffix 'e' of arene is replaced by amine.

Importance of diazonium salts in synthesis of aromatic compounds

In preparation of substituted aromatic compounds which cannot be prepared by direct substitution in benzene/ substituted benzene.

Chemical reactions

(i) Basic character of amines

- React with acids to form salts $R-NH_2 + HX \rightleftharpoons R-NH_3X$ (salt)
- React with base to regenerate parent amines $RN^+H_3X^- + OH^- \longrightarrow RNH_2 + H_2O + X$
- Order of stability of ions : 1° > 2° > 3°

(ii) $C_2H_5-\underset{C_2H_5}{\underset{|}{N}}H+CH_3-\overset{}{\underset{O}{\underset{\|}{C}}}-Cl \xrightarrow{Base} C_2H_5-\underset{C_2H_5}{\underset{|}{N}}-\overset{O}{\overset{\|}{C}}-CH_3+HCl$

(iii) Carbylamine reaction : $R-NH_2 + CHCl_3 + 3KOH \xrightarrow{\Delta} R-NC + 3KCl + 3H_2O$

(iv) With nitrous acid

$RNH_2 + HNO_2 \xrightarrow{NaNO_2+HCl} [R-N_2Cl] \xrightarrow{H_2O} ROH + N_2 + HCl$

$C_6H_5NH_2 \xrightarrow[273\text{-}278K]{NaNO_2+HCl} C_6H_5N_2Cl + NaCl + 2H_2O$

(v)

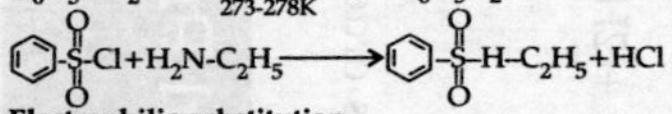

(vi) Electrophilic substitution

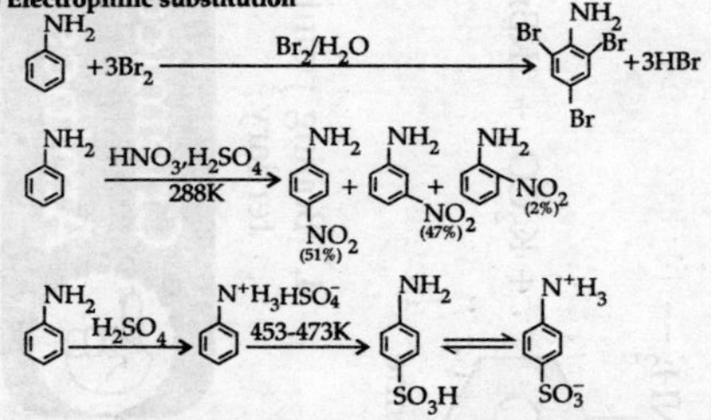

Diazonium Salts (RN_2X)

Preparation :

$C_6H_5NH_2 + NaNO_2 + 2HCl \xrightarrow{273\text{-}278K} C_6H_5N_2^+Cl^- + NaCl + 2H_2O$

Physical properties : Colourless crystalline solid, soluble in water, stable in cold but reacts with water on warming.

Chemical properties :

(i) Sandmeyer reaction: $ArN_2^+X^-$ $\xrightarrow{Cu_2Cl_2/HCl} ArCl + N_2$; $\xrightarrow{Cu_2Br_2/HBr} ArBr + N_2$; $\xrightarrow{CuCN/KCN} ArCN + N_2$

Gattermann reaction :

$ArN_2^+X^-$ $\xrightarrow{Cu/HCl} ArCl + N_2 + CuX$; $\xrightarrow{Cu/HBr} ArBr + N_2 + CuX$

(ii) $ArN_2^+Cl^- + KI \longrightarrow ArI + KCl + N_2$

(iii) $ArN_2^+Cl^- + HBF_4 \longrightarrow ArN_2^+BF_4^- \xrightarrow{\Delta} ArF + BF_3 + N_2$

(iv) $ArN_2^+Cl^- + H_3PO_2 + H_2O \longrightarrow ArH + N_2 + H_3PO_3 + HCl$

(v) $ArN_2^+Cl^- + H_2O \longrightarrow ArOH + N_2 + HCl$

(iv) **Coupling reaction :**

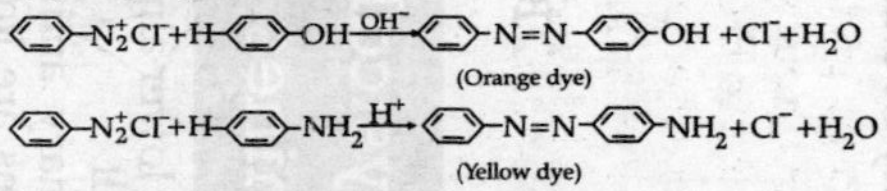

Trace the Mind Map
- First Level
- Second Level
- Third Level

(iv) Gabriel phthalimide synthesis:

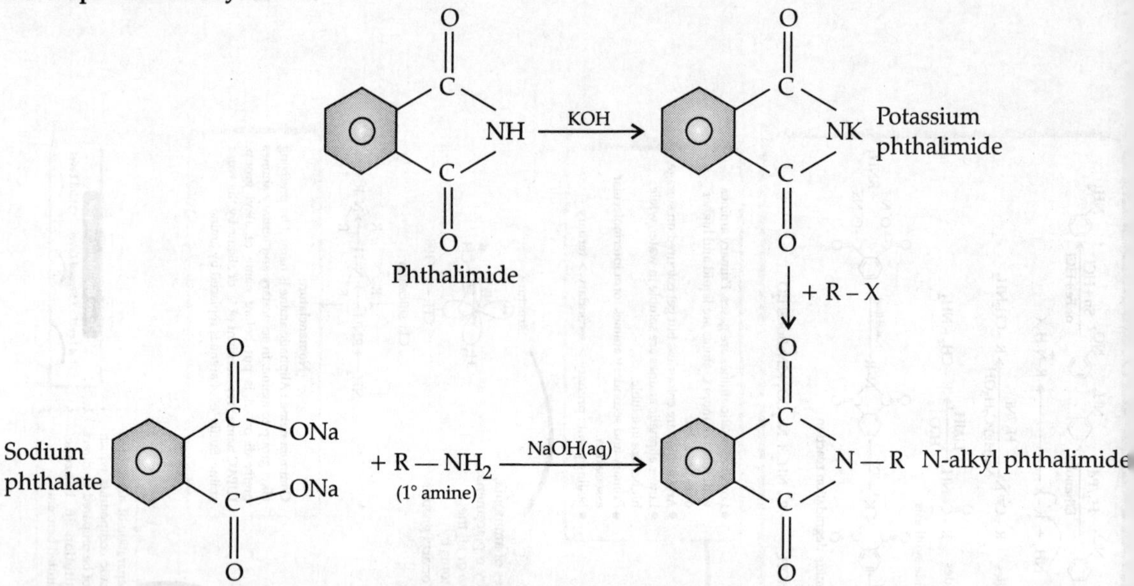

Note: Aromatic primary amines can not be prepared by this method because it does not undergo nucleophlic substitution reaction.

(v) By reduction of amides:

$$R-\overset{O}{\overset{\|}{C}}-NH_2 \xrightarrow[\text{(ii) } H_2O]{\text{(i) } LiAlH_4} R-CH_2-NH_2$$

Amine

(vi) By Hoffmann bromamide degradation reaction:

$$R-\overset{O}{\overset{\|}{C}}-NH_2 + Br_2 + 4NaOH \longrightarrow R-NH_2 + Na_2CO_3 + 2NaBr + 2H_2O$$

1° amine

Basic Strength of Amines:

Amines act as Lewis bases due to the presence of lone pair of electrons on the nitrogen atom.

More the K_b (dissociation constant of base), higher is the basicity of amines. Lesser the pK_b higher is the basicity of amines.

Aliphatic amines (CH_3NH_2) are stronger bases than NH_3 due to the electron releasing +I effect of the alkyl group. Among aliphatic methyl amines, the order of basic strength in aqueous solution is as follows :

$$(C_2H_5)_2NH > (C_2H_5)_3N > C_2H_5NH_2 > NH_3$$
$$(CH_3)_2NH > CH_3NH_2 > (CH_3)_3N > NH_3$$

Aromatic amines are weaker bases than aliphatic amines and NH_3, due to the fact that the electron pair on the nitrogen atom is involved in resonance with the π-electron pairs of the ring.

Electron releasing groups (e.g., $-CH_3$, $-OCH_3$, $-NH_2$, etc.) increase the basic strength of aromatic amines while electron withdrawing groups (like – NO_2, –X, –,CN, etc.) tend to decrease the same.

o-substituted aromatic amines are usually weaker bases, than aniline irrespective of the nature of substituent whether electron releasing or electron withdrawing. This is called ortho effect and is probably due to steric and electronic factors.

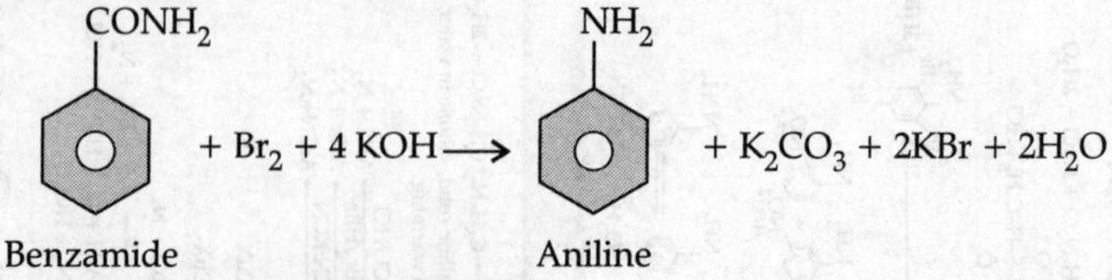

Physical Properties of Amines

1. The lower aliphatic amines are gases with fishy smell.
2. Primary amines with three or more carbon atoms are liquid and higher members are all solids.
3. Lower aliphatic amines are water soluble because they can form hydrogen bonds with water molecules, however the solubility decreases with increase in hydrophobic alkyl group.
4. Boiling points order: primary > secondary > tertiary.

Chemical Properties of Amines

(i) Alkylation:

All the three types of amines react with alkyl halides to form quaternary ammonium salt as the final product provided alkyl halide is present in excess. Aromatic amines also undergo this reaction.

$$C_2H_5NH_2 + C_2H_5Br \xrightarrow{-HBr} (C_2H_5)_2NH \xrightarrow[-HBr]{C_2H_5Br} (C_2H_6)_3\ddot{N} \xrightarrow{C_2H_5Br} (C_2H_5)_4\overset{+}{N}Br$$

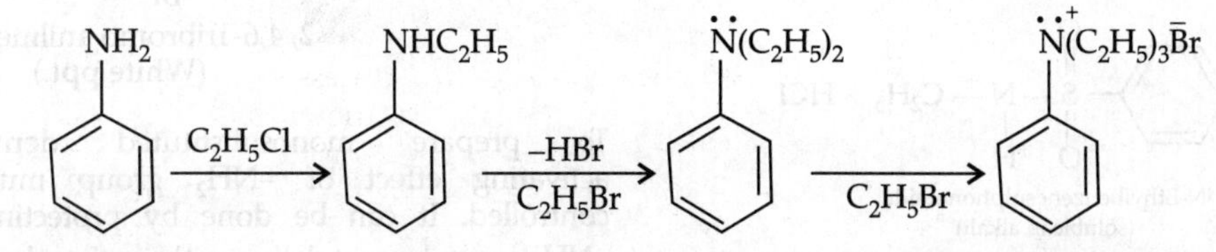

Triethylanilinium bromide

(ii) Acylation:

Aliphatic and aromatic primary and secondary amines react with acid chlorides, anhydrides and esters by nucleophilic substitution reaction. This reaction is known as acylation. The products obtained by acylation reaction are known as amides. The reaction is carried out in the presence of a base stronger than the amine, like pyridine, which removes HCl so formed and shifts the equilibrium to the right hand side.

$$\underset{\text{Ethylamine}}{CH_3-CH_2-NH_2} + \underset{\text{Acetic anhydride}}{(CH_3-CO)_2O} \longrightarrow \underset{\text{N-Ethylacetamide}}{CH_3-\overset{O}{\overset{\|}{C}}-NH-CH_2-CH_3} + CH_3-COOH$$

$$\underset{\text{Benzenamine}}{C_6H_5-\ddot{N}H-H} + \underset{\text{Ethanoic anhydride}}{CH_3-\overset{O}{\overset{\|}{C}}-O-\overset{O}{\overset{\|}{C}}-CH_3} \longrightarrow \underset{\text{N-Phenylethanamide or Acetanilide}}{C_6H_5-NH-\overset{O}{\overset{\|}{C}}-CH_3} + CH_3COOH$$

Benzoylation: Amines also react with benzoyl chloride (C_6H_5COCl). This reaction is known as benzoylation.

$$\underset{\text{Methyl amine}}{CH_3NH_2} + \underset{\text{Benzoyl chloride}}{C_6H_5COCl} \rightarrow \underset{\text{N-Methyl benzamide}}{CH_3NHCOC_6H_5} + HCl$$

(iii) Carbylamine reaction: Secondary and tertiary amines do not give this reaction. This reaction is used as a test for primary amines. Aliphatic and aromatic primary amines on heating with chloroform and ethanolic potassium hydroxide form isocyanides or carbylamines which are foul smelling substances.

$$R-NH_2 + CHCl_3 + \underset{(alc.)}{3KOH} \xrightarrow{Heat} R-NC + 3KCl + 3H_2O$$

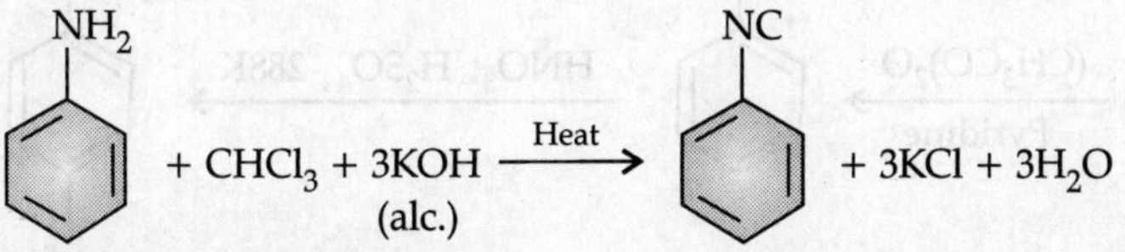

(iv) Reaction with nitrous acid: Three classes of amines react differently with nitrous acid which is prepared *in situ* from a mineral acid and sodium nitrite.

$$\underset{1° \text{ amine}}{R-NH_2} + HNO_2 \xrightarrow{NaNO_2+HCl} [R-\overset{+}{N_2}\overset{-}{Cl}] \xrightarrow{H_2O} ROH + N_2 + HCl$$

$$\underset{2° \text{ amine}}{R_2NH} + HNO_2 \longrightarrow \underset{\text{N-Nitrosamine}}{R_2N-N=O} + H_2O$$

$$\underset{3° \text{ amine}}{R_3N} + HNO_2 \longrightarrow \underset{\text{Trialkyl ammonium nitrite}}{R_3NHNO_2}$$

Aromatic amines react with nitrous acid at low temperatures (273-278 K) to form diazonium salts, a very important class of compounds used for synthesis of a variety of aromatic compound.

$$\underset{\text{Aromatic amine (Aniline)}}{C_6H_5-NH_2} \xrightarrow[273-278K]{NaNO_2+HCl} \underset{\text{Benzenediazonium chloride}}{C_6H_5-\overset{+}{N_2}\overset{-}{Cl}} + NaCl + 2H_2O$$

(v) Reaction with arylsulphonyl chloride: (Hinsberg Reagent)

(a) The reaction of benzenesulphonyl chloride with primary amine yields N-ethylbenzenesulphonyl amide. The hydrogen attached to nitrogen in sulphonamide is strongly acidic due to the presence of strong electron withdrawing sulphonyl group. Hence, it is soluble in alkali.

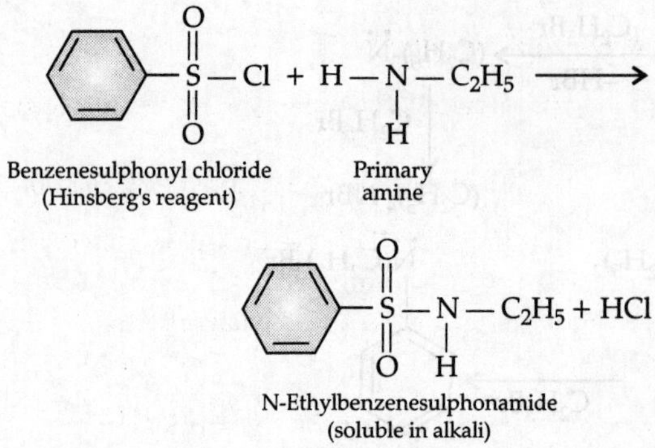

(b) Since N, N-diethylbenzene sulphonamide does not contain any hydrogen atom attached to nitrogen atom, it is not acidic and hence insoluble in alkali.

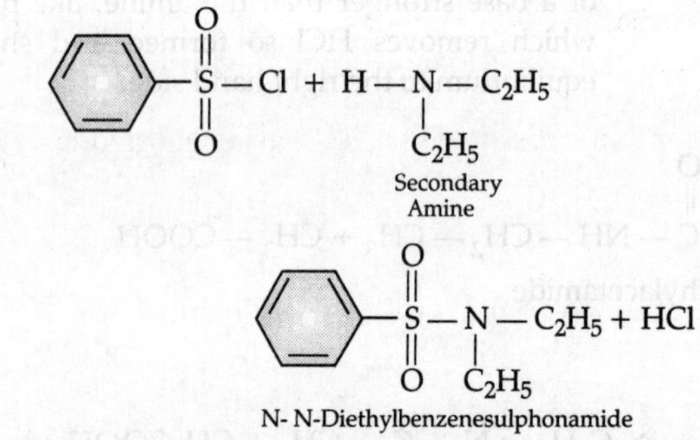

Tertiary amines do not react with benzenesulphonyl chloride. This property of amines is used for the distinction of primary, secondary and tertiary amines and also for the separation of a mixture of amines.

(vi) Bromination: Electrophilic substitution reaction and it will have sub parts.

(a) Bromination: Aniline is *ortho* and *para* directing towards electrophilic substitution reaction due to high electron density at *ortho* and *para*-positions.

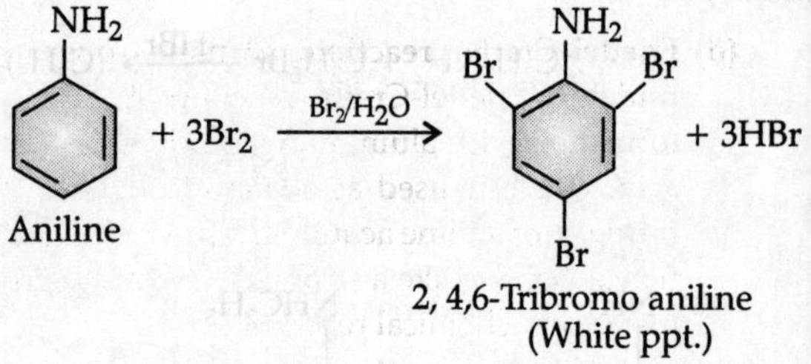

To prepare monosubstituted derivativ activating effect of $-NH_2$ group must b controlled. It can be done by protecting th $-NH_2$ group by acetylation with acetic anhydrid

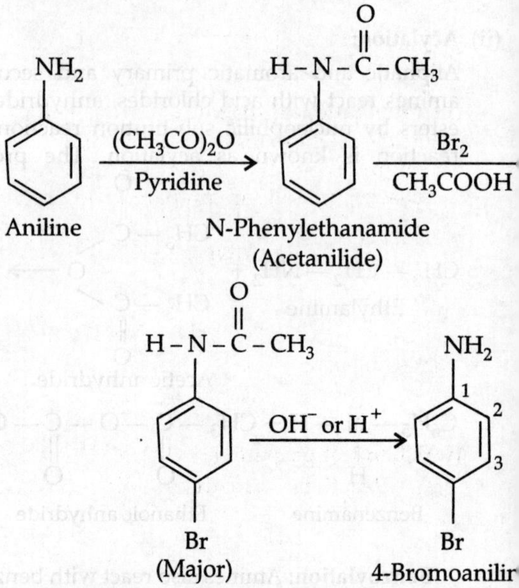

(b) Nitration: Direct nitration of aniline is no possible as it is susceptible to oxidation, thu amino group is first protected by acetylatio otherwise significant amount of *meta*-derivat is also formed along with *ortho*- and *par* directives.

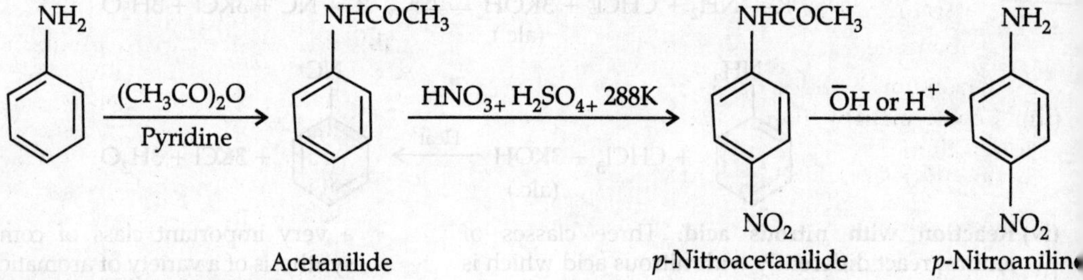

(c) Sulphonation: Aniline reacts with concentrated sulphuric acid to form anilinium hydrogensulphate which on heating with sulphuric acid at 453-473K produces sulphanili acid, as the major product.

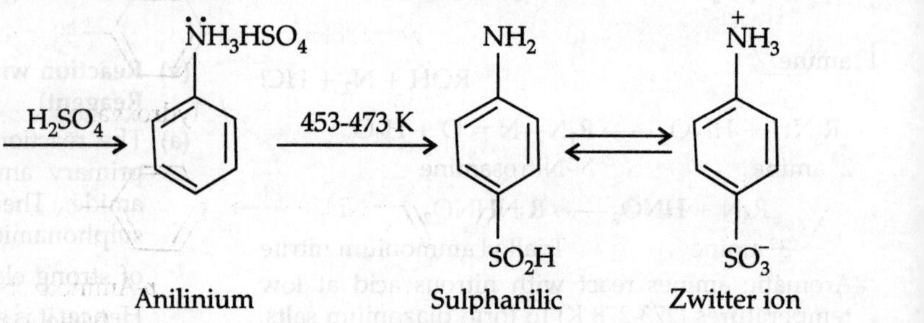

(d) Friedel-Crafts reaction: Aniline does not undergo Friedel-Crafts reaction due to salt formation with aluminium chloride, the Lewis acid, which is used as a catalyst. Due to this, nitrogen of aniline acquires positive charge and hence, behave like a strong deactivating group for further chemical reaction.

- **Diazonium salts:**

(i) General formula: $R\overset{+}{N_2}\overset{-}{X}$ where R stands for an aryl group and X^- ion may be Cl^-, Br^-, HSO_4^-, BF_4^- etc. The $\overset{+}{N_2}$ group is called diazonium group.

(ii) Stability of diazonium salts: Arenediazonium salts are more stable than alkyl diazonium salts due to the dispersal of the positive charge over the benzene ring.

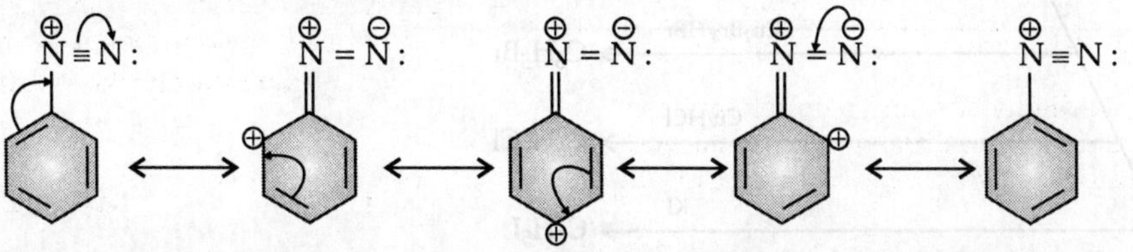

(iii) Preparation of diazonium salts: The excess acid in diazotisation reaction is necessary to maintain proper acidic medium for the reaction and to prevent combination of diazonium salt formed with the undiazotised amine.

Diazonium salts are prepared and used in aqueous solutions because in solid state, they explode.

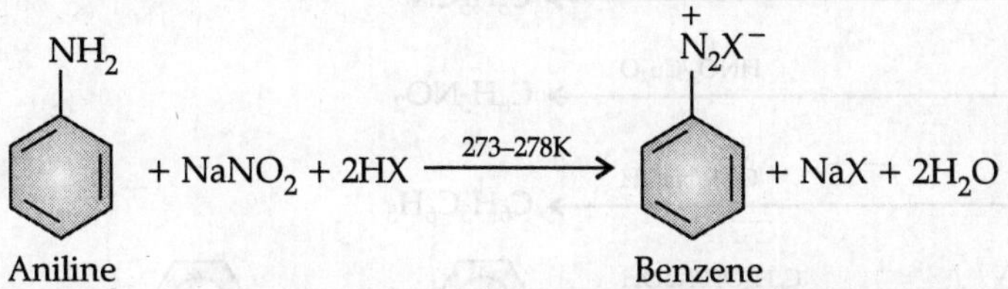

Aniline　　　Benzene diazonium salt

(iv) Chemical properties:

(a) Reactions involving displacement of nitrogen:

(i) Replacement by halide or cyanide ion–

$$Ar\overset{+}{N_2}\overset{-}{X} \xrightarrow{Cu_2Cl_2/HCl} ArCl + N_2$$
$$Ar\overset{+}{N_2}\overset{-}{X} \xrightarrow{Cu_2Br_2/HBr} ArBr + N_2$$
$$Ar\overset{+}{N_2}\overset{-}{X} \xrightarrow{CuCN/KCN} ArCN + N_2$$
} Sandmeyer's reaction

$$Ar\overset{+}{N_2}\overset{-}{X} \xrightarrow{Cu/HCl} ArCl + N_2 + CuX$$
$$Ar\overset{+}{N_2}\overset{-}{X} \xrightarrow{Cu/HBr} ArBr + N_2 + CuX$$
} Gattermann's reaction

(ii) Replacement by iodide ion–

$$Ar\overset{+}{N_2}\overset{-}{Cl} + KI \longrightarrow ArI + KCl + N_2$$

Benzene diazonium chloride　　Iodobenzene

(iii) Replacement by fluoride ion— (Balz-Schiemann reaction)

(a) $ArN_2^+Cl^- + HBF_4 \longrightarrow ArN_2^+BF_4^-$

(b) $Ar\overset{+}{N_2}\overset{-}{BF_4} \xrightarrow{\Delta} Ar-F + BF_3 + N_2$

(iv) Replacement by H—

(a) $Ar\overset{+}{N_2}\overset{-}{Cl} + H_3PO_2 + H_2O \longrightarrow ArH + N_2 + H_3PO_3 + HCl$

(b) $Ar\overset{+}{N_2}\overset{-}{Cl} + CH_3CH_2OH \longrightarrow ArH + N_2 + CH_3CHO + HCl$

(b) Retention of diazo group: The azo products obtained have an extended conjugate system having both the aromatic rings joined through the –N=N– bond. Benzene diazonium chloride reacts with phenol in which the phenol molecule at its *para* position is coupled with the diazonium salt to form *p*-hydroxyazobenzene. This type of reaction is known as coupling reaction. Similarly, the reaction of diazonium salt with aniline yields *p*-aminoazobenzene. This is an example of electrophilic substitution reaction.

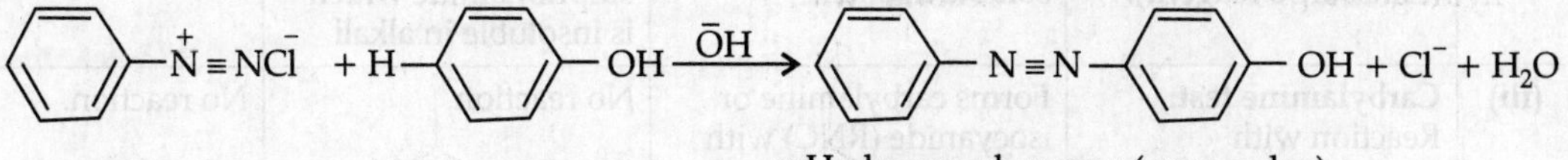

p-Hydroxyazobenzene (orange dye)

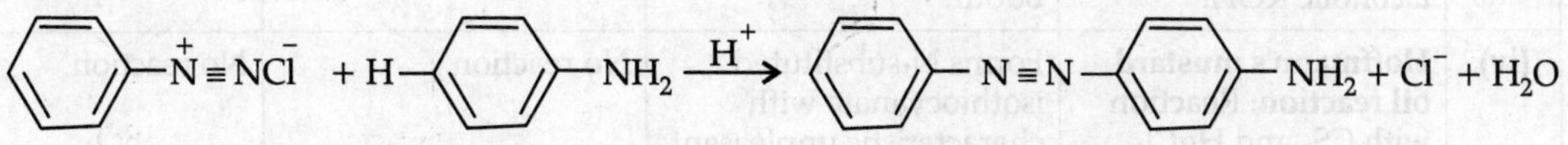

p-Aminoazobenzene (yellow dye)

- **Synthesis of organic compounds from diazonium salts:**

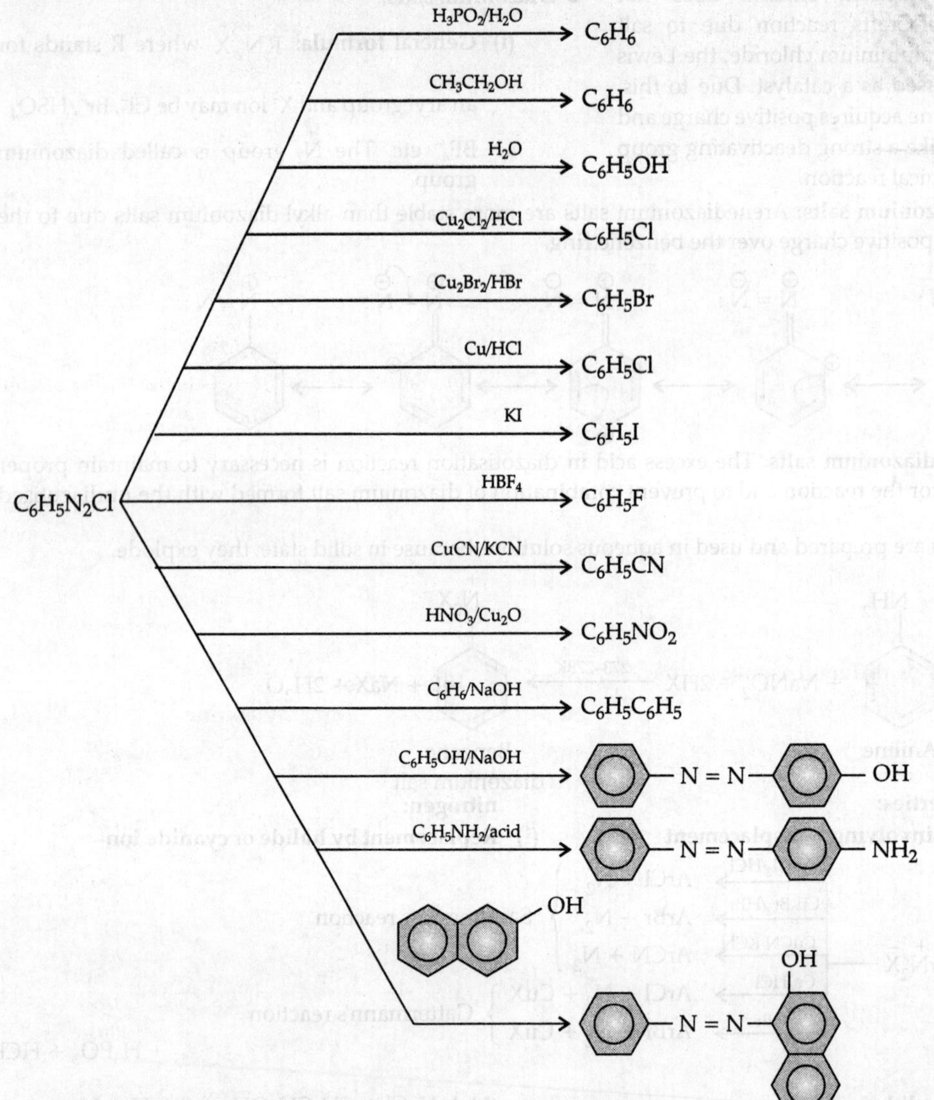

Identification of Primary, Secondary and Tertiary Amines

S.No.	Test	Primary amine	Secondary amine	Tertiary amine
(i)	Reaction with nitrous acid.	Gives alcohol with effervescence of N_2 gas.	Gives oily nitrosoamine which gives Liebermann's nitrosoamine test.	Forms nitrite in cold soluble in water and on heating gives nitrosoamine
(ii)	Reaction with benzene sulphonyl chloride (Hinsberg's reagent).	Gives N-alkyl benzene-sulphonamide which is soluble in alkali.	Gives N, N-dialkyl benzene sulphonamide which is insoluble in alkali.	No reaction.
(iii)	**Carbylamine test:** Reaction with chloroform and alcoholic KOH.	Forms carbylamine or isocyanide (RNC) with characteristic unpleasant odour.	No reaction.	No reaction.
(iv)	**Hoffmann's mustard oil reaction:** Reaction with CS_2 and $HgCl_2$.	Forms N-substituted isothiocyanate with characteristic unpleasant smell of mustard oil.	No reaction.	No reaction.

NCERT CORNER

Intext Questions

Page - 262

Q. 9.1. Classify the following amines as primary, secondary or tertiary.

(i) 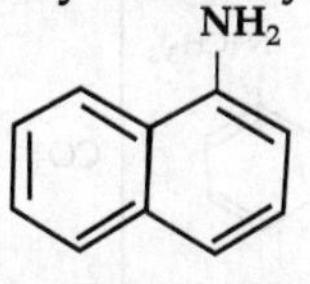

(ii) 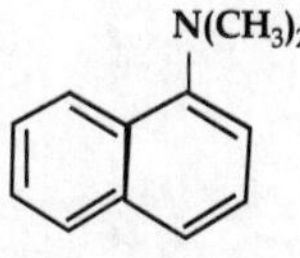

(iii) $(C_2H_5)_2CHNH_2$ (iv) $(C_2H_5)_2NH$

Ans. (i) 1° (primary amines)

(ii) 3° (tertiary amines)

(iii) 1° (primary amines)

(iv) 2° (secondary amines)

Q. 9.2. (i) Write structures of different isomeric amines corresponding to the molecular formula, $C_4H_{11}N$.

(ii) Write IUPAC names of all the isomers.

(iii) What type of isomerism is exhibited by different pairs of amines?

Ans. (i), (ii) The structures and their IUPAC names of different isomeric amines corresponding to the molecular formula, $C_4H_{11}N$ are given below:

(a) $CH_3–CH_2–CH_2–CH_2–NH_2$

Butanamine (1°)

(b) $CH_3—CH_2—CH(NH_2)—CH_3$

Butan-2-amine (2°)

(c) $CH_3—CH(CH_3)—CH_2—NH_2$

2-Methylpropanamine (1°)

(d) $CH_3—C(CH_3)_2—NH_2$

2-Methylpropan-2-amine (1°)

(e) CH_3-CH_2-CH_2-NH-CH_3

N-Methylpropanamine (2°)

(f) CH_3-CH_2-NH-CH_2-CH_3

N-Ethylethanamine (2°)

(g) $CH_3—CH(CH_3)—NH—CH_3$

N-Methylpropan-2-amine (2°)

(h) $CH_3—CH_2—N(CH_3)—CH_3$

N, N-Dimethylethanamine (3°)

(iii) The pairs (a) — (b) and (e) — (g) exhibit position isomerism.

The pairs (a) — (c), (a) — (d), (b) — (c), (b) — (d) exhibit chain isomerism.

The pairs (e) — (f) and (f) — (g) exhibit metamerism.

All *primary* amines exhibit functional isomerism with *secondary* and *tertiary* amines and vice-versa.

Page - 265

Q. 9.3. How will you convert

(i) Benzene into aniline

(ii) Benzene into N, N-dimethylaniline

(iii) $Cl-(CH_2)_4-Cl$ into hexane-1, 6-diamine?

Ans. (i)

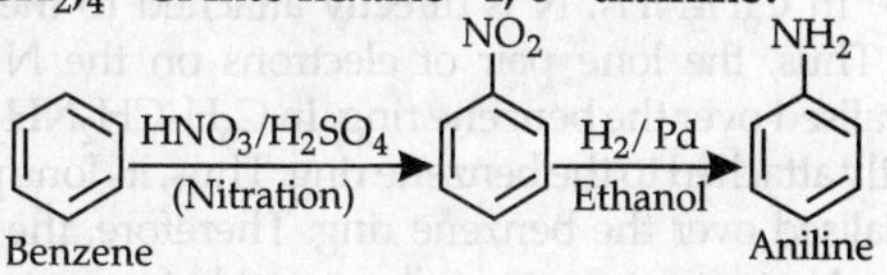

(ii)

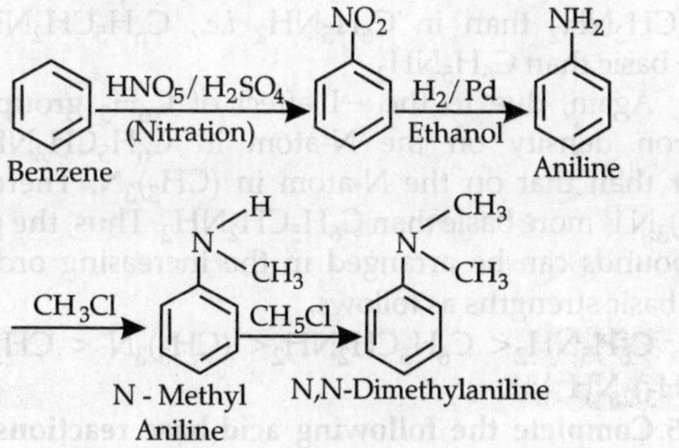

(iii) $Cl–(CH_2)_4–Cl \xrightarrow{\text{Ethanolic NaCN}} N≡C–(CH_2)_4–C≡N$

1, 4–Dichlorobutane

$\downarrow H_2/Ni$

$H_2N–CH_2–(CH_2)_4–CH_2–NH_2$

Hexane – 1,6 - Diamine

Page - 274

Q. 9.4. Arrange the following in increasing order of their basic strength:

(i) $C_2H_5NH_2$, $C_6H_5NH_2$, NH_3, $C_6H_5CH_2NH_2$ and $(C_2H_5)_2NH$

(ii) $C_2H_5NH_2$, $(C_2H_5)_2NH$, $(C_2H_5)_3N$, $C_6H_5NH_2$

(iii) CH_3NH_2, $(CH_3)_2NH$, $(CH_3)_3N$, $C_6H_5NH_2$, $C_6H_5CH_2NH_2$.

Ans. (i) Considering the inductive effect of alkyl groups, NH_3, $C_2H_5NH_2$, and $(C_2H_5)_2NH$ can be arranged in the increasing order of their basic strengths as:

$$NH_3 < C_2H_5NH_2 < (C_2H_5)_2NH$$

Again, $C_6H_5NH_2$ has proton acceptability less than NH_3. Thus, we have:

$$C_6H_5NH_2 < NH_3 < C_2H_5NH_2 < (C_2H_5)_2NH$$

Due to the $-I$ effect of C_6H_5 group, the electron density on the N-atom in $C_6H_5CH_2NH_2$ is lower than that on the N-atom in $C_2H_5NH_2$, but more than that in NH_3. Therefore, the given compounds can be arranged in the order of their basic strengths as:

$$C_6H_5NH_2 < NH_3 < C_6H_5CH_2NH_2 < C_2H_5NH_2 < (C_2H_5)_2NH$$

(ii) Considering the inductive effect and the steric hindrance of the alkyl groups, $C_2H_5NH_2$, $(C_2H_5)_2NH$, and their basic strengths as follows:

$$C_6H_5NH_2 < (C_2H_5)_3N < (C_2H_5)_2NH$$

Again, due to the $-R$ effect of C_6H_5 group, the electron density on the N atom in $C_6H_5NH_2$ is lower than that on the N atom in $C_2H_5NH_2$. Therefore, the basicity of $C_6H_5NH_2$ is lower than that of $C_2H_5NH_2$. Hence, the given compounds can be arranged in the increasing order of their basic strengths as follows:

$$C_6H_5NH_2 < C_2H_5NH_2 < (C_2H_5)_3N < (C_2H_5)_2NH$$

(iii) Considering the inductive effect and the steric hindrance of alkyl groups, CH_3NH_2, $(CH_3)_2NH$, and $(CH_3)_3N$ can be arranged in the increasing order of their basic strengths as:

$$(CH_3)_3N < CH_3NH_2 < (CH_3)_2NH$$

In $C_6H_5NH_2$, N is directly attached to the benzene ring. Thus, the lone pair of electrons on the N–atom is delocalised over the benzene ring. In $C_6H_5CH_2NH_2$, N is not directly attached to the benzene ring. Thus, its lone pair is not delocalised over the benzene ring. Therefore, the electrons on the N atom are more easily available for protonation in $C_6H_5CH_2NH_2$ than in $C_6H_5NH_2$ *i.e.*, $C_6H_5CH_2NH_2$ is more basic than $C_6H_5NH_2$.

Again, due to the $-I$ effect of C_6H_5 group, the electron density on the N-atom in $C_6H_5CH_2NH_2$ is lower than that on the N-atom in $(CH_3)_3N$. Therefore, $(CH_3)_3N$ is more basic than $C_6H_5CH_2NH_2$. Thus, the given compounds can be arranged in the increasing order of their basic strengths as follows.

$$C_6H_5NH_2 < C_6H_5CH_2NH_2 < (CH_3)_3N < CH_3NH_2 < (CH_3)_2NH$$

Q. 9.5. Complete the following acid-base reactions and name the products :

(i) $CH_3CH_2CH_2NH_2 + HCl \rightarrow$

(ii) $(C_2H_5)N + HCl \rightarrow$

Ans.

(i) $CH_3CH_2CH_2NH_2 + HCl \rightarrow CH_3CH_2CH_2NH_3^+ Cl^-$

n-propyl ammonium chloride

(ii) $(C_2H_5)N + HCl \rightarrow C_2H_5N^+ Cl^-$

tri-ethyl ammonium chloride

Q. 9.6. Write reactions of the final alkylation product of aniline with excess of methyl iodide in the presence of sodium carbonate solution.

Ans. Aniline reacts with methyl iodide to produce N, N-dimethylaniline.

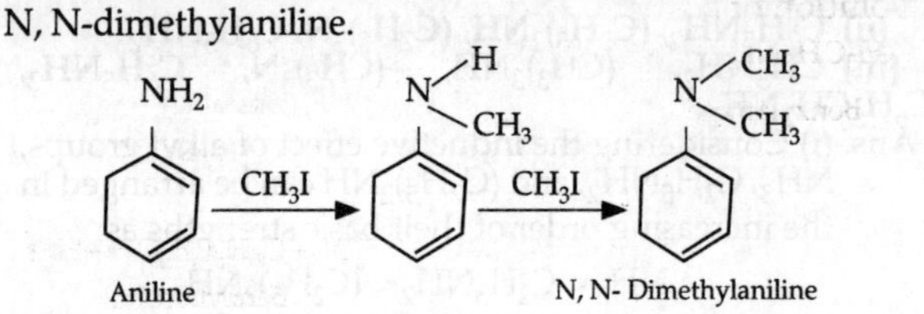

With excess methyl iodide, in the presence of Na_2CO_3 solution, N, N-dimethylaniline produces N, N, N-trimethylanilinium carbonate.

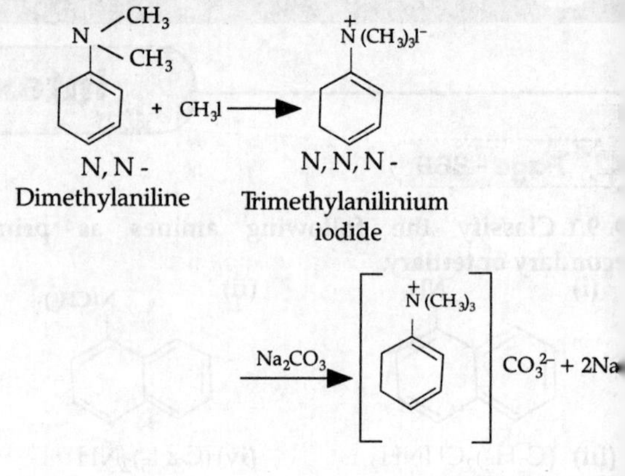

Q. 9.7. Write chemical reaction of aniline with benzoyl chloride and write the name of the product obtained.

Ans.

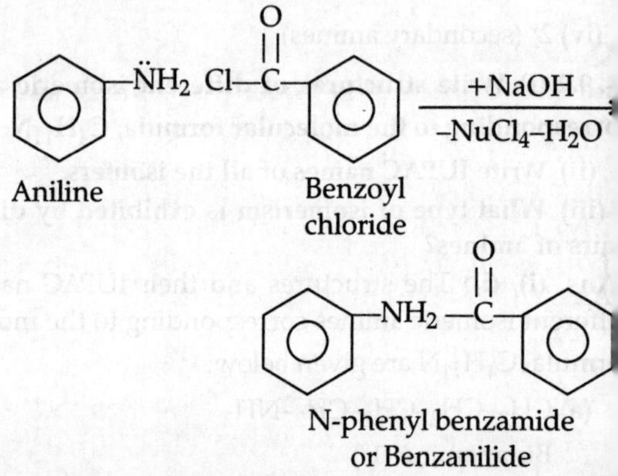

Q. 9.8. Write structures of different isomers corresponding to the molecular formula, C_3H_9N. Write IUPAC names of the isomers which will liberate nitrogen gas on treatment with nitrous acid.

Ans. The structures of different isomers corresponding to the molecular formula, C_3H_9N are given below:

(a) $CH_3–CH_2–CH_2–NH_2$

Propan-1-amine (1°)

(b) $CH_3—CH(NH_2)—CH_3$

Propan-2-amine (1°)

(c) $CH_3–NH–C_2H_5$

N-methylethanamine (2°)

(d) $CH_3—N(CH_3)—CH_3$

N,N-Dimethylmethanamine (3°)

1° amines, (a) propan-1-amine, and (b) Propan-2-amine will liberate nitrogen gas on treatment with nitrous acid.

$$CH_3CH_2CH_2NH_2 + HNO_2 \rightarrow CH_3CH_2CH_2OH + N_2 + HCl$$

Propan - 1 - amine → Propan - 1 - ol

$$CH_3-CH(NH_2)-CH_3 + HNO_2 \rightarrow CH_3-CH(OH)-CH_3 + N_2 + HCl$$

Propan - 1 - amine → Propan - 2 - ol

Page - 277

Q. 9.9. Convert

(i) 3-Methylaniline into 3-nitrotoluene.

(ii) Aniline into 1,3,5-tribromobenzene.

Ans. (i)

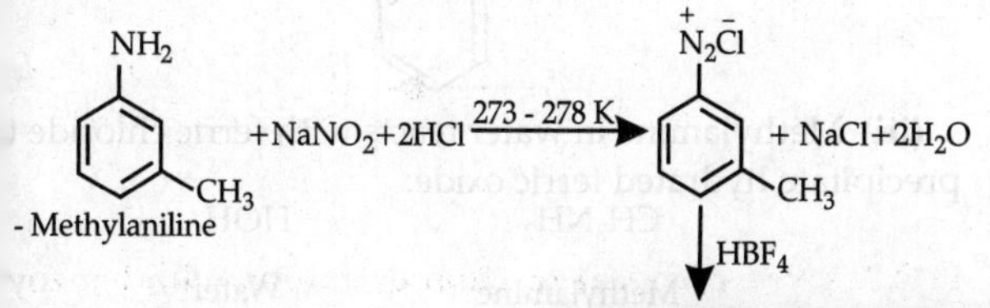

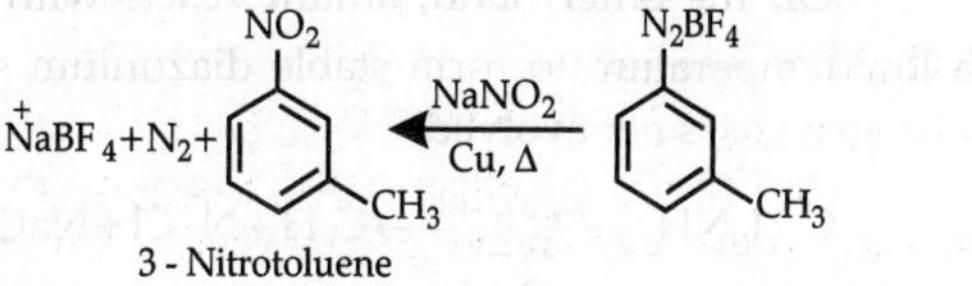

3 - Nitrotoluene

(ii)

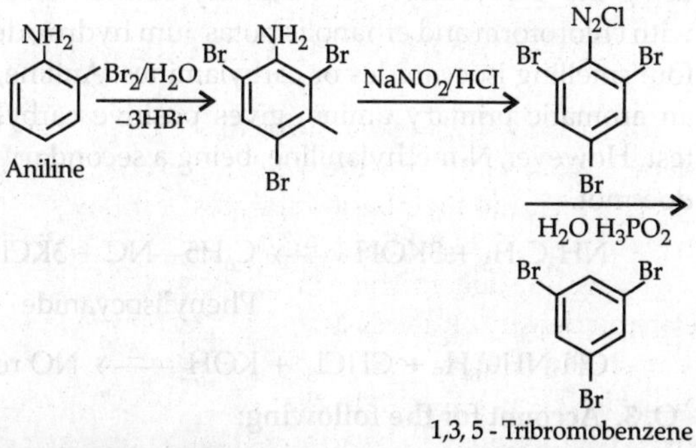

1,3, 5 - Tribromobenzene

Exercise Questions

Q. 1. Write IUPAC names of the following compounds and classify them into primary, secondary and tertiary amines.

(i) $(CH_3)_2$ $CHNH_2$ **(ii) $CH_3(CH_2)_2NH_2$**

(iii) $CH_3NHCH(CH_3)_2$ **(iv) $(CH_3)_3CNH_2$**

(v) $C_6H_5NHCH_3$ **(vi) $(CH_3CH_2)_2NCH_3$**

(vii) *m*-$BrC_6H_4NH_2$ **[NCERT Ex. Q. 9.1, Page 278]**

Ans. (i) 1-Methylethanamine (1° amine)

(ii) Propan-1-amine (1° amine)

(iii) N-Methyl-2-methylethanamine (2° amine)

(iv) 2-Methylpropan-2-amine (1° amine)

(v) N-Methylbenzamine or N-methylaniline (2° amine)

(vi) N-Ethyl-N-methylethanamine (3° amine)

(vii) 3-Bromobenzenamine or 3-bromoaniline (1° amine)

Q. 2. Give one chemical test to distinguish between the following pairs of compounds.

(i) Methylamine and dimethylamine

(ii) Secondary and tertiary amines

(iii) Ethylamine and aniline

(iv) Aniline and benzylamine

(v) Aniline and N-methylaniline.

[NCERT Ex. Q. 9.2, Page 278]

Ans. (i) Methylamine and dimethylamine can be distinguished by the carbylamine test.

Carbylamine test: Aliphatic and aromatic primary amines on heating with chloroform and ethanolic potassium hydroxide form foul-smelling isocyanides or carbylamines. Methylamine (being an aliphatic primary amine) gives a positive carbylamine test, but dimethylamine does not.

$$CH_3\text{–}NH_2 + CHCl_3 + 3KOH \xrightarrow{\Delta} C_6H_5\text{–}NC + 3KCl + 3H_2O$$

Benzylamine (l°) → Benzylisocyanide (foul smell)

$$C_6\text{–}H_5NHCH_3 + CHCl_3 + 3KOH \xrightarrow{\Delta} \text{No reaction}$$

N-Methylaniline

(ii) Secondary and tertiary amines can be distinguished by allowing them to react with Hinsberg's reagent (benzenesulphonyl chloride, $C_6H_5SO_2Cl$).

Secondary amines react with Hinsberg's reagent to form a product that is insoluble in an alkali. For example, N, N-diethylamine reacts with Hinsberg's reagent to form N, N–diethylbenzenesulphonamide, which is insoluble in an alkali. Tertiary amines, however, do not react with Hinsberg's reagent.

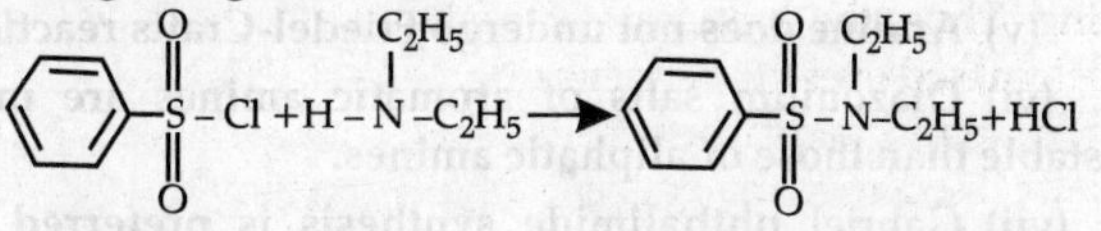

nzenesulphonyl chloride N, N - Diethylbenzenesulphonamide

(iii) Ethylamine and aniline can be distinguished using the azo-dye test. A dye is obtained when aromatic amines react with HNO_2 ($NaNO_2$ + dil.HCl) at 0-5°C, followed by a reaction with the alkaline solution of 2-naphthol. The dye is usually yellow, red, or orange in colour. Aliphatic amines gives a brisk effervescence due (to the evolution of N_2 gas) under similar conditions.

Benzenediazoniumchloride

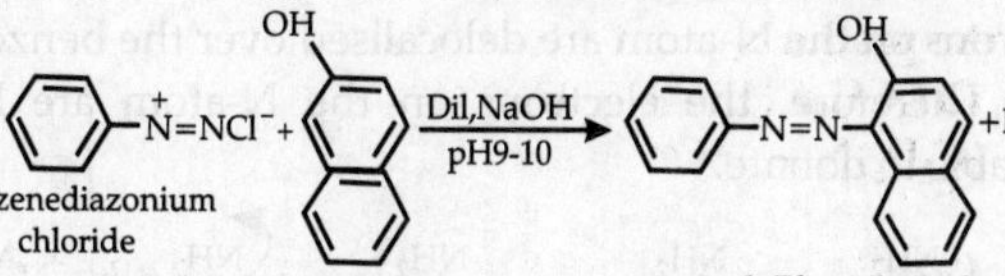

Benzenediazonium chloride 2 - Naphthol 1- Phenylazo - 2 - napthol (orangedye)

$$CH_3CH_2\text{–}NH_2 + HONO \xrightarrow{0\text{-}5°C} C_2H_5OH + N_2 + H_2O$$

(iv) Aniline and benzylamine can be distinguished by their reactions with the help of nitrous acid, which is prepared in situ from a mineral acid and sodium nitrite. Benzylamine reacts with nitrous acid to form unstable diazonium salt, which in turn gives alcohol with the evolution of nitrogen gas.

$$C_6H_5CH_2NH_2 + HNO_2 \xrightarrow{NaNO_2 + HCl} C_6H_5C_2H_2N^+Cl^-$$

Benzylamine (Unstable)

$$\downarrow H_2O$$

$$\uparrow N_2 + C_6H_5CH_2OH + HCl$$

Benzylalcohol

On the other hand, aniline reacts with HNO_2 at a low temperature to form stable diazonium salt. Thus, nitrogen gas is not evolved.

$$C_6H_5NH_2 \xrightarrow[273\text{-}278K]{NaNO_2+HCl} C_6H_5\text{-}\overset{+}{N_2}\overset{-}{Cl} + NaCl + 2H_2O$$

(v) Aniline and N-methylaniline can be distinguished using the Carbylamine test. Primary amines, on heating with chloroform and ethanolic potassium hydroxide, form foul smelling isocyanides or carbylamines. Aniline, being an aromatic primary amine, gives positive carbylamine test. However, N-methylaniline, being a secondary amine does not.

$$NH_2C_6H_5 + 3KOH \xrightarrow{\Delta} C_6H5\text{—}NC + 3KCl + 3H_2$$

Phenylisocyanide

$$CH_3NHC_6H_5 + CHCl_3 + KOH \xrightarrow{\Delta} \text{NO reaction}$$

Q. 3. Account for the following:

(i) pK_b of aniline is more than that of methylamine.

(ii) Ethylamine is soluble in water whereas aniline is not.

(iii) Methylamine in water reacts with ferric chloride to precipitate hydrated ferric oxide.

(iv) Although amino group is *o, p*-directing in aromatic electrophilic substitution reactions, aniline on nitration gives a substantial amount of *m*-nitroaniline.

(v) Aniline does not undergo Friedel-Crafts reaction.

(vi) Diazonium salts of aromatic amines are more stable than those of aliphatic amines.

(vii) Gabriel phthalimide synthesis is preferred for synthesising primary amines.

[NCERT Ex. Q. 9.3, Page 278]

Ans. (i) pK_b of aniline is more than that of methylamine:

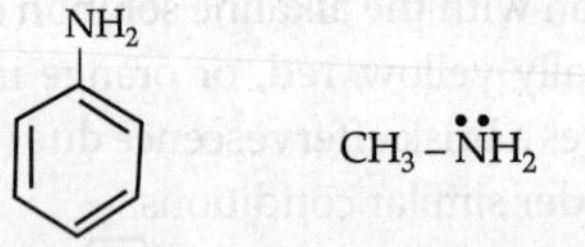

Aniline Methylamine

Aniline undergoes resonance and as a result, the electrons on the N-atom are delocalised over the benzene ring. Therefore, the electrons on the N-atom are less available to donate.

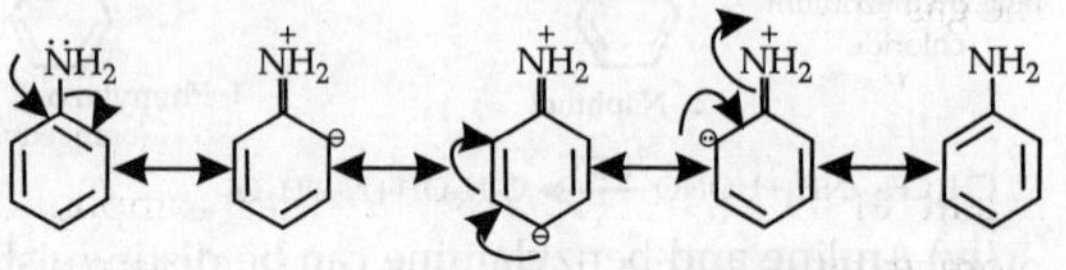

On the other hand, in case of methylamine (due to the +I effect of methyl group), the electron density on the N-atom is increased. As a result, aniline is less basic than methylamine. Thus, pK_b of aniline is more than that of methylamine.

(ii) Ethylamine is soluble in water whereas aniline is not.

Ethylamine when added to water forms intermolecular H−bonds with water. Hence, it is soluble in water.

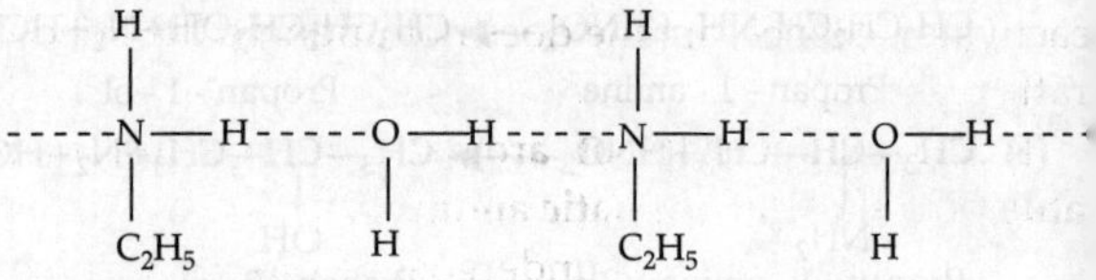

Ethylamine

But aniline does not undergo H-bonding with water to a very large extent due to the presence of a large hydrophobic $-C_6H_5$ group. Hence, aniline is insoluble in water.

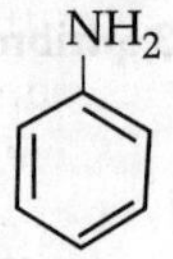

(iii) Methylamine in water reacts with ferric chloride to precipitate hydrated ferric oxide:

CH_3NH_2 HOH

Methylamine Water

Due to the +I effect of $-CH_3$ group, methylamine is more basic than water. Therefore, in water, methylamine produces OH^- ions by accepting H^+ ions from water.

$$CH_3-NH_2 + H-OH \rightarrow CH_3-\overset{+}{N}H_3 + OH^-$$

Ferric chloride ($FeCl_3$) dissociates in water to form Fe^{3+} and Cl^- ions.

$$FeCl_3 \rightarrow Fe^{3+} + 3Cl^-$$

Then, OH^- ion reacts with Fe^{3+} ion to form precipitate of hydrated ferric oxide.

$$2Fe^{3+} + 6OH^- \longrightarrow \underset{\text{Hydrated ferric oxide}}{Fe_2O_3 \cdot 3H_2O}$$

(iv) Although amino group is *o, p*-directing in aromatic electrophilic substitution reactions, aniline on nitration gives a substantial amount of *m*-nitroaniline.

Nitration is carried out in an acidic medium. In an acidic medium, aniline is protonated to give anilinium ion (which is *meta*-directing).

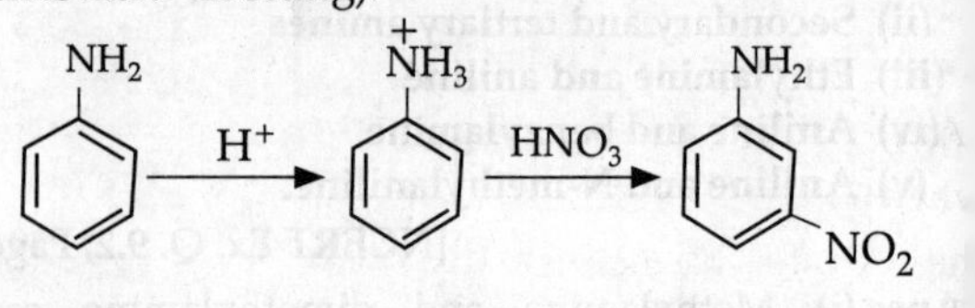

Aniline **Anilinium ion** ***m*-Nitroaniline (47%)**

For this reason, aniline on nitration gives substantial amount of *m*-nitroaniline.

(v) Aniline does not undergo Friedel-Crafts reaction:

A Friedel-Crafts reaction is carried out in the presence of $AlCl_3$. But $AlCl_3$ is acidic in nature, while aniline is a strong base. Thus, aniline reacts with $AlCl_3$ to form a salt (as shown in the following equation):

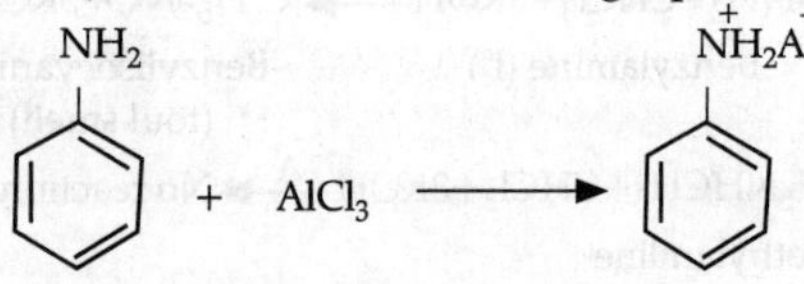

Aniline Salt

Due to the positive charge on the N-atom, electrophilic substitution in the benzene ring is eactivated. Hence, aniline does not undergo the Friedel-rafts reaction.

(f) Diazonium salts of aromatic amines are more able than those of aliphatic amines:

The diazonium ion undergoes resonance as shown elow:

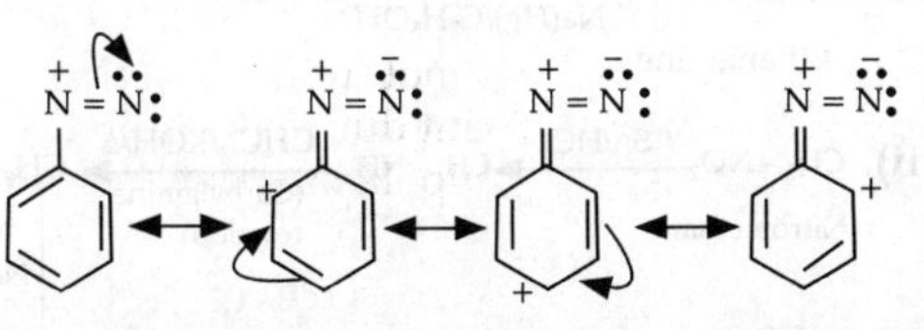

This resonance accounts for the stability of the iazonium ion. Hence, diazonium salts of aromatic amines re more stable than those of aliphatic amines.

(g) Gabriel phthalimide synthesis is preferred for ynthesising primary amines:

Gabriel phthalimide synthesis results in the formation f 1° amine only. 2° or 3° amines are not formed in this ynthesis. Thus, a pure 1° amine can be obtained. Therefore, abriel phthalimide synthesis is preferred for synthesizing rimary amines.

Q. 4. Arrange the following:

(i) In decreasing order of the pK_b values:

$C_2H_5NH_2$, $C_6H_5NHCH_3$, $(C_2H_5)_2NH$ and $C_6H_5NH_2$

(ii) In increasing order of basic strength:

$C_6H_5NH_2$, $C_6H_5N(CH_3)_2$, $(C_2H_5)_2NH$ and CH_3NH_2

(iii) In increasing order of basic strength:

(a) Aniline, *p*-nitroaniline and *p*-toluidine

(b) $C_6H_5NH_2$, $C_6H_5NHCH_3$, $C_6H_5CH_2NH_2$.

(iv) In decreasing order of basic strength in gas phase:

$C_2H_5NH_2$, $(C_2H_5)_2NH$, $(C_2H_5)_3N$ and NH_3

(v) In increasing order of boiling point:

C_2H_5OH, $(CH_3)_2NH$, $C_2H_5NH_2$

(vi) In increasing order of solubility in water:

$C_6H_5NH_2$, $(C_2H_5)_2NH$, $C_2H_5NH_2$.

[NCERT Ex. Q. 9.4, Page 278]

Ans. (i) In $C_2H_5NH_2$, only one $-C_2H_5$ group is present hile in $(C_2H_5)_2NH$, two $-C_2H_5$ groups are present. Thus, he +I effect is more in $(C_2H_5)_2NH$ than in $C_2H_5NH_2$. herefore, the electron density over the N-atom is more in $(C_2H_5)_2NH$ than in $C_2H_5NH_2$. Hence, $(C_2H_5)_2NH$ is more asic than $C_2H_5NH_2$.

Also, both $C_6H_5NHCH_3$ and $C_6H_5NH_2$ are less basic han $(C_2H_5)_2NH$ and $C_2H_5NH_2$ due to the delocalization f the lone pair in the former of the two. Further, among $C_6H_5NHCH_3$ and $C_6H_5NH_2$, the former will be more basic ue to the + I effect of $-CH_3$ group. Hence, the order of ncreasing basicity of the given compounds is as follows:

$$C_6H_5NH_2 < C_6H_5NHCH_3 < C_2H_5NH_2 < (C_2H_5)_2NH$$

We know that the higher the basic strength, the ower is the pK_b values.

$$C_6H_5NH_2 > C_6H_5NHCH_3 > C_2H_5NH_2 > (C_2H_5)_2NH$$

(ii) $C_6H_5N(CH_3)_2$ is more basic than $C_6H_5NH_2$ due o the presence of the +I effect of two $-CH_3$ groups in $C_6H_5N(CH_3)_2$. Further, CH_3NH_2 contains one $-CH_3$ group while $(C_2H_5)_2NH$ contains two $-C_2H_5$ groups. Thus, $(C_2H_5)_2NH$ is more basic than $C_2H_5NH_2$.

Now, $C_6H_5N(CH_3)_2$ is less basic than CH_3NH_2 because of the – R effect of $-C_6H_5$ group.

Hence, the increasing order of the basic strengths of the given compounds is as follows:

$$C_6H_5NH_2 < C_6H_5N(CH_3)_2 < CH_3NH_2 < (C_2H_5)_2NH$$

(iii) (a)

NH₂ NH₂ NH₂

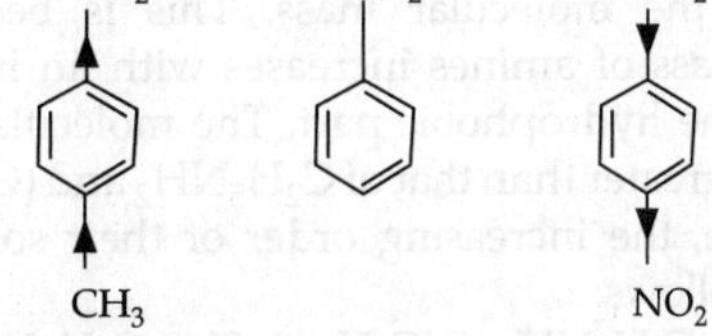

CH₃ NO₂

p- Toluidine Aniline *p*-Nitroaniline

In *p*-toluidine, the presence of electron-donating $-CH_3$ group increases the electron density on the N-atom. Thus, *p*-toluidine is more basic than aniline.

On the other hand, the presence of electron-withdrawing $-NO_2$ group decreases the electron density over the N-atom in *p*-nitroaniline. Thus, p-nitroaniline is less basic than aniline.

Hence, the increasing order of the basic strengths of the given compounds is as follows: p-Nitroaniline < Aniline < p-Toluidine.

(b) $C_6H_5NHCH_3$ is more basic than $C_6H_5NH_2$ due to the presence of electron-donating $-CH_3$ group in $C_6H_5NHCH_3$.

Again, in $C_6H_5NHCH_3$, $-C_6H_5$ group is directly attached to the N-atom. However, it is not so in $C_6H_5CH_2NH_2$. Thus, in $C_6H_5NHCH_3$, the –R effect of $-C_6H_5$ group decreases the electron density over the N-atom. Therefore, $C_6H_5CH_2NH_2$ is more basic than $C_6H_5NHCH_3$. Hence, the increasing order of the basic strengths of the given compounds is as follows:

$$C_6H_5NH_2 < C_6H_5NHCH_3 < C_6H_5CH_2NH_2.$$

(iv) In the gas phase, there is no solvation effect. As a result, the basic strength mainly depends upon the +I effect. The higher the +I effect, the stronger is the base. Also, the greater the number of alkyl groups, the higher is the +I effect. Therefore, the given compounds can be arranged in the decreasing order of their basic strengths in the gas phase as follows:

$$(C_2H_5)_3N > (C_2H_5)_2NH > C_2H_5NH_2 > NH_3$$

(v) The boiling points of compounds depend on the extent of H-bonding present in that compound. The more extensive the H-bonding in the compound, the higher is the boiling point. $(CH_3)_2NH$ contains only one H-atom whereas $C_2H_5NH_2$ contains two H-atoms. Then, $C_2H_5NH_2$ undergoes more extensive H-bonding than $(CH_3)_2NH$. Hence, the boiling point of $C_2H_5NH_2$ is higher than that of $(CH_3)_2NH$.

Further, *o* – is more electronegative than N. Thus, C_2H_5OH forms stronger H-bonds than $C_2H_5NH_2$. As a result, the boiling point of C_2H_5OH is higher than that of $C_2H_5NH_2$ and $(CH_3)_2NH$.

Now, the given compounds can be arranged in the increasing order of their boiling points as follows:

$$(CH_3)_2NH < C_2H_5NH_2 < C_2H_5OH$$

(vi) The more extensive the H-bonding, the higher is the solubility. $C_2H_5NH_2$ contains two H-atoms whereas $(C_2H_5)_2NH$ contains only one H-atom. Thus, $C_2H_5NH_2$ undergoes more extensive H−bonding than $(C_2H_5)_2NH$. Hence, the solubility in water of $C_2H_5NH_2$ is more than that of $(C_2H_5)_2NH$.

Further, the solubility of amines decreases with increase in the molecular mass. This is because the molecular mass of amines increases with an increase in the size of the hydrophobic part. The molecular mass of $C_6H_5NH_2$ is greater than that of $C_2H_5NH_2$ and $(C_2H_5)_2NH$.

Hence, the increasing order of their solubility in water is as follows:

$$C_6H_5NH_2 < (C_2H_5)_2NH < C_2H_5NH_2$$

Q. 5. How will you convert

(i) Ethanoic acid into methanamine
(ii) Hexanenitrile into 1-aminopentane
(iii) Methanol to ethanoic acid
(iv) Ethanamine into methanamine
(v) Ethanoic acid into propanoic acid
(vi) Methanamine into ethanamine
(vii) Nitromethane into dimethylamine
(viii) Propanoic acid into ethanoic acid

[NCERT Ex. Q. 9.5, Page 279]

Ans.

(i) $$\underset{\text{Ethanoic acid}}{CH_3COOH} \xrightarrow{SOCl_2} CH_3COCl \xrightarrow{NH_3(\text{excess})} CH_3CONH_2 \xrightarrow{Br_2/NaOH} \underset{\text{Methanamine}}{CH_3NH_2}$$

(ii) $$\underset{\text{Hexanenitrile}}{C_5H_{11}CN} \xrightarrow{H^+/H_2O} C_5H_{11}-COOH \xrightarrow{SOCl_2} C_5H_{11}-COCl \xrightarrow{NH_3(\text{excess})} C_5H_{11}-CONH_2 \xrightarrow{Br_2/KOH} \underset{\text{1-Aminopentane}}{C_5H_{11}-NH_2}$$

(iii) $$\underset{\text{Methanol}}{CH_3OH} \xrightarrow{PCl_5} CH_3Cl \xrightarrow{\text{Ethanoic NaCN}} CH_3CN \xrightarrow{H^+/H_2O} \underset{\text{Ethanoic acid}}{CH_3COOH}$$

(iv) $$\underset{\text{Ethanamine}}{CH_3-CH_2-NH_2} \xrightarrow{NaNO_2/HCl} [CH_3-CH_2-\overset{+}{N_2}\overset{-}{Cl}] \xrightarrow{H_2O} CH_3-CH_2-OH \xrightarrow{KMnO_4/H^+} CH_3COOH \xrightarrow[\Delta]{NH_3\text{ (excess)}} CH_3CONH_2 \xrightarrow{Br_2/NaOH} \underset{\text{Methanamine}}{CH_3-NH_2}$$

(v) $$\underset{\text{Ethanoic acid}}{CH_3COOH} \xrightarrow[\text{(ii) } H_3O^+]{\text{(i) } LiAlH_4/\text{ether}} CH_3CH_2OH \xrightarrow{PCl_5} CH_3CH_2Cl \xrightarrow{\text{Ethanolic NaCN}} CH_3CH_2CN \xrightarrow{H^+/H_2O} \underset{\text{Propanoic acid}}{CH_3CH_2COOH}$$

(vi) $$\underset{\text{Methanamine}}{CH_3-NH_2} \xrightarrow{NaNO_2/HCl} [CH_3-\overset{+}{N_2}\overset{-}{Cl}] \xrightarrow{H_2O} CH_3OH \xrightarrow{PCl_5} CH_3Cl \xrightarrow{\text{Ethanolic NaCN}} CH_3CN \xrightarrow[Na(Hg)/C_2H_5OH]{H_2/Ni} \underset{\text{Ethanamine}}{CH_3CH_2NH_2}$$

(vii) $$\underset{\text{Nitromethane}}{CH_3-NO_2} \xrightarrow{Sn/HCl} CH_3-NH_2 \xrightarrow[\text{(Carbylamine reaction)}]{CHCl_3/KOH/\Delta} CH_3-NC \xrightarrow{Na/C_2H_5OH} \underset{\text{Dimethylamine}}{CH_3-NH-CH_3}$$

(viii) $$\underset{\text{Propanoic acid}}{CH_3CH_2COOH} \xrightarrow[\Delta]{NH_3(\text{excess})} CH_3CH_2CONH_2 \xrightarrow[\text{(Hoffmann bromamide reaction)}]{Br_2/KOH} CH_3CH_2NH_2 \xrightarrow{NaNO_2/HCl} [CH_3CH_2\overset{+}{N_2}\overset{-}{Cl}] \xrightarrow{H_2O} CH_3CH_2OH \xrightarrow{KMnO_4/H^+} \underset{\text{Ethanoic acid}}{CH_3COOH}$$

Q. 6. Describe a method for the identification of primary, secondary and tertiary amines. Also write chemical equations of the reactions involved.

[NCERT Ex. Q. 9.6, Page 279]

Ans. *Primary, secondary* and *tertiary* amines can be identified and distinguished by Hinsberg's test. In this test the amines are allowed to react with Hinsberg's reagent benzenesulphonyl chloride ($C_6H_5SO_2Cl$). The three types of amines react differently with Hinsberg's reagent. Therefore, they can be easily identified using Hinsberg's reagent. Primary amines react with benzenesulphonyl chloride to form N-alkylbenzenesulphonyl amide which is soluble in alkali.

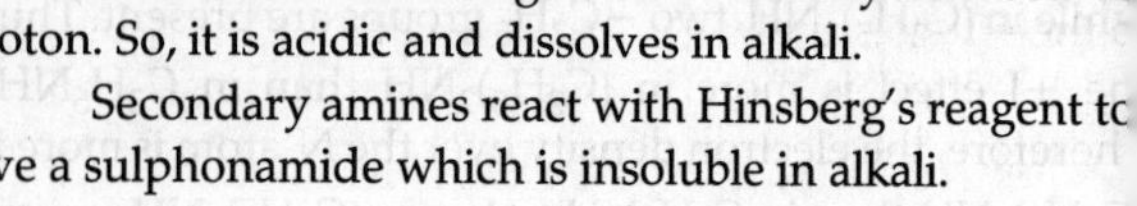

Benzenesulphonyl chloride — Propanamine — N - Propylbenzenesulphonamide

Due to the presence of a strong electron-withdrawing sulphonyl group in the sulphonamide, the H−atom attached to nitrogen can be easily released as proton. So, it is acidic and dissolves in alkali.

Secondary amines react with Hinsberg's reagent to give a sulphonamide which is insoluble in alkali.

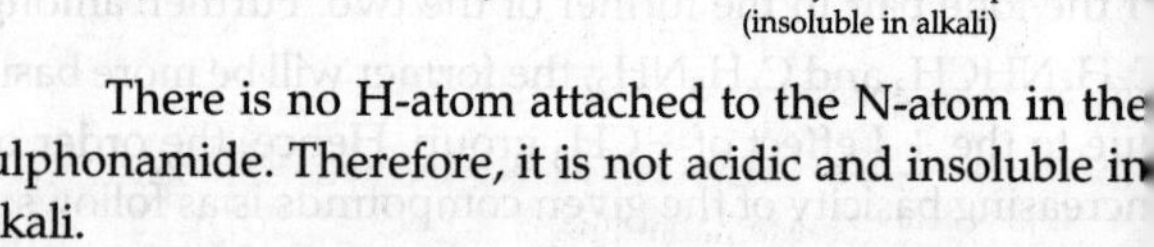

Benzenesulphonyl chloride — Dimethylamine — N, N - Dimethylbenzenesulphonamide (insoluble in alkali)

There is no H-atom attached to the N-atom in the sulphonamide. Therefore, it is not acidic and insoluble in alkali.

On the other hand, tertiary amines do not react with Hinsberg's reagent at all.

Q. 7. Write short notes on the following:

(i) Carbylamine reaction
(ii) Diazotisation
(iii) Hoffmann bromamide reaction

(iv) Coupling reaction
(v) Ammonolysis
(vi) Acetylation
(vii) Gabriel phthalimide synthesis.

[NCERT Ex. Q. 9.7, Page 279]

Ans. (i) Carbylamine reaction: It is used as a test for ꞏe identification of primary amines. When aliphatic and romatic primary amines are heated with chloroform nd ethanolic potassium hydroxide, carbylamines (or ocyanides) are formed. These carbylamines have very npleasant odours. Secondary and tertiary amines do not espond to this test.

$$-NH_2 + CHCl_3 + 3KOH(alc.) \xrightarrow{\Delta} R-NC + 3KCl + 3H_2O$$

rimary mine   Chloroform   Potasium hydroxide   carbylamine

$$H_3-NH_2 + CHCl_3 + 3KOH(alc.) \xrightarrow{\Delta} CH_3-NC + 3KCl + 3H_2O$$

Methanamine   Methyl carblylamine or methyl isocyanide

(ii) Diazotisation: Aromatic primary amines react with itrous acid (prepared *in situ* from $NaNO_2$ and a mineral cid such as HCl) at low temperatures (273-278 K) to form iazonium salts. This conversion of aromatic primary mines into diazonium salts is known as diazotization. For xample, on treatment with $NaNO_2$ and HCl at 273-278 K, niline produces benzenediazonium chloride, with NaCl nd H_2O as by-products.

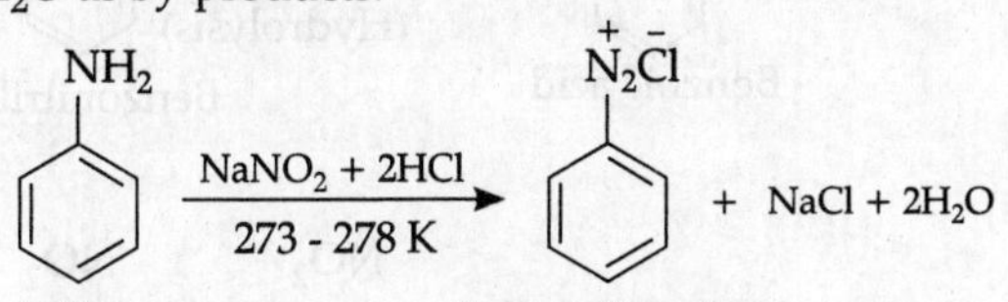

Aniline   Benzenediazonium chloride

(iii) Hoffmann bromamide reaction: When an amide is reated with bromine in an aqueous or ethanolic solution f sodium hydroxide, a primary amine with one carbon tom less than the original amide is produced. This egradation reaction is known as Hoffmann bromamide eaction. This reaction involves the migration of an alkyl r aryl group from the carbonyl carbon atom of the amide o the nitrogen atom.

$$\underset{\text{Amide}}{R-\overset{O}{\overset{\|}{C}}-NH_2} + Br_2 + 4NaOH \longrightarrow \underset{\text{Primay amine}}{R-NH_2} + Na_2CO_3 + 2NaBr + 2H_2O$$

$$\underset{\text{Ethanamide}}{CH_3-\overset{O}{\overset{\|}{C}}-NH_2} + Br_2 + 4NaOH \longrightarrow \underset{\text{Methanamine}}{CH_3-NH_2} + Na_2CO_3 + 2NaBr + 2H_2O$$

$$\underset{\text{Benzamide}}{C_6H_5-\overset{O}{\overset{\|}{C}}-NH_2} + Br_2 + 4NaOH \longrightarrow \underset{\text{Aniline}}{C_6H_5-NH_2} + Na_2CO_3 + 2NaBr + 2H_2O$$

(iv) Coupling reaction: The reaction of joining two aromatic rings through the $-N=N-$ bond is known as coupling reaction. Arene diazonium salts such as benzene diazonium salts react with phenol or aromatic amines to form coloured azo compounds.

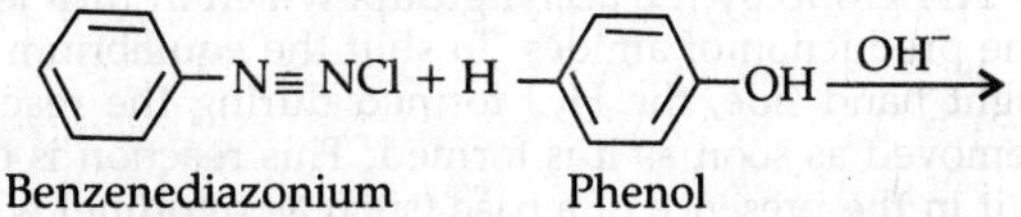

Benzenediazonium chloride   Phenol

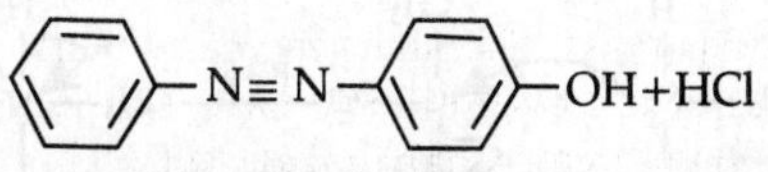

p-Hydroxyazobenzene (Orange dye)

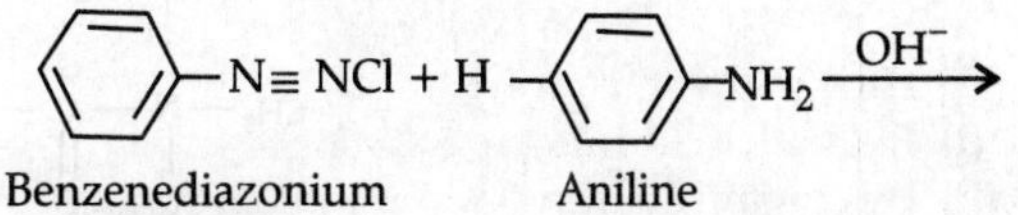

Benzenediazonium chloride   Aniline

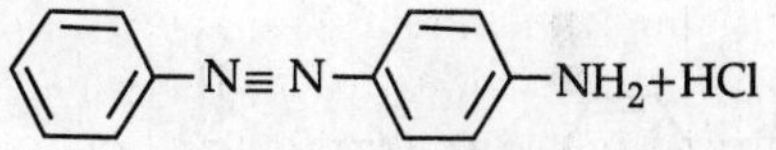

p-Aminoazobenzene (Yellow dye)

It can be observed that, the para-positions of phenol and aniline are coupled with the diazonium salt. This reaction proceeds through electrophilic substitution.

(v) Ammonolysis: When an alkyl or benzyl halide is allowed to react with an ethanolic solution of ammonia, it undergoes nucleophilic substitution reaction in which the halogen atom is replaced by an amino $(-NH_2)$ group. This process of cleavage of the carbon-halogen bond is known as ammonolysis.

$$\underset{\text{(Nucleophile)}}{\underset{\text{Ammonia}}{\ddot{N}H_3(alc)}} + \underset{\text{Alkyl halide}}{R-X} \quad \underset{\text{ammonium salt}}{\underset{\text{Substituted}}{R-\overset{+}{N}H_3\overset{-}{X}}}$$

When this substituted ammonium salt is treated with a strong base such as sodium hydroxide, amine is obtained.

$$R-\overset{+}{N}H_3\overset{-}{X} + NaOH \rightarrow \underset{\text{Amine}}{R-NH_2} + H_2O + NaX$$

Though primary amine is produced as the major product, this process produces a mixture of primary, secondary and tertiary amines, and also a quaternary ammonium salt as shown.

$$\underset{(1^\circ)}{RNH_2} \xrightarrow{RX} \underset{(2^\circ)}{R_2NH} \xrightarrow{RX} \underset{(3^\circ)}{R_3N} \xrightarrow{RX} \underset{\text{Quaternary ammonium salt}}{R_4\overset{+}{N}\overset{-}{X}}$$

(vi) Acetylation : Acetylation (or ethanoylation) is the process of introducing an acetyl group into a molecule.

Aliphatic and aromatic *primary* and *secondary* amines undergo acetylation reaction by nucleophilic substitution when treated with acid chlorides, anhydrides or esters. This reaction involves the replacement of the hydrogen atom of $-NH_2$ or $> NH$ group by the acetyl group, which in turn leads to the production of amides. To shift the equilibrium to the right hand side, the HCl formed during the reaction is removed as soon as it is formed. This reaction is carried out in the presence of a base (such as pyridine) which is stronger than the amine.

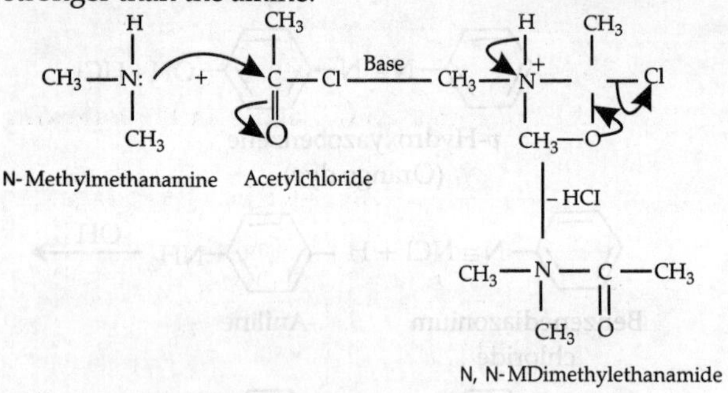

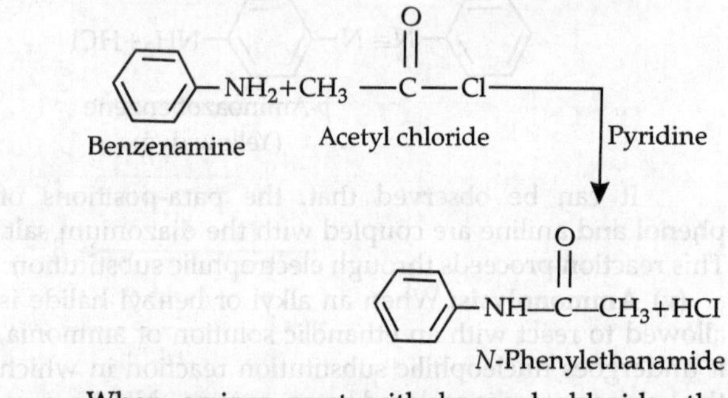

When amines react with benzoyl chloride, the reaction is also known as benzoylation.

For example,

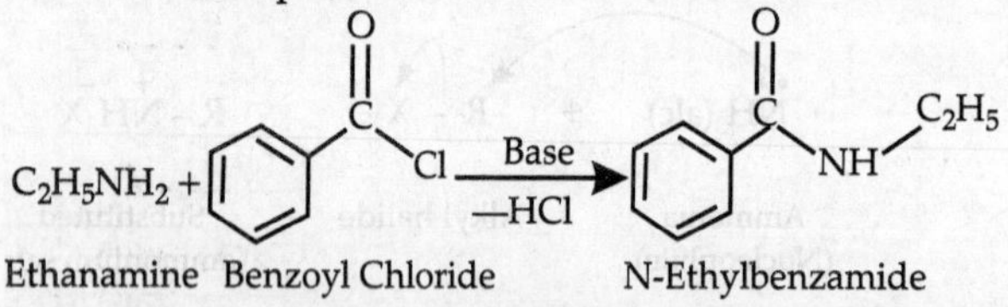

(vii) Gabriel phthalimide synthesis: Gabriel phthalimide synthesis is a very useful method for the preparation of aliphatic primary amines. It involves the treatment of phthalimide with ethanolic potassium hydroxide to form potassium salt of phthalimide. This salt is further heated with alkyl halide, followed by alkaline hydrolysis to yield the corresponding primary amine.

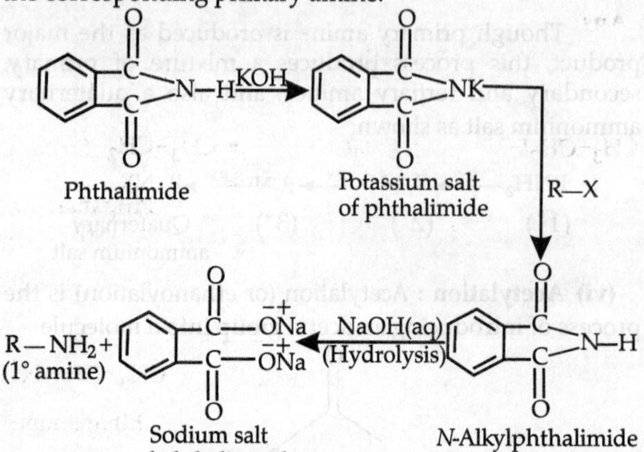

Q. 8. Accomplish the following conversions:

(i) Nitrobenzene to benzoic acid

(ii) Benzene to m-bromophenol

(iii) Benzoic acid to aniline

(iv) Aniline to 2,4,6-tribromofluorobenzene

(v) Benzyl chloride to 2-phenylethanamine

(vi) Chlorobenzene to p-chloroaniline

(vii) Aniline to p-bromoaniline

(viii) Benzamide to toluene

(ix) Aniline to benzyl alcohol.

[NCERT Ex. Q. 9.8, Page 27

Ans.

(i)

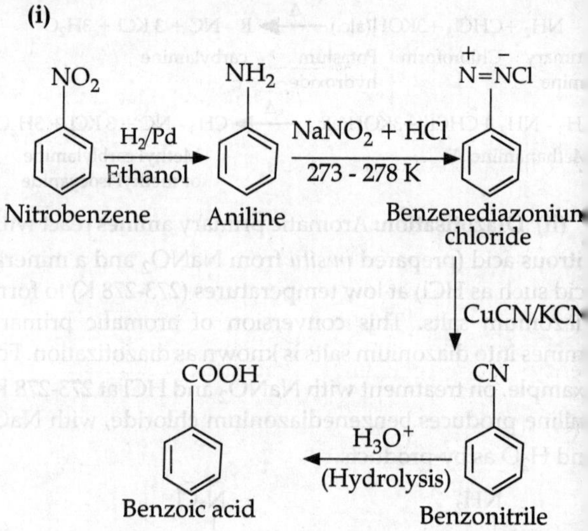

(ii)

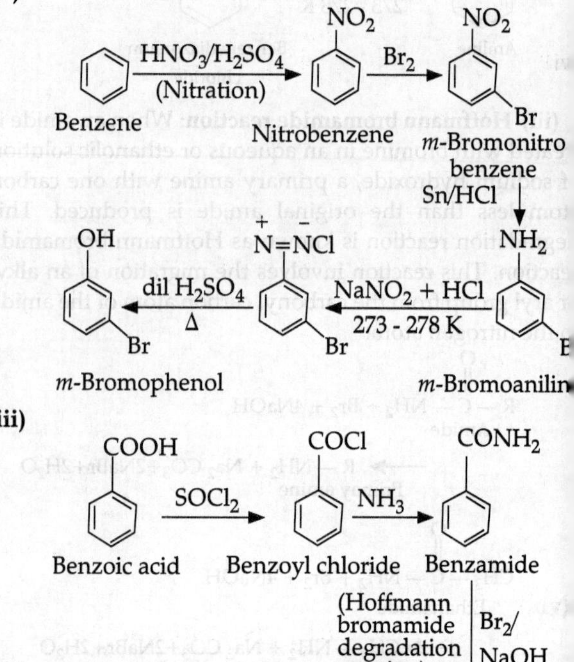

(iii)

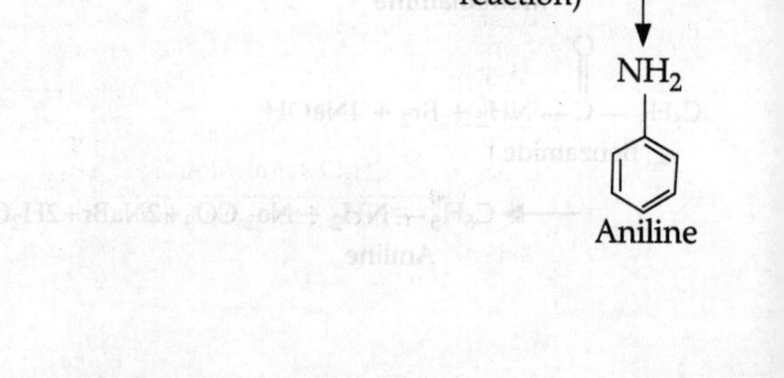

(v)

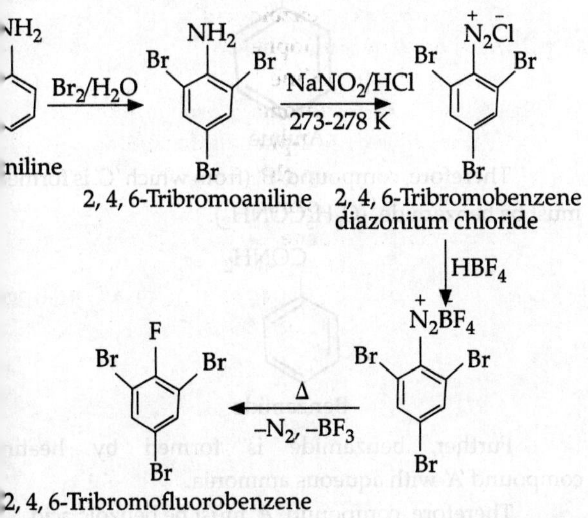

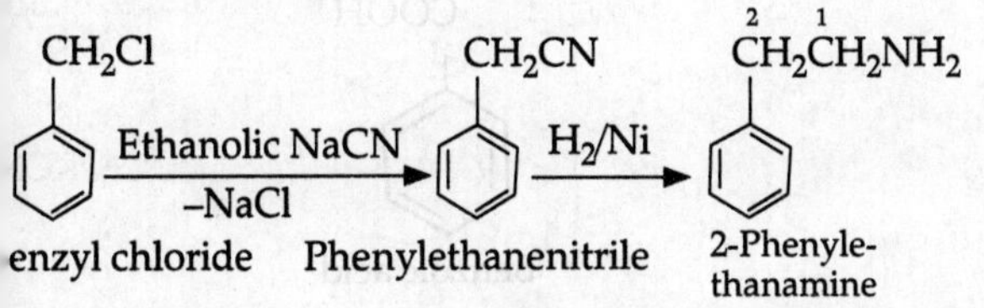

(vi)

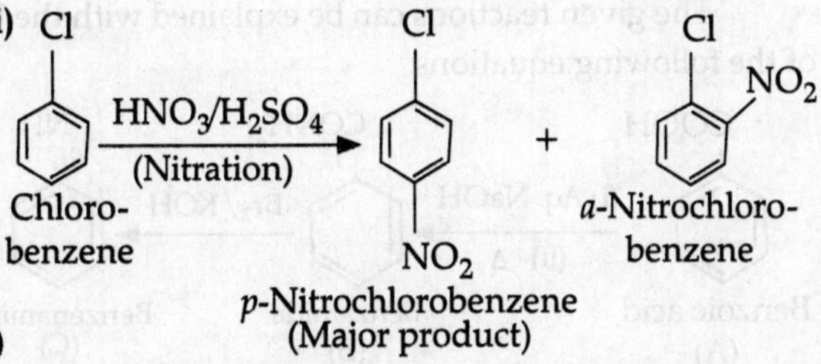

(vii)

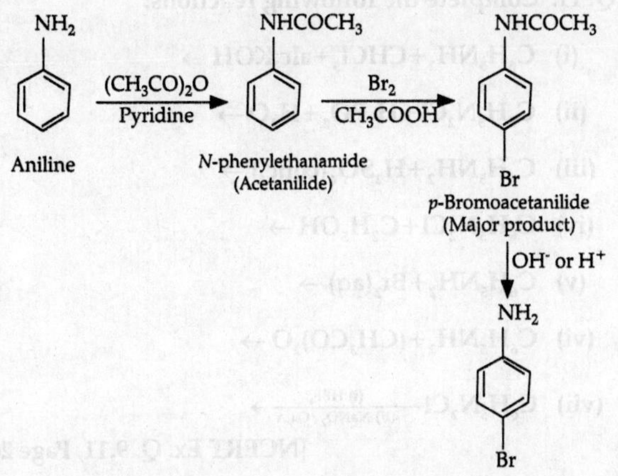

(viii)

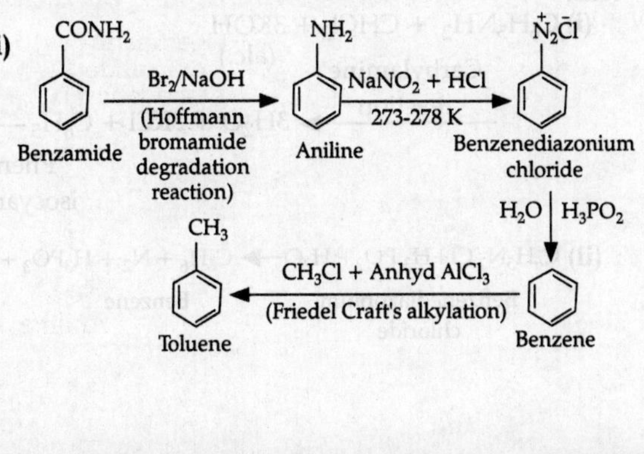

(ix)

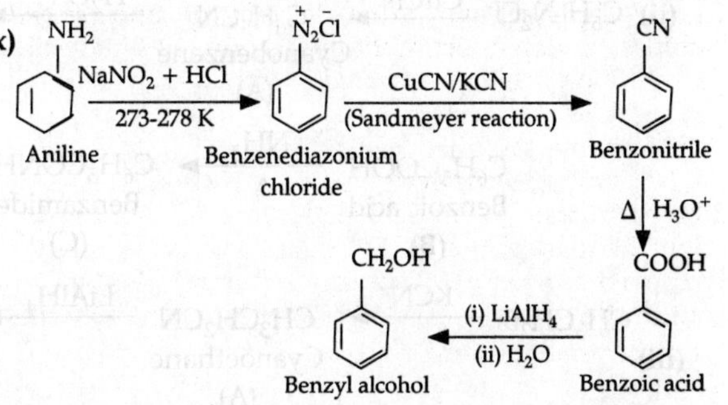

Q. 9. Give the structures of *A*, *B* and *C* in the following reactions: **[NCERT Ex. Q. 9.9, Page 279]**

(i) $CH_3CH_2I \xrightarrow{NaCN} A \xrightarrow[\text{partial hydrolysis}]{OH^-} B \xrightarrow[H_2O]{NaOH+BR_2} C$

(ii) $C_6H_5N_2Cl \xrightarrow{CuCN} A \xrightarrow{H_2O/H^+} B \xrightarrow{NH_3} C$

(iii) $CH_3CH_2Br \xrightarrow{KCN} A \xrightarrow{LiAlH_4} B \xrightarrow[O°C]{HNO_2} C$

(iv) $C_6H_5NO_2 \xrightarrow{Fe/HCl} A \xrightarrow[273K]{NaNO_2+HCl} B \xrightarrow[\Delta]{H_2O/H^+} C$

(v) $CH_3COOH \xrightarrow[\Delta]{NH_3} A \xrightarrow{NaOBr} B \xrightarrow[\Delta]{NaNO_2+HCl} C$

(vi) $C_6H_5NO_2 \xrightarrow[\Delta]{Fe/HCl} A \xrightarrow[273K]{HNO_2} B \xrightarrow{C_6H_5OH} C$

Ans.

$$\underset{\text{Propanenitrile (A)}}{CH_3-CH_2I \xrightarrow{NaCN} CH_3CH_2CN} \xrightarrow[\text{partial hydrolysis}]{OH^-} \underset{\text{Propanamide (B)}}{CH_3-CH_2-\overset{O}{\overset{\|}{C}}-NH_2}$$

$$\xrightarrow{NaOH + Br_2} \underset{\text{Ethanamine (C)}}{CH_3-CH_2-NH_2}$$

(ii) $C_6H_5N_2Cl \xrightarrow{CuCN} \underset{\text{Cyanobenzene (A)}}{C_6H_5CN} \xrightarrow{H_2O/H^+}$

$\underset{\text{Benzoic acid (B)}}{C_6H_5COOH} \xrightarrow[\Delta]{NH_3} \underset{\text{Benzamide (C)}}{C_6H_5CONH_2}$

(iii) $CH_3CH_2Br \xrightarrow{KCN} \underset{\text{Cyanoethane (A)}}{CH_3CH_2CN} \xrightarrow{LiAlH_4}$

$\underset{\text{Propan-1-amine (B)}}{CH_3CH_2CH_2NH_2} \xrightarrow[0°C]{HNO_2} \underset{\text{Propan-1-ol (C)}}{CH_3CH_2CH_2OH}$

(iv) $C_6H_5NO_2 \xrightarrow{Fe/HCl} \underset{\text{Aniline (A)}}{C_6H_5NH_2} \xrightarrow[273\ K]{NaNO_2 + HCl}$

$\underset{\text{Benzenediazorium chloride (B)}}{C_6H_5-\overset{+}{N_2}\overset{-}{Cl}} \xrightarrow[\Delta]{H_2O/H^+} \underset{\text{Phenol (C)}}{C_6H_5OH}$

(v) $CH_3COOH \xrightarrow[\Delta]{NH_3} \underset{\text{Ethanamide (A)}}{CH_3CONH_2} \xrightarrow{NaOBr}$

$\underset{\text{Methanamine (B)}}{CH_3NH_2} \xrightarrow{NaNO_2/HCl} \underset{\text{Methanol (C)}}{CH_3OH}$

(vi)

$C_6H_5NO_2 \xrightarrow{Fe/HCl} \underset{\text{Aniline (A)}}{C_6H_5NH_2} \xrightarrow[273\ K]{HNO_2}$

$\underset{\text{Benzenediazonium chloride (B)}}{C_6H_5-\overset{+}{N_2}\overset{-}{Cl}} \xrightarrow{C_6H_5OH}$

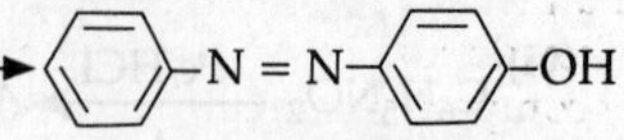

p- Hydroxyazobenzene
(C)

Q. 10. An aromatic compound 'A' on treatment with aqueous ammonia and heating forms compound 'B' which on heating with Br_2 and KOH forms a compound 'C' of molecular formula C_6H_7N. Write the structures and IUPAC names of compounds A, B and C.

[NCERT Ex. Q. 9.10, Page 280]

Ans. It is given that compound 'C' having the molecular formula, C_6H_7N is formed by heating compound 'B' with Br_2 and KOH. This is a Hoffmann bromamide degradation reaction. Therefore, compound 'B' is an amide and compound 'C' is an amine. The only amine having the molecular formula, C_6H_7N is aniline, $(C_6H_5NH_2)$.

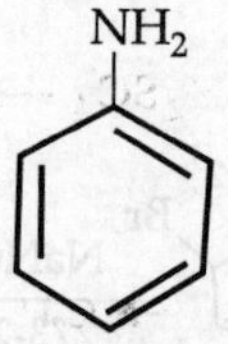

Aniline

Therefore, compound 'B' (from which 'C' is formed) must be benzamide, $(C_6H_5CONH_2)$.

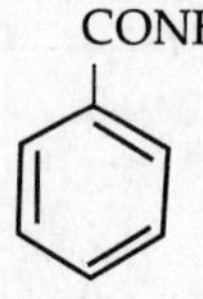

Benzamide

Further, benzamide is formed by heating compound 'A' with aqueous ammonia.

Therefore, compound 'A' must be benzoic acid.

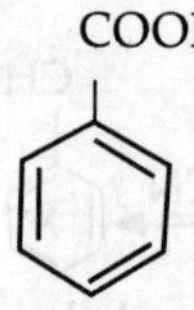

Benzoic acid

The given reactions can be explained with the help of the following equations:

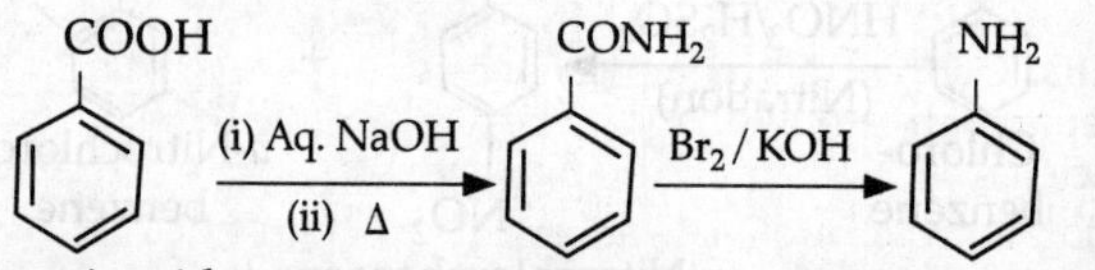

Benzoic acid (A) | Benzamide (B) | Benzenamine (C)

Q. 11. Complete the following reactions:

(i) $C_6H_5NH_2 + CHCl_3 + alc.KOH \rightarrow$

(ii) $C_6H_5N_2Cl + H_3PO_2 + H_2O \rightarrow$

(iii) $C_6H_5NH_2 + H_2SO_4(conc.) \rightarrow$

(iv) $C_6H_5N_2Cl + C_2H_5OH \rightarrow$

(v) $C_6H_5NH_2 + Br_2(aq) \rightarrow$

(vi) $C_6H_5NH_2 + (CH_3CO)_2O \rightarrow$

(vii) $C_6H_5N_2Cl \xrightarrow[(ii)\ NaNO_2/Cu,\Delta]{(i)\ HBF_4}$

[NCERT Ex. Q. 9.11, Page 280]

Ans.

(i) $C_6H_5NH_2 + CHCl_3 + \underset{(alc.)}{3KOH} \xrightarrow{\text{Carbylamine reaction}} 3H_2O + 3KCl + \underset{\text{Phenyl isocyanide}}{C_6H_5-NC}$

(ii) $\underset{\text{Benzenediazonium chloride}}{C_6H_5N_2Cl} + H_3PO_2 + H_2O \longrightarrow \underset{\text{Benzene}}{C_6H_6} + N_2 + H_3PO_3 + HCl$

(iii) $C_6H_5NH_2 + conc.H_2SO_4 \longrightarrow C_6H_6\overset{+}{N}H_3H\overset{-}{S}O_4$
Aniline — Anilinium hydrogen sulphate

(iv) $C_6H_5N_2Cl + C_2H_5OH \longrightarrow C_6H_6 + CH_3CHO + N_2 + HCl$
Benzene-diazonium chloride — Ethanol — Benzene — Ethanal

(v) $C_6H_5NH_2 + 3Br_2(aq) \longrightarrow$ 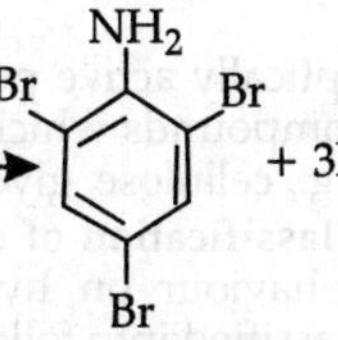 $+ 3HBr$
Aniline — 2,4,6 – Tribromoanilne

(vi) $C_6H_5NH_2 + (CH_3CO)_2O$
Aniline — acetic anhydride

$$\longrightarrow C_6H_5-\underset{H}{N}-\underset{O}{\overset{}{C}}-CH_3 + CH_3COOH$$
acetic acid

N-Phenylethanamide

vii)
$C_6H_5N_2Cl \xrightarrow[\text{(ii) } NaNO_2/Cu,\Delta]{\text{(i) } HBF_4} C_6H_5NO_2 + N_2 + NaBF_4$
enzenediazonium chloride — Nitrobenzene

. 12. Why cannot aromatic primary amines be prepared Gabriel phthalimide synthesis?
[NCERT Ex. Q. 9.12, Page 280]

Ans. Gabriel phthalimide synthesis is used for the eparation of aliphatic primary amines. It involves cleophilic substitution (S_{N2}) of alkyl halides by the ion formed by the phthalimide.

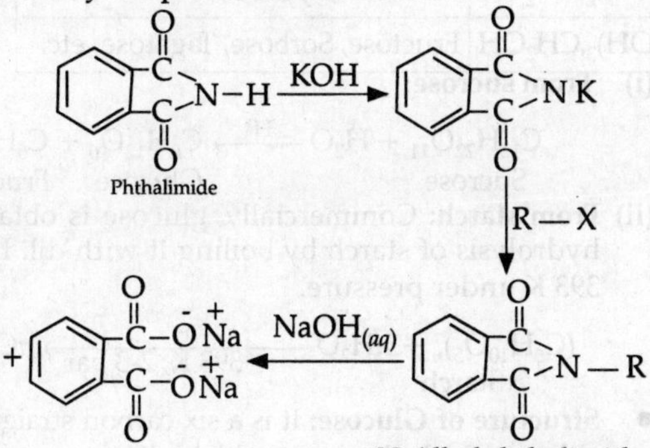

N-Alkylphthalimide

But aryl halides do not undergo nucleophilic bstitution with the anion formed by the phthalimide.

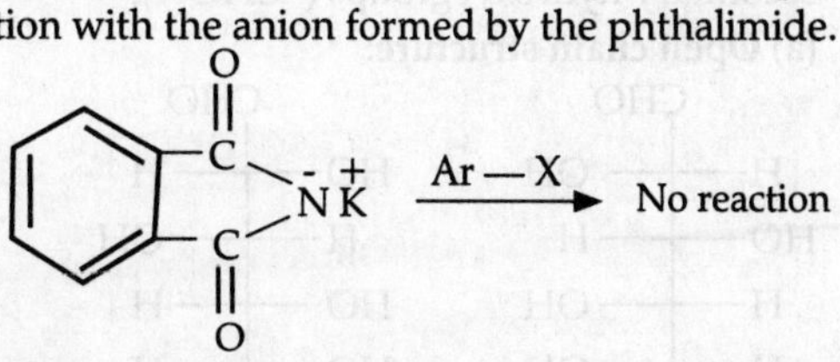

Hence, aromatic *primary* amines cannot be repared by this process.

. 13. Write the reactions of (i) aromatic and (ii) aliphatic rimary amines with nitrous acid.
[NCERT Ex. Q. 9.13, Page 280]

Ans. (i) Aromatic amines react with nitrous acid repared *in situ* from $NaNO_2$ and a mineral acid such as HCl) at 273 – 278 K to form stable aromatic diazonium salts *i.e.*, NaCl and H_2O.

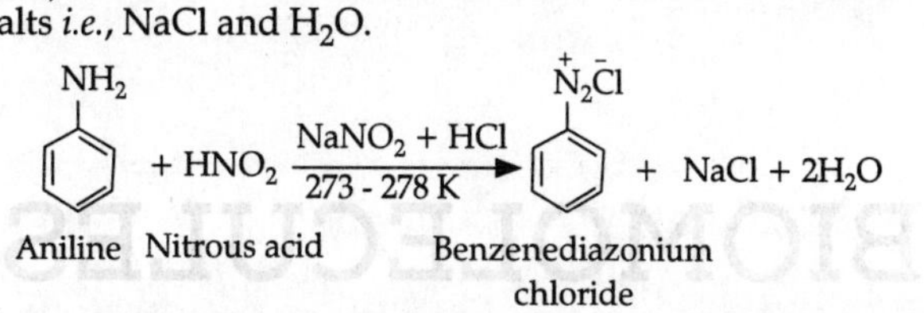

(ii) Aliphatic primary amines react with nitrous acid (prepared in situ from $NaNO_2$ and a mineral acid such as HCl) to form unstable aliphatic diazonium salts, which further produce alcohol and HCl with the evolution of N_2 gas.

$$R-NH_2 + HNO_2 \xrightarrow{NaNO_2 + HCl} [R\overset{+}{N_2}Cl^-] \xrightarrow{H_2O} N_2\uparrow + HCl + ROH$$
Aliphatic primary alcohol — Nitrous acid — Aliphatic diazonium salt — alcohol

Q. 14. Give plausible explanation for each of the following:

(i) Why are amines less acidic than alcohols of comparable molecular masses?

(ii) Why do primary amines have higher boiling point than tertiary amines?

(iii) Why are aliphatic amines stronger bases than aromatic amines? **[NCERT Ex. Q. 9.14, Page 280]**

Ans (i) Amines undergo protonation to give amide ion.

$$R-NH_2 \longrightarrow R-\overset{-}{N}H + H^+$$
Amide ion

Similarly, alcohol loses a proton to give alkoxide ion.

$$R-OH \longrightarrow R-\overset{-}{O} + H^+$$
Alcohol — Alkoxide ion

In an amide ion, the negative charge is on the N-atom whereas in alkoxide ion, the negative charge is on the O-atom. Since, O is more electronegative than N, O can accommodate the negative charge more easily than N. As a result, the amide ion is less stable than the alkoxide ion. Hence, amines are less acidic than alcohols of comparable molecular masses.

(ii) In a molecule of *tertiary* amine, there are no H-atoms whereas in primary amines, two hydrogen atoms are present. Due to the presence of H-atoms, primary amines undergo extensive intermolecular H-bonding.

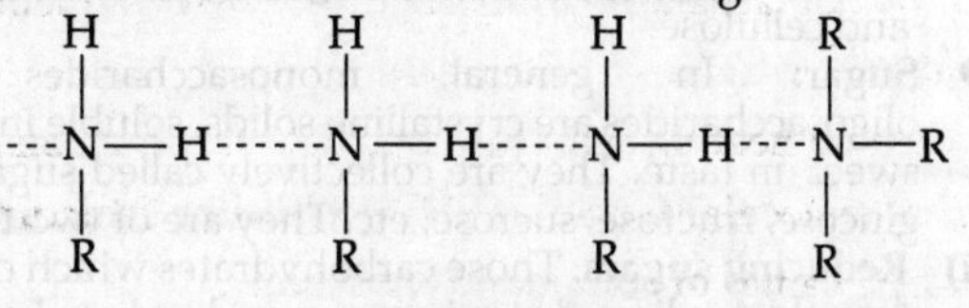

Primary amine — Tertiary amine

As a result, extra energy is required to separate the molecules of primary amines. Hence, primary amines have higher boiling points than tertiary amines.

(iii) Due to the – R effect of the benzene ring, the electrons on the N- atom are less available in case of aromatic amines. Therefore, the electrons on the N-atom in aromatic amines cannot be donated easily. This explains why aliphatic amines are stronger bases than aromatic amines.

CHAPTER 10

BIOMOLECULES

- **Biomolecules:** Biomolecules are the naturally occurring organic compounds present as essential constituents of living organism in different cells. e.g., polysaccharides, proteins, etc. They are also called saccharides.
- **Carbohydrates:** Carbohydrates may be defined as optically active polyhydroxy aldehydes or ketones or compounds which produce such units on hydrolysi e.g., cellulose, glycogen, starch, etc.
- **Classification of carbohydrates:** On the basis of the behaviour on hydrolysis, carbohydrates have bee classified into following four types:

(i) Monosaccharides: Monosaccharides include non-hydrolysable carbohydrates. They are soluble in water. Thos containing aldehydic group are called aldoses, while other containing a ketonic group are called ketoses. Som monosaccharides with example are given in the table as shown below:

Table 1 : Carbohydrates

Class	Molecular Formula	Structural formula	Example
		Aldoses	
Aldotriose	$C_3H_6O_3$	$CH_2OH.CHOH.CHO$	Glyceraldehyde
Aldotetrose	$C_4H_8O_4$	$CH_2OH.(CHOH)_2.CHO$	Erythrose, Threose
Aldopentose	$C_5H_{10}O_5$	$CH_2OH.(CHOH)_3.CHO$	Arabinose, Ribose, Xylose, Lyxose
Aldohexose	$C_6H_{12}O_6$	$CH_2OH.(CHOH)_4.CHO$	Glucose, Mannose, Galactose, Talose, Idose, llose, Altrose
		Ketoses	
Ketotriose	$C_3H_6O_3$	$CH_2OH.CO.CH_2OH$	Dihydroxyacetone
Ketotetrose	$C_4H_8O_4$	$CH_2OH.COCHOH.CH_2OH$	Erythrulose
Ketopentose	$C_5H_{10}O_5$	$CH_2OH.CO(CHOH)_2.CH_2OH$	Ribulose, Xylulose
Ketohexose	$C_6H_{12}O_6$	$CH_2OH.CO(CHOH)_3.CH_2OH$	Fructose, Sorbose, Tagatose, etc.

(ii) Disaccharides: Those carbohydrates which on hydrolysis yield two molecules of monosaccharides are called disaccharides. They are crystalline, soluble in water and sweet in taste. e.g., cane sugar, maltose, etc.

(iii) Oligosaccharides: Those carbohydrates which yield 2 to 10 monosaccharide molecules on hydrolysis are called oligosaccharides. e.g., raffinose on hydrolysis gives glucose, fructose and galactose.

(iv) Polysaccharides: Those carbohydrates which produce large number of monosaccharide units on hydrolysis are called polysaccharides. They are formed by linking together a large number of monosaccharide units through glycosidic linkage. e.g., starch, amylose and cellulose.

- **Sugar:** In general, monosaccharides and oligosaccharides are crystalline solids, soluble in water, sweet in taste. They are collectively called sugar. e.g., glucose, fructose, sucrose, etc. They are of two types:

(i) Reducing sugars: Those carbohydrates which contain free aldehydic or ketonic group and reduce Fehling's solution and Tollen's reagent are known as reducing sugars. e.g., all monosaccharides, maltose.

(ii) Non-reducing sugars: Those carbohydrates which do not have free aldehydic or ketonic group and do not reduce Fehling's solution or Tollen's reagent are known as non-reducing sugars. e.g., sucrose.

- **Glucose:** Glucose occurs in nature in free as well as in the combined form. It is present in sweet fruits and honey.
- **Methods of preparation of Glucose:**

(i) From sucrose:

$$\underset{\text{Sucrose}}{C_{12}H_{22}O_{11}} + H_2O \xrightarrow{H^+} \underset{\text{Glucose}}{C_6H_{12}O_6} + \underset{\text{Fructose}}{C_6H_{12}O_6}$$

(ii) From starch: Commercially, glucose is obtained b hydrolysis of starch by boiling it with dil. H_2SO_4 a 393 K under pressure.

$$\underset{\text{Starch}}{(C_6H_{10}O_5)_n} + nH_2O \xrightarrow[393\text{ K, 2-3 bar}]{H^+} \underset{\text{Glucos}}{nC_6H_{12}O_6}$$

- **Structure of Glucose:** It is a six carbon straight chai aldose which has one aldehydic group (–CHO one primary hydroxyl group ($-CH_2OH$) and fou secondary hydroxyl groups (–CHOH).

(a) **Open chain structure:**

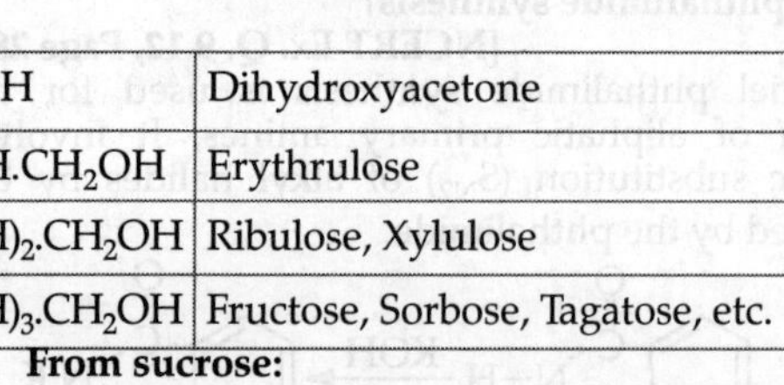

D–(+)–Glucose L–(–)–Glucose

(b) **Cyclic structure:**

1. Despite having the aldehyde group, glucose doe not give Schiff's test and it does not form th hydrogensulphite addition product with $NaHSO_3$.

Biomolecules

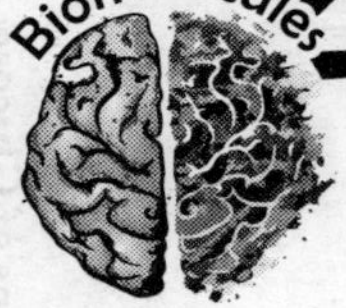

Carbohydrates

Optically active polyhydroxy aldehydes or ketones or compounds which produce units with specific functional groups on hydrolysis.

- **Classification :**

(I) **Monosaccharides :** (Aldehyde group – aldose, keto group –ketose)

Glucose : Preparation :

(a) **From sucrose :** $C_{12}H_{22}O_{11} + H_2O \xrightarrow{H^+} \underset{\text{Glucose}}{C_6H_{12}O_6} + \underset{\text{Fructose}}{C_6H_{12}O_6}$ (Sucrose)

(b) **From starch :** $(C_6H_{10}O_5)_n + nH_2O \xrightarrow[393K;\ 2\text{-}3\ atm]{H^+} nC_6H_{12}O_6$

- **Structure :**

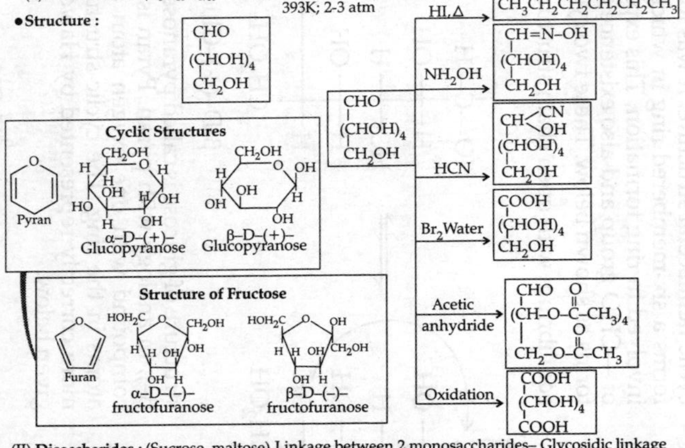

(II) **Disaccharides :** (Sucrose, maltose) Linkage between 2 monosaccharides– Glycosidic linkage

(III) **Polysaccharides :** Large number of monosaccharides units joined by glycosidic linkages. e.g.,

(a) Starch : Polymer of α–glucose with two components amylose and amylopectin

(b) Cellulose

(c) Glycogen

Importance :

- Form a major portion of food.
- As storage molecules.
- Cellulose forms cell wall of bacteria and plants.
- Raw materials for industries like textiles, paper, lacquers and breweries.

Proteins

-(Polymers of amino acids)

-Amino acids contain $-NH_2$ and –COOH group.

Classification :

- **On the basis of relative number of $-NH_2$ and –COOH group:**
  - (i) Neutral : Equal number of $-NH_2$ and –COOH group.
  - (ii) Basic : More number of $-NH_2$ than –COOH group.
  - (iii) Acidic : More number of –COOH than $-NH_2$ group.
- **On the basis of place of synthesis :**
  - (i) Essential – cannot be synthesized in the body.
  - (ii) Non-essential – synthesized in the body.
- **On the basis of shape :**
  - (I) Fibrous : Fibre-like structure
  - (ii) Globular : Spherical

Structure : $H_2N-CH_2-\boxed{CO-NH}-\underset{CH_3}{CH}-COOH$ (Peptide linkage)

Denaturation of protein :

When a protein in its native form is subjected to physical change, globules unfold, helix get uncoiled and protein loses its biological activity.

Vitamin

Organic compounds required in diet in small amounts to perform specific biological functions for maintenance and growth.

Classification :

(i) **Fat soluble :** Soluble in fats and oils but insoluble in water. (Vitamins A,D,E and K)

(ii) **Water soluble :** B group and vitamin C are soluble in water.

Nucleic Acids

Chromosomes : Particles in nucleus responsible for heredity. Chromosomes are made up of proteins and nucleic acid.

Two types : Deoxyribonucleic acid (DNA), ribonucleic acid (RNA)

Composition : In DNA, sugar is β–D–2–deoxyribose whereas in RNA is β–D–ribose. DNA contains A,G,C,T whereas RNA has A,G,C,U.

Structure :

Nucleoside : Formed by attachment of a base to 1′ of sugar

Nucleotide : Formed by link to phosphoric acid at 5′ of sugar.

–Sugar(Base)–Phosphate–[Sugar(Base)–Phosphate]–Sugar(Base)–

Types of RNA : m–RNA, r–RNA, t–RNA

Biological Functions :

- Chemical basis of heredity.
- Responsible for identity of different species of organisms.
- Nucleic acids are responsible for protein synthesis in cell.

DNA Fingerprinting : Unique sequence of bases on DNA

A sequence of bases on DNA is unique for a person and information regarding this is called DNA fingerprinting. It is same for every cell and cannot be altered by any known treatment. DNA fingerprinting is now used

(i) in forensic laboratories for identification of criminals.

(ii) to determine paternity of an individual.

(iii) to identify the dead bodies in any accident by comparing the DNA's of parents or children.

(iv) to identify racial groups to rewrite biological evolution.

Enzymes

Globular proteins specific for particular reaction and for particular substrate. Mechanism : Reduces the magnitude of activation energy

Trace the Mind Map

- First Level
- Second Level
- Third Level

2. The pentaacetate of glucose does not react with hydroxylamine indicating the absence of free —CHO group.
3. Glucose is found to exist in two different crystalline forms which are named as α and β. The α-form of glucose (m.p. 419 K) is obtained by crystallisation from concentrated solution of glucose at 303 K while the β-form (m.p. 423 K) is obtained by crystallisation from hot and saturated aqueous solution at 371 K. This behaviour could not be explained by the open chain structure

(I) For glucose—It was proposed that one of the —C groups may add to the —CHO group and form cyclic hemiacetal structure. It was found that gluc forms a six-membered ring in which —OH at C-5 involved in ring formation. This explains the abser of —CHO group and also existence of glucose in tw forms as shown below. These two cyclic forms exist equilibrium with open chain structure.

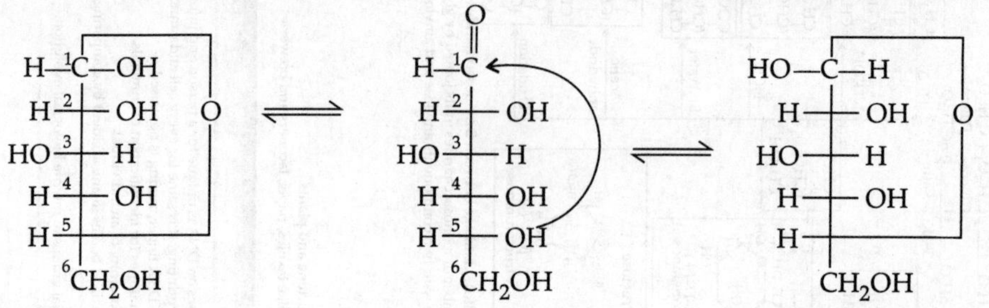

α-D-(+)-Glucose β-D-(+)-Glucose

(c) Haworth structure: The two cyclic hemiacetal forms of glucose differ only in the configuration of the hydroxyl group at C1, called anomeric carbon (aldehyde carbon before cyclisation). Such isomers, i.e., α-form and β-form, are called anomers. The six membered cyclic structure of glucose is called pyranose structure (α– β–), in analogy with pyran. Pyran is a cyclic orgar compound with one oxygen atom and five carb atoms in the ring. The cyclic structure of glucose more correctly represented by Haworth structure given below.

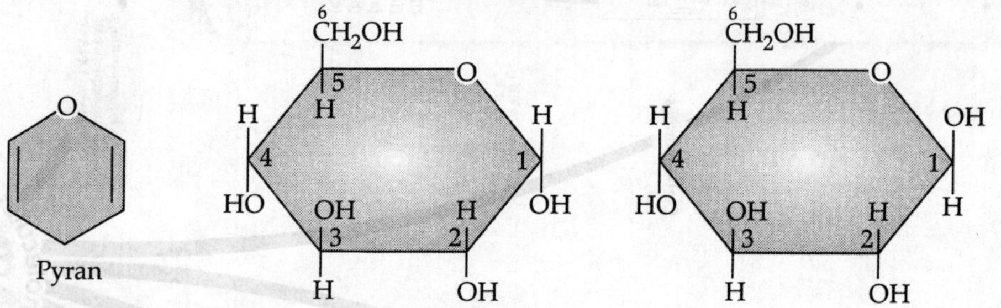

Pyran α-D-(+)-Glucopyranose β-D-(+)-Glucopyranose

- **Reactions of Glucose:** It suggests all the six carbon atoms are linked in a straight chain.

(i) With HI:

$$\underset{\text{Glucose}}{CHO-(CHOH)_4-CH_2OH} \xrightarrow[\Delta]{HI} \underset{n\text{-Hexane}}{CH_3-CH_2-CH_2-CH_2-CH_2-CH_3}$$

(ii) Reactions showing the presence of carbonyl group (>C = O):

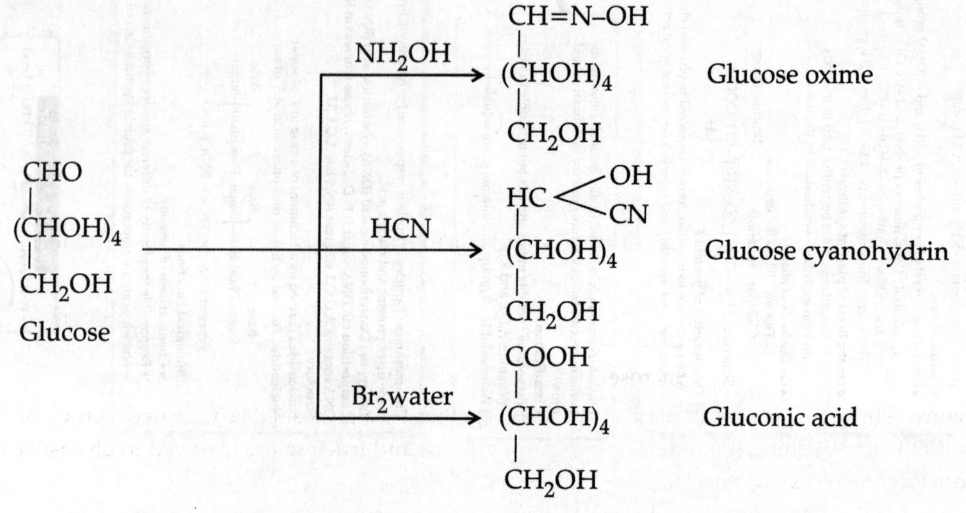

(iii) Acetylation of glucose: It confirms the presence of 5 –OH groups. Since, it exists as a stable compound, five –OH groups should be attached to different carbon atoms.

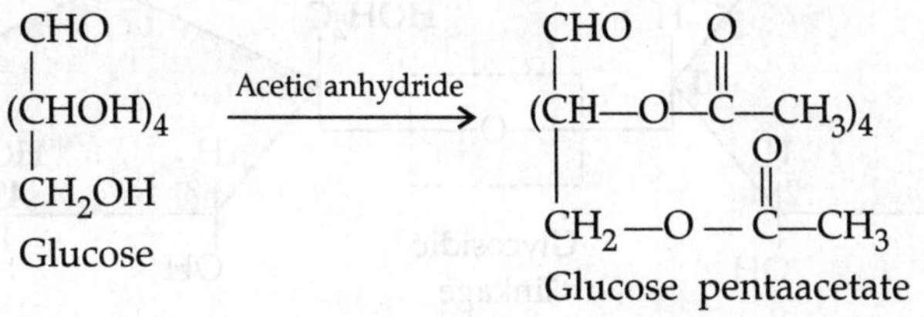

(iv) Reaction showing the presence of primary alcoholic (– OH) group:

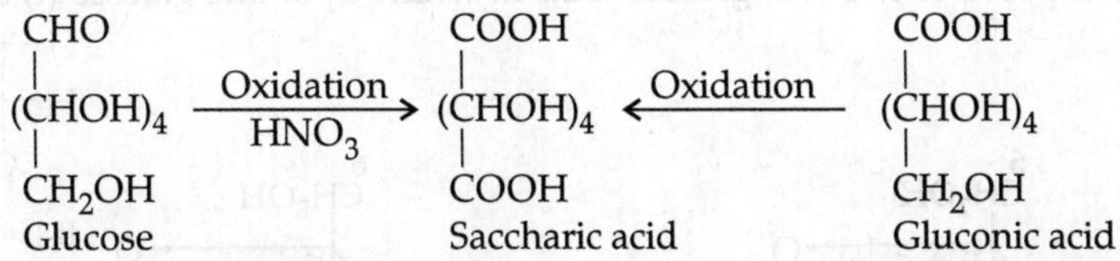

Fructose: It is a ketohexose obtained by the hydrolysis of disaccharide.

Structure of Fructose: Fructose also has the molecular formula $C_6H_{12}O_6$ and on the basis of its reactions it was found to contain a ketonic functional group at carbon number 2 and six carbons in straight chain as in the case of glucose. It belongs to D-series and is a laevorotatory compound. It is appropriately written as D-(–)-fructose.

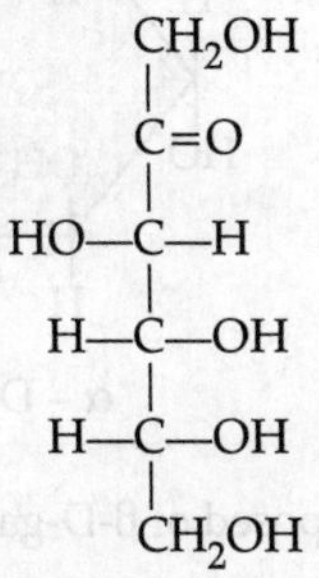

a) Open chain structure **(b) Cyclic structure:**

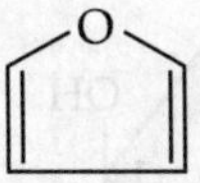

Furan

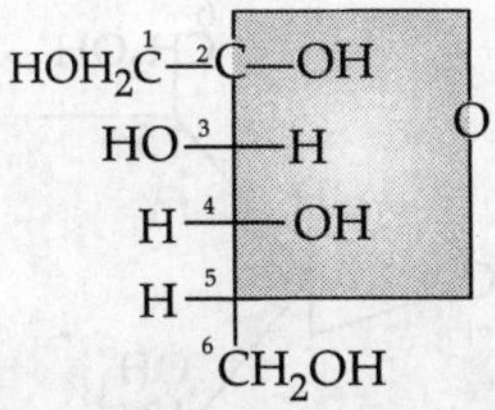

α-D-(–)-Fructofuranose

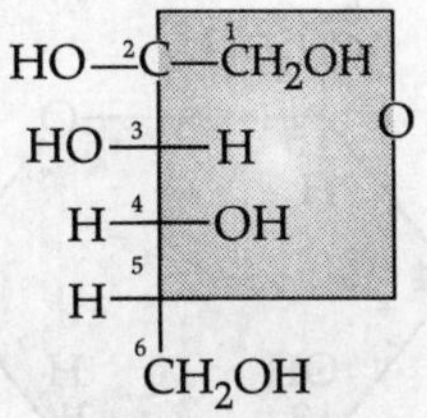

β-D-(+)-Fructofuranose

c) Haworth structure:

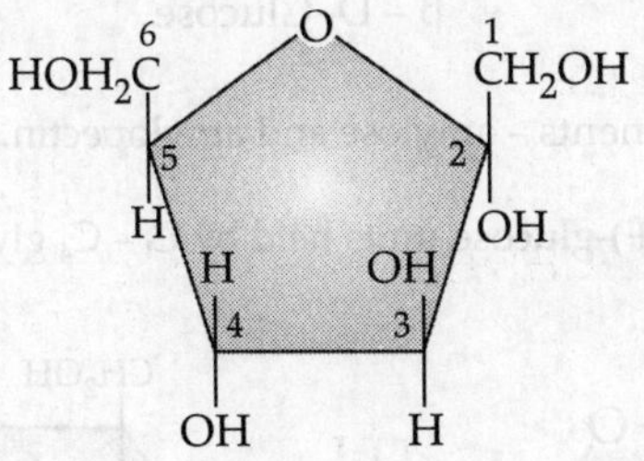

α-D-(–)-Fructofuranose

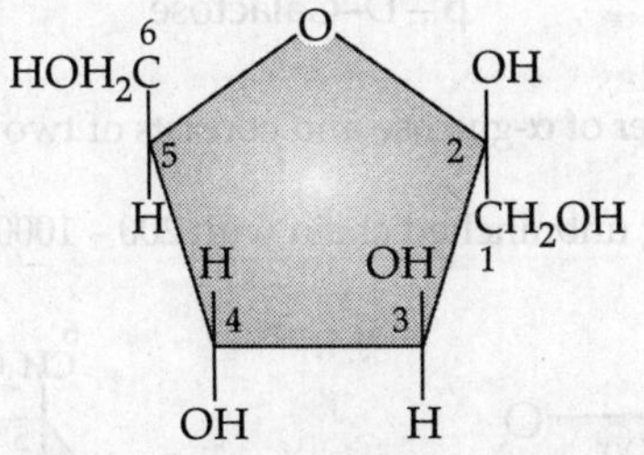

β-D-(–)-Fructofuranose

- **Sucrose:** Since, the reducing groups of glucose and fructose are involved in glycosidic bond formation, sucrose is a non reducing sugar.

$$\underset{\text{Sucrose}}{C_{12}H_{22}O_{11}} + H_2O \xrightarrow{H^+} \underset{\text{D–(+)–Glucose}}{C_6H_{12}O_6} + \underset{\text{D–(–)–Fructose}}{C_6H_{12}O_6}$$

- **Structure:** These two monosaccharides are held together by a glycosidic linkage between C_1 of α-D-glucose and C_2 of β-D-fructose. Since, the reducing groups of glucose and fructose are involved in glycosidic bond formation, sucrose is a non reducing sugar.

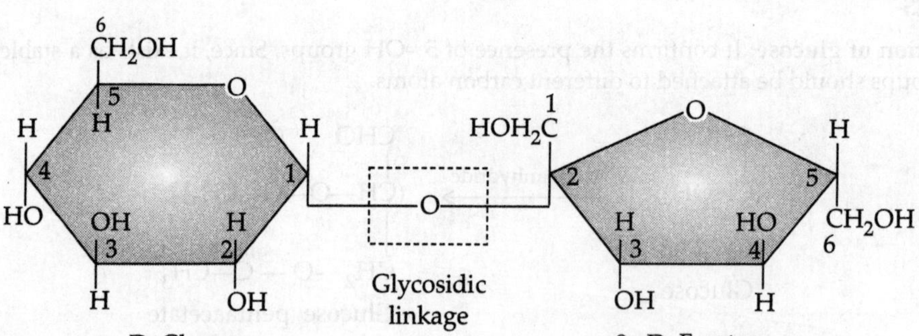

- **Maltose** molecule is composed of two α-D-glucose units in which C_1 of one glucose (I) is linked to C_4 of another glucose unit (II).

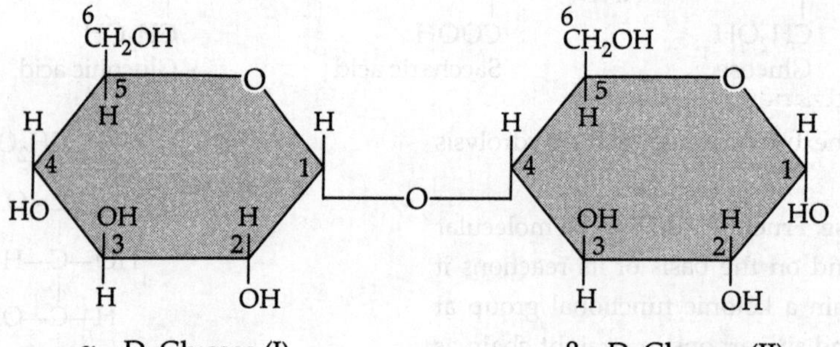

- **Lactose:** It is composed of β-D-galactose and β-D-glucose. The linkage is between C_1 of galactose and C_4 of glucose. Free aldehyde group may be produced at C-1 of glucose unit, hence it is also a reducing sugar

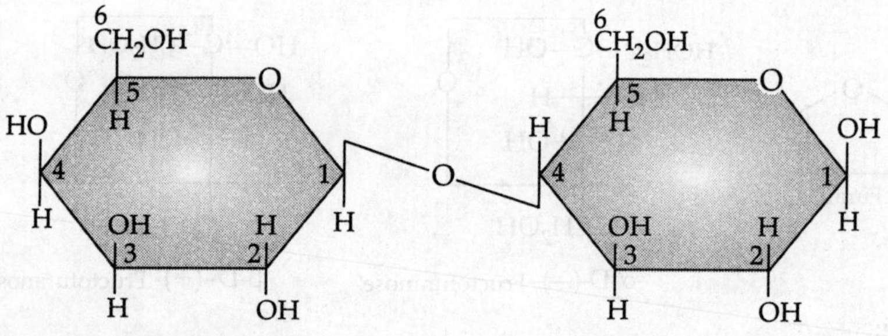

- **Starch** is a polymer of α-glucose and consists of two components – amylose and amylopectin.
- **Amylose** is a long unbranched chain with 200 – 1000 α-D-(+)-glucose units held by $C_1 – C_4$ glycosidic linkage.

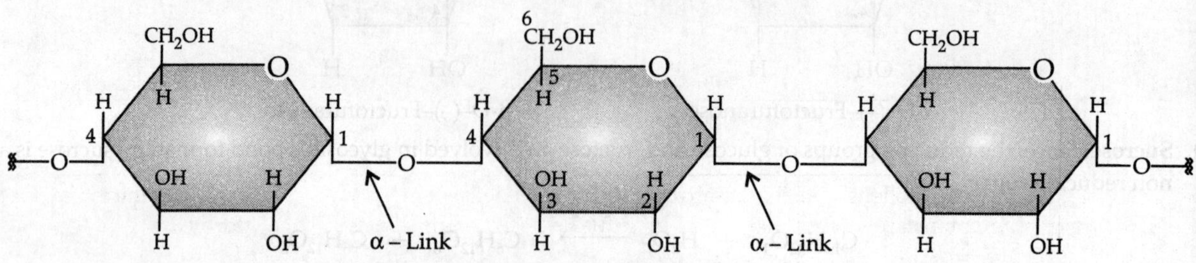

Amylose

Amylopectin is a branched chain polymer of α-D-glucose units in which the chain is formed by $C_1 – C_4$ glycosidic linkage whereas branching occurs by $C_1 – C_6$ glycosidic linkage.

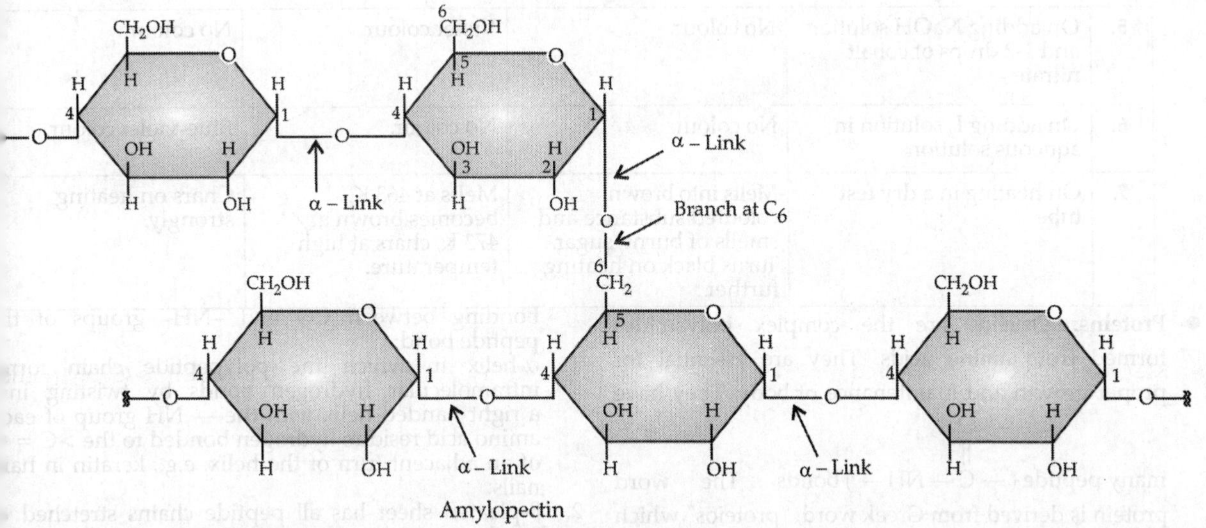

Amylopectin

Cellulose is a polysaccharide whose fundamental structural unit is β-D-glucose joined by glycosidic linkage between C_1 of one glucose unit and C_4 of the next glucose unit.

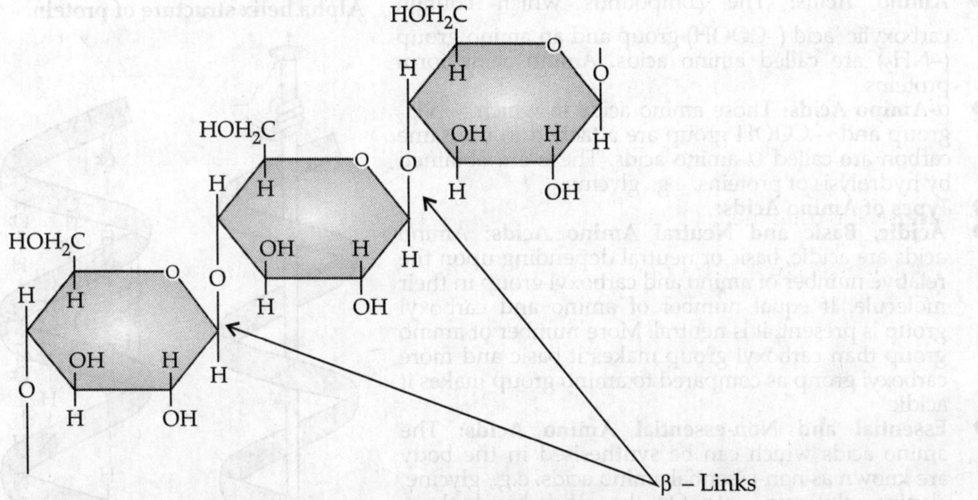

Glycogen is an animal starch with structure similar to amylopectin and has more branches.

Importance of Carbohydrates:

(i) They are essential for plants and animals as a source of energy.

(ii) They form structural materials for cells.

(iii) They provide raw materials for textile, paper and alcohol industry.

(iv) Monosaccharides are also present in nucleic acids which control the transmission of hereditary effects from one generation to other and biosynthesis of proteins as well.

- **Distinction between Glucose (monosaccharide), Sucrose (disaccharide) and Starch (polysaccharide):**

Table 2 : Important Distinctions

S. No.	Test	Glucose (Monosaccharide)	Sucrose (Disaccharide)	Starch (Polysaccharide)
1.	On heating with Fehling's solution	Red precipitate is obtained.	No precipitate.	No precipitate.
2.	On heating with Tollens' reagent (ammonical $AgNO_3$)	Silver mirror is formed.	No silver mirror is formed.	No silver mirror is formed.
3.	On heating with phenyl hydrazine	Yellow coloured crystals of osazone are formed.	No osazone is formed.	No osazone is formed.
4.	On heating with resorcinol and HCl	No colour.	Wine red colour.	No colour.

5.	On adding NaOH solution and 1-2 drops of cobalt nitrate	No colour.	Violet colour.	No colour.
6.	On adding I_2 solution in aqueous solution	No colour.	No colour.	Blue-violet colour.
7.	On heating in a dry test tube	Melts into brown coloured substance and smells of burnt sugar. Turns black on heating further.	Melts at 463 K, becomes brown at 473 K, chars at high temperature.	Chars on heating strongly.

- **Proteins:** Proteins are the complex polyamides formed from amino acids. They are essential for proper growth and maintenance of body. They have many peptide ($-\overset{\overset{\displaystyle O}{\|}}{C}-NH-$) bonds. The word protein is derived from Greek word, "proteios" which means primary or of prime importance. All proteins are polymers of α-amino acids.
- **Amino Acids:** The compounds which contain carboxylic acid (–COOH) group and an amino group ($-NH_2$) are called amino acids. Amino acids form proteins.
- **α-Amino Acids:** Those amino acids in which $-NH_2$ group and —COOH group are attached to the same carbon are called α-amino acids. These are obtained by hydrolysis of proteins. e.g., glycine.
- **Types of Amino Acids:**
- **Acidic, Basic and Neutral Amino Acids:** Amino acids are acidic, basic or neutral depending upon the relative number of amino and carboxyl group in their molecule. If equal number of amino and carboxyl group is present, it is neutral. More number of amino group than carboxyl group makes it basic and more carboxyl group as compared to amino group makes it acidic.
- **Essential and Non-essential Amino Acids:** The amino acids which can be synthesised in the body are known as non-essential amino acids. e.g., glycine, alanine, glutamine, etc. On the other hand, those which cannot be synthesised in the body and must be obtained by diet are known as essential amino acids.
- **Zwitter ion:** In aqueous solution, the carboxyl group can lose proton and amino group can accept a proton, giving rise to a dipolar ion known as zwitter ion. This is neutral but contains both positive and negative charges. In zwitter ionic form, amino acids show amphoteric behaviour as they react both with acids and bases.
- **Classification of Proteins:** Proteins are classified as follows:

(a) Based on molecular shape:

(i) Fibrous proteins: They have thread like molecules which tend to lie side by side to form fibres. e.g., keratin, collagen, etc.

(ii) Globular proteins: They have molecules which are folded into compact units that often approach spheroidal shape. e.g., insulin, albumin, haemoglobin, etc.

(b) Based on structure and shape:

(i) Primary structure: Each polypeptide in a protein has amino acids linked with each other in a specific sequence. This sequence of amino acids is called as primary structure of proteins.

(ii) Secondary structure: It refers to the shape in which a long polypeptide chain exists. They are of two types. These structures arise due to the regular folding of the backbone of the polypeptide chain due to hydrogen bonding between CO and –NH– groups of th peptide bond:

1. α-helix in which the polypeptide chain form intramolecular hydrogen bonds by twisting int a right handed helix with the — NH group of eac amino acid residue hydrogen bonded to the >C = of an adjacent turn of the helix. e.g., keratin in ha nails.
2. β-pleated sheet has all peptide chains stretched nearly maximum extension and then arranged sid by side held together with intermolecular hydroge bonding. e.g., silk.

Alpha helix structure of protein

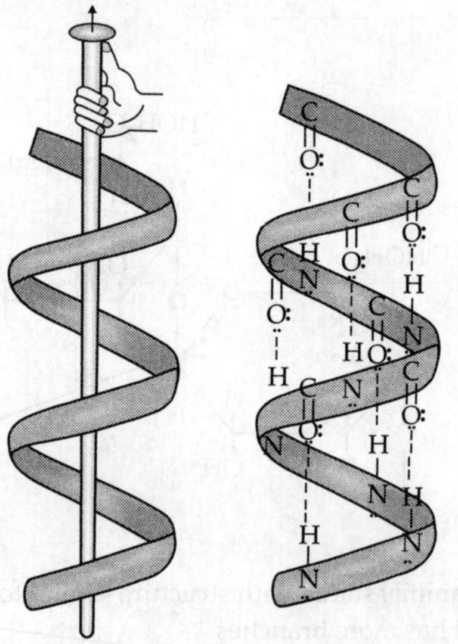

Scan to know more about this topic

Classification of Proteins

Beta pleated structure of protein

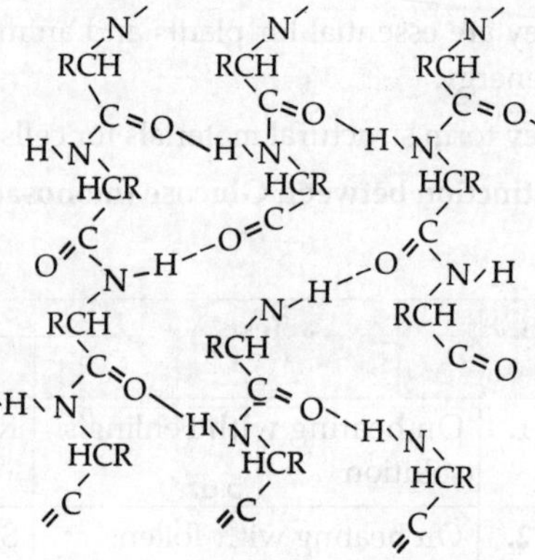

(iii) Tertiary structure: It represents overall folding of polypeptide chains by H-bonds, disulphide linkages, van der Waals and electrostatic form of attraction. e.g., fibrous and globular proteins.

(iv) Quaternary structure: The spatial arrangement of two or more polypeptide chains with respect to each other is known as quaternary structure.

Name and structure of some naturally occurring α-Amino Acids: ($H_2N-\underset{\displaystyle R}{\underset{|}{CH}}-COOH$)

Table 3 : Amino Acids

S. No.	Amino acids	Isoelectric point (Hydrophobic)	One alphabet code	Three alphabet code	—R (Side chain)
1.	**Non-polar** Glycine	5.97	G	Gly	—H
2.	Alanine	6.02	A	Ala	$-CH_3$
3.	Valine*	5.97	V	Val	$-CH(CH_3)_2$
4.	Leucine*	5.90	L	Leu	$-CH_2-CH(CH_3)_2$
5.	Isoleucine*	6.02	I	Ile	$-CH(CH_3)-CH_2-CH_3$
6.	Phenylalanine*	5.84	F	Phe	$-CH_2-Ph$
7.	Methionine*	5.06	M	Met	$-CH_2-CH_2-S-CH_3$
8.	Tryptophan*	5.88	W	Trp	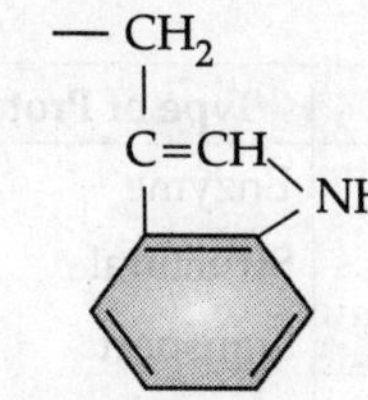
9.	Proline	6.30	P	Pro	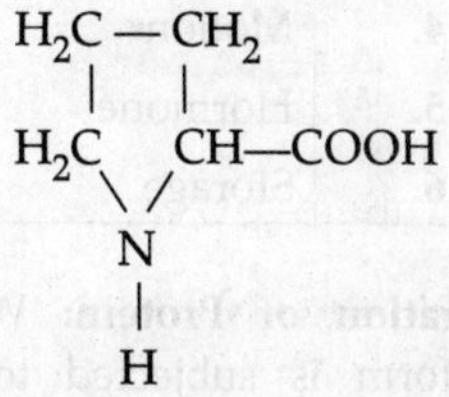
10.	**Polar (Neutral)** Serine	5.68	S	Ser	$-CH_2OH$
11.	Cysteine	5.02	C	Cys	$-CH_2-SH$
12.	Asparagine	5.41	N	Asn	$-CH_2\overset{O}{\overset{\parallel}{C}}NH_2$
13.	Glutamine	5.70	Q	Gln	$-CH_2-CH_2-\overset{O}{\overset{\parallel}{C}}-NH_2$
14.	Threonine*	5.60	T	Thr	$-CH(OH)-CH_3$
15.	Tyrosine	5.67	Y	Tyr	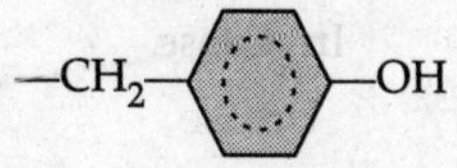
16.	**Acidic** Aspartic acid	2.98	D	Asp	$-CH_2-COOH$
17.	Glutamic acid	3.22	E	Glu	$-CH_2CH_2COOH$
18.	**Basic** Lysine*	9.47	K	Lys	$-CH_2-(CH_2)_3-NH_2$

19.	Arginine*	10.76	R	Arg	$-CH_2-(CH_2)_2-NH-\overset{\overset{\large NH}{\|\|}}{C}-NH_2$
20.	Histidine*	7.59	H	His	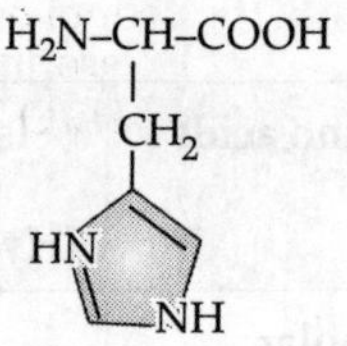

* These are essential amino acids.

Mnemonics

Concept: Essential Amino Acids
Mnemonics: PVT TIM HALL
Interpretations: **P**henylalanine, **V**aline, **T**hreonine, **T**ryptophan, **I**soleucine, **M**ethionine, **H**istidine, **A**rginine, **L**eucine, **L**ysine

- **Different Proteins and their functions:**

Table 4: Proteins

S. No.	Type of Protein	Example	Function
1.	Enzyme	Trypsin, Pepsin	As a catalyst in biochemical reactions.
2.	Structural	Collagen, Keratin	Structural and protective action in teeth, nails and hairs.
3.	Transport	Haemoglobin	Transport of oxygen from lungs by blood stream to different tissues.
4.	Motion	Myosin, Actin	For motion of muscles.
5.	Hormone	Insulin	Regulate body metabolism.
6.	Storage	Ferritin, Casein	Store nutrients.

- **Denaturation of Protein:** When a protein in its native form is subjected to change, like change in temperature or pH, the hydrogen bonds are disturbed. Due to this, globules unfold and helix gets uncoiled and protein loses its biological activity. During denaturation, secondary and tertiary structures are destroyed but primary structure remains intact. It is called denaturation of protein. e.g., coagulation of egg white on boiling, curdling of milk etc.
- **Enzymes:** Enzymes are essential biological catalyst which are needed to catalyse the biochemical reactions e.g., maltase, lactase, invertase, etc. Almost all enzyme are globular proteins. They are generally named after the reaction or the compounds on which they work upon.
- **Some specific Enzymes and the reactions catalysed by them:**

Table 5: Enzyme

Enzyme	Reaction catalysed
Maltase	Maltose $\rightarrow$ Glucose
Lactase	Lactose $\rightarrow$ Glucose + Galactose
Amylase or Ptyalin	Starch $\rightarrow$ Glucose
Invertase	Sucrose $\rightarrow$ Glucose + Fructose
Urease	Urea $\rightarrow$ $NH_3 + CO_2$
Trypsin, Pepsin	Protein $\rightarrow$ Amino acid

- **Vitamins:** Vitamins are the group of organic compounds which are required in a very small amount for the healthy growth and functioning of the body. They are stored in liver and adipose organism. They cannot be made by organism and so have to be part of our diet.
- **Types of Vitamins:**

(i) Fat soluble vitamins: Vitamins A, D, E and K are fat soluble but insoluble in water.

(ii) Water soluble vitamins: Vitamins belonging to group B (B_1, B_2, B_6, B_{12}, etc.) and vitamin C are soluble in water.

Different Vitamins:

Table 6: Vitamins

Vitamin	Name and Formula	Sources	Function	Deficiency Diseases
Vitamin A	Retinol or Excerophytol $C_{20}H_{30}O$	Milk, butter, egg, fish, spinach, green vegetables, carrot, etc.	Essential for vision and growth. Develops resistance against diseases.	Night blindness, xerophthalmia, retarded growth and decreases the immunity of body towards various diseases.
Vitamin B_1	Thiamine or Aneurin $C_{12}H_{17}N_4OS$	Egg, fish, meat, rice, wheat, yeast, etc.	For proper functioning of nervous system.	Beri-beri, anaemia, weakness of muscles, etc.
Vitamin B_2	Riboflavin or Lactoflavin $C_{17}H_{20}N_4O_6$	Milk, cheese, egg, meat, green vegetables, liver, etc.	Essential for growth of body.	Cracking skin particularly at the corners of mouth (Cheilosis), glossitis, dermatitis.
Vitamin B_6	Pyridoxine $C_8H_{11}O_3N$	Wheat, maize, husk of rice, meat, fish, egg, etc.	In blood formation.	Convulsions, paralysis.
Vitamin B_{12}	Cyanocobalamin $C_{63}H_{88}CoN_{14}O_{14}P$	Liver, egg, fish, meat, etc.	In blood formation.	Macrocytic anaemia or pernicious anaemia.
Vitamin C	Ascorbic acid $C_6H_8O_6$	Citrus fruits such as lemon, orange, tomatoes, amla, etc.	For bones, teeth and healing of wounds, healthy skin.	Scurvy, pyria, pain in joints, loosening of teeth, mental depression, anaemia, bleeding of gums.
Vitamin D	Calciferol or Ergocalciferol or Vitamin D_2, $C_{28}H_{44}O$	Egg, meat, fish, liver oil, butter, etc.	Control of metabolism of calcium and phosphorus in the formation of bones.	Rickets, osteomalacia.
Vitamin E	α-Tocopherol $C_{29}H_{50}O_2$	Milk, egg, meat, pulses, green vegetables, seeds, beans, etc.	Anti sterility or reproduction.	Loss of reproductive ability or infertility.
Vitamin K (Vitamin K_1 or K_2)	Vitamin K_1 or Phylloquinone $C_{31}H_{46}O_2$, Vitamin K_2, $C_{41}H_{56}O_2$	Cabbage, spinach, green vegetables, egg, fish, etc.	Helps in clotting of blood.	Delay in blood clotting (Haemophilia).

- **Hormones:** Hormones are the chemical substances produced by ductless glands called endocrine glands such as thyroid, adrenals, etc. They find their way into the blood stream and influence and regulate the functions of the other organs of the body. Hormonal deficiency leads to specific biological disorders which can be cured by the administration of the specific hormones.
- **Steroid hormones:** Those hormones which have structure similar to steroids. e.g., cortisone, testosterone, estrogen and progesterone.
- **Various hormones, gland of secretion and their functions:**

Table 7: Hormones

S. No.	Hormones	Gland	Function
1.	**Steroid hormones:**		
	(i) Testosterone (androgens)	Testes	Responsible for development of male sex organs.
	(ii) Estrogen and progesterone	Ovary	Influences development of female sex organs, maintains pregnancy.
	(iii) Cortisone	Adrenal cortex	Regulates metabolism of water, mineral salts.
2.	**Amine hormones:**		

	(i) Adrenalin	Adrenal medulla	Increases blood pressure and pulse rate. It also releases glucose from glycogen and fatty acids from fats.
	(ii) Thyroxine	Thyroid	Stimulates rate of oxidative metabolism and regulates general growth and development.
3.	**Peptide hormones:**		
	(i) Oxytocin	Posterior pituitary	Causes construction of some smooth muscles. It causes contraction of uterus during child birth.
	(ii) Vasopressin (ADH)	Posterior pituitary	Controls the re-absorption of water in kid-neys.
	(iii) Insulin	Pancreas	Controls blood glucose level.
	(iv) Glucagon	Pancreas	Increases blood glucose level.

- **Nucleic acid:** The particles in nucleus of the cell, responsible for heredity, are called chromosomes which are made up of proteins and another type of biomolecules called nucleic acids. Complete hydrolysis of DNA (or RNA) yields a pentose sugar, phosphoric acid and nitrogen containing heterocyclic compounds (called bases). The polymers of nucleotides help in synthesis of protein and transfer genetic traits.

  Nucleic acids are of two types:

  (i) Deoxyribonucleic acid (DNA)

  (ii) Ribonucleic acid (RNA)

  Constituents of nucleic acids: The complete hydrolysis of nucleic acid releases—Pentose sugar, phosphoric acid and nitrogenous bases.

- **Nitrogen containing bases:**
- **Pyrimidines:** These are three bases derived from pyrimidines. These are cytosine (C), thymine (T) and uracil (U). In DNA, T is present but in RNA, U is present.
- **Purines:** There are two bases derived from purine. These are adenine (A) and guanine (G).
- **DNA & RNA:** In DNA molecules, the sugar moiety is β-D-2-deoxyribose whereas in RNA molecule, it is β-D-ribose. DNA contains four bases viz. adenine (A), guanine (G), cytosine (C)and thymine (T). RNA also contains four bases, the first three bases are same as in DNA but the fourth one is uracil (U).
- **Nucleoside:** A unit formed by the attachment of base to 1′-position of sugar is known as nucleoside.

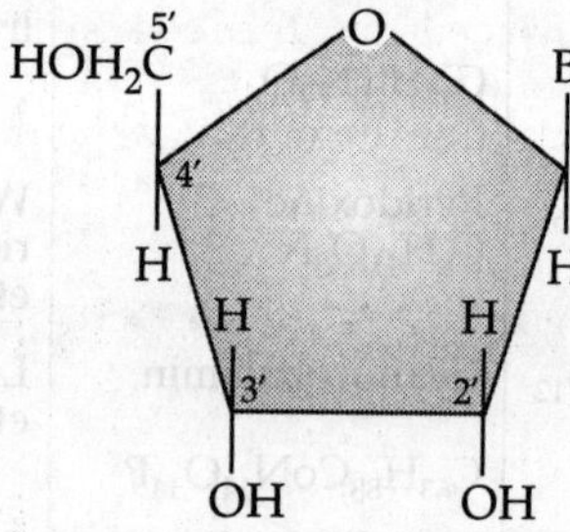

- **Nucleotide:** When nucleoside is linked to phosphoric acid at 5′-position of sugar the unit obtained is called nucleotide.

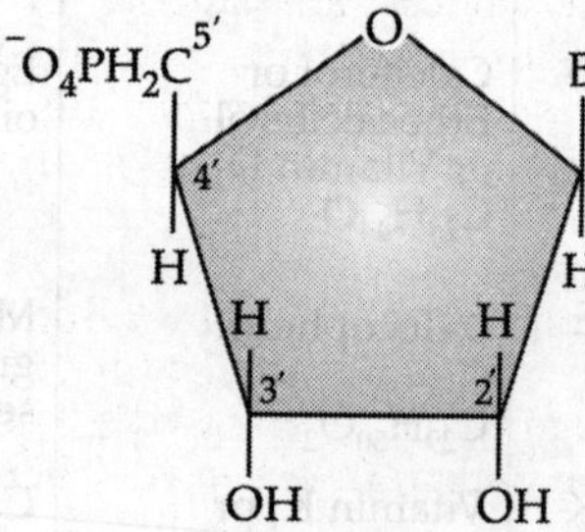

- **Simple structure of nucleic acid chain:**

$$\begin{matrix} \text{Base} & & \text{Base} & & \text{Base} \\ | & & | & & | \\ \text{— Sugar — Phosphate} & \Big[& \text{Sugar — Phosphate} & \Big]_n & \text{Sugar —} \end{matrix}$$

- **DNA: James Watson and Francis Crick gave double helix structure of DNA.**

Nucleic acid (DNA)
↓ hydrolysis
Nucleotide
↓ hydrolysis
Phosphoric acid + Nucleoside
↓ hydrolysis

Sugar (2-deoxy ribose)	Purine base (Adenine + Guanine)	Pyrimidine base (Cytosine + Thymine)

- **RNA: (i)** *m*-RNA (Messenger RNA)

  (ii) *r*-RNA (Ribosomal RNA)

  (iii) *t*-RNA (Transfer RNA)

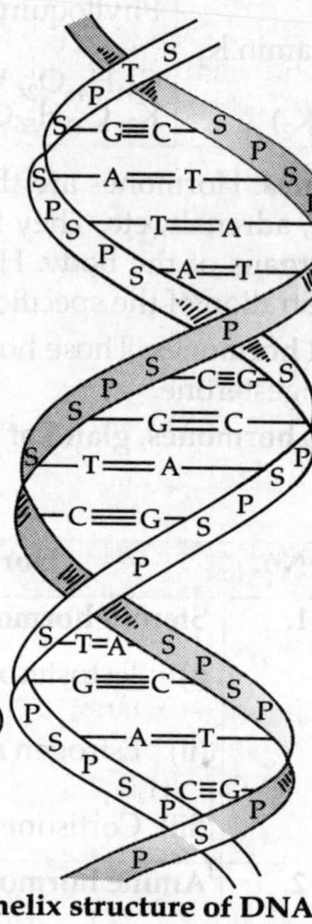

Double helix structure of DNA molecule

Nucleic acid (RNA)

↓ hydrolysis

Nucleotide

↓ hydrolysis

Phosphoric acid — Nucleoside

Nucleoside ↓ hydrolysis

Sugar (Ribose) — Purine base (Adenine + Guanine) — Pyrimidine base (Cytosine + Uracil)

operties of Nucleic Acids:

Nucleic acids are very important constituents (polynucleotide) found in nucleus of cell which help in biosynthesis of protein and act as carriers for transfer of hereditary characters.

) A molecule formed by the combination of one pentose sugar unit, a purine or pyrimidine base and a phosphate nucleotides combine among themselves to manufacture polynucleotide (nucleic acid).

(iii) A polynucleotide (DNA) which has a thymine base but not a uracil base. It contains deoxyribose sugar but not ribose sugar. It has double helix structure.

(iv) A polynucleotide (RNA) which contains uracil base and ribose sugar but thymine base and deoxyribose sugar are absent. It has single stranded structure.

NCERT CORNER

Intext Questions

Page - 290

). 1. Glucose or sucrose are soluble in water, but 'clohexane or benzene (simple six membered ring ›mpounds) are insoluble in water. Explain.

Ans. Glucose or sucrose contain several hydroxyl groups, their molecules which form hydrogen bonding with ater molecules due to which they dissolve in water. On e other hand, compounds like benzene or cyclohexane nnot form hydrogen bonds with water molecules, so ey are insoluble in water.

. 10.2. What products are expected when lactose is ydrolysed ?

Ans. Lactose ($C_{12}H_{22}O_{11}$) on hydrolysis with dilute acid elds an equimolar mixture of D-glucose and D-galactose.

$$\underset{\text{Lactose}}{C_{12}H_{22}O_{11}} + H_2O \xrightarrow{H^+} \underset{D\text{-Glucose}}{C_6H_{12}O_6} + \underset{D\text{-Glactose}}{C_6H_{12}O_6}$$

Q. 10.3. How do you explain the absence of aldehyde group in pentaacetate of glucose ?

Ans. The cyclic hemiacetal form of glucose contains an OH group at C-1 which gets hydrolysed in the aqueous solution to produce the open chain aldehydic form which then reacts with NH_2OH to form the corresponding oxime. Therefore, glucose contains an aldehydic group. On the other hand, when glucose is reacted with acetic anhydride, the OH group at C-1, along with the four other OH groups at C-2, C-3, C-4 and C-6 form a pentacetate. As the pentaacetate of glucose does not contain a free OH group at C-1, it cannot get hydrolysed in aqueous solution to produce the open chain aldehydic form and thus glucose pentaacetate does not react with NH_2OH to form glucose oxime. Hence, glucose pentaacetate does not contain the aldehdye group.

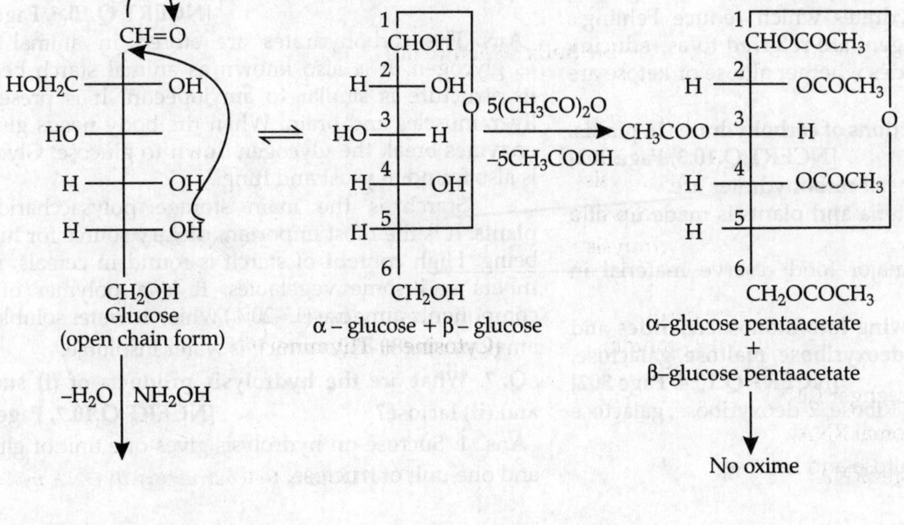

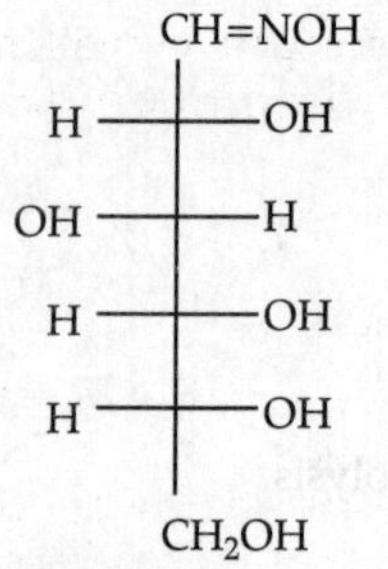

Glucose oxime

Page - 295

Q. 10.4. The melting points and solubility in water of amino acids are higher than those of the corresponding haloacids. Explain.

Ans. The amino acids exist as zwitter ions, H_3N^+ CHR – COO^-. Because of this dipolar salt like character they have strong dipole- dipole attractions. So, their melting points are higher than halo acids which do not have salt like character. Moreover, due to this salt like character, they interact strongly with H_2O. Thus, solubility of amino acids in water is higher than that of the corresponding halo acids which do not have salt like character.

Q. 10.5. Where does the water present in the egg go after boiling the egg?

Ans. The boiling of an egg is a common example of denaturation of proteins present in the white portion of an egg. The albumin present in the white of an egg gets coagulated when the egg is boiled hard. The soluble globular protein present in it is denatured resulting in the formation of insoluble fibrous protein.

Q. 10.6. Why vitamin C cannot be stored in our body?

Ans. Vitamin C is a water-soluble vitamin. Water-solub vitamins when supplied regularly in the diet cannot b stored in our body because they are readily excreted i urine.

Q. 10.7. What products would be formed when nucleotide from DNA containing thymine is hydrolyse

Ans. When a nucleotide from DNA containing thymir is completely hydrolysed, the products obtained are:

1. **2-deoxy-D(-)ribose.**
2. **Two pyrimidine,** i.e., guanine (G) and adenine (A
3. **Two purines,** i.e., thymine (T) and cytosine (C) an
4. Phosphoric acid.

Page -301

Q. 10.8. When RNA is hydrolysed, there is no relationshi among the quantities of different bases obtained? Wha does this fact suggest about the structure of RNA?

Ans. RNA also contains four bases, the first three ar same as in DNA but the fourth one is uracil (U).

As in RNA there is no relationship between th quantities of four bases (C, G, A and U) obtained, therefor the base-pairing principle, viz., (A) pairs with (U) and (C pairs with (G) is not followed. So, unlike DNA, RNA has single strand.

Exercise Questions

Q. 1. What are monosaccharides?
[NCERT Q.10.1, Page 302]

Ans. A carbohydrate that cannot be hydrolysed further to give simpler unit of polyhydroxy aldehyde or ketone is called a monosaccharide. With a few exceptions they have general formula, $C_nH_{2n}O_n$. About 20 monosaccharides are known to occur in nature. Some common examples are glucose, fructose, ribose, etc.

Q. 2. What are reducing sugars?
[NCERT Q.10.2, Page 302]

Ans. All those carbohydrates which reduce Fehling's solution and Tollen's reagent are referred to as reducing sugars. All monosaccharides whether aldose or ketose are reducing sugars.

Q. 3. Write two main functions of carbohydrates in plants.
[NCERT Q.10.3, Page 302]

Ans. Two main functions of carbohydrates are

1. Cell wall of bacteria and plants is made up of a polysaccharide, cellulose.
2. Starch is the major food reserve material in plants.

Q. 4. Classify the following into monosaccharides and disaccharides. Ribose, 2-deoxyribose, maltose, galactose, fructose and lactose. **[NCERT Q.10.4, Page 302]**

Ans. Monosaccharides: Ribose, 2-deoxyribose, galactose and fructose

Disaccharides: Maltose and Lactose

Q. 5. What do you understand by the term glycosidi linkage? **[NCERT Q.10.5, Page 302**

Ans. Disaccharides on hydrolysis with dilute acid or enzymes yield two molecules of either the same o different monosaccharides. The two monosaccharide are joined together by an oxide linkage formed by th loss of a water molecule. Such a linkage between tw monosaccharides units through oxygen atom is calle glycosidic linkage.

Q. 6. What is glycogen? How is it different from starch
[NCERT Q.10.6, Page 302

Ans. The carbohydrates are stored in animal bod as glycogen. It is also known as animal starch becaus its structure is similar to amylopectin. It is present i liver, muscles and brain. When the body needs glucose enzymes break the glycogen down to glucose. Glycoge is also found in yeast and fungi.

Starch is the main storage polysaccharide o plants. It is the most important dietary source for huma being. High content of starch is found in cereals, roots tubers and some vegetables. It is a polymer of tw components-amylose (15-20%) which is water soluble and amylopectin(80-85%) which is water insoluble.

Q. 7. What are the hydrolysis products of (i) sucros and (ii) lactose? **[NCERT Q.10.7, Page 302]**

Ans. 1. Sucrose on hydrolysis gives one unit of glucose and one unit of fructose.

$$C_{12}H_{22}O_{11} + H_2O \xrightarrow{\text{Invertase}} C_6H_{12}O_6 + C_6H_{12}O_6$$

Sucrose → Glucose + Fructose

2. Lactose on hydrolysis with dilute acids yields an uimolar mixture of D-glucose and D-galactose.

). 8. What is the basic structural difference between arch and cellulose ? [NCERT Q.10.8, Page 302]

Ans. The basic structural difference between starch and llulose is of linkage between the glucose units. In starch, ere is α-D-glycosidic linkage. Both the components of arch-amylose and amylopectin are polymer of α-D-ucose. On the other hand, cellulose is a linear polymer of D-glucose in which C_1 of one glucose unit is connected C_4 of the other through β-D-glycosidic linkage.

). 9. What happens when D-glucose is treated with the llowing reagents? [NCERT Q.10.9, Page 302]

(i) HI

(ii) Bromine water

(iii) HNO_3

ns. (i)

$$\begin{array}{l} CHO \\ | \\ (CHOH)_4 \\ | \\ CH_2OH \end{array} \xrightarrow[\Delta]{HI} CH_3-CH_2-CH_2-CH_2-CH_2-CH_3$$

D-Glucose → *n*-Hexane

i)

$$\begin{array}{l} CHO \\ | \\ (CHOH)_4 \\ | \\ CH_2OH \end{array} \xrightarrow{Br_2\ water} \begin{array}{l} COOH \\ | \\ (CHOH)_4 \\ | \\ CH_2OH \end{array}$$

D-glucose → D-gluconic acid

ii)

$$\begin{array}{l} CHO \\ | \\ (CHOH)_4 \\ | \\ CH_2OH \end{array} \xrightarrow{HNO_3} \begin{array}{l} COOH \\ | \\ (CHOH)_4 \\ | \\ COOH \end{array}$$

D-glucose → Saacharic acid

). 10. Enumerate the reactions of D-glucose which annot be explained by its open chain structure. [NCERT Q.10.10, Page 302]

Ans. The open chain structure of D-glucose)HC – $(CHOH)_4$ – CH_2OH fails to explain the following eactions:

(i) Though it contains the aldehyde (-CHO) group, lucose does not give 2,4-DNP test, Schiff's test and it loes not form the hydrogen sulphite addition product vith $NaHSO_3$.

(ii) The pentaacetate of glucose does not react with ydroxylamine (NH_2OH) to form' the oxime indicating he absence of free -CHO group.

(iii) The formation of two anomeric methyl glycosides y glucose on reaction with CH_3OH and dry HCl can be xplained in terms of the cyclic structure. The equilibrium mixture of α-and β-glucose react separately with methanol in the presence of dry HCl gas to form the corresponding methyl D-glucosides.

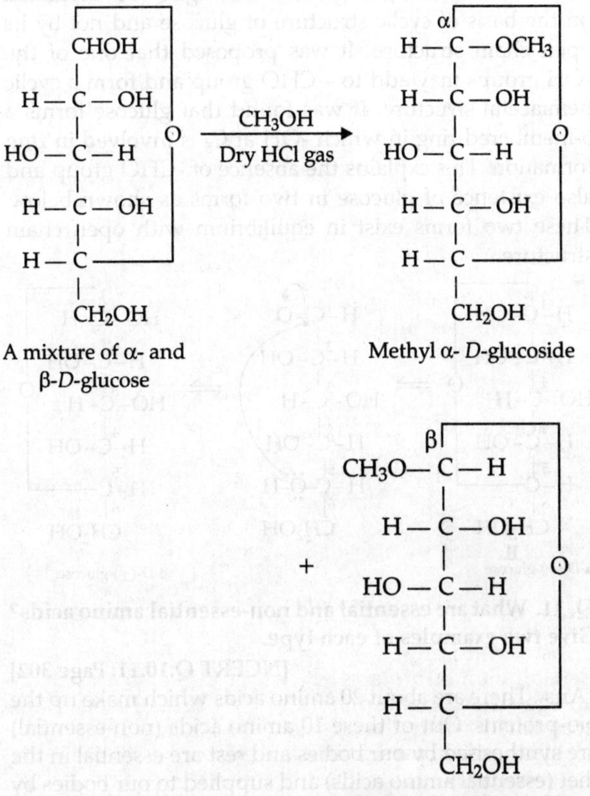

A mixture of α- and β-*D*-glucose → Methyl α- *D*-glucoside + Methyl β- *D*-glucoside

(iv) Like methyl glycosides, glucose pentaacetate also exists in two anomeric forms as explained below:

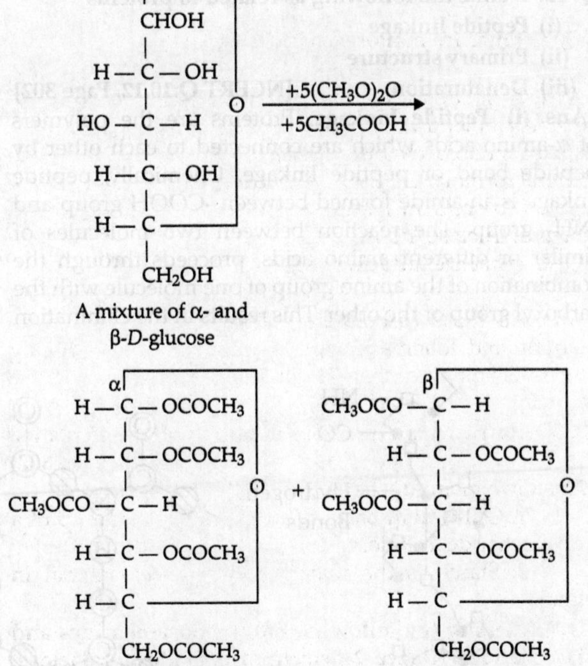

A mixture of α- and β-*D*-glucose → α- *D*-glucoside pentaacetate + β- *D*-Glucose pentaacetate

These pentaacetates do not have a free -OH group at C_1 and hence are not hydrolysed in aqueous solution to produce the open chain aldehyde form and hence do not react with NH_2OH to form glucose oxime.

(v) The existence of glucose in two crystalline forms termed as α and β-D-glucose can again be explained on the basis of cyclic structure of glucose and not by its open chain structure. It was proposed that one of the -OH groups may add to – CHO group and form a cyclic hemiacetal structure. It was found that glucose forms a 6-membered ring in which -OH at C_5 is involved in ring formation. This explains the absence of -CHO group and also existence of glucose in two forms as shown below. These two forms exist in equilibrium with open chain structure.

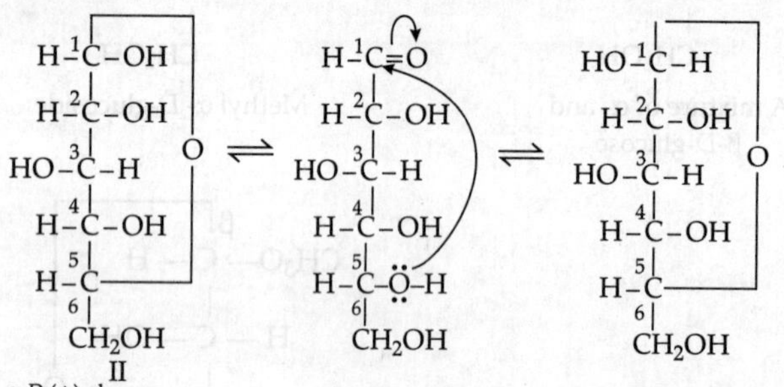

α-D-(+)-glucose β-D-(+)-glucose

Q. 11. What are essential and non-essential amino acids? Give two examples of each type.
[NCERT Q.10.11, Page 302]

Ans. There are about 20 amino acids which make up the bio-proteins. Out of these 10 amino acids (non-essential) are synthesised by our bodies and rest are essential in the diet (essential amino acids) and supplied to our bodies by food which we take because they cannot be synthesised in our body.

e.g., Essential amino acid – Valine and Leucine
Non-essential amino acid – Glycine and Alanine

Q. 12. Define the following as related to proteins
(i) Peptide linkage
(ii) Primary structure
(iii) Denaturation. **[NCERT Q.10.12, Page 302]**

Ans. (i) Peptide Linkage: Proteins are the polymers of α-amino acids which are connected to each other by peptide bond or peptide linkage. Chemically, peptide linkage is an amide formed between -COOH group and $-NH_2$ group. The reaction between two molecules of similar or different amino acids, proceeds through the combination of the amino group of one molecule with the carboxyl group of the other. This results in the elimination of a water molecule and formation of a peptide bond -CC NH-. The product of the reaction is called a dipeptic because it is made up of two amino acids. For exampl when carboxyl group of glycine combines with the amir group of alanine we get a dipeptide, glycylalanine.

(ii) Primary Structure: Proteins may have one or mo polypeptide chains. Each polypeptide in a protein ha amino acids linked with each other in a specific sequenc and it is this sequence of amino acids that is said to b the primary structure of that protein. Any change in th primary structure, i.e., the sequence of amino acids create a different protein.

(iii) Denaturation: Protein found in a biological syste with a unique three-dimensional structure and biologic activity is called a native protein. When a protein in i native form, is subjected to physical change like chang in temperature or chemical change in pH, the hydroge bonds are disturbed. Due to this, globules unfold and heli get uncoiled and protein loses its biological activity. Th is called denaturation of protein. During denaturation 2 and 3° structures are destroyed but 1° structure remair intact. The coagulation of egg white on boiling is common example of denaturation. Another example i curdling of milk which is caused due to the formation c lactic acid by the bacteria present in milk.

Q. 13. What are the common types of secondary structur of proteins? **[NCERT Q.10.13, Page 302]**

Ans. The secondary structure of protein refers to th shape in which a long polypeptide chain can exist. The are found to exist in two different types of structures vi α-helix and β-pleated sheet structure. These structure arise due to the regular folding of the backbone of th polypeptide chain due to hydrogen bonding betwee >C=O and –NH– groups of the peptide bond. α-Heli is one of the most common ways in which a polypeptid chain forms all possible hydrogen bonds by twisting int a right handed screw (helix) with the –NH group of eac amino acid residue hydrogen bonded to the >C=O o an adjacent turn of the helix. In β-structure all peptid chains are stretched out to nearly maximum extensior and then laid side by side which are held together by intermolecular hydrogen bonds. The structure resemble the pleated folds of drapery and therefore is known a β-pleated sheet

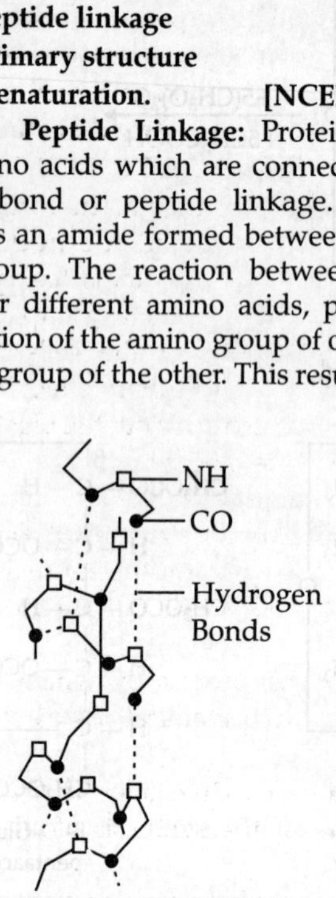

α-helix structure of a protein

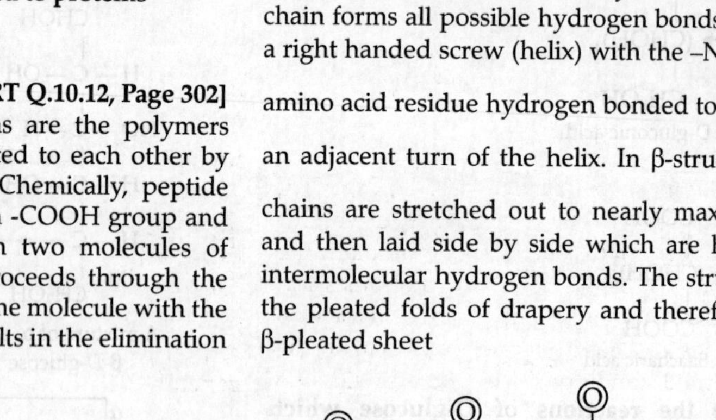

β-pleated sheet structure of a protein

14. What type of bonding helps in stabilising the elix structure of proteins? [NCERT Q.10.14, Page 302]

ns. α–Helix is one of the most common ways in which olypeptide chain forms all possible hydrogen bonds by isting into a right handed screw (helix) with the -NH oup of each amino acid residue hydrogen bonded to the = O of an adjacent turn of the helix.

15. Differentiate between globular and fibrous oteins. [NCERT Q.10.15, Page 302]

ns. Difference between Globular and Fibrous protein:

S. No.	Globular protein	Fibrous protein
1.	Polypeptide chains are arranged as coils.	Polypeptide chains are run parallel to each other.
2.	They have spherical shape.	They have thread like stucture.
3.	These are water soluble.	These are insoluble in water.

16. How do you explain the amphoteric behaviour of nino acids? [NCERT Q.10.16, Page 302]

ns. Due to dipolar or Zwitter ionic structure, amino ids are amphoteric in nature. The acidic character of e amino acids is due to the NH_3^+ group while the basic aracter is due to the COO^- group.

$$\overset{+}{N}H_3-\underset{\underset{R}{|}}{CH}-COO^- + OH^- \longrightarrow H_2N-\underset{\underset{R}{|}}{CH}-COO^- + H_2O$$

Acidic part

$$\overset{+}{N}H_3-\underset{\underset{R}{|}}{CH}-COO^- + H^+ \longrightarrow \overset{+}{N}H_3-\underset{\underset{R}{|}}{CH}-COOH$$

Basic part

17. What are enzymes? [NCERT Q.10.17, Page 302]

ns. Life is possible due to the coordination of various emical processes in living organisms. An example is the gestion of food, absorption of appropriate molecules and timately production of energy. This process involves a quence of reactions and all these reactions occur in the ody under very mild conditions. This occurs with the elp of certain biocatalysts called enzymes. Almost all e enzymes are globular proteins. Enzymes are specific r a particular reaction and for a particular substrate. hey are generally named after the compound or class compounds upon which they work. For example, the zyme that catalyses hydrolysis of maltose into glucose is amed as maltose.

$$\underset{\text{Maltose}}{C_{12}H_{22}O_{11}} \xrightarrow{\text{Maltase}} \underset{\text{Glucose}}{2C_6H_{12}O_6}$$

. 18. What is the effect of denaturation on the structure f proteins? [NCERT Q.10.18, Page 302]

Ans. Proteins are very sensitive to the action of heat, ineral acids, alkalies, etc. On heating or on treatment with mineral acids, soluble forms of proteins such as globular proteins often undergo coagulation or precipitation to give fibrous proteins which are insoluble in water. This coagulation also results in the loss of the biological activity of the protein. That is why the coagulated proteins so formed are called denatured proteins. Chemically, denaturation does not change the primary structure but brings about changes in the secondary and tertiary structure of proteins.

Q. 19. How are vitamins classified? Name the vitamin responsible for the coagulation of blood. [NCERT Q.10.19, Page 302]

Ans. Vitamins are classified into two groups depending upon their solubility in water or fat.

(i) Fat soluble vitamins: Vitamins which are soluble in fats and oils but insoluble in water are kept in this group. These are vitamins A, D, E and K. They are stored in liver and adipose (fat storing) tissues.

(ii) Water soluble vitamins: Vitamin B and vitamin C are soluble in water so they are grouped together. Water soluble vitamins must be supplied regularly in diet because they are readily excreted in urine and cannot be stored (except vitamin B_{12}) in our body.

Q. 20. Why are vitamin A and vitamin C essential to us? Give their important sources. [NCERT Q.10.20, Page 302]

Ans. Deficiency of vitamin A causes Xerophthalmia (hardening of cornea of the eye) and night blindness. So its use is essential to us. It is available in fish liver oil, carrots, butter and milk. It promotes growth and increases resistance to diseases. Vitamin C is very essential to us because its deficiency causes Scurvy (bleeding of gums) and pyorrhea (loosening and bleeding of teeth). Vitamin C increases resistance of the body towards diseases. Maintains healthy skin and helps cuts and abrasions to heal properly. It is soluble in water. It is present in citrus fruits, e.g., oranges, lemons, amla, tomato, green vegetables (Cabbage) chillies, sprouts pulses and germinated grains.

Q. 21. What are nucleic acids? Mention their two important functions. [NCERT Q.10.21, Page 302]

Ans. Nucleic acids: They constitute an important class of biomolecules which are found in the nuclei of all living cells in the form of nucleoproteins (i.e., proteins containing nucleic acid as the prosthetic group). Nucleic acids are the genetic materials of the cells and are responsible for transmission of hereditary effect from one generation to the other and also carry out the biosynthesis of proteins. Nucleic acids are biopolymers (i.e., polymers present in the living system). The genetic information coded in nucleic acids controls the structure of all proteins including enzymes and thus governs the entire metabolic activity in the living organism. Two important functions of nucleic acids are:

1. **Replication:** The process by which a single DNA molecule produces two identical copies of itself is called replication.

2. **Protein Synthesis:** DNA may be regarded as the instrument manual for the synthesis of all proteins present in the cell.

Q. 22. What is the difference between a nucleoside and a nucleotide? [NCERT Q.10.22, Page 302]

Ans. Nucleoside: A nucleoside contains only two basic components of nucleic acids, i.e., a pentose sugar and a nitrogenous base. It may be represented as sugar-base. Depending upon the type of sugar present, nucleosides are of two types:

1. Ribonucleosides and
2. Deoxyribonucleosides.

Nucleotides: A nucleotide contains all the three basic components of nucleic acids, i.e., a phosphoric acid group, a pentose sugar and a nitrogenous base. In other words, nucleotides are nucleoside monophosphates.

Depending upon the type of sugar present, nucleotides like nucleosides are of two types:

1. Ribonucleotides and
2. Deoxyribonucleotides.

Q. 23. The two strands in DNA are not identical but are complementary. Explain. [NCERT Q.10.23, Page 302]

Ans. Two nucleic acid chains are wound about each other and held together by hydrogen bonds between pairs of bases. The strands are complementary to each other because the hydrogen bonds are formed between specific pairs of bases. Adenine forms hydrogen bonds with thymine whereas cytosine forms hydrogen bonds with guanine.

Q. 24. Write the important structural and functional differences between DNA and RNA. [NCERT Q.10.24, Page 302]

Ans. Difference between DNA and RNA.

	DNA	RNA
1.	It usually occurs inside nucleus and some cell organelles	Very little RNA occurs inside nucleus. Most of it is found in the cytoplasm.
2.	DNA is the genetic material.	RNA is not the genetic material except in certain viruses, e.g., TMV, retorvirus.
3.	It is double stranded with α-helix structure in which two stands are coiled spirally.	RNA is single stranded with the exception of some viruses (e.g., double standard in retrovirus).
4.	DNA shows regular helical coiling.	There is no regular coiling except in par of *t*RNA.
5.	DNA is of only two types, nuclear and extra-nuclear.	There are at least three types of RNA- *m*-RNA, *r*-RNA and *t*-RNA.
6.	It contains deoxyribose sugar.	It contains ribose sugar.
7.	Nitrogen base thymine occurs in DNA along with three other adenine, cytosine and guanine.	Thymine is replaced by uracil in RNA. The other three are adenine, cytosine an guanine.
8.	It has a unique property of replication	It does not replicate.
9.	DNA transcribes genetic information to RNA.	RNA translates the transcribed message for forming polypeptides.
10.	DNA controls heredity, evolution, metabolism, structure and differentiation.	RNA controls only protein synthesis.
11.	DNA controls metabolism and genetics including variations.	It only controls metabolism under instructions from DNA.

Q. 25. What are the different types of RNA found in th cell? [NCERT Q.10.25, Page 30

Ans. RNA molecules are of three types and they perfor different functions. They are named as messenger RN (m-RNA), ribosomal RNA (r-RNA) and transfer RN (t-RNA).

□□